Visual C++
Windows Shell Programming

Dino Esposito

Wrox Press Ltd. ®

Visual C++ Windows Shell Programming

© 1998 Wrox Press

wrox
PROGRAMMER TO PROGRAMMER

Published by Wrox Press Ltd. 30 Lincoln Road, Olton, Birmingham, B27 6PA
Printed in USA
ISBN 1-861001-8-43

Trademark Acknowledgements

Wrox has endeavored to provide trademark information about all the companies and products mentioned in this book by the appropriate use of capitals. However, Wrox cannot guarantee the accuracy of this information.

Credits

Author
Dino Esposito

Development Editor
John Franklin

Editors
Jon Hill
Chris Hindley

Technical Reviewers
Davide Marcato
Tommy Riddle
Kenn Scribner
Marc Simkin
Mark Stiver
Julian Templeman

Cover
Andrew Guillaume
Concept by Third Wave

Design/Layout
Noel Donnelly

Index
Andrew Criddle

Keep it simple: as simple as possible, but no simpler.
Albert Einstein

Photo of the ammonite courtesy of Claren Kidd at the
Laurence S Youngblood Energy Library, University of Oklahoma.
http://www-lib.ou.edu/depts/geol/lammonite.html

About the Author

Dino Esposito is a senior consultant who specializes in Windows and COM development. At present, his work for Andersen Consulting focuses on the development of Web-based applications. He's a frequent speaker at industry conferences such as Microsoft Developer Days and occasionally holds seminars for Mondadori Informatica Education.

He also has extensive experience developing commercial Windows-based software, especially for the photography world, and was part of the team who designed and realized one of the first European image databanks.

Dino loves writing, and is a contributing editor to *Microsoft Internet Developer* for which he runs the Cutting Edge column. He contributes to a number of magazines including *Microsoft Systems Journal, MSDN News, Windows Developer's Journal, Dr. Dobb's Journal* and a number of Italian magazines. He co-authored *Professional IE4 Programming* and authored *Instant DHTML Scriptlets*, both published by Wrox Press.

Dino lives in Rome (Italy) with his wife Silvia and a six-month-old son, Francesco. Feel free to contact him at desposito@infomedia.it.

Acknowlegements

Even though I appear smiling and relaxed on the cover, believe me, doing this book was no picnic. It's been a pleasure, though. I've really enjoyed presenting my development experience and telling you about all the pitfalls I've found along the way. My hope is that, with this book, your coding will progress more quickly.

I said it wasn't easy, and didn't just mean for myself. Silvia, my wife, was incredibly patient with me and many nights, at the end of a chapter, I found her solicitously awake. This book considerably increased her capacity to sleep in spite of the typical but annoying noise of a programmer: the unremitting clicking, plop and plonk, dialing and so on. There's nothing to do, I really love you – and it's rhymed too!

No, Francesco, don't cry! Daddy loves you too. Francesco is now six months old and shows a great interest for everything with buttons, from keyboards to remote controls and from telephones to cameras. He's a very lively and precocious baby. Although his name doesn't appear among the technical reviewers, he really gave a considerable contribution to the last two chapters. (Jon, now you know the real reason why you got them so late...)

Jon Hill was the lead technical editor of this book and, let me say, did an excellent job testing and re-testing the source code, providing countless pieces of good advice and, above all, addressing the weak points in the original text. You'll never know about them, but believe me, the book is now far more readable, rich and enjoyable. Thank you, Jon!

And thanks also to all the guys that reviewed the various chapters. In particular, I'd like to mention Kenn Scribner who led me to discover and consider a number of neglected topics. Thank you, Kenn; I appreciated your ideas very much.

Other people contributed to this book with their suggestions and technical tips. I want to say thanks to Marco Losavio, Graziano Lorusso, Giuseppe Dimauro, Francesco Balena, Carlo Pescio and Antonio Derossi.

Writing a book related to Windows necessarily involves pinging people at Microsoft, searching for help, tips, references and so forth. Among others, I'd like to mention Scott Roberts, Andrew Clinick and Michael Edwards who clarified a number of obscure points and helped me to find up-to-date information. Scott was incredibly kind and patient and even answered my questions over some weekends. I'm really grateful. I'll write it in Italian too: *Te ne sono veramente molto grato.*

Other people at Microsoft provided assistance, directly or indirectly. In no particular order: Josh Trupin and Joe Flanigen, for their appreciation and continued encouragement, and with them all the staff at *MIND* and *MSJ*. Paula Ladenburg, for giving me the opportunity to appear on *MSDN* and astound friends and colleagues with public full-text search engines. Joanne Steinhart, for providing me with the colorful *MIND* mousepad that many times has captured Francesco's attention and allowed me to work a bit more quietly.

Writing a book is just one aspect of my daily activity. Thus, I want to reserve a special mention for the people at Andersen Consulting. In particular, I want to thank Bruno Ronchetti and Giorgio Di Paolo for the opportunities they offered me and the patience they always demonstrated.

Thanks also to Natale Fino and Roberto Palumbo at Infomedia. Their magazines are probably the only chance I have not to forget how to write in Italian!

I love writing, but speaking is another thing that lets you touch what's going on in development today. For this, I wish to mention Stefano Maruzzi and Alessandro Pedone at Mondadori Informatica Education.

A word written a few lines above now is striking me: *weekend.* What's that? I think I'll have to do some research to figure it out. When you work so hard month after month, sooner or later you end up neglecting friends. To try to partially remedy this, I want to embrace in a common thought Marco Lucani, Raffaele D'Orsogna, Roberto Raschetti and my brother Telly.

Last but not least, I would like to thank the person who is somewhat *responsible* for this book: John Franklin. I enjoyed writing this book, despite the hard work. You and your team made it really pleasant.

Thanks to you all

Dino

Table of Contents

Table of Contents

v

Introduction

Welcome to *Visual C++ Windows Shell Programming*! With this book, you'll learn how to program the Windows Shell, customize its behavior and integrate your applications with it. You'll discover how to use and modify its features to best effect, and the way to call shell API functions whose documentation is scant. Programming the shell isn't difficult, but few books explain the subject in its entirety.

Everything Changes

In Windows 95 and Windows NT 4.0, Microsoft made the operating system's shell programmable and highly customizable through a variety of different extensions, of which shell and namespace extensions are just the tip of the iceberg. What's commonly understood by the expression '*shell programming*' also includes a bunch of API functions and registry keys that can transform your Win32 application.

The integrated web browser has blurred the distinction between local and remote objects – it presents everything on your desktop using the same metaphor, which can be extended to encompass user applications and documents. Integration with the new parts of the Windows shell is a key part of that process.

So, the shell today doesn't just mean COM, extensions, and a user interface, but also a window on the Internet, Dynamic HTML and scripting. The shell has become the meeting-point of a large number of client-side technologies. Every programmer who is developing Windows-based code sooner or later needs concrete and insightful samples of how to exploit the built-in features of the Windows shell.

This book covers the whole range of API functions in detail, often revealing bugs and undocumented features. It delves deep into the world of Explorer, bringing to light things like hooks, the registry, browser helper objects, shell extensions, namespace extensions and web views. It also looks at Windows Scripting Host extensions and Shell Scriptable Objects.

Introduction

This book is for professional and home developers alike, and has three main goals:

- Providing a better understanding of the existing and often poorly documented shell API
- Giving ideas for new applications
- Showing what's new in Internet Explorer 4.*x*, the Active Desktop and Windows 98, and how these fit with the existing shell

What Does this Book Cover?

In this book, I shall attempt to answer the following common questions:

- What is the shell API and how do I use it?
- How do I customize the Windows shell using the registry?
- How can I create special directories like the Recycle Bin or My Briefcase?
- What are the different ways to insert code into Explorer's address space?
- How do I handle icons, the taskbar and the Recycle Bin?
- What is the Windows Scripting Host and how can I use it?
- What are Shell Scripting Objects and Browser Helper Objects?
- How can I implement shell support for the documents my application handles?
- How can I customize the context menu of my documents?
- How do I use COM and ATL to alter shell behavior with shell and namespace extensions?
- How do I debug shell extensions?
- Can you explain the principles and techniques necessary for creating successful shell-integrated applications?
- How do I customize a folder with Dynamic HTML?

Each aspect of shell programming will be clearly explained with the help of concrete examples written using Visual C++ 6.0 and ATL 3.0. Some of the most interesting examples in this book are:

- Subclassing the Start button
- Creating and installing a new and enhanced shortcut handler
- New objects to work with the Windows Scripting Host
- A shell extension for assigning different icons to bitmap files according to the palette size
- Press a key and create a new folder in Explorer
- Showing open windows as a node in Explorer

What You Need to Use this Book

It goes almost without saying that in order to run the code in this book, you need a computer running Windows 98, Windows 95 or Windows NT 4.0 (with Service Pack 4.0). With regard to the last two of these, some of the examples require you to have installed the Active Desktop update that first shipped with version 4.0 of Internet Explorer.

The code was developed and tested using Visual C++ 6.0 and ATL 3.0, although you should find few problems using Visual C++ 5 if that's what is on your machine. The book also makes use of the Windows Scripting Host and Internet Explorer 4.01 as hosts for some of the applications developed.

Conventions Used

We use a number of different styles of text and layout in the book to help differentiate between different kinds of information. Here are some examples of the styles we use and an explanation of what they mean:

> These boxes hold important, not-to-be forgotten, mission critical details that are directly relevant to the surrounding text.

Background information, asides and references to information located elsewhere appear in text like this.

- **Important Words** are in a bold font
- Words that appear on the screen, such as menu options, are in a similar font to the one used on the screen – the File menu, for example
- Keys that you press on the keyboard, like *Ctrl* and *Delete*, are in italics
- All filenames are in this style: Pidl.cpp
- Function names look like this: SHBrowseForFolder()

Code that's new, important or relevant to the current discussion will be presented like this:

```
void CALLBACK TimerProc(HWND hwnd, UINT uMsg, UINT idEvent, DWORD dwTime)
{
   HWND hwndOK = GetDlgItem(g_hwndDlg, IDOK);

   // Simulate the Close button being pressed
   if(IsWindowEnabled(hwndOK))
      PostMessage(g_hwndDlg, WM_COMMAND, IDCANCEL, 0);
}
```

However, code that you've seen before, or which has little to do with the matter at hand, looks like this:

```
void CALLBACK TimerProc(HWND hwnd, UINT uMsg, UINT idEvent, DWORD dwTime)
{
   HWND hwndOK = GetDlgItem(g_hwndDlg, IDOK);

   // Simulate the Close button being pressed
   if(IsWindowEnabled(hwndOK))
      PostMessage(g_hwndDlg, WM_COMMAND, IDCANCEL, 0);
}
```

Tell Us What You Think

We've tried to make this book as accurate and enjoyable as possible, but what really matters is what the book actually does for you. Please let us know your views, either by returning the reply card in the back of the book, or by contacting us via e-mail at feedback@wrox.com

Source Code

All the source code from the examples in this book is available for download from the Wrox Press web site:

http://www.wrox.com
ftp://ftp.wrox.com/professional
ftp://ftp.wrox.co.uk/professional

Support

We've made every effort to make sure there are no errors in the text or the code. However, to err is human and as such we recognize the need to keep you, the reader, informed of any mistakes as they're spotted and corrected. The web site acts as a focus for providing the following information and support:

- ❑ Errata sheets
- ❑ Information about current and forthcoming titles
- ❑ Sample chapters
- ❑ Source code downloads
- ❑ An e-mail newsletter
- ❑ Developer's Journal subscription
- ❑ Articles and opinion on related topics
- ❑ Subscription to the COMDeveloper newsletter

Errata sheets are available for all our books – please download them, or take part in the continuous improvement of our products and upload a 'fix' or a pointer to the solution.

What is the Windows Shell?

A good definition of an operating system's shell is that it's the user interface provided by the system to allow the user to carry out common tasks, such as accessing the file system, launching programs, changing system-wide settings, and so on. MS-DOS had the ubiquitous `command.com` prompt to play this role, but Windows has always been a graphical environment, and therefore its shell is, of necessity, graphical too. Before the advent of Windows 95, the default Windows shell was the Program Manager.

Program Manager was a kind of central console from which you could start applications, reorder and regroup icons, and perform a few other duties. In other words, Program Manager was exactly what its name suggests — a manager for all the programs gathered under the Windows umbrella. Existing side by side with Program Manager was the File Manager, a system tool designed specifically for the purpose of maintaining the file system.

With the advent of Windows 95, Explorer superseded these two old tools and encompassed the functionality of both. If you want to, you can still find the File Manager buried deep in the folds of Windows' system directory, but it's seldom used these days because it is considerably less user-friendly than its successor.

A common misconception is that Explorer is just the program that starts up when you attempt to browse the file system by clicking on My Computer or right-clicking the Start button. In fact, Explorer is *always* up and running, from boot time until you switch off your machine. The thing commonly perceived as being 'Explorer' is actually just a window created in a new thread that is added to the Explorer process. Explorer is the executable module (called `explorer.exe`) that implements the Windows shell.

In this chapter, my aim is to briefly introduce the shell and Explorer. More precisely, I'll cover:

❑ The components of the shell
❑ The structure of Explorer

The Components of the Shell

There are many distinct components that contribute to the shell, but let's begin with the most obvious ones: the **desktop** and the **taskbar**. From a conceptual point of view, the desktop is intended to be the parent of all the objects that populate the Windows shell. In terms of implementation, the desktop is a window of a particular system-defined window class (whose name is "#32769") and is the ancestor of all windows that are created. The 'top-level' windows in which running applications are rendered are (in most cases) children of the desktop window. Among the desktop's children, there is also an interesting little sub-tree of windows, the root of which is called "Program Manager" – the name is no accident.

You can examine the stack of existing windows, including those of the Windows shell and any other application, at any time by using a tool such as Microsoft Spy++, which comes bundled with Microsoft Visual C++.

The Program Manager window has been retained for compatibility purposes only, as you'll see in a moment. It envelops a structure like the one shown in the figure:

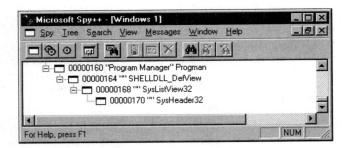

Immediately below the Program Manager, there's a window whose class name is `SHELLDLL_DefView`. This window encompasses the default view object in Windows 95 and Windows NT 4.0. In practice, this window is responsible for enumerating the content of a standard folder, which is always rendered through a **ListView** control – one of the Windows 95 and NT 3.51+ common controls. In fact, the `SHELLDLL_DefView` window includes a ListView (whose class name is `SysListView32`) and a Header control (whose class name is `SysHeader32`) that is used only for the ListView's report view.

With the introduction of the Active Desktop in Internet Explorer 4.0 and Windows 98, the default view object has changed, gaining some Internet-based browsing capability. We'll be looking more closely at view objects and the changes they have undergone in the next chapter.

The Program Manager

As I mentioned earlier, the Program Manager window is still present for reasons of compatibility. It's just possible that an application inadvertently ported from 16-bit to 32-bit could be broken in the absence of such a window (of class `Progman`). In the Win16 (that is, the Windows 3.1*x*) world, the only way to communicate with the shell was through **Dynamic Data Exchange** (**DDE**). This layer of code has been maintained in Windows 95 and even Windows 98. Why? Once again, it's for compatibility purposes.

For more details about DDE interface programming and the shell, I recommend that you have a look at the documentation available with the Internet Client SDK, which contains the most up-to-date information. DDE is an old technology, and Microsoft has supplied plenty of documentation for it, which is the reason why I won't be covering it here.

The Taskbar

A primary component of the Windows shell is the taskbar, but this is really just a window owned by the Explorer process. Each time you need to kill the Explorer process (I'll say more about this in Chapter 9), you'll cause the taskbar to disappear and reappear. Each time it reappears it is a brand new window, with a different HWND handle. Thus, it is advisable that you never store its HWND for future reference. The taskbar is also the window that owns the Start menu, the tray area with the clock, and even those button-like controls that represent running applications.

The taskbar really is nothing more than a window, so you can perform upon it any action you might carry out on any other window — moving, hiding, subclassing, etc. In Chapter 7, I'll show how to subclass the taskbar and the Start button, while in Chapter 9, I'll address how to hide the taskbar and programmatically restart the shell. This latter feature turns out to be really useful when you're developing shell and namespace extensions, which we'll look at briefly in the next chapter and thoroughly in Chapters 15 and 16.

The Desktop

Have you ever wondered where the shortcuts on the desktop come from, and who owns them? I must confess that I was initially quite convinced that an Explorer module took care of regularly drawing the icons, taking account of user settings for their placement, color, status, and so on. This module would have drawn on top of the desktop background, over any wallpaper that the user might have set.

That's not the way it works. Instead, the shortcuts are just icons displayed by an ordinary ListView. Of course, this ListView has a variety of rather unusual styles, but it's definitely just a ListView. A consequence of this is that it's not hard to grab a handle to it and send some messages, as I'll prove in an example in Chapter 9.

The Structure of Explorer

Explorer is the application that plays the role of the system's shell. When we talk about shell extensions, we're talking about blocks of code that are detected, loaded and ultimately executed by Explorer.

Explorer can be considered as a sort of development environment — a kind of microcosm of the Windows environment. Think about it for a moment: it has its own set of functions and dialogs; it lets you write specific applications that integrate with the existing infrastructure; it can host applications and documents. It can even be scripted with any of the Active Scripting-compatible languages (VBScript, JScript, Perl, and so on). I'll be covering all of these features in this book.

Injection Points for Extensions

The File Manager that shipped with Windows 3.1 had a very nice but underused feature: it was capable of loading a DLL at runtime, and executing a registered function with a specific prototype. This means that there were well-defined points in the source where the code itself was 'aware' of some possible actions that could be carried out by the user. Put another way, it means that the File Manager had support for extensions – when executing certain actions, it looked for registered extensions, and loaded and ran them.

We find exactly the same principle behind Explorer's shell and namespace extensions – the difference is purely one of detail. File Manager used to load global functions from traditional DLLs with predefined prototypes, but Explorer makes this process more elegant. Specifically, it employs COM interfaces (which can be thought of as a collection of predefined and fixed function prototypes) and in-process servers (essentially DLLs).

> *Of course, COM interfaces and in-process servers are more than just a collection of functions and DLLs but their use makes Explorer's process more elegant and powerful than the old, DLL-based process.*

Extensions to Explorer

Basically, there are two types of extensions in Explorer's world: shell and namespace extensions. Their names are a little confusing. Explorer *is* the Windows shell, so both types could be considered shell extensions. On the other hand, while shell and namespace extensions both contribute to 'extending' the capabilities of Explorer, there are some differences between them.

A shell extension is a custom behavior that applies to all files of a given type when they are displayed in Explorer's view. Given this, we could call them, "shell view extensions". The custom behavior is triggered by a number of specific events such as dragging-and-dropping, right clicking to bring up a context-menu, drawing an icon, or displaying the Properties dialog. You can define your own handler for any of these events. For example, you can decide the icon to be displayed for a given .bmp file, add a preview page to the Properties dialog for all Windows metafiles, or even add a new function to an executable's context menu. I'll cover all these examples in Chapter 15.

A namespace extension can be one of two types, depending upon what you link it to. If you associate a namespace extension with a type of file, then it is functionally equivalent to a context menu extension, albeit with significantly more complicated code. However, if you associate a namespace extension with a folder, then that folder will become a custom folder. Your code will decide the content, the icon for Explorer to display, subfolders, sorting, context menus, and so on.

Why Program the Shell?

This is a very reasonable question. The simple answer is, "To make our applications better and richer," but that's a bit glib. We do it to integrate our modules with the system, or to automate some tasks for which there's no key combination, interface, or menu command. We do it to administer the system in a more flexible and powerful way. We do it to deliver more user-friendly applications. At least, these are the reasons why *I* program the Windows shell; I'm sure that, in time, you'll find there are many other reasons to do it.

Where This Book Will Take You

There are two ways to program the shell: using API functions and using COM interfaces. The two methods are not mutually exclusive, nor do they overlap. They are two different approaches and address two different areas of functionality. I'll say more about this in the next chapter, but in the meantime let's take a look at the direction the book will be taking in later chapters.

You know that shell programming requires the use of both API functions and COM interfaces. The API functions let you access the basic functionality of the shell, such as working with files, browsing folders, executing programs, and handling icons and shortcuts. The COM approach springs into life when you want to enhance and refine the basic shell's behavior with custom extensions.

This book will cover the API functionality first, digging deep into function prototypes, possible gaps in the documentation, and uncovering bugs. In general, my goal is to shed light on all the obscurities that you might have found. Chapters 3 to 9 are devoted to specific groups of APIs that span across the range of typical shell operations. In particular, Chapter 3 will tell you about SHFileOperation() – a function for copying, moving, deleting, or renaming files. Chapter 4 unveils the secrets of SHGetFileInfo(), the system-provided means to get both system and shell information about files (attributes, icons, type, display name). Chapter 5 in turn provides you with a crash-course on the internal organization of folders, covering settings, browsing, and special folders like Favorites and SendTo.

Shortcuts are featured in Chapter 6, where you will learn about creating and resolving shortcuts, and infrequently used fields. In Chapter 7 we enter Explorer's address space and discuss the other side of customization: what you can do safely without Explorer being aware of it. In particular, I'll show you how to replace the Start button with a new button and a different menu! Once you have done this, you have full control over the Windows system. The remaining chapters, 8 and 9, will tell you about program spawning, icons and the taskbar. I'll demonstrate how to add new buttons with their own menu to the taskbar, programmatically.

The second part of the book is based on those Explorer features that require COM interfaces, but this doesn't begin until Chapter 12. In the middle there are two chapters that bridge the gap between the shell functions and Explorer's interfaces. Chapter 10 covers the new SDKs that have been added with the most recent shell updates and requires Windows 98, or Windows 95/Windows NT 4.0 with Active Desktop installed. Chapter 11 provides an overview of shell objects such as My Briefcase, Control Panel and Printers and prepares you for the concept of custom folders. Scrap objects and the RunDLL32 utility are also covered in this chapter, and there is a full description of Explorer's command line.

In Chapter 12 I'll introduce the shell's object model – the first attempt to move a small subset of API functions into (dual) COM interfaces. This is a feature that, as a minimum, requires Active Desktop to be installed. What's interesting is that this object model allows you to access some functions (mostly system dialogs) that are otherwise unavailable.

Chapter 13 introduces the Windows Scripting Host. In a nutshell, this is the runtime engine that (at last!) lets you write Windows batch files. Technically speaking, it is a separate entity from the shell but there's a strict logical relationship between them. The Windows Scripting Host exposes an object model that you can program using VBScript, JScript or any other scripting language. I shall extend this model by adding useful new objects.

In Chapter 14 I shall begin to focus on the application and the reasons that might lead you to adopt shell or namespace extensions. I shall explain what a shell-integrated application actually is, and why shell extensions represent the best way to fuse your modules to the system's shell. In Chapter 15 I'll show how to write shell extensions to customize context menus, icons and properties, and how to debug them. Chapter 16 covers namespace extensions and includes an example that adds a new expandable node to Explorer's tree view, rendering the entire stack of currently extant windows in terms of folders.

Our trip around the Windows shell ends with a look at folder customization with Dynamic HTML and scripting. This is not purely for fun — it appears to be the easiest way to create namespace extensions!

The Plethora of Shell Versions

These days, you can't write a book about shell programming without first explaining the range of shell versions covered. In this case, it's easy — I'll cover every version that has appeared on Earth, from August 25, 1995 (the date that Windows 95 shipped) onwards. My approach will generally be task-based so I'll concentrate on functionality and warn you when a given feature requires a specific shell version. If you're running Windows 98, or IE 4.0x and the Active Desktop shell update on either Windows 95 or Windows NT 4.0, you won't have problems with any of the examples. Some of them may not work properly, however, if you haven't installed the Active Desktop updates, whether or not you have IE 4.0x installed.

The following table summarizes the shell version numbers for each platform. The version numbers refer to the `shell32.dll` file. You can check the version yourself by looking at the Version page of the DLL's Properties dialog, or dropping `shell32.dll` into the version testing utility that I'll build in Chapter 10!

System	Internet Explorer	Active Desktop	Version
Windows 95, NT 4	–	–	4.00
Windows 95, NT 4	IE 4.0	–	4.00
Windows 95, NT 4	IE 4.0x	–	4.00
Windows 95, NT 4	IE 4.0	Yes	4.71
Windows 95, NT 4	IE 4.01	Yes	4.72
Windows 95, NT 4	IE 4 SP1	Yes	4.72
Windows 98	–	–	4.72

The greater part of the functions and COM interfaces are already available with version 4.00 of the shell. More interesting is to see what changes with the newer versions. Version 4.71, which corresponds to the first release of the Active Desktop, bundled with IE 4.0, added functions such as:

- ❑ `SHGetSettings()`
- ❑ `SHGetSpecialFolderPath()`
- ❑ `SHInvokePrinterCommand()`
- ❑ `SHEmptyRecycleBin()`

- ❑ SHGetFreeDiskSpace()
- ❑ SHQueryRecycleBin()
- ❑ SHGetNewLinkInfo()

And some new COM interfaces, including:

- ❑ IURLSearchHook
- ❑ IQueryInfo
- ❑ IPersistFolder2
- ❑ IContextMenu3
- ❑ IInputObject
- ❑ ITaskbarList
- ❑ IDeskBand

Version 4.72 seems not to have changed anything in the programming interface.

There are some strange anomalies, however. For example, IShellView2 is commonly associated with Web View and the Active Desktop, but it's defined in the shlobj.h file that came with Visual Studio 97 in early March 1997. (IE 4.0 and Active Desktop shipped in fall '97.) Is IShellView2 supported by version 4.00, then? The answer is probably yes, but I really don't know for certain.

SHGetSettings(), SHEmptyRecycleBin(), and SHQueryRecycleBin() aren't marked as version 4.71 functions, even in the Visual Studio 6 documentation. Nevertheless, they aren't version 4.00 functions – just try to use them on the retail version of Windows 95, and see what happens!

A complete list of the currently supported interfaces and functions can be found in the Visual C++ online documentation and the Internet Client SDK. See the next section for more information on documentation.

Where is the Official Documentation?

To conclude, I'll point out where you can find the relevant official Microsoft documentation. Function prototypes, a syntax overview, and a few samples can be found in the MSDN library (under Platform SDK\User Interface Services\Shell and Common Controls\Windows Shell API). Also, the Internet Client SDK (which is, at the time of writing, available from http://www.microsoft.com/workshop/essentials) is a good source of information on all the most recent changes and version differences. Finally, the MSDN library also includes a few examples taken from MSJ and MIND articles and reprinted from books. (See the *Further Reading* sections at the end of each chapter.)

Summary

In this chapter I've outlined what we're going to be doing in the forthcoming chapters, and why. In particular, I've tried to explain:

- ❑ The nature and the structure of the shell
- ❑ Differences between the various shell versions
- ❑ Where to find the documentation that I'm aiming to extend

The Structure of the Shell

Under the umbrella of 'shell programming' are a number of API functions and COM interfaces. This heterogeneous collection of 'commands' allows you to program the Windows shell in different ways. Functions and interfaces are *not* two equivalent approaches that provide the same functionality. Instead, they provide different functionality at different logical levels.

API functions cover the basic operations a user might want to perform on the objects that populate the shell: files and folders. The COM interfaces give you the chance to extend, enhance and even customize the standard behavior of the various constituent objects, including that of the shell itself.

Grouping the functions and interfaces in a task-oriented manner will give us the chance to look at the shell as a whole. We can consider it rather as we would an object, with properties and methods. In this chapter, I'll attempt to identify what functional group each function or interface falls into. As a result, you should gain a better grasp of the shell's programming interface that will help when you're looking for that 'missing' piece of functionality.

In this chapter, we'll be covering:

- ❑ Definitions that we'll be using throughout the rest of the book
- ❑ Functional groups of shell API functions
- ❑ Functional groups of COM interfaces implemented by the shell and its inhabitants
- ❑ How the structure of the shell has evolved with the introduction of Active Desktop

By the end, you should have a better understanding of where the book is taking you, and a clear picture of how the kind of functionality that is available to you as a shell programmer.

The Pieces of the Shell

While we can't say that the Windows shell is object-oriented in practice, there are certainly some 'objects' that we can identify when looking at its structure. These 'objects' have attributes that sound like 'properties', and can they perform actions that sound like 'methods'. It's just that they rely on API functions to let you get and set them. A typical object is the folder.

If the shell isn't object-oriented, then neither is there an all-encompassing object model, although once again we can draw analogies. We can imagine a certain infrastructure that *looks like* a hierarchy of objects. Put another way, we have a collection of objects that work together in a manner represented by the following diagram:

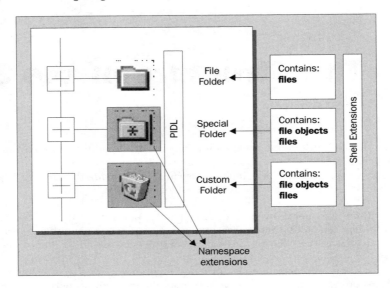

Basically, the shell is composed of **folders**. A folder is a container of child elements, including sub-folders — these elements are usually called **folder items**. The root folder is called Desktop, and its children include things like My Computer, Network Neighborhood, Recycle Bin, and possibly others depending on your PC's settings. The collection of all folders is called the shell's **namespace**.

The Shell's Namespace

Conceptually, a folder is something fairly similar to a directory in a file system, but it may or may not be bound to a real, physical directory. If it isn't bound in this fashion, it's called a **virtual folder**. We can distinguish two main categories of folders: ordinary folders (also named "file folders" or "directories"), and **custom folders**. Naturally enough, the items contained in a file folder are files, and their attributes are name, type, size, date last modified, and so forth. The items contained in any other type of folder *may* be files — usually with another, extended set of attributes — but could also be something completely different, like printers or network nodes.

Folders

How is a folder implemented? A folder is actually a shell 'object' whose behavior is coded into a COM module that exposes a common interface to the Windows shell. By means of this connection, a folder can tell the shell how to design its content, what icon to use to identify it, and what text to employ to describe it. This is what, for example, My Computer does to look like a folder. It has a layer of code that detects all the drives available on the PC, and adds a sub-tree to the Explorer's view for each one.

Each different type of folder has a different layer of code to provide its behavior. For file folders, this means scanning the file system, retrieving files and sub-folders, and displaying them through a list view control. The Printers folder, on the other hand, counts the connected and installed printers and displays an icon for each of them. You can have folders of virtually any type and with any behavior. File folders (that is, directories) are just one of all the possible types.

From all the folders that aren't file folders, the shell documentation picks up on a relatively small subset that it calls **special folders**. In fact, these are custom folders that the Windows shell provides by default, and they differ from file folders in the following ways:

- ❑ They can contain files *and* other 'objects'
- ❑ They can provide a different view of their content
- ❑ They can choose not to be bound to a physical directory
- ❑ They are part of a system-defined group for which the SDK offers a specific set of functions

A list of the special folders can be found in the Win32 SDK documentation, and later on in Chapter 5 of this book. Just as I said earlier, a special folder is a folder of a particular type with its own COM module to provide its behavior. Because this COM module is the reason for a new node being added to the shell's namespace, it is termed a **namespace extension**.

A special folder is intended to make system information available via a suitable user interface. In most cases, this means that the folder provides a view of its content that's more or less consistent with the typical view offered by a file folder. The precise kind of information, of course, depends upon the type of the folder.

Like ordinary file folders, special folders can contain files. However, they usually represent them in a slightly different way, showing different attributes. This occurs because a special folder assigns a special meaning to a file, and isn't treating it as a normal entry in the file system. (If this wasn't true, they wouldn't be that special...) The Recycle Bin, for example, holds ordinary but hidden files. Because the folder is intended to show the current list of files marked for deletion, it brings attributes like the original location, and the date of deletion to the fore.

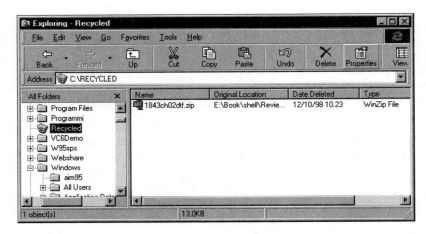

Most (but not all) of the special folders are tied to a physical directory on one of your disks. Normally this is a read-only directory whose content is all that is needed to display the intended information in the most suitable way.

Another way to look at it is this: most of the special folders need a directory in which to store their data. This directory may be located *anywhere* in the disk, and represents the junction between the folder and the rest of the shell – the location in the namespace where the special folder is placed. The content of this directory is not necessarily shown as a list of files. Instead, the code associated with the folder takes care of interpreting and displaying it in a way that best suits its intended role.

The ability to have a folder that can contain absolutely anything leads us to another couple of important concepts that we'll be dealing with extensively in the chapters to come: **file objects** and **PIDLs**.

File Objects

A 'file object' is an item contained in a generic folder – a file, a record, a block of memory, a connected device, and so on. 'Folder items', 'elements of a folder', and 'file objects' are all equivalent expressions to refer to the individual items within a folder. If the folder is a file folder, then a file object is nothing more than a file. The word 'file' is therefore a bit more specific than 'file object', because it refers to a precise entry in the file system. A file is a file object, but a file object is not always a file.

There's a subtle problem hidden behind these generalized concepts of folders and folder items. How can we safely and uniquely identify each item in the shell's namespace? If the shell coincides with the file system (as it does in Windows 3.*x*) then the fully qualified name of the file is an excellent guarantee of uniqueness. You can't possibly have two files with the same name and path. However, when a folder becomes something more general than a directory of files, a more general way of identifying its items is needed.

The Structure of the Shell

PIDLs

A **PIDL** is a data structure that's meant to identify an item contained in a folder uniquely. A PIDL – the acronym stands for **p**ointer to an **id**entifier **l**ist – is more versatile than a fully qualified file name. It has to guarantee the uniqueness of the item not just within the folder, but also throughout the shell's namespace. More importantly, it must be able to handle files and file objects transparently. To understand the structure and the role of PIDLs, let's analyze the binary structure and compare it with the path names that they replace.

A fully qualified file name is just a string, but it's a string with a very particular format. It's a concatenation of substrings, each of which identifies a level in the file system's hierarchy. You have the drive name, then the directory name(s), the filename, and finally the extension, all separated by backslashes. What you perceive to be a fully qualified file name is no more than a pointer to these concatenated elements – a pointer to a string in this case. Conceptually, you could see it as a pointer to an array of structures, each of which identifies an element of the path name.

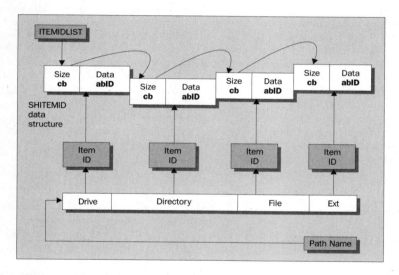

The figure illustrates the relationship between a path name and a PIDL. At the same time, it gives an idea of how an identifier list is organized in memory. From the programmer's point of view, a PIDL is implemented using an `LPITEMIDLIST` type, which is just a pointer to an `ITEMIDLIST` structure.

```
typedef struct _ITEMIDLIST
{
    SHITEMID mkid;
} ITEMIDLIST, *LPITEMIDLIST;
```

The intermediate objects that make up the various parts of a path name map to the **item identifiers** of a PIDL. They're rendered through a `SHITEMID` structure:

```
typedef struct _SHITEMID
{
    USHORT cb;
    BYTE   abID[1];
} SHITEMID, *LPSHITEMID;
```

19

The first two bytes of this structure denote the size of the item identifier — that is, the number of bytes taken up by the data associated with the element and used to identify it. The cb value must include also its own size. Mapping to path names, cb would be the length of the string representing the drive or the directory, plus the length of an unsigned short variable. Following that in the structure is the first byte of the data.

A fundamental point to bear in mind is that a PIDL must be a 'flat' structure, and can't include pointers. All the data that comes together to form a PIDL must be explicitly embedded, rather than linked through a pointer. This means that we can't use the typical schema of a list composed of structures whose final member points to the next element in the chain. There's another point, however. As you can see, the address of the next element in the list can be calculated by adding cb bytes to the address of the current SHITEMID object. This is by design, but it still requires that consecutive SHITEMIDs be contiguously allocated.

Defining the rules for constructing PIDLs is up to the code that implements the behavior of the folder whose items they represent. This code should also decide what data must be used to identify each item identifier. For example, suppose that you wanted to implement a folder that renders the Windows registry as if it were a file system. Your 'subfolders' will be the registry keys, and your 'file objects' will be the registry values. A possible way of identifying each element in this folder would be to use the names of keys involved. Here's how that PIDL may look using the same diagrammatic format as we had in the previous figure. Notice that HKEY_CLASSES_ROOT is a long value, so it takes four bytes plus the two bytes of an unsigned short.

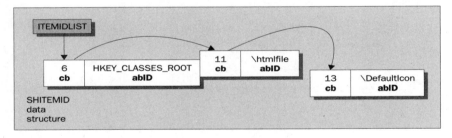

The chain of item identifiers traces the path from the root of the namespace to a specific item in a specific folder. The identifier list gathers all the elements of the chain and represents a way of distinguishing an element that's unique throughout the shell. Making sure that two item identifiers are contiguously allocated in memory is the responsibility of the code that wraps the folder object.

While path names and PIDLs are similar, they certainly aren't equivalent, and they can't be used interchangeably. They are different data structures.

There are a actually a few other issues to take into account when it comes to defining the rules for a PIDL, and we'll be examining them in detail when we look at namespace extensions at greater length in Chapter 16.

The Shell's View

The content of any folder is displayed inside Windows Explorer through an object called a **shell view**. Each folder defines its own shell view object, and delegates to it all the tasks that relate to its user interface. The shell view object for a file folder is implemented using a list view control whose items are the names of the files and the subfolders. The default shell view object assigns an icon, a **display name** and a **type name** to each file it is called upon to treat.

The icon may be determined in several ways, depending on the nature of the file in question. Usually, icon files (.ico) are rendered using the icon they define, while programs (.exe) display the first icon defined in their resources. If no icon is present, a default one is used. For all other files, the shell *usually* employs the icon defined for the class that the file belongs to. However, this behavior can be customized, as I'll explain in a while.

Throughout the shell, files are grouped together by types that are specified using file extensions. The set of files of a certain type is often referred as a **file class**, which is associated with an icon and a descriptive string that's shown under the Type column in the Details view of Windows Explorer. For this to take place, however, the file class needs to be registered in the system registry, from where the shell will read the information about the type, and its icon.

Once you've defined a file class (as described in Chapter 14), you can write code that affects and modifies the default behavior of the shell in response to some events that take place on files of a certain class. These include drawing the icon for a file, popping up the context menu, and displaying the Properties dialog. By defining a **shell extension**, you can decide dynamically what to do when those events take place. It's possible, for example, to add new items to a context menu and handle the user clicking on them, and to determine dynamically, on a per-file basis, what icon to display.

Hooking the Shell

In general, shell extensions can be seen as **hooks** that are set throughout the shell. In Win32, a 'hook' is a piece of code defined by an application that the system calls back when a certain event is about to occur. There are about a dozen different types of hook, and they can vary widely in their scope: some affect only the application that installed them, while others impact upon all the applications running in the system.

A typical example of this kind of thing is the keyboard hook that allows your code to be informed of a keypress before the corresponding message is sent to the interested window. Other activities subject to hooking are mouse actions (movements, clicking), window management (creation, destruction, activation), and message handling. See the Win32 SDK documentation for a complete list.

From the programmer's perspective, a hook is a **callback function** with a fixed and predefined syntax. As a callback function, the system calls it on the basis of a well-known prototype. A shell extension is a COM interface rather than a callback function, but the principle behind it is the same: both allow you to specify some code the system will execute while in the process of some predefined action.

The subject of scope is particularly interesting for Windows hooks. By setting a local hook, you catch only the events that occur within the context of the application, but the result of setting a global hook is that you'll get informed when the hooked event occurs in *any* running application. Setting a global hook means that your application is defining a piece of code that other applications, running in the context of other processes, will execute. In fact, this is the easiest way under Win32 of breaking process boundaries and injecting your own code into the address space of another process. It is also the only approach that works on all platforms, from Windows 95 to Windows 98 and NT 4.

> *Process memory separation is a huge topic that's not among the goals of this book. Excellent coverage, however, may be found in the 3rd edition of Jeffrey Richter's* Advanced Windows *(Microsoft Press).*

The Shell's Address Space

Injecting code into the context of another process is important because it allows you to gain access to the unexposed objects of the other process, and this is particularly important and interesting for shell programmers. When you successfully insert your code into the shell's address space, you can query for the shell's interfaces, change the user interface, and even replace the ubiquitous Start button (as I'll show you in Chapter 7).

Global hooks are one way of letting your code run in the shell's address space, but a more powerful and flexible mechanism is provided by **browser helper objects** – COM objects that Explorer and Internet Explorer both load automatically each time their main window starts up.

The Shell's Memory Allocator

Sooner or later, working with the shell is going to require you to allocate memory within its address space for your own purposes, and to this end the shell provides you with the **memory allocator**. This service, which is a wrapper built around the `IMalloc` interface, can be used as a replacement for `new` or `GlobalAlloc()`.

To get a reference to this object, you should call `SHGetMalloc()`. What you're returned is not a new pointer to the `IMalloc` interface – you can get one of those using `CoGetMalloc()` – but a reference to the `IMalloc` object held by the system's shell. With this pointer you can safely free memory that has been allocated by the shell, and have the shell free your memory. It might sound a little strange, but these practices are not so uncommon in shell programming.

The Shell's Taskbar

The taskbar window is a well-known part of the Windows user interface, if for no other reason then because it contains the Start button. What we call the "Windows taskbar", however, is actually a special case of a family of windows called 'application desktop toolbars', the best-known example of which is probably the Office 97 shortcut bar. There's a specific set of functions and messages that address desktop toolbars, but interestingly only a very few of them affect the Windows taskbar. As a result, even if it is not clearly pointed out by the documentation, the system taskbar and desktop toolbar may be considered different objects.

Another common misconception about the taskbar is that it contains as many buttons as there are running applications, but this is untrue for two reasons:

- ❑ Not all the running applications show up in the taskbar
- ❑ The only child of the taskbar that's a button is the Start button

Believe it or not, what appears to be a collection of buttons is actually a tab control with a special, button-like style.

The role of the taskbar is that of a system console, giving you access to all the running programs. In many cases, it would be desirable to be able to limit the functionality of the taskbar – this is a typical requirement of applications intended to run on publicly available PCs, where you don't want users to be able to run other programs or browse the file system. The Win32 API doesn't provide a rich set of functions to work on the taskbar, but I'll try to remedy this in Chapter 9.

The Shell API Functions

The version of the MSDN library that ships with Visual C++ 6.0 lists over 100 functions in its shell reference section. However, a good number of these deal with very specific areas that sometimes are at the margin of what is commonly perceived as being the Windows shell – I'm referring in particular to the routines that deal with parsing files, and with the screen saver.

You won't find an exhaustive guide to every single one of those functions in this book. Instead, we'll concentrate on the core functions that work on files and folders, and try to shed light on their often obscure and poor documentation. To help in categorizing them further, I've identified five different functional groups.

Group	Functions
General Windows Functions	Functions to deal with screen savers, Control Panel applets, context-sensitive help, and shell drag-and-drop. (*Not* OLE drag-and-drop.)
Shell Internals	Functions to access Explorer's address space, get the shell's memory allocator, launch executables, and detect changes in the user interface.
Taskbar	Functions that deal with the tray area and communicate with the Windows taskbar.
Files	Functions that operate on files. They execute system actions like 'copy', 'move', 'delete' and 'get information', and add files to special system folders like Recent Documents.
Folders	Functions that work on folders. By the means of these functions, you can browse for folders, get the path of a system folder, or discover the settings of a folder.

Along with these groups, there are a few others whose functions are not explicitly referred to as being part of the shell's programming interface, but in my opinion they definitely deserve to appear in the list.

Group	Functions
Icons	Functions to extract icons from executable files.
Environment	Functions to manipulate environment variables.
Shell Lightweight API	Functions to access the registry easily, for reading and writing, to handle path names, and to manipulate strings.

In particular, there are functions for working with icons and environment strings in the `shellapi.h` header file, which is the main reason that led me to include them here. As for the Shell Lightweight API (which is examined in detail in Chapter 10), let's say the functions it provides could be placed in any number of categories, but that they apply particularly well to programming the shell.

The tables that follow this section list and describe some of the functions in the categories I've defined here. I do this so that you get a better idea of the kinds of operations we'll be looking at over the course of the book, and to provide you with a place that you can come to look up quickly any function I use later on whose purpose temporarily slips your mind.

General Windows Functions

As the name suggests, these functions affect the Windows shell only marginally. In most cases, the functions come directly from the Windows 3.1*x* API – they handle things like help files and drag-and-drop. All of them are well supported in any 32-bit version of the shell.

Function	Description
DragAcceptFiles()	Toggles the style that enables a window to accept drag-and-drop.
DragFinish()	Frees the memory allocated to move a list of file names from the shell.
DragQueryFile()	Extracts file names from the memory block the shell allocated to hold dragged files.
DragQueryPoint()	Obtains the point where the drop occurred.
CPlApplet()	Main procedure for a Control Panel applet.
GetMenuContextHelpId()	Returns the ID of the help context for a given menu.
GetWindowContextHelpId()	Returns the ID of the help context for a given window.
SetMenuContextHelpId()	Sets the ID of the help context for a given menu.
SetWindowContextHelpId()	Sets the ID of the help context for a given window.
WinHelp()	Opens a help file.
ShellAbout()	Displays a default and partially customizable About box.

Shell Internals

This category contains functions that work with the shell at the lowest level. Also, they let you enter the address space of the shell in order that you may do work alongside it, and gain access to its memory.

Function	Description
ShellExecute()	Executes the specified operation on the specified file.
ShellExecuteEx()	The same as above, but with more options.
SHChangeNotify()	Through this function, a program can let the shell know about changes that require it to refresh the information it holds.
SHGetInstanceExplorer()	Returns Explorer's IUnknown interface pointer.
SHGetMalloc()	Returns a pointer to the shell memory allocator.
SHLoadInProc()	Loads the specified COM object into Explorer's address space.

Taskbar Functions

The Windows shell doesn't define many functions to work with the taskbar, so you often end up having to do most of the work yourself. (I'll show you how in Chapter 9.) However, there are a couple of functions related to the taskbar:

Function	Description
Shell_NotifyIcon()	Displays and manages icons in the tray area, near the clock.
SHAppBarMessage()	Sends messages to the system's taskbar.

File Functions

The file is one of the most important elements in the Windows shell. A graphical environment requires a file to have many different attributes, which in turn means specific functions to deal with them. Note the appearance in this table of the **Version** column; some of the functions in this and later categories were introduced in recent versions of the shell, and this column reflects that fact.

Function	Description	Version
FindExecutable()	Returns the path of the executable file registered to handle a file of given name.	Any
SHAddToRecentDocs()	Adds a link to a given file to the system's Recent Documents folder.	Any

Table Continued on Following Page

Function	Description	Version
SHFileOperation()	Used to copy, move, delete or rename one or more files at a time.	Any
SHFreeNameMappings()	Frees a memory structure returned by SHFileOperation() under certain circumstances.	Any
SHGetFileInfo()	Returns various pieces of information about a given file.	Any
SHGetNewLinkInfo()	Creates the proper name for a new shortcut file.	4.71

Folder Functions

As we've discussed, a folder is a little more general than a directory: it can contain more than just files. Furthermore, the software behind a folder is directly involved in returning a unique identifier for each of its items. Under the Active Desktop, a folder can also have its own set of graphical attributes.

Function	Description	Version
SHBrowseForFolder()	Displays a dialog that lets you choose a folder.	Any
SHEmptyRecycleBin()	Destroys the content of the Recycle Bin folder.	4.71
SHGetDataFromIDList()	Retrieves data from an identifier list.	Any
SHGetDesktopFolder()	Returns the IShellFolder pointer for the Desktop folder.	Any
SHGetDiskFreeSpace()	Returns the amount of free disk space for a specified drive.	4.71
SHGetPathFromIDList()	Returns the path name (if any) for the specified identifier list.	Any
SHGetSpecialFolder Location()	Returns the identifier list for the specified system folder.	4.71
SHGetSpecialFolderPath()	Returns the path name (if any) for the specified system folder.	Any
SHGetSettings()	Returns a value denoting the current settings for that folder.	4.71
SHInvokePrinterCommand()	Allows you to send commands to the printer.	4.71
SHQueryRecycleBin()	Returns the amount of space the Recycle Bin is currently taking up.	4.71

Icon Functions

Icons are central to a graphical environment like Windows, and the shell is the most visible part of the operating system. Consequently, in my opinion, icons are central to the Windows shell programming interface.

Function	Description
ExtractIcon()	Returns an icon handle from an executable file.
ExtractIconEx()	The same as above, but with more options.
ExtractAssociatedIcon()	Returns the icon handle for the specified file, based on the file class.

The COM Interfaces

We can perform a similar trick with the COM interfaces involved with the shell as we did with the API functions. Once again, using the version of the MSDN library that ships with Visual C++ 6.0 as a reference, we can count up to four different categories of shell-related COM interfaces.

Group	Interfaces
Shell extensions	The COM interfaces that get involved in all the shell's activities, from icons to context menus, and from UI activation to file viewers.
Namespace extensions	The COM interfaces usually involved with namespace extensions.
Hook	The interfaces that let you 'hook' onto something. Specifically, program execution, URL translation and the creation of Internet shortcuts.
Miscellaneous	Interfaces to customize the taskbar, to communicate with the **Open** common dialog, and to program the My Briefcase object.

Not all of these interfaces always have to be implemented by developers – in some cases, you only need to know enough about them to be able to invoke their methods properly. Let's see them in a bit more detail.

Shell Interfaces

Under this heading, I've put all the COM interfaces that eventually have something to do with the shell and its extensions.

Interface	Description	Version
IFileViewer, IFileViewerSite	Let you define modules to provide **Quick View** handlers for a given type of file.	Any
IInputObject, IInputObjectSite	These interfaces are used to handle UI activation and process accelerators for objects contained in the shell that can accept input from the user.	4.71

Table Continued on Following Page

Interface	Description	Version
IShellIconOverlay, IShellIconOverlay Identifier	Used to manage the icon overlay for files, letting you know which overlay is used for a given file. An icon overlay is a bitmap the shell draws over an icon better to qualify it, like the hand that indicates a shared folder.	4.71
IContextMenu, IContextMenu2	Allows you to add new items to the context menu for a particular type of file. IContextMenu2 handles owner-drawn menus.	Any
IContextMenu3	The same as IContextMenu2, but allowing better keyboard control.	4.71
IShellExtInit	Takes care of initializing a shell extension.	Any
IShellChangeNotify	The shell extension counterpart of the SHChangeNotify() API function. Basically, it allows you to write a module that hooks on the changes at the shell level notified through SHChangeNotify().	4.71
IExtractIcon	Enables you to obtain icon information for any folder item.	Any
IShellIcon	Provides an alternative way of getting icons for any folder item that is superior to IExtractIcon under certain circumstances.	Any
IShellLink	Allows you to create and resolve shortcuts to files and folders.	Any
IShellPropSheetExt	Used to add new pages to the Properties dialog for a given file class.	Any

Namespace Interfaces

To write namespace extensions (as we will in Chapter 16), you will need to acquaint yourself with a considerable number of COM interfaces. Here are the most important and necessary ones.

Interface	Description	Version
IShellView, IShellView2	Used to define a view object for a namespace extension. IShellView2 is still not documented, but it's used in Web-based views.	Any
IShellBrowser	Represents the browser, be it Explorer or Internet Explorer.	Any
IEnumIDList	Provides methods to let the shell enumerate the content of a folder.	Any

Interface	Description	Version
IShellFolder	Provides methods to let the shell handle a custom folder in a standard way. IShellFolder hides custom code from Explorer.	Any
IPersistFolder	Lets you initialize some shell extensions and any namespace extension.	Any
IPersistFolder2	The same as above, plus some enhancements to support Web-based views.	4.71
IQueryInfo	Retrieves flags and infotip text for items in a folder.	4.71

Hook Interfaces

The Windows shell gives our modules the opportunity to detect a certain number of events, and to add our own custom code in the middle.

Interface	Description	Version
ICopyHook	Lets you hook onto any file operation (copy, move, delete, rename) in the shell.	Any
IURLSearchHook	Lets you hook while Explorer is trying to translate an unknown URL protocol.	4.71
INewShortcutHook	Lets you hook while Explorer is trying to create a new Internet shortcut.	4.71
IShellExecuteHook	Lets you hook up to the startup of any new process instigated through ShellExecute() or ShellExecuteEx().	Any

Miscellaneous Interfaces

The remaining interfaces cover specific areas of shell programming: My Briefcase, common dialogs, and the taskbar.

Interface	Description	Version
INotifyReplica, IReconcilableObject, IReconcileInitiator	All these interfaces are involved in the file reconciliation process that ends up with a new and unique updated version of the same document.	Any
ICommDlgBrowser	Provides special behavior when a custom folder is hosted inside the common dialog boxes.	Any
ITaskbarList	Enables you to add new buttons to the system's taskbar.	4.71

Why the API? Why COM?

Now that we've looked at the functionality provided by the Windows shell, it's time to give a little thought to the roles played by API functions and COM interfaces. Essentially, the whole set of shell functionality can be divided up into two areas: basic functions and extensions. From this point of view, it's easy to see which approach addresses which area.

At present, much of the functionality offered through API calls can be seen as the 'methods' of a pseudo-object called "the shell". This pseudo-object enables you to move or copy files, or to browse for folders. You can also retrieve information about a given document, and so on. The first signs of an object model begin to delineate themselves.

On the other hand, Windows was originally designed in pure C, and it has never really been re-thought in terms of an object-oriented design. From that perspective, it's not surprising at all that we have basic functionality exposed through straight API calls.

COM allows components to be written and then used through interfaces they choose to expose, and by no other means. Using interfaces, it's easy to gather related functions and provide access to a given object. From the shell's point of view, COM interfaces are an evolution of the API calls – you can see this in the ITaskbarList interface, which is one of the first examples of a system component whose programming interface is exposed through COM, and not through API calls.

Other examples of this pattern are the hook interfaces we met above. The Win32 SDK is full of hooks, but they are programmed through callback functions, not COM interfaces. The shell programming interface, on the other hand, contains hooks that require you to write, and properly register, a COM server. In practice, the difference is not that great, but architecturally speaking they're a world apart.

In summary, there's a wind of change blowing through the Windows shell, and COM is its source. Aside from the examples already mentioned, all the remaining COM interfaces are used to extend Explorer's behavior. Because Explorer requires in-process servers by design, they all fall into a kind of parallel container that is just as important as the one that contains API calls and a few COM interfaces here and there. They can be seen as the two sides of the same coin (the coin being the shell), but they are definitely distinct.

What Changed with Active Desktop

The Active Desktop shell update brought with it some new features and changed several aspects of the Windows shell. It encourages the use of HTML wherever possible, and introduces the concept of a Web view, folder customization, scripting capabilities, a simplified but effective object model, and a handful of new functions and COM interfaces.

The last item in the above list is particularly interesting: we now have the very first shell object model, exposing some of the shell's functionality through COM objects. This has been done primarily with the benefit of Visual Basic programmers in mind, and so far the model is incomplete and not as flexible as you might expect, but it's an important first step.

Apart from the changes in the shell API, Active Desktop represents a noteworthy evolution of the structure of the desktop and the folders. In particular, it has changed:

- ❑   The shell view object
- ❑   The structure of the taskbar

In addition, and as a consequence of the enhanced shell view object, we now have the possibility of executing script code at the folder level, even exploiting the facilities of Dynamic HTML and Scriptlets.

The New Shell View Object

Originally, the shell view object was rendered and implemented through a stack of windows at the top of which was one of class SHELLDLL_DefView. You have already seen this in Chapter 1:

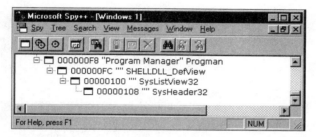

The screenshot shows the view object of the desktop, but it is exactly the same for any other folder. The picture below, for example, shows the stack of windows for the My Computer folder:

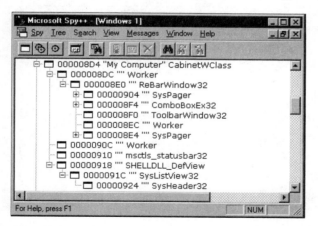

Most of the windows you see here collaborate to form the overall framework of the folder window (rebar windows, combo box, toolbars, etc.). What provides the actual *content* of the folder (namely, the shell view object) is always a window of class SHELLDLL_DefView, with its child list view.

With Active Desktop, however, there's the possibility of another kind of view object that includes support for HTML and scripting too. This is called the **Web view**, and it can be turned on and off from the folder's View I as Web Page menu. Here's how the My Computer window looks when the Web view is active:

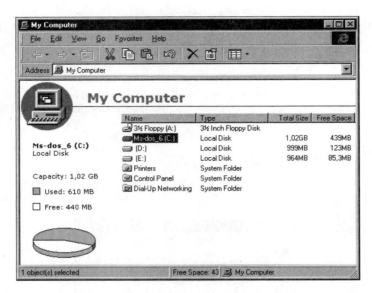

The content of the folder appears to be merged into an HTML-based template, of which the list view containing details of the file objects is just a component. The corresponding stack of windows is:

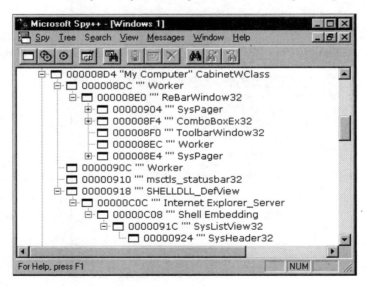

The big difference you'll notice almost immediately is the window of class `Internet Explorer_Server` that has a child window of class `Shell Embedding`. The former of these is the window through which the WebBrowser control displays its output, while `Shell Embedding` is a window that wraps the list view that contains the file list.

WebBrowser is the ActiveX component used by Internet Explorer 3.0 and higher to display their content: HTML files, GIF and JPEG images, and even Active documents.

To summarize, when a Web view is enabled on a file folder, then

❑ A folder is seen through an HTML page rendered by a WebBrowser control

❑ The HTML page is generated starting with an HTML template that you can customize if necessary

❑ The list view containing the files is embedded into an ActiveX control hosted in the HTML page

A Web view could also be enabled on a custom folder, but in this case the namespace extension that wraps the folder would be required to implement specific and additional interfaces.

On the desktop, things go in much the same way. You can turn on and off the Web view by using the context menu:

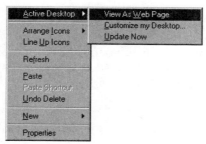

When this view is active, the desktop's view object also makes use of a WebBrowser control to show the desktop content. The desktop icons are drawn in a different, 'higher' layer than the background, and although this 'icon layer' existed before Active Desktop, the Web view adds some underlying HTML 'wallpaper' whose content is always drawn underneath the icons.

Customizing a Folder

When the Web view mode is turned on, the folders you visit are displayed using an HTML template. There's a standard folder template called `folder.htt` stored in the `Web` subdirectory of Windows, and unless you specify another one, it is used by default. If you want to study its source code, note that it is a hidden file, so you won't see it until you turn on your Show all files setting.

By right clicking on any folder, you get a menu like the one shown in the screenshot:

Choosing <u>C</u>ustomize this Folder... allows you to run a fairly straightforward Wizard that ends up editing the content of the `folder.htt` file that I've already mentioned. More precisely, what you actually edit is a copy of the original template created by the Wizard in the folder in question. If you need to, you can alter the look of the folder completely simply by editing the HTML file – despite the `.htt`, extension it is a perfectly normal HTML file. If you want to, you can also remove or replace the file list component, showing only what you want the user to see.

Since the folder template is an HTML file viewed through the Internet Explorer's WebBrowser, you can exploit all the features that XML, data binding, Dynamic HTML, and Scriptlets bring to you, and transform a simple folder into something that looks like an application. (I presented an example of this in the March 1998 issue of MIND.) After a fashion, this kind of customization is rather like a rough and ready namespace extension.

The New Taskbar Layout

As well as the changes in the view object, Active Desktop also introduced a number of changes to the layout of the taskbar. We will examine it in more detail in Chapter 9, but the following diagram should give you an idea of what to expect, and a comparison of the new structure with the old one:

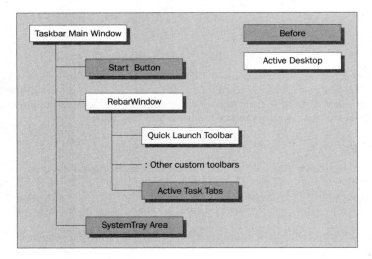

Summary

In this chapter, we addressed:

- ❏ Task-based groups of API functions and COM interfaces in the Windows shell
- ❏ How this maps to the book's layout
- ❏ An overview of the shell structure and its objects

As we progress through this book, I'll always try to make sure the structure of the shell programming interface stays clear in your mind. Thus, in the next few chapters, you'll find details about the most tricky-to-use and poorly documented API functions. The code presented will mostly involve calls to SDK functions using 'vanilla' C++.

After that, we'll start moving towards shell and namespace extensions, looking at some useful COM interfaces for hooking and programming along the way, and examining the primitive shell object model. There's a long way to go, and we haven't even looked at any code yet. It's about time we put that right.

3

Working with Files

I still remember when the first betas of Windows 95 were on the way, and rumors were spreading amongst my friends and colleagues. How cool was the new File Manager? It was full of icons, it was colorful, it was customizable, and it had little animations that could make your life easier and happier when it came to copying or deleting files!

As real software maniacs, we started a competition (with a pizza as the prize) to be the first person able to figure out how to reproduce that behavior programmatically – that is, how to copy files with animation. It took a few hours to extricate SHFileOperation() from the heap of new functions. SHFileOperation() is the API function responsible for animated copying, and more generally, for all the file operations performed by Explorer.

One of the criteria for the competition was to create a demonstration program with the sole goal of impressing colleagues, which was simple enough; the real problems with this function appeared later on. In fact, they cropped up exactly when I decided to adopt it as the standard function for any file operation in my programs! To do this, I needed a thorough knowledge of the function's prototype and its capabilities, and it is at this point that the really interesting part of the story begins.

In this chapter, I'm going to show you the inner secrets of SHFileOperation():

- ❑ How to use the flags and commands that it supports correctly
- ❑ How to use the source and target buffers correctly
- ❑ What its 'most probable' return codes are
- ❑ The problems you may encounter with long file names (yes, really!)
- ❑ The (previously) unrevealed story of file name mappings

Also included in this chapter – as in any other of this book – you'll find helper functions to facilitate your work with Windows common controls, dialogs, and the like.

What Can SHFileOperation() do for You?

To get an answer to this question, let's have a look at the declaration of SHFileOperation(), taken from shellapi.h:

```
int WINAPI SHFileOperation(LPSHFILEOPSTRUCT lpFileOp);
```

This tells us little more than we knew already. To find out more, let's snoop inside SHFILEOPSTRUCT, which is a data structure also defined in shellapi.h:

```
typedef struct _SHFILEOPSTRUCT
{
    HWND            hwnd;
    UINT            wFunc;
    LPCSTR          pFrom;
    LPCSTR          pTo;
    FILEOP_FLAGS    fFlags;
    BOOL            fAnyOperationsAborted;
    LPVOID          hNameMappings;
    LPCSTR          lpszProgressTitle;
} SHFILEOPSTRUCT, FAR* LPSHFILEOPSTRUCT;
```

Through this structure, SHFileOperation() can be instructed to do everything we want. In brief, the function can:

- ❑ Copy one or more files from a source to a target path
- ❑ Delete one or more files, sending them to the Recycle Bin
- ❑ Rename files
- ❑ Move one or more files from a source to a target path

So far, then, we've seen nothing new – or at least, nothing particularly exciting. In fact, the Win32 API (and the C runtime library) already provide the means to do the same thing. Specifically, the Win32 API provides CopyFile(), DeleteFile(), and MoveFile() to perform these tasks.

The strength of SHFileOperation(), however, comes in all its accessory parameters which let you arrange for multiple copies and the creation of missing directories with a single command. It also supports 'undo', and automatic renaming in the case of target name collisions. Last (but probably not least), it provides, for free, an animation that shows blank sheets of paper, fluttering from one folder to another.

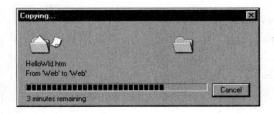

Undoubtedly, you could obtain the same functionality from the low-level Win32 APIs mentioned above, but you would have a large amount of work to do.

How SHFileOperation() Works

Like all functions that take only a data structure as an input parameter, SHFileOperation() is quite a flexible routine. It can perform many different actions by combining various flags in the appropriate manner, and by using (or not using) the various members of SHFILEOPSTRUCT. Let's see what role each member of this structure plays.

Name	Description
hwnd	The handle of the parent window for any dialog generated by this function.
wFunc	Indicates the operation to perform. (See later.)
pFrom	The buffer containing the source file names.
pTo	The buffer containing the target file names. (Ignored in case of deletion.)
fFlags	Flags that can affect the operation. (See later.)
fAnyOperationsAborted	A return value that will contain TRUE or FALSE depending on whether the user aborted any file operations before completion. By testing this member you can determine whether the operation completed normally, or if it was manually interrupted.
hNameMappings	The documentation describes it as a "Handle to a file name mapping object that contains an array of SHNAMEMAPPING structures." (See later for a better explanation.)
lpszProgressTitle	A string that is used, under certain conditions, as the title of the dialog box being displayed.

In short, there are four members that definitely require some investigation. They are:

- ❑ wFunc (**and indirectly,** pFrom **and** pTo)
- ❑ fFlags
- ❑ hNameMappings
- ❑ lpszProgressTitle

Available Operations

The wFunc member specifies the operation to be performed on the files specified in pFrom and pTo. The possible values of wFunc (defined in shellapi.h) are:

Code	Value	Description
FO_MOVE	0x0001	All the files specified in pFrom are moved to the location stored in pTo, which must be a directory name.
FO_COPY	0x0002	All the files specified in pFrom are copied to the location stored in pTo. The latter can be a directory name or even a collection of files with a 1:1 correspondence to the ones in pFrom.
FO_DELETE	0x0003	All the files specified in pFrom are sent to the Recycle Bin. pTo is ignored.
FO_RENAME	0x0004	All the files specified in pFrom are renamed as the file names specified in pTo. A 1:1 correspondence must exist between the names in pFrom and pTo.

Both pFrom and pTo are buffers that contain one or more file names. If they include more than one file name, then the various names must be separated with NULL characters (\0) and the whole string must be terminated with a double NULL character (\0\0), regardless of how many file names it contains.

If pFrom and pTo don't include directory information (that is, they are unqualified names) then the function assumes that it should use the drive and the directory returned by GetCurrentDirectory(). pFrom can also contain wildcard characters, and can be a string such as "*.*".

Any of these operations can be affected by the flags that you set in the fFlags member of the SHFILEOPSTRUCT structure. The online documentation lists all these flags in alphabetical order, which is not always a good thing. When I discuss them shortly, I'll try to follow a slightly different approach in which the flags are grouped together according to the actual operations they can affect. If you just want a crude list, refer to the online documentation.

Pay Attention to the Double-NULL

In my opinion, the documentation doesn't place sufficient emphasis on the fact that pFrom and pTo are actually pointers to lists of strings, rather than generic buffers. This means that SHFileOperation() always expects a double NULL character at the end of the string passed, and this is true even when you're passing a single file name, or a single string with wildcards.

If you don't use a double NULL character to terminate the strings in both pFrom and pTo, the chances are that the function will fail when parsing their contents. In this case, it returns a 'Cannot Copy/Move File' error (error code 1026). Without a double NULL, the function may consider the bytes that it finds at the end of the string, after the single NULL character, as a file name to be copied or moved. These bytes could be anything and are unlikely to be a valid file name, so an error arises.

This error is more frequent with pFrom, simply because pFrom is always interpreted as a list of file names, whereas pTo is parsed as a list of file names only if the FOF_MULTIDESTFILES flag is specified (we'll be discussing this and other similar flags shortly). In all other cases, SHFileOperation() assumes that pTo refers to a single file name. In this case, a single NULL terminator suffices – the double NULL is required only for terminating a list containing more than one file name. Unless you explicitly say that there are multiple target files, the parsing of the content of pTo stops at the first NULL terminator.

The way the content is parsed depends upon whether the pointer is the reference to a list of strings or a simple buffer. Consequently, for safety's sake, you should always remember to add an additional terminator at the end of the strings you're going to assign to pFrom. Do the same to pTo if you have multiple destination files. If you're using literals, then you can add an explicit \0 at the end (the string is, of course, automatically terminated with a single NULL character):

```
shfo.pFrom = "c:\\demo\\one.txt\0c:\\demo\\two.txt\0";
```

If you're using variables, then you can adopt the following approach:

```
pszFrom[lstrlen(pszFrom) + 1] = 0;
```

Moving and Copying Files

To move or copy files from one location to another, we need to specify:

- ❑ A buffer containing the source file names. This can be a sequence of names (separated and qualified as shown above), a single name, a string that includes wildcards, or even a sequence of strings that include wildcards.
- ❑ A target directory. If we're moving a well-defined list of files, then we could also prepare a target list of names, taking care to preserve a 1:1 correspondence with the source names. In other words, each source file name must have a target file name in order for the move or copy to take place. If there *are* multiple target files, then we *must* specify the FOF_MULTIDESTFILES flag in the fFlags member.

The flags (defined in shellapi.h) that can affect these operations are:

Flag	Value	Description
FOF_MULTIDESTFILES	0x0001	The pTo member contains multiple target files, one for each source file.
FOF_SILENT	0x0004	The operation occurs without feedback to the user, which means that the progress dialog isn't displayed. Any relevant message boxes will still appear, however.
FOF_RENAMEONCOLLISION	0x0008	If the target location already contains a file with the same name as one being moved or copied, this flag instructs the function to change the target name automatically and silently.
FOF_NOCONFIRMATION	0x0010	This flag causes the function to assume that the answer to any message box it may encounter is always "Yes". An exception is the dialog that asks you to create a missing directory. To deal with it you need to resort to the flag called FOF_NOCONFIRMMKDIR. (See later in table.)

Table Continued on Following Page

Flag	Value	Description
FOF_FILESONLY	0x0080	This flag applies only when you specify wildcards (say, *.*) that can contain sub-directories. With this flag set, the function deals only with files and never goes down to directories.
FOF_SIMPLEPROGRESS	0x0100	This results in a simplified user interface: there's animation, but the names of the files involved are not displayed. Instead of the names, it will display the text you specified through the lpszProgressTitle member.
FOF_NOCONFIRMMKDIR	0x0200	If the target directory doesn't exist, this flag causes the function to create what's missing silently. Without this flag, you'll be prompted to authorize the creation of the full destination path. This flag has a subtle relationship with the next one that I shall explain later.
FOF_NOERRORUI	0x0400	If this flag is set, any error that occurs will not result in a message box being displayed. All you'll get is a return code describing the error. This flag has a subtle relationship with the previous one.
FOF_NOCOPYSECURITYATTRIBS	0x0800	Applies to Windows NT, shell version 4.71 (Windows NT 4.0 with IE 4.0 and Active Desktop) and higher. This flag prevents copying of the security attributes that a given file may have.

Let's take a look at these options in more detail. When moving or copying files, you have two main concerns: correctly identifying the files to be transferred, and making sure that the flags you set produce the behavior you're expecting.

Avoiding Unwanted Dialog Boxes

If you want the operation to occur as silently as possible, without dialogs or even any system error messages, then you may think that FOF_NOERRORUI | FOF_SILENT is a good choice. This is not true, as I'll show in a moment. Using FOF_NOERRORUI only hides the message boxes that originate from errors. On the other hand, using FOF_SILENT alone doesn't prevent all the possible message boxes that the function can display from appearing. In fact, FOF_SILENT only affects the progress dialog – that is, the one that shows the names of the files being copied or moved, along with the usual animation. If the function finds that a given file or directory already exists in the target location, it will prompt you anyway. To avoid this behavior, you need to add FOF_NOCONFIRMATION to the flags. This will cause SHFileOperation() to behave as though an invisible user clicks Yes at each step. However, this is far from the end of the story.

All of these flags are useless if the target path includes a missing directory. Before continuing with copying or moving a file, the function tries to make sure that the given target path exists. You could legitimately have specified a directory that doesn't exist, and the function *will* take care of creating it, but first it requires an explicit authorization from you.

To skip this dialog, you need to set `FOF_NOCONFIRMMKDIR`. If this bit is set, then the function automatically creates any missing directories without prompting you.

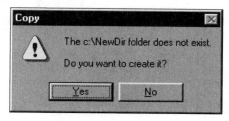

In summary, if you want the copy (or the move) to be completed without the user's intervention, then you can set the `fFlags` member of `SHFILEOPSTRUCT` with the following combination of flags:

- ❑ `FOF_SILENT`
- ❑ `FOF_NOCONFIRMATION`
- ❑ `FOF_NOERRORUI`
- ❑ `FOF_NOCONFIRMMKDIR`

However, there's one point regarding the use of the `FOF_NOERRORUI` and `FOF_NOCONFIRMMKDIR` flags at the same time that still needs clarifying.

Missing Directories

Interestingly, a missing directory is considered as a system error for which a system dialog should be shown. Although you can skip over the dialog by setting the `FOF_NOCONFIRMMKDIR` flag, the `FOF_NOERRORUI` flag takes precedence over `FOF_NOCONFIMMKDIR`, effectively suppressing the dialog before the latter flag gets a chance to deal with it. If both flags are specified, therefore, you *won't* be prompted to authorize the creation of a directory that doesn't exist, and a directory *won't* be created on your behalf. Instead, the function will continue as if you refused to create it, and you'll get:

- ❑ An error code of 117 (I'll say more about error codes later)
- ❑ The abort flag `fAnyOperationsAborted` set to `TRUE`
- ❑ No files moved, or copies made

Does this mean that you should avoid using `FOF_NOERRORUI`? It depends. If you want an absolutely silent operation, you can't avoid using it – it prevents *all* error message boxes from being displayed. The problem is that it also prevents a new directory from being silently created, causing an unnecessary and bothersome error. Fortunately, there's a way to work around this by making sure that the full directory path stored in `pTo` exists before calling `SHFileOperation()` with the flags that make it silent. The Win32 SDK provides a function for exactly this purpose:

```
BOOL MakeSureDirectoryPathExists(LPCSTR DirPath);
```

To use it, you need to `#include` the `imagehlp.h` file, and link to the `imagehlp.lib` library.

Renaming Files

One of the questions that `SHFileOperation()` could pose concerns replacing an existing file:

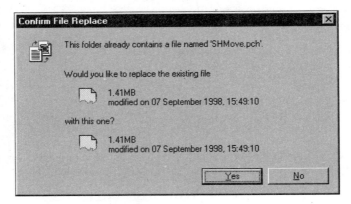

Or, similarly, it could pose a question about an existing directory:

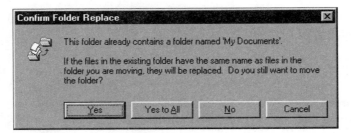

By setting `FOF_NOCONFIRMATION`, you implicitly enable the function to replace the old object, but there is a second possibility. You know that if you select a file in Windows Explorer and hit *Ctrl-C* followed by *Ctrl-V*, then a new file appears in the same folder with a name like `Copy of Xxxx`, where `Xxxx` is the file you selected. Explorer automatically renamed the new file to avoid collisions. `SHFileOperation()` provides this feature too, as long as you set the `FOF_RENAMEONCOLLISION` flag. Both `FOF_RENAMEONCOLLISION` and `FOF_NOCONFIRMATION` suppress the confirmation dialog for replacing things, but in the latter case your file or directory will be unavoidably overwritten. In the pathological case that you specify both, `FOF_RENAMEONCOLLISION` takes precedence.

Relationships Between Flags

What I've said so far should have raised a couple of questions in your mind. Firstly, what are the relationships between the various flags? Secondly, which flag affects which class of dialogs?

The following table explains which flag overrides which others, and which dialog each flag suppresses.

Flag	Dialog Suppressed	Dependency and Precedence
FOF_MULTIDESTFILES	None.	None.
FOF_FILESONLY	None.	None.
FOF_SILENT	If set, the progress dialog won't appear.	Takes precedence over the FOF_SIMPLEPROGRESS flag.
FOF_SIMPLEPROGRESS	None.	Suppressed by FOF_SILENT.
FOF_RENAMEONCOLLISION	If set, the replace dialog never appears when a file with the same name as one being copied or moved already exists.	In the case of name collisions (and *only* then) it works as if FOF_NOCONFIRMATION was set. It takes precedence over FOF_NOCONFIRMATION if both are set. This means that the files are duplicated, given new names and are not overwritten.
FOF_NOCONFIRMATION	If set, no confirmation dialog will appear in any case.	In case of name collisions, it causes the files to be overwritten unless FOF_RENAMEONCOLLISION is specified.
FOF_NOCONFIRMMKDIR	Suppresses the dialog that asks for your permission to create a new folder.	A missing directory is considered a fatal error requiring an error message box. The directory creation confirmation dialog is considered to be an error message box. For this reason the flag depends upon FOF_NOERRORUI.
FOF_NOERRORUI	Suppresses all the error message boxes.	Takes precedence over the previous flag. If set then a missing directory raises an unhandled exception and the function returns an error code.

An Example Program

To help you get to grips with the features of SHFileOperation(), I've put together a simple example program called SHMove. Like many of the other examples that we'll create over the course of this book, it will start its life as a skeleton generated by the Wrox AppWizard, a custom Wizard that is developed and documented in Appendix A. You should go and take a look at that now, if you haven't done so already!

45

Once you have the AppWizard safely installed on your machine, either by typing in all the code or (preferably) by downloading the source from the Wrox web site (http://www.wrox.com), you should use it (on this occasion) to generate a dialog-based application. Here's the user interface you then need to create:

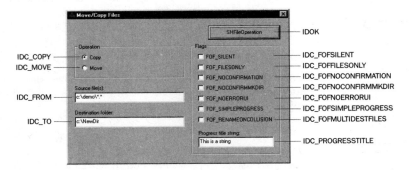

The default settings you can see are put in place in the `OnInitDialog()` function that you'll find in `SHMove.cpp`. The new lines just set the radio buttons and place strings in the edit boxes:

```cpp
void OnInitDialog(HWND hDlg)
{
    // Set the icons (T/F as to Large/Small icon)
    SendMessage(hDlg, WM_SETICON, FALSE, reinterpret_cast<LPARAM>(g_hIconSmall));
    SendMessage(hDlg, WM_SETICON, TRUE, reinterpret_cast<LPARAM>(g_hIconLarge));

    // Initialize the 'to' and 'from' edit fields
    SetDlgItemText(hDlg, IDC_TO, "c:\\NewDir");
    SetDlgItemText(hDlg, IDC_FROM, "c:\\demo\\*.*");

    // Take care of the 'progress' title
    SetDlgItemText(hDlg, IDC_PROGRESSTITLE, "This is a string");

    // Select the default operation
    CheckRadioButton(hDlg, IDC_COPY, IDC_MOVE, IDC_COPY);
}
```

In order to make this dialog issue calls to `SHFileOperation()`, we simply need to implement the skeleton `OnOK()` function that executes when someone clicks the **SHFileOperation** button. The contents of the `pTo` and `pFrom` members and the relevant `FOF_` flags are set in this function.

```cpp
void OnOK(HWND hDlg)
{
    SHFILEOPSTRUCT shfo;
    WORD wFunc;
    TCHAR pszTo[1024] = {0};
    TCHAR pszFrom[1024] = {0};
    TCHAR pszTitle[MAX_PATH] = {0};

    // Set the operation to perform
    if(IsDlgButtonChecked(hDlg, IDC_COPY))
        wFunc = FO_COPY;
    else
        wFunc = FO_MOVE;
```

```
        // Get the 'progress' string
    GetDlgItemText(hDlg, IDC_PROGRESSTITLE, pszTitle, MAX_PATH);
        // Get the 'from' buffer
    GetDlgItemText(hDlg, IDC_FROM, pszFrom, MAX_PATH);
    pszFrom[lstrlen(pszFrom) + 1] = 0;

        // Get the 'to' buffer
    GetDlgItemText(hDlg, IDC_TO, pszTo, MAX_PATH);

        // Get the flags
    WORD wFlags = 0;

    if(IsDlgButtonChecked(hDlg, IDC_FOFSILENT))
        wFlags |= FOF_SILENT;
    if(IsDlgButtonChecked(hDlg, IDC_FOFNOERRORUI))
        wFlags |= FOF_NOERRORUI;
    if(IsDlgButtonChecked(hDlg, IDC_FOFNOCONFIRMATION))
        wFlags |= FOF_NOCONFIRMATION;
    if(IsDlgButtonChecked(hDlg, IDC_FOFNOCONFIRMMKDIR))
        wFlags |= FOF_NOCONFIRMMKDIR;
    if(IsDlgButtonChecked(hDlg, IDC_FOFSIMPLEPROGRESS))
        wFlags |= FOF_SIMPLEPROGRESS;
    if(IsDlgButtonChecked(hDlg, IDC_FOFRENAMEONCOLLISION))
        wFlags |= FOF_RENAMEONCOLLISION;
    if(IsDlgButtonChecked(hDlg, IDC_FOFFILESONLY))
        wFlags |= FOF_FILESONLY;

        // Call SHFileOperation()
    ZeroMemory(&shfo, sizeof(SHFILEOPSTRUCT));
    shfo.hwnd = hDlg;
    shfo.wFunc = wFunc;
    shfo.lpszProgressTitle = pszTitle;
    shfo.fFlags = static_cast<FILEOP_FLAGS>(wFlags);
    shfo.pTo = pszTo;
    shfo.pFrom = pszFrom;

    int iRC = SHFileOperation(&shfo);
    if(shfo.fAnyOperationsAborted)
    {
        Msg("Aborted!");
        return;
    }

        // Display the result of the operation
    SPB_SystemMessage(iRC);
}
```

The function gathers all the data it needs from the dialog's controls, and then fills in the SHFILEOPSTRUCT structure. If any operation was aborted, the fAnyOperationsAborted member is filled with the Boolean value TRUE. In the code above, you may have noticed two strange names: Msg() and SPB_SystemMessage(). These functions are just wrappers for MessageBox() that were added by the Wrox AppWizard, and I'll discuss them in the *Two Poor Man's Utilities for Surviving Error Messages* section, when delving into what SHFileOperation() actually returns. For now, I'll concentrate on the source and target buffers, so add a #include for resource.h to SHMove.cpp, and build the project.

Source and Target

When moving or copying files from a source to a target, you have the following possibilities:

- ❑ A group of files to a single folder
- ❑ Many single files to a single folder
- ❑ A single file to a single file
- ❑ Many single files to many single files

By the expression 'single file' I mean a fully qualified file – that is, a file for which you know the complete name. By contrast, a 'group of files' means all the files you indicate through wildcards, which you do not know the names of. Only in the last of the four cases above you do need to use FOF_MULTIDESTFILES.

A possible way to copy or move files is by assigning a string such as c:\demo*.* to pFrom, as is done by default in the code. In this situation, you must indicate a specific folder as the destination. Everything you pass through the pTo buffer is considered to be a folder name, unless it contains an invalid character. In that case you'll get an error, as shown below (coversheet is the first file in the directory being copied):

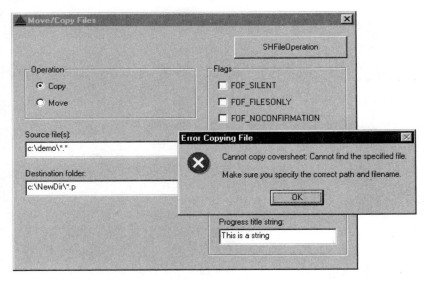

As explained earlier, you can work on multiple files by passing a double NULL terminated string whose items are separated by single NULL characters. For example, you could hard-code the following into OnOK():

```
shfo.pFrom = "c:\\demo\\one.txt\0c:\\two.txt\0c:\\three.txt\0";
shfo.pTo = "c:\\NewDir";
```

Here, we're attempting to move/copy three files at a time: one.txt, two.txt, and three.txt. All three files will be copied into a new directory called NewDir located under the root, c:\. The first source file is located in the c:\demo directory, while the other two are in c:\.

If the `pFrom` buffer contains just one file name, the `SHFileOperation()` function can deal with the content of `pTo` in two ways.

```
shfo.pFrom = "c:\\demo\\one.txt\0";
shfo.pTo = "c:\\NewDir";
```

If a directory or a file called `c:\NewDir` already exists, then it will be treated properly. That is, the file `c:\demo\one.txt` gets copied to the directory or replaces the existing file. On the other hand, if `c:\NewDir` doesn't exist, then it is considered to be the name of a new file, and is no longer considered to be a folder name.

If you want to copy a single file to a new folder, then you might think that adding a final backslash \ to the content of `pTo` would work.

```
shfo.pFrom = "c:\\demo\\one.txt\0";
shfo.pTo = "c:\\NewDir\\";
```

Curiously, this will cause the missing folders to be created, but it fails to copy or move the file. If you retry it, then it works as expected because on the second attempt the folder already exists! So what do you have to do to copy a single file to a non-existent folder? The only approach that will always work is to add a * at the end of the file. In doing so, you fool the function into thinking it is working on a wildcard expression.

```
shfo.pFrom = "c:\\demo\\one.txt*\0";
shfo.pTo = "c:\\NewDir";
```

Another possible circumstance is where you want to copy many single files to the same number of single files. You must meet two requirements. First, you should add the `FOF_MULTIDESTFILES` flag. Second, make sure you have a destination file for each source file – you need a perfect, 1:1 correspondence. The *n*th file in the source list will be copied/moved to the *n*th file in the target list.

```
shfo.fFlags |= FOF_MULTIDESTFILES;
shfo.pFrom = "c:\\one.txt\0c:\\two.txt\0";
shfo.pTo = "c:\\New one.txt\0c:\\New two.txt\0";
```

What if you fail to meet these criteria? What happens, for example, if you attempt to execute code such as the following?

```
shfo.fFlags |= FOF_MULTIDESTFILES;
shfo.pFrom = "c:\\one.txt\0c:\\two.txt\0c:\\three.txt\0";
shfo.pTo = "c:\\New one.txt\0c:\\New two.txt\0";
```

If this happens, the first item of the target list (that is, `c:\New one.txt`) is considered to be the folder name where all the source files go. In practice, it is handled as if it were a many-to-one operation.

When you make use of wildcards, the source buffer can implicitly refer to both files and directories. If you want the function to handle only files, add the `FOF_FILESONLY` flag. If you want to copy an entire directory, you need to add `\*.*` to the end of its path.

Unless you specify the FOF_SILENT flag, SHFileOperation() always displays a progress dialog with an animated control, a progress bar, and some labels to show the files being copied or moved. By using FOF_SIMPLEPROGRESS you can hide these labels, replacing them with the text you provide in the lpszProgressTitle member. This may be of help if, for any reason, you want to hide the names of the files being copied or moved.

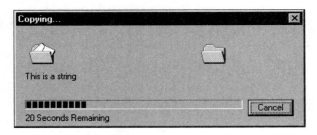

Deleting Files

File deletion is a simpler operation, as it only affects the input buffer pFrom – the pTo buffer is ignored. As before, the details of its operation depend which flags are set. The flags of interest are:

Flag	Value	Description
FOF_SILENT	0x0004	The operation occurs without feedback to the user, which means that the progress dialog isn't displayed. Any relevant message boxes will still appear, however.
FOF_NOCONFIRMATION	0x0010	This flag causes the function to assume "Yes" is always the answer to any message box it may encounter.
FOF_ALLOWUNDO	0x0040	If set, this flag forces the function to move the files being deleted to the Recycle Bin. Otherwise, the files will be physically removed from the disk.
FOF_FILESONLY	0x0080	Setting this flag results in the function deleting only files, and skipping directories. It applies only when you specify wildcards.
FOF_SIMPLEPROGRESS	0x0100	This results in a simplified user interface, with animation but without reporting the names of the files being deleted. Instead of the names, it will display the text you specified through the lpszProgressTitle member.
FOF_NOERRORUI	0x0400	If this flag is set, any error that occurs will not result in a message box being displayed. All you'll get is a return code.

The most striking thing here is the new flag FOF_ALLOWUNDO, which allows the programmer to decide whether the files should be deleted once and for all, or stored in the Recycle Bin awaiting possible restoration. If FOF_ALLOWUNDO is set, the files are moved to the Recycle Bin, and the operation may be undone (though you can only do this manually). The API that deals with the Recycle Bin is covered in Chapter 10. The 'undo' feature is available only for deletion – there's no equivalent for copy and move operations.

The presence of the FOF_ALLOWUNDO flag affects the user interface of the function, as I'm about to demonstrate. It wouldn't be too difficult to modify our sample project to accept requests for deletions as well as for copies and moves, but for the sake of brevity I'll just put the code straight into the OnOK() function:

```
ZeroMemory(&shfo, sizeof(SHFILEOPSTRUCT));
shfo.hwnd = hDlg;
shfo.wFunc = FO_DELETE;
shfo.lpszProgressTitle = pszTitle;
shfo.fFlags = FOF_NOERRORUI;
shfo.pFrom = "c:\\demo\\*.*\0";
```

The above code attempts to delete the entire content of the c:\demo directory, and results in the following dialog:

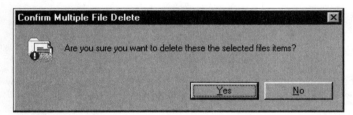

As you can see, there's no mention of the Recycle Bin in the message because we haven't specified the FOF_ALLOWUNDO flag. By doing so, the files would instead be sent directly to the Recycle Bin:

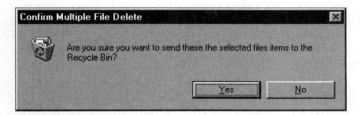

The other flags listed above work in much the same way as they did for copy and move. Accordingly, you can hide the names of the files being deleted with FOF_SIMPLEPROGRESS or FOF_SILENT, and delete *only* files with FOF_FILESONLY. Note that FOF_FILESONLY doesn't go down into sub-directories.

The dialogs shown above don't mention how many files are about to be deleted, but this is simply because the command that originated the figures included wildcards (the number of files would otherwise be displayed) so the function can't easily figure out the number of files. This might also be one of the reasons why it returns successfully even if there are no files to delete.

It is accepted practice that an operating system will ask for confirmation before deleting files. If you find such dialogs useless, then you can hide them by answering "Yes" to all questions automatically through use of the FOF_NOCONFIRMATION flag. Typically, an FO_DELETE operation will look something like this:

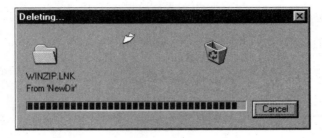

Renaming Files

The first thing I must do in this section is to confess that I have been unable to make SHFileOperation() rename files through wildcards. It seems that the only way to change the name of a file is by specifying a single source file name as pFrom, and a single target file name as pTo:

```
ZeroMemory(&shfo, sizeof(SHFILEOPSTRUCT));
shfo.wFunc = FO_RENAME;
shfo.pFrom = "c:\\demo\\one.txt\0";
shfo.pTo = "c:\\demo\\one.xxx";
```

Obviously, there are a couple of things that it's quite reasonable for you not to be allowed to do when you're renaming files. Specifically, these are:

- ❑ Changing the destination folder. Renaming just means changing the name, not the folder!
- ❑ Overwriting an existing file.

If you attempt to perform such operations, then it's natural that you'll get errors. Searching for all the error codes I could find, I tried passing parameters like those shown below to the function:

```
shfo.pFrom = "c:\\demo\\*.*\0";
shfo.pTo = "c:\\newdir";
```

This is obviously nonsense, and the function duly returns a message like this:

The message is clear enough, although paradoxically the command ends up returning success (a value of 0)! The *implication* of the message, however, is that the syntax used by MS-DOS will also work here. In other words, we should be able to rename, say, `*.txt` to `*.xtt`. With MS-DOS this works just fine; with `SHFileOperation()` it doesn't. If you try, the message you'll get is:

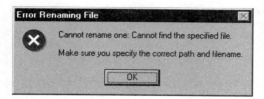

The message you can see originated from these two lines of code:

```
shfo.pFrom = "c:\\demo\\*.txt\0";
shfo.pTo = "c:\\demo\\*.xtt";
```

For this example, the `c:\demo` directory contained two files: `one.txt` and `two.txt`. Hence, **one** in this case is just the name of one of the files involved, without the extension. The return code behind this message is 2 – 'file not found'. I'll say more about return values later on.

Since the `FO_RENAME` command seems to be successful only with single files, the flags that affect the user interface of the dialog lose importance – the speed of the operation is such that the user interface simply won't be seen. The flags that still make sense are:

Flag	Value	Description
FOF_RENAMEONCOLLISION	0x0008	If the target location already contains a file with the same name as one being renamed, this flag instructs the function to change the target name automatically to `Copy of Xxx`, where `Xxx` is the original file name without the extension. If you don't set this flag, you still won't be prompted, but you'll get an error message instead.
FOF_NOERRORUI	0x0400	If this flag is set, any error that occurs will not result in a message box being displayed. All you'll get is a return code.

SHFileOperation() Return Values

The online documentation states that `SHFileOperation()` will return 0 if the function succeeded, and a nonzero value in case of failure. Obviously this is true, but it's not the most helpful information. By testing and re-testing the function, I have become convinced that there are very many possible ways for the function to terminate. In fact, I have often run into system errors, suggesting that somewhere in the code the function is simply returning what it gets from other routines that are closer to the file system.

Nevertheless, here's a table (that almost certainly isn't exhaustive) of the most common errors returned by `SHFileOperation()`. More precisely, it's a table of the most common errors I got while I was testing the function!

Error Code	Description
2	As mentioned above, you run into this message if you're trying to rename multiple files. The description is quite straightforward – *The system cannot find the file specified* – but I don't understand why it can't find the file.
7	This is returned if you click Cancel when you're asked whether you want to replace a given file. It has a rather ambiguous description: *The storage control blocks were destroyed.*
115	A file system error that occurs when you attempt to rename files to a different folder. Renaming a file just means changing the file name, not the folder too.
117	An IOCTL (Input/Output Control) error that appears when there's something wrong with the destination path, or you canceled the creation of a new directory.
123	You're trying to rename a file, but you're giving it the name of an existing file. Once again, we have an unhelpful description: *The file name, directory name, or volume label syntax is incorrect.*
1026	A file system error that's raised when you try to move/copy a file that doesn't exist. More generally, it warns you that something should be changed in the source buffer. The code causes an error box to appear – you can prevent this by setting `FOF_NOERRORUI`.

Error code 117 is returned in many cases, all of which relate to problems with the target directory. For example, it's returned (but there's no system message box) if you cancel the creation of a required directory. If there's an obvious error in a directory name that you've specified then an error box is provided which you can prevent from appearing by using `FOF_NOERRORUI`.

Two Poor Man's Utilities for Surviving Error Messages

Error messages are a curse for most programmers. Either you are given a numeric code but want a textual description, or else it's the other way around. Frameworks like MFC provide some facilities, but you certainly wouldn't want to move your code to MFC just to exploit such features.

Given this, I've made the Wrox AppWizard (see Appendix A) generate a file containing a couple of utility functions that we'll be using regularly, as we progress through the book. The first one is a revised version of `MessageBox()` that extends the standard functionality by adding the formatting capabilities of the evergreen `printf()`. I called the function `Msg()`, and it looks like this:

```
#include <stdarg.h>

void WINAPI Msg(char* szFormat, ...)
{
    va_list argptr;
    char szBuf[MAX_PATH];
    HWND hwndFocus = GetFocus();

    // init va_ functions
    va_start(argptr, szFormat);

    // format output string
    wvsprintf(szBuf, szFormat, argptr);

    // read title and show
    MessageBox(hwndFocus, szBuf, NULL, MB_ICONEXCLAMATION | MB_OK);

    // close va_ functions
    va_end(argptr);
    SetFocus(hwndFocus);
}
```

Basically, the code exploits the `va_` functions that are included through the `stdarg.h` header. The variable list of arguments is then formatted via `wvsprintf()`, and finally displayed by the ordinary `MessageBox()` function. Now you can write code such as this:

```
iRC = CallFunc(p1, p2);
Msg("The error code returned is: %d", iRC);
```

The second utility is called `SPB_SystemMessage()`. (The SPB prefix stands for Shell Programming Book, and is intended to differentiate these functions from yours!) It accepts an error code and passes it down to `FormatMessage()`, a Win32 API function capable of returning descriptive text for all system errors (at least, all those defined in `winerror.h`). The string that `FormatMessage()` provides is then aggregated with the numeric code, and displayed:

```
void WINAPI SPB_SystemMessage(DWORD dwRC)
{
    LPVOID lpMsgBuf;
    DWORD rc;

    rc = FormatMessage(FORMAT_MESSAGE_ALLOCATE_BUFFER |
                       FORMAT_MESSAGE_FROM_SYSTEM |
                       FORMAT_MESSAGE_IGNORE_INSERTS,
                    NULL, dwRC,
                    MAKELANGID(LANG_NEUTRAL, SUBLANG_DEFAULT),
                    reinterpret_cast<LPTSTR>(&lpMsgBuf), 0, NULL);

    Msg("%s: %ld.\n\n\n%s:\n\n%s", "This is the error code", dwRC,
        "This is the system's explanation", (rc == 0 ? "<unknown>" : lpMsgBuf));
    LocalFree(lpMsgBuf);
}
```

Did Everything Really Work Properly?

Undoubtedly, `SHFileOperation()` has some problems with its return codes. In particular, it can return 0 (that is, success) even when, due to an error in the input parameters, the requested operation couldn't be completed:

Try this code that is intended to copy/move files:

```
shfo.pFrom = "c:\\demo\\one.txt\0";
shfo.pTo = "c:\\NewDir";
```

If the `one.txt` file exists in the original folder, everything works fine. If the file doesn't exist, error 1026 is raised. That's just what you'd expect, and there's nothing else to say. However, now see what happens if you try *this* code (making sure that no files match the pattern):

```
shfo.pFrom = "c:\\demo\\x.*\0";
shfo.pTo = "c:\\NewDir";
```

The function will still return zero, even if no file actually gets processed. The same thing occurs with deletion. Even if there's no file to delete, the return code indicates success. To be honest, I don't know whether this should be considered a bug, or whether this behavior was intended. There's no quick way to verify whether the desired result has been achieved. The solution that comes to mind is to check for the existence of the file in question, after the function returns.

Long File Names

Although the Windows shell has been designed and coded with the idea of bringing information to the user's fingertips, one of the most important shell functions seems to have some problems with long file names. Yes, that's right – with *long file names*. Let's see what's going on.

In all the samples you saw above, we specified a fully qualified name for the target folder (we often used `c:\NewDir`). The documentation says that if you don't provide a full pathname, the function assumes it should use the current directory returned by the API function `GetCurrentDirectory()`. Well, let's test it. Try to use this code with `SHFileOperation()`:

```
shfo.pFrom = "c:\\demo\\*.*\0";
shfo.pTo = "NewDir";
```

We're attempting to copy/move all the files found in the `c:\demo` directory into a new or existing directory called `NewDir`, located under the current directory. All goes well, provided that there are no long file names among the files to be transferred. If there are any, this dialog will appear:

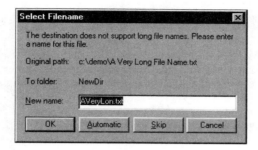

What's happening is that the function is trying to shorten a long file name to make sure it will be correctly stored on the target drive. This is a perfectly natural action if you're moving files across a network where the destination machine is running Windows 3.1, for example. Unfortunately, we're trying to copy/move files on a single machine running a 32-bit – and long file name compliant – operating system. If we weren't, SHFileOperation() itself wouldn't work!

Curiously, if you add a drive to what the function perceives to be the target folder, everything will work properly again. As if that wasn't strange enough, you will be surprised to know that if you use a relative path, such as .\ANewDir, all will be well. Curiously though, the floppy drive is accessed for reading. What on earth is going on?

It appears that if the path begins with a letter that is also the logical representation of one of the available drives, then SHFileOperation() works well with long file names. Otherwise, it thinks that you're attempting to connect to a remote drive, for which the check for long file name support failed. (If there isn't an N: drive, it will surely fail...) On my home machine, for example, it works well up to the letter F, which is the CD-ROM drive.

It's likely that there's an error somewhere in the code that is used to figure out the destination drive for the files. The workaround is fairly simple: always use fully qualified paths.

File Name Mapping Objects

Reading the official documentation for SHFileOperation(), you'll have noticed the discreet presence of a thing called a **file name mapping object**. In particular, the documentation speaks of such objects when describing the hNameMappings member of the SHFILEOPSTRUCT structure.

hNameMappings is a pointer to a block of memory that contains a certain number of SHNAMEMAPPING structures – it is declared as LPVOID. A SHNAMEMAPPING data structure looks like this:

```
typedef struct _SHNAMEMAPPING
{
    LPSTR pszOldPath;
    LPSTR pszNewPath;
    int   cchOldPath;
    int   cchNewPath;
} SHNAMEMAPPING, FAR* LPSHNAMEMAPPING;
```

The structure identifies a file being copied, moved, or even renamed. More precisely, it stores both the original and the new (fully qualified) filename. Put this way, it suggests an interesting possibility: you could have a complete report of what happened during the execution of SHFileOperation(). Sadly, things don't quite work out like that.

First of all, to have SHFileOperation() fill the hNameMappings member, you must specify an additional flag: FOF_WANTMAPPINGHANDLE. However, even that isn't enough, because the member only gets filled if you *also* set the FOF_RENAMEONCOLLISION flag. Furthermore, for it to be anything other than zero, it's necessary that some files really do get renamed to avoid collisions. In all other cases, the hNameMappings handle simply points to NULL.

Demonstrating File Mapping

Using the Wrox AppWizard once again as my starting point, I created a dialog-based application called FileMap to test out some aspects of file mapping. Here's its user interface:

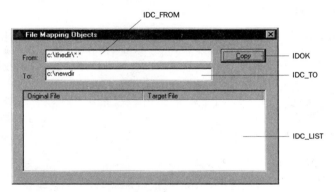

To set up the dialog with the values shown, and to initialize the list view, it's necessary to adjust the OnInitDialog() function as follows (remember to add a #include for resource.h):

```
void OnInitDialog(HWND hDlg)
{
    HWND hwndList = GetDlgItem(hDlg, IDC_LIST);

    // Set up the report view
    LV_COLUMN lvc;
    ZeroMemory(&lvc, sizeof(LV_COLUMN));

    lvc.mask = LVCF_TEXT | LVCF_WIDTH;
    lvc.cx = 200;

    lvc.pszText = "Original File";
    ListView_InsertColumn(hwndList, 0, &lvc);

    lvc.pszText = "Target File";
    ListView_InsertColumn(hwndList, 1, &lvc);

    // Initialize the edit fields
    SetDlgItemText(hDlg, IDC_FROM, "c:\\thedir\\*.*");
    SetDlgItemText(hDlg, IDC_TO, "c:\\newdir");
```

```
    // Set the icons (T/F as to Large/Small icon)
    SendMessage(hDlg, WM_SETICON, FALSE, reinterpret_cast<LPARAM>(g_hIconSmall));
    SendMessage(hDlg, WM_SETICON, TRUE, reinterpret_cast<LPARAM>(g_hIconLarge));
}
```

Now you can edit OnOK(), adding code that demonstrates how to acquire and test a handle to a file name mapping object:

```
void OnOK(HWND hDlg)
{
    TCHAR pszFrom[1024] = {0};
    TCHAR pszTo[MAX_PATH] = {0};

    GetDlgItemText(hDlg, IDC_FROM, pszFrom, MAX_PATH);
    GetDlgItemText(hDlg, IDC_TO, pszTo, MAX_PATH);

    SHFILEOPSTRUCT shfo;
    ZeroMemory(&shfo, sizeof(SHFILEOPSTRUCT));
    shfo.hwnd = hDlg;
    shfo.wFunc = FO_COPY;
    shfo.pFrom = pszFrom;
    shfo.pTo = pszTo;
    shfo.fFlags = FOF_NOCONFIRMMKDIR |
                  FOF_RENAMEONCOLLISION |
                  FOF_WANTMAPPINGHANDLE;

    int iRC = SHFileOperation(&shfo);
    if(iRC)
    {
        SPB_SystemMessage(iRC);
        return;
    }

    // Trace the value of the handle
    Msg("hNameMappings is: %x", shfo.hNameMappings);

    // Free the object, as recommended
    if(shfo.hNameMappings)
        SHFreeNameMappings(shfo.hNameMappings);
}
```

Pay particular attention to the last line in this code – freeing a file name mapping object is the simplest operation you can perform on it, but it's also one of the most important. You just have to call SHFreeNameMapping(), passing the handle you received from SHFileOperation(). Everything works properly, and it's perfectly understandable. Perhaps one day, all the Windows documentation will be this clear!

Anyway, by running this code, you'll discover that the hNameMappings handle is always NULL unless and until the operation you're performing (copy, move, rename) causes name collisions. If renaming occurs, the handle serves the purpose of giving you a report of what files have actually been renamed to avoid overwriting other files, indicating both their new and original names.

So, a file name mapping object has nothing to do with memory-mapped files or other mechanisms for interprocess communication. It's just a chunk of memory that allows the shell (and you) to keep track of what files have been renamed in order to avoid name collisions.

If the target directory (c:\newdir in the sample) doesn't exist, or if it contains files whose names are all different from those in the source path (c:\thedir*.* in the sample), then, despite the flags we specified, the handle is NULL:

On the other hand, if at least one rename-on-collision occurred, the handle refers to a meaningful block of data, and you're returned a valid memory address.

Using the Object

Obtaining a handle to a file name mapping object is only half the battle – now you have to figure out how to use it! The documentation simply says that (when it isn't NULL) hNameMappings points to an array of SHNAMEMAPPING structures. There's no mention, for example, of how to get the size of this array. Even worse, the LPVOID member that SHFileOperation() uses to store the handle is anything but a pointer to an array of data structures. The obvious method of walking the array via a loop simply doesn't work here.

In some old MSDN documentation, you will find mention of a couple of functions called SHGetNameMappingCount() *and* SHGetNameMappingPtr()*. However, these now seem to be not only undocumented, but unexported as well. No version of* shell32.dll *(from Internet Explorer 4.0 onwards) has any trace of them. This is a shame, since they were exactly the kinds of functions I'm going to write right now! I really don't understand why these functions have been removed, but support for the* hNameMappings *member has been neither withdrawn nor declared obsolete.*

An Undocumented Structure

What the documentation claims is true, but incomplete. The problem is that it neglects to mention a data structure that sits in the middle, between hNameMappings and the array, desperately calling you. There were two clues that put me on the right track, the first of which was the output from code like this:

```
TCHAR* pNM = static_cast<TCHAR*>(shfo.hNameMappings);
Msg(pNM);
```

When I tried this, I was resigned to getting yet another access violation error, but to my surprise it just dumped a number (such as 9) instead. Could that be the number of renames-on-collision? I checked the directories and found that it was. Of course, I immediately performed another test with a different number of files, and that confirmed my theory. Whatever it is that hNameMappings points to, it begins with the total number of file name mapping objects.

So what's the next step? Well, looking through the Internet Client SDK and MSDN documentation, I ran into some unknown (at least, to me) clipboard formats. They are mentioned in:

❑ Windows Shell API I Dragging and Dropping, for the Internet Client SDK
❑ Knowledge Base Article Q154123, for the MSDN Library

These formats (among which there's an encouraging one called "FileNameMap") are used internally by the shell when you request copy and paste operations, or when you drag-and-drop file objects from one folder to another. More interestingly (at least for our purposes), many of these formats are stored in the clipboard as a block of data, comprising a number and a pointer to an array of custom data structures. The number denotes the size of the array, and the pointer refers to its first element.

Towards a Solution

Happily, the same pattern applies to mapping objects, so I defined an intermediate structure called SHNAMEMAPPINGHEADER:

```
struct SHNAMEMAPPINGHEADER
{
    UINT cNumOfMappings;
    LPSHNAMEMAPPING lpNM;
};

typedef SHNAMEMAPPINGHEADER* LPSHNAMEMAPPINGHEADER;
```

The structure has exactly the same format as the data pointed to by hNameMappings. This is illustrated in the diagram below, which also demonstrates the way to access the array of SHNAMEMAPPING structures:

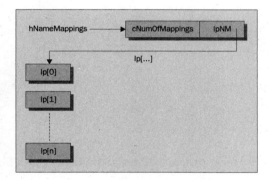

With this done, writing a function that enumerates all of the file name mapping objects is pretty straightforward; I called mine SHEnumFileMapping(). Before we look at the function itself, though, we need to extend our earlier listing for OnOK() to incorporate a call to it:

```
void OnOK(HWND hDlg)
{
    ...

    // Trace the value of the handle
    Msg("hNameMappings is: %x", shfo.hNameMappings);

    // Enumerate the file mapping objects
    SHEnumFileMapping(shfo.hNameMappings, ProcessNM,
                      reinterpret_cast<DWORD>(GetDlgItem(hDlg, IDC_LIST)));

    // Free the object, as recommended
    if(shfo.hNameMappings)
        SHFreeNameMappings(shfo.hNameMappings);
}
```

`SHEnumFileMapping()` accepts the handle, a callback procedure, and a generic buffer. It enumerates all the `SHNAMEMAPPING` structures, passing them one by one to the callback function for further processing.

```
int WINAPI SHEnumFileMapping(
                    HANDLE hNameMappings, ENUMFILEMAPPROC lpfnEnum, DWORD dwData)
{
    SHNAMEMAPPING shNM;

    // Check the handle
    if(!hNameMappings)
        return -1;

    // Get the header of the structure
    LPSHNAMEMAPPINGHEADER lpNMH =
                            static_cast<LPSHNAMEMAPPINGHEADER>(hNameMappings);
    int iNumOfNM = lpNMH->cNumOfMappings;

    // Check the function pointer; if NULL, just return the number of mappings
    if(!lpfnEnum)
        return iNumOfNM;

    // Enumerate the objects
    LPSHNAMEMAPPING lp = lpNMH->lpNM;
    int i = 0;

    while(i < iNumOfNM)
    {
        CopyMemory(&shNM, &lp[i++], sizeof(SHNAMEMAPPING));        if(!lpfnEnum(&shNM,
dwData))
            break;
    }

    // Returns the number of objects actually processed
    return i;
}
```

`SHEnumFileMapping()` follows the same pattern as most of the other 'enum-like' Windows functions. It accepts a callback function and a generic `DWORD` buffer that's used to pass custom data from the calling program to the callback. Furthermore, it expects the callback to return 0 if the enumeration should stop. I defined the callback function to be of type `ENUMFILEMAPPROC`:

```
typedef BOOL (CALLBACK *ENUMFILEMAPPROC)(LPSHNAMEMAPPING, DWORD);
```

The function receives a pointer to a `SHNAMEMAPPING` object, together with any custom data the calling program wants to send.

Of course, creating an 'enum-like' function for listing all the structures is a matter of personal preference. I could equally have defined a navigational interface, by providing functions like `FindFirstSHNameMapping()` *and* `FindNextSHNameMapping()`.

In practice, pretty much all the work is carried out by the callback function. The one I've used here (`ProcessNM()`) extracts the `pszOldPath` and `pszNewPath` fields from any `SHNAMEMAPPING` structure it receives, and adds them to the report list view:

```
BOOL CALLBACK ProcessNM(LPSHNAMEMAPPING pshNM, DWORD dwData)
{
    TCHAR szBuf[1024] = {0};
    TCHAR szOldPath[MAX_PATH] = {0};
    TCHAR szNewPath[MAX_PATH] = {0};
    OSVERSIONINFO os;

    // We need to know the underlying OS
    os.dwOSVersionInfoSize = sizeof(OSVERSIONINFO);
    GetVersionEx(&os);
    BOOL bIsNT = (os.dwPlatformId == VER_PLATFORM_WIN32_NT);

    // Under NT the SHNAMEMAPPING structure includes UNICODE strings
    if(bIsNT)
    {
        WideCharToMultiByte(CP_ACP, 0, reinterpret_cast<LPWSTR>(pshNM->pszOldPath),
            MAX_PATH, szOldPath, MAX_PATH, NULL, NULL);
        WideCharToMultiByte(CP_ACP, 0, reinterpret_cast<LPWSTR>(pshNM->pszNewPath),
            MAX_PATH, szNewPath, MAX_PATH, NULL, NULL);
    }
    else
    {
        lstrcpy(szOldPath, pshNM->pszOldPath);
        lstrcpy(szNewPath, pshNM->pszNewPath);
    }

    // Save the list view handle
    HWND hwndListView = reinterpret_cast<HWND>(dwData);

    // Create a \0 separated string
    LPTSTR psz = szBuf;
    lstrcpyn(psz, szOldPath, pshNM->cchOldPath + 1);
    lstrcat(psz, __TEXT("\0"));

    psz += lstrlen(psz) + 1;

    lstrcpyn(psz, szNewPath, pshNM->cchNewPath + 1);
    lstrcat(psz, __TEXT("\0"));

    // Add the strings to the report view
    LV_ITEM lvi;
    ZeroMemory(&lvi, sizeof(LV_ITEM));
    lvi.mask = LVIF_TEXT;
    lvi.pszText = szBuf;
    lvi.cchTextMax = lstrlen(szBuf);
    lvi.iItem = 0;
    ListView_InsertItem(hwndListView, &lvi);

    psz = szBuf + lstrlen(szBuf) + 1;
    ListView_SetItemText(hwndListView, 0, 1, psz);

    return TRUE;
}
```

Note that under Windows NT, the strings in the SHNAMEMAPPING structure are in Unicode format. Here, if the operating system is NT, I convert the strings to ANSI format in order to use them in the example. Also notice that the dwData buffer I added to the prototype is used to pass the handle of the list view to the callback function.

With all this code in place, the basic example I put together earlier in the chapter is now able to give details of the files renamed by the call to SHFileOperation(). A test, in typical circumstances, might result in something like this:

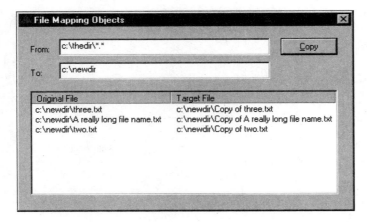

Summary

This chapter was devoted entirely to a single function. Each aspect of SHFileOperation() was thoroughly examined, starting with the commands that let you copy, move, rename or delete files, and the flags you can set to make the function work as you'd like it to. Then I spent some time talking about the undocumented return codes, bugs, and pitfalls of the function. In summary, in this chapter I've shown you:

❑ How to program SHFileOperation()
❑ The most common programming errors
❑ The shortcomings of the function's documentation
❑ How to take advantage of file name mapping

Further Reading

It's difficult to find reference material for a single function like SHFileOperation(), but there are at least a couple of brief articles on MSDN that are worth a glance. They are:

❑ Knowledge Base Article Q133326: *SHFILEOPSTRUCT pFrom and pTo Fields Incorrect*
❑ Knowledge Base Article Q142066: *SHGetNameMappingPtr() and SHGetNameMappingCount ()*

In addition to these, MSDN is full of tips and quick examples on how to use SHFileOperation() with Visual Basic. Good suggestions can be found in *Manipulating Files with the SHFileOperation Function in Visual Basic 4.0* by Deborah L. Cooper, which can be found under *Technical Articles | Visual Tools | Visual Basic | Visual Basic 4.0*. The documentation for CreateFile() contains details of the security attributes of files.

Investigating the Nature of Files

Once upon a time, all files and directories had a limited and well-defined set of attributes: time, date, size, and a set of flags denoting their status, which could be 'read-only', 'hidden', 'archive' or 'system'. However, Windows 95 (and then Windows NT 4.0) brought with it a number of changes, the most important of which is that the concept of a 'file' has been widened. A file is now *any* object that's a part of the shell – it doesn't necessarily have to be a part of the file system.

To give a precise definition, any object that's part of the shell namespace is called a **file object**. Note once again that in this context, the word 'namespace' has nothing to do with the C++ keyword. By 'shell namespace', I just mean the collection of all the named items that actually form the shell. They all appear in the Explorer's tree view.

Not all file objects are entries in the file system, as items like `Printers` and `My Computer` demonstrate. A file object that contains other, child file objects is called a **folder object**. Files and directories are only the most common of the file objects.

> *In all probability this change has been made as a first step towards what some years ago was known as 'Cairo' – Microsoft's fully object-oriented operating system that would have fused Windows 9x and Windows NT into a single product. From what we mere mortals can see today, a unified operating system is still a project* in divenire, *even if the hype about its object-oriented nature has disappeared.*

How many attributes can a file object have today? It will come as no surprise that the complete set comprises all the attributes a file had under MS-DOS, plus a few others due to the graphical nature of the Windows 9x and Windows NT shells. The shell API provides a composite and quite rich function for investigating the properties of a given file object, be it an ordinary file, a directory, or even a system folder or a system object like a printer or a dial-up connection. This function is `SHGetFileInfo()`.

In this chapter, my aim is to examine carefully the prototype of this routine, emphasizing for a given file object:

- How to get its type name
- How to get a handle to its Explorer icon
- How to get the target platform for an executable
- How to retrieve the attributes that define what you can do and what you cannot do with it from within the Explorer

You might be surprised at the diversity of the information you can get through SHGetFileInfo(). I still remember the reader who once asked me how to determine whether a given .exe file was a 16-bit or a 32-bit module (without the hassle of mapping the EXE header structures). My answer was SHGetFileInfo(). A few days later, he came back to me again with a question about getting hold of the icon for a given drive. Once again, my answer was SHGetFileInfo(). A weekend went by, and he sent me a third message with lots of excuses for being so boring. Now he was searching for a clever way to determine whether a folder had sub-folders. My answer was the same as before. The last message I got from him asked what arguments he should pass SHGetFileInfo() to get a good cup of coffee!

What SHGetFileInfo() Can Do for You

As usual, let's start with the function's prototype, which is located in shellapi.h. The function takes five arguments:

```
DWORD SHGetFileInfo(LPCTSTR        pszPath,
                    DWORD          dwFileAttributes,
                    SHFILEINFO FAR* psfi,
                    UINT           cbFileInfo,
                    UINT           uFlags);
```

Basically, SHGetFileInfo() provides information about an object in the file system. As explained earlier, this object can be a file, a folder, a directory or a drive root. The DWORD it returns has a meaning that can vary quite a lot, depending upon the contents of the uFlags argument. In a nutshell, by means of this function you can expect to:

- Determine the target platform of an executable file (Win32, Win16, MS-DOS)
- Get the various flavors of the file icon (small, large, with the link overlay, selected, opened)
- Retrieve other display attributes, such as the file type (the short description shown by Explorer in the Type column) and the display name (what appears in the Name column)
- Retrieve any other attribute that can characterize the file, such as whether it can be copied, moved, deleted or renamed; whether it can originate a shortcut; whether it has sub-folders; whether it is shared, is a drop target or has additional property pages, and much more

How SHGetFileInfo() Works

To understand exactly what the function can do for you, a tour of all the possible ways to call it is mandatory. To begin, let's examine the arguments it requires:

Name	Description
pszPath	A buffer that contains the relative or absolute path to the file for which information is required. It can handle short and long file names.
dwFileAttributes	The documentation says that this parameter is used only if uFlags includes the SHGFI_USEFILEATTRIBUTES flag. If so, it should be a combination of file attribute constants: archive, read-only, directory, system and the like. (See later)
psfi	Points to a SHFILEINFO structure that will receive the data.
cbFileInfo	This is simply the size of the above structure.
uFlags	The brains of the function. Through all the possible flags, you can drive the behavior and the information actually retrieved. (See later)

The SHFILEINFO structure is defined like this:

```
typedef struct _SHFILEINFO
{
    HICON hIcon;
    int iIcon;
    DWORD dwAttributes;
    char szDisplayName[MAX_PATH];
    char szTypeName[80];
} SHFILEINFO;
```

With a single exception, this structure is always used to transfer data back to the calling program, and never needs initialization. The only member that may sometimes contain information that affects the behavior of the function is dwAttributes, and I'll have more to say on this later in the chapter.

It's clear that all the interesting uses to which SHGetFileInfo() can be put depend upon the value you put in the uFlags argument. In most cases, information is returned via the psfi buffer, but there are circumstances where the answer can be packed efficiently in the DWORD return value of the function.

Specifying the Input File

A function that retrieves information about files first requires the name of the file on which to operate, and the pszPath parameter serves this purpose. However, there are some points about even this that need to be clarified. For one thing, it can be a path name (as you'd expect) *or* a PIDL, which we discussed in Chapter 2.

If you want to pass a PIDL instead of an ordinary path name, then you should set the SHGFI_PIDL flag in the uFlags argument. The converse is true as well: if you set the SHGFI_PIDL flag, then the pszPath *must* be a pointer to an ITEMIDLIST structure (in other words, a PIDL). Of course, pszPath can also be a folder name or a drive name, in which cases you need to leave a final backslash in the path name. That is, you should specify 'c:\' rather than 'c:' to avoid errors when retrieving information about the C drive.

Using Wildcards with SHGetFileInfo()

The documentation doesn't say anything about using SHGetFileInfo() with wildcards, and from that you might expect that wildcards aren't recognized. However, I've discovered that if you pass a string with wildcards then provided that at least one file matches the pattern, the function works correctly. The next figure shows the output from a sample program that we'll discuss in detail later on:

The program lets you select a file name or a path name, and retrieves the information you checked beneath. It can return the icon, the display name, the type name and a list of all the other attributes. Also, you can ask the program to determine the type of executable of the file in question. Checking the **EXE Type** box suppresses all the other options. The **Return Code** label shows the return code of the function (or a textual representation of it), and by checking **Accept any file name** you can force the function to accept *anything* as the input file.

On this occasion, the program has called SHGetFileInfo() with the path e:\mssdk\doc\misc*.txt, and you can see the response: the icon and the type name are both correct (on my PC, a text file is described as a **Text Document**). Curiously though, despite specifying a wildcard, we also have non-null file attributes and a display name! While the icon and the type name may be obtained from the file extension, the same can't be true for display names and attributes — those are clearly only relevant to a particular file.

To examine what was happening here, I tried calling the function with a different path: e:\mssdk\doc\misc\g*.*. As you can see, there's now a wildcard for the extension as well as for the name of the file. The resulting dialog looked like this:

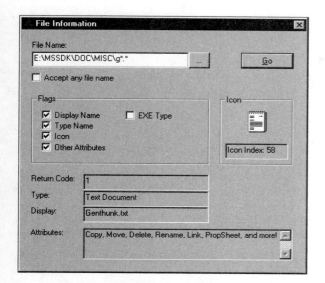

As you can see, we've got the same file as before, and the clear implication of this is that if you pass wildcards, `SHGetFileInfo()` takes the first file that matches the string and works with it. If no file matches the pattern, the function does nothing but return zero.

The other possibility we need to check is what happens when you pass a path name ending in * . *. As you can see in the screenshot opposite, when I tried it, the function returned information about a folder:

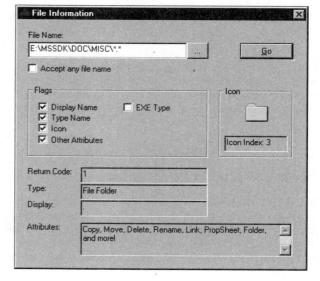

What's going on now? Well, stop for a while, and have a closer look at the output. In the Display field, you can see a dot (.), just like in an old DOS directory listing! This result confirms what I stated earlier: `SHGetFileInfo()` operates on the first file object whose name matches the pattern. In fact, if you try to enumerate the content of a folder using * . * as the matching string, the first item you get is the dot. If you still aren't convinced, try this code when you next get the chance:

```
WIN32_FIND_DATA wff;
FindFirstFile("*.*", &wff);
Msg(wff.cFileName);
```

In summary, even though it's an undocumented feature, you can use wildcards with
`SHGetFileInfo()` provided that:

❑   You specify a pattern string that matches at least one file
❑   You are aware that the function stops at the first file found

It's likely that somewhere in its internal code, `SHGetFileInfo()` gets hold of a
`WIN32_FIND_DATA` structure. This is filled with low-level file information, and its use wouldn't be at
all surprising here. Incidentally, this structure is also involved in another shell function that we'll
examine in a later chapter – `SHGetDataFromIDList()` – that can also return information about a
file object.

The Display Name

Looking at the screenshots above and running the same program on your machine, you may notice a
slight difference in what is returned as the 'display name'. In my screenshots, the display name is
composed of the filename plus the extension, but it may be that you only see the filename. It all
depends upon the settings in Explorer's View | Folder Options... dialog, in which you can choose to
'Hide file extensions for known file types'.

Here, a "known file type" is simply a registered file type. We'll discuss thoroughly how file type
registration works in Chapter 14, but for now it's enough to know that this is just a class of documents
the shell knows how to handle. If you double-click a file of a known type, the chances are that the
document will open up in a program that knows how to deal with it. To retrieve this kind of setting
programmatically, you need to use a function called `SHGetSettings()` that will be covered in the
next chapter.

The Sample Program

It's about time we had a look at the sample program that I've been using for the tests so far, and
which you'll see a few more times before the end of this chapter. Once again, it's a dialog-based
application built from the Wrox AppWizard, and this time I called my project `FileInfo`. The
operational part of the sample is built around `SHGetFileInfo()`, and works as a generic executor
of queries about the state and the attributes of a given file or folder. This is what its user interface
looks like:

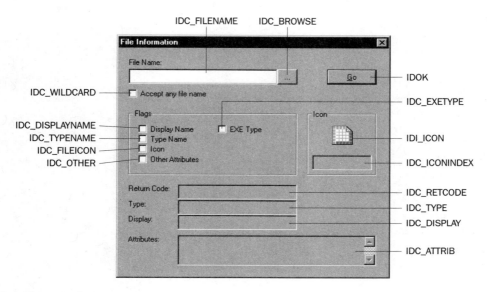

As you can see, the user interface is composed of an edit field with an associated browse button that lets you choose a file. Unfortunately, you can't select a directory in this fashion; if you want to pass in a folder name, you must type its name by hand. The checkboxes allow you to select which flags you want to add to the call; if you check the **EXE Type** box, all the others will be discarded. This is due to a feature of SHGetFileInfo() that requires the flag for specifying the executable type to be specified alone. The icon for the file will be drawn in a static control, while the attributes are parsed and transformed into a descriptive string.

Most of the significant code goes in the OnOK() method, which executes when the user clicks on the **G**o button. In order to successfully compile the code after these changes, remember to #include "resource.h" to keep track of the dialog's control IDs, and <shlobj.h> for the prototype of SHGetFileInfo().

```
void OnOK(HWND hDlg)
{
    TCHAR szFile[MAX_PATH] = {0};
    TCHAR szBuf[1024] = {0};

    // Get the file name
    GetDlgItemText(hDlg, IDC_FILENAME, szFile, MAX_PATH);

    /////////////////////////////////////////
    // Collect Flags
    //
    DWORD dwFileAttributes = 0;
    UINT uFlags = 0;

    if(IsDlgButtonChecked(hDlg, IDC_FILEICON))
        uFlags |= SHGFI_ICON;
    if(IsDlgButtonChecked(hDlg, IDC_DISPLAYNAME))
        uFlags |= SHGFI_DISPLAYNAME;
```

```
    if(IsDlgButtonChecked(hDlg, IDC_TYPENAME))
        uFlags |= SHGFI_TYPENAME;
    if(IsDlgButtonChecked(hDlg, IDC_OTHER))
        uFlags |= SHGFI_ATTRIBUTES;
    if(IsDlgButtonChecked(hDlg, IDC_WILDCARD))
        uFlags |= SHGFI_USEFILEATTRIBUTES;
    if(IsDlgButtonChecked(hDlg, IDC_EXETYPE))
        uFlags = SHGFI_EXETYPE;

    //////////////////////////////////////
    // Call the function
    //
    SHFILEINFO sfi;
    ZeroMemory(&sfi, sizeof(SHFILEINFO));
    DWORD dwRC = SHGetFileInfo(
                    szFile, dwFileAttributes, &sfi, sizeof(SHFILEINFO), uFlags);

    //////////////////////////////////////
    // Deal with the UI
    //
    wsprintf(szBuf, "%d", dwRC);
    SetDlgItemText(hDlg, IDC_RETCODE, szBuf);

    wsprintf(szBuf, "Icon Index: %d", sfi.iIcon);
    SetDlgItemText(hDlg, IDC_ICONINDEX, szBuf);

    SetDlgItemText(hDlg, IDC_DISPLAY, sfi.szDisplayName);
    SetDlgItemText(hDlg, IDC_TYPE, sfi.szTypeName);

    //////////////////////////////////////
    // Parse attributes and display
    //
    DWORD dwAttrib = sfi.dwAttributes;
    lstrcpy(szBuf, "");
    if(dwAttrib != 0)
    {
        if(dwAttrib & SFGAO_CANCOPY)
            lstrcat(szBuf, "Copy, ");
        if(dwAttrib & SFGAO_CANMOVE)
            lstrcat(szBuf, "Move, ");
        if(dwAttrib & SFGAO_CANDELETE)
            lstrcat(szBuf, "Delete, ");
        if(dwAttrib & SFGAO_CANRENAME)
            lstrcat(szBuf, "Rename, ");
        if(dwAttrib & SFGAO_CANLINK)
            lstrcat(szBuf, "Link, ");
        if(dwAttrib & SFGAO_HASPROPSHEET)
            lstrcat(szBuf, "PropSheet, ");
        if(dwAttrib & SFGAO_GHOSTED)
            lstrcat(szBuf, "Ghosted, ");
        if(dwAttrib & SFGAO_SHARE)
            lstrcat(szBuf, "Shared, ");
        if(dwAttrib & SFGAO_HASSUBFOLDER)
            lstrcat(szBuf, "SubFolders, ");
        if(dwAttrib & SFGAO_REMOVABLE)
            lstrcat(szBuf, "On removable media, ");
        if(dwAttrib & SFGAO_FOLDER)
            lstrcat(szBuf, "Folder, ");

        lstrcat(szBuf, "and more!");
    }
```

```
    SetDlgItemText(hDlg, IDC_ATTRIB, szBuf);

    ////////////////////////////////////////
    // Show the icon
    //
    HICON hIcon = sfi.hIcon;
    SendDlgItemMessage(
               hDlg, IDI_ICON, STM_SETICON, reinterpret_cast<WPARAM>(hIcon), 0);
}
```

This code is enough to reproduce the behavior you've seen so far, although we will be adding more functionality as we go. The two most important sections are the `if` blocks, and while it may not be immediately clear what they do, we'll be focusing on them for the majority of the rest of the chapter.

The only other function we need to implement at this stage is the handler for the browse (...) button. This involves adding an extra `case` to the `switch` in `APP_DlgProc()`, and the `OnBrowse()` function itself, which looks like this:

```
void OnBrowse(HWND hDlg)
{
    TCHAR szFile[MAX_PATH] = {0};

    OPENFILENAME ofn;
    ZeroMemory(&ofn, sizeof(OPENFILENAME));
    ofn.lStructSize = sizeof(OPENFILENAME);
    ofn.lpstrFilter = "All files\0*.*\0";
    ofn.nMaxFile = MAX_PATH;
    ofn.lpstrFile = szFile;

    if(GetOpenFileName(&ofn))
        SetDlgItemText(hDlg, IDC_FILENAME, ofn.lpstrFile);
}
```

To make use of common dialogs (in this case, the **Open** dialog), you need to link against `comdlg32.lib` and `#include <commdlg.h>`. The screenshot shows typical output from the program. It's been asked to provide information about the icon, type, display name, and attributes for the `Favorites` folder:

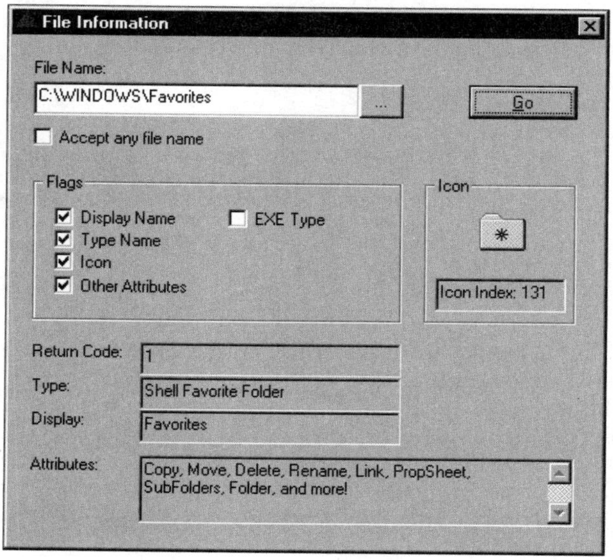

Note that in this case we're referring to the folder by its physical name rather than its PIDL. On my home PC, this directory is `C:\WINDOWS\Favorites`, but it wouldn't have mattered if the file I was looking for were on a network drive – such details are transparent to `SHGetFileInfo()`.

The Flags of the Function

It's clear that the `uFlags` argument is absolutely central to `SHGetFileInfo()`. It can be constructed from almost any combination of the following values, some of which you've already seen in the code we've put together so far:

Code	Value	Description
SHGFI_ICON	0x0100	Stores the HICON handle to the file icon in the hIcon member of the SHFILEINFO structure.
SHGFI_DISPLAYNAME	0x0200	Stores a pointer to the display name string for the file in the szDisplayName member of the SHFILEINFO structure.
SHGFI_TYPENAME	0x0400	Stores a pointer to the type string for the file in the szTypeName member of the SHFILEINFO structure.
SHGFI_ATTRIBUTES	0x0800	Stores a DWORD with all the settings retrieved for the file in the dwAttributes member of the SHFILEINFO structure.
SHGFI_ICONLOCATION	0x1000	Stores a pointer to the name of the file that contains the icon the shell is using for the specified object in the szDisplayName member of the SHFILEINFO structure. Because of this, you can't use it together with SHGFI_DISPLAYNAME. Strangely, it seems to work only if you specify a folder name; if you specify a file name, the return buffer is always empty.
SHGFI_EXETYPE	0x2000	Causes the function to return a value denoting the binary format of an executable file, and its target platform.
SHGFI_SYSICONINDEX	0x4000	Causes the function to return the handle of the system image list that contains the icon. The index of the icon is stored in the iIcon field of the SHFILEINFO structure.

By using the test program described earlier, I've discovered an interesting thing. It seems that there exists a relationship between `SHGFI_ICON` and `SHGFI_ATTRIBUTES`: the former implies the latter. This means that the `dwAttributes` member of the `SHFILEINFO` structure is always filled in when you specify `SHGFI_ICON`, regardless of whether you also specify `SHGFI_ATTRIBUTES`.

All the above are flags that make the function perform some kind of useful task for the programmer. There are other flags, but these play a secondary role. In some cases, they refine one of the flags from the above table. This is true for:

Code	Value	Description
SHGFI_LARGEICON	0x00000	Causes the function to retrieve the file's large icon.
SHGFI_SMALLICON	0x00001	Causes the function to retrieve the file's small icon.
SHGFI_OPENICON	0x00002	For a folder, this causes the function to retrieve the icon displayed when it's open.
SHGFI_SHELLICONSIZE	0x00004	Causes the function to retrieve an icon with the size that's set in the **Appearance** tab of the **Display** Control Panel applet.
SHGFI_SELECTED	0x10000	The icon retrieved is the one displayed when the file is selected (blended with the highlight color).
SHGFI_LINKOVERLAY	0x08000	The icon retrieved is the one displayed when the file is a shortcut (with that little arrow over it).

The flags in this table affect SHGFI_ICON, and only work in conjunction with it. As you can see, it's possible to get every flavor of icon.

Another flag that refines one of the earlier ones is SHGFI_ATTR_SPECIFIED, which applies to SHGFI_ATTRIBUTES. It means that the dwAttributes field of the SHFILEINFO structure is *already* initialized with the attributes flags the caller wants SHGetFileInfo() to retrieve. In other words, if dwAttributes has a particular flag set, say SFGAO_SHARE, the function must check that flag (and only that flag) on the file being operated upon. By default, dwAttributes contains 0xFFFFFFFF, which means that all the attributes must be checked. I'll have more to say about file attributes a little later on.

To complete the list of the flags, there are just two that I haven't yet mentioned: SHGFI_PIDL and SHGFI_USEFILEATTRIBUTES. We'll discuss more about these two, and the flags that modify SHGFI_ICON, in the forthcoming sections.

> *Provided that there's a way to return data, you can specify several flags at the same time. In other words, you can request (say) the icon, the display and the type name together, but not the large and the small icon, since these are both returned through the same buffer.*

Getting Information for a Given File Type

If you want to know the icon and the type name that the system uses for a certain *kind* of document, you have no need to resort to wildcards. Instead, you can exploit a feature of SHGetFileInfo() that's well documented.

By setting the SHGFI_USEFILEATTRIBUTES flag in the uFlags parameter, you force the function to assume that the file you passed in through pszPath exists. In this case, it just takes the extension and searches the registry for information about the icon and the type name. This is a really interesting feature because it allows you to ask, for example, for the icon of a given family of files simply by specifying *.ext.

Of course, if you're using SHGFI_USEFILEATTRIBUTES, you can't expect other flags like
SHGFI_EXETYPE, SHGFI_ATTRIBUTES or SHGFI_PIDL to work properly, since they are specific to
a particular, file that *exists*.

In my opinion, the oddest thing in this procedure is the name of the constant. Why did they use
SHGFI_USEFILEATTRIBUTES? The name and the documentation seem to suggest a link between
this flag and the dwFileAttributes argument of SHGetFileInfo(): the idea is that the function
behaves as if a file exists with the name specified in pszPath and the attributes set in
dwFileAttributes. However, the role played by the file attributes here appears to be somewhat
tenuous. All the samples I wrote worked fine, regardless of the value assigned to
dwFileAttributes.

To see this flag in action, you can check the **Accept any file name** box in the sample application and
enter something like *.htm as the **File Name**. Alternatively, here's a helper function that you can use
in isolation to get the icon and type name for any type of file:

```
HICON GetFileTypeIcon(LPCTSTR szFileType, LPTSTR szTypeName)
{
    SHFILEINFO sfi;
    ZeroMemory(&sfi, sizeof(SHFILEINFO));
    SHGetFileInfo(szFileType, 0, &sfi, sizeof(SHFILEINFO),
                        SHGFI_USEFILEATTRIBUTES | SHGFI_ICON | SHGFI_TYPENAME);

    lstrcpy(szTypeName, sfi.szTypeName);
    return sfi.hIcon;
}
```

Shell Icon Size

The SHGFI_SHELLICONSIZE flag forces the function to retrieve a large icon with the size specified
in the Shell Icon Size value of the following registry path:

HKEY_CURRENT_USER\Control Panel\desktop\WindowMetrics

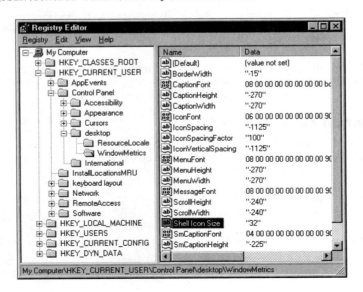

This value may be set through the Control Panel's Display applet, by selecting the **Appearance** tab. It affects the size of large icons throughout the desktop, and inside folders:

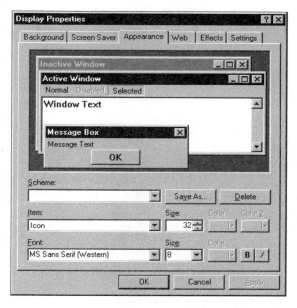

If the key doesn't exist, or if the SHGFI_SHELLICONSIZE flag is not specified, then the size of the icon retrieved by SHGetFileInfo() follows the default window metric, which is 32 x 32 pixels. Each time you change the Shell Icon Size key, the Explorer refreshes its internal cache of icons, which is simply the system image list that's returned by SHGFI_SYSICONINDEX. To get the real size of the icon retrieved, you should use the ImageList_GetIconSize() function.

Using a PIDL

SHGFI_PIDL simply informs the system that the item being passed as if it were a file name is actually a PIDL, and therefore needs special treatment. This code, for example, demonstrates how to get the icon of the My Computer folder:

```
LPITEMIDLIST pidl;
SHGetSpecialFolderLocation(NULL, CSIDL_DRIVES, &pidl);
DWORD dwRC = SHGetFileInfo(reinterpret_cast<LPCTSTR>(pidl),
        dwFileAttributes, &sfi, sizeof(SHFILEINFO), uFlags | SHGFI_PIDL);
```

My Computer is a special folder that doesn't map to a physical directory on your disks. Rather, it's a virtual folder whose underpinnings are coded into a namespace extension. Since such a folder doesn't have a matching path name, we need to identify it to SHGetFileInfo() by some other means. The obvious approach is to use its PIDL.

Since version 4.71, the shell API has defined a function called SHGetSpecialFolderLocation() that takes a symbol identifying a special folder, and returns the corresponding PIDL. For My Computer, this symbol is CSIDL_DRIVES. In earlier versions of the shell, getting the PIDL of a special folder was still possible, but it was a complex task. However, it's exactly the kind of code we'll have to deal with ourselves if we want the PIDL of an object that isn't part of the file system and isn't a special folder. Such code is presented in Chapter 5, where we'll be writing a custom routine to walk the content of *any* folder.

If you replace the call to SHGetFileInfo() with the three lines of code you see above, the resulting output will be:

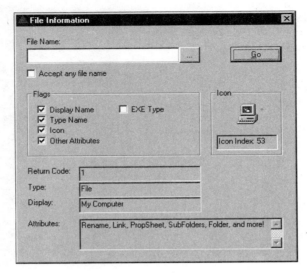

Getting Attributes for a File

There's a long list of attributes you can retrieve for a given file object, many of which appeared in the second if block of our OnOK() implementation. The attributes you can obtain using SHGetFileInfo() are the same as those you can retrieve through using the GetAttributesOf() method of the IShellFolder interface. In other words, SHGetFileInfo() acts as a wrapper for the IShellFolder interface in this case. The attributes you can read are all defined in the shlobj.h header file. Here's a list of the ones you're most likely to have to deal with:

Attribute	Description
SFGAO_CANCOPY	The file object can be copied through drag-and-drop or the clipboard.
SFGAO_CANDELETE	The file object can be deleted through the shell.
SFGAO_CANLINK	It is possible to create shortcuts for the file object.
SFGAO_CANMOVE	The file object can be moved through drag-and-drop or the clipboard.
SFGAO_CANRENAME	The file object can be renamed through the shell.
SFGAO_HASPROPSHEET	The file object has at least one property sheet.
SFGAO_GHOSTED	The file object is displayed using a ghosted icon (normally, this is a hidden file).
SFGAO_LINK	The file object is a shortcut.
SFGAO_READONLY	The file object is read-only.

Attribute	Description
SFGAO_SHARE	The specified folder is shared.
SFGAO_HASSUBFOLDER	The specified folder has at least one sub-folder.
SFGAO_COMPRESSED	The file object resides on a compressed drive.
SFGAO_FILESYSTEM	The file object is part of the file system and not a virtual folder. This also means that a physical object (drive, directory or file) exists for it.
SFGAO_FOLDER	The specified object is a folder.
SFGAO_REMOVABLE	The file object resides on removable media (typically a floppy disk).

Given this, it's easy to arrange quick functions to test such conditions. For example, a question I'm often asked is, "How can I know whether a given directory is shared?" Determining this is simply a matter of checking the contents of the dwAttributes field of the SHFILEINFO structure returned by SHGetFileInfo() against SHGAO_SHARE:

```
BOOL IsDirectoryShared(LPCTSTR szDirName)
{
    SHFILEINFO sfi;
    ZeroMemory(&sfi, sizeof(SHFILEINFO));
    SHGetFileInfo(szDirName, 0, &sfi, sizeof(SHFILEINFO), SHGFI_ATTRIBUTES);
    return(sfi.dwAttributes & SFGAO_SHARE);
}
```

If a given folder *is* shared, you might want the function to return the icon in which a hand is holding the object:

After all, SHGetFileInfo() can return 'selected' icons for folders, so ours isn't a far-fetched demand. Unfortunately, the function doesn't support this feature, but that's no good reason to give up! Let's see how we can work around this problem.

Creating the 'Hand-held' Folder Icon

The 'holding hand' icon is the 29th icon in shell32.dll (with a zero-based index of 28):

Rather than resorting to hard work with device contexts, XOR and AND masks, and the like, we can exploit the power of an underused Windows 95 common control: the **image list**.

An image list is a collection of images (icons and bitmaps) that are kept in memory in a very special and efficient way: they are stored as a *single* bitmap that's created by putting all the constituent images side-by-side. Think of it as a comic strip or, better yet, as a film roll. A fundamental constraint of image lists is that all the images have the same size, allowing the system to access any image by index quickly and easily. Image lists are generally used to manage large numbers of small images, and many of the Windows 9x and Windows NT common controls (list views and tree views, for example) require you to provide icons through an image list.

From the programmer's standpoint, an image list is an invisible control with its own set of messages and styles, and a specific handle (HIMAGELIST). Image lists have a very rich programming interface, though, and there are functions to manage the list (extract, add, copy), to support drag-and-drop and especially to support drawing. For more information about image lists, and for a complete programming guide, you can refer to the documentation under Platform SDK I User Interface Services I Shell and Common Controls I Image Lists.

The aspect of image lists we're interested in here is their substantial, built-in support for overlaying and combining icons and small bitmaps. Explorer itself uses image lists when it comes to displaying a composite icon for certain types of file objects, such as shortcuts and shared folders: it first gets hold of the right 'basic' icon, and then, if necessary, processes it in one of the following ways:

❑ Blending with the highlight color (selected state)
❑ Blending with the gray color (ghosted state, for a hidden file)
❑ Overlaying the icon with others, such as the link or the 'holding hand'

If all you want to do is simply to produce output, then ImageList_SetOverlayImage() is the function that does the job. It works in conjunction with ImageList_Draw() to combine two icons in a given device context. Here's an example:

```
HICON hiFolder;
HICON hiHand;

// Load the icons
// hiFolder = ...;
// hiHand = ...;

// Get the DC to draw into
HDC hdc = GetDC(GetFocus());

// Create the image list
HIMAGELIST himl = ImageList_Create(32, 32, ILC_MASK, 1, 0);

// Add icons to the image list
ImageList_AddIcon(himl, hiFolder);      // Icon index of 0
ImageList_AddIcon(himl, hiHand);        // Icon index of 1

// Icon 1 (hand icon) is the overlay mask #1
ImageList_SetOverlayImage(himl, 1, 1);

// Icon 0 (the folder) must be overlaid by mask #1 in the device context
ImageList_Draw(himl, 0, hdc, 0, 0, INDEXTOOVERLAYMASK(1));
```

```
// Free the icons
DestroyIcon(hiFolder);
DestroyIcon(hiHand);

// Clean up and exit
ReleaseDC(GetFocus(), hdc);
ImageList_Destroy(himl);
```

The source code employs a number of functions from the image list API. In particular, `ImageList_Create()` gives you a brand new image list with the specified size for the images (32 x 32 in the sample above). When you've finished, you destroy it using `ImageList_Destroy()`. As its name suggests, `ImageList_AddIcon()` adds icons to the given image list. For these and other functions, documentation is available in Visual C++ Books Online.

The call to `ImageList_SetOverlayImage()` in the above code defines the second icon in the image list (index 1, the 'holding hand') as overlay mask #1. Then, in the device context specified by hdc, the icon with index 0 (that is, the folder) is overlaid with mask #1. Take care here, because the indexes for icons and masks are different – the former are 0-based, while the latter are 1-based.

Version 4.71 of the shell has increased the number of overlay masks available from 4 to 15.

Although the code presented so far works fine and does what we asked it to, it would be more useful if we could return a brand new icon to a caller, and so we need to find something *like* `ImageList_Draw()`, but which creates an icon that can be addressed by an `HICON` handle. We can then return that handle to the caller. In fact, we don't have to look very far for help, because `ImageList_Merge()` does just what we need.

```
HIMAGELIST ImageList_Merge(HIMAGELIST himl1,
                           int        i1,
                           HIMAGELIST himl2,
                           int        i2,
                           int        dx,
                           int        dy);
```

The function takes two images from two image lists (it can be the same image list in both cases, if you wish), and merges them by drawing the second over the first. The new image is stored in a new image list, and the mask for the resulting image is obtained by ORing the masks (if any) of the two constituent images. The documentation is not completely clear what the dx and dy parameters do, but a moment's experimentation reveals that they indicate the position relative to the first image at which you want the overlaying image to be drawn. The offset is calculated from the top-left pixel, but I bet that in most cases you'll set both parameters to 0.

Here, then, is the source code for a reusable function called `GetSharedFolderIcon()` that takes an `HICON` and returns a handle to a new icon in which the original image has been overlaid with the 'holding hand' icon:

```
HICON GetSharedFolderIcon(HICON hiFolder)
{
    HICON hiShared;
    HICON hiHand;

    // Get the 'holding hand' icon
    ExtractIconEx("shell32.dll", 28, &hiHand, NULL, 1);
```

```
    // Create an image list to merge the folder and hand icons
    HIMAGELIST himl = ImageList_Create(32, 32, ILC_MASK, 1, 0);

    // Add icons to the image list
    ImageList_AddIcon(himl, hiFolder);
    ImageList_AddIcon(himl, hiHand);

    // Merge the icons to a new image list
    HIMAGELIST himlNew = ImageList_Merge(himl, 0, himl, 1, 0, 0);

    // Extract the icon from the new image list
    hiShared = ImageList_ExtractIcon(0, himlNew, 0);

    // Free the 'holding hand' icon. We don't free the 'folder' icon
    //  because we received it from the caller, who may still need it.
    DestroyIcon(hiHand);

    // Clean up the image lists and exit
    ImageList_Destroy(himl);
    ImageList_Destroy(himlNew);
    return hiShared;
}
```

The function receives the icon whose 'shared' version is required from the caller, so the first thing we have to do is get hold of the 'holding hand' icon, which (as explained earlier) is stored in shell32.dll with an index of 28. To extract the icon, we use ExtractIconEx(). This is not the only possibility (ExtractIcon() is fine as well), but it's the more flexible choice: it lets you extract more icons in more sizes at the same time.

```
    ExtractIconEx("shell32.dll", 28, &hiHand, NULL, 1);
```

This single line instructs the function to load only the large version of the 29th icon (remember that 0-based index) in shell32.dll. We want neither the small version, nor more icons. See the Visual C++ Books Online for further details about ExtractIconEx().

With both icons in our possession, we create an image list and fill it with the two icons to combine. Then, we merge the icons and save the result into another new list that has just one icon – the syntax of ImageList_Merge() requires you to identify the icons through an <image list, icon index> pair. After calling ImageList_Merge(), we have a brand new image list from which to extract the composite icon. You can now amend the code in OnOK() so that this new function is called if the object on which SHGetFileInfo() operates is shared:

```
    ////////////////////////////////////////////
    // Show the icon
    //
    HICON hIcon;
    if(dwAttrib & SFGAO_SHARE)
        hIcon = GetSharedFolderIcon(sfi.hIcon);
    else
        hIcon = sfi.hIcon;

    SendDlgItemMessage(
              hDlg, IDI_ICON, STM_SETICON, reinterpret_cast<WPARAM>(hIcon), 0);
```

The following screenshot shows how the function works:

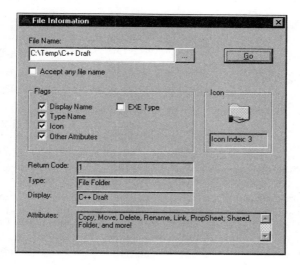

Binary Format of Executables

Another interesting feature of `SHGetFileInfo()` is its ability to return the binary format of an executable file. By specifying the correct flag, you can discover whether a given .exe is a 32-bit or 16-bit module, and even which is the minimum Windows platform it requires. Typical scenarios when this might be necessary are when you're:

❑ Writing a system-wide routine to analyze processes and windows, or to scan files. You might want to indicate whether a 16-bit or a 32-bit program has created that process or window.

❑ Detecting programmatically whether your customers have upgraded from the old 16-bit version of your tool.

❑ Writing low-level tools to spy on the system and its files.

❑ Implementing interprocess communication, as this may also require knowledge of the type of an executable.

If you're in one of these situations, it looks at first like there's only one way out: learn about the binary format of Windows (and possibly DOS) executables, and manually scan the binary code looking for identifying characteristics. Fortunately, `SHGetFileInfo()` saves us from having to do so. In order to decide which generation of Windows platform a given program was designed for, you just need to specify the `SHGFI_EXETYPE` flag. Note, though, that to work properly, this flag cannot be combined with any other.

Retrieving information about the executable format is one of the few cases where you must analyze the *return code* of the function to extrapolate the result. `SHGetFileInfo()` returns a DWORD value, and in this case the *low order word* is the signature of the executable, which is given by the following strings:

File Signature	Hex Code	Meaning
PE	0x4550	Win32 Portable Executable format, as adopted by all the 32-bit Microsoft operating systems.
NE	0x454E	Windows 3.*x* New Executable format, which is typical of all 16-bit Windows programs.
MZ	0x5A4D	DOS executable format. This value is also returned if you interrogate a `.com` or a `.bat` file.

The hexadecimal codes correspond exactly to the letters in the 'file signature' column. For example, 0x50 is the P, 0x45 is the E, and so on.

The two bytes of the *high order word*, on the other hand, contain the version number of the minimum release of the operating system required to run the program. This information isn't strictly necessary if your goal is just to know whether a given module is 16- or 32-bit, but you'll find it to be 0x030A in the case of old Windows 3.1 programs, and 0x0400 for all the other 32-bit platforms. The only exceptions to this are programs specifically targeted to Windows NT 3.5*x*, where the value is less than 0x0400 even if they're 32-bit programs – in this case, the number is 0x0350. It's also possible that there will be a zero value in the high order word, which means you're looking at a 32-bit console application.

So while `SHGetFileInfo()` can give you all the information you could ever want to know about a file, its programming interface has considerable room for improvement. Given a file name, for example, it's quite a complex process to arrange a test to determine whether it is a 32-bit, a 16-bit or a DOS program. Calling the function is only half the job; you then have to check the result and decide what to do about it.

We will round off this discussion by implementing the code that deals with the **EXE Type** box being checked in our sample application. It involves defining constants for the three different types of file at the top of `FileInfo.cpp`, and then testing the return value of `SHGetFileInfo()` in the fashion described above. The results of these tests are then used to modify the output of the application:

```
// Constants
const int PE_SIGN = 0x4550;
const int NE_SIGN = 0x454E;
const int MZ_SIGN = 0x5A4D;

...

/////////////////////////////////////////////
// Deal with the UI
//
if(uFlags == SHGFI_EXETYPE)
{
    if(dwRC == 0)
        lstrcpy(szBuf, "Not an executable file.");
    else
        lstrcpy(szBuf, "");

    if(LOWORD(dwRC) == PE_SIGN)
    {
        lstrcat(szBuf, "32-bit");
        if(HIWORD(dwRC))
```

```
                lstrcat(szBuf, " Windows executable");
            else
                lstrcat(szBuf, " Console executable");
        }
        else if(LOWORD(dwRC) == NE_SIGN)
            lstrcat(szBuf, "16-bit executable");
        else if(LOWORD(dwRC) == MZ_SIGN)
            lstrcat(szBuf, "DOS executable");
    }
    else
        wsprintf(szBuf, "%d", dwRC);
```

The screenshot below illustrates what happens with `Explorer.exe`:

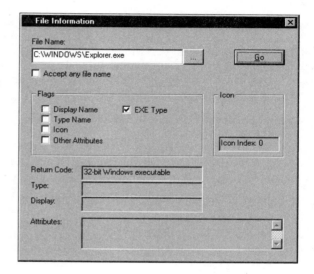

Curiously, `SHGetFileInfo()` *doesn't recognize a DLL or a VxD as an executable file, and doesn't return its binary format. There's therefore no way to know about the binary format of a DLL other than delving into the file. This means that the explanation above works well only for stand-alone executables with the* `.exe` *extension. In fact, the function even fails with screen savers, despite files with* `.scr` *extensions being no more than ordinary stand-alone executables. This may (or may not) be a bug, depending upon the definition of 'executable file' you want to adopt.*

SHGetFileInfo() Return Values

If the function returns 0, then an error occurred somewhere. In most cases, this means that you passed an invalid file name or PIDL, or that you specified a faulty combination of flags. The latter of these is the more likely of the two.

Unless the flags specified instruct it to do otherwise, the function returns 1 if everything went well. One example of where this is not the case is when the `SHGFI_EXETYPE` flag is set, as we have been discussing. A second situation in which the return code means something more than just 'success' is when the `SHGFI_SYSICONINDEX` flag is set. In this case, the function returns the handle of the system image list that contains the icon for the specified file or folder.

Interestingly, `SHGetFileInfo()` may even be used successfully to retrieve the icon associated with a CD-ROM. While the icons for other drives are almost always standard, the icon shown by the Explorer for the CD-ROM often depends upon the content of the `autorun.inf` file. Having a function capable of returning the correct icon is a great help whenever you need such an icon.

Summary

`SHGetFileInfo()` doesn't have any obvious bugs, but once again it suffers from documentation that is at the survival level. If you spend a few hours studying what's there and testing all the possible combinations, it's likely that you will eventually find what you need, but that's hardly the point — good documentation must emphasize clearly what a function can and cannot do. At least three of the questions I get asked most frequently are answered by `SHGetFileInfo()`, but discovering that fact was a far from easy business.

To redress the balance a little, this chapter showed you:

❑ How to get the various icons associated with a given file or folder
❑ How to discover the binary format of executable (`.exe`) files
❑ How to determine the system attributes of a given file or folder may have
❑ How to merge two icons using image lists, instead of XOR masks and device contexts

Further Reading

Unfortunately, I don't have a list of books or magazine articles for you on this occasion – this is a subject for which there's a very limited range of material. There are a few things I can recommend, but as you can see, most of them are errata in the official documentation or accessory articles and examples.

The sources listed here are among those I used in researching this chapter, so you might not find anything new. Then again, four eyes are better than two, and you could just notice something that I missed. In particular, I'd like to point you towards a couple of Knowledge Base articles:

- ❑ **Knowledge Base Article ID Q132750:** *Convert a File Path to an ITEMIDLIST*
- ❑ **Knowledge Base Article ID Q128786:** *How to Shade Images to Look Like Windows 95 Active Icon*

The first one touches upon a topic we'll cover later on, and shows how to create PIDLs from scratch, and for non-folder objects. The second may help if you need to do some quick graphical processing of your windows' client areas.

We talked briefly about the size of shell icons, and there are a couple of articles to read on that topic. One of these, a piece by Bret Pehrson, appeared in the April 1998 issue of the Windows Developer's Journal (WDJ) under the title *Rebuilding the Internal Shell Icon Cache*. It shows how to force the system programmatically to recognize that the user has changed the current default size for large icons. This same topic (along with many others) is covered by John Hornick in an article called *Icons in Win32*, which appears in the MSDN library under Technical Articles | Windows Platform | User Interface.

5

Browsing for Folders

I provided an overview of folders and their place in the Windows shell in Chapter 2, but in this chapter we're going to look at them in detail. We'll focus on the shell functions that deal with folders at any level, and all the underlying machinery that makes sure everything is working properly. In doing so, we'll run into two things that play very important roles: shortcuts and PIDLs. The former will be the subject of the next chapter, but we'll examine PIDLs in this one, covering:

- ❑   The use of the SHBrowseForFolder() function
- ❑   More about what PIDLs are, and how to work with them
- ❑   Virtual folders and special locations
- ❑   How to get the settings of a folder

The examples we'll discuss include an enhanced version of the SHBrowseForFolder() API function, some helper functions to make it easier to work with PIDLs, and some samples of how to enumerate the contents of some special locations, such as SendTo, Favorites, and My Documents.

Choosing a Folder

Let's begin our trip with a look at the various ways there are to select a folder. It's a common requirement for an application to be able to allow the user to choose a particular directory from a specific drive. The Windows 3.x API didn't provide any built-in facility for this, so you had to create your own helper function, and there was a pretty common technique for doing so. It consisted of modifying the common dialog template, leaving out some unnecessary controls like the list box that contained the file names.

Porting this solution to Win32 has a drawback, however: you have to renounce the new Explorer-style user interface and instead remain faithful to the old one:

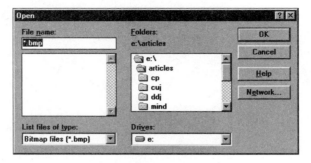

On Win32 platforms, the Explorer-style Open dialog is a single entity, and you can't just 'get rid' of any of its components (like the file list, for example...).

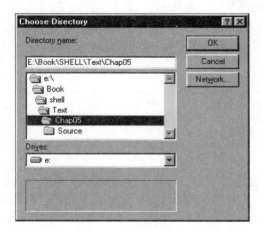

Another option that's open if you elect to adopt the old Windows 3.*x* interface is to arrange a dialog like the one shown by Visual C++ when it asks you to specify a folder for your new project. Check out the Win32 documentation for GetOpenFileName() to discover more about it.

A More Modern Approach

Starting with Windows 95, the Win32 SDK finally delivered a system-provided solution for browsing folders: the function called SHBrowseForFolder(). Its main feature is that it uses a tree view that's similar to the one we know and love from using Explorer:

Like the functions we've examined in the last two chapters, SHBrowseForFolder() has a prototype that *looks* simple, but which actually involves a structure with lots of settings and flags. Unlike those others, however, it may be considered a more 'focused' function — its one purpose in life is to let you choose a folder from those available in your desktop's namespace.

The Prototype of SHBrowseForFolder()

Let's have a look at the prototype of SHBrowseForFolder(), which can be found in shlobj.h:

```
LPITEMIDLIST WINAPI SHBrowseForFolder(LPBROWSEINFO lpbi);
```

It takes a single pointer to a BROWSEINFO structure, which is declared in the same file:

```
typedef struct _browseinfo
{
    HWND hwndOwner;
    LPCITEMIDLIST pidlRoot;
    LPSTR pszDisplayName;
    LPCSTR lpszTitle;
    UINT ulFlags;
    BFFCALLBACK lpfn;
    LPARAM lParam;
    int iImage;
} BROWSEINFO, *PBROWSEINFO, *LPBROWSEINFO;
```

Let's see what each member is for.

Name	Description
hwndOwner	Handle of the window that owns the dialog.
pidlRoot	Identifies the root node for the hierarchy of objects to be presented. This is a PIDL.
pszDisplayName	Must be a pointer to an allocated buffer that will contain the display name of the selected object.
lpszTitle	Must be a pointer to a buffer that contains the string to be assigned to the label just above the tree view.
ulFlags	Specifies the appearance and behavior of the window. (See later for permitted values.)
lpfn	Callback function used to hook the dialog.
lParam	32-bit custom data to be passed to the callback function. Usually a pointer or a handle.
IImage	Buffer that will contain the index of the icon for the selected folder or file. This index is relative to the system image list.

The very simplest way to call SHBrowseForFolder() is:

```
BROWSEINFO bi;
ZeroMemory(&bi, sizeof(BROWSEINFO));
bi.hwndOwner = hDlg;
LPITEMIDLIST pidl = SHBrowseForFolder(&bi);
```

This code will display a dialog box like the one in the figure you saw earlier in the chapter, and it retrieves a PIDL to the selected folder. If the folder has a corresponding path, you can get it through this code:

```
TCHAR szPath[MAX_PATH] = {0};
SHGetPathFromIDList(pidl, szPath);
Msg(szPath);
```

There are, however, a number of interesting issues connected with using SHBrowseForFolder(). We can summarize them as follows, and over the next sections, we'll be looking at them in detail.

❑ The function handles both PIDLs and path names transparently.
❑ The function allows you to browse even into special system folders.
❑ The function returns a great deal of information, not unlike SHGetFileInfo(). (See the previous chapter.)
❑ The dialog is slightly customizable, which is always good news.

Using SHBrowseForFolder()

What you can do with SHBrowseForFolder() is strongly bound to the ulFlags member of BROWSEINFO, whose legal values are combinations of the following flags:

Flag	Description
BIF_RETURNONLYFSDIRS	If set, the function enables the **OK** button only if the user selects a file system directory. If, for example, you were to select the **Network Neighborhood** node with this flag set, the **OK** button would be grayed out.
BIF_DONTGOBELOWDOMAIN	Do not show network folders, only nodes with the domain name.
BIF_STATUSTEXT	The dialog template contains a label where you can display any text you want, especially if you subclass the dialog window. (More on this later on.)
BIF_EDITBOX	This is a new feature (shell version 4.71 and above) that allows you to have an edit box from which to choose a folder manually.
BIF_VALIDATE	This is another new feature (shell version 4.71) that complements BIF_EDITBOX. If you set this flag and subclass the dialog window, then you'll be notified each time the user enters and confirms an incorrect file or folder name in the edit box. (More on this later on.)

Flag	Description
BIF_BROWSEFORCOMPUTER	Allows the user to choose only a computer name. The browse takes place as usual, but the **OK** button that enables the selection is always disabled, except when a computer name is selected.
BIF_BROWSEFORPRINTER	The same as above, but for printer names.
BIF_BROWSEINCLUDEFILES	If this flag is set, then despite the function's name, the tree view shows and lets you select file names and not just folder names. This offers a great chance to set up dialogs with all the printers or the fonts available in the system.

When calling SHBrowseForFolder(), there are two ways in which you can customize the look of the final dialog. The more powerful requires you to subclass the window via a callback function, and we'll cover this later in the chapter. A far simpler way to get a limited degree of customization is by modifying the text above the tree view. The lpszTitle member of BROWSEINFO is responsible for this; it is declared as a pointer, so you just have to pass a 32-bit pointer to an existing memory buffer:

```
TCHAR szBuf[MAX_PATH] = {0};
lstrcpy(szBuf, __TEXT("Choose a folder:"));
bi.lpszTitle = static_cast<LPCSTR>(szBuf);
```

The same holds true for pszDisplayName, which is a return buffer. If you're interested in the display name of the selected folder, then you need to pass a valid buffer to be filled. First declare or allocate it, and then assign the pointer to pszDisplayName:

```
TCHAR szDisp[MAX_PATH] = {0};
bi.pszDisplayName = static_cast<LPSTR>(szDisp);
```

The function assumes that pszDisplayName is at least MAX_PATH bytes in size. Of course, this field may be NULL, in which case you won't receive the display name of the folder.

As explained in earlier chapters, the display name of the folder is the name used by Explorer to display that folder. On my machine, for example, (C:) is the display name of C:\.

What the Function Returns

Technically, the return value of SHBrowseForFolder() is a PIDL that identifies the selected file or folder. If you cancel the dialog, then the function returns NULL. Simple as ever.

However, the function is capable of returning other useful information through the BROWSEINFO structure that you pass to it. Specific examples of this include the display name of the selected object (as I've already mentioned), and even the icon that represents it.

Getting the Folder Icon

Even though SHBrowseForFolder() seems to be reproducing functionality we've already observed in SHGetFileInfo(), there's quite a bit of work you have to do on your own to get and display the icon.

When the function returns, the iImage member of the BROWSEINFO structure contains a number that is the index to the position the icon occupies in the system image list. Thus, if you want to draw the icon – or more simply, if you want the HICON handle to it – you must first get a handle to the image list.

I talked about this in the previous chapter, so it's fairly easy to employ the method here. If you call SHGetFileInfo() with the SHGFI_ICON and (above all) SHGFI_SYSICONINDEX flags set, the function returns a handle to the system image list.

```
HICON SHGetSystemIcon(int iIconIndex)
{
    SHFILEINFO sfi;
    ZeroMemory(&sfi, sizeof(SHFILEINFO));

    // We aren't specifying a file name, since all we want is the handle...
    HIMAGELIST himl = reinterpret_cast<HIMAGELIST>(SHGetFileInfo(
        "*.*", 0, &sfi, sizeof(SHFILEINFO), SHGFI_ICON | SHGFI_SYSICONINDEX));

    HICON hIcon = ImageList_ExtractIcon(0, himl, iIconIndex);
    return hIcon;
}
```

The above code is a helper routine that given an index, returns the corresponding icon in the system image list. To run this code, you need to include shellapi.h and to initialize the common controls library by calling either InitCommonControls() or InitCommonControlsEx(). As discussed in Appendix A, the first is the approach to use for old versions of the shell, while the second is recommended for shell versions 4.71 and above.

Using a Callback Function

The most interesting things you can do with SHBrowseForFolder() require a callback function. This kind of thing is well supported and, once in a while, even pretty well documented. To subclass the dialog box created by the function, you need to assign a valid function pointer to the lpfn field of BROWSEINFO. The pointer must point to a function with a prototype like this:

```
int CALLBACK BrowseCallbackProc(HWND    hwnd,
                                UINT    uMsg,
                                LPARAM  lParam,
                                LPARAM  dwData);
```

As I'm sure you've guessed, hwnd is the handle of the hooked window, while uMsg is the code of the message being received. lParam is a value that can have different meanings according to uMsg, and finally dwData is user-defined data – the same data you specified through the lParam member of BROWSEINFO. If you need the callback function to work on data created by the calling program instead of using global variables, you can fill the BROWSEINFO structure's lParam member with a 32-bit value and be sure that it will automatically be passed to the callback via the dwData argument. To fit more data in those 32 bits, you can use pointers or, better yet, allocate a handle to a block of memory, lock it, package everything you need, unlock it, and store it as the lParam field.

The figure shows the situation once the callback has been set up: SHBrowseForFolder() calls a function that you define, passing in some data and notifying some events.

Events You Can Detect

The dialog box created by SHBrowseForFolder() can notify the callback function of the following events:

- ❑ Dialog initialization has completed
- ❑ The selection has changed
- ❑ The user entered some invalid file or folder name in the edit box

It does this by sending the following messages:

- ❑ BFFM_INITIALIZED
- ❑ BFFM_SELCHANGED
- ❑ BFFM_VALIDATEFAILED

These messages are received by the callback function through its uMsg parameter. Each message carries with it a LPARAM value, which evaluates to the lParam argument. Let's see how lParam is configured message by message.

Message	lParam **Meaning**
BFFM_INITIALIZED	Unused – it is always NULL. This message is sent after the dialog's window procedure has finished processing the WM_INITDIALOG message.
BFFM_SELCHANGED	Points to the identifier list of the newly selected folder. Note that, like other Windows controls, this event is notified when the selection has already changed.
BFFM_VALIDATEFAILED	Points to the current contents of the edit box, which means that like its subject, this message is supported only with shell version 4.71. By returning zero, the callback can force the browsing dialog to close. By returning a non-zero value, on the other hand, the dialog is kept active.

Messages You Can Send

There are a few messages that a callback function can send to the dialog window to have it execute certain actions. Specifically, they are:

Message	Description
BFFM_ENABLEOK	This enables or disables the OK button, according to the value of lParam. If non-zero, the button is enabled so you can confirm the currently selected folder. wParam is unused.
BFFM_SETSELECTION	Selects the specified file or folder. A pointer to the PIDL or the path name is stored in lParam, while wParam dictates how to interpret the pointer. FALSE means it is a PIDL, TRUE stands for a path name.
BFFM_SETSTATUSTEXT	Sets the text you provide in the dialog's status area. The actual text is pointed by lParam, while wParam is unused.

These messages are sent using the ordinary SendMessage() function, and by combining them you can really enhance the behavior of SHBrowseForFolder().

Customizing the User Interface

By using a callback function, you can intervene and make changes to the dialog's user interface so that it suits your needs perfectly. Suppose, for example, that you don't want the ? button on the caption bar, or that you want to give a more marked 3D look to some controls. In this section, I'll explain how such things can be done.

Removing the Context Help Button

Removing the context help button from the caption bar is simply a matter of style. That's right: you just have to turn off the bit that causes Windows to draw and handle it! The button appears when the extended style of *any* window has the WS_EX_CONTEXTHELP bit set.

> *Extended styles were first introduced with Windows 3.1, and reinforced with the SDK version that shipped with Windows 95. To the best of my knowledge, the only difference between 'ordinary' styles and 'extended' styles lies in the memory area where they are stored. There are no conceptual differences and no hidden meanings.*

You need to use different code to access 'extended' styles than you do to access window styles. To turn off the bit that makes the help button appear, what you have to do in your callback function in response to the BFFM_INITIALIZED message is the following:

```
DWORD dwStyle = GetWindowLong(hwnd, GWL_EXSTYLE);
SetWindowLong(hwnd, GWL_EXSTYLE, dwStyle & ~WS_EX_CONTEXTHELP);
```

First, you get the current extended style (using GWL_EXSTYLE instead of GWL_STYLE), and then you turn off the specified bit. Finally, save the style back again.

Adding a 3D Border to the Status Text

Doing this is only a little more complex and requires just one more line of code than the last example. However, you should be aware that doing things like we're about to do doesn't guarantee that your code will work on all existing and future versions of Windows. You can only be sure it works where you have successfully tested it.

That warning aside, we want to draw the status label with a 3D border, just like any other status bar. The `BIF_STATUSTEXT` flag is somewhat misleading — it doesn't add a real status bar to the bottom of the window as you might expect it to. Instead, it adds a static label just above the tree view and below the title. This window has a control ID that we can discover through a utility like Spy++:

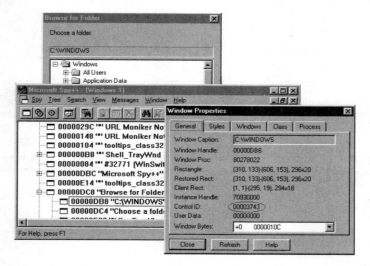

When you know the control ID, and once the callback function has brought you inside the dialog's code, getting the handle of any child window is as easy as calling:

```
HWND hwndChild = GetDlgItem(hDlg, controlID);
```

You can see from the screenshots above that the label we're interested in has a control ID of 0x3743, so:

```
HWND hwndLabel = GetDlgItem(hwnd, 0x3743);
dwStyle = GetWindowLong(hwndLabel, GWL_EXSTYLE);
SetWindowLong(hwndLabel, GWL_EXSTYLE, dwStyle | WS_EX_STATICEDGE);
SetWindowPos(hwndLabel, NULL, 0, 0, 0, 0,
                          SWP_NOSIZE | SWP_NOMOVE | SWP_DRAWFRAME);
```

The above code just adds a slightly inset edge to the window, making it look like this:

Note that in order to see the change, you need to force the window to redraw its non-client area, which is where `SetWindowPos()` comes in. Once again, all this is done in your callback function responding to the `BFFM_INITIALIZED` message.

I warned you earlier about the potentially temporary nature of this code. Today, it works well on all Win32 platforms, but what if some day Microsoft decides to change that ID? A good workaround might be the following.

```
HWND hwndLabel = GetDlgItem(hwnd, 0x3743);
```

```
// Check if it is a valid window
if(IsWindow(hwndLabel))
{
    // Now check if it is window of class 'static'
    TCHAR szClass[MAX_PATH] = {0};
    GetClassName(hwndLabel, szClass, MAX_PATH);
    if(lstrcmpi(szClass, __TEXT("static")))
        return;
}
else
    return;
```

We perform a double check against the window handle returned from `GetDlgItem()`. Firstly, we check that it's a valid window using `IsWindow()`. Secondly, we verify that the window really is a label – a window of class 'static'. If either of these tests fails, we should exit the procedure to avoid access violation errors.

Changing the Dialog Caption

A more useful (and rather safer) action than adding a 3D border might be to change the caption of the dialog window – you have just to call `SetWindowText()` with the new string. Again, this code will execute in response to `BFFM_INITIALIZED`.

```
SetWindowText(hwnd, szNewCaption);
```

Moving the Dialog Window

Another thing you might want to do during the initialization step, responding to BFFM_INITIALIZED, is to position the window wherever it suits your needs. Typically, you would move the dialog to the center of the screen:

```
RECT rc;
GetClientRect(hwnd, &rc);
SetWindowPos(hwnd, NULL,
             (GetSystemMetrics(SM_CXSCREEN) - (rc.right - rc.left)) / 2,
             (GetSystemMetrics(SM_CYSCREEN) - (rc.bottom - rc.top)) / 2,
             0, 0, SWP_NOZORDER | SWP_NOSIZE);
```

Animating the Status Label

A typical use for the status label is displaying the name of the file or folder that's currently selected, as shown in the previous figure. The mechanism that makes this possible is built around the BFFM_SELCHANGED message.

```
TCHAR szText[MAX_PATH] = {0};
SHGetPathFromIDList(reinterpret_cast<LPITEMIDLIST>(lParam), szText);
SendMessage(hwnd, BFFM_SETSTATUSTEXT, 0, reinterpret_cast<LPARAM>(szText));
```

When you receive it, the lParam argument points to the PIDL of the newly selected folder or file. Then, *provided that one exists for that folder*, you can get the path name in displayable form by calling the SHGetPathFromIDList() function. The reason for this proviso is that not all folders map to a physical directory — My Computer, for example, appears to be a folder without actually being one. If you call SHGetPathFromIDList() with a PIDL that points to My Computer, you'll get an empty string as a result.

The string retrieved by SHGetPathFromIDList() can then be sent to the status window using the BFFM_SETSTATUSTEXT message.

Validating Manual Editing

Since 4.71 version of the shell, which was bundled with Internet Explorer 4.0, it has been possible to add an edit box to the user interface of this dialog, and it's not even necessary to resort to callbacks in order to do so. It suffices simply that you specify the BIF_EDITBOX flag when calling SHBrowseForFolder(). The result is the following:

The edit box allows you to type in the name of a folder to select. When you confirm it by clicking OK, the function will validate your input. The content of the edit box is correct if it contains the full path name for a folder, or the name of the currently selected folder, as in the figure above.

If the BIF_VALIDATE flag is specified and the function finds the contents of the edit box to be incorrect, then SHBrowseForFolder() will invoke your callback function specifying the BFFM_VALIDATEFAILED message. The string in the edit box is passed via the callback's lParam argument (the third one). Any data it receives from the user in the BROWSEINFO structure's lParam member becomes the fourth argument to the callback. Thus, if you want to select a folder by typing its name into the edit box you absolutely need to type in the full path name.

The following listing presents a sample callback procedure that encompasses all the examples we've looked at so far. We'll look at an application that uses it later in the chapter, so keep it in mind until then!

```
int CALLBACK BrowseCallbackProc(
                       HWND hwnd, UINT uMsg, LPARAM lParam, LPARAM dwData)
{
    switch(uMsg)
    {
    case BFFM_INITIALIZED:
        {
            // Remove the ? from the caption
            DWORD dwStyle = GetWindowLong(hwnd, GWL_EXSTYLE);
            SetWindowLong(hwnd, GWL_EXSTYLE, dwStyle & ~WS_EX_CONTEXTHELP);

            // Add a 3D border to the status text
            HWND hwndLabel = GetDlgItem(hwnd, 0x3743);

            // Check if it is a valid window
            if(IsWindow(hwndLabel))
            {
                // Now check if it is window of class 'static'
                TCHAR szClass[MAX_PATH] = {0};
                GetClassName(hwndLabel, szClass, MAX_PATH);
                if(lstrcmpi(szClass, __TEXT("static")))
                    break;
            }
            else
                break;

            dwStyle = GetWindowLong(hwndLabel, GWL_EXSTYLE);
            SetWindowLong(hwndLabel, GWL_EXSTYLE, dwStyle | WS_EX_STATICEDGE);
            SetWindowPos(hwndLabel, NULL, 0, 0, 0, 0,
                                    SWP_NOSIZE | SWP_NOMOVE | SWP_DRAWFRAME);
        }
        break;

    case BFFM_SELCHANGED:
        {
            TCHAR szText[MAX_PATH] = {0};
            SHGetPathFromIDList(reinterpret_cast<LPITEMIDLIST>(lParam), szText);
            SendMessage(hwnd, BFFM_SETSTATUSTEXT, 0,
                                        reinterpret_cast<LPARAM>(szText));
        }
        break;
```

```
case BFFM_VALIDATEFAILED:
    Msg("\"%s\" is a wrong path name.", reinterpret_cast<LPTSTR>(lParam));
    return 1;
}

return 0;
}
```

Specifying the Initial Folder

A significant flaw in the design of SHBrowseForFolder() is that there isn't an easy way to specify the initial directory from which to start browsing. You can specify the root of the hierarchy being *displayed*, but even this is not so simple if you want a regular directory instead of a special folder. To set the folder to be selected initially in code, we have to resort to callbacks. In particular, we can exploit the BFFM_SETSELECTION message and ask the function to move the focus over a specific folder. The best place to do this is in response to the BFFM_INITIALIZED notification.

After reading the previous sections, working out how to select an initial folder shouldn't worry you. The code required looks like this:

```
int CALLBACK BrowseCallbackProc(
                    HWND hwnd, UINT uMsg, LPARAM lParam, LPARAM dwData)
{
    switch(uMsg)
    {
    case BFFM_INITIALIZED:
        {
            ...

            SendMessage(hwnd, BFFM_SETSELECTION, TRUE, dwData);

        }
        break;
    ...
    }

    return 0;
}
```

The BFFM_SETSELECTION message needs to know whether *its* lParam argument is a PIDL or a path name. In the fragment above, we're saying dwData points to a path name by setting *our* lParam (the third parameter) to TRUE. Had dwData been a PIDL, the third parameter would have been FALSE.

Specifying the Root Node

As I hinted in the previous section, SHBrowseForFolder() allows you to specify which node of the desktop's hierarchy you want to be the root of the tree. In other words, you can choose which sub-tree of the Explorer view you want to browse. The parameter that lets you do this is the pidlRoot member of the BROWSEINFO structure. If this parameter is set to NULL, the tree view has the desktop as its root.

The figure shows a browsing dialog where the root has been set to `Printers` and the `BIF_BROWSEINCLUDEFILES` bit has been set:

Incidentally, this sample demonstrates how powerful the `BIF_BROWSEINCLUDEFILES` flag can be. The code involved in the figure is:

```
LPITEMIDLIST pidl = NULL;
BROWSEINFO bi;
ZeroMemory(&bi, sizeof(BROWSEINFO));
bi.lpszTitle = __TEXT("Choose a printer:");
SHGetSpecialFolderLocation(NULL, CSIDL_PRINTERS, &pidl);
bi.pidlRoot = pidl;
bi.ulFlags = BIF_BROWSEINCLUDEFILES;
SHBrowseForFolder(&bi);
```

If you check out the declaration of the `BROWSEINFO` structure, you'll see that the `pidlRoot` member *must* be of type `LPCITEMIDLIST` – that is, a PIDL. In the sample above, we've obtained a value to assign to it by passing `CSIDL_PRINTERS` as the second argument to `SHGetSpecialFolderLocation()`, which we'll discuss a little later on. For now, in summary, you *can* specify the root of the displayed tree, but you need to provide its PIDL.

Using a Directory as the Root

If our goal is just to browse into some special system folder, like `Printers` or `Fonts` or `Favorites`, there's no further problem – just take the code fragment shown above and replace `CSIDL_PRINTERS` with the ID of the folder you want. If you want an ordinary directory to be the root of the tree view, however, things get a little trickier.

For a list of special folder IDs, check out `SHGetSpecialFolderLocation()` 's documentation or snoop around the source code of `shlobj.h`, where you'll even find some undocumented IDs. (I'll have more to say on this later in the chapter, in the section dedicated to special folders.)

Converting Path Names to PIDLs

There's nothing else for it: you have to convert your path name into a PIDL. Now, you might expect that somewhere in the shell API there would exist a function that does this for you, but unfortunately you'd be quite wrong. Happily though, there's an MSDN article (See the *Further Reading* section at the end of the chapter) that shows the way. To convert the name of a directory to a PIDL, you need to follow two steps:

❑   Get a pointer to an `IShellFolder` interface
❑   Call its `ParseDisplayName()` method

The `ParseDisplayName()` method of the `IShellFolder` interface does exactly what we need: it takes a path name and converts it to a PIDL. The problem, of course, is how we get hold of a pointer to an `IShellFolder` interface in the first place!

`IShellFolder` is an interface that you need to implement when you're writing namespace extensions (see Chapter 16), and Explorer uses it when working with folders to ask them to draw and enumerate their contents. A pointer to an `IShellFolder` interface is returned by the `SHGetDesktopFolder()` function – more precisely, it returns the `IShellFolder` of the desktop folder. For the case we're considering here, we just need a pointer to an object that provides a 'real' implementation of `ParseDisplayName()`, and the one returned by `SHGetDesktopFolder()` is fine.

Here's the source code for a new shell function that takes a path name and returns its PIDL. In the spirit of Microsoft's naming conventions, I've called it `SHPathToPidl()`:

```
HRESULT SHPathToPidl(LPCTSTR szPath, LPITEMIDLIST* ppidl)
{
   LPSHELLFOLDER pShellFolder = NULL;
   OLECHAR wszPath[MAX_PATH] = {0};
   ULONG nCharsParsed = 0;

   // Get an IShellFolder interface pointer
   HRESULT hr = SHGetDesktopFolder(&pShellFolder);
   if(FAILED(hr))
      return hr;

   // Convert the path name to Unicode
   MultiByteToWideChar(CP_ACP, MB_PRECOMPOSED, szPath, -1, wszPath, MAX_PATH);

   // Call ParseDisplayName() to do the job
   hr = pShellFolder->ParseDisplayName(
                       NULL, NULL, wszPath, &nCharsParsed, ppidl, NULL);

   // Clean up
   pShellFolder->Release();
   return hr;
}
```

The prototype of `ParseDisplayName()` looks like this:

```
HRESULT ParseDisplayName(HWND           hwndOwner,
                         LPBC           pbcReserved,
                         LPOLESTR       lpszDisplayName,
                         ULONG*         pchEaten,
                         LPITEMIDLIST*  ppidl,
                         ULONG*         pdwAttributes);
```

The first argument is the handle of a window to be used as the parent of any message box the function might need to show. The second, pbcReserved, is unused at present and must be NULL. The first *significant* argument is lpszDisplayName, which basically represents the name to convert and must be in Unicode format. pchEaten is a buffer that will contain the number of characters actually processed, while pdwAttributes (if not NULL) will contain the shell attributes of the folder item specified in lpszDisplayName. These attributes are the SHGAO_ constants we examined in Chapter 4, but if you don't care about this, you can just pass NULL. Finally, ppidl is the return buffer for the newly generated PIDL.

Once you've successfully generated a PIDL for a path name, you can limit the user to browsing a specific sub-tree without the ability to go up a level, like this:

The figure shows what happened on my PC when I chose C:\Program Files as the root.

Putting it all Together

So far, we've been discussing aspects of SHBrowseForFolder() in isolation, always providing single pieces of code to solve specific problems. It's about time we constructed a whole application that puts together all the features you've seen above.

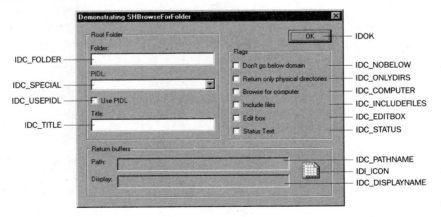

The dialog rendered in the figure is the interface of the program I've been using throughout this chapter to test the features of the SHBrowseForFolder() function. Called SHBrowse, I generated it using the Wrox AppWizard, and it allows you to decide which should be the root folder to use by choosing a path name (the **Folder** edit box) or a PIDL (the **PIDL** combo box) — the **Use PIDL** check box determines which. You can also set the title of the dialog (the **Title** edit box), and a few flags whose names roughly match the constants used by SHBrowseForFolder(). The results are shown in the area at the bottom: display name, path name, and folder icon.

The first code I added to the Wizard-generated skeleton was to the OnInitDialog() function, in order to set up the **PIDL** combo box with the names of some special folders:

```
void OnInitDialog(HWND hDlg)
{
    // Set the icons (T/F as to Large/Small icon)
    SendMessage(hDlg, WM_SETICON, FALSE, reinterpret_cast<LPARAM>(g_hIconSmall));
    SendMessage(hDlg, WM_SETICON, TRUE, reinterpret_cast<LPARAM>(g_hIconLarge));

    // Fill the combo box
    HWND hwndCbo = GetDlgItem(hDlg, IDC_SPECIAL);
    int i = ComboBox_AddString(hwndCbo, "Control Panel");
    ComboBox_SetItemData(hwndCbo, i, CSIDL_CONTROLS);
    i = ComboBox_AddString(hwndCbo, "Favorites");
    ComboBox_SetItemData(hwndCbo, i, CSIDL_FAVORITES);
    i = ComboBox_AddString(hwndCbo, "Printers");
    ComboBox_SetItemData(hwndCbo, i, CSIDL_PRINTERS);
    i = ComboBox_AddString(hwndCbo, "Fonts");
    ComboBox_SetItemData(hwndCbo, i, CSIDL_FONTS);
    i = ComboBox_AddString(hwndCbo, "SendTo");
    ComboBox_SetItemData(hwndCbo, i, CSIDL_SENDTO);
    ComboBox_SetCurSel(hwndCbo, 0);
}
```

With this in place, you'll be able to choose (say) the SendTo folder from the list, and depending on the other options you've set, you'll be presented with something like:

Of course, the dialog you'll obtain on your own computer will probably differ from this, due to the different shortcuts in your `SendTo` directory. Select **Outlook Express** at this point, though, and here's the result:

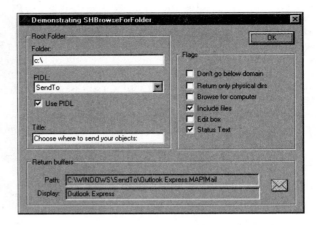

The entire project is available on our web site; the code includes the `BrowseCallbackProc()` `SHGetSystemIcon()` and `SHPathToPidl()` functions we defined earlier in the chapter. Before compiling, don't forget to `#include shlobj.h` and `resource.h`. The function reproduced here executes when the user clicks the **OK** button:

```c
void OnOK(HWND hDlg)
{
    BROWSEINFO bi;
    TCHAR szTitle[MAX_PATH] = {0};
    TCHAR szPath[MAX_PATH] = {0};
    TCHAR szDisplay[MAX_PATH] = {0};
    LPITEMIDLIST pidl = NULL;
    LPMALLOC pMalloc = NULL;

    // Prepare the call
    ZeroMemory(&bi, sizeof(BROWSEINFO));
    bi.hwndOwner = hDlg;

    // Title and display name
    GetDlgItemText(hDlg, IDC_TITLE, szTitle, MAX_PATH);
    bi.lpszTitle = szTitle;
    bi.pszDisplayName = szDisplay;

    // Initial directory
    if(IsDlgButtonChecked(hDlg, IDC_USEPIDL))
    {
        HWND hwndCbo = GetDlgItem(hDlg, IDC_SPECIAL);
        int i = ComboBox_GetCurSel(hwndCbo);
        int nFolder = ComboBox_GetItemData(hwndCbo, i);

        SHGetSpecialFolderLocation(NULL, nFolder, &pidl);
        bi.pidlRoot = pidl;
    }
```

```
    else
    {
        // Convert a path name to a PIDL
        GetDlgItemText(hDlg, IDC_FOLDER, szPath, MAX_PATH);
        if(lstrlen(szPath) == 0)
            GetCurrentDirectory(MAX_PATH, szPath);
        SHPathToPidl(szPath, &pidl);
        bi.pidlRoot = pidl;
    }

    // Collect the flags
    UINT uiFlags = 0;
    if(IsDlgButtonChecked(hDlg, IDC_NOBELOW))
        uiFlags |= BIF_DONTGOBELOWDOMAIN;
    if(IsDlgButtonChecked(hDlg, IDC_ONLYDIRS))
        uiFlags |= BIF_RETURNONLYFSDIRS;
    if(IsDlgButtonChecked(hDlg, IDC_INCLUDEFILES))
        uiFlags |= BIF_BROWSEINCLUDEFILES;
    if(IsDlgButtonChecked(hDlg, IDC_EDITBOX))
        uiFlags |= BIF_EDITBOX | BIF_VALIDATE;
    if(IsDlgButtonChecked(hDlg, IDC_STATUS))
        uiFlags |= BIF_STATUSTEXT;
    if(IsDlgButtonChecked(hDlg, IDC_COMPUTER))
        uiFlags |= BIF_BROWSEFORCOMPUTER;
    bi.ulFlags = uiFlags;

    // Set up the callback
    bi.lpfn = BrowseCallbackProc;
    bi.lParam = 0;

    // Call the function
    LPITEMIDLIST pidlFolder = SHBrowseForFolder(&bi);
    if(pidlFolder == NULL)
        return;

    // Display the results...
    // Show the display name
    SetDlgItemText(hDlg, IDC_DISPLAYNAME, bi.pszDisplayName);

    // Show the path name
    SHGetPathFromIDList(pidlFolder, szPath);
    SetDlgItemText(hDlg, IDC_PATHNAME, szPath);

    // Show the folder icon
    HICON hIcon = SHGetSystemIcon(bi.iImage);
    SendDlgItemMessage(
                hDlg, IDI_ICON, STM_SETICON, reinterpret_cast<WPARAM>(hIcon), 0);

    // Free
    SHGetMalloc(&pMalloc);
    pMalloc->Free(pidl);
    pMalloc->Free(pidlFolder);
    pMalloc->Release();
}
```

The way that the above function works should be pretty clear to you — except, perhaps for the very last section. In order to explain what's going on there, though, we need to dig a little deeper into the world of the PIDL.

That Crazy Little Thing Called PIDL

We examined the basics of PIDLs in Chapter 2, but here we have a specific application for them: we want to use them to browse the contents of a folder, whatever that content may be. *Every* element in the Windows shell has its own PIDL and is contained in some kind of folder. For each element, therefore, there's a piece of code that wraps the folder and provides the PIDL according to the folder's own rules and requirements. This means that we can never make assumptions about the structure of a PIDL or the data it is composed of. We must use common interfaces to deal with PIDLs.

If, for example, you want to follow the chain of SHITEMID structures, you should check the length of the next chunk of data at every step. As you've already seen, an ITEMIDLIST – or a PIDL, if you prefer – is made up of one or more SHITEMID structures allocated consecutively. This chain is terminated by an element whose cb field is set to 0. Here's a function excerpted from MSDN that demonstrates how to walk an item identifier list. It's not very different from navigating an 'ordinary' list:

```
LPITEMIDLIST GetNextItemID(LPITEMIDLIST pidl)
{
    // Get the size of the specified item identifier
    int cb = pidl->mkid.cb;

    // If the size is zero, it is the end of the list
    if(cb == 0)
        return NULL;

    // Add cb to pidl (casting to increment by bytes)
    pidl = (LPITEMIDLIST)(((LPBYTE)pidl) + cb);

    // Return NULL if it is null-terminating, or a pidl otherwise
    return (pidl->mkid.cb == 0) ? NULL : pidl;
}
```

You can't make assumptions about the format of a PIDL. An approach that works well for one folder may fail with another. To make sure two items are identical, for example, you must ask the folder itself to compare them through the IShellFolder::CompareIDs() method.

Freeing PIDLs

Before we go any further, let's just take a moment to explain that code at the end of the last example. While it's true that folders create PIDLs, they usually have to be destroyed by another module, and that's what I was doing at the end of the OnOK() function. The memory for identifier lists is taken from the allocator for shell applications, and as you also saw in Chapter 2, you can get a pointer to that by calling the SHGetMalloc() function. In general, the sequence of calls will look something like this:

```
LPMALLOC pMalloc;
SHGetMalloc(&pMalloc);      // Get a pointer to the IMalloc interface
pMalloc->Free(pidl);        // Free the identifier list
pMalloc->Release();         // Release the IMalloc interface
```

How to Use PIDLs

Returning to our theme of putting PIDLs to some practical uses, we have two main goals. First, we want to be able to enumerate the content of any folder; second, we'd like to reproduce a nice feature of Explorer that's supported by shell versions 4.71 and higher. To show you what I mean, here's a screenshot of Explorer that I produced by typing Printers into the Address Bar and hitting *Return*:

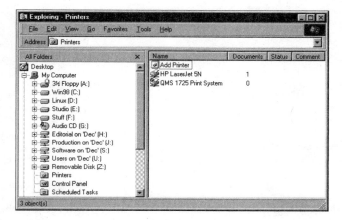

Explorer is allowing you to use the name Printers as if it were the name of a regular folder. In other words, it blurs the distinction between physical and virtual folders. To be accurate, Printers is the display name of the virtual folder that contains the available printers.

For my example, I used our custom AppWizard to create a demonstration program called `Pidl` with a user interface that looks like this:

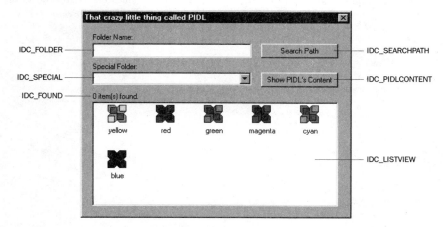

The Search Path button will take the contents of the edit box and attempt to identify a folder with that name. The string in the edit box is intended to be the display name of a folder (keep in mind that a path name is also a display name). If successful, the application will display all the file objects found inside the folder in a list view. The Show PIDL's Content button, on the other hand, will enumerate in the list view all the file objects found in the special folder that you select using the combo box.

Searching by Display Name

Let's begin by looking at the code that executes when you click the **Search Path** button. Of course, both the new buttons need to be handled by `APP_DlgProc()`, so we can add code for both of them here:

```
case WM_COMMAND:
   switch(wParam)
   {

   case IDC_SEARCHPATH:
      DoSearchPath(hDlg);
      return FALSE;

   case IDC_PIDLCONTENT:
      DoEnumeratePidl(hDlg);
      return FALSE;


   case IDCANCEL:
      EndDialog(hDlg, FALSE);
      return FALSE;
   }
   break;
```

The function we're dealing with first, then, is `DoSearchPath()`. It will retrieve the name you entered in the **Folder Name** edit box, and treat it as if it's a path name to search for. If it really *is* a path name, everything will be fine, but what if it's the display name of a folder? We want the function to be able to deal with, say, `C:\` and `(C:)`. This implementation will be able to handle correctly all the path names and display names whose associated folders are children of either `Desktop` or `My Computer`, although the limitation is purely by design.

> *Note that normally, the display name of a drive is given by its label followed the drive letter in brackets. An example is* `Ms-dos_6 (C:)`. *However, if you don't have a label, then consider that there's a leading blank in* `(C:)`.

`DoSearchPath()` starts by enumerating the content of the `Desktop` folder:

```
void DoSearchPath(HWND hDlg)
{
    LPITEMIDLIST pidl = NULL;
    LPSHELLFOLDER pFolder = NULL;
    LPSHELLFOLDER pSubFolder = NULL;

    // Get the memory allocator
    LPMALLOC pMalloc = NULL;
    SHGetMalloc(&pMalloc);

    // Get the name to search
    TCHAR szName[MAX_PATH] = {0};
    GetDlgItemText(hDlg, IDC_FOLDER, szName, MAX_PATH);

    // Get the IShellFolder interface for the desktop
    SHGetDesktopFolder(&pFolder);
```

```
// Try to find a match under Desktop
int iNumOfItems = SHEnumFolderContent(pFolder, NULL, 0, NULL);
int rc = SHEnumFolderContent(
            pFolder, SearchText, reinterpret_cast<DWORD>(szName), &pidl);
```

SHEnumFolderContent() is a user-defined function that takes a PIDL to a folder and a callback function as input, and then enumerates all the items in the folder, passing them to the function for further processing. We'll discuss it more thoroughly later on, but in order to understand its use here you need to know that if no callback function is specified, it returns the number of items found:

```
int iNumOfItems = SHEnumFolderContent(pFolder, NULL, 0, NULL);
```

Otherwise, it returns the number of items actually processed. These two values aren't necessarily the same, because the callback function could stop the enumeration at a point of its own choosing. The SearchText() function, for example, causes SHEnumFolderContent() to stop when it finds the name you're looking for.

SHEnumFolderContent() begins its search by checking whether the name we typed in the edit box corresponds to the display name of a folder under Desktop. This is the case if at the end of the above code, rc and iNumOfItems are not equal. If they *are* equal, we start a new search under the My Computer node:

```
// If not found, try under My Computer
if(rc == iNumOfItems)
{
    // Bind to My Computer
    LPITEMIDLIST pidlMyComp;
    SHGetSpecialFolderLocation(NULL, CSIDL_DRIVES, &pidlMyComp);
    pFolder->BindToObject(pidlMyComp, NULL, IID_IShellFolder,
                                reinterpret_cast<LPVOID*>(&pSubFolder));

    // Free the pointer to the desktop folder
    pFolder->Release();
    pMalloc->Free(pidlMyComp);
    pFolder = pSubFolder;

    // Scan My Computer
    iNumOfItems = SHEnumFolderContent(pFolder, NULL, 0, NULL);
    rc = SHEnumFolderContent(
                pFolder, SearchText, reinterpret_cast<DWORD>(szName), &pidl);
```

Before calling SHEnumFolderContent() again to work on the My Computer folder, we need to get a IShellFolder pointer for it. What we have at the moment is the *desktop's* IShellFolder, but we can get the one we want by using the BindToObject() method of this interface. This lets you bind to the IShellFolder interface of a child folder that you identify to the method using a PIDL:

```
HRESULT IShellFolder::BindToObject(
    LPCITEMIDLIST pidl,         // PIDL of the folder you want
    LPBC          pbcReserved,  // Reserved; must be NULL
    REFIID        riid,         // Must be IID_IShellFolder
    LPVOID*       ppvOut        // Receives the IShellFolder pointer
);
```

If the display name has been found under neither `Desktop` nor `My Computer`, we take a shortcut and decide that we aren't able to locate it at all. Don't think this is a system limitation, though — it's quite possible to set up a recursive search on folders to locate the name wherever it is. The approach to follow might be outlined as follows:

- ❏ Enumerate the content of the `Desktop` folder, as we do above
- ❏ For each folder found (not just `My Computer`), repeat the search

However, a fully recursive search could lead us to try to identify by name a folder that is not unique — it's quite possible, of course, to have two folders with a display name of `MyDir`, one under `c:\` and one under `d:\`. The above algorithm would stop at the first occurrence.

A better approach would be to accept and parse fully qualified folder names, like the following:

```
My Computer\ (c:)\Windows
Control Panel\Add New Hardware
```

To do this, we would need only a little extra code to parse the folder name and search for the first item in the desktop, the next item in the folder reached by the previous step, and so on. The code seen above could be generalized slightly, and enclosed in a loop.

If you think about it, this is really no different from searching for a directory within the file system. It's just that instead of using `FindFirstFile()` *and* `FindNextFile()` *to enumerate the contents of a directory, you have to use the methods of a COM interface exposed by the folder object.*

Prior to giving up completely, it could be that the display name entered is a full path name, like `c:\`. It's worth taking this one last chance before outputting a message box — we just have to convert the name into a PIDL and see what happens. If there are no errors, then a path name was entered.

```
if(rc == iNumOfItems)
{
    // Make the last attempt: is it a path name?
    HRESULT hr = SHPathToPidlEx(szName, &pidl, pFolder);
    if(FAILED(hr))
    {
        Msg("\"%s\" not found under Desktop or My Computer.", szName);
        pMalloc->Free(pidl);
        pFolder->Release();

        // Call a helper function to refresh the UI
        ClearUI(hDlg);
        return;
    }
}
```

Finally, if the function hasn't returned before this point, we know that we have a PIDL we can use to output the icons in the folder it points to. In other words, we had a string entered in the edit box, referred to in the source code above as `szName`. We identified the folder object with that name and obtained its PIDL. Now, to enumerate the content of this folder we need to get its `IShellFolder` interface and pass it to `SHEnumFolderContent()`.

The **Search Path** button handler therefore ends like this:

```
    // If here, then:
    //   pidl points to the folder we need to bind to enumerate the content
    //   pFolder points to the IShellFolder of the pidl's parent folder

    // Bind to the subfolder we're searching for
    // pFolder can point to Desktop's or My Computer's IShellFolder
    pFolder->BindToObject(pidl, NULL, IID_IShellFolder,
                                    reinterpret_cast<LPVOID*>(&pSubFolder));

    // Refresh UI (empty list view, image list and the like)
    ClearUI(hDlg);

    // Enumerate the content of the folder in the listview
    HWND hwndListView = GetDlgItem(hDlg, IDC_LISTVIEW);
    SHEnumFolderContent(pSubFolder, ShowFolderContent,
                                    reinterpret_cast<DWORD>(hwndListView), NULL);

    // Clean up
    pFolder->Release();
    pSubFolder->Release();
    pMalloc->Free(pidl);
    pMalloc->Release();
    return;
}
```

Converting Path Names to PIDLs (again)

Looking at the source code above, you'll notice that I used a function called `SHPathToPidlEx()` to convert a path name into a PIDL. Now, earlier in this chapter we developed the `SHPathToPidl()` helper function for the same purpose – it used the `ParseDisplayName()` method of the `IShellFolder` interface in order to do so. The code in `SHPathToPidl()` boiled down to this, which gets a PIDL relative to the desktop – that is, the root of the hierarchy

```
    SHGetDesktopFolder(&pFolder);
    pFolder->ParseDisplayName(NULL, NULL, wszPath, &n, ppidl, NULL);
```

Unfortunately, this PIDL is relative to the folder that is providing the `IShellFolder` interface, the desktop. In the new case, we need a PIDL that's relative to the parent of the folder we're considering. The reason for this is that when you're using `BindToObject()` to get the `IShellFolder` interface for a sub-folder, you're required to pass in a PIDL that is relative to the *same* folder from which you're calling `BindToObject()`.

Given this, we need an extra step between getting a pointer to an `IShellFolder` interface and calling `ParseDisplayName()`. This extra step must ensure that the `IShellFolder` used to call `ParseDisplayName()` is the one of the folder we want to work with.

The code becomes:

```
HRESULT SHPathToPidlEx(
            LPCTSTR szPath, LPITEMIDLIST* ppidl, LPSHELLFOLDER pFolder)
{
    OLECHAR wszPath[MAX_PATH] = {0};
    ULONG nCharsParsed = 0;
    LPSHELLFOLDER pShellFolder = NULL;
    BOOL bFreeOnExit = FALSE;
```

```
    MultiByteToWideChar(CP_ACP, MB_PRECOMPOSED, szPath, -1, wszPath, MAX_PATH);
    // Use the desktop's IShellFolder by default
    if(pFolder == NULL)
    {
        SHGetDesktopFolder(&pShellFolder);
        bFreeOnExit = TRUE;
    }
    else
        pShellFolder = pFolder;

    HRESULT hr = pShellFolder->ParseDisplayName(
                        NULL, NULL, wszPath, &nCharsParsed, ppidl, NULL);

    if(bFreeOnExit)
        pShellFolder->Release();

    return hr;
}
```

This function is a bit more general than `SHPathToPidl()`, and requires you also to pass in the folder that the PIDL will be relative to. If you pass `NULL` instead of a valid `IShellFolder` pointer, the desktop's `IShellFolder` interface is used and then released. In the sample program, the code that invokes the conversion function is:

```
        HRESULT hr = SHPathToPidlEx(szName, &pidl, pFolder);
```

Try passing `NULL` instead of `pFolder`, specify a path name to search, and see what happens: whatever the path name, you'll be always enumerating the contents of the `Desktop` folder.

Clearing the User Interface

Apart from the details of `SHEnumFolderContent()`, which are coming up in the next section, the only other function you've seen in the code so far is the simple helper `ClearUI()`:

```
void ClearUI(HWND hDlg)
{
    HWND hwndListView = GetDlgItem(hDlg, IDC_LISTVIEW);
    ListView_DeleteAllItems(hwndListView);
    ImageList_RemoveAll(g_himl);
    SetDlgItemText(hDlg, IDC_FOUND, __TEXT("0 item(s) found."));
}
```

This just resets the application's dialog, deleting all items from the list view, and emptying the image list that will be created by `SHEnumFolderContent()` in order to fill the list view in the first place. The latter task is done by means of `g_himl`, a global variable of type `HIMAGELIST` that should be initialized to zero in `WinMain()`.

Building an Enumerator Function

There's still plenty to say about enumerating the content of a given folder, whether it's a physical directory or a virtual folder like `Printers`. The source code you've seen so far makes considerable use of a user-defined function called `SHEnumFolderContent()`, which is responsible for asking the folder itself to enumerate its items one after another.

There are folders whose content is given by a collection of files. There are other folders whose visible items might be the records of a single file, or hardware devices of some kind. In general, only the folder knows exactly what its content is. There's no safe way for either Explorer or programmers to enumerate the items contained in a folder without 'asking' the folder itself about it. It will come as no surprise to you that this communication is based on a COM interface.

In my design, `SHEnumFolderContent()` interrogates a folder for its contents, and passes the name of each item it finds to another function for further processing. You've seen a couple of these functions named in the listing above: `SearchText()` and `ShowFolderContent()`. To understand their roles properly, however, it is better first to study how the enumeration of items occurs.

Reading the Folder's Content

The purpose of the code linked to the **Search Path** (and the **Show PIDL's Content**) button is that it should read the content of a folder. To allow the enumeration of its items, a folder implements the `IEnumIDList` interface, which exposes four functions to move back and forth within a given collection: `Next()`, `Skip()`, `Reset()` and `Clone()`. We'll be interested mainly in `Next()`, whose prototype is:

```
HRESULT IEnumIDList::Next(ULONG         celt,
                          LPITEMIDLIST* rgelt,
                          ULONG*        pceltFetched);
```

The first argument is the number of items required, the second is a pointer to an array of PIDLs, and the third is an output parameter set with the number of items actually copied. The `IEnumIDList` interface itself is responsible for allocating the memory to hold the PIDLs.

A piece of software that wants to know about the content of a specific folder must begin by getting a pointer to `IEnumIDList`, and the `IShellFolder` interface exposes the `EnumObjects()` method with exactly this task in mind. Its prototype looks like this:

```
HRESULT IShellFolder::EnumObjects(
    HWND          hwndOwner,      // Handle to an owner window
    DWORD         grfFlags,       // A set of flags (see below)
    LPENUMIDLIST* ppenumIDList    // Receives the IEnumIDList pointer
);
```

The second parameter to this method allows you to dictate the type of the items to be enumerated. It takes a combination of the values defined in the following enumerated type:

```
typedef enum tagSHCONTF
{
    SHCONTF_FOLDERS = 32,
    SHCONTF_NONFOLDERS = 64,
    SHCONTF_INCLUDEHIDDEN = 128,
} SHCONTF;
```

The mnemonic names are almost self-explanatory: you can decide to enumerate folders, non-folder objects, and even hidden objects.

> *By necessity, we'll be discussing rather more about the details of these interfaces later on, when we begin writing namespace extensions. For now, I recommend you take a look at the Visual C++ help files for clarification of any issues regarding method names and prototypes.*

```
LPENUMIDLIST pEnumIDList = NULL;
LPITEMIDLIST pItem = NULL;
ULONG ulFetched = 0;

pFolder->EnumObjects(
            NULL, SHCONTF_FOLDERS | SHCONTF_NONFOLDERS, &pEnumIDList);
while(pEnumIDList->Next(1, &pItem, &ulFetched) == NOERROR)
{
    ...
}
```

The above fragment represents the 'engine' of a function that enumerates the items of a folder. Each time the loop passes the condition, pItem is a PIDL to a single item. Once we have that, there are two things we might need: its display name, and possibly its icon.

Getting an Item's Display Name

Even though you have the PIDL, getting the display name of an item is not as easy as you might think. Despite an ideal-sounding function like IShellFolder::GetDisplayNameOf(), there's additional work to be done. The problem is that this method *doesn't* provide a normal string in ANSI or Unicode format. Instead, it returns a pointer to a STRRET structure, defined as follows:

```
typedef struct _STRRET
{
    UINT uType;
    union
    {
        LPWSTR pOleStr;
        LPSTR pStr;     // Unused
        UINT uOffset;
        char cStr[MAX_PATH];
    } DUMMYUNIONNAME;
} STRRET, *LPSTRRET;
```

As you can see, the structure is formed from a flag that denotes the type of the string that follows it. This might be a Unicode string (pOleStr), an ANSI string (cStr), or even an offset to the address of the string (uOffset). This means that you need to write your own wrapper routine that returns the kind of string you need, regardless of the original type. The one I wrote looks like this:

```
void StrretToString(LPITEMIDLIST pidl, LPSTRRET pStr, LPSTR pszBuf)
{
    lstrcpy(pszBuf, "");

    switch(pStr->uType)
    {
    case STRRET_WSTR:               // Unicode string
        WideCharToMultiByte(
                CP_ACP, 0, pStr->pOleStr, -1, pszBuf, MAX_PATH, NULL, NULL);
        break;

    case STRRET_OFFSET:             // Offset
        lstrcpy(pszBuf, reinterpret_cast<LPSTR>(pidl) + pStr->uOffset);
        break;
```

```
    case STRRET_CSTR:              // ANSI string
lstrcpy(pszBuf, pStr->cStr);
        break;
    }
}
```

`StrretToString()` accepts the PIDL and a pointer to the `STRRET` structure, and returns an `LPSTR` via its third argument. Incidentally, the above listing also shows the legal values for `uType`.

Moving back to the main thrust of our discussion, the prototype of `GetDisplayNameOf()` is:

```
HRESULT IShellFolder::GetDisplayNameOf(LPCITEMIDLIST pidl,
                                       DWORD         uFlags,
                                       LPSTRRET      lpName);
```

Where the flags to be used in `uFlags` come from the `SHGNO` enumerated type:

```
typedef enum tagSHGDN
{
    SHGDN_NORMAL = 0,
    SHGDN_INFOLDER = 1,
    SHGDN_INCLUDE_NONFILESYS = 0x2000,
    SHGDN_FORADDRESSBAR = 0x4000,
    SHGDN_FORPARSING = 0x8000,
} SHGNO;
```

The descriptions of these flags in the documentation seem to be clear enough, and so you build your expectations as to the ultimate behavior of the function. However, all the samples I tried worked in the same way, regardless of what flags I set. Frankly, don't know where the bug resides, if bug it is. My advice is always to use 0 for this parameter.

```
    STRRET sName;
    CHAR szBuf[MAX_PATH] = {0};
    pFolder->GetDisplayNameOf(pItem, 0, &sName);
    StrretToString(pItem, &sName, szBuf);
```

This code fragment provides the display name of the item in human-readable format. Note once more that this holds true for file folders as well as for special folders like `Fonts`, `Favorites`, `Printers`, `Control Panel`, and so on. This means that in a while, we'll be able to list all the applets in the Control Panel.

Personally, I've no argument with a structure like `STRRET`, *but I would have very much appreciated a 'conversion' function like* `StrretToString()` *to have been provided natively by the shell libraries.*

Getting an Item's Icon

At first glance, programming the shell seems a huge task. However, once you've survived for the first three or four months, the chances are that you'll start to know the answer to any question on the subject in advance. To demonstrate the point, how do you think you get an item's icon? Once again, you just have to ask the folder to provide it. The `IShellFolder::GetUIObjectOf()` method returns all the interfaces you could need to deal with the user interfaces of folders and file objects.

```
HRESULT IShellFolder::GetUIObjectOf(
    HWND            hwndOwner,    // Handle to the owner window
    UINT            cidl,         // Number of elements in the next parameter
    LPCITEMIDLIST*  apidl,        // Pointer to an array of PIDLs
    REFIID          riid,         // ID of the interface to return
    UINT*           prgfInOut,    // Reserved (must be NULL)
    LPVOID*         ppvOut        // Receives the interface pointer
);
```

What's interesting about this declaration is that you can request a number of different interface pointers that affect UI tasks. For example, you may ask for `IContextMenu` to get the `HMENU` handle of the context menu being displayed for that element. In our case, we'll be requiring `IExtractIcon` in order to find out about the icon. (We'll see more about `GetUIObjectOf()` in Chapter 16, and you should also take a look at the references listed in *Further Reading*.)

```
pFolder->GetUIObjectOf(NULL, 1, const_cast<LPCITEMIDLIST*>(&pItem),
        IID_IExtractIcon, NULL, reinterpret_cast<LPVOID*>(&pExtractIcon));
```

The `IExtractIcon` interface has just two new methods: `GetIconLocation()` and `Extract()`. The first of these lets you know about the location and index of the icon, while the second returns an `HICON` handle. When a client calls `GetIconLocation()`, it will be returned the name of the file that contains the icon, and the 0-based index of the icon in the file's resources.

```
HRESULT IExtractIcon::GetIconLocation(UINT   uFlags,
                                      LPSTR  szIconFile,
                                      INT    cchMax,
                                      LPINT  piIndex,
                                      UINT*  pwFlags);
```

`Extract()` in turn extracts the given icon from the specified file and returns its `HICON`. This method is nearly identical to the API function `ExtractIconEx()`.

```
HRESULT IExtractIcon::Extract(LPCSTR pszFile,
                              UINT   nIconIndex,
                              HICON* phiconLarge,
                              HICON* phiconSmall,
                              UINT   nIconSize);
```

The documentation for these functions suffers from a few little omissions. For instance, you need to know that `pwFlags` can't be `NULL`, even if you don't care about its contents. Similarly, even if you need only, say, the large icon, you must still pass a valid, non-zero `HICON` for the small icon as well. Here's a brief example of how to call them:

```
pExtractIcon->GetIconLocation(0, szIconFile, MAX_PATH, &iIconIndex, &u);
pExtractIcon->Extract(
            szIconFile, iIconIndex, &hIcon, &hIconSm, MAKELONG(32, 16));
pExtractIcon->Release();
```

When developing this sample code, I ran into another interesting side effect, whose causes are frankly beyond me. In some cases, the handle returned by `Extract()` is `NULL`, even when the icon's location and index are known and correct. Curiously, calling the API function `ExtractIconEx()` with the same parameters works perfectly!

The workaround, of course, is immediate:

```
    if(hIcon == NULL)
        ExtractIconEx(szIconFile, iIconIndex, &hIcon, NULL, 1);
```

At this point, we finally have all we need to create a new shell function that takes a pointer to IShellFolder and loops over its items, invoking a callback function for each one. Just like many other functions called 'Enum', our SHEnumFolderContent() function will provide a user-defined buffer (dwData) to send program-level variables down to the callback function. Furthermore, if the callback returns FALSE, the function will stop working. Here's the prototype:

```
int SHEnumFolderContent(LPSHELLFOLDER pFolder,
            FOLDERCONTENTPROC pfn, DWORD dwData, LPITEMIDLIST* ppidl);
```

Where FOLDERCONTENTPROC is a user-defined function pointer declared this way:

```
typedef BOOL (CALLBACK *FOLDERCONTENTPROC)(LPCSTR, HICON, DWORD);
```

The first argument here is the display name of the element. After that comes the handle to the icon, and then the user-defined buffer. As already mentioned, this function will return FALSE to abort enumeration, and TRUE otherwise.

The last parameter of SHEnumFolderContent() is a pointer to a PIDL. This isn't strictly necessary; it's just that sometimes (as in our sample application), knowing the last processed PIDL can be of considerable help. If the argument passed is NULL, then it is ignored. At long last, here's the source code for SHEnumFolderContent().

```
int SHEnumFolderContent(LPSHELLFOLDER pFolder,
            FOLDERCONTENTPROC pfn, DWORD dwData, LPITEMIDLIST* ppidl)
{
    int iNumOfItems = 0;

    // Enumerates the content
    LPENUMIDLIST pEnumIDList = NULL;
    pFolder->EnumObjects(
            NULL, SHCONTF_FOLDERS | SHCONTF_NONFOLDERS, &pEnumIDList);

    ULONG ulFetched = 0;
    LPITEMIDLIST pItem = NULL;
    while(NOERROR == pEnumIDList->Next(1, &pItem, &ulFetched))
    {
        STRRET sName;
        TCHAR szBuf[MAX_PATH] = {0};
        pFolder->GetDisplayNameOf(pItem, 0, &sName);
        StrretToString(pItem, &sName, szBuf);

        // Invoke callback
        if(pfn)
        {
            // Get the icon
            UINT u = 0;
            int iIconIndex = 0;
            HICON hIcon = NULL;
            HICON hIconSm = NULL;
            TCHAR szIconFile[MAX_PATH] = {0};
            LPEXTRACTICON pExtractIcon = NULL;
```

```
        pFolder->GetUIObjectOf(NULL, 1, const_cast<LPCITEMIDLIST*>(&pItem),
        IID_IExtractIcon, NULL, reinterpret_cast<LPVOID*>(&pExtractIcon));
        pExtractIcon->GetIconLocation(
                            0, szIconFile, MAX_PATH, &iIconIndex, &u);
        pExtractIcon->Extract(
              szIconFile, iIconIndex, &hIcon, &hIconSm, MAKELONG(32, 16));
        pExtractIcon->Release();

        if(hIcon == NULL)
           ExtractIconEx(szIconFile, iIconIndex, &hIcon, NULL, 1);

        if(!pfn(szBuf, hIcon, dwData))
        {
           // Returns the current PIDL
           if(ppidl != NULL)
              *ppidl = pItem;
           break;
        }
     }
     ++iNumOfItems;
   }
   return iNumOfItems;
}
```

The Callback Functions

Typically, callback functions are used to accomplish some tasks on a collection of items. In this case, SHEnumFolderContent() calls such functions on the various folder items. SearchText() simply reports whether the two strings you pass it are equal:

```
BOOL CALLBACK SearchText(LPCSTR pszItem, HICON hIcon, DWORD dwData)
{
   return static_cast<BOOL>(lstrcmpi(
                         pszItem, reinterpret_cast<LPCSTR>(dwData)));
}
```

And ShowFolderContent() is used to build up an image list of the icons passed to it, inserting them in the list view it was also supplied with as it does so:

```
BOOL CALLBACK ShowFolderContent(LPCSTR pszItem, HICON hIcon, DWORD dwData)
{
   // Create the imagelist
   int iIconWidth = GetSystemMetrics(SM_CXICON);
   int iIconHeight = GetSystemMetrics(SM_CYICON);
   if(g_himl == NULL)
      g_himl = ImageList_Create(iIconWidth, iIconHeight, ILC_MASK, 1, 0);
   int iIconPos = ImageList_AddIcon(g_himl, hIcon);

   HWND hwndListView = reinterpret_cast<HWND>(dwData);
   ListView_SetImageList(hwndListView, g_himl, LVSIL_NORMAL);

   LV_ITEM lvi;
   ZeroMemory(&lvi, sizeof(LV_ITEM));
   lvi.mask = LVIF_TEXT | LVIF_IMAGE;
   lvi.pszText = const_cast<LPSTR>(pszItem);
   lvi.cchTextMax = lstrlen(pszItem);
   lvi.iImage = iIconPos;
   ListView_InsertItem(hwndListView, &lvi);
```

```
    // Update count
    TCHAR s[MAX_PATH] = {0};
    wsprintf(s, "%d item(s) found.", ListView_GetItemCount(hwndListView));
    SetDlgItemText(GetParent(hwndListView), IDC_FOUND, s);
    return TRUE;
}
```

The Sample Program

Make sure that your main source file contains #includes for shlobj.h and resource.h, and the following figures show what you can do with the sample program at this stage in its development. By typing Printers, you can fill the list view and have it look just like a standard folder window:

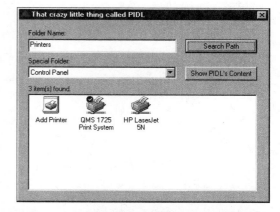

Alternatively, by specifying a path name you'll have files and folders, just as you'd get in Explorer:

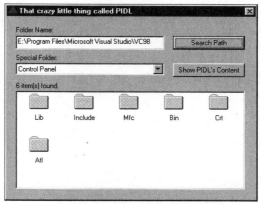

Remember that if you want the contents of the root directory of any drive, you must include the final backslash. For example, c:\ works fine, but c: produces this result:

Searching by PIDL

With all our helper functions in place, writing the handler for the Show PIDL's Content button won't be too onerous a task. The combo box that the button relates to is initialized with the names and the IDs of some special folders, which involves exactly the same code as we had in the SHBrowse example earlier in the chapter.

That just leaves the DoEnumeratePidl() function that executes when you click on Show PIDL's Content and fills in the list view:

```
void DoEnumeratePidl(HWND hDlg)
{
    LPITEMIDLIST pidl = NULL;

    // Get the special folder and its PIDL
    HWND hwndCbo = GetDlgItem(hDlg, IDC_SPECIAL);
    int i = ComboBox_GetCurSel(hwndCbo);
    int nFolder = ComboBox_GetItemData(hwndCbo, i);
    SHGetSpecialFolderLocation(NULL, nFolder, &pidl);

    // Get the IShellFolder interface
    LPSHELLFOLDER pFolder = NULL;
    SHGetDesktopFolder(&pFolder);

    // Bind to subfolder
    LPSHELLFOLDER pSubFolder = NULL;
    pFolder->BindToObject(pidl, NULL, IID_IShellFolder,
                                reinterpret_cast<LPVOID*>(&pSubFolder));
    pFolder->Release();
    pFolder = pSubFolder;

    // Clear the program's UI
    ClearUI(hDlg);

    // Enumerate the content
    HWND hwndListView = GetDlgItem(hDlg, IDC_LISTVIEW);
    SHEnumFolderContent(pFolder, ShowFolderContent,
                              reinterpret_cast<DWORD>(hwndListView), NULL);

    // Clean up
    LPMALLOC pMalloc = NULL;
    SHGetMalloc(&pMalloc);
    pMalloc->Free(pidl);
    pMalloc->Release();
    pFolder->Release();
}
```

The function starts by getting the ID of the special folder that was selected through the combo box, and then calls `SHGetSpecialFolderLocation()` to get the PIDL of that folder. From the PIDL, we obtain the `IShellFolder` interface to pass to `SHEnumFolderContent()`. The figure shows how the application can now enumerate the applets in Control Panel:

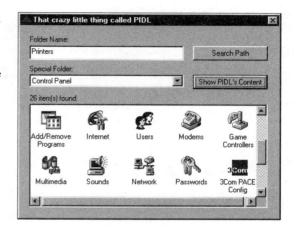

Special Folders

We first looked at special folders and their underpinnings in Chapter 2, and there are three basic types. Almost all of them have a corresponding directory, but these are split between ordinary file folders and custom folders. The third category consists of the folders without directories: the virtual folders.

Virtual folders are *perceived* as folders, but their location and content can't be mapped in terms of files and directories. `Control Panel`, `Printers`, `Network Neighborhood` and `My Computer` are all examples of virtual folders. The Control Panel, for instance, may be considered as a folder containing all the installed applets.

Despite appearances, however, there's no physical directory called `Control Panel` containing anything that could be associated with, say, Add New Hardware or Modems. All the icons listed in the folder come from `.cpl` files located in the `System` directory. They are gathered and presented as a virtual folder by a namespace extension. (See Chapter 2 for an overview, and Chapter 16 for examples of namespace extensions.)

System Support for Special Folders

The Windows API defines a number of special folders and a bunch of functions to work with them. These routines identify each special folder through a number that works like an ID, but has nothing to do with PIDLs or CLSIDs.

The IDs are defined in `shlobj.h` and have rather odd symbolic names: they all begin with `CSIDL_`. What follows is a table of the available special folders.

Folder ID	Virtual	Description
CSIDL_DESKTOP	Yes	Desktop
CSIDL_DRIVES	Yes	My Computer

Table Continued on Following Page

125

Folder ID	Virtual	Description
CSIDL_BITBUCKET	Yes	Recycle Bin
CSIDL_CONTROLS	Yes	Control Panel
CSIDL_NETWORK	Yes	Network Neighborhood
CSIDL_INTERNET	Yes	The Internet Explorer node that appears in shell version 4.71 and above
CSIDL_PRINTERS	Yes	Printers
CSIDL_DESKTOPDIRECTORY		Directory with all the desktop shortcuts
CSIDL_FAVORITES		Shortcuts to favorite folders
CSIDL_FONTS		Installed fonts
CSIDL_NETHOOD		References to network domains
CSIDL_PRINTHOOD		References to printers
CSIDL_PERSONAL		Shortcuts to personal files
CSIDL_PROGRAMS		The shortcuts in the **Programs** menu
CSIDL_RECENT		Shortcuts to recently used documents
CSIDL_SENDTO		Shortcuts for the **SendTo** menu
CSIDL_STARTMENU		User-defined items for the **Start** menu
CSIDL_STARTUP		Shortcuts to the programs that run at boot time
CSIDL_COOKIES		Cookies
CSIDL_TEMPLATES		Shortcuts to document templates
CSIDL_HISTORY		Shortcuts to visited web pages
CSIDL_INTERNET_CACHE		Internet Explorer's temporary Internet files
CSIDL_APPDATA		A folder for application-specific data
CSIDL_ALTSTARTUP		The non-localized **StartUp** group

The documentation mentions other folders labeled as CSIDL_COMMON_XXX. They are:

CSIDL_COMMON_STARTUP	CSIDL_COMMON_STARTMENU
CSIDL_COMMON_PROGRAMS	CSIDL_COMMON_FAVORITES
CSIDL_COMMON_DESKTOPDIRECTORY	CSIDL_COMMON_ALTSTARTUP

These work in the same way as the ones whose names don't contain COMMON, except that they point to physical folders that are visible to all users. Even though this is not mentioned explicitly in the documentation, these folders seem to make sense only under Windows NT, as I'll demonstrate in the next section.

Getting the Path to a Folder

Non-virtual folders have a path somewhere in the machine. You can obtain the path for a special folder by calling the SHGetSpecialFolderPath() API function, which I'll have more to say about shortly. The link between special folders and their paths is stored in the registry, under this key:

```
HKEY_CURRENT_USER
   \Software
      \Microsoft
         \Windows
            \CurrentVersion
               \Explorer
                  \Shell Folders
```

The same key under the HKEY_LOCAL_MACHINE node stores paths for all the available COMMON folders, but not all the COMMON folders have their paths stored under Windows 95 and Windows 98. In fact, it only happens with CSIDL_COMMON_DESKTOPDIRECTORY and CSIDL_COMMON_STARTUP.

Assuming that C:\Windows is your Windows directory, the paths listed are located inside the C:\Windows\All Users folder. However, under Windows 95 and Windows 98, SHGetSpecialFolderPath() doesn't return a value for any of them. Using the same function under Windows NT, on the other hand, returns the correct path.

Functions

We can approach SHGetSpecialFolderPath() by looking at an API function that we've already made use of: SHGetSpecialFolderLocation(). This retrieves a *PIDL* to the special folder you specify, and has the following prototype:

```
HRESULT SHGetSpecialFolderLocation(HWND        hwndOwner,
                                   int         nFolder,
                                   LPITEMIDLIST* ppidl);
```

hwndOwner is the parent window for any popup window to be displayed, nFolder is the identifier of a special folder and can be one of the constants listed above, and ppidl is a pointer to the buffer that will contain the PIDL for the folder. SHGetSpecialFolderPath(), which is intended to retrieve the *path* of a given folder, is very similar:

```
HRESULT SHGetSpecialFolderPath(HWND     hwndOwner,
                               LPTSTR   lpszPath,
                               int      nFolder,
                               BOOL     fCreate);
```

lpszPath will contain the path name, while fCreate is a Boolean value that denotes whether the folder should be created if it doesn't already exist. Of course, you can't specify the ID of a virtual folder in this case. Note that unlike SHGetSpecialFolderLocation(), SHGetSpecialFolderPath() is only supported by shell versions 4.71 and higher.

Folder Settings

Internet Explorer 4.0 and Active Desktop greatly increased the number of settings for system folders. The Folder Options dialog is now full of boxes to check or uncheck in order to have folders look the way you want them to:

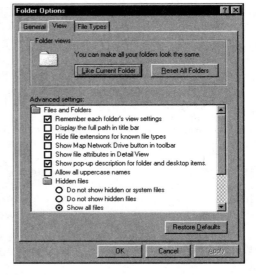

The dialog shown in the figure is one that everyone uses once in a lifetime (or once every time they install Windows, whichever comes sooner) to make all the system and hidden files visible throughout Explorer. Some (but not all) of these settings can be read programmatically through the SHGetSettings() function, which naturally enough is only available in version 4.71 of the shell.

You can easily read about the details of each setting in the Visual C++ documentation. What you won't find there, however, is an example.

SHGetSettings()

Actually, using SHGetSettings() is quite simple. The function requires just two arguments:

```
void SHGetSettings(LPSHELLFLAGSTATE lpsfs, DWORD dwMask);
```

SHELLFLAGSTATE is a very compact structure defined in this way:

```
typedef struct
{
    BOOL fShowAllObjects : 1;
    BOOL fShowExtensions : 1;
    BOOL fNoConfirmRecycle : 1;
    BOOL fShowSysFiles : 1;
    BOOL fShowCompColor : 1;
    BOOL fDoubleClickInWebView : 1;
    BOOL fDesktopHTML : 1;
    BOOL fWin95Classic : 1;
    BOOL fDontPrettyPath : 1;
    BOOL fShowAttribCol : 1;
    BOOL fMapNetDrvBtn : 1;
    BOOL fShowInfoTip : 1;
    BOOL fHideIcons : 1;
    UINT fRestFlags : 3;
} SHELLFLAGSTATE, *LPSHELLFLAGSTATE;
```

The `dwMask` parameter is a binary bitmask — you have to set the appropriate bit for each of the above fields you're interested in and want the function to retrieve. The possible values are:

Field	Mask bit	Setting in the Folder Options dialog
`fShowAllObjects`	`SSF_SHOWALLOBJECTS`	Show all files
`fShowExtensions`	`SSF_SHOWEXTENSIONS`	Hide file extensions for known file types
`fNoConfirmRecycle`	`SSF_NOCONFIRMRECYCLE`	None
`fShowSysFiles`	`SSF_SHOWSYSFILES`	Do not show hidden files
`fShowCompColor`	`SSF_SHOWCOMPCOLOR`	None
`fDoubleClickInWebView`	`SSF_DOUBLECLICKINWEBVIEW`	Double-Click to Open an Item option on the General I Custom Settings dialog
`fWin95Classic`	`SSF_WIN95CLASSIC`	Classic Style option in the General page
`fDontPrettyPath`	`SSF_DONTPRETTYPATH`	Allow all uppercase names
`fMapNetDrvBtn`	`SSF_MAPNETDRVBUTTON`	Show Map Network Drive button in toolbar
`fShowAttribCol`	`SSF_SHOWATTRIBCOL`	Show file attributes in the Detail View
`fShowInfoTip`	`SSF_SHOWINFOTIP`	Show pop-up description for folders and desktop items
`fDesktopHTML`	`SSF_DESKTOPHTML`	View as Web Page on the Active Desktop context menu
`fHideIcons`	`SSF_HIDEICONS`	Hide icons when desktop is viewed as a Web page

The documentation erroneously states that `fHideIcons` is not used, when in fact it works perfectly: it indicates whether the icons on the desktop will be shown when the desktop view is set to Web mode. Let's have a look at some possible applications for the information you can get from these flags.

Watch the File Extension

The first use that comes to my mind relates to whether programmers want to show file extensions in the user interface of their applications. If your program displays file names for any reason, then you should take the user's preferences into account and decide whether to display the extension according to the status of this flag.

Make the Desktop More Active

The fHideIcons flag lets you know whether the icons on the desktop are viewable when the view mode is set to **As a Web Page**. fDesktopHTML, on the other hand, tells you if the desktop uses an HTML page as its background. If the desktop is in Web mode, *and* the icons aren't viewable, then you might not want to create new shortcuts on the desktop.

The combined use of both fDesktopHTML and fHideIcons would be very useful if only we could *set* these settings, and not just get their status. Consider the following scenario: there are many ways of clearing the desktop in order to stop users of publicly available computers from browsing or running applications other than yours. However, a new possibility is offered by the combination of fDesktopHTML and fHideIcons. The first of these allows you to set the flag that displays an HTML page as the desktop background, while the second one hides all the icons on the desktop. In this way, you can transform the Windows desktop (and the machine) into a dedicated server on which a single HTML-based application is running. Admittedly, the taskbar will still be there, but you can easily hide that by getting its HWND and then calling ShowWindow() with the SW_HIDE flag:

```
// The taskbar is a window of class 'Shell_TrayWnd'
HWND hwnd = FindWindow("Shell_TrayWnd", NULL);
if(IsWindow(hwnd))
    ShowWindow(hwnd, SW_HIDE);
```

At the time of writing, there was no documented way to set the flags we're interested in. However, there's almost always an undocumented way to work around these things! I'll have more to say on this subject in a while.

How to Click a List View

Among the numerous folder settings in shell version 4.71, there's the possibility of arranging things so folders are underlined when they're selected, and one click is enough to open them. You can set these options through the **General** page of the **Folder Options** dialog. Interestingly, these styles are also available for list views in version 4.70 of the common controls library, so you might want to modify the activation modality and the mouse-tracking capability of your list views according to the fDoubleClickInWebView flag. The styles to take into account are:

- ❑ LVS_EX_ONECLICKACTIVATE   (4.70)
- ❑ LVS_EX_TWOCLICKACTIVATE   (4.70)
- ❑ LVS_EX_UNDERLINECOLD   (4.71)
- ❑ LVS_EX_UNDERLINEHOT   (4.71)

In this list, the version numbers refer to the *common controls library*, and not to the shell. Version 4.70 of comctl32.dll shipped with Internet Explorer 4.0 (regardless of whether Active Desktop is installed), while 4.71 shipped with IE 4.01.

To set the extended styles for a list view, you need ListView_SetExtendedListViewStyle(), which is a new macro built around the LVM_SETEXTENDEDLISTVIEWSTYLE message. The meaning of the first two styles listed above is straightforward, while the others deal with hot items, a term used to describe an item that the mouse is passing over. LVS_EX_UNDERLINECOLD causes 'non-hot' items to be underlined, while LVS_EX_UNDERLINEHOT underlines only the hot item.

Delete Confirmation

The fNoConfirmRecycle flag informs you whether or not the confirmation dialog will be shown before deleting files. As you might imagine, this applies only to deletions that go through the Recycle Bin and the shell. However, even if you aren't deleting files via shell functions like SHFileOperation() that we saw in Chapter 3, wouldn't it be nice to ask for confirmation if the user is expecting such questions to be asked? Reading fNoConfirmRecycle is a big step towards making this possible.

The Sample Program

The interface for this, the final example in this chapter, looks something like the one in the screenshot I wonder if you can guess what I used to create the skeleton?

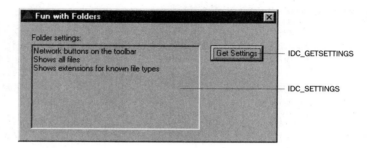

The code for this example is very easy indeed: you just need to add a handler for the Get Settings button, which will cause the current shell option settings to be read. The following source code produces the effect you can see in the screenshot. As always, remember to #include shlobj.h and resource.h at the top of the source file.

```
void OnSettings(HWND hDlg)
{
    SetDlgItemText(hDlg, IDC_SETTINGS, "");

    SHELLFLAGSTATE sfs;
    SHGetSettings(&sfs, SSF_DESKTOPHTML | SSF_SHOWALLOBJECTS |
                  SSF_MAPNETDRVBUTTON | SSF_SHOWATTRIBCOL | SSF_SHOWEXTENSIONS);

    TCHAR szBuf[MAX_PATH] = {0};
    if(sfs.fDesktopHTML)
        lstrcat(szBuf, __TEXT("Active Desktop - View as Web page is active\r\n"));

    if(sfs.fMapNetDrvBtn)
        lstrcat(szBuf, __TEXT("Network buttons on the toolbar\r\n"));

    if(sfs.fShowAllObjects)
        lstrcat(szBuf, __TEXT("Shows all files\r\n"));

    if(sfs.fShowAttribCol)
        lstrcat(szBuf, __TEXT("Shows attributes in Detail view\r\n"));

    if(sfs.fShowExtensions)
        lstrcat(szBuf, __TEXT("Shows extensions for known file types\r\n"));

    SetDlgItemText(hDlg, IDC_SETTINGS, szBuf);
}
```

Setting Preferences

Reading these kinds of settings might indeed be helpful in a range of circumstances, but rather more interesting would be the ability to *set* these attributes programmatically. Unfortunately, a SHSetSettings() routine is yet to appear, but in this section I'll demonstrate that there's plenty you can do to achieve this goal without Microsoft's help.

Where are Preferences Stored?

As you could probably have guessed, all the settings you can read through SHGetSettings() are stored somewhere in the registry, and that means there's a relatively secure way to set preferences programmatically.

> **Before going any further, let me make clear an important point. In the absence of official documentation, Microsoft is free to change the registry keys it uses in future versions of the operating system, indirectly causing your code to break. At the time of writing, the technique I'm presenting here worked perfectly under version 4.71 of the shell and Windows 98.**

With that warning out of the way, on with the show! While snooping in the registry, I ran across the following key:

```
HKEY_CURRENT_USER
    \Software
        \Microsoft
            \Windows
                \CurrentVersion
                    \Explorer
                        \Advanced
```

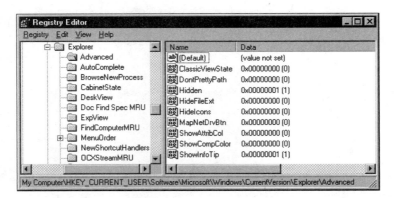

It seemed that I had found what I was looking for. Would it be enough simply to modify these registry entries? Unfortunately, this was not to be – I soon noticed that the list of values was missing a number of entries, in particular the 'Web view' settings.

At this point, I remembered the golden rule of trying to reverse-engineer registry settings: always compare the contents of the same key under HKEY_CURRENT_USER and HKEY_LOCAL_MACHINE. Here's what I found:

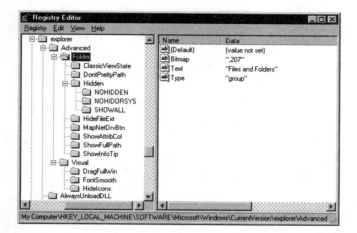

As you can see, there's an entire hierarchical structure that reproduces the same tree as the Folder Options dialog. The main nodes are of type "group", and have their own bitmap, and a display name. The 'leaves' of the structure hold a collection of attributes, from which stand out a couple of values: RegPath and HKeyRoot:

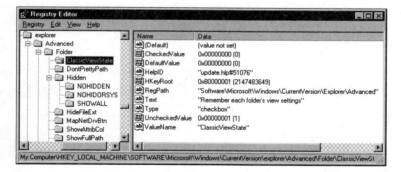

What this means is that every entry in this sub-tree points to another key in the registry where the actual value is stored, via a path constructed from HKeyRoot\RegPath\ValueName. The attributes of the leaf determine the text to be shown, the type of the option (checkbox or radio button), the value when checked or unchecked, the default value, and even the file name and topic ID for any available help.

Given all this, arranging a custom SHSetSettings() function is simply a matter of reading and writing some data from and to the registry.

Adding Custom Options to the Standard Dialog

Since there seemed to be a perfect correspondence between the layout of the registry sub-tree and the structure of the Folder Options dialog, I immediately suspected that adding a new key in the registry would cause a new, custom option to appear in the standard dialog. To prove it, there was only one thing to do: add a new key to that registry sub-tree!

I started by defining a
new key called
MySetting under
Folder. Then, I defined
all the values that I'd seen
the other leaves have:

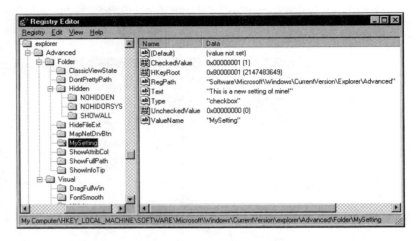

After saving the changes to the registry, I opened the **Folder Options** dialog expectantly, but nothing new appeared. In fact, though, there's an obvious reason for this: the code behind the dialog adds a new item only if it is able to read its stored value. As I mentioned earlier, this value is in another area of the registry – it's where HKeyRoot, RegPath and ValueName point.

The extra step required is the creation of a new value called MySetting under this key:

```
HKEY_CURRENT_USER
    \Software
        \Microsoft
            \Windows
                \CurrentVersion
                    \Explorer
                        \Advanced
```

It should be set to the default value you expect for
the option. When I saved the changes and reopened
the **Folder Options** dialog, the new setting appeared,
as this screenshot demonstrates:

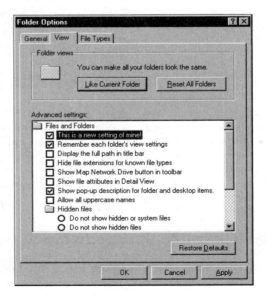

When Custom Options Are Helpful

Adding new, custom options to the Folder Options dialog is not just a trick to impress colleagues — rather, it could represent a very convenient way of allowing your users to customize your programs. I don't suggest that you should use this dialog for all the settings an application can have, but it's well worth considering for those options that revolve around the user interface and the folders. In my opinion, the module that could best exploit this feature is a namespace extension.

The choice of the registry path to use is completely up to you, but it would seem to make sense to store your settings away from the standard ones. An excellent choice could be to use an application-specific registry key.

Summary

Folders are an extensive topic that this chapter has attempted to cover in detail. You've seen how to browse for specific folders and how to work with them, enumerating their contents and setting preferences. In particular, this chapter showed you:

- ❑ How to make best use of `SHBrowseForFolder()`
- ❑ How to enumerate the content of any folder
- ❑ The functions to deal with special system folders
- ❑ Which folder settings are available for reading, and how to set them programmatically

Along the way, we've built some potentially useful functions to extend the set of tools provided by the API. Examples of such helper routines are `SHEnumFolderContent()` and `SHPathToPidlEx()`. Moreover, I also revealed how the shell stores the folder settings, and addressed an undocumented way of adding new options to the standard Folder Options dialog.

Further Reading

Complementary to this chapter is my article *The Windows 98 Shell* that appeared in MIND, in August 1998. It discusses how to take advantage of the scriptable objects of the Windows 9x shell, a topic that will be covered in detail later in this book. That article also shows how to build an ActiveX control that browses for folders. A similar subject was discussed in the August 1998 issue of MSJ, where ADSI (Active Directory Service Interface) and namespace extensions combine to arrange a 'web view' for a folder.

I picked up some tips on how to go about writing the code that I presented in this chapter from Knowledge Base articles such as:

❑ **Knowledge Base Article ID Q179378:** *Browse for Folders from the Current Directory*
❑ **Knowledge Base Article ID Q132750:** *Convert a File Path to an ITEMIDLIST*

A quick but useful definition of the role played by the memory allocator can be found in the *Ask Dr Gui* column of MSDN News, Sept/Oct 97. The book *Programming the Windows 95 User Interface* by Nancy Cluts (Microsoft Press, available on the MSDN Library CDs) is still the only source I know to provide some code that allows you to form an idea about PIDLs.

As for PIDLs and folder content, there's a good article in Jeff Prosise's *Wicked Code* column in the December 1997 issue MSJ, in which he illustrates how to get the handle of the context menu for a given file object.

The Shortest Path to Shortcuts

The Windows shell allows you to store references to any object you might come across anywhere in the system. When you drag-and-drop executables from one folder to another, for example, the mouse cursor automatically changes its shape to offer a third choice in addition to those of copying and moving the file.

Unless you specify otherwise, executables are not copied or moved. Instead, each time you attempt such an operation, what actually gets copied or moved is a reference to their physical location. What actually gets created is not a copy of the file, but a link to its original location.

All these are samples of **shortcuts**. Things of this kind have been around for a while in older versions of Windows – the icons in Program Manager, for example, were a sort of 'early version' of shortcuts. Don't be confused, however – they aren't the same, and the main difference lies in the fact that a shortcut is a general mechanism that can point to *file objects*: not just executables, and not just files.

Shortcuts are everywhere in the Windows 9*x* and Windows NT shell. You can find them in any folder, but most of all you find them in the special system folders. If you want your application to do impressive things like adding items to the Favorites or SendTo folders, or even to the Start menu, then creating shortcuts is the way to go. They are an important piece of the shell jigsaw that we need to discuss thoroughly.

In this chapter, we're going to cover:

- ❑ Exactly what shortcuts are
- ❑ How the system stores and reloads them
- ❑ How you can create or delete shortcuts
- ❑ Examples of useful functions that you can code for shortcuts

The examples we'll examine along the way assume a certain familiarity with topics that might be considered at the margin of shell programming, but which will demonstrate more clearly the flexibility of shortcuts. In this chapter, for instance, we'll be using hotkey controls and drag-and-drop as built-in features of the sample applications.

What are Shortcuts?

A shortcut represents a link to a particular file object, and is implemented as a tiny binary file with a .lnk extension. When I say, "tiny," I really mean it – the size of a shortcut file rarely reaches 1 KB. Not all shortcuts have exactly the same size, but they do possess a fixed set of attributes: the target file object, a description, an hotkey, an icon, and more. We'll examine all of these shortly.

Shortcuts pervade the whole of the Windows shell, and may be perceived as a service that the shell provides you with. From the software point of view, shortcuts are implemented through a COM server that exposes the IShellLink interface and is identified by the mnemonic CLSID_ShellLink. By means of this interface, you're allowed to set the various attributes of a shortcut, and call the methods that save it to or load it from disk.

The Shortcut File Type

When all is said and done, a shortcut is a file, but it's a kind of file that the shell handles in a particular way. The shell knows that a file of type 'shortcut' is a reference to something else, so that when you double-click it (or click it – it depends on your Active Desktop settings, as shown in Chapter 5!) you're returned the object being pointed to, not the file you clicked on.

Creating Shortcuts

Although shortcuts are often associated with executable programs, this is by no means a rule – you can create shortcuts to directories and non-executable files. From a software perspective, there's absolutely no difference. However it's *also* possible to create shortcuts to non-file system objects (such as printers); in this case there *is* a small difference, and you should use a different method for this purpose.

To create a new .lnk file, you have two choices. The first one relies on the shell DDE interface, which is inherited directly from the old Program Manager. We won't be covering it here, but more details on shell DDE and full documentation of the syntax are available in the Internet Client SDK and the MSDN Library. If you used to program using DDE but haven't been back to it recently, it may interest you to know that there have been changes since Windows 3.x, and there are some relatively new features in the DDE interface.

Using the IShellLink Interface

The second and recommended way of creating shortcuts is by means of the IShellLink COM interface, and it's a surprisingly painless process.

The steps involved are:

- ❑ Creating the appropriate COM server
- ❑ Getting a pointer to the `IShellLink` interface

- ❑ Setting some attributes through the methods of `IShellLink`
- ❑ Getting a pointer to the `IPersistFile` interface
- ❑ Saving the shortcut to a file using methods of `IPersistFile`

Creating the server is just a matter of calling `CoCreateInstance()`, making sure to have initialized the COM libraries properly (with `CoInitialize()`) beforehand:

```
IShellLink* pShellLink = NULL;
HRESULT hr = CoCreateInstance(CLSID_ShellLink, NULL, CLSCTX_INPROC_SERVER,
                 IID_IShellLink, reinterpret_cast<LPVOID*>(&pShellLink));
if(FAILED(hr))
   return hr;
```

The CLSID is defined in the `shlobj.h` header file, and the above call returns a pointer to the `IShellLink` interface, which is the key to handling shortcuts. The following table presents a list of all its methods, with brief descriptions of each. I'll point out some possible pitfalls a little later on, in the course of writing a sample program.

Method	Description
GetArguments() SetArguments()	Returns/sets the command-line arguments.
GetDescription() SetDescription()	Returns/sets the description string.
GetHotkey() SetHotkey()	Returns/sets the hot key for the shortcut.
GetIconLocation() SetIconLocation()	Returns/sets the path and index of the icon.
GetIDList() SetIDList()	Returns/sets the PIDL of the linked object. Use these methods instead of `GetPath()` and `SetPath()` if you're working with non-file system objects.
GetPath() SetPath()	Returns/sets the path and filename of the linked object.
GetShowCmd() SetShowCmd()	Returns/sets the SW_XXX flag of the linked object.
GetWorkingDirectory() SetWorkingDirectory()	Returns/sets the working directory.
SetRelativePath()	Sets a relative path to the linked object.
Resolve()	Retrieves the file object pointed to by the shortcut.

Once you have a pointer to `IShellLink`, you can start configuring the shortcut by setting the target object (a file, a directory, or a PIDL to a non-file object), and a list of optional attributes. You can set a description, a hotkey to access the file quickly, a specific icon, a working directory, command-line arguments, and a value that denotes how the window (if any) should be created. Here's a typical code fragment:

```
pShellLink->SetPath(pszTarget);
pShellLink->SetDescription(pszDesc);
pShellLink->SetHotkey(wHotKey);
pShellLink->SetIconLocation(pszIconPath, wIconIndex);
```

At this point, the object only exists in memory. To make it persistent, we need to store it in a file. For this reason, the COM server we're working with (the one identified by `CLSID_ShellLink`) implements the `IPersistFile` interface together with `IShellLink`. The former is an interface that comprises methods to read from and write to disk, and therefore serves the purpose of providing callers with a common programming interface to load and save files.

```
IPersistFile* pPF;
pShellLink->QueryInterface(IID_IPersistFile, reinterpret_cast<LPVOID*>(&pPF));
MultiByteToWideChar(CP_ACP, 0, szLnkFile, -1, wszLnkFile, MAX_PATH);
pPF->Save(wszLnkFile, TRUE);
```

`IPersistFile`'s two most important methods, `Load()` and `Save()`, both require Unicode strings, and therefore we need to convert the buffer containing the filename to wide characters.

A Global Function for Shortcuts

We can already put this information together to form a new shell helper function that creates shortcuts – remarkably, the Windows shell API doesn't provide a simple and direct function to create (or resolve) a shortcut. In another feat of imagination, I'm going to call ours `SHCreateShortcutEx()`.

> *In fact, although the Win32 API doesn't have one, the Windows CE SDK does include a function called* `SHCreateShortcut()`, *with the following prototype:*
>
> `BOOL SHCreateShortcut(LPTSTR szShortcut, LPTSTR szTarget);`

As input, our function will take the name of the target `.lnk` file, and a structure that will contain all the attributes requested for the shortcut:

```
struct SHORTCUTSTRUCT
{
    LPTSTR pszTarget;
    LPTSTR pszDesc;
    WORD wHotKey;
    LPTSTR pszIconPath;
    WORD wIconIndex;
};

typedef SHORTCUTSTRUCT* LPSHORTCUTSTRUCT;
```

Here's the source code for the function, which we'll be using in a sample program that we'll create and discuss later on:

```
HRESULT SHCreateShortcutEx(LPCTSTR szLnkFile, LPSHORTCUTSTRUCT lpss)
{
    WCHAR wszLnkFile[MAX_PATH] = {0};
    IShellLink* pShellLink = NULL;
    IPersistFile* pPF = NULL;

    // Validate SHORTCUTSTRUCT pointer
    if(lpss == NULL)
        return E_FAIL;

    // Create the COM server assuming CoInitialize() has already been called
    HRESULT hr = CoCreateInstance(CLSID_ShellLink, NULL,
                                  CLSCTX_INPROC_SERVER, IID_IShellLink,
                                  reinterpret_cast<LPVOID*>(&pShellLink));
    if(FAILED(hr))
        return hr;

    // Set attributes
    pShellLink->SetPath(lpss->pszTarget);
    pShellLink->SetDescription(lpss->pszDesc);
    pShellLink->SetHotkey(lpss->wHotKey);
    pShellLink->SetIconLocation(lpss->pszIconPath, lpss->wIconIndex);

    // Get the IPersistFile interface to save
    hr = pShellLink->QueryInterface(
                        IID_IPersistFile, reinterpret_cast<LPVOID*>(&pPF));
    if(FAILED(hr))
    {
        pShellLink->Release();
        return hr;
    }

    // Save to a LNK file (Unicode name)
    MultiByteToWideChar(CP_ACP, MB_PRECOMPOSED,
                                szLnkFile, -1, wszLnkFile, MAX_PATH);
    hr = pPF->Save(wszLnkFile, TRUE);

    // Clean up
    pPF->Release();
    pShellLink->Release();
    return hr;
}
```

Shell Scriptable Objects

A better possibility for working with shortcuts is offered by **shell scriptable objects**. These were introduced with Internet Explorer 4.0, and are a standard part of Windows 98. In a nutshell, they are Automation servers that expose a programming interface for creating and resolving shortcuts. (They also do many other interesting things...)

Most interestingly, these components can be used from desktop applications, HTML pages, and also throughout the **Windows Scripting Host** (WSH). We'll be covering these objects and WSH in detail in Chapter 12.

Giving Shortcuts the Right Name

Since version 4.71 of the shell, a new function called SHGetNewLinkInfo() has been available to programmers. Despite what you might expect, though, this function doesn't actually *create* a shortcut. Instead, it is useful when the time comes to arrange a correct name for a shortcut:

```
BOOL SHGetNewLinkInfo(LPCTSTR pszLinkTo,
                      LPCTSTR pszDir,
                      LPTSTR  pszName,
                      BOOL*   pfMustCopy,
                      UINT    uFlags);
```

The function takes either a pointer to the path name, or the PIDL of the target object; this is stored in pszLinkTo. Whether it gets considered as a PIDL or a path name depends upon the value in uFlags. The destination folder is pszDir.

This routine will suggest the name for the shortcut file you're about to create. This name is returned in pszName, which assumes a buffer of MAX_PATH characters. When you create shortcuts to existing shortcuts, the shell doesn't create a new link, but simply copies and modifies the target. The pfMustCopy flag serves the purpose of returning a Boolean value that denotes whether the shell will create a shortcut file from scratch, or proceed with a copy. TRUE means that pszLinkTo is an existing shortcut, in which case the shell will make a copy and modify it appropriately. A value of FALSE means that a completely new shortcut will be created. Finally, the available flags are:

Flag	Description
SHGNLI_PIDL	If set, the pszLinkTo argument will be considered as a PIDL, otherwise as a string.
SHGNLI_NOUNIQUE	If set, the shell will first determine the shortcut name and then check for possible collisions. If the name collides with others in the same folder, it gets updated iteratively until a unique name is found.
SHGNLI_PREFIXNAME	If set, the name will always be prefixed by 'Shortcut to'.

In practice, SHGetNewLinkInfo() endeavors to provide a consistent name for the shortcut to the given target. This means, for example, that it will have a .pif extension if it points to a DOS executable and a .lnk extension otherwise. Another check the function performs regards the target drive's support for long filenames. If the drive doesn't support long names, then it will return a name in 8.3 format.

> *As for any other function that's available only from version 4.71 onwards, it's a good idea not to link this function through the* shell32.lib *import library. Instead, you should consider loading it dynamically by calling* LoadLibrary("shell32.dll") *and* GetProcAddress().

Deleting Shortcuts

Deleting shortcuts is as easy as deleting a file. More importantly, you don't have to worry about the destiny of the file being pointed to, because all you delete is the reference. The object being pointed to remains completely unaffected.

Resolving Shortcuts

Creating shortcuts is only half the job. It's completely plausible that sooner or later, you (and not just the system) will need to read the contents of a shortcut file. While resolving shortcuts is not *that* different from reading a file, the operation is usually referred as 'resolving' rather than 'reading'.

There are reasons for this difference in nomenclature. A shortcut points to a file object, but this is just a link – it's not embedded. When you create your shortcut, the object is supposed to exist, but no such assumption can be made when the time comes to read it. When you need to access the referenced object, there is nothing to guarantee that it hasn't been deleted, moved, or renamed in the meantime.

Reading a shortcut simply means that you will try to access the object specified in the .lnk file. *Resolving* a shortcut means that the system will try to understand where the referenced object has been moved to, or how it has been renamed.

How Explorer Resolves Shortcuts

We could say that, to begin with, each resolution of a shortcut *is* a reading. However, if Explorer doesn't find a valid file object at the location specified in the .lnk file, then it will perform a recursive search on all the drives and directories in the disk until it finds a file with the same size, creation date and attributes as the one pointed to by the shortcut. If that search fails, Explorer will display a dialog box like this one:

This dialog can be suppressed by setting the appropriate flag when calling `IShellLink::Resolve()`. Of course, if you have deleted the referenced object, it's impossible for Explorer to find it, even if it's still in the Recycle Bin.

A Function for Resolving Shortcuts

The shell API also lacks a function to resolve shortcuts, so once again we'll be writing our own. The steps involved are:

- Creating the necessary COM server
- Getting a pointer to the `IPersistFile` interface
- Loading the shortcut from the .lnk file using methods of `IPersistFile`
- Getting a pointer to the `IShellLink` interface
- Resolving the shortcut

The core of the whole operation is the call to `Resolve()`. This method has the following syntax:

```
HRESULT IShellLink::Resolve(HWND hwnd, DWORD fFlags);
```

The first parameter is the handle of the parent window for any dialog box the function should need to show. More interesting from our point of view is the `dwFlags` argument, which can be a combination of the following values:

Flag	Description
SLR_NO_UI	The function won't display any dialog box, even if it fails to locate the file pointed to. In this case, the function returns after 3 seconds by default; this timeout can be customized by specifying the number of desired milliseconds in the high-order word of the argument.
SLR_ANY_MATCH	Try to resolve the link, and display a dialog box if it fails.
SLR_UPDATE	If this flag is set, and the referenced object has been moved or renamed, then the shortcut is updated to point to the new location. This behavior is not the default.

Notice here that updating the shortcut to have it point to the new location (if any) of the file object is not automatic. It must be requested explicitly by passing the `SLR_UPDATE` flag to `IShellLink::Resolve()`.

Here's the complete source code for our `SHResolveShortcut()` function. Like its sister routine `SHCreateShortcutEx()`, it will be used extensively in our sample program to illustrate shortcut programming.

```
HRESULT SHResolveShortcut(LPCTSTR szLnkFile, LPSHORTCUTSTRUCT lpss)
{
    WCHAR wszLnkFile[MAX_PATH] = {0};
    IShellLink* pShellLink = NULL;
    IPersistFile* pPF = NULL;

    // Create the appropriate COM server
    HRESULT hr = CoCreateInstance(CLSID_ShellLink, NULL,
                                  CLSCTX_INPROC_SERVER, IID_IShellLink,
                                  reinterpret_cast<LPVOID*>(&pShellLink));
    if(FAILED(hr))
        return hr;

    // Get the IPersistFile interface to load the LNK file
    hr = pShellLink->QueryInterface(
                        IID_IPersistFile, reinterpret_cast<LPVOID*>(&pPF));
    if(FAILED(hr))
    {
        pShellLink->Release();
        return hr;
    }
```

```
// Load the shortcut (Unicode name)
   MultiByteToWideChar(CP_ACP, 0, szLnkFile, -1, wszLnkFile, MAX_PATH);
   hr = pPF->Load(wszLnkFile, STGM_READ);
   if(FAILED(hr))
   {
      pPF->Release();
      pShellLink->Release();
      return hr;
   }

   // Resolve the link
   hr = pShellLink->Resolve(NULL, SLR_ANY_MATCH);
   if(FAILED(hr))
   {
      pPF->Release();
      pShellLink->Release();
      return hr;
   }

   // Extract the information to fill lpss
   if(lpss != NULL)
   {
      TCHAR szPath[MAX_PATH] = {0};
      TCHAR szDesc[MAX_PATH] = {0};
      TCHAR szIcon[MAX_PATH] = {0};
      WORD w = 0;
      WORD wIcon = 0;
      WIN32_FIND_DATA wfd;

      pShellLink->GetPath(szPath, MAX_PATH, &wfd, SLGP_SHORTPATH);
      pShellLink->GetDescription(szDesc, MAX_PATH);
      pShellLink->GetHotkey(&w);
      pShellLink->GetIconLocation(
                     szIcon, MAX_PATH, reinterpret_cast<int*>(&wIcon));

      lpss->pszTarget = szPath;
      lpss->pszDesc = szDesc;
      lpss->pszIconPath = szIcon;
      lpss->wHotKey = w;
      lpss->wIconIndex = wIcon;
   }

   pPF->Release();
   pShellLink->Release();
   return hr;
}
```

To load the file, we use the Load() method of IPersistFile, which takes two arguments. The first one is the Unicode version of the .lnk file name to work with, while the second parameter denotes the access mode with which the file should be opened.

Shortcuts and Special Folders

In most cases, if you need to create a shortcut programmatically, you need to create it in a special folder. However, this is not a complication – it's just a matter of specifying the right path to the folder. The sample program that we'll discuss in the next section allows you to create shortcuts in many of the 'usual' special folders: My Documents, Desktop, Start Menu, Programs, SendTo and Favorites. As we saw in Chapter 5, the SHGetSpecialFolderPath() function can discover the path to a non-virtual folder.

The Sample Program: Shortcut Manager

The application you can see in the figure below was generated by the Wrox AppWizard, and is intended to work as a simple console to create and resolve shortcuts. Its dialog window is divided in two parts: the upper for resolving shortcuts, and the lower to create new ones.

The user interface will let you select .lnk files to open, and it will work as a drop target too — that is, you can drag-and-drop shortcuts from wherever you like, and have it resolve them.

Each shortcut that is resolved by the program will be reported in the view. The example we'll develop here will only show target, description and hotkey information, but enhancing this aspect should not pose you problems if you choose to do so.

Selecting a Shortcut

The first potential pitfall we have to consider arises when you try to arrange an **Open** dialog to select a shortcut to resolve. The trouble is that by default, the **Open** dialog dereferences shortcuts, so you'll never be returned the names of any .lnk files! To work around this, you must specify the OFN_NODEREFERENCELINKS flag to the GetOpenFileName() function, as shown below in the handler function that deals with *both* the browse buttons on the application dialog:

```
void OnBrowse(HWND hDlg, WPARAM wID)
{
    TCHAR szFile[MAX_PATH] = {0};

    OPENFILENAME ofn;
    ZeroMemory(&ofn, sizeof(OPENFILENAME));
    ofn.lStructSize = sizeof(OPENFILENAME);
    if(wID == IDC_SHORTCUT)
    {
        ofn.lpstrFilter = __TEXT("Shortcuts\0*.lnk\0");
        ofn.Flags = OFN_NODEREFERENCELINKS;
    }
    else
        ofn.lpstrFilter = __TEXT("All files\0*.*\0");

    ofn.nMaxFile = MAX_PATH;
    ofn.lpstrInitialDir = __TEXT("c:\\");
    ofn.lpstrFile = szFile;
```

```
    if(!GetOpenFileName(&ofn))
        return;
    else
        SetDlgItemText(hDlg, wID, ofn.lpstrFile);
    return;
}
```

By this technique, if you double click on a `.lnk` file, Explorer will stop there and return the name of *that* file instead of going down to the referenced file.

Shell Drag-and-Drop

All right, I admit it: even though we're in the land of shell programming, this is not a strictly related topic. Just in case you haven't seen it before, though, it is worth a look. The Visual C++ Resource Editor allows you to assign a drop-target attribute (by turning on the `WS_EX_ACCEPTFILES` bit) to literally any window. However, it's then completely up to you to figure out how and when you can handle drop events. We want to limit drag-and-drop to the list view, but if we assign it the attribute, then we're faced with having to subclass the window in order to detect drop-related events.

Instead, we're going to use a simpler approach: the whole dialog will be drop-enabled, but when it catches a `WM_DROPFILES` message, it will verify that the event occurred within the list view. If not, it will ignore the event. The functions that handle drag-and-drop from the shell are all defined in `shellapi.h`, and go by the names of `DragQueryPoint()`, `DragQueryFile()` and `DragFinish()`. I'll have more to say on this subject later on.

Displaying the Results

This program has a report-style list view in its user interface, and to make using it a little easier, I've created a couple of helper functions to assist with adding columns and strings to such views. Keep them in mind, because we'll be using them again later on.

The first function is called `MakeReportView()`, and is meant to transform any list view window into a report-style list view with the columns you specify. Its prototype requires you to pass in the handle of the list view, an array of strings with name and width of each column, and the total number of columns. To make the prototype as compact as possible, I've assumed that the array you pass contains names in the even entries (0, 2, 4, and so forth) and numbers in the odd positions.

The array is actually an array of pointers to strings – namely, an array of 32-bit values. Provided that you're aware of this, you can use an array like the following:

```
LPTSTR psz[] = {"Target",      reinterpret_cast<TCHAR*>(170),
                "Description", reinterpret_cast<TCHAR*>(170),
                "Hotkey",      reinterpret_cast<TCHAR*>(100)};
MakeReportView(hwndList, psz, 3);
```

`MakeReportView()` always treats the entries as name/width pairs, so the number of columns should always be equal to half the size of the array.

```
void MakeReportView(HWND hwndList, LPTSTR* psz, int iNumOfCols)
{
    RECT rc;
    DWORD dwStyle = GetWindowStyle(hwndList);
    SetWindowLong(hwndList, GWL_STYLE, dwStyle | LVS_REPORT);
    GetClientRect(hwndList, &rc);
```

```
    // Handle pairs of entries. Array size is assumed to be 2 * iNumOfCols
    for(int i = 0 ; i < 2 * iNumOfCols ; i = i + 2)
    {
       LV_COLUMN lvc;
       ZeroMemory(&lvc, sizeof(LV_COLUMN));
       lvc.mask = LVCF_TEXT | LVCF_WIDTH;
       lvc.pszText = psz[i];
       if(reinterpret_cast<int>(psz[i + 1]) == 0)
          lvc.cx = rc.right / iNumOfCols;
       else
          lvc.cx = reinterpret_cast<int>(psz[i + 1]);

       ListView_InsertColumn(hwndList, i, &lvc);
    }
    return;
}
```

The companion routine for `MakeReportView()` is `AddStringToReportView()`, which adds a new row to the specified list view. Due to the low-level programming interface, filling all the columns of a report-style list view requires you to go through several steps. You should add the new item specifying the text for the first column (the main one), and then iterate on the remaining columns to set the text in those. All these steps are executed by `AddStringToReportView()`; you just pass a null-separated string that contains all the necessary substrings, and indicate how many there are in `iNumOfCols`.

```
void AddStringToReportView(HWND hwndList, LPTSTR psz, int iNumOfCols)
{
    LV_ITEM lvi;
    ZeroMemory(&lvi, sizeof(LV_ITEM));
    lvi.mask = LVIF_TEXT;
    lvi.pszText = psz;
    lvi.cchTextMax = lstrlen(psz);
    lvi.iItem = 0;
    ListView_InsertItem(hwndList, &lvi);

    // Other columns
    for(int i = 1 ; i < iNumOfCols ; i++)
    {
       psz += lstrlen(psz) + 1;
       ListView_SetItemText(hwndList, 0, i, psz);
    }
    return;
}
```

In this example, the list view will have three columns: **Target**, **Description**, and **Hotkey**. The first two of these are straightforward, but the third makes use of a common control that you may not have used before, so it's worth just a little more explanation.

The Hotkey Common Control

Windows 95 introduced a new common control that lets you choose a key combination 'graphically' (see the figure):

To use the control, you hit the key combination you want, and it interprets the code and converts it into text. Clearly, this control is perfect for creating a more pleasant user interface around shortcut creation.

When it comes to *resolving* shortcuts, on the other hand, all you have is the number (a WORD to be precise) that gets returned by `IShellLink::GetHotkey()`. It's up to you to translate it into a well-formed string.

The word that identifies a hotkey is split into two bytes. The high-order byte is the modifier (*Alt*, *Ctrl*, *Shift*, or a combination of the three), while the low-order byte is the code of the key you hit. Note that if you press *A*, for example, the code is 65 (upper case letter) and not 97 (lower case).

To arrange a `HotkeyToString()` routine, then, we just need to check the bits of the high byte against some known constants. Here's another function to join the ranks of those that make up our project:

```
void HotkeyToString(WORD wHotKey, LPTSTR pszBuf)
{
    BYTE bKey = LOBYTE(wHotKey);
    BYTE bMod = HIBYTE(wHotKey);

    if(bMod & HOTKEYF_CONTROL)
        lstrcpy(pszBuf, __TEXT("Ctrl"));

    if(bMod & HOTKEYF_SHIFT)
        if(lstrlen(pszBuf))
            lstrcat(pszBuf, __TEXT(" + Shift"));
        else
            lstrcpy(pszBuf, __TEXT("Shift"));

    if(bMod & HOTKEYF_ALT)
        if(lstrlen(pszBuf))
            lstrcat(pszBuf, __TEXT(" + Alt"));
        else
            lstrcpy(pszBuf, __TEXT("Alt"));
```

```
    TCHAR s[2] = {0};
    wsprintf(s, __TEXT("%c"), bKey);
    if(lstrlen(pszBuf))
    {
        lstrcat(pszBuf, __TEXT(" + "));
        lstrcat(pszBuf, s);
    }
    else
        lstrcpy(pszBuf, s);
}
```

As input, the `HotkeyToString()` function takes the hotkey and a buffer to fill with the resulting string. It checks the modifier and builds the first part of the string – say, *Ctrl + Alt*. Then, it completes the job by concatenating the character of the key pressed – say, *Ctrl + Alt + X*. The next picture shows how the application looks when it has resolved a shortcut:

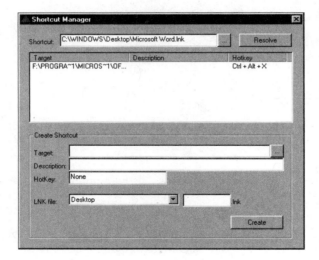

Collecting Arguments for Creation

The portion of the dialog that provides shortcut creation wouldn't be noteworthy if it weren't for a little subtlety. Open an existing shortcut (one of the ones you have on the desktop is fine) and try to assign it a new hotkey. You'll find that in some cases, the hotkey control corrects the key you pressed. Try it with *A*, and it will become *Ctrl + Alt + A*.

"Just a feature," you might say, but it's an *important* feature, because if you try to assign a hotkey that's *not* in the form *Ctrl + Alt + ...* programmatically, the hotkey will never be recognized. If you think about it for a moment, this behavior isn't *that* strange – *Ctrl + Alt + ...* shouldn't conflict with other possible accelerators. However, it took me a considerable amount of time to figure out what was wrong with the *Alt + Z* combination of my first few examples!

Giving Rules to the Hotkey

To instruct a hotkey control to replace some wrong or invalid key combination automatically, you must use **key rules**. Despite the important-sounding name, this just reduces to sending a simple message to the hotkey window.

To force it to accept only *Ctrl + Alt* prefixed keys, you must:

```
SendMessage(hwndHotkey, HKM_SETRULES,
            HKCOMB_NONE | HKCOMB_S | HKCOMB_A | HKCOMB_C,
            HOTKEYF_CONTROL | HOTKEYF_ALT);
```

The 'rule' can be rephrased like this:

❑ Invalid key combinations are all those that have one of the modifiers listed in wParam
❑ Replace each invalid key combination with those specified in lParam

If your hotkey combination begins with nothing (HKCOMB_NONE), *Shift* (HKCOMB_S), *Alt* (HKCOMB_A) or *Ctrl* (HKCOMB_C), then discard them and replace with *Ctrl + Alt*. The following picture shows the program when it's about to create a shortcut:

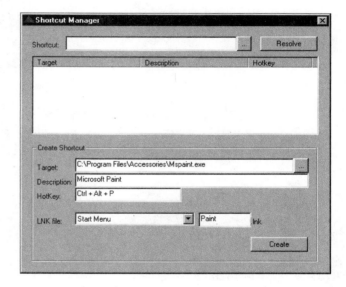

The Source Code

Let's now have a look at the remaining source code for this chapter's sample program. To compile it correctly, make sure that you include shlobj.h, resource.h and commdlg.h, and that you're linking against comdlg32.lib and ole32.lib. Also, because we're using COM, you'll need to bracket the call to DialogBox() in WinMain() with calls to CoInitialize(NULL) and CoUninitialize().

DoCreateShortcut()

This function is invoked when the user clicks on the **Create** button. It collects parameters from the other controls and arranges a call to SHCreateShortcutEx(). The combo box with the names of some special folders uses the same technique as we employed in Chapter 5.

```
void DoCreateShortcut(HWND hDlg)
{
    SHORTCUTSTRUCT ss;
    ZeroMemory(&ss, sizeof(SHORTCUTSTRUCT));
    TCHAR szTarget[MAX_PATH] = {0};
    TCHAR szDesc[MAX_PATH] = {0};
```

```
      // Get the hotkey
      ss.wHotKey = static_cast<WORD>(SendDlgItemMessage(
                                hDlg, IDC_HOTKEY, HKM_GETHOTKEY, 0, 0));

      // Get target and description
      GetDlgItemText(hDlg, IDC_TARGET, szTarget, MAX_PATH);
      GetDlgItemText(hDlg, IDC_DESCRIPTION, szDesc, MAX_PATH);
      ss.pszTarget = szTarget;
      ss.pszDesc = szDesc;

      // Determine the shortcut file name
      // Get the target folder & final backslash
      HWND hwndCbo = GetDlgItem(hDlg, IDC_SPECIAL);
      int i = ComboBox_GetCurSel(hwndCbo);
      DWORD nFolder = ComboBox_GetItemData(hwndCbo, i);

      TCHAR szPath[MAX_PATH] = {0};
      SHGetSpecialFolderPath(hDlg, szPath, nFolder, FALSE);
      if(szPath[lstrlen(szPath) - 1] != '\\')
         lstrcat(szPath, __TEXT("\\"));

      TCHAR szLnkFile[MAX_PATH] = {0};
      GetDlgItemText(hDlg, IDC_LNKFILE, szLnkFile, MAX_PATH);
      lstrcat(szPath, szLnkFile);
      lstrcat(szPath, __TEXT(".lnk"));

      // Create
      SHCreateShortcutEx(szPath, &ss);

      // Update UI
      SetDlgItemText(hDlg, IDC_SHORTCUT, szPath);
      return;
   }
```

DoResolveShortcut()

This function gets called in response to a click on the **Resolve** button, although it also takes an additional parameter `pszFile` that can be used to denote the file to resolve. If this parameter is NULL, then the function works on the file name specified in the **Shortcut** edit box. The reason for this argument is that it makes it easier to resolve any files dropped onto the program's window. `DoResolveShortcut()` first resolves the shortcut calling our `SHResolveShortcut()`, and then updates the user interface of the program, adding a new row to the report list view.

```
   void DoResolveShortcut(HWND hDlg, LPTSTR pszFile)
   {
      TCHAR szLnkFile[MAX_PATH] = {0};
      if(pszFile == NULL)
        GetDlgItemText(hDlg, IDC_SHORTCUT, szLnkFile, MAX_PATH);
      else
        lstrcpy(szLnkFile, pszFile);

      // Resolve the shortcut
      SHORTCUTSTRUCT ss;
      HRESULT hr = SHResolveShortcut(szLnkFile, &ss);
      if(FAILED(hr))
         return;
```

```
    /////////////////////////////////////////////////
// Update UI

    // Create the string for the listview
    TCHAR pszBuf[1024] = {0};
    LPTSTR psz = pszBuf;

    lstrcpy(psz, ss.pszTarget);
    lstrcat(psz, __TEXT("\0"));
    psz += lstrlen(psz) + 1;

    lstrcpy(psz, ss.pszDesc);
    lstrcat(psz, __TEXT("\0"));
    psz += lstrlen(psz) + 1;

    // Try to get the text version of the hotkey
    TCHAR szKey[30] = {0};
    HotkeyToString(ss.wHotKey, szKey);

    lstrcpy(psz, szKey);
    lstrcat(psz, __TEXT("\0"));

    // Add a new item to the report list view (3 columns)
    HWND hwndList = GetDlgItem(hDlg, IDC_VIEW);
    AddStringToReportView(hwndList, pszBuf, 3);
    return;
}
```

HandleFileDrop()

Called in response to WM_DROPFILES, this function defines what the program must do when the user drops files on its client area. Accepted data must be of type CF_HDROP, which is the interchange format used by the shell to move files around when you drag-and-drop files from the Explorer window or from the desktop. Any window with the WS_EX_ACCEPTFILES style set (we discussed this earlier), is sensitive only to drag-and-drop operations that involve data in this format. In other words, our program will accept drag-and-drop only if the source is the Windows shell, or another program that transfers data in the CF_HDROP format.

CF_HDROP is a clipboard format intended to exchange data items that are basically file names – you can look at the Visual C++ help files for more information about clipboard formats and the internal structure of CF_HDROP data. What's important for us is that there are a number of functions capable of reading data held in this format, through a type of memory handle called an HDROP.

When you drop files from the shell, the target window receives a WM_DROPFILES message in which one of the arguments is the HDROP handle. Our HandleFileDrop() function first checks the window onto which the drop occurred, and if this window is the list view, then it proceeds with extracting and resolving the various file names. You can drop any file onto the list view, but only shortcuts are handled correctly.

```
void HandleFileDrop(HWND hDlg, HDROP hDrop)
{
    // Check the window being dropped on
    POINT pt;
    DragQueryPoint(hDrop, &pt);
    ClientToScreen(hDlg, &pt);
    HWND hwndDrop = WindowFromPoint(pt);
```

```
   if(hwndDrop != GetDlgItem(hDlg, IDC_VIEW))
   {
      Msg(__TEXT("Sorry, you have to drop over the list view control!"));
      return;
   }

   // Now check the files
   int iNumOfFiles = DragQueryFile(hDrop, -1, NULL, 0);
   for(int i = 0 ; i < iNumOfFiles; i++)
   {
      TCHAR szFileName[MAX_PATH] = {0};
      DragQueryFile(hDrop, i, szFileName, MAX_PATH);
      DoResolveShortcut(hDlg, szFileName);
   }

   DragFinish(hDrop);
}
```

`DragQueryPoint()` lets you know the client coordinates of the point where the drop occurred, while `DragQueryFile()` extracts all the files packed in the HDROP handle, one after another. You can also use this function to discover how many files have been dropped. Finally, `DragFinish()` must be called when you've finished with the HDROP handle.

APP_DlgProc()

This is the window procedure of the application's main window, and because there are few more than we've had to deal with in previous examples, it's worth a look at the handlers that need to be added to the AppWizard code:

```
BOOL CALLBACK APP_DlgProc(HWND hDlg, UINT uiMsg, WPARAM wParam, LPARAM lParam)
{
   switch(uiMsg)
   {
   case WM_INITDIALOG:
      OnInitDialog(hDlg);
      break;

   case WM_DROPFILES:
      HandleFileDrop(hDlg, reinterpret_cast<HDROP>(wParam));
      break;

   case WM_COMMAND:
      switch(wParam)
      {
      case IDC_RESOLVE:
         DoResolveShortcut(hDlg, NULL);
         return FALSE;

      case IDC_CREATE:
         DoCreateShortcut(hDlg);
         return FALSE;

      case IDC_BROWSE:
         OnBrowse(hDlg, IDC_SHORTCUT);
         return FALSE;
```

```
                    case IDC_BROWSETARGET:
                        OnBrowse(hDlg, IDC_TARGET);
                        return FALSE;


                    case IDCANCEL:
                        EndDialog(hDlg, FALSE);
                        return FALSE;
                    }
                    break;
                }

            return FALSE;
        }
```

OnInitDialog()

There are a few more things to be initialized on the dialog in this project, as well. While dealing with the combo box should be a familiar process by now, we also need to set up the list view control, and to program the hotkey control to use the *Ctrl + Alt + ...* form:

```
void OnInitDialog(HWND hDlg)
{
    // Set the icons (T/F as to Large/Small icon)
    SendMessage(hDlg, WM_SETICON, FALSE, reinterpret_cast<LPARAM>(g_hIconSmall));
    SendMessage(hDlg, WM_SETICON, TRUE, reinterpret_cast<LPARAM>(g_hIconLarge));

    // Initialize the report view
    HWND hwndList = GetDlgItem(hDlg, IDC_VIEW);
    LPTSTR psz[] = {"Target",        reinterpret_cast<TCHAR*>(170),
                    "Description", reinterpret_cast<TCHAR*>(170),
                    "Hotkey",        reinterpret_cast<TCHAR*>(100)};
    MakeReportView(hwndList, psz, 3);

    // Special folders available
    HWND hwndCbo = GetDlgItem(hDlg, IDC_SPECIAL);
    int i = ComboBox_AddString(hwndCbo, "Desktop");
    ComboBox_SetItemData(hwndCbo, i, CSIDL_DESKTOP);
    i = ComboBox_AddString(hwndCbo, "Favorites");
    ComboBox_SetItemData(hwndCbo, i, CSIDL_FAVORITES);
    i = ComboBox_AddString(hwndCbo, "Programs");
    ComboBox_SetItemData(hwndCbo, i, CSIDL_PROGRAMS);
    i = ComboBox_AddString(hwndCbo, "My Documents");
    ComboBox_SetItemData(hwndCbo, i, CSIDL_PERSONAL);
    i = ComboBox_AddString(hwndCbo, "SendTo");
    ComboBox_SetItemData(hwndCbo, i, CSIDL_SENDTO);
    i = ComboBox_AddString(hwndCbo, "Start Menu");
    ComboBox_SetItemData(hwndCbo, i, CSIDL_STARTMENU);
    ComboBox_SetCurSel(hwndCbo, 0);

    // Initialize the hotkey control to prefix everything with Ctrl + Alt
    SendDlgItemMessage(hDlg, IDC_HOTKEY, HKM_SETRULES,
                    HKCOMB_NONE | HKCOMB_S | HKCOMB_A | HKCOMB_C,
                    HOTKEYF_CONTROL | HOTKEYF_ALT);

    SetDlgItemText(hDlg, IDC_TARGET, __TEXT("C:\\"));
}
```

Creating Shortcuts in System Folders

The sample program, which you should now be able to compile and run, makes it easy to create shortcuts in system folders – all you have to do is choose a folder name from a combo box and press a button. If you need to do this silently from within one of your own programs, then once you know which folder you're dealing with, all that remains is to format a string with the full path name.

Here's a simple function that does exactly this. As arguments, it takes the name of the .lnk file to be created, the ID of the special folder (one of the CSIDL_XXX constants you saw earlier), and the name of the file being pointed to. The code is an evolution of the SHCreateShortcutEx() function that I presented above.

```
HRESULT SHCreateSystemShortcut(LPCTSTR szLnkFile, int nFolder, LPCTSTR szFile)
{
    WCHAR wszLnkFile[MAX_PATH] = {0};

    TCHAR szPath[MAX_PATH] = {0};

    IShellLink* pShellLink = NULL;
    IPersistFile* pPF = NULL;

    // Create the proper COM server
    HRESULT hr = CoCreateInstance(CLSID_ShellLink, NULL,
                                  CLSCTX_INPROC_SERVER, IID_IShellLink,
                                  reinterpret_cast<LPVOID*>(&pShellLink));
    if(FAILED(hr))
        return hr;


    // Set attributes
    pShellLink->SetPath(szFile);


    // Get the IPersistFile interface to save
    hr = pShellLink->QueryInterface(
                            IID_IPersistFile, reinterpret_cast<LPVOID*>(&pPF));
    if(FAILED(hr))
    {
        pShellLink->Release();
        return hr;
    }


    // Prepare the name of the shortcut
    SHGetSpecialFolderPath(NULL, szPath, nFolder, FALSE);
    if(szPath[lstrlen(szPath) - 1] != '\\')
        lstrcat(szPath, __TEXT("\\"));
    lstrcat(szPath, szLnkFile);


    // Save to a LNK file (Unicode name)

    MultiByteToWideChar(CP_ACP, MB_PRECOMPOSED, szPath, -1, wszLnkFile, MAX_PATH);

    hr = pPF->Save(wszLnkFile, TRUE);

    // Clean up
    pPF->Release();
    pShellLink->Release();
    return hr;
}
```

With the help of the above function, creating shortcuts on the Desktop, in the Start menu, in
`Program Files`, or in `Favorites` is really easy. To prove it, the code needed to add a new item in
the Start menu that points to Notepad is now just:

```
SHCreateSystemShortcut(
    __TEXT("Notepad.lnk"), CSIDL_STARTMENU, __TEXT("c:\\windows\\notepad.exe"));
```

Obviously, the `c:\windows\` *path should be replaced with the actual path to your own Windows
directory. Also notice that under NT,* `notepad.exe` *is stored in the* `System` *directory.*

You can create shortcuts to directories and non-executable files as well. In fact, to refer to *any* file
system object, just pass the path to `IShellLink::SetPath()`, or call
`IShellLink::SetIDList()` passing the PIDL.

The SendTo Folder

The `SendTo` folder isn't as notable for shortcuts as it is for a couple of *non*-shortcut objects it hosts. If
you install Internet Explorer 4.0 on Windows 95 or Windows NT 4.0, or if you have Windows 98,
then it's likely that your `SendTo` folder will contain references to a mail recipient and to the desktop.
Using this mechanism, you can send a given file directly from the shell to your outbox as attachment
in a new message, or as a shortcut to the desktop.

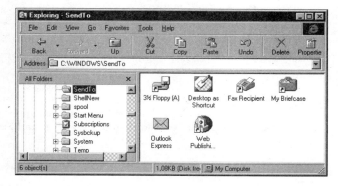

The screenshot shows a couple of items that don't have the typical overlaid arrow. What are they?
Well, **Desktop as Shortcut** is an empty `.DeskLink` file with a length of 0 bytes. If you search the
registry for this extension, you'll find that there's a COM object behind it.

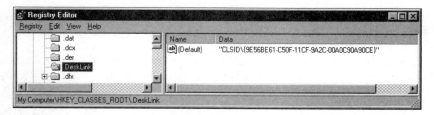

Knowing that it's a COM object is great news, but what kind of COM object? What interfaces does it
implement? In fact, it's a shell extension; more precisely, it's a **drop handler**. We'll cover shell
extensions in Chapter 15; for now, this just demonstrates that the `SendTo` folder doesn't only host
shortcuts. The `.DeskLink` extension is purely indicative, and could have been any other string.

The Recent Folder

The `Recent` folder collects recently opened documents. The contents of this directory can be verified by clicking on the <u>D</u>ocuments item in the Start menu, and its physical location is under the Windows directory. Curiously, however, there isn't a 1:1 correspondence between the shortcuts it contains and the items displayed through the menu.

The shell API exposes a function called `SHAddToRecentDocs()` solely for the purpose of letting programmers store links to their documents in this folder.

```
void SHAddToRecentDocs(UINT uFlags, LPCVOID pv);
```

The first argument qualifies the type of the second: PIDL or pointer to path name. Accordingly, it can take the value `SHARD_PATH` or `SHARD_PIDL`. If you use this function, you'll succeed in adding a reference to your document in the menu. The same isn't true if you simply create a new shortcut in the folder – in other words, creating a shortcut is necessary but not sufficient. `SHAddToRecentDocs()` is clearly doing something more.

Ultimately, `SHAddToRecentDocs()` adds the item to the global MRU (Most Recently Used) list that the Start menu uses; simply adding the file to the `Recent` folder, on the other hand, does not. The function also handles duplicate shortcuts in the folder, and deals with the ordering of the menu for you. For all these reasons, you should stick to using `SHAddToRecentDocs()` in case the method of implementation changes at some point in the future.

Summary

This chapter covered shortcuts, a primary topic for any book or article that attempts to discuss the Windows shell. Shortcuts are relatively simple and quick to write, but there is no single function to create and resolve them. In this chapter, we discussed and then did just this, and also looked at:

- ❑ The role of shortcuts
- ❑ How to create and resolve them
- ❑ Some useful functions to work with shortcuts
- ❑ Drag-and-drop and hotkey controls (albeit briefly)
- ❑ The relationship between shortcuts and system folders

Further Reading

The lack of a direct function for creating or resolving shortcuts has originated many articles. Although Windows 98 provides some COM facilities to create shortcuts programmatically, the lack of an equivalent API function is arguably an oversight.

In this chapter, I've presented functions for creating and resolving shortcuts. Another function to create shortcuts was presented by Ron Burk, in the December 1996 issue of WDJ. More recently, a short piece on shortcut dereferencing, written by Bret Pehrson, appeared in the April 98 edition of WDJ.

7

Shell Invaders

Like any other Win32 process, the shell has its own memory address space that is completely unknown to other applications. To enter this space, we have to pass a number of control points, as if we were crossing the frontier of a country. What's interesting in the land of the Windows shell? Is it a kind of Garden of Eden? Are there rich gold mines? Or is it a fiscal paradise? Unfortunately, it's none of these things. Getting inside the shell simply enables our code to carry out tasks that are impossible to perform from outside. By injecting code into the memory address of a Win32 process, we are able to control the behavior of that program. We can filter its events, have a look at the flow of messages, and even force it to do (or not to do) certain actions.

To get this result, we can take a number of different roads. There's the brute-force approach that exploits some Windows features (or weaknesses) to enter another process's address space and subclass windows. There are programs that explicitly allow external modules to be hosted and work together. In this case, what we have to do is write a module (usually a COM in-process server) with the required interface, and register it wherever the host module requires.

A third road, however, leaves each process running in its own space, but establishes a 'channel' through which they can communicate. You can imagine a situation in which one program legitimately does something that can affect the behavior of another one — or rather, one program could do something that another program should be aware of. In this case, an underlying channel that links the modules is useful — it's something like this that allows Explorer to know about any changes you might have made to files or folders.

In this chapter, you'll be seeing examples of the three models listed above in practice. I'm going to show you:

- ❏ How the shell detects changes in the file system
- ❏ How you can notify the shell of your events
- ❏ How to get into the shell's address space
- ❏ How to subclass Explorer's window
- ❏ As a consequence of all this, how to alter the behavior of the Start button

Along the way, I'll be emphasizing the use of two basic Win32 software components: **hooks** and **notification objects**. They are part of the hidden machinery in many of the scenarios we'll be examining.

Notifying the Shell of Events

You will certainly have noticed that Explorer is very quick at detecting any changes in the file system. Periodically, it refreshes the current view and reflects any changes that other applications may have caused. For example, if you open a DOS window and an Explorer window, select the same directory in both, and then create a directory in the former, the latter will be updated without intervention shortly afterwards.

It seems that something is telling Explorer that a new folder has been created. Under the hood, the levers making all this possible are **notification objects**.

Notification Objects

A notification object is a kernel object that you can synchronize your threads on. The idea is that you create such an object and assign to it some properties that configure an event. Then, you block your threads on it, waiting for the event to occur. If you like, you can think of notification objects as highly specialized events that automatically get signaled when they detect a change in the file system.

By means of a notification object, you can put a directory, a sub-tree, or even a whole drive under control and watch for several events that relate to files and folders – creation, renaming, deletion, attribute changes, and so on.

Using Notification Objects

The Win32 SDK defines three functions to work with notification objects. They are:

- ❏ `FindFirstChangeNotification()`
- ❏ `FindNextChangeNotification()`
- ❏ `FindCloseChangeNotification()`

Despite the misleading name, the first function *creates* a new change notification object, while the last one deletes it. Curiously, you don't have to use `CloseHandle()` to release a notification object, as you would do with all the other kernel objects.

As stated earlier, behind a notification object lies one of the standard Win32 synchronization objects, but it has been specialized by adding specific behavior that takes care of file system changes. Behind the façade, the `FindFirstChangeNotification()` and `FindNextChangeNotification()` functions have the secret task of toggling the signaled state of this hidden kernel object.

When it first gets created by a call to `FindFirstChangeNotification()`, the object is in a non-signaled state. When it detects an action that meets its filter condition, the state changes to signal any waiting thread. To continue looking for events, it must be explicitly reset to the initial state, which is what `FindNextChangeNotification()` does. Let's have a closer look at the details of the prototypes.

> *Synchronization objects include mutexes, semaphores, events and critical sections, amongst others, and are fully described in the Visual C++ help files. They have different behaviors, but essentially they are all used to stop and then resume thread execution in order to synchronize actions. From a high-level perspective, you can look at them as control points that a thread encounters during execution.*
>
> *There are two states that synchronization objects can be in: signaled and non-signaled. The thread is stopped when the object is non-signaled, and resumes when the state is toggled to signaled.*

Creation Parameters

The `FindFirstChangeNotification()` function is declared as follows:

```
HANDLE FindFirstChangeNotification(LPCTSTR lpPathName,
                                   BOOL    bWatchSubtree,
                                   DWORD   dwNotifyFilter);
```

`lpPathName` is a pointer to a buffer containing the name of the directory to watch. The Boolean value `bWatchSubtree` is quite self-explanatory and specifies whether or not the path should include the sub-tree below it. More interestingly, `dwNotifyFilter` lets you set the criteria that will actually trigger a change notification; by combining the flags available for `dwNotifyFilter`, you can decide which types of file system events you want to monitor. The flags available are:

Flag	Description
FILE_NOTIFY_CHANGE_FILE _NAME	A file has been created, deleted, or removed.
FILE_NOTIFY_CHANGE_DIR _NAME	A folder has been created, deleted, or removed.
FILE_NOTIFY_CHANGE _ATTRIBUTES	Any attribute for a file or folder has changed.
FILE_NOTIFY_CHANGE_SIZE	The size of a file or folder has changed. This is detected only when any caches have been flushed to disk.
FILE_NOTIFY_CHANGE_LAST _WRITE	The time of last writing for a file or folder changed. This is detected only when any caches have been flushed to disk.
FILE_NOTIFY_CHANGE _SECURITY	Any security descriptor for a file or folder changed.

Obviously, these events must occur within the watched path. For example, if you issued a call like this:

```
HANDLE hNotify = FindFirstChangeNotification(__TEXT("c:\\"), TRUE,
      FILE_NOTIFY_CHANGE_FILE_NAME | FILE_NOTIFY_CHANGE_DIR_NAME |
      FILE_NOTIFY_CHANGE_ATTRIBUTES | FILE_NOTIFY_CHANGE_SIZE);
```

Any new file created on the C drive will awaken a thread waiting on the notification object. If you specify FALSE as the second argument, then only changes in the root directory of drive C will be detected.

Calling FindFirstChangeNotification() causes the returned object to be in a non-signaled state, meaning that a thread required to synchronize with that object will be stopped.

Watching Directories

Now that you know how to create a change notification object, another question arises: is this sufficient to do a bit of directory watching? Actually, it's not. As with any other watching activity you may practice, directory watching requires a bit of patience. Above all, you must be ready to catch the event at *any* time. In software terms this means that you need to set up some kind of loop in your code. Each time you've dealt with one event, you must promptly notify that you're ready for another one to occur, or for any event that has occurred in the meantime. FindNextChangeNotification() is the function to use.

```
BOOL FindNextChangeNotification(HANDLE hChangeHandle);
```

The following is a code snippet, taken from the sample application that I'll create shortly, which shows a typical way of using it.

```
// Note that the Boolean guard is actually set outside this thread.
// This code snippet, in fact, is pulled from a worker thread.
while(g_bContinue)
{
    // Wait for the change to occur
    WaitForSingleObject(hNotify, INFINITE);

    // A change has occurred, so notify the main window of the fact.
    // This gives us a chance to refresh the UI of the program.
    // WM_EX_XXX is a custom message defined by the application for internal use.
    PostMessage(ci.hWnd, WM_EX_CHANGENOTIFICATION, 0, 0);

    // Get ready for the next change to arrive
    FindNextChangeNotification(hNotify);

    // NB:
    // At this point the underlying synchronization object wrapped by hNotify, is
    // non-signaled, so when this thread executes WaitForSingleObject() again,
    // it will be stopped until a new change occurs and makes the state signaled.
}
```

As you can see, there is no event inside the loop that can cause the loop to terminate. The Boolean guard g_bContinue is a global variable set *outside* the thread executing the above code. In other words, this code fragment implies the presence of two threads: the main application's thread, and a worker thread to deal with the notification object (I'll say more on this shortly).

Since this code is supposed to execute after a call to `FindFirstChangeNotification()`, the thread executing the fragment above will stop on the call to `WaitForSingleObject()` because the object will be non-signaled. When an event that satisfies the `hNotify` notification object occurs, the status of the object changes so that it becomes signaled. Consequently, the thread continues and posts a custom message to a specified window to give it a chance to refresh the user interface, or do further processing. Then, it stops again for a new event. After the call to `FindNextChangeNotification()`, the status of the synchronization object whose handle is contained in `hNotify` is changed to non-signaled.

When dealing with notification objects, it's advisable that you isolate all the code that will wait for an event in a separate worker thread. This is to avoid your main program blocking indefinitely. If you don't want a multithreaded application, you should resort to `MsgWaitForMultipleObjects()` instead of `WaitForSingleObject()` and wait for either a message *or* an event.

It's quite possible to set multiple notification objects at the same time. For example, you might want to run separate watches on different directories in the same or different drives. If you need to do so, `WaitForMultipleObjects()` can help you to synchronize all the notification objects together.

Stopping Watching

To release a notification object, you must call `FindCloseChangeNotification()`. The single argument you pass should be the handle previously created by `FindFirstChangeNotification()`:

```
BOOL FindCloseChangeNotification(HANDLE hChangeHandle);
```

Putting it all Together

Let's see a sample application that should give you an idea of what Explorer is doing behind the scenes. The program lets you choose a path and creates a notification object that watches the whole sub-tree. All the change notification handling is done in a separate thread. Each time an event is detected, the application's main window is posted a message. For the purposes of this demonstration, we don't need to do much more than simply add a line containing the current time to a report list view. In a real-world scenario you might want to do rather more, although as I'll show you in a while, you can't *actually* do that much under Windows 9*x* anyway.

The worker thread receives the path to watch and the handle of the window to which it should send messages through a user-defined structure. The program's user interface is shown in the figure; as ever, it's the front-end of an application generated with the Wrox AppWizard – I called mine `Notify`.

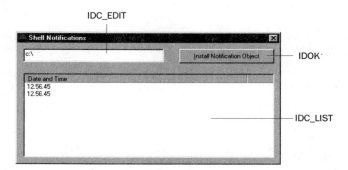

When you click the button, a notification object is installed with the same attributes as in the sample call above: `FILE_NOTIFY_CHANGE_FILE_NAME`, `FILE_NOTIFY_CHANGE_DIR_NAME`, `FILE_NOTIFY_CHANGE_ATTRIBUTES` and `FILE_NOTIFY_CHANGE_SIZE`. Here's the code you need to add to the skeleton provided, starting with the 'global' section:

```
// Data
HICON g_hIconLarge;
HICON g_hIconSmall;
bool g_bContinue;    // Should be set to false in WinMain()
const int WM_EX_CHANGENOTIFICATION = WM_APP + 1;

// Custom data to be passed to the thread
struct CUSTOMINFO
{
    HWND hWnd;
    TCHAR pszDir[MAX_PATH];
};

typedef CUSTOMINFO* LPCUSTOMINFO;
```

In the code above, I've explicitly declared the `WM_EX_CHANGENOTIFICATION` message as a constant. In general, when defining constants to be used as Windows messages you should use `RegisterWindowMessage()` to make sure that the number is unique throughout the system. However, in the context of a single application, if you're not broadcasting the message, using an explicit constant based on `WM_APP` is safe. `WM_APP` is the base constant from which custom messages must be generated so they don't clash with Windows messages. As you can see, the only risk is a conflict with custom messages from other applications, and that can't occur in this example.

There's a new handler to add to `APP_DlgProc()` that will be invoked when the notification object detects a change. You also need to make a small change to the `IDCANCEL` handler to terminate the new thread on shutdown:

```
BOOL CALLBACK APP_DlgProc(HWND hDlg, UINT uiMsg, WPARAM wParam, LPARAM lParam)
{
    switch(uiMsg)
    {
    case WM_INITDIALOG:
        OnInitDialog(hDlg);
        break;

    case WM_EX_CHANGENOTIFICATION:
        UpdateView(hDlg);
        break;

    case WM_COMMAND:
        switch(wParam)
        {
        case IDOK:
            OnOK(hDlg);
            return FALSE;

        case IDCANCEL:
            g_bContinue = false;
            EndDialog(hDlg, FALSE);
            return FALSE;
        }
        break;
```

```
    }
    return FALSE;
}
```

Next, the handler for the Install Notification Object button, which is still called OnOK() because I didn't change its ID, only the label for the button!

```
void OnOK(HWND hDlg)
{
    TCHAR szDir[MAX_PATH] = {0};
    GetDlgItemText(hDlg, IDC_EDIT, szDir, MAX_PATH);
    SHInstallNotifier(hDlg, szDir);
}
```

OnOK() calls SHInstallNotifier(), a function that creates a CUSTOMINFO object and passes it to a thread function called Notify():

```
HANDLE SHInstallNotifier(HWND hwndParent, LPCTSTR pszDir)
{
    DWORD dwID = 0;

    CUSTOMINFO ci;
    ZeroMemory(&ci, sizeof(CUSTOMINFO));
    ci.hWnd = hwndParent;
    lstrcpy(ci.pszDir, pszDir);

    // Create a new worker thread
    g_bContinue = true;
    HANDLE hThread = CreateThread(NULL, 0, Notify, &ci, 0, &dwID);

    return hThread;
}
```

Notify() itself is where the calls to FindXXXChangeNotification() are made, and is the location of the loop that keeps its eye on the directory tree you've specified:

```
DWORD WINAPI Notify(LPVOID lpv)
{
    CUSTOMINFO ci;
    ci.hWnd = static_cast<LPCUSTOMINFO>(lpv)->hWnd;
    lstrcpy(ci.pszDir, static_cast<LPCUSTOMINFO>(lpv)->pszDir);

    HANDLE hNotify = FindFirstChangeNotification(ci.pszDir, TRUE,
                FILE_NOTIFY_CHANGE_FILE_NAME | FILE_NOTIFY_CHANGE_DIR_NAME |
                FILE_NOTIFY_CHANGE_ATTRIBUTES | FILE_NOTIFY_CHANGE_SIZE);
    if(hNotify == INVALID_HANDLE_VALUE)
    {
        SPB_SystemMessage(GetLastError());
        return 0;
    }

    while(g_bContinue)
    {
        WaitForSingleObject(hNotify, INFINITE);
        PostMessage(ci.hWnd, WM_EX_CHANGENOTIFICATION, 0, 0);
        FindNextChangeNotification(hNotify);
    }
```

```
        FindCloseChangeNotification(hNotify);
        return 1;
}
```

When the event becomes signaled, a message of type WM_EX_CHANGENOTIFICATION is sent, resulting in a call to UpdateView():

```
void UpdateView(HWND hDlg)
{
    TCHAR szTime[100] = {0};

    HWND hwndList = GetDlgItem(hDlg,IDC_LIST);
    GetTimeFormat(LOCALE_SYSTEM_DEFAULT, 0, NULL, NULL, szTime, 100);
    AddStringToReportView(hwndList, szTime, 1);
}
```

You can see that this code uses the AddStringToReportView() function that we developed in the last chapter to send strings to a report view. Its partner function, MakeReportView() (also developed in the previous chapter), is called in OnInitDialog() to set up the report view in the first place:

```
void OnInitDialog(HWND hDlg)
{
    // Set the icons (T/F as to Large/Small icon)
    SendMessage(hDlg, WM_SETICON, FALSE, reinterpret_cast<LPARAM>(g_hIconSmall));
    SendMessage(hDlg, WM_SETICON, TRUE, reinterpret_cast<LPARAM>(g_hIconLarge));

    LPTSTR psz[] = {__TEXT("Date and Time"), reinterpret_cast<LPTSTR>(400)};
    MakeReportView(GetDlgItem(hDlg, IDC_LIST), psz, 1);
}
```

Add a #include for resource.h to the top of the source file, and build the application When you run it, you'll notice that if you copy a file, you get two notifications. You get *three* notifications for each deletion. If you remove all the flags except FILE_NOTIFY_CHANGE_FILE_NAME, and repeat the copy, you'll find that the number of notifications is reduced to 1, since we are no longer interested in attribute or size changes. Curiously, though, there are *still* two notifications when you delete a file.

To see why this is, try deleting a file while holding down the *Shift* key – you'll find that there is now just one notification. The difference is that deleting a file in this fashion destroys the file *without* saving it in the Recycle Bin, thus eliminating the file copy step from the normal, two step, 'copy-to-Recycle-Bin-and-then-delete' action. Simply deleting the file results in a single notification when the file is actually deleted.

Explorer and Notification Objects

Explorer behaves in roughly the same way as the application I've just created: it sets a notification object on the folder currently being displayed. Each time it receives a notification that something has changed, it reloads the folder content to reflect those changes. If you think it over for a while, you'll realize that the mechanism of the notification objects seems to be tailored precisely to the needs of Explorer.

170

Explorer is not a file system monitoring utility; it needs to know whether something in the folder currently being viewed has changed, in case that change affects the displayed data: file and sub-folder names, attributes, sizes, dates, security, etc. Whatever the exact operation, what matters is that *something* has occurred. This seems to be a good compromise between the performance concerns of Explorer and those of the system itself.

Towards a File System Monitoring Utility

As we have seen, the greatest drawback of notification objects is the poor information they provide about the event that actually occurred. A notification object is like a bell that's connected to a burglar alarm and a fire alarm: when it rings, you don't know whether your house is being robbed, burned down, or both! This restriction makes it difficult (if not impossible) to exploit this feature to create, say, a file system monitoring utility to let us know which files are being manipulated by programs throughout the system.

Later in the book, I'll consider a different approach to the same problem, which makes use of the `ICopyHook` shell extension. I can say in advance, though, that this will still leave us some distance from that ultimate objective, even if it is a significant step towards it.

What about Windows NT?

So far, I haven't said anything about different operating systems. You might have been led to think that there are no significant differences between Windows 95, Windows 98, and Windows NT 4.0, but in fact what we just wished for is a reality under Windows NT 4.0 and higher. The Win32 SDK for Windows NT exports and documents a function called `ReadDirectoryChangesW()` that has a prototype similar to `FindFirstChangeNotification()`, but with one big difference: it fills a buffer with specific information about the action that took place, and the actors involved.

> *More information about* `ReadDirectoryChangesW()`*, and about notification objects in general, can be found in Jeff Richter's excellent book,* Advanced Windows. *(See the Further Reading section.)*

SHChangeNotify()

When things about the system change, Explorer can detect some of them itself (changes to files in particular), but must be told explicitly about changes carried out by programs.

To make this easy, the shell API defines a function called `SHChangeNotify()`. Its only purpose in life is to notify Explorer that some system setting has been modified. Conceptually, `SHChangeNotify()` produces the same effect as notification objects, but it follows a different logic. In this case, an external application notifies Explorer of some changes it has made. In response to such notifications, Explorer will refresh its user interface. This is a clear example of what I referred to earlier as a 'channel' between applications and the shell.

Calling SHChangeNotify()

The function is defined in `shlobj.h` with the following prototype:

```
void WINAPI SHChangeNotify(LONG    wEventId,
                           UINT    uFlags,
                           LPCVOID dwItem1,
                           LPCVOID dwItem2);
```

The wEventId parameter specifies an event of which the system should be notified. It takes one or more of a collection of possible values, the most frequently used of which are listed below:

Event	Description
SHCNE_ASSOCCHANGED	A file type association has changed; which one is not specified.
SHCNE_NETSHARE	A local folder is being shared via the network. This causes an icon change. dwItem1 should contain the folder name. A folder name can be either a fully qualified path name or PIDL. (See below.)
SHCNE_NETUNSHARE	A local folder is no longer shared. This causes an icon change. dwItem1 should contain the folder name (a fully qualified path name or PIDL).
SHCNE_SERVERDISCONNECT	The PC has been disconnected from a server. dwItem1 should contain the name of that server.
SHCNE_UPDATEDIR	The content of a given folder has changed, but the changes don't affect the file system. dwItem1 should contain the folder name (a full path name or a PIDL).
SHCNE_UPDATEIMAGE	An icon in the system image list has changed. dwItem1 should contain the index of the icon. This causes Explorer to refresh the user interface to draw the new icon where needed. All the icons used by Explorer are stored in a global structure referred to as the 'system image list' or the 'Explorer internal icon cache'. I showed how to get the handle of this image list in Chapter 4.
SHCNE_UPDATEITEM	A non-folder item has changed. dwItem1 should contain the full file name or the PIDL.

This list of events is not complete, and I'll cover the remaining flags later on. For the complete list of flags right now, you can refer to the MSDN library.

The other three parameters to SHChangeNotify() are affected by the event identifier specified by the wEventId argument. The dwItem1 and dwItem2 variables contain event-dependent values. The uFlags parameter is used to denote the *type* of dwItem1 and dwItem2. It can indicate a DWORD number (SHCNF_DWORD), a PIDL (SHCNF_IDLIST), a string (SHNCF_PATH) or a printer name (SHCNF_PRINTER). In addition, uFlags can indicate whether the function should wait for the notification to be handled completely. SHCNF_FLUSH is the constant to use if you want to wait; SHCNF_FLUSHNOWAIT, on the other hand, causes the function to return immediately.

The Role of SHChangeNotify()

What does SHChangeNotify() do that makes it complementary to notification objects? Put another way, when do you absolutely need to use SHChangeNotify()? Basically, this function attempts to provide the same functionality as notification objects (although it follows a different logic), but it isn't restricted only to file system objects.

As we saw in Chapter 5, the Windows shell is composed of file objects, and while most of them map to a physical entity in the file system, that isn't always the case. File objects such as `My Computer` and `Printers` don't have a corresponding directory. Furthermore, even if you have folders linked to a directory, the items that they contain are not necessarily files. This means that you can add new items to (or delete items from) such a folder without any impact on the file system. In this scenario, how can Explorer detect the changes?

There are deeper aspects to this question. Is it plausible to plan a software module that is capable of monitoring this whole range of possible actions? As we'll see later in this book, a namespace extension can be used to display pretty much anything through a folder-style interface. The Internet Client SDK, for example, comes with a sample called `RegView` that adds a new node to Explorer's hierarchy, just like an ordinary folder. The one little peculiarity is that what it 'contains' is the contents of the system registry, which is really just a file or two! How could Explorer, or indeed any other tool, detect changes here? You could write a piece of software to hook for registry activity, but what if someone replaces `RegView` with another namespace extension that does completely different things?

Once we've gone beyond the context of the traditional file system, we need to change the way in which notification occurs. It's no longer a matter of Explorer detecting changes itself, but of applications sending notifications. This is the scenario into which `SHChangeNotify()` fits.

Some of the events defined for use in calls to `SHChangeNotify()` may appear redundant. For example, an event like `SHCNE_CREATE` might *seem* useless – it indicates that a new file has been created, but Explorer already knows about that, thanks to notification objects. However, if the item is not a file system object, you absolutely must call `SHChangeNotify()` to let Explorer know about this change:

```
SHChangeNotify(SHCNE_CREATE, SHCNF_IDLIST, pidl, NULL);
```

SHChangeNotify()'s Other Events

The rationale for `SHChangeNotify()` now a little clearer, it's time to make amends for the earlier omissions. Here all the other events you can pass as the `wEventId` argument of the function:

Event	Description
SHCNE_ATTRIBUTES	Attributes of a file or folder changed. `dwItem1` is the file or folder name (a fully qualified path name or PIDL).
SHCNE_CREATE	A file object has been created. `dwItem1` is the name of the file object.
SHCNE_DELETE	A file object has been deleted. `dwItem1` is the name of the file object.
SHCNE_DRIVEADD	A drive has been added. `dwItem1` is the root of the drive in the form `C:\`.
SHCNE_DRIVEADDGUI	A drive has been added and a new window is needed. `dwItem1` is the root of the drive in the form `C:\`.

Table Continued on Following Page

Event	Description
SHCNE_DRIVEREMOVED	A drive has been removed. dwItem1 is the root of the drive.
SHCNE_FREESPACE	The amount of free space on a drive changed. dwItem1 is the root of the drive in the form C:\.
SHCNE_MEDIAINSERTED	Storage media has been inserted into a drive. dwItem1 is the root of the drive in the form C:\.
SHCNE_MEDIAREMOVED	Storage media has been removed from a drive. dwItem1 is the root of the drive in the form C:\.
SHCNE_MKDIR	A folder has been created. dwItem1 is the name of the file object.
SHCNE_RENAMEFOLDER	A folder has been renamed. dwItem1 is the old name and dwItem2 is the new one. These names can be either fully qualified path names or PIDLs.
SHCNE_RENAMEITEM	A file object has been renamed. dwItem1 is the old name and dwItem2 is the new one.
SHCNE_RMDIR	A file object has been deleted. dwItem1 is the name of the file object.

Using SHChangeNotify()

SHChangeNotify() will be very useful when we begin writing namespace extensions, because it lets you hide from Explorer the fact that an item or a folder might not be a real file system object. In Chapter 16, I'll be developing a namespace extension that presents information about the windows currently in existence on the system as if the windows themselves are the contents of a folder. By combining that extension with, say, a global hook module that detects whenever a new window is created and calls SHChangeNotify() with the SHCNE_CREATE flag, we will also be able to have Explorer regularly refreshing the contents of our custom folder.

I'm not going to cover Windows hooks here, though I mentioned them in Chapter 2. You might want to refer to the MSDN library for more information.

Ordinary applications, on the other hand, rarely need to exploit the services of SHChangeNotify(). An example, though, might be a program that dynamically changes a file type association — that is, it changes the program that's used to handle documents of a particular kind. This information is stored in the registry at the following location:

```
HKEY_LOCAL_MACHINE
    \Software
        \Microsoft
            \Windows
                \CurrentVersion
                    \Extensions
```

To inform Explorer of the update, you could call:

```
SHChangeNotify(SHCNE_ASSOCCHANGED, 0, NULL, NULL);
```

Invading the Shell's Memory Space

If you're a seasoned Win32 programmer, you'll be well aware that every process runs in its own address space, and that a memory address has a consistent value only within the space in which it originates. This means, for example, that you can't subclass a window created by another process because the address of your new window procedure could be pointing absolutely anywhere if you look at it from another address space. In fact, attempting this kind of thing is prevented by SetWindowLong(), which returns zero instead of working if you try it.

It requires a few steps, but having your code programmatically mapped into another application's process space is definitely possible. Microsoft discourages the practice because the potential for making errors is higher than it is for other, more common programming techniques, but accessing another application's address space *is* safe, provided that you know what you're doing and – above all – what you have to do! There's nothing prohibited or intrinsically dangerous about breaking process boundaries. It's just like working with pointers – they can introduce bugs if you handle them badly.

The shell is just another Win32 process, and you can invade its memory space in the same way you would do with, say, Notepad. (I don't know why, but the unfortunate victim of the foulest experiments in software genetic manipulation always seems to be Notepad!)

Why do we need to invade the shell? The reasons are the same ones that can lead you to enter any other Win32 or Win16 process: the need to alter (or just filter) the behavior of a program. Have you ever noticed that the copy of Notepad that ships with Windows NT 4.0 has the capability to maintain some settings across sessions? If you run it and check the 'word wrap' mode, the setting is made persistent and restored each time you launch it. If you plan to realize something like this under Windows 95 or Windows 98, you have to customize the standard behavior of Notepad. In other words, you need to invade its address space with your code.

In the remainder of this chapter, I'll show you three ways to get into Explorer's address space. The first one relies on traditional SDK techniques such as hooks and subclassing. The second exploits a little-known shell API function called SHLoadInProc(). Both these techniques work under all Win32 platforms, except Windows CE. The third option is available only with version 4.71 (or higher) of the shell, and exploits a feature that Explorer shares with Internet Explorer: **browser helper objects**.

The Brute Force Approach

I started to think about subclassing the Explorer window when I realized that there was no way to create folders other than by going through a couple of menus. Because I don't believe I'm the only person on Earth not to have found a magical key combination, I endeavored to add a keyboard accelerator that creates a new folder on the fly. Even in Knowledge Base article Q126449, which contains the list of keyboard shortcuts for Windows, there's no mention of new folders.

I don't know about you, but I find all that work rather frustrating: right clicking (or clicking the File menu), then selecting a couple of items, and finally clicking again.

I decided to do something about it. My strategy was to develop a little application to put in the `StartUp` folder, which installs a system-wide hook for keeping track of the creation of windows belonging to a certain class. The class in question is that of the Explorer window, `ExploreWClass`.

In case you're wondering, I found the name of the class by snooping around the stack of existing windows with Spy++.

Once I've obtained the handle to Explorer's window, I can install a keyboard hook on the specific thread that created that window. This second hook is responsible for catching keyboard activity, and creating a folder when a key combination meets the allotted criteria. The task can be split into two parts:

- ❑ Getting inside Explorer
- ❑ Creating a folder in the same way as Explorer does

In Win32, there aren't many ways to have your own code mapped into another process's address space. If you want your code to work unchanged on both Windows 9x and Windows NT, then you have just one possibility: system-wide hooks.

Why Hooks?

Even if your eventual goal is not to hook but simply to subclass a window, if the window belongs to another process, you must install a hook before you do your subclassing work. Regardless of the hook you use, what matters is that it applies to all the threads in the system.

As mentioned in Chapter 2, where I briefly introduced the concept, using a hook means that you specify a callback function that the system will invoke when a certain event, relevant to the hook, occurs. If you want to watch *all* the threads across *all* running processes, your function must necessarily reside in a DLL, because the system needs to map it into those processes.

Getting inside Explorer

The utility I have in mind will look for a window (specifically, an Explorer window) being created. A hook procedure of type `WH_CBT`, which is triggered when the system is about to perform any action on a window (creation, deletion, activation, and so on), therefore needs to be installed at program startup:

```
g_hShellHook = SetWindowsHookEx(WH_CBT, ShellDll_MainHook, g_hThisDll, 0);
```

The hook must be removed before exiting:

```
if(g_hShellHook != NULL)
    UnhookWindowsHookEx(g_hShellHook);
```

Obviously, there's a concern that having a hook throughout the system may affect its performance. Any system-wide hook will affect performance simply because it exists! It causes the system to do additional work, and this undoubtedly introduces a proportional reduction in performance. For this reason, it's highly recommended that you keep system-wide hooks as small as possible. Mine is a minimal one, and this greatly reduces the risk of significant performance loss. Furthermore, I've tested the utility under Windows 95 on several machines, with processors ranging from a 486 to a P166 and achieved good results – far better than I expected, in fact. The code for the hook procedure looks like this:

```
LRESULT CALLBACK ShellDll_MainHook(int nCode, WPARAM wParam, LPARAM lParam)
{
    TCHAR szClass[MAX_PATH] = {0};

    // Typical beginning for any hook procedure
    if(nCode < 0)
        return CallNextHookEx(g_hShellHook, nCode, wParam, lParam);

    // The system is creating a window. Notice that the hook is invoked
    //  from within the code of both CreateWindow() and CreateWindowEx().
    // At this point the window already exists and its HWND is a valid one,
    //  even if we're still in the middle of the creation process.
    if(nCode == HCBT_CREATEWND)
    {
        // Get the HWND of the window
        HWND hwndExplorer = reinterpret_cast<HWND>(wParam);

        // Compare it to 'ExploreWClass' and install the keyboard hook
        GetClassName(hwndExplorer, szClass, MAX_PATH);
        if(!lstrcmpi(szClass, __TEXT("ExploreWClass")))
            InstallKeyboardHook(hwndExplorer);
    }

    return CallNextHookEx(g_hShellHook, nCode, wParam, lParam);
}
```

This code executes each time a window is created. If the window class name matches the Explorer window class name (which is ExploreWClass) then a keyboard hook is installed. At this point, we're already inside Explorer's address space. Notice that the *keyboard* hook can be local to the Explorer thread that owns the window of class ExploreWClass. There's no need to hook the keyboard activity throughout the system, because when we're about to create a new folder it's natural that the input focus is on Explorer (I'll say more about this in the section entitled *Writing a Helper Object*).

The next picture shows a diagram that illustrates inter-process window subclassing. Keep this in mind, as it will help you to understand the forthcoming code.

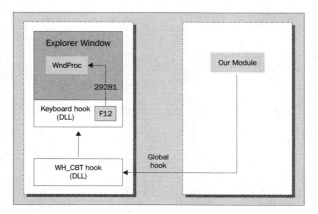

How to Create a New Folder

To have hook code mapped into a process's address space, it's sufficient that a system-wide hook procedure is invoked from within that process. The problem is now reduced to that of creating a new folder. Clearly, we would like to get the same result as we do by manual intervention, and so the easiest way would be to duplicate exactly what Explorer does when you click the New | Folder menu item.

> *You may be wondering why I chose not to employ a method that made use of the theory we've been discussing up to this point in the book — in other words, why not get the current directory and create a new one using the Shell API? The reason is that the method has flaws in this situation.*
>
> *First, how do you know what folder is currently displayed in Explorer? It's not necessarily the name returned by* GetCurrentDirectory(). *Second, many special folders don't allow you to create sub-folders, and you could really cause problems if you tried.*

I reasoned that Explorer must create new folders in response to a WM_COMMAND message being sent to the main window procedure. To investigate, I wrote a program that subclassed the ExploreWClass window in order to spy on the parameters of each processed WM_COMMAND message. By this means, I discovered that in order to ask Explorer to create a new folder, you just need to send its window a message like this:

```
PostMessage(hwndExplorer, WM_COMMAND, 29281, 0);
```

The magic number 29281 is the ID of the New | Folder menu item. This is unofficial information, and it may be subject to change in newer versions of the shell, but for now it works well with Windows 9x and Windows NT 4.0. However, if this number changes in upcoming releases, and unless there are radical alterations to the structure of the shell, you should simply have to find out the new number. The number didn't change from shell version 4.00 to 4.71.

The keyboard hook is installed so that the shell creates a new folder in response to a key. I've chosen the *F12* key out of personal preference — there is no particular reason for it, so feel free to employ any other key you wish. When the keyboard hook procedure detects that *F12* has been pressed, it simply retrieves the Explorer window and posts it a message.

The Sample Program

As I've explained, the sample program necessarily comes in two parts: a DLL and an executable. First, here's the source code for the DLL that contains both the hooks. It's based on the skeleton DLL generated by the Wrox AppWizard, and I called my project ExpHook.

Here are the global variables and function declarations to add to ExpHook.h:

```
/*-------------------------------------------------------------*/
//                     PROTOTYPES section
/*-------------------------------------------------------------*/
HHOOK g_hShellHook;
HHOOK g_hKeybHook;
HWND g_hwndExplorer;
```

```
void InstallKeyboardHook(HWND hwnd);
void APIENTRY ShellDll_Hook();
void APIENTRY ShellDll_Unhook();
LRESULT CALLBACK ShellDll_KeybHook(int nCode, WPARAM wParam, LPARAM lParam);
LRESULT CALLBACK ShellDll_MainHook(int nCode, WPARAM wParam, LPARAM lParam);
```

And naturally enough, the implementations go in `ExpHook.cpp`. These functions are just the realization of the theory we've discussed to this point:

```
// Sets up a hook to detect when Explorer starts
void APIENTRY ShellDll_Hook()
{
    g_hShellHook = SetWindowsHookEx(WH_CBT, ShellDll_MainHook, g_hThisDll, 0);
}


void APIENTRY ShellDll_Unhook()
{
    if(g_hKeybHook != NULL)
        UnhookWindowsHookEx(g_hKeybHook);

    if(g_hShellHook != NULL)
        UnhookWindowsHookEx(g_hShellHook);
}
```

```
// Insert the code for ShellDll_MainHook() from the listing above
```

```
LRESULT CALLBACK ShellDll_KeybHook(int nCode, WPARAM wParam, LPARAM lParam)
{
    // Typical beginning for any hook procedure
    if(nCode < 0)
        return CallNextHookEx(g_hKeybHook, nCode, wParam, lParam);

    // Normally this code executes both when the key is pressed and released.
    // The information about the transition state is stored in the 2 most
    // significant bits of lParam. In this way we process the key only once.
    if((lParam & 0x80000000) || (lParam & 0x40000000))
        return CallNextHookEx(g_hKeybHook, nCode, wParam, lParam);

    if(wParam == VK_F12)
    {
        // Get the Explorer window handle and post the message
        g_hwndExplorer = FindWindow("ExploreWClass", NULL);
        PostMessage(g_hwndExplorer, WM_COMMAND, 29281, 0);
    }

    return CallNextHookEx(g_hKeybHook, nCode, wParam, lParam);
}
```

```
// Install a keyboard hook
void InstallKeyboardHook(HWND hwnd)
{
    g_hwndExplorer = hwnd;
    DWORD dwThread = GetWindowThreadProcessId(g_hwndExplorer, NULL);
    g_hKeybHook = SetWindowsHookEx(WH_KEYBOARD, ShellDll_KeybHook,
                                    g_hThisDll, dwThread);
}
```

To make the library export the functions we'll need, you should add these lines to the `.def` file, which was also generated for you by the Wizard:

```
EXPORTS
    ShellDll_Hook      @2
    ShellDll_Unhook    @3
    ShellDll_KeybHook  @4
    ShellDll_MainHook  @5
```

That's all we need for the DLL, so you can build that and move on to the main program, which will add an icon to the tray notification area to allow you to uninstall the hook easily, at any time.

Apart from creating a tray icon, the main program restricts itself to installing and uninstalling the WH_CBT hook. You can use the Wrox AppWizard for the skeleton, although you'll find that because of the nature of this application, there's rather more customization required than usual. First, create a dialog-based application called `ExpFold`, and add a `#include` for the header that contains the definitions of our DLL functions:

```
/*---------------------------------------------------------------*/
//                        INCLUDE section
/*---------------------------------------------------------------*/
#include "ExpFold.h"
#include "ExpHook.h"
```

Next, you need a couple of new constants: one for the custom message that will be sent when the tray icon is clicked on, and one for the ID of the icon itself.

```
// Data
const int WM_MYMESSAGE = WM_APP + 1;        // For the tray icon
const int ICON_ID = 13;

HICON g_hIconLarge;
HICON g_hIconSmall;
HINSTANCE g_hInstance;
```

The new global variable will be used to store a handle to this instance of the application, which will be necessary in a later call to `LoadMenu()`. In the meantime, here are the changes you need to make to `WinMain()`:

```
int APIENTRY WinMain(HINSTANCE hInstance, HINSTANCE hPrevious,
                     LPTSTR lpsz, int iCmd)
{
    // Save global data
    g_hInstance = hInstance;
    g_hIconSmall = static_cast<HICON>(LoadImage(hInstance, "APP_ICON",
                                 IMAGE_ICON, GetSystemMetrics(SM_CXSMICON),
                                 GetSystemMetrics(SM_CXSMICON), 0));

    // Create an invisible dialog to get messages from the icon
    HWND hDlg = CreateDialog(hInstance, "DLG_MAIN", NULL, APP_DlgProc);

    // Show the icon in the tray area
    TrayIcon(hDlg, NIM_ADD);
```

```
    // Install Explorer's hook
    ShellDll_Hook();

    MSG msg;
    while(GetMessage(&msg, NULL, 0, 0))
    {
        if(!IsDialogMessage(hDlg, &msg))
        {
            TranslateMessage(&msg);
            DispatchMessage(&msg);
        }
    }

    // Uninstall the hook
    ShellDll_Unhook();

    // Remove the icon
    TrayIcon(hDlg, NIM_DELETE);

    DestroyWindow(hDlg);
    DestroyIcon(g_hIconSmall);
    return 1;
}
```

Rather than showing a dialog, this application creates an invisible one by calling `CreateDialog()` instead of `DialogBox()`. The dialog procedure to go with it looks like this:

```
BOOL CALLBACK APP_DlgProc(HWND hDlg, UINT uiMsg, WPARAM wParam, LPARAM lParam)
{
    switch(uiMsg)
    {
    case WM_COMMAND:
        switch(wParam)
        {
        case IDCANCEL:
            PostQuitMessage(0);
            return FALSE;
        }
        break;

    case WM_MYMESSAGE:
        if(wParam == ICON_ID)
        {
            switch(lParam)
            {
            case WM_RBUTTONUP:
                ContextMenu(hDlg);
                break;
            }
        }
        break;
    }

    return FALSE;
}
```

The `TrayIcon()` function is called by `WinMain()` after the dialog has been set up. It displays an icon in (and later removes it from) the taskbar tray:

```
// Shows an icon in the tray area
BOOL TrayIcon(HWND hWnd, DWORD msg)
{
    NOTIFYICONDATA nid;
    ZeroMemory(&nid, sizeof(NOTIFYICONDATA));
    nid.cbSize = sizeof(NOTIFYICONDATA);
    nid.hWnd = hWnd;
    nid.uID = ICON_ID;
    nid.uFlags = NIF_TIP | NIF_ICON | NIF_MESSAGE;
    nid.uCallbackMessage = WM_MYMESSAGE;
    nid.hIcon = g_hIconSmall;
    lstrcpyn(nid.szTip, __TEXT("Explorer's Hook"), 64);
    return Shell_NotifyIcon(msg, &nid);
}
```

Finally, `ContextMenu()` is called when the user clicks on the icon in the tray. To make this work, you'll need to add a menu resource called `IDR_MENU` to your project; the menu should contain a single item called **Close**, whose ID is `IDCANCEL`.

```
// Shows up the context menu for the icon
void ContextMenu(HWND hwnd)
{
    POINT pt;
    GetCursorPos(&pt);

    HMENU hmenu = LoadMenu(g_hInstance, MAKEINTRESOURCE(IDR_MENU));
    HMENU hmnuPopup = GetSubMenu(hmenu, 0);
    SetMenuDefaultItem(hmnuPopup, IDOK, FALSE);
    SetForegroundWindow(hwnd);
    TrackPopupMenu(hmnuPopup, TPM_LEFTALIGN, pt.x, pt.y, 0, hwnd, NULL);
    SetForegroundWindow(hwnd);
    DestroyMenu(hmnuPopup);
    DestroyMenu(hmenu);
}
```

The Program in Action

Once you've compiled the program (you'll need to `#include "resource.h"` and link to `exphook.lib`), you will have `.exe` and `.dll` files. You can then create a shortcut to the executable, and copy it to the `Startup` folder.

The program can be removed by right-clicking its tray-icon and selecting <u>C</u>lose. Once it is installed, it hooks each Explorer window that's created and installs a keyboard hook in that thread. The keyboard procedure looks for *F12* and then posts a message to the window.

Invited into the Shell's Memory Space

There are basically two ways to inject external code into the shell's address space. There's invasion (which we've already seen), and invitation (which is much friendlier, if only we can find a way to do it). In the former case, the host program is completely unaware of what's going on. With the latter, on the other hand, everything happens under its direct control.

The Windows shell *does* offer a means to get into its memory space by invitation rather than invasion – the shell API provides an often-underestimated function called SHLoadInProc() that is defined in shlobj.h, and is surprisingly powerful. I hadn't given it a great deal of thought myself until I saw an article that appeared in Windows Developer's Journal. (See *Further Reading*.) Before that time, I had only browsed its declaration and documentation without going any further.

Let me say, however, that the documentation is poor, and that even once you've read it you're still miles away from even suspecting the real power of this function. To demonstrate just what it's capable of, the example we're going to create in this section is a DLL that will enable us to retrieve and replace the ubiquitous Windows Start button. Before we can begin that task, though, a little more explanation is in order.

SHLoadInProc()

In a nutshell, SHLoadInProc() loads one of your modules into the shell's address space. This is exactly the kind of thing we tried so hard to achieve in the previous section. SHLoadInProc() loads the module and then leaves it alone to do whatever it wants. Here's how the documentation (in the Internet Client SDK) available at the time of writing describes it:

```
WINSHELLAPI HRESULT WINAPI SHLoadInProc(
    REFCLSID rclsid
);
```

Creates an instance of the specified object class from within the context of the shell's process.

Returns NOERROR if successful, or an OLE-defined error result otherwise.

rclsid
CLSID of the object class to be created.

Now, I'm the first in line to state that the documentation is absolutely correct. The trouble is, there's no mention at all about the structure of this 'object class'. Is there some interface that it must implement? Is there some special policy it must follow? Does a COM server with no specific interface to implement really make sense? If no particular interface is required, how can the object start working?

All these are questions that arise almost immediately, but they have no answer in the documentation, which is as concise as ever. Be honest: at this point, do *you* have a clear understanding of what's needed to put this function to work?

A Minimal COM Object

Let me try to make things clearer. To begin, SHLoadInProc() is a quick and effective way to get our code inside the shell's address space, and this code should be a COM object. To exploit the function, however, we don't *necessarily* need a fully-fledged COM object – we can get by with something halfway between that and an ordinary DLL. It must fulfill the criteria for a COM server (and therefore needs to register itself and have a CLSID), but in practice it will look more like an old-fashioned DLL than an in process COM object server.

How a COM Object is Made

An in-process COM object is a DLL, which means that it has a `DllMain()` function. More importantly, a COM object exports four other global functions that are the handles by which *any* container works with *any* COM in-process object. These functions are:

- ❑ `DllGetClassObject()`
- ❑ `DllCanUnloadNow()`
- ❑ `DllRegisterServer()`
- ❑ `DllUnregisterServer()`

The last two of these are for automatic registration and unregistration, so provided that you promise to do this manually, you can avoid implementing them. Our COM object is now reduced to a bare DLL with two global, exported functions: `DllGetClassObject()` and `DllCanUnloadNow()`.

The Role of DllGetClassObject()

Any client of a COM object must first load the library that contains it, and then get a pointer to the interface it requires through `DllGetClassObject()`:

```
STDAPI DllGetClassObject(REFCLSID rclsid, REFIID riid, LPVOID* ppv);
```

Details aside, the important point is that this function always gets called, and shortly afterwards the class object is loaded. In other words, the code we place here *always* gets executed. More interestingly still, it executes in the shell's context (that is, its address space).

Meeting the Client's Expectations

Typically, the module that loads a class object will call `DllGetClassObject()` asking for the `IClassFactory` interface. Our client – in this case, Explorer – will expect some interface pointer to be returned via `DllGetClassObject()`. Since we don't implement this interface, how can we cope with such expectations?

It's enough for us to state explicitly that the required class is not available, which simply involves returning the appropriate error code:

```
STDAPI DllGetClassObject(REFCLSID rclsid, REFIID riid, LPVOID* ppv)
{
    return CLASS_E_CLASSNOTAVAILABLE;
}
```

The above is a possible implementation for `DllGetClassObject()` that makes sense for those circumstances in which there's no specific interface to support.

Using the Shell's Address Space

Besides returning an error code, the function can do whatever it wants with any of the objects that populate the shell's address space. When `DllGetClassObject()` is called, we're already in the shell's context, and that's what will enable us to subclass the Start button. I'll begin that demonstration very soon, but not before we take a little time to discuss `DllCanUnloadNow()`.

The Role of DllCanUnloadNow()

A module that loaded a COM object through `DllGetClassObject()` calls `DllCanUnloadNow()` to make sure that the DLL can be safely unloaded and freed. Explorer performs this check periodically, although the period itself can range from ten seconds to ten minutes. I'll be expanding on this point later on, when I cover shell extensions in Chapter 15.

If `DllCanUnloadNow()` returns `S_OK`, then the DLL that hosts it will be unloaded. If it always returns `S_FALSE`, or if the DLL doesn't export a function with this name, the library will be released when the host application calls `CoUninitialize()` to close the COM library. Because the host application in this case is Explorer, it might be some time before this happens!

Source Code for the COM Object

What follows is the minimal source code for a 'fake' COM object to be used in conjunction with `SHLoadInProc()`, and we can use it as the seed for an example that will grow to become the Start button-subclassing application I keep promising! In Visual C++, create a new Win32 Dynamic-Link Library called `Start` (I chose the Simple DLL option), and add this code to `start.cpp`:

```
#include "start.h"

HINSTANCE g_hInstance;

BOOL APIENTRY DllMain(HINSTANCE hInstance,
                      DWORD  ul_reason_for_call,
                      LPVOID lpReserved
                     )
{
    g_hInstance = hModule;
    return TRUE;
}


/*-------------------------------------------------------------------------*/
// DllGetClassObject
// Main function for a COM in-proc object like this
/*-------------------------------------------------------------------------*/
STDAPI DllGetClassObject(REFCLSID rclsid, REFIID riid, LPVOID* ppv)
{
    // Do something here
    return CLASS_E_CLASSNOTAVAILABLE;
}


/*-------------------------------------------------------------------------*/
// DllCanUnloadNow
// Confirm the unload for a COM library
/*-------------------------------------------------------------------------*/
STDAPI DllCanUnloadNow()
{
    return S_OK;
}
```

The `start.h` header file that gets `#include`'d in the above file defines the CLSID of our 'fake' COM object and incorporates some `#include` directives of its own:

```
#include <windows.h>
#include <windowsx.h>
#include <objbase.h>
#include <shlobj.h>

DEFINE_GUID(CLSID_NewStart, 0x20051998, 0x0020,
                      0x0005, 0x19, 0x98, 0x00, 0x00, 0x00, 0x00, 0x00, 0x00);
```

So that the DLL exports the functions we need it to, you should also create a short `start.def` file:

```
LIBRARY START

EXPORTS
    DllCanUnloadNow      @1 PRIVATE
    DllGetClassObject    @2 PRIVATE
```

To conclude this section, here's an idea of the kind of code that a sample program would use to load this COM object into Explorer's address space via `SHLoadInProc()`:

```
void DoGoInsideExplorer()
{
    const CLSID clsid = {0x20051998,0x0020,0x0005,
                      {0x19,0x98,0x00,0x00,0x00,0x00,0x00,0x00}};
    SHLoadInProc(clsid);
}
```

Registering the COM Object

There are essentially two ways in which you can register COM objects: by inserting code through `DllRegisterServer()`, or manually – best done by means of a registration script. Let's take a look at both the approaches, starting with the simpler one: a registration script.

What follows is the content of a script REG file that is automatically handled by the Registry Editor. It adds two keys that register the CLSID under the `CLSID` node of `HKEY_CLASSES_ROOT`, and store the name of the executable that implements it.

```
REGEDIT4

[HKEY_CLASSES_ROOT\CLSID\{20051998-0020-0005-1998-000000000000}]
@= "Start Button"
[HKEY_CLASSES_ROOT\CLSID\{20051998-0020-0005-1998-000000000000}\InProcServer32]
@= "C:\\Chap07\\Source\\Start\\start.dll"
"ThreadingModel" = "Apartment"
```

You should, of course, ensure that the path is replaced with the actual directory you're using. In practice, a key needs to be added under `CLSID` with the name of the CLSID enclosed in brackets:

```
HKEY_CLASSES_ROOT
    \CLSID
       \{20051998-0020-0005-1998-000000000000}
```

Furthermore, we need to add another key under this one called `InProcServer32`, whose default value points to the actual name of the server. The value `ThreadingModel` specifies the threading model required. To register this server, it suffices that you double-click the REG file from Explorer, or import it using the Registry Editor.

A neater approach is to code all this in the `DllRegisterServer()` function; doing so requires us to program using the Win32 registry API. As I'll show you in Chapter 10, version 4.71 of the shell contains a new set of high-level functions for dealing with the registry, and we could employ them here, but then the code would work only on shell version 4.71 or higher. The following code makes use of the traditional Win32 registry API:

```
STDAPI DllRegisterServer()
{
    TCHAR szSubKey[MAX_PATH] = {0};
    TCHAR szCLSID[MAX_PATH] = {0};
    TCHAR szModule[MAX_PATH] = {0};
    HKEY hKey;
    DWORD dwDisp;

    // Set the CLSID
    lstrcpy(szCLSID, __TEXT("{20051998-0020-0005-1998-000000000000}"));

    // Get the module name
    GetModuleFileName(g_hInstance, szModule, MAX_PATH);

    // HKCR: CLSID\{...}
    wsprintf(szSubKey, __TEXT("CLSID\\%s"), szCLSID);
    LRESULT lResult = RegCreateKeyEx(HKEY_CLASSES_ROOT, szSubKey, 0, NULL,
                REG_OPTION_NON_VOLATILE, KEY_WRITE, NULL, &hKey, &dwDisp);
    if(lResult == NOERROR)
    {
        TCHAR szData[MAX_PATH] = {0};
        wsprintf(szData, __TEXT("Start Button"), szModule);
        lResult = RegSetValueEx(hKey, NULL, 0, REG_SZ,
                    reinterpret_cast<LPBYTE>(szData), lstrlen(szData) + 1);
        RegCloseKey(hKey);
    }

    // HKCR: CLSID\{...}\InProcServer32
    wsprintf(szSubKey, __TEXT("CLSID\\%s\\InProcServer32"), szCLSID);
    lResult = RegCreateKeyEx(HKEY_CLASSES_ROOT, szSubKey, 0, NULL,
                REG_OPTION_NON_VOLATILE, KEY_WRITE, NULL, &hKey, &dwDisp);
    if(lResult == NOERROR)
    {
        lResult = RegSetValueEx(hKey, NULL, 0, REG_SZ,
                    reinterpret_cast<LPBYTE>(szModule), lstrlen(szModule) + 1);
        TCHAR szData[MAX_PATH] = {0};
        lstrcpy(szData, __TEXT("Apartment"));
        lResult = RegSetValueEx(hKey, __TEXT("ThreadingModel"), 0, REG_SZ,
                    reinterpret_cast<LPBYTE>(szData), lstrlen(szData) + 1);
        RegCloseKey(hKey);
    }

    return S_OK;
}
```

A COM object that exposes `DllRegisterServer()` via its DEF file may be registered via a call to the system utility `regsvr32.exe`:

```
regsvr32.exe <full_server_name>
```

Deregistering the Object

The REG script doesn't allow you to *de*register settings, so if this is the method you've chosen, the only way to do it is through manual deletion with the help of the Registry Editor. If you have the Windows Scripting Host (WSH) installed (more on this in Chapter 13) then an alternative solution would be to write a small VBScript or JavaScript function that uses the WSH registry object to delete keys and values. Because using a scripting language is more flexible and versatile than using REG files, you can bet that this will become a popular approach in the future.

Speaking of scripting languages, it's worth noting that a COM object written with ATL may use RGS files to provide registration and deregistration. RGS scripts look rather like an enhanced version of the Registry Editor's REG files, and when I begin writing COM objects with ATL, I will examine the features of RGS scripts in case you haven't had cause to manipulate them before.

Returning to the discussion at hand and our API functions, to make a COM object self-deregistering, you can use code like this:

```
STDAPI DllUnregisterServer()
{
    TCHAR szSubKey[MAX_PATH] = {0};
    TCHAR szCLSID[MAX_PATH] = {0};
    TCHAR szModule[MAX_PATH] = {0};
    HKEY hKey;
    DWORD dwDisp;

    // Set the CLSID
    lstrcpy(szCLSID, __TEXT("{20051998-0020-0005-1998-000000000000}"));

    // Open HKCR
    LRESULT lResult = RegCreateKeyEx(HKEY_CLASSES_ROOT, "", 0, NULL,
                REG_OPTION_NON_VOLATILE, KEY_WRITE, NULL, &hKey, &dwDisp);
    if(lResult == NOERROR)
    {
        wsprintf(szSubKey, __TEXT("CLSID\\%s\\InProcServer32"), szCLSID);
        RegDeleteKey(hKey, szSubKey);
        wsprintf(szSubKey, __TEXT("CLSID\\%s"), szCLSID);
        RegDeleteKey(hKey, szSubKey);
        RegCloseKey(hKey);
    }

    return S_OK;
}
```

In this function, we open the `HKEY_CLASSES_ROOT` node and delete the keys, starting with the innermost. The `RegDeleteKey()` function works slightly differently under Windows 9*x* and Windows NT. The former allows you to delete keys even if they contain sub-keys, but recursive deletion isn't supported under NT, and the function fails if the given key isn't empty. Notice that by 'empty' I mean 'without sub-keys', regardless of whether values are present. Since the code shown above deletes the innermost key first, it works unchanged on both platforms.

A COM object exposing `DllUnregisterServer()` may be deregistered via a call to the system utility `regsvr32.exe`:

```
regsvr32.exe /u <full_server_name>
```

A Brand New Start Button

To demonstrate the power of `SHLoadInProc()`, I'm going to show you how to expand the code of `DllGetClassObject()` so that it creates a brand new **Start** button, with a different bitmap and a different menu. We'll reach this result by following these steps:

- ❑ Getting the handle of the **Start** button
- ❑ Replacing its bitmap
- ❑ Subclassing the button window to change the menu and the cursor
- ❑ Creating a customized menu to display

You will then be able to control both the *Windows* key and the *Ctrl+Esc* key combination. You can neutralize them, leaving them to display the standard **Start** menu, or associate them with the new, customized menu. The screenshot shows the desired outcome:

The first thing to do is create a main function that will be called from within `DllGetClassObject()`. This procedure will be our point of departure into the unexplored territory of the shell.

```
STDAPI DllGetClassObject(REFCLSID rclsid, REFIID riid, LPVOID* ppv)
{
    InstallHandler();
    return CLASS_E_CLASSNOTAVAILABLE;
}

/*----------------------------------------------------------*/
// InstallHandler
// Replace the Start button and install the hooks
/*----------------------------------------------------------*/
void InstallHandler()
{
    if(g_bInstalled)
    {
        int irc = MessageBox(HWND_DESKTOP,
            __TEXT("The extension is installed. Would you like to uninstall?"),
            __TEXT("Start"), MB_ICONQUESTION | MB_YESNO | MB_SETFOREGROUND);

        if(irc == IDYES)
            UninstallHandler();
        return;
    }
```

```
    // Remember whether the handler is installed
    g_bInstalled = TRUE;

    // Set a new Start button
    SetNewStartButton(TRUE);
}
```

When we've finished with it and want to restore the standard behavior, we call the uninstaller:

```
void UninstallHandler()
{
    // Restore the Start settings
    SetNewStartButton(FALSE);

    // The handler is now uninstalled
    g_bInstalled = FALSE;
}
```

The presence of the handler is now the critical factor when Explorer calls `DllCanUnloadNow()` to discover whether our library can be unloaded. The last thing we need to do in this section, then, is to make sure that nothing nasty happens while the handler is installed:

```
STDAPI DllCanUnloadNow()
{
    return (g_bInstalled ? S_FALSE : S_OK);
}
```

Given that we can now go through the motions of installing and uninstalling a handler for the Start button, let's see how to accomplish the various steps required to complete our task.

Getting the Button Handle

The results are striking because we're altering such a familiar component of the Windows interface, but in fact we've already done the hardest part of the job, which was to get inside the shell's address space. What remains are simply Win32 programming techniques applied to some shell objects. Remember, what's really important here is that our minimal COM object (which I've placed in start.dll) is working in the same environment as Explorer.

The Start button is an ordinary window of class Button, as the following Spy++ screenshot demonstrates:

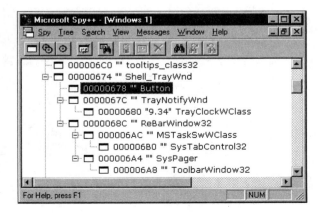

Locating the button among the enormous stack of windows is as easy as using the Spy++ finder tool: just drag the finder over the desired window, and it will be selected in the list of windows. The finder tool is available via the S_earch I F_ind Window... menu item.

If you want to retrieve the handle for a child window programmatically, you should use `FindWindowEx()` rather than `FindWindow()`, the difference being that the former lets you specify the root window from which the search should begin. In this case, we know that the Start button is a child of the taskbar, which is the only window of class `Shell_TrayWnd` anywhere in the system.

```
hwndTray  = FindWindowEx(NULL, NULL, "Shell_TrayWnd", NULL);
hwndStart = FindWindowEx(hwndTray, NULL, "Button", NULL);
```

The above fragment first retrieves a handle to the taskbar window, and then a handle to the first child of class `Button`.

Despite appearances, all the other 'buttons' you see on the taskbar aren't buttons. In fact, they aren't windows at all — they're simply the button-like tabs of a tab control. I'll say more about this in Chapter 9.

Replacing the Bitmap

Looking once again at the screenshot from Spy++, you'll notice that the Start button has no caption. This means that the famous word Start (which is localized for non-English versions of Windows) is just a bitmap. However, you won't find any trace of this bitmap in `shell32.dll`, or `explorer.exe`, or indeed any other system module. The bitmap is built dynamically by merging the Windows logo bitmap with a text string read from the resources. Both resources are stored in `explorer.exe`.

The Windows logo is the bitmap with an ID of 143, while the Start string evaluates to an entry in the string table with an ID of 578.

The composite bitmap is created in a memory device context by copying the Windows logo and drawing the text.

Reverse Engineering Explorer's Resources

If you look at Explorer's resources, you'll find that many of the bitmaps that populate the various configuration dialogs (for instance, the bitmap that's displayed in the Taskbar Properties dialog) are created dynamically in order to save space. In fact, the `explorer.exe` file only contains some constituent bitmaps; not the final, displayed result.

If you want to browse through some application resources on your own, here are some suggestions on how to go about it:

- ❑ Create a copy of the file you want to look into. This is necessary because the file could be in use.
- ❑ Open it with Visual C++, making sure to specify Resources in the Open as combo box.
- ❑ The IDE will warn you that under Windows 9x, you can't update the resources. Don't worry about it!

Once your display has changed to the tree of all the resources, saving them as separate files is easy too. Just right-click the desired resource and select Export.... This feature is available only for the resources that map to a file, such as bitmaps, icons and cursors, and for custom resources like AVI files. Curiously, you can't save a dialog template to a text file. (See *Further Reading.*)

Styles of the Start Button

The Start button has the `BS_BITMAP` style that means its surface is covered by a bitmap instead of the more usual text. (You can confirm this by right clicking on the window in the Spy++ list, then selecting Properties... I Styles). Getting the handle to this bitmap is as easy as calling:

```
g_hbmStart = reinterpret_cast<HBITMAP>(SendMessage(hwndStart,
                                        BM_GETIMAGE, IMAGE_BITMAP, 0));
```

Replacing the bitmap is no more difficult. First we use `LoadImage()` to load a new bitmap image from the resources of our application. Next, `SendMessage()` allows us to assign the bitmap to a button with the `BS_BITMAP` style. The `lParam` parameter refers to the handle returned by `LoadImage()`.

```
HBITMAP hbm = reinterpret_cast<HBITMAP>(LoadImage(g_hInstance,
          MAKEINTRESOURCE(IDB_NEWSTART), IMAGE_BITMAP, 0, 0, LR_DEFAULTSIZE));
SendMessage(hwndStart, BM_SETIMAGE,
                            IMAGE_BITMAP, reinterpret_cast<LPARAM>(hbm));
```

Here's the bitmap I used in the sample. Its ID is `IDB_NEWSTART`, which is defined in `resource.h`:

For this demonstration, I chose a bitmap that simulates a hyperlink, and for simplicity I also hard-coded the bitmap into the module's resources. The bitmap is the same size as the actual Start button bitmap (48 x 16). You can use whatever bitmap you like, but I recommend that you stick to this size.

Simply changing the bitmap does not necessarily result in an immediate refresh of the button interface. The button needs to redraw its non-client area in order to reflect the changes we've made. We can force that action by calling `SetWindowPos()`, like this:

```
SetWindowPos(hwndStart, NULL, 0, 0, 0, 0,
                    SWP_NOSIZE | SWP_NOZORDER | SWP_NOMOVE | SWP_DRAWFRAME);
```

To see the effects of the things we've done so far, we need to implement `SetNewStartButton()`, which strings together all the snippets of code that we looked at earlier in this section in order to do its job. Here's how it goes:

```
void SetNewStartButton(BOOL fNew)
{
    // Get the handle to the Start button
    HWND hwndTray = FindWindowEx(NULL, NULL, "Shell_TrayWnd", NULL);
    HWND hwndStart = FindWindowEx(hwndTray, NULL, "Button", NULL);

    // Change the bitmap
    g_hbmStart = NewStartBitmap(hwndStart, fNew);
}
```

Getting a handle to the button is a trivial affair, but replacing the bitmap in a way the allows the process to be reversed requires a little more logic, which is why I moved the code off into a helper function called `NewStartBitmap()`:

```
HBITMAP NewStartBitmap(HWND hwndStart, BOOL fNew)
{
    if(!fNew)
    {
        if(g_hbmStart)
            SendMessage(hwndStart, BM_SETIMAGE, IMAGE_BITMAP,
                                        reinterpret_cast<LPARAM>(g_hbmStart));

        // Refresh the button to reflect the change
        SetWindowPos(hwndStart, NULL, 0, 0, 0, 0,
                        SWP_NOSIZE | SWP_NOZORDER | SWP_NOMOVE | SWP_DRAWFRAME);
        return NULL;
    }

    // Save the current bitmap
    g_hbmStart = reinterpret_cast<HBITMAP>(
                        SendMessage(hwndStart, BM_GETIMAGE, IMAGE_BITMAP, 0));

    // Load and set the new bitmap
    HBITMAP hbm = reinterpret_cast<HBITMAP>(LoadImage(g_hInstance,
            MAKEINTRESOURCE(IDB_NEWSTART), IMAGE_BITMAP, 0, 0, LR_DEFAULTSIZE));
    SendMessage(hwndStart, BM_SETIMAGE, IMAGE_BITMAP,
                                        reinterpret_cast<LPARAM>(hbm));

    // Refresh the button to reflect the change
    SetWindowPos(hwndStart, NULL, 0, 0, 0, 0,
                        SWP_NOSIZE | SWP_NOZORDER | SWP_NOMOVE | SWP_DRAWFRAME);
    return g_hbmStart;
}
```

You now have all the code you need to build a working DLL. Once it has been registered, you should be able to use a function like `DoGoInsideExplorer()` that I presented earlier to invoke `SHLoadInProc()` and have your 'fake' COM object loaded into Explorer's address space.

Chapter 7

Subclassing the Window

Changing the Start button bitmap is a great result, but more can be achieved. My next goal is to change the behavior of the button, which means:

- Setting a hand-shaped cursor instead of the ordinary arrow
- Removing the context menu
- Customizing the tooltip text

By far the most impressive thing that I'll demonstrate, though, is to make clicking on the Start button produce a *different menu*.

A Hand-Shaped Cursor

Since we've made the button look like an HTML hyperlink, it would be nice to change the shape of the cursor to the pointing finger that usually appears on HTML links. I got hold of this cursor from Internet Explorer's resources by using the same technique as I discussed above for Explorer, and called it IDC_HAND.

Every time Windows needs to display a cursor for a window, it sends a WM_SETCURSOR message. If the application doesn't process it, then Windows sets up the predefined cursor for that class. The cursor for a class is defined when you register the class using RegisterClass() or RegisterClassEx() — it's one of the fields of a WNDCLASS (or WNDCLASSEX) structure. For system controls (like buttons), the predefined cursor is the standard arrow; the only exceptions to this are edit controls.

If we're going to start processing messages sent by the system that were intended for the Start button, we do now need to subclass it. We can begin the operation by adding code to SetNewStartButton() that will install (and uninstall) a custom window procedure called NewStartProc():

```
void SetNewStartButton(BOOL fNew)
{
    // Get the handle to the Start button
    HWND hwndTray = FindWindowEx(NULL, NULL, "Shell_TrayWnd", NULL);
    HWND hwndStart = FindWindowEx(hwndTray, NULL, "Button", NULL);

    // Change the bitmap
    g_hbmStart = NewStartBitmap(hwndStart, fNew);

    // Subclass the button
    if(fNew)
    {
        if(!g_bSubclassed)
        {
            g_pfnStartProc = SubclassWindow(hwndStart, NewStartProc);
            g_bSubclassed = TRUE;
        }
    }
    else
    {
        if(g_pfnStartProc != NULL)
            SubclassWindow(hwndStart, g_pfnStartProc);
        g_bSubclassed = FALSE;
    }
}
```

194

To have a different cursor appear when the mouse pointer is over the area of the window, you just need now to specify it in response to the WM_SETCURSOR message when it's received by the window procedure we're writing to subclass the Start button:

```
LRESULT CALLBACK NewStartProc(
                        HWND hwnd, UINT uMsg, WPARAM wParam, LPARAM lParam)
{
    switch(uMsg)
    {
    case WM_SETCURSOR:
        SetCursor(LoadCursor(g_hInstance, MAKEINTRESOURCE(IDC_HAND)));
        return 0;
    }

    return CallWindowProc(g_pfnStartProc, hwnd, uMsg, wParam, lParam);
}
```

It's extremely important that you return from the window procedure after dealing with the WM_SETCURSOR message. If you don't, Windows will end up executing the default code for the message and restore the arrow cursor!

Removing the Standard Context Menu

Hiding the standard context menu is even simpler. All you need to do is return 0 whenever you receive a WM_CONTEXTMENU message:

```
    switch(uMsg)
    {
    case WM_SETCURSOR:
        SetCursor(LoadCursor(g_hInstance, MAKEINTRESOURCE(IDC_HAND)));
        return 0;
    case WM_CONTEXTMENU:
        // Create your own pop-up menu here!
        return 0;
    }
```

Of course, there's nothing to prevent you from displaying your own pop-up menu in place of the standard one – just replace the comment in the above snippet with code of your own.

Customizing the Tooltip

Another possible form of customization might involve tooltips – you could consider changing the default message, Click here to begin. If you've ever worked with tooltips in Win32 programs, though, you'll know that they are hard nuts to crack. There's no easy way to detect which tooltips are currently active, and even if you catch the TTN_SHOW notification (a notification message sent when a tooltip window is about to be displayed), you can't cancel the tip.

The Start button tooltip is handled away from the code for the button itself. At startup, the taskbar creates a tooltip window and sets up some tools. Therefore, to get the handle of the window used for displaying the Start button's tooltip, a possible approach is to walk all the windows created by the current thread by using the EnumThreadWindows() function. The chances are that there's only one tooltip window: the right one. The following code shows how to get the tooltip window and the tool that relate to the Start button. (A **tool** here is the area in which you want the tip to appear – the client area in the case of the Start button.)

```
void RemoveTooltip(HWND hwndStart)
{
    EnumThreadWindows(GetCurrentThreadId(), EnumThreadWndProc,
                                reinterpret_cast<LPARAM>(hwndStart));
}


// This thread created just one tooltip window. All the windows that belong
//  to the thread are enumerated in order to find the tooltip. This
//  callback receives the handle of all the windows the thread created. The
//  lParam is the handle (hwndStart) of the Start button.
BOOL CALLBACK EnumThreadWndProc(HWND hwnd, LPARAM lParam)
{
    TCHAR szClass[MAX_PATH] = {0};
    GetClassName(hwnd, szClass, MAX_PATH);
    if(0 == lstrcmpi(szClass, TOOLTIPS_CLASS))
    {
        // Tooltip window found, so try to locate the tool
        int iNumOfTools = SendMessage(hwnd, TTM_GETTOOLCOUNT, 0, 0);
        for(int i = 0 ; i < iNumOfTools ; i++)
        {
            // Get information about the ith tool
            TOOLINFO ti;
            ti.cbSize = sizeof(TOOLINFO);
            SendMessage(hwnd, TTM_ENUMTOOLS, i, reinterpret_cast<LPARAM>(&ti));
            if(ti.uId == static_cast<UINT>(lParam))
            {
                // Tool for the Start button found.
                ti.lpszText = __TEXT("Buy this book!");
                SendMessage(hwnd, TTM_UPDATETIPTEXT, 0,
                                            reinterpret_cast<LPARAM>(&ti));
            }
        }
        return FALSE;
    }
    return TRUE;
}
```

Once we have the tooltip window handle, we use the programming interface of tooltips to enumerate the various tools. A **tool** is a rectangular region that originates a tip if the mouse hovers over it for a while, and is described by a TOOLINFO structure. During the enumeration of the tools, the tool for the Start button is found by comparing the uId field of TOOLINFO with the handle of the Start button. It can then be removed, or better still, the text can be replaced through the TTM_UPDATETIPTEXT message.

There are a couple of aspects of this code that I deduced by trial and error. First, the current thread creates just one tooltip window. Second, the tool that relates to the Start button has the TTF_IDISHWND flag set. This means that the tool relates to the client area of a window, and not to a generic rectangle. Third, the uId member of the TOOLINFO structure contains the HWND of that window. This is actually not surprising at all, since it's common practice to assign the TTF_IDISHWND flag when you want to define a tooltip for an entire window. Knowing these things greatly simplifies our work, since we can easily identify (and even remove) the tool for the Start button. TOOLTIPS_CLASS is a window class name provided by the common control library − these controls (believe it or not!) display tooltips.

If it's your intention to change the tooltip text, remember that this change is not tied to the module being run. It will continue to appear even when the module that installed it has been unloaded. The only way to restore the old tip is by changing the tool back to its previous settings.

A New Menu

The default **Start** menu appears when the user clicks on the button. More precisely, it is shown when the button receives the `BM_SETSTATE` message with the `wParam` argument set to `TRUE`. `BM_SETSTATE` is a button-specific message that's used to ask the button to draw in 'pressed' or 'released' mode; a `wParam` value of `TRUE` means that the button is required to be pressed, while a value of `FALSE` means it should be released. If your goal is simply to hide the standard menu, just process the `BM_SETSTATE` message and return 0.

When you hit the Windows *key or press* Ctrl-Esc, *you cause a* BM_SETSTATE *message to be sent to the button. By acting on the handler for that message, you have trapped those key combinations too.*

Correct Behavior

Suppose that you have your own menu to display. You might try to show it by processing the `WM_LBUTTONDOWN` message:

```
TrackPopupMenu(hmnuPopup, uFlags, ix, iy, 0, hwnd, NULL);
```

Provided that you specify the correct coordinates, the menu will appear near the button. However, the button will not be drawn 'pressed'.

To fix this, you need to send `BM_SETSTATE` messages to 'press' and 'release' the button. However, if you send the button itself such a message, it ends up being handled by the original window procedure, which we've just replaced. As a result, the standard **Start** menu appears!

The trouble is that the **Start** button is a child window of the taskbar. Each time you click on it (or send a `BM_SETSTATE` message), Windows automatically notifies the *parent* window of the event. For buttons, this means a `BN_CLICKED` message. By handling this `BN_CLICKED` message, the *taskbar* (not the button) displays the standard menu.

We want the *button* to provide the menu, but need a way to draw it 'pressed'. How can we obtain this behavior? What we need is an 'independent' function to draw the button with that look, and the solution is to resort to the *original* button procedure – the one that just draws the button in the normal way, without doing anything else or causing anything else to happen. The address of this function may be found in the `WNDCLASS` structure retrieved by `GetClassInfo()`:

```
switch(uMsg)
{
case WM_SETCURSOR:
    SetCursor(LoadCursor(g_hInstance, MAKEINTRESOURCE(IDC_HAND)));
    return 0;
case WM_CONTEXTMENU:
    return 0;
```

```
case WM_LBUTTONDOWN:
    {
        WNDCLASS wc;
        GetClassInfo(NULL, "Button", &wc);
        CallWindowProc(wc.lpfnWndProc, hwnd, BM_SETSTATE, TRUE, 0);

        // Call TrackPopupMenu() here

        CallWindowProc(wc.lpfnWndProc, hwnd, BM_SETSTATE, FALSE, 0);
        return 0;
    }
}
```

The code above ensures that our Start button behaves correctly and appears 'pressed' when the menu is up. This line:

```
CallWindowProc(wc.lpfnWndProc, hwnd, BM_SETSTATE, TRUE, 0);
```

now works as if it's an external function that takes the Start button handle as an argument.

In case you're wondering, there is an alternative way to do all this: I could have subclassed the taskbar window and intercepted the BN_CLICKED *message. However, I prefer the approach detailed here, as it minimizes the number of subclassed windows.*

How to Trap Ctrl-Esc and the Windows Key

When pressed, both *Ctrl-Esc* and the *Windows* key send a BM_SETSTATE message (with wParam set to TRUE) to the Start button, causing it to display the Start menu. By subclassing the Start button, we can decide to ignore that event:

```
case BM_SETSTATE:
    return 0;
```

Or we could choose to display our own menu instead:

```
case BM_SETSTATE:
case WM_LBUTTONDOWN:
    {
        ...
    }
```

Creating Owner-Drawn Menus

TrackPopupMenu() is fine for displaying a menu at a certain screen position, but Start has two additional features that differentiate it from ordinary menus. Firstly, it is an owner-drawn menu, and secondly, it must appear at rigorously defined positions that depend on the edge of the taskbar and the absolute location of the Start button.

If the taskbar is docked at the bottom of the screen, the menu must be displayed *above* the Start button; if it's at the top, the menu should go *below* it. Therefore, to determine the correct coordinates for the menu, we first need to know the position of the system taskbar.

Determining the Menu's Screen Position

`TrackPopupMenu()` needs a position expressed in (x, y) screen coordinates. Interestingly, you can tell the function how to interpret each coordinate, and how to align the menu accordingly. For example, if you specify the `TPM_BOTTOMALIGN` flag, then the y-coordinate is intended to be the bottom of the menu. If you set `TPM_RIGHTALIGN`, the x-coordinate is where the right edge of the menu will lie.

The position of a pop-up menu depends on these three pieces of information: x- and y-coordinates, and alignment flags. I packed them into a custom structure called `STARTMENUPOS`, and defined a helper function that checks the position of the taskbar and fills the structure accordingly:

```
struct STARTMENUPOS
{
    int ix;
    int iy;
    UINT uFlags;
};

typedef STARTMENUPOS* LPSTARTMENUPOS;


void GetStartMenuPosition(LPSTARTMENUPOS lpsmp)
{
    // Get the taskbar's edge and position
    APPBARDATA abd;
    abd.cbSize = sizeof(APPBARDATA);
    SHAppBarMessage(ABM_GETTASKBARPOS, &abd);

    switch(abd.uEdge)
    {
    case ABE_BOTTOM:
       lpsmp->ix = 0;
       lpsmp->iy = abd.rc.top;
       lpsmp->uFlags = TPM_LEFTALIGN | TPM_BOTTOMALIGN;
       break;

    case ABE_TOP:
       lpsmp->ix = 0;
       lpsmp->iy = abd.rc.bottom;
       lpsmp->uFlags = TPM_LEFTALIGN | TPM_TOPALIGN;
       break;

    case ABE_LEFT:
       lpsmp->ix = abd.rc.right;
       lpsmp->iy = 0;
       lpsmp->uFlags = TPM_LEFTALIGN | TPM_TOPALIGN;
       break;

    case ABE_RIGHT:
       lpsmp->ix = abd.rc.left;
       lpsmp->iy = 0;
       lpsmp->uFlags = TPM_RIGHTALIGN | TPM_TOPALIGN;
       break;
    }
}
```

`SHAppBarMessage()` is an API function defined in `shellapi.h` that can return the edge and the position of the system taskbar. It can also serve other purposes that I'll look at in Chapter 9.

The `GetStartMenuPosition()` function allows us to display the **Start** menu in the correct position relative to the taskbar. The code to display the pop-up menu may then look like this:

```
case WM_LBUTTONDOWN:
    {
        WNDCLASS wc;
        GetClassInfo(NULL, __TEXT("Button"), &wc);
        CallWindowProc(wc.lpfnWndProc, hwnd, BM_SETSTATE, TRUE, 0);

        STARTMENUPOS smp;
        GetStartMenuPosition(&smp);
        HMENU hmenu = LoadMenu(g_hInstance, MAKEINTRESOURCE(IDR_MENU));
        HMENU hmnuPopup = GetSubMenu(hmenu, 0);

        TrackPopupMenu(hmnuPopup, smp.uFlags, smp.ix, smp.iy, 0, hwnd, NULL);
        CallWindowProc(wc.lpfnWndProc, hwnd, BM_SETSTATE, FALSE, 0);
        return 0;
    }
```

Each menu item you select sends a `WM_COMMAND` message to the `hwnd` window, which is none other than the button itself! Thus, our subclassing procedure is also handling the user's selections, which I'll process further in a moment.

Loading a New Menu

I created a very simple, predefined menu to be used as a replacement for the standard menu called `IDR_MENU` (as above). You could do this yourself, loading and displaying it through `TrackPopupMenu()`, but you'll soon realize that it is rather uninspiring. What you'll get, in fact, is a traditional, text-based menu:

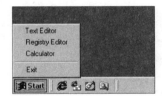

The Windows **Start** menu, on the other hand, is an owner-drawn menu, in which each item is drawn separately by a user-defined procedure. Unfortunately, Visual C++'s resource editor doesn't allow you to create owner-drawn menus in a 'visual' fashion, so you have to do everything programmatically.

If the menu you want to draw already exists (if it's stored in the module's resources, say), then your first step should be to walk through all the items and assign each one the special `MF_OWNERDRAW` attribute. This flag qualifies it as an item whose contents must be drawn by a user-defined procedure. Here's a piece of code that takes a pop-up menu and sets the owner-drawn style for each item:

```
// Maximum size allowed item names in an owner-drawn menu
const int ITEMSIZE = 100;

struct MENUSTRUCT
{
    TCHAR szText[ITEMSIZE];
    int iItemID;
    TCHAR szFile[MAX_PATH];
};
typedef MENUSTRUCT* LPMENUSTRUCT;
```

```
void MakePopupOwnerDraw(HWND hwnd, HMENU hmnuPopup)
{
    // Iterate over all popup items
    for(int i = 0 ; i < GetMenuItemCount(hmnuPopup) ; i++)
    {
        // Saves some data for the owner-draw functions
        LPMENUSTRUCT lpms = GlobalAllocPtr(GHND, sizeof(MENUSTRUCT));
        int iItemID = static_cast<int>(GetMenuItemID(hmnuPopup, i));
        GetMenuString(hmnuPopup, iItemID, lpms->szText, ITEMSIZE, MF_BYCOMMAND);
        lpms->iItemID = iItemID;

        UINT uiState = GetMenuState(hmnuPopup, iItemID, MF_BYCOMMAND);
        ModifyMenu(hmnuPopup, iItemID, uiState | MF_BYCOMMAND | MF_OWNERDRAW,
                iItemID, reinterpret_cast<LPCTSTR>(lpms));
    }
}
```

When you assign the owner-drawn style to a menu item, you might want to store some per-item information, such as the string to be displayed. In our case, this is done through the custom structure MENUSTRUCT, a pointer to which is passed as the final parameter to ModifyMenu(). This memory buffer is then passed to the functions that actually draw the items. This memory must be freed by a similar routine that should be called when you have finished with the menu.

Owner-Drawn Separators

If we're really going to produce a menu that's akin to the standard Windows Start menu, we'll also need to make owner-drawn separators. That's because the Start menu contains a continuous vertical band at one edge that can't be broken by separators, effectively reducing the horizontal area available for items *and* separators. By default, a separator is drawn as an inset line that runs from edge to edge. This means that we need to consider separators as items to be drawn as well.

Collecting Menu Items Dynamically

For this example, I decided not to load the new menu from project resources. The Start menu is a semi-dynamic menu, in the sense that the menu items are partially determined at runtime. If you create shortcuts in the Start Menu special folder (see Chapter 6), you can cause a new item to appear on the menu. I will define a similar mechanism for this custom handler.

I created a directory (hard-coded to C:\MyStartMenu) to be filled with the shortcuts to add to the menu. Apart from these dynamic items, my Start menu will always contain a 'fixed' command to restore the previous settings and the original menu. A click on a shortcut will call the target file, while a click on the fixed item causes the handler to uninstall.

The following function, GetMenuHandle(), creates the menu to be displayed by the new Start button. It scans the C:\MyStartMenu directory searching for LNK files, resolves them, and adds the relevant icon and name to the menu.

```
HMENU GetMenuHandle(LPTSTR szPath)
{
    LPMENUSTRUCT lpms;
    int iItemID = 1;

    // These globals are a reminder that the menu drawing is starting now
    g_bAlreadyDrawn = FALSE;      // Not already drawn
    g_bFirstTime = TRUE;          // First time we enter
```

```
// Creates an empty menu
HMENU hmenu = CreatePopupMenu();

// Filter string for *.lnk
TCHAR szDir[MAX_PATH] = {0};
lstrcpy(szDir, szPath);
if(szDir[lstrlen(szDir) - 1] != '\\')
    lstrcat(szDir, __TEXT("\\"));

TCHAR szBuf[MAX_PATH] = {0};
wsprintf(szBuf, __TEXT("%s*.lnk"), szDir);

// Search for .lnk files
WIN32_FIND_DATA wfd;
HANDLE h = FindFirstFile(szBuf, &wfd);
while(h != INVALID_HANDLE_VALUE)
{
    // Resolve the shortcut
    SHORTCUTSTRUCT ss;
    ZeroMemory(&ss, sizeof(SHORTCUTSTRUCT));
    wsprintf(szBuf, __TEXT("%s\\%s"), szDir, wfd.cFileName);
    SHResolveShortcut(szBuf, &ss);

    // Prepare per-item data using ID, description and target file
    lpms = reinterpret_cast<LPMENUSTRUCT>(
                            GlobalAllocPtr(GHND, sizeof(MENUSTRUCT)));
    lpms->iItemID = iItemID;
    if(!lstrlen(ss.pszDesc))
        lstrcpy(lpms->szText, wfd.cFileName);
    else
        lstrcpy(lpms->szText, ss.pszDesc);
    lstrcpy(lpms->szFile, ss.pszTarget);

    // Add the item
    AppendMenu(hmenu, MF_OWNERDRAW,
                            iItemID++, reinterpret_cast<LPTSTR>(lpms));

    // Next file
    if(!FindNextFile(h, &wfd))
    {
        FindClose(h);
        break;
    }
}

// Add the separator and the 'Restore' item
AppendMenu(hmenu, MF_OWNERDRAW | MF_SEPARATOR, 0, NULL);

lpms = reinterpret_cast<LPMENUSTRUCT>(
                        GlobalAllocPtr(GHND, sizeof(MENUSTRUCT)));
lpms->iItemID = ID_FILE_EXIT;
lstrcpy(lpms->szText, __TEXT("Restore Previous Settings"));
lstrcpy(lpms->szFile, "");
AppendMenu(hmenu, MF_OWNERDRAW, ID_FILE_EXIT,
                                    reinterpret_cast<LPTSTR>(lpms));
return hmenu;
}
```

As you can see, this function introduces two new global, Boolean variables. g_bAlreadyDrawn is used to remember whether the bitmap has already been drawn in the vertical band, because we need to do this only once. g_bFirstTime, on the other hand, is used to remember whether this is the first time items have been drawn in the menu. If this variable is TRUE, the top edge of the menu item rectangle is saved, in order to determine the height of the menu. You'll see these values being changed in later functions.

Items are drawn from top to bottom, and the last item in this implementation is determined by ID – it's my fixed item that will uninstall the handler. It relies on the existence in the DLL's resources of an appropriate 32 x 32-pixel icon with the identifier ID_FILE_EXIT. The *other* thing that this code relies on is the function called SHResolveShortcut() that we put together in the previous chapter.

Setting the Measurements

Owner-drawn resources cause two messages to be sent to their parent's window procedure. In this case, these messages will reach our new Start button procedure. They are:

- ❑ WM_MEASUREITEM
- ❑ WM_DRAWITEM

The first of these is intended to obtain the width and height (in pixels) of a single menu item, which we must do by filling in a structure that comes with the message. The second requires you to do any painting work that needs to be done. Here's a typical example of a function for handling the WM_MEASUREITEM message:

```
// These are absolute constants (expressed in pixels) that define
//  measurements for the items to draw
const int DEFBITMAPSIZE = 32; // 32 x 32 is the area reserved for bitmaps
const int DEFBANDSIZE = 25;   // Width of the vertical band
const int DEFSEPSIZE = 6;     // Height of the area reserved for separators
const int DEFBORDERSIZE = 2;  // Gap between item text and edge of the menu

void MeasureItem(HWND hwnd, LPMEASUREITEMSTRUCT lpmis)
{
    SIZE size;
    int iItemID = lpmis->itemID;
    LPMENUSTRUCT lpms = reinterpret_cast<LPMENUSTRUCT>(lpmis->itemData);

    // Calculate the size of the item string
    HDC hdc = GetDC(hwnd);
    GetTextExtentPoint32(hdc, lpms->szText, lstrlen(lpms->szText), &size);
    ReleaseDC(hwnd, hdc);

    // Set width and height for the item
    lpmis->itemWidth = DEFBITMAPSIZE + DEFBANDSIZE + size.cx;

    // A separator has a zero ID
    if(iItemID)
        lpmis->itemHeight = DEFBITMAPSIZE;
    else
        lpmis->itemHeight = DEFSEPSIZE;
}
```

The `lParam` argument of a `WM_MEASUREITEM` message points to a `MEASUREITEMSTRUCT` structure, the `itemHeight` and `itemWidth` fields of which must be filled with the actual size of the item. In the code above, the height is set to 32 pixels, while the width depends on the length of the text, the space reserved for bitmaps (icons), and the band that runs up the edge of the menu (the 'Windows 98' banner, for example).

Note that explicit constants are used here so that the appearance of the Start menu will remain the same whatever the display settings are.

> *For more information about the structures employed here, and the owner-drawn mechanism, you should take a look at the official documentation in the MSDN library, or read the suggestions in the* Further Reading *section of this chapter.*

Drawing the Items

The `WM_DRAWITEM` message is sent each time Windows needs to paint a given menu item. The `lParam` argument of the message points to a `DRAWITEMSTRUCT` structure that provides all the information you need to do the work. Basically, we want a menu window with a vertical band on the left and then, for each item, an icon and a string. The most interesting feature is that the area on the left will be filled with a bitmap.

Drawing icons and strings is quite straightforward, and can be accomplished by common APIs such as `DrawIcon()` and `ExtTextOut()`. (See *Further Reading*.) When you draw items, you work on a per-item basis and see only a slice of the menu window. When it comes to drawing a bitmap along the edge of the menu window, it's a bit different. The drawing procedures are called item by item when selection changes, but we need to find out a way of drawing the bitmap only once, and the global variable that remembers we have already drawn it was my solution. However, there's more to drawing a bitmap than that!

How would you draw the bitmap at all? Using `BitBlt()` is probably as good a method as any. Windows paints its owner-drawn menus using top-down logic, so if we pass (0, 0) as the origin of the destination device context, the bitmap will be aligned with the top of the menu.

If you look at the Start menus of Windows 95, 98 and NT, you'll see that the bitmap is always aligned with the *bottom* of the menu. This introduces further complications – what are the correct coordinates to pass to `BitBlt()`? The x coordinate will be 0, or an absolute offset from the left edge. The y coordinate should be given by the height of the menu window, minus the height of the bitmap we're using. Because `BitBlt()` draws from top to bottom, the bitmap will be aligned with the bottom.

There's a fairly simple solution to the problem of finding the height of the menu window. We know that the `DRAWITEMSTRUCT` contains the rectangle for the current item, so if we remember the top of the first element and the bottom of the last one, the height of the window must be the difference between the two.

So, we know the height of the bitmap, and we know the height of the window. That makes it easy to determine the correct y-coordinate for `BitBlt()` to work. Things should now work in the same way as they do in the standard Start menu. The necessary code is shown on the next page:

```
void DrawItem(LPDRAWITEMSTRUCT lpdis)
{
    TCHAR szItem[ITEMSIZE] = {0};
    TCHAR szFile[MAX_PATH] = {0};
    COLORREF crText, crBack;
    HICON hIcon = NULL;

    LPMENUSTRUCT lpms = reinterpret_cast<LPMENUSTRUCT>(lpdis->itemData);
    int iItemID = lpdis->itemID;
    int iTopEdge = 0;

    // Save the item text and target file
    if(lpms)
    {
        lstrcpy(szItem, lpms->szText);
        lstrcpy(szFile, lpms->szFile);
    }

    // Manage how to draw
    if(lpdis->itemAction & (ODA_DRAWENTIRE | ODA_SELECT))
    {
        COLORREF clr;
        RECT rtBand, rtBmp, rtText, rtItem, rt;
        SIZE size;

        // Defines rectangles for further use:
        //    lpdis->rcItem is the menu item rectangle
        //    rtBand: portion of the menu item area for vertical band
        //    rtBmp: portion of the menu item area for item icon
        //    rtText: portion of the menu item area for item text
        CopyRect(&rt, &(lpdis->rcItem));
        CopyRect(&rtBand, &rt);
        rtBand.right = rtBand.left + DEFBANDSIZE;
        CopyRect(&rtBmp, &rt);
        rtBmp.left = rtBand.right + DEFBORDERSIZE;
        rtBmp.right = rtBmp.left + DEFBITMAPSIZE;
        CopyRect(&rtText, &rt);
        rtText.left = rtBmp.right + 2 * DEFBORDERSIZE;
        CopyRect(&rtItem, &rt);
        rtItem.left += DEFBANDSIZE + DEFBORDERSIZE;

        // If it is the first item, store the y-coordinate
        if(g_bFirstTime)
        {
            iTopEdge = rtBand.top;
            g_bFirstTime = FALSE;
        }

        // Draw the band rectangle and the vertical bitmap
        if(!g_bAlreadyDrawn)
        {
            // Draw the band area in blue
            clr = SetBkColor(lpdis->hDC, RGB(0, 0, 255));
            ExtTextOut(lpdis->hDC, 0, 0,
                         ETO_CLIPPED | ETO_OPAQUE, &rtBand, NULL, 0, NULL);
            SetBkColor(lpdis->hDC, clr);

            // If the last item, determine menu height, load bitmap, and draw
            if(iItemID == ID_FILE_EXIT)
            {
                int iMenuHeight = rtBand.bottom - iTopEdge;
```

```
            HBITMAP hbm = LoadBitmap(g_hInstance, MAKEINTRESOURCE(IDB_LOGO));
            DrawBitmap(lpdis->hDC, 0, iMenuHeight, hbm);
            DeleteObject(hbm);
            g_bAlreadyDrawn = TRUE;
        }
    }

    // Everything so far is unaffected by selection state. Now need to
    //  draw icon and text with respect to this and hence backgnd color
    if(lpdis->itemState & ODS_SELECTED)
    {
        crText = SetTextColor(lpdis->hDC, GetSysColor(COLOR_HIGHLIGHTTEXT));
        crBack = SetBkColor(lpdis->hDC, GetSysColor(COLOR_HIGHLIGHT));
    }

    // Clear the area with the correct background color
    ExtTextOut(lpdis->hDC, rtText.left, rtText.left,
                        ETO_CLIPPED | ETO_OPAQUE, &rtItem, NULL, 0, NULL);

    // Get icon to draw. Load it from resources if it is the last item.
    //  Otherwise, determine system icon for the shortcut's target file.
    if(iItemID == ID_FILE_EXIT)
        hIcon = LoadIcon(g_hInstance, MAKEINTRESOURCE(iItemID));
    else
    {
        SHFILEINFO sfi;
        ZeroMemory(&sfi, sizeof(SHFILEINFO));
        SHGetFileInfo(szFile, 0, &sfi, sizeof(SHFILEINFO), SHGFI_ICON);
        hIcon = sfi.hIcon;
    }

    // Draw the icon (transparence is automatic)
    if(hIcon)
    {
        DrawIcon(lpdis->hDC, rtBmp.left, rtBmp.top, hIcon);
        DestroyIcon(hIcon);
    }

    // Draw the text (one line centered vertically)
    if(!iItemID)
    {
        // It's a separator
        rt.top++;
        rt.bottom = rt.top + DEFBORDERSIZE;
        rt.left = rt.left + DEFBANDSIZE + DEFBORDERSIZE;
        DrawEdge(lpdis->hDC, &rt, EDGE_ETCHED, BF_RECT);
    }
    else
    {
        // Get the size of the text according to the font
        GetTextExtentPoint32(lpdis->hDC, szItem, lstrlen(szItem), &size);

        // Center it vertically
        int iy = ((lpdis->rcItem.bottom - lpdis->rcItem.top) - size.cy) / 2;
        iy = lpdis->rcItem.top + (iy >= 0 ? iy : 0);
        rtText.top = iy;
        DrawText(lpdis->hDC, szItem, lstrlen(szItem),
                                    &rtText, DT_LEFT | DT_EXPANDTABS);
    }
}
}
```

The large but relatively straightforward function above deals with drawing text and icons, but it passes off the drawing of the bitmap with the vertical logo (which it expects to find in a 25 pixel wide resource called IDB_LOGO) to the next routine, DrawBitmap():

```
void DrawBitmap(HDC hdc, int x, int iHeight, HBITMAP hbm)
{
    // This function calculates the y-coordinate based on the height
    // of the area to cover. The bitmap will be aligned with the bottom
    BITMAP bm;

    // Creates a memory device context and selects the bitmap in it
    HDC hdcMem = CreateCompatibleDC(hdc);
    HBITMAP hOldBm = static_cast<HBITMAP>(SelectObject(hdcMem, hbm));

    // Obtains information about the bitmap
    GetObject(hbm, sizeof(BITMAP), &bm);

    // Determine the y-coordinate
    int y = iHeight - bm.bmHeight;
    y = (y < 0 ? 0 : y);

    // Transfer the bitmap from memory DC to the menu DC
    BitBlt(hdc, x, y, bm.bmWidth, bm.bmHeight, hdcMem, 0, 0, SRCCOPY);

    // Free the memory DC
    SelectObject(hdcMem, hOldBm);
    DeleteDC(hdcMem);
}
```

Finally, you need to amend our button-subclassing window procedure so that it correctly constructs our custom menu, and so that it can process the WM_MEASUREITEM and WM_DRAWITEM messages:

```
switch(uMsg)
{
case WM_SETCURSOR:
    SetCursor(LoadCursor(g_hInstance, MAKEINTRESOURCE(IDC_HANDY)));
    return 0;
case WM_MEASUREITEM:
    MeasureItem(HWND_DESKTOP, reinterpret_cast<LPMEASUREITEMSTRUCT>(lParam));
    break;
case WM_DRAWITEM:
    DrawItem(reinterpret_cast<LPDRAWITEMSTRUCT>(lParam));
    break;
case WM_CONTEXTMENU:
    return 0;
case BM_SETSTATE:
case WM_LBUTTONDOWN:
    {
        WNDCLASS wc;
        GetClassInfo(NULL, "Button", &wc);
        CallWindowProc(wc.lpfnWndProc, hwnd, BM_SETSTATE, TRUE, 0);

        STARTMENUPOS smp;
        GetStartMenuPosition(&smp);
        HMENU hmnuPopup = GetMenuHandle("c:\\myStartMenu");
        int iCmd = TrackPopupMenu(hmnuPopup,
                            smp.uFlags | TPM_RETURNCMD | TPM_NONOTIFY,
                            smp.ix, smp.iy, 0, hwnd, NULL);
```

```
        // Handle the user's mouse clicks
        HandleResults(hmnuPopup, iCmd);

        // Free memory
        DestroyMenu(hmnuPopup);

        CallWindowProc(wc.lpfnWndProc, hwnd, BM_SETSTATE, FALSE, 0);
        return 0;
    }
}
```

Executing Commands

The menu is now complete and operational, with only the slight drawback that none of the items we add to it actually does anything! From the listing above, you can see that the answer will have something to do with the `HandleResults()` function, but a question arises as to what kinds of item we expect on the menu. Will they just be application commands, or shortcuts to documents and programs?

Of course, this ultimately depends on your requirements. I've chosen to read the contents of a directory on disk and arrange a menu dynamically. (This is exactly what the shell does when you add shortcuts to the **Start** or **Programs** menus.) As mentioned earlier, the assumption is that the handler will find shortcuts to file objects, which it then resolves and appends to the menu. Finally, it adds a separator and a standard 'quit' item.

A shortcut's description becomes the menu item's text. If the shortcut hasn't got a description (a common situation), then the file name is used. When the item is clicked, the module simply calls the file pointed to by the shortcut:

```
void HandleResults(HMENU hmenu, int iCmd)
{
    MENUITEMINFO mii;
    LPMENUSTRUCT lpms;

    if(iCmd <= 0)
        return;

    if(iCmd == ID_FILE_EXIT)
    {
        UninstallHandler();
        return;
    }

    mii.cbSize = sizeof(MENUITEMINFO);
    mii.fMask = MIIM_DATA;
    GetMenuItemInfo(hmenu, iCmd, FALSE, &mii);
    lpms = reinterpret_cast<LPMENUSTRUCT>(mii.dwItemData);
    ShellExecute(NULL, __TEXT("open"), lpms->szFile, NULL, NULL, SW_SHOW);
}
```

If the item clicked on was **Restore Previous Settings** then `UninstallHandler()` is called and the function exits. For any other selection, the path to the file to be executed is extracted from the item data, and then the `ShellExecute()` API function, which we will examine in detail in the next chapter, is used to execute the file. Our custom **Start** menu is complete!

Browser Helper Objects

SHLoadInProc() is the lever that allows your programs to insert COM objects into the shell. I've used a minimal COM object for this purpose, but you can, of course, use normal COM objects as well. The point is that you don't have to be an expert COM programmer to exploit this function. What you are required to build is something that *presents itself* as a COM object: it must have a CLSID, it must be registered, and it must implement the minimum functions of any COM server. You aren't required to implement any interfaces, but nothing prevents you from doing so if you need to.

Browser helper objects, on the other hand, are fully qualified, in-process COM servers that Internet Explorer (and Explorer too, if you're running shell version 4.71) loads whenever a new instance of itself is created. Note that these objects always need an instance of a browser to be open in order to come into play, as I'll explain in the *Activation Mechanism* section, shortly.

With SHLoadInProc(), it's your program that decides when and if it should head off into Explorer's address space. The big difference with browser helper objects is that it's the browser (Explorer or Internet Explorer) that automatically loads all the modules that are registered in a particular area of the registry.

> *As their name implies, browser helper objects affect only a specific part of Explorer — the browser, which lets you browse for files and folders.*

You can now choose between two complementary methods — it's down to you to decide which of the two options best suits your specific needs. In order to assist you in your choice, I shall examine the relative merits of the two approaches. The main points of difference are:

- ❑ Backward compatibility
- ❑ Activation mechanism
- ❑ Registration
- ❑ Structure of the COM object
- ❑ Communication with the host
- ❑ Usage

It is important to keep in mind that both options are valid means of loading a COM object into the shell's memory space, and I shall evaluate them in those terms. Technically speaking, the two are completely different: SHLoadInProc() is a function, while a browser helper object is a COM object.

Backward Compatibility

While SHLoadInProc() is supported from shell version 4.00 onwards, browser helper objects are specific to shell 4.71 — they were introduced with Internet Explorer 4.0. Both work well on all Win32 platforms, with the exception of Windows CE.

> *Remember that shell version 4.71 means that you must have Internet Explorer 4.0 or higher and Active Desktop. Both are included in Windows 98.*

Activation Mechanism

The two methods are quite different from this point of view. SHLoadInProc() allows your application to load a COM object into the shell's context programmatically. Browser helper objects, on the other hand, are registered objects that are loaded into memory by Internet Explorer and Explorer each time a new instance is started. You can't control when browser helper objects are loaded into memory.

To have helper objects in action, you *must* open an instance of Explorer or Internet Explorer. Furthermore, an instance of the helper is associated with every instance of Explorer or Internet Explorer – the helper will be unloaded as soon as the instance with which it is associated is closed.

Registration

SHLoadInProc() can load any COM object that is correctly registered as such. A browser helper object must also be registered in a specific registry path so that Explorer and Internet Explorer can see it. (See the *Registering Helper Objects* section for more information on this.)

Structure of the COM Object

As shown above, SHLoadInProc() can manage and successfully load any COM object – even fake objects that don't implement interfaces. A browser helper object must have a well-defined format, which is verified by the browser (both IE and Explorer). There's just one rule: implement the IObjectWithSite interface.

Communication with the Host

Objects loaded via SHLoadInProc() don't receive a pointer to the IUnknown interface of the shell. This might constitute a significant limitation, but if your goal is simply 'subclassing' shell objects, then you don't need that pointer. By 'subclassing' I mean any technique that allows you to modify and filter the behavior of an object (the Start button, for example) using brute force, in such a way that the object is 'unaware' of your actions.

Having a reference to the objects of the host environment, on the other hand, allows contact with them through their public programming interface, which is a much neater (and almost certainly safer) approach. This also opens up a new range of exploitable functionality, of which **event handling** is the most useful. A helper object loaded by the browser can retrieve a pointer to IWebBrowser2, and handle all the events that the browser fires. (See *Further Reading*.) This communication is supported by the IObjectWithSite interface.

Usage

SHLoadInProc() has the advantage that it can be used to load a variety of objects, including 'fake' objects as shown earlier. In principle, you can use SHLoadInProc() to load helper objects too. Unfortunately, though, it doesn't allow you to communicate with the shell through the latter's IUnknown interface, so in this respect browser helper objects are more versatile, although they can't be loaded programmatically. SHLoadInProc() works only with Explorer, whereas helper objects work with both Internet Explorer and Explorer, but SHLoadInProc() doesn't *require* an instance of Explorer or Internet Explorer to be open.

I took the fake COM module that I developed earlier and tried registering it as a helper object, and it worked fine! In this scenario, the 'minimal' COM object works in the same way and for the same reasons as it does with `SHLoadInProc()`: it exports `DllGetClassObject()`, which is always invoked.

Registering Helper Objects

A browser helper object is a COM module that must register itself under the following path:

```
HKEY_LOCAL_MACHINE
    \Software
        \Microsoft
            \Windows
                \CurrentVersion
                    \Explorer
                        \Browser Helper Objects
```

The CLSIDs of all the enabled modules are listed under the **Browser Helper Objects** key. Explorer (and Internet Explorer) loads them one after another. Remember that a new instance of the browser is also created when you open the Recycle Bin or the `Printers` folder, which means that the helper objects get called *very* frequently – or at least, more frequently than you might expect. (Look out for dialog boxes or modal windows...) The list of the helpers is never cached, and always re-read from disk, so it only takes a second to get rid of modules that are no longer useful – you just have to remove the corresponding CLSID line in the registry. Happily, removing an object from this sub-tree doesn't affect the server's global registration status. Other applications will find it the same as they did before.

The IObjectWithSite Interface

With `SHLoadInProc()`, a module gets loaded into Explorer's address space, but there is no COM-based connection to it. In other words, it doesn't receive the `IUnknown` pointer of the browser, and it can't access the object model. Helper objects fix this by implementing the `IObjectWithSite` interface.

When the browser loads one of the COM servers listed in the registry, it queries for the `IObjectWithSite` interface. If it is found, the module is passed a pointer to the browser's `IUnknown` interface via the `SetSite()` method.

The `IObjectWithSite` interface includes just two methods in addition to the `IUnknown` triplet: `SetSite()` and `GetSite()`.

```
HRESULT IObjectWithSite::SetSite(IUnknown* pUnkSite);
HRESULT IObjectWithSite::GetSite(REFIID riid, void** ppvSite);
```

`SetSite()` is called by the browser and may be considered to be a kind of entry point. `GetSite()` works much like `QueryInterface()`, and returns a pointer to the specified interface on the site last set by `SetSite()`.

Writing a Helper Object

If you plan to write a browser helper object, ATL can provide considerable assistance. Once you've created a skeleton DLL with the ATL COM AppWizard, you can add a new simple object with the Object Wizard and derive it from `IObjectWithSiteImpl`. All that remains then is to fill the body of `SetSite()` with the helper's logic.

To demonstrate this, I'll rewrite the tool that creates a new folder when a specific key is pressed as a helper object. Browser helper objects are more applicable to creating small utilities that enhance Explorer than to generic extensions to shell objects, and so a browser helper object seems to be the ideal means to add new accelerators to Explorer. We no longer need an application to inject code into Explorer's context; instead, we have to create a COM object that implements `IObjectWithSite`.

There are two points to consider:

❑ Finding the handle of Explorer's window
❑ The keyboard hook to detect the accelerator

My previous solution was based on a global hook on window creation. When the hook procedure detected the creation of a window of a certain class (`ExploreWClass`), it installed a local hook on keyboard activity. When *F12* was pressed, Explorer's window received the command message that caused it to create a new folder. A helper object, on the other hand, is loaded when an Explorer window *already exists*. However, `FindWindow()` is not necessarily the right function for finding the handle of Explorer's window, because it returns the handle of the *top level* window of the specified class. Consequently, if multiple copies of Explorer are running at the same time, we can't be sure it is *our* window.

If multiple copies of Explorer *are* running at the same time, each of them runs in its own thread. For browser helper objects, a better approach to finding the handle of Explorer's window is to enumerate the windows owned by the current thread, like this:

```
EnumThreadWindows(GetCurrentThreadId(), WndEnumProc,
                            reinterpret_cast<LPARAM>(&m_hwndExplorer));
if(!IsWindow(m_hwndExplorer))
   return E_FAIL;
```

`EnumThreadWindows()` is an API function that enumerates all the windows created by the specified thread. Each window is then processed by the callback function passed as the second argument, which in this case is `WndEnumProc()`:

```
BOOL CALLBACK CNewFolder::WndEnumProc(HWND hwnd, LPARAM lParam)
{
   TCHAR szClassName[MAX_PATH] = {0};
   GetClassName(hwnd, szClassName, MAX_PATH);
   if(!lstrcmpi(szClassName, __TEXT("ExploreWClass")))
   {
      HWND* phWnd = reinterpret_cast<HWND*>(lParam);
      *phWnd = hwnd;
      return FALSE;
   }

   return TRUE;
}
```

The third parameter of `EnumThreadWindows()` is a 32-bit value that can be used by the caller in whatever way it sees fit. In this case, we need a way to get the handle of the Explorer window (if there is one) returned, and for this reason we use the third parameter to pass a pointer to an `HWND` variable. When `WndEnumProc()` finds a window of type `ExploreWClass`, it copies a handle to it to the pointer, and then stops the enumeration process by returning `FALSE`.

Despite appearances, Explorer's window is actually composed of a whole stack of windows; the figure should give you a better idea of its layout. Refer to Spy++ for the exact window classes and styles.

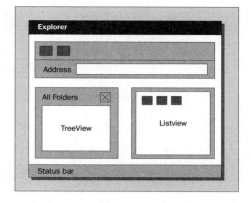

Each keypress is processed differently according to which window has the input focus. By installing a local keyboard hook, we can process each key before it enters the traditional channels for distribution among the windows.

An ATL COM Object

Let's have a look at the source code for the browser helper object. Here, the ATL COM AppWizard has been used to generate the skeleton of the code, and a new **Simple Object** called `NewFolder` has been added. The code for the header file `newfolder.h` looks like this:

```
#ifndef __NEWFOLDER_H_
#define __NEWFOLDER_H_

#include "resource.h"                // main symbols

//////////////////////////////////////////////////////////////////////////
// Constants
const int NEWFOLDERMSG = 29281;      // WM_COMMAND to send
const int NEWFOLDERKEY = VK_F12;     // Key to detect

//////////////////////////////////////////////////////////////////////////
// CNewFolder
class ATL_NO_VTABLE CNewFolder :
    public CComObjectRootEx<CComSingleThreadModel>,
    public CComCoClass<CNewFolder, &CLSID_NewFolder>,
    public IObjectWithSiteImpl<CNewFolder>,
    public IDispatchImpl<INewFolder, &IID_INewFolder, &LIBID_OBJFOLDERLib>
{
public:
    CNewFolder()
    {
        m_bSubclassed = false;
    }
    ~CNewFolder();

DECLARE_REGISTRY_RESOURCEID(IDR_NEWFOLDER)

DECLARE_PROTECT_FINAL_CONSTRUCT()
```

```
BEGIN_COM_MAP(CNewFolder)
    COM_INTERFACE_ENTRY(INewFolder)
    COM_INTERFACE_ENTRY(IDispatch)

    COM_INTERFACE_ENTRY_IMPL(IObjectWithSite)
END_COM_MAP()

// INewFolder
public:
    STDMETHOD(SubclassExplorer)(bool bSubclass);

// IObjectWithSite
public:
    STDMETHOD(SetSite)(IUnknown* pUnkSite);

private:
    bool m_bSubclassed;
    HWND m_hwndExplorer;

// Callback functions
    static BOOL CALLBACK WndEnumProc(HWND, LPARAM);
    static LRESULT CALLBACK KeyboardProc(int, WPARAM, LPARAM);
    static LRESULT CALLBACK NewExplorerWndProc(HWND, UINT, WPARAM, LPARAM);
};

#endif //__NEWFOLDER_H_
```

I've derived NewFolder from the standard implementation that ATL provides for IObjectWithSite. The only change we need to make to it is an override for SetSite(), which is the key function for a helper object.

The code below figures out which is Explorer's window and installs the keyboard hook. Even though it's not strictly necessary for *this* sample, I've subclassed Explorer's window so that the code is ready for further enhancements.

```
#include "stdafx.h"
#include "ObjFolder.h"
#include "NewFolder.h"

// These constants are used inside the static members of the class
static WNDPROC g_pfnExplorerWndProc = NULL;
static HHOOK g_hHook = NULL;
static HWND g_hwndExplorer;

//////////////////////////////////////////////////////////////////////////
// CNewFolder

CNewFolder::~CNewFolder()
{
    if(m_bSubclassed)
    {
        SubclassExplorer(false);
        m_bSubclassed = false;
    }
}
```

```
/*------------------------------------------------------------------*/
// SetSite
// Called by Explorer/IExplorer to get in touch
/*------------------------------------------------------------------*/
STDMETHODIMP CNewFolder::SetSite(IUnknown* pUnkSite)
{
   HRESULT hr = SubclassExplorer(true);
   if(SUCCEEDED(hr))
      m_bSubclassed = true;

   return S_OK;
}



/*------------------------------------------------------------------*/
// SubclassExplorer
// Subclass the Explorer window and install the keyboard hook
/*------------------------------------------------------------------*/
STDMETHODIMP CNewFolder::SubclassExplorer(bool bSubclass)
{
   // Get the HWND of the Explorer's window
   EnumThreadWindows(GetCurrentThreadId(), WndEnumProc,
                              reinterpret_cast<LPARAM>(&m_hwndExplorer));

   if(!IsWindow(m_hwndExplorer))
      return E_FAIL;
   else
      g_hwndExplorer = m_hwndExplorer;

   // Subclass Explorer's window
   if(bSubclass && !m_bSubclassed)
   {
      g_pfnExplorerWndProc = reinterpret_cast<WNDPROC>(SetWindowLong(
                         m_hwndExplorer, GWL_WNDPROC,
                         reinterpret_cast<LONG>(NewExplorerWndProc)));

      // Set a keyboard hook to detect F12
      g_hHook = SetWindowsHookEx(
                  WH_KEYBOARD, KeyboardProc, NULL, GetCurrentThreadId());
   }

   // Unsubclass Explorer's window
   if(!bSubclass && m_bSubclassed)
   {
      SetWindowLong(m_hwndExplorer, GWL_WNDPROC,
                         reinterpret_cast<LONG>(g_pfnExplorerWndProc));

      // Remove the hook
      UnhookWindowsHookEx(g_hHook);
   }

   return S_OK;
}



/*------------------------------------------------------------------*/
// WndEnumProc
// Static member to enumerate thread windows
/*------------------------------------------------------------------*/

// Insert this code as given in the above discussion.
```

```
/*-----------------------------------------------------------------*/
// NewExplorerWndProc
// Static member to replace Explorer's wndproc
/*-----------------------------------------------------------------*/
LRESULT CALLBACK CNewFolder::NewExplorerWndProc(
                        HWND hwnd, UINT uMsg, WPARAM wParam, LPARAM lParam)
{
    // This does nothing, so just call into the standard procedure
    return CallWindowProc(g_pfnExplorerWndProc, hwnd, uMsg, wParam, lParam);
}



/*-----------------------------------------------------------------*/
// KeyboardProc
// Static member to handle keys
/*-----------------------------------------------------------------*/
LRESULT CALLBACK CNewFolder::KeyboardProc(
                            int nCode, WPARAM wParam, LPARAM lParam)
{
    // Typical start-off for any hook
    if(nCode < 0)
        return CallNextHookEx(g_hHook, nCode, wParam, lParam);

    // Process the key only once
    if((lParam & 0x80000000) || (lParam & 0x40000000))
        return CallNextHookEx(g_hHook, nCode, wParam, lParam);

    if(wParam == NEWFOLDERKEY)
        PostMessage(g_hwndExplorer, WM_COMMAND, NEWFOLDERMSG, 0);

    return CallNextHookEx(g_hHook, nCode, wParam, lParam);
}
```

Another thing you might wish to do when writing a helper object is to make it completely self-registering. In order to register the browser helper object correctly, you need to add the following code to the RGS script:

```
HKLM
{
    SOFTWARE
    {
        Microsoft
        {
            Windows
            {
                CurrentVersion
                {
                    Explorer
                    {
                        'Browser Helper Objects'
                        {
                            {B4F8DE53-65F4-11D2-BC00-B0FB05C10627}
                        }
                    }
                }
            }
        }
    }
}
```

A problem with browser helper objects is that while they aren't completely undocumented, they are certainly under-documented. In the Further Reading section, I'll point out a good article that includes useful code.

That completes the code for this project; you should now be able to build the project, registering the browser helper object in the process. Any new instances of Explorer that you invoke after installing the object will have the keyboard hook, and pressing *F12* will once again produce a new folder in the directory being displayed.

Helper Objects under Windows NT

Browser helper objects work the in the same way under Windows NT as they do under Windows 9*x*. The registration process is identical, as is the design logic that you should follow. There's just one pitfall to avoid: Unicode. Under Windows NT, helper objects really need to be Unicode modules. If they aren't, the code will still work after a fashion, but some strings in Explorer's user interface will be truncated!

Fortunately, because we're using ATL, recompiling for Unicode is just a matter of choosing the appropriate setting from the **Active Configuration** combo box on the **Build** menu. For browser helper objects, then, you need to create and deploy two different versions: ANSI for Windows 9*x*, and Unicode for Windows NT.

Glossary of Techniques for Entering the Shell

I've now explored three ways to access the shell's address space. Below is a table that summarizes the techniques, and allows you to cross-reference them.

Parameter	Brute force	SHLoadInProc()	Helper Object
Backward compatibility	Shell 4.00	Shell 4.00	Shell 4.71
Activation mechanism	Programmatically	Programmatically	Loaded automatically by the shell
Registry impact	None	Ordinary COM object registration	Ordinary COM object registration plus specific registration for helpers
Structure of the code	Based on global hooks	A COM object with no specific interface	A COM object implementing `IObjectWithSite`
Communication with the host	Through subclassing	Through subclassing	Through the site's `IUnknown` interface
Required knowledge	Win32 programming	Win32 programming and minimal COM competence	Win32 programming and good knowledge of COM

Summary

In this chapter, I've examined various ways of invading the shell's territory and modifying the behavior and the look of the shell. I started with **notification objects**, which enable Explorer to become aware of changes in the file system, and then touched upon **shell notifications**, which are a more general way to achieve the same result. (In fact, they are quite different, but they share the same goal.)

Next, I covered the topic of interprocess communication, talked about subclassing and hooking, and demonstrated a utility that adds a keyboard accelerator to Explorer and allows you to create new folders by pressing a single key. I showed you how a single shell API can be used to take your code straight into the shell's context. Later on I looked at how to replace the Start button, and scratched the surface of many Win32 programming topics, including owner-drawn controls, tooltips and button styles. Finally, I introduced browser helper objects – a new way to enhance the behavior of both Explorer and Internet Explorer. In summary, I demonstrated:

- ❑ How to get file system notifications
- ❑ How to get into the shell's address space
- ❑ How to subclass the Start button
- ❑ How to implement a fully customized menu
- ❑ The differences between SHLoadInProc() and Browser Helper Objects

Further Reading

I've covered many topics in this chapter, so I'll revisit them in order and address additional sources of information. First, notification objects, of which an example may be found in the *Wicked Code* column of the October 1996 edition of MSJ. The author, Jeff Prosise, shows how to build an MFC class that works in roughly the same way as Explorer's tree view – that is, it loads and displays drives and folders. This class uses notification objects to detect changes.

Notification objects are also covered in Jeff Richter's *Advanced Windows* book (Microsoft Press, ISBN 1-57231-548-2). Additionally, you'll find information about file monitoring under Windows NT, an explanation of the whys and wherefores of separate address spaces in Win32, and three examples of how to break process boundaries.

When it comes to fundamental techniques like subclassing, owner-drawing, and hooks, I'd recommend Petzold's *Programming Windows 95* book (Microsoft Press, ISBN 1-55615-676-6). If you're more oriented towards MFC programming, then Mike Blaszczak's *Professional MFC with Visual C++* (Wrox Press, ISBN 1-861000-14-6) is a good choice. (I'd also recommend my first Win32 book, but unfortunately it only exists in Italian! If you're interested, the title is *Progettare applicazioni per Win32* (McGraw-Hill, 88386-0444-4.)

Earlier in the chapter, I mentioned an article that stimulated my curiosity in `SHLoadInProc()`. It was written by Eric Heimburg, and appeared in the February 1998 edition of WDJ under the title *Monitoring System Events by Subclassing the Shell*. Similarly, I heard about browser helper objects from an article published in the May 1998 issue of MIND. Scott Roberts' piece *Controlling Internet Explorer 4.0 with Browser Helper Objects* shows how to build an ATL-based COM server that will be loaded each time a new instance of (Internet) Explorer executes. Specifically, the sample provided displays a log window to trace all the events fired. Other related material, more oriented to Internet Explorer and its object model, are my article *Hooking the IE 4.0 Object Model*, which appeared in the December 1997 edition of MIND, and Scott Roberts' *Keeping an Eye on your Browser by Monitoring IE 4.0 Events*, which appeared in MSJ, June 1998.

To conclude, here are a few Knowledge Base articles that I found useful:

- ❑ **Knowledge Base Article Q142276**: *Icon Handlers in Start Menu Don't Match Those in Explorer*
- ❑ **Knowledge Base Article Q160976**: *Controlling the Currently Running Instance of IE3 via DDE*
- ❑ **Knowledge Base Article Q176792**: *Connecting to a Running Instance of Internet Explorer*

8

Program Executors

With the advent of Windows 95, the concept of a 'document' gained importance. Behind this word there are more than just bare ASCII text files, and I'm not just talking about more complex Word or Excel files. By 'document', I mean a more general object that is part of the system's namespace, and for which there is (or may be) a program that can 'open', 'print', 'explore', or 'find' it. In other words, a document is an item upon which a program can execute **verbs** – command strings such as, "Open," "Print," and "Explore."

The ability to be executed is no longer a privilege only of the small category of files with extensions like .exe, .com, .pif or .bat. From Windows 95 on, *all* files with an associated set of verbs have become executable.

A direct consequence of this is that today there is less and less sense in having a function that only executes programs. Programs are just files, and running them is just an action that you perform on a file. When it comes to finding a way to spawn an external program, we now have a range of choices, but as I will show, the correct choices are fairly obvious. There has been some evolution, but essentially we're moving from one single function – WinExec() – to another – ShellExecuteEx() – through a couple of intermediate stages.

In this chapter, I will present the various options that you have for starting applications, creating processes and opening documents. In particular, I'll cover:

- ❑ The differences between WinExec() and CreateProcess()
- ❑ How ShellExecute() and ShellExecuteEx() supersede the other functions
- ❑ Verbs, documents and policies
- ❑ How to customize the execution process via hooking

I'll also present some quick code examples that illustrate things such as:

- How to detect the default browser
- How to run programs and wait for them to terminate
- How to display the Properties dialog box for a file
- How to display the Find dialog box
- How to prevent users from accessing certain folders or running certain applications

To begin, let's see how and why `CreateProcess()` is far superior to dear old `WinExec()`.

From WinExec() to CreateProcess()

Under Windows 3.1, `WinExec()` was the only way to run an external program. It has the world's simplest prototype – one of very few that you can remember on the fly, without even a quick glance at the online help. You want to launch another program? All you need to do is specify its name, and the attribute that you want the new window to have:

```
UINT WinExec(LPCSTR lpCmdLine, UINT uCmdShow);
```

The `lpCmdLine` parameter is a pointer to a `NULL`-terminated string that contains the command line of the application that you want to start: the program name and any arguments you want it to receive. `uCmdShow` is one of the well-known `SW_` constants that determine whether the resulting window should be iconic, maximized, hidden, visible, etc.

The major drawback of `WinExec()` is that you can't detect whether the newly started process has terminated, when many of the real-world uses of this functionality require exactly that sort of synchronization. What `WinExec()` returns is a value that's an error code if it's less than 32, and something related to the task otherwise. While it's possible to find a way of establishing a minimum level of communication between caller and callee, doing so is an unofficial, unnatural, and potentially unsafe road to follow. See *Further Reading* for more information on these topics.

Externally, `WinExec()` has changed little in the process of being ported from Win16 to Win32, but internally it now calls `CreateProcess()` to help with its duties. This latter function should be the first one you consider when you need to create a new process.

A Comparison of WinExec() with CreateProcess()

A good measure of the differing powers of `WinExec()` and `CreateProcess()` can be obtained by comparing their respective prototypes. You've already seen the one for `WinExec()`, so let's now take a look at that of `CreateProcess()`:

```
BOOL CreateProcess(
   LPCTSTR lpApplicationName,       // Pointer to name of executable module
   LPTSTR lpCommandLine,            // Pointer to command line string
   LPSECURITY_ATTRIBUTES lpPA,      // Pointer to process security attributes
   LPSECURITY_ATTRIBUTES lpTA,      // Pointer to thread security attributes
   BOOL bInheritHandles,            // Handle inheritance flag
   DWORD dwCreationFlags,           // Creation flags
   LPVOID lpEnvironment,            // Pointer to new environment block
   LPCTSTR lpCurrentDir,            // Pointer to current directory name
   LPSTARTUPINFO lpStartupInfo,     // Pointer to STARTUPINFO
   LPPROCESS_INFORMATION lpPI       // Pointer to PROCESS_INFORMATION
);
```

As you can see, there are a great many new features here. However, `CreateProcess()` is well documented in the MSDN Library (see also the *Further Reading* section at the end of the chapter), so I won't be covering it in detail here. Something that is worth doing, though, is examining what a minimal call to `CreateProcess()` looks like:

```
ZeroMemory(&si, sizeof(STARTUPINFO));
bResult = CreateProcess(NULL, szPrgName, NULL, NULL, TRUE,
                        NORMAL_PRIORITY_CLASS, NULL, NULL, &si, &pi);
```

Whichever way you look at it, it's a lot more complex than `WinExec()`. However, `CreateProcess()` has at least one interesting practical advantage. While spawning a new process requires a bit of work, as the above code demonstrates, waiting for it to terminate is really easy and relatively inexpensive.

```
BOOL WinExecEx(LPCSTR lpCmdLine, UINT uCmdShow)
{
    PROCESS_INFORMATION pi;
    STARTUPINFO si;

    // Create a new process
    ZeroMemory(&si, sizeof(STARTUPINFO));
    BOOL b = CreateProcess(NULL, const_cast<LPTSTR>(lpCmdLine), NULL,
                NULL, TRUE, NORMAL_PRIORITY_CLASS, NULL, NULL, &si, &pi);
    if(!b)
        return FALSE;

    // Block the caller thread
    WaitForSingleObject(pi.hProcess, INFINITE);
    return TRUE;
}
```

The above code shows a function that falls somewhere between `CreateProcess()` and `WinExec()`. Once the new process has been created, it blocks the caller thread waiting for the process handle to become signaled. The process handle `hPROCESS`, returned by `CreateProcess()` through the `PROCESS_INFORMATION` structure, is a kernel object that becomes signaled only when the handle itself becomes `NULL`. The handle becomes `NULL` only when the process has terminated.

If the program that calls the above function has a user interface, it would be better if it first minimized or hid itself in order to prevent painting problems. When an application is suspended, it stops responding to the system and rejects all messages. If painting messages are being ignored, the window won't be able to redraw itself properly if you move it around or overlap it with another window.

Is CreateProcess() Manna from Heaven?

Apparently, `CreateProcess()` has solved all the problems we identified with `WinExec()`. We can run programs, we can synchronize them, and we've gained great control over the entire startup 'process'. Is there anything else we could want? Considering things from the point of view of wanting to launch applications, the answer is no, but what about documents? More specifically, what about documents that have benefited from updates to the shell? If you think it over, the things that `CreateProcess()` does, albeit very well, are just a fraction of the whole. Executable programs, in the traditional sense of the term, are just one type of document.

The evolution of the Windows 9x shell follows a document-centric vision, in which the verb "Execute" is a synonym of "Use." In general, you and your users will be using documents of all types, not just programs.

ShellExecute()

ShellExecute() was a wrapper for WinExec() that originally appeared in Windows 3.x, and was the first example of a function that tried to put a kind of document-centric vision of Windows into practice. It has been ported to Windows 95 and later systems, preserving the same prototype for compatibility purposes. Under Win32 it became a wrapper for both WinExec() and CreateProcess() because as I said earlier, WinExec() makes internal use of CreateProcess(). Its prototype is:

```
HINSTANCE ShellExecute(HWND     hwnd,
                       LPCTSTR  lpOperation,
                       LPCTSTR  lpFile,
                       LPCTSTR  lpParameters,
                       LPCTSTR  lpDirectory,
                       INT      nShowCmd);
```

It accepts more arguments than WinExec(), but at first sight it looks less powerful than CreateProcess(). What *really* makes ShellExecute() different, though, is that it is capable of handling **file type associations**. In other words, when you pass in the name of a non-executable file, the function scans the registry and searches for an executable program capable of handling documents of that type. As long as such a handler exists, the function will work.

I'll return to this important concept later in the chapter. In the meantime, let's take a closer look at the function's prototype.

Parameter	Description
hwnd	The parent window for any message box that the function should display.
lpOperation	A string denoting the operation you want to perform on the file. (See below.)
lpFile	The name of the file on which the function is called to operate. It may be an executable or a document.
lpParameters	A string containing all the parameters you want to be passed to the executable. Ignored if lpFile is a document file.
lpDirectory	A string with the working directory for the executable. Ignored if lpFile is a document file.
nShowCmd	The display attributes for the newly created window – one of the SW_ constants. This flag *isn't* ignored if lpFile is a document file. (See *A Frustrating Documentation Error.*)

The operations (also called **verbs**) you can execute on a file vary quite a bit according to the file type. Common operations include those listed in the following table:

Operation	Applies to
Open	Programs, documents, folders
Explore	Folders
Print	Documents
Print to	Documents
Find	Folders

Note that by, "Common operations," I simply mean that those verbs that are commonly supported by all types of file for which they make sense. It's a bit odd, for example, to imagine an executable being printed. Likewise, the 'Applies to' column indicates only the types of documents to which the command *normally* applies. There are no fixed and rigorous rules. Provided that you write the necessary code, there's nothing preventing you from implementing a print operation for executables that dumps the file header, or a find operation for a certain type of document that retrieves pieces of information.

The default operation is open, and this is the action that takes place if you set the lpOperation argument to NULL. Accepting the operation name, however, doesn't automatically mean that the operation will execute. The function needs to figure out which command line to execute in response to that verb, and this information is stored in the registry. Before we get on to that, though, let's examine in a bit more detail how each of the 'common' operations works.

The Open Operation

You can call open to open a document, to run a program, or to dereference a shortcut. In doing so, you may need the other parameters to have specific values:

```
ShellExecute(hwnd, __TEXT("open"), __TEXT("c:\\prg.exe"),
                    __TEXT("/nologo"), __TEXT("d:\\"), SW_SHOW);
```

The above line runs c:\prg.exe, passing /nologo as its command line and specifyng d:\ as its working directory. If the document to be opened is not an executable, then both lpParameters and lpDirectory are ignored. As I'll show in a moment, the same doesn't hold true for nCmdShow. The following code snippet shows how to open a .txt file in the program registered for handling them. (Normally, notepad.exe.):

```
ShellExecute(hwnd, __TEXT("open"), __TEXT("c:\\file.txt"),
                                    NULL, NULL, SW_SHOW);
```

The important thing here is that `ShellExecute()` is capable of opening documents if and only if there's a program registered to handle them. If no program is registered, then the function will prompt you for the program to use:

There are file types for which the concept of 'opening' is ambiguous. For example, suppose you have a VBScript `.vbs` file. When we talk of opening this file, are we intending to edit its contents, or to run it? Within the context of the shell, the second option is appropriate.

The Explore Operation

The `explore` operation applies only to folders; it displays the given folder inside Explorer. In the case of folders, there's a subtle difference between the `explore` and `open` operations. Both let you see the contents of a folder through Explorer, but with the latter you get a new, single folder window, while the former causes the creation of a two-paned window:

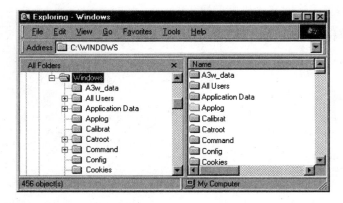

The `explore` operation is automatically enabled for folders − that is, for documents of type **File Folder**. This setting is saved during the Windows installation process. However, if an `explore` operation makes sense for your documents, you can register it as well. The following code causes the window in the picture to appear:

```
ShellExecute(hwnd, __TEXT("explore"), __TEXT("c:\\windows"),
                                        NULL, NULL, SW_SHOW);
```

The Print Operation

The `print` operation is meant to print documents, but it relies on the information stored in the registry to identify the program and command line capable of printing the specified document. The snippet of code here demonstrates how to print a text file:

```
ShellExecute(hwnd, __TEXT("print"), __TEXT("c:\\file.txt"),
                                    NULL, NULL, SW_SHOW);
```

In this configuration, the function searches for the program registered to handle text files and sees whether it supports a command for printing. Normally, this program is `notepad.exe` and the command line is:

```
notepad.exe /p <file_name>
```

Note that specifying /p is a widely supported way of issuing a print command using the command line.

By default, the `print` operation tries to use the default printer. Throughout the Windows shell, however, users can print documents by dropping the file onto a printer's icon. In this case, the code that the shell executes looks like this

```
ShellExecute(NULL, __TEXT("printto"), filename, NULL, NULL, SW_SHOW);
```

As you can see, there's another operation called `printto`. If this is supported by the document, then the registered command line is executed. Otherwise, you'll be prompted by the following dialog:

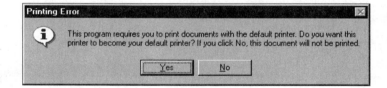

Unlike the `open` and `explore` operations, folders don't have native support for `print` and `printto`.

The `printto` operation is intended to allow you to print documents from the shell using non-default printers. Apart from the file name, there are three additional parameters that you have to pass, and these are formatted in the `lpParameter` argument. The first is the name of the printer as it appears in the `Printers` folder, while the other two are the name of the driver for it, and the name of the port. If you're adding support for the `printto` command, then the command line will look something like this:

```
MyProgram.exe  %1 %2 %3 %4
```

Here, the first parameter is the name of the file. Consider also that it's common practice for a Windows program to specify the printer port with the `/pt` option. In other words, if you're writing an application and want it to print its documents on different printers connected on different ports, it's recommended that you detect this option on the application's command line, via a `/pt` prefix:

```
MyProgram.exe  /pt %1 %2 %3 %4
```

Once again, however, this is only a convention, not a rule.

Printing to Ports

The additional three command line parameters are required to allow the system to build a device context (DC) for the required printer. A device context is a kind of logical surface where the Windows GDI functions send their output, and you need a specific DC for each printer you want to print to. A printer DC is created using the CreateDC() API function, whose prototype is:

```
HDC CreateDC(LPCTSTR       lpszDriver,    // Driver name (e.g. wspuni.drv)
             LPCTSTR       lpszDevice,    // Device name (e.g. OKIPage 4W)
             LPCTSTR       lpszOutput,    // Do not use; set to NULL
             CONST DEVMODE* lpInitData);  // Optional printer data
```

Interestingly, this function has maintained the same prototype it had in Windows 3.1 despite the fact that in practice it needs just one argument: lpszDevice. Under Win32, printers are identified by their descriptive names and you don't need to handle information such as the driver name and the port name explicitly. In Windows 3.1, lpszOutput was a pointer to a string with the name of the port. (LPT1:, for example.) Under Win32, this information remains important, but for a less direct reason. The functions use the device name as a search key to find the registry entries where the other information is kept.

The Find Operation

Apart from the operations mentioned above, there's another one that is completely ignored by the documentation but hinted at by a recent Knowledge Base article in the MSDN Library (Q183903). This new operation is find, and it applies to folders. Its effect is to run the Find: All Files system dialog box, starting from the specified folder:

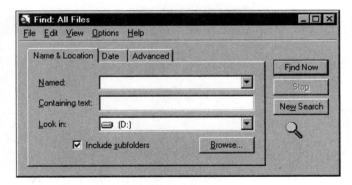

The important point to take away from this section is that ShellExecute() *isn't limited to a finite set of strings as the content of* lpOperation. *By editing the registry, you can add new verbs and associate them with command lines. We'll see this in action later in the chapter.*

A Frustrating Documentation Error

I don't use calls to `ShellExecute()` everyday, and I must confess that sometimes I don't read the documentation from top to bottom. In many cases, I feel confident once I have understood the *role* of the function. Over time, the impression formed in my mind that `ShellExecute()` was a highly specialized version of `WinExec()`, and so when I wrote calls to it I relied on memory rather than consulting the documentation. For this reason, I always passed `SW_SHOW` as the value of the `nCmdShow` argument.

Then, one day, I *did* look at the documentation, and discovered that `nCmdShow` should be 0 if `lpFile` isn't pointing to an executable. "Why should that be?" I wondered, "Presumably, they're forcing `SW_SHOW` to be the only possible value."

To be faithful to the documentation, I replaced `SW_SHOW` with 0 wherever applicable, but from then on I was able only to spawn programs. `ShellExecute()` appeared no longer able to open documents. It took me a few days to realize what had happened, and the more I tested the function, the more the system's performance slowed down.

The documentation notwithstanding, the value you pass through `nCmdShow` is *not* ignored if the target is a file and not an executable. By passing 0, you're actually telling the function to show the new window with the `SW_HIDE` attribute (which evaluates to 0). After running a bunch of test applications and discovering this, I summoned up the courage to look at the Task Manager and counted 23 Notepad, 12 WScript and 3 MSPaint instances running perfectly, but hidden from view!

> *This is definitely an error in the documentation, but there's still no mention of it on the MSDN. Happily, I have found reference to it in WDJ Notes (available from* http://www.wdj.com/utilities.html*), and this is a confirmation of my findings.*

More Details of the Verbs

All the operations (also known as verbs) I have examined so far have an intuitive implementation. To `open` a program, for example, means calling `CreateProcess()`. Exploring or even opening a folder usually means calling `explorer.exe` with some specific flags on the command line, and the Find dialog also appears due to the magic of an internal shell function — the folder name is merely an argument that you pass. All this is simple, and somewhat 'static'.

When it comes to opening a generic document, however, things start to get complicated. Earlier in the chapter, I mentioned VBScript files, so which program knows about those? Does it require a specific command line? More importantly, how can the shell know about it? This is where the twin concepts of **verbs** and **file handlers** come into play.

Verbs and File Handlers

As I mentioned earlier, a verb is a string that denotes an action that a program is capable of executing on a particular type of file. The program can be called a 'file handler', since it knows how to deal with that type of document.

Chapter 8

The association between file types, verbs and handlers can be seen in the system registry, under the key HKEY_CLASSES_ROOT:

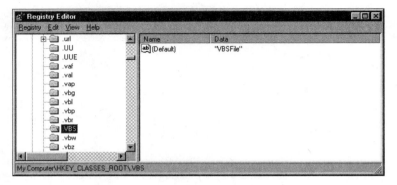

The figure shows a view of the sub-tree that contains a list of all the file extensions for which it's *likely* that a proper handler is correctly registered. The *presence* of a node — say, .xyz — is not sufficient to have that type of file perfectly managed by the system's shell. To demonstrate this point, let's consider the VBScript files with extension .vbs, which are simply ASCII files that contain VBScript source code.

A .vbs key under HKEY_CLASSES_ROOT is only the first step. In its Default entry, the node contains a string that points to another key in the same sub-tree. In this case, it is:

```
HKEY_CLASSES_ROOT
    \VBSFile
```

The Default entry of *this* node defines the string that Explorer considers as a description of the file type, and below it is the section that's relevant to us here. It contains all the verbs that are defined, along with their command lines. In the case of VBScript (and on my home PC), the situation is as depicted in the figure:

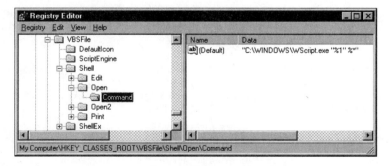

Every 'verb' key has a sub-key called Command whose Default entry points to the command line. It's this string that will determine the actual behavior of the shell. In this case, to open (or run) a VBScript file, the shell must use a file called wscript.exe. (I'll cover wscript.exe in Chapter 13, when I talk about the Windows Scripting Host.) Printing a VBScript file, on the other hand, just requires a call to Notepad with the conventional /p option:

```
C:\WINDOWS\Notepad.exe /p %1
```

As you may have realized by now, these verbs are the main components of the context menu for a particular type of file:

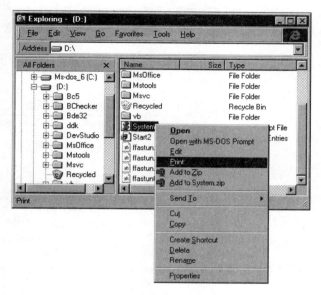

The contents of these verbs are decided by programs and by expert end-users. After all, there's no rule that tells you how to print a document: it's up to you (or the programs you install) to know the way to do it, and to save that command line to the registry. From the shell's point of view, all that matters is that it can find a `print` key under `HKEY_CLASSES_ROOT\DocumentType\Shell`, and that `print` has a sub-key called `command`.

Notice here that `print` is *not* a keyword handled by `ShellExecute()`, but simply a word that you would reasonably want to associate with a command line in the registry that's able to print a given type of document.

Executing a Verb

Let's see in practice how `ShellExecute()` handles a sample call. This should clarify how to use the function, and how to edit the registry if you need to do so. The call we're analyzing is:

```
ShellExecute(hwnd, __TEXT("OpenWithIE"), __TEXT("file.txt"),
                                      NULL, NULL, SW_SHOW);
```

The verb here is the rather strange `OpenWithIE`, and the intention of the call is that it be applied to a text file. The verb is no problem for `ShellExecute()`, though, which just follows its normal process:

❑ Find out the path to the `shell` registry key for the document
❑ Search for an `OpenWithIE` key
❑ Read the `Command` sub-key
❑ Execute the specified command line using `CreateProcess()`, passing the name of the document as an argument

First of all, let's assume that someone has created the key shown in this figure:

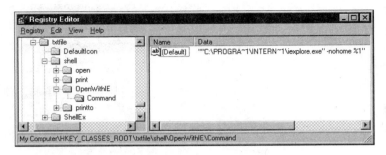

The function ends up calling this command line:

```
"C:\PROGRA~1\INTERN~1\iexplore.exe" -nohome %1
```

As it does so, it replaces %1 with the file name, file.txt. Then it's the turn of CreateProcess():

```
CreateProcess(NULL, const_cast<LPTSTR>(lpCmdLine), NULL, NULL, TRUE,
                    NORMAL_PRIORITY_CLASS, NULL, NULL, &si, &pi);
```

Where the lpCmdLine argument will be:

```
"C:\PROGRA~1\INTERN~1\iexplore.exe" -nohome file.txt
```

Ultimately, as a result of the call, Internet Explorer will open the text file in read-only mode.

Static and Dynamic Verbs

All the keys found in the registry should be considered **static verbs**, and they are the only sorts of verbs that we can expect a function like ShellExecute() to recognize. However, there are also **dynamic verbs**, which are context menu items that are added at runtime under conditions that may vary on the fly, or on a per-file basis. To handle static verbs, the shell always needs to create a new process, starting from the command line that you stored in the registry. Dynamic verbs, on the other hand, are handled by shell extensions that exist in the same process as the shell.

Getting the Executable Name for a File

If your goal is simply to open a particular file, then ShellExecute() is what you need. All that you then need to know is the name of the file to open. However, there may be other circumstances in which you need to know the exact name of the program registered to handle files of a given type on a given computer. Let's see an example of that.

Have you ever wondered how browsers detect when they are no longer your default browser, and promptly complain about this? Roughly speaking, they try to read the name of the executable file registered to handle HTML files. If they don't find their name, they realize that you have changed your allegiance, and feel authorized to reproach you officially!

The Windows SDK defines a function that returns the name of the executable file that's registered to handle a given file type. Its name is FindExecutable(), and it's declared in shellapi.dll:

```
HINSTANCE FindExecutable(LPCTSTR lpFile, LPCTSTR lpDirectory, LPTSTR lpResult);
```

The prototype is quite self-explanatory. It accepts the name of the document, and a base directory if the name isn't fully qualified. If the file name is complete (specifies both drive and directory) then lpDirectory is redundant. The name of the file is returned through lpResult.

FindExecutable() searches the registry for the file extension provided, and returns the contents of the shell\open\command\default entry.

Flaws in FindExecutable()

There are a few points about this function that need clarification: FindExecutable() isn't perfect, and it suffers from at least one known bug. For a start, the documentation claims that the return value should be greater than 32 to denote success, but I have no idea of what it *really* means – is it an HINSTANCE (of what?), a DDE conversation ID (why does it need DDE?) or a just a random number (I hope not!). On Win32 platforms, I would have found a Boolean value far more reasonable.

The File Must Exist

FindExecutable() has a couple of other, more interesting, flaws. The first one regards the file name: even though this is not clearly pointed out in the documentation, the file name you're passing *must* exist. I suspect that this behavior is forced by backward compatibility; in my opinion, there's no reason for not retrieving the executable associated with a file name just because the file itself doesn't exist. The information you're seeking is only tied to the *extension* of that file name. If I want to know the name of the default browser, I should be able to call FindExecutable() and pass *.htm as the file name. To demonstrate that these are not far-fetched ideas, let me say that SHGetFileInfo() (which we examined in Chapter 4) lets you do just this.

Avoiding Spaces in Path Names

Last but not least, FindExecutable() has real problems with long file names that include spaces. There's an MSDN article (See *Further Reading*) about this with a few workarounds, and I suggest that you pay close attention. This is a definite bug in the code, and this time Microsoft appears to be fully aware of the problem.

When you ask FindExecutable() to retrieve a path name, it reads the registry and returns the string. The problem is that sometimes, these strings include command line arguments, but it's not easy for the function to determine where they begin. A good rule of thumb to follow is that you should enclose the file name in quotes, so that the function can assume everything after the last quote to be arguments:

```
Default = "c:\my Dir\theApp.exe" \n
```

If you don't do this, the chances are that the function will cut off a portion of the string while trying to locate possible command line arguments, because it will assume that the arguments begin after the first space. Thus, if the path name includes spaces, it will be truncated. For example, if the string to be retrieved is:

```
c:\My Dir\theapp.exe
```

Then what actually gets returned to you is:

```
c:\My
```

I have noticed that Internet Explorer (see above) registers its 8.3 name in the registry (under the `HKEY_CLASSES_ROOT\htmlfile\shell\command` key), rather than its long file name. Many other Microsoft programs do the same thing, and the problems with long file names when using `FindExecutable()` are the reason.

Using Long File Names without Rules

This bug has been known since December 1995, but nearly 3 years later it is still waiting for a fix. However, `FindExecutable()` is only partially responsible for problem – it simply inherits the complexity that derives from using long file names without rules. Let me emphasize again that if you enclose the path name in quotes, everything works perfectly.

The MSDN article that describes the bug (see *Further Reading* for references) points out that you can just replace the terminating `\0` of the string returned to you with a space (ASCII 32), and the string will then be fixed. Unfortunately, this is not quite true; let's see why.

Microsoft is right when it claims that replacing the null character that truncated the string with a space restores the string to its initial state. This occurs because the memory buffer hasn't actually been changed or set to zero. The function shown below should work fine:

```
HINSTANCE FindExecutableEx(LPCTSTR lpFile, LPCTSTR lpDirectory, LPTSTR lpResult)
{
    HINSTANCE hi = FindExecutable(lpFile, lpDirectory, lpResult);

    lpResult[lstrlen(lpesult)] = 32;      // 32 is the ASCII value of space

    return hi;
}
```

Or rather, it would do, if it weren't for a small problem. As a result of this modification, what you're returned is the string read from the registry. The trouble is that this is the string with the command line arguments that originated the problem! For example, suppose that the `shell\command` string is:

```
c:\My Dir\theapp.exe %1
```

Now suppose further that the file name for which you want the executable is `c:\myFile.xyz`. Normally, `FindExecutable()` would return:

```
c:\My
```

By applying the suggested workaround (by using `FindExecutableEx()`), the string returned becomes:

```
c:\My Dir\theapp.exe c:\myFile.xyz
```

Now it's up to you to extract the real file name! Remember that you can't rely on spaces to break the string into its component parts, because it might be one long file name with spaces everywhere, even in the extension.

A More Reliable Workaround for FindExecutable()

If you use the faithful old _splitpath() function to break a file name like the one above into its component parts, your directory item will be \My Dir\theapp.exe c:\

_splitpath() extracts whatever is between the first and the final backslash in the string you pass to it. If there's a file name as an argument, then there will always be a ':' in the extracted string. Thus, it suffices to truncate the string at that point and then split it again. Here's the code:

```
HINSTANCE FindExecutableEx(LPCTSTR lpFile, LPCTSTR lpDirectory, LPTSTR lpResult)
{
    // These _MAX constants defined in stdlib.h
    TCHAR drive[_MAX_DRIVE];
    TCHAR dir[_MAX_DIR];
    TCHAR dir1[_MAX_DIR];
    TCHAR file[_MAX_FNAME];
    TCHAR ext[_MAX_EXT];

    HINSTANCE hi = FindExecutable(lpFile, lpDirectory, lpResult);
    lpResult[lstrlen(lpResult)] = 32;

    _splitpath(lpResult, drive, dir, file, ext);

    // Search for : in the directory name, and truncate the string
    LPTSTR p = strchr(dir, ':');
    if(p != NULL)
    {
        --p;
        dir[p - dir] = 0;

        // Now split what remains again to get file and extension
        _splitpath(dir, NULL, dir1, file, ext);
        _makepath(lpResult, drive, dir1, file, ext);
    }

    return hi;
}
```

It works! Or rather, it works provided that there's nothing on the command line between the program name and the file. In other words, if the layout is like this, then you're OK:

```
c:\My Dir\theapp.exe %1 [whatever you want]
```

But if it's like this, you still have a problem:

```
c:\My Dir\theapp.exe [option list] %1
```

Unfortunately, this isn't an unusual choice, and I can't offer you a 100% safe solution – I'm not at all sure that a solution is even possible. If you've ever worked with long file names, you will know that when it comes to free parsing, they are really hard nuts to crack.

What happens is that the option list is automatically appended to the file extension, and unless it contains invalid long file name characters, an extension containing a space like .exe -p is perfectly acceptable. Moreover, _splitpath() and _makepath() just handle strings and don't check the components for long file name compatibility.

To cut a long story short, I think that truncating the file extension to the first space would be a good first approximation. In my experience, I've never seen a real-world use of spaces in file extensions. In conclusion, then, the final `FindExecutableEx()` function looks like this:

```
HINSTANCE FindExecutableEx(LPCTSTR lpFile, LPCTSTR lpDirectory, LPTSTR lpResult)
{
    ...

    // Search for : in the directory name, and truncate the string
    LPTSTR p = strchr(dir, ':');
    if(p != NULL)
    {
        --p;
        dir[p - dir] = 0;

        // Now split what remains again to get file and extension
        _splitpath(dir, NULL, dir1, file, ext);
        p = strchr(ext, 32);
        ext[p - ext] = 0;
        _makepath(lpResult, drive, dir1, file, ext);
    }

    return hi;
}
```

The `FindExecutable()` bug is a long story that began a few months after the release of Windows 95, and is still far from ending. The bug lives on in Windows 98!

You may be aware that shell versions 4.71 and later support a new library called `shlwapi.dll` *that's full of apparently useful functions for string and path name manipulation. You might be wondering whether such functions, with promising names like* `PathRemoveArgs()`, *could have helped here. Unfortunately, they don't – I tried them out, but they aren't smart enough to handle long file names successfully. (I'll cover* `shlwapi.dll` *in Chapter 10.)*

ShellExecute() Tips and Tricks

I mentioned earlier that `ShellExecute()` is a very useful function for performing operations on files and system objects. In addition to this, when used in conjunction with `FindExecutable()`, it can help you to perform some tricky tasks more quickly. Here's a collection of examples.

Detecting the Default Browser

To determine the default browser for a machine, you need to specify the name of an existing `.htm` file to `FindExecutable()`. A self-contained routine might create an empty file on the fly, call `FindExecutable()`, and then delete the file again:

```
void GetDefaultBrowser(LPTSTR szBrowserName)
{
    HFILE h = _lcreat("dummy.htm", 0);
    _lclose(h);

    FindExecutable("dummy.htm", NULL, szBrowserName);
    DeleteFile("dummy.htm");
}
```

Of course, to detect whether *your* default browser is Internet Explorer or Netscape Communicator, you can simply check the value of the Default entry in the HKEY_CLASSES_ROOT\.htm key. It will be htmlfile if the browser is Internet Explorer or NetscapeMarkup if the browser comes from Netscape. Each browser writes (and leaves) its own settings in a separate registry sub-tree. Then, just by changing the magic word in the .htm key, the default browser is switched.

Connecting to a URL

If you need to know the browser's name in order to connect to a remote URL, or to view a HTML file, then there's a quicker solution: ShellExecute().

```
ShellExecute(NULL, NULL, __TEXT("http://www.wrox.com"), NULL, NULL, SW_SHOW);
```

The function itself does the job of retrieving and launching the browser (if one is installed). When the file name is prefixed by http, ShellExecute() searches under HKEY_CLASSES_ROOT\ http\shell\open\command.

Sending e-mail Messages

To send e-mail messages programmatically, you have a number of choices: there are Collaborative Data Objects (CDO), the Messaging API, or you can rely on the services of other applications like Microsoft Outlook. I always envied the simplicity of this task in HTML pages, where you just need a link through the specialized mailto protocol:

```
<A href=mailto:desposito@infomedia.it>Dino Esposito</A>
```

Well, thanks to ShellExecute(), the same simplicity is available also to Windows programs:

```
ShellExecute(NULL, NULL, __TEXT("mailto:desposito@infomedia.it"),
                                          NULL, NULL, SW_SHOW);
```

Once more, the key is in the registry:

```
HKEY_CLASSES_ROOT
    \mailto
        \shell
            \open
                \command
```

http and mailto are examples of pluggable protocols – custom URL protocols built into an in-process COM server that guide the browser through the process of accessing the resource. With ShellExecute(), you can invoke resources through any registered protocol, even a custom protocol like res: or about:. (See *Further Reading*.)

Printing Documents

As long as a program that enables printing via the command line for certain kinds of documents exists, you can issue a command like this:

```
ShellExecute(NULL, __TEXT("print"), szDocName, NULL, NULL, SW_SHOW);
```

A common convention is to enable printing of a document by using the /p option on the command line, but it *is* just a convention – feel free to use any option you want to denote printing.

Finding Files and Folders

If you need to run the Find dialog, starting from a specific folder, it's as easy as calling:

```
ShellExecute(NULL, __TEXT("find"), szDirName, NULL, NULL, SW_SHOW);
```

If you specify NULL or the empty string as the folder name, the dialog will appear ready to work on drive C. If you pass a non-zero string that points to a non-existent folder, you'll get an error.

ShellExecute() vs. CreateProcess()

I have now said enough about ShellExecute() for us to be able to hazard a comparison with CreateProcess(). The point is not to determine which function is better (they are quite different, and both are very useful), but which function to use when it comes to creating a process.

The first thing to take into account is that internally, ShellExecute() calls CreateProcess(), and so ShellExecute() is necessarily a smaller and simpler-to-use wrapper for CreateProcess(). On the other hand, ShellExecute() is flexible enough to let you open and print documents, not to mention more specific verbs that are available to document classes.

Unless you need to create processes that exploit the advanced features CreateProcess() makes available (debug mode, priority, environment settings, startup information and the like), I recommend that you always choose ShellExecute(), which has a simpler syntax.

Why You Should Use ShellExecute() to Run Programs

Another argument that tilts the balance in favor of using ShellExecute() is a guideline from Microsoft that forms part of the current draft for the new Logo Requirements – that hefty tome you should depend upon when creating logo-compliant Microsoft Windows 98 and Windows NT applications.

Microsoft recommends that you use ShellExecute() to run external applications because it ensures that any restrictive policy adopted by the system administrator will be carefully checked. System policies allow administrators to decide which applications can or can't be started from Windows. ShellExecute() takes this blacklist into account, whereas CreateProcess() does not.

Policies

A **policy** is simply a collection of related settings that's normally saved in the system registry. One of the most interesting of these collections is called Shell Restrictions, which contains registry entries that let you control the functionality of the Start menu and Explorer.

One of the things you can do is to prevent the shell from displaying the Run or the Find item in the Start menu. In the same way, you can forbid the changing of settings through the Control Panel, or through the taskbar Properties dialog. Let's see how to set such things up.

The Shell Restrictions Policy

The registry key involved in the Shell Restrictions policy is:

```
HKEY_CURRENT_USER
    \Software
        \Microsoft

            \Windows
                \CurrentVersion
                    \Policies
                        \Explorer
```

To do what was outlined above, you need to create some new entries that don't exist by default, setting them to 0 or 1 as appropriate:

Entry	Description
NoRun	If the entry is set to 1, this hides the Run... command from the Start menu
NoFind	If 1, hides the Find command from the Start menu
NoSetFolders	If 1, hides all the standard Settings commands from the Start menu
NoSetTaskbar	If 1, hides the Taskbar Properties dialog

For the update to take place, all the entries must be DWORDs. When you remove commands in this way, the changes take place immediately, but the user interface isn't updated until next time you reboot the machine. If you try to use one of the commands during this period, you'll get a message box like this:

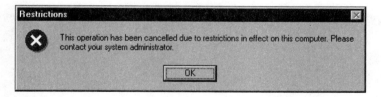

A good source of information about the registry keys to use for implementing policies may be found in the Platform SDK area of the MSDN Library. In particular, check out the Windows Logo and Programming Guidelines.

Extending ShellExecute()

Despite supporting policies, ShellExecute() has a significant drawback that can make using it difficult: it doesn't return, or let you know, the handle of the newly created process. This means that we can't, for example, spawn a program and wait for it to terminate before continuing execution. In other words, ShellExecute() suffers from its 16-bit origins that allow it to exploit only a subset of the new and more powerful features of CreateProcess() – the one that's also supported by WinExec().

However, a new function was introduced with shell version 4.0: ShellExecuteEx(). It has a compact prototype that is typical of many shell functions, supports many flags, and, above all, extends ShellExecute() by providing support for process synchronization and PIDLs.

ShellExecuteEx()

ShellExecuteEx() clearly supersedes ShellExecute(). It is declared in shellapi.h:

```
BOOL ShellExecuteEx(LPSHELLEXECUTEINFO lpExecInfo);
```

The SHELLEXECUTEINFO structure has the following layout:

```
typedef struct _SHELLEXECUTEINFO
{
    DWORD cbSize;
    ULONG fMask;
    HWND hwnd;
    LPCTSTR lpVerb;
    LPCTSTR lpFile;
    LPCTSTR lpParameters;
    LPCTSTR lpDirectory;
    int nShow;
    HINSTANCE hInstApp;

    // Optional members
    LPVOID lpIDList;
    LPCSTR lpClass;
    HKEY hkeyClass;
    DWORD dwHotKey;
    HANDLE hIcon;
    HANDLE hProcess;
} SHELLEXECUTEINFO, FAR *LPSHELLEXECUTEINFO;
```

Before using this structure, it's highly recommended that you fill it with zeros and set cbSize to the actual length, like this:

```
SHELLEXECUTEINFO sei;
ZeroMemory(&sei, sizeof(SHELLEXECUTEINFO));
sei.cbSize = sizeof(SHELLEXECUTEINFO);
```

As you can see from the comment inside the declaration, the members are divided into two groups. In practice, the first group makes ShellExecuteEx() functionally equivalent to ShellExecute(), while the collection of optional members makes it more powerful and justifies the 'Ex' suffix.

The hwnd, lpVerb, lpFile, lpParameters, lpDirectory and nShow members are identical in intention to the parameters for ShellExecute() that we have already seen. The hInstApp member, however, is an output buffer that will be filled with what was formerly the return value of ShellExecute().

The nShow member *always* denotes the style of the created window, even though the documentation says that it only specifies how the application is to be displayed if lpFile is an executable. Whether lpFile is an executable or a document file, nShow must always be assigned the SW_ constant that you require. Be aware that if you set it to 0, you'll have a hidden window.

Here's the simplest way to call `ShellExecuteEx()`:

```
SHELLEXECUTEINFO sei;
ZeroMemory(&sei, sizeof(SHELLEXECUTEINFO));
sei.cbSize = sizeof(SHELLEXECUTEINFO);
sei.lpFile = __TEXT("explorer.exe");
sei.nShow = SW_SHOW;
sei.lpVerb = __TEXT("open");
ShellExecuteEx(&sei);
```

The Optional Members

One of the members that doesn't have a corresponding entry in the parameter list of `ShellExecute()` is fMask. This can be a combination of one or more of the following values:

Flag	Description
SEE_MASK_CLASSKEY	The hkeyClass member should be used.
SEE_MASK_CLASSNAME	The lpClass member should be used.
SEE_MASK_CONNECTNETDRV	lpFile will be interpreted as a file name expressed in UNC (Universal Naming Convention) format.
SEE_MASK_DOENVSUBST	Any environment variables specified in the lpDirectory and lpFile members will be expanded. %WINDIR%, for example, opens the Windows folder.
SEE_MASK_FLAG_DDEWAIT	If the function starts a DDE conversation, wait for it to terminate before returning.
SEE_MASK_FLAG_NO_UI	Don't display a message box in the case of errors.
SEE_MASK_HOTKEY	The dwHotkey member should be used.
SEE_MASK_ICON	The hIcon member should be used.
SEE_MASK_IDLIST	Forces the function to use the contents of lpIDList instead of lpFile.
SEE_MASK_INVOKEIDLIST	Causes the function to use the PIDL specified in lpIDList. If the member is NULL, a PIDL to lpFile is created on the fly and used. This flag overrides SEE_MASK_IDLIST.
SEE_MASK_NOCLOSEPROCESS	Sets the hProcess member with the handle to the process.

The lpIDList member can contain a PIDL that will be used instead of lpFile. hProcess returns the HPROCESS handle of the new process spawned.

Additional Features

The optional fields serve to implement some additional functionality over ShellExecute(). First and foremost, you can use PIDLs to run applications and open folders. Here's the code to open the Printers folder:

```
LPITEMIDLIST pidl;
SHGetSpecialFolderLocation(NULL, CSIDL_PRINTERS, &pidl);
SHELLEXECUTEINFO sei;
ZeroMemory(&sei, sizeof(SHELLEXECUTEINFO));
sei.cbSize = sizeof(SHELLEXECUTEINFO);
sei.nShow = SW_SHOW;
sei.lpIDList = pidl;
sei.fMask = SEE_MASK_INVOKEIDLIST;
sei.lpVerb = __TEXT("open");
ShellExecuteEx(&sei);
```

If you also specify the SEE_MASK_DOENVSUBST flag, then you can use any environment variable in either lpFile or lpDirectory. To open the Windows directory, for example, you can just indicate %WINDIR%.

Lastly, we have the ability to synchronize an application launched by ShellExecuteEx()! Provided that you turn on the SEE_MASK_NOCLOSEPROCESS bit in the fMask member, you will be returned the handle of the new process via the hProcess member. That means the line:

```
WaitForSingleObject(sei.hProcess, INFINITE);
```

will cause the calling application to block while waiting for the other one to terminate.

Displaying a File's Properties Dialog

The SEE_MASK_INVOKEIDLIST flag is important because it gives ShellExecuteEx() another big advantage over ShellExecute(): it enables the function to invoke dynamic verbs as well as static ones. As I explained earlier, dynamic verbs are added at runtime by context menu shell extensions.

It works like this: if ShellExecuteEx() is unable to find the verb in the list of static verbs, it tries to locate the context menu for the given file. This search results in a pointer to the IContextMenu interface. The dynamic verb is then invoked through the functions exposed by the interface.

> *I'll deal with context menu and shell extensions later on, in Chapter 15. To discover how to get the handle of the context menu for a given file, see* Further Reading.

As a consequence of this, you can easily display the file's Properties dialog box – the same dialog that shows up when you right-click on a file and choose Properties. Here's a simple function that does just that:

```
void ShowFileProperties(LPCTSTR szPathName)
{
    SHELLEXECUTEINFO sei;
    ZeroMemory(&sei, sizeof(SHELLEXECUTEINFO));
    sei.cbSize = sizeof(SHELLEXECUTEINFO);
```

```
        sei.lpFile = szPathName;
        sei.nShow = SW_SHOW;
        sei.fMask = SEE_MASK_INVOKEIDLIST;
        sei.lpVerb = __TEXT("properties");
        ShellExecuteEx(&sei);
}
```

ShellExecuteEx() Return Values

The function returns a Boolean value that describes the success of the call: TRUE if successful, and FALSE in the case of failure. GetLastError() and the value returned in hInstApp can be used to gain more information about what has happened when something goes wrong.

Example: Program Executors

The screenshot below shows the interface of a simple demonstration program called Execute that allows you to test verbs. As usual, it's based on the skeleton for dialog-based applications generated by the Wrox AppWizard.

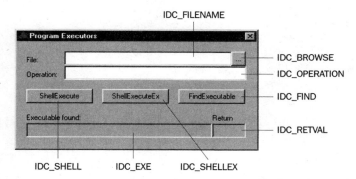

You can choose the file to test either by typing its name, or by browsing for it with the ... button. In the **Operation** edit box, you should write the name of the verb you want to execute on the file.

The first two buttons – **ShellExecute** and **ShellExecuteEx** – allow you to test the respective functions. The **FindExecutable** button, on the other hand, calls that function to return the name of the executable registered to open (always the verb open) the specified file. This name is then displayed in the **Executable found** edit box, while **Return** shows FindExecutable()'s return code.

Implementing the application's functionality is simply a matter of providing handlers for the four buttons on the dialog. OnBrowse() is the easiest, so let's start with that.

```
void OnBrowse(HWND hDlg)
{
    TCHAR szFile[MAX_PATH] = {0};
    TCHAR szWinDir[MAX_PATH] = {0};
    GetWindowsDirectory(szWinDir, MAX_PATH);

    OPENFILENAME ofn;
    ZeroMemory(&ofn, sizeof(OPENFILENAME));
```

```
    ofn.lStructSize = sizeof(OPENFILENAME);
    ofn.lpstrFilter = __TEXT("All files\0*.*\0");
    ofn.nMaxFile = MAX_PATH;
    ofn.lpstrInitialDir = szWinDir;
    ofn.lpstrFile = szFile;
    if(!GetOpenFileName(&ofn))
        return;
    else
        SetDlgItemText(hDlg, IDC_FILENAME, ofn.lpstrFile);
}
```

Next comes `OnShellExecute()`, while simply extracts the file name and the operation from the dialog, assembles a call to `ShellExecute()` itself, and displays the return value:

```
void OnShellExecute(HWND hDlg)
{
    TCHAR sFile[MAX_PATH] = {0};
    TCHAR sOp[MAX_PATH] = {0};
    TCHAR sRC[MAX_PATH] = {0};

    GetDlgItemText(hDlg, IDC_FILENAME, sFile, MAX_PATH);
    GetDlgItemText(hDlg, IDC_OPERATION, sOp, MAX_PATH);
    HINSTANCE h = ShellExecute(NULL, sOp, sFile, NULL, NULL, SW_SHOW);

    wsprintf(sRC, __TEXT("%ld"), h);
    SetDlgItemText(hDlg, IDC_RETVAL, sRC);
    return;
}
```

Thirdly, there's `OnShellExecuteEx()`, which does pretty much the same thing, but using a `SHELLEXECUTEINFO` structure:

```
void OnShellExecuteEx(HWND hDlg)
{
    TCHAR sFile[MAX_PATH] = {0};
    TCHAR sOp[MAX_PATH] = {0};
    TCHAR sRC[MAX_PATH] = {0};

    GetDlgItemText(hDlg, IDC_FILENAME, sFile, MAX_PATH);
    GetDlgItemText(hDlg, IDC_OPERATION, sOp, MAX_PATH);

    SHELLEXECUTEINFO sei;
    ZeroMemory(&sei, sizeof(SHELLEXECUTEINFO));
    sei.cbSize = sizeof(SHELLEXECUTEINFO);
    sei.lpFile = sFile;
    sei.nShow = SW_SHOW;
    sei.fMask = SEE_MASK_DOENVSUBST | SEE_MASK_INVOKEIDLIST;
    sei.lpVerb = sOp;
    DWORD rc = ShellExecuteEx(&sei);

    wsprintf(sRC, __TEXT("%ld"), rc);
    SetDlgItemText(hDlg, IDC_RETVAL, sRC);
    return;
}
```

Finally, `OnFindExec()` uses the `FindExecutableEx()` function that we put together earlier in the chapter to do its work:

```
void OnFindExec(HWND hDlg)
{
   TCHAR sFile[MAX_PATH] = {0};
   TCHAR sPrg[MAX_PATH] = {0};
   TCHAR sRC[MAX_PATH] = {0};

   GetDlgItemText(hDlg, IDC_FILENAME, sFile, MAX_PATH);
   HINSTANCE h = FindExecutableEx(sFile, NULL, sPrg);

   wsprintf(sRC, __TEXT("%ld"), h);
   SetDlgItemText(hDlg, IDC_RETVAL, sRC);
   SetDlgItemText(hDlg, IDC_EXE, sPrg);
   return;
}
```

Add `#includes` for `shlobj.h`, `commdlg.h` and `resource.h` to the top of your source file, make sure that you're linking to `comdlg32.h`, and you should be able to compile and link the application. The screenshot below shows it getting to grips with the **Properties** dialog of a GIF file:

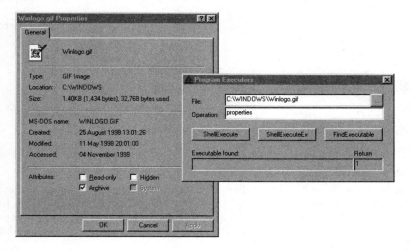

Multi-Monitor Support

To conclude our discussion of the `ShellExecute()` and `ShellExecuteEx()` functions, I want to say a few words about a cool feature that was new in Windows 98. I'm talking about **multi-monitor** support, which is the ability programmatically to span the output of programs across multiple monitors. Personally, I find the new Windows 98 function called `MonitorFromPoint()` amazing, although at the time of writing I've yet to meet a program who has really experimented with it.

What's the relationship between multi-monitor support and `ShellExecute()`? Well, the Windows 98 version of this function supports multiple monitors. This means, for instance, that any child process will be shown on the same monitor as the parent. However, this is only the default behavior. If you specify an `hwnd` parameter, then you can redirect the new window to the same monitor as the window that has that `hwnd` parameter.

Hooking on ShellExecute()

Have you ever heard of the IShellExecuteHook interface? As its name rather suggests, its logic follows the traditional Windows hook model, while the practical implementation requires you to write an in-process COM server. Methods of the interface are called from the code of both ShellExecute() and ShellExecuteEx() in order to let the user gain more control of the startup process. By using IShellExecuteHook, a module can parse (in a customized way) the command line that is being executed, and resolve it to the right program.

When using MS DOS, for example, we sometimes write small batch procedures with very short or easy-to-type names. In this way we can run a program, or perform a repetitive task, quickly and easily. Well, IShellExecuteHook gives us the ability to do roughly the same thing under Windows. A module implementing IShellExecuteHook is invoked whenever ShellExecute() or ShellExecuteEx() is about to execute a verb on a file, no matter what kind of file it is. The module is in the middle, and can do whatever suits it, such as:

- ❑ Trace (and log in a file) all the applications started through the shell
- ❑ Prevent unauthorized access to certain programs or folders
- ❑ Implement **named objects** – that is, keywords that map to a specific program or action

Implementing the IShellExecuteHook interface really is quick and easy. Unfortunately, there's no mention anywhere in the documentation of how to let the shell know that you've done so, and it's this point that I shall address in the next section.

Registering an IShellExecuteHook Handler

First and foremost, an IShellExecuteHook handler is a COM server, and must be registered properly under the following path:

```
HKEY_CLASSES_ROOT
    \CLSID
```

Of course, this is far from the end of the matter. The Windows shell must know that the handler exists, and where it is located. Since an IShellExecuteHook handler isn't very different from the Browser Helper Objects that I examined in Chapter 7, I guessed and hoped that the registration pattern was similar in this case, and I was right. Both helper objects and shell execute hooks must also be registered under:

```
HKEY_LOCAL_MACHINE
    \Software
        \Microsoft
            \Windows
                \CurrentVersion
                    \Explorer
```

Helpers go under a key named `Browser Helper Objects`, while hooks are located under `ShellExecuteHooks`:

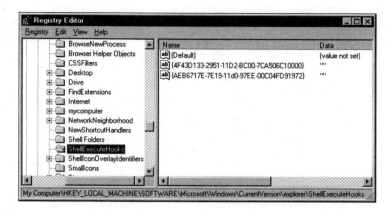

As shown in the figure, each key may contain a collection of strings that each evaluate to a CLSID. The shell just walks that list, and attempts to load the servers.

The IShellExecuteHook Interface

`IShellExecuteHook` is one of the simplest COM interfaces I've ever seen. It's composed of a single function called `Execute()`, which is declared as follows:

```
HRESULT Execute(LPSHELLEXECUTEINFO pei);
```

`SHELLEXECUTEINFO` is the same structure we met earlier when talking about `ShellExecuteEx()`. This function is invoked by the system just before a new application or document is opened through the shell interface. In other words, this hook gets involved when you run a new application, or you invoke a verb on a document in one of the following ways:

❑ Programmatically, through `ShellExecute()` or `ShellExecuteEx()`
❑ Through the Run dialog box
❑ Double-clicking from the Explorer

If you run another program through `CreateProcess()` or `WinExec()`, the hook module won't be notified. The same problem occurs if you run a program or open documents via a DOS box, or use any other low-level techniques.

Thanks to the structure passed as an argument, the `Execute()` method receives a verb, a file name, arguments, a directory and whatever else the user has passed to `ShellExecute()` or its sister function.

As mentioned earlier, both `ShellExecute()` *and* `ShellExecuteEx()` *end up calling* `CreateProcess()`. *However, they do much more than simply obtaining the command line and passing it to* `CreateProcess()`. *For a start, they handle policies and support this hook!*

Returning from the Hook

The hook will return S_FALSE if the shell can proceed as usual and create the required process. If no further processing is required, however – that is, the hook doesn't want the shell to start the process – then the hook will return a value of S_OK. This *may* happen because the hook checked some conditions and wants to prevent the currently logged user to run that program or document, but another possibility is that the hook code wants to run the document itself, giving (say) a non-standard priority to the thread. This requires that you arrange the call to CreateProcess() yourself. More importantly, if we return S_OK to the shell, we also need to set the hInstApp member of SHELLEXECUTEINFO properly.

"Setting the hInstApp member properly," means assigning it a value that denotes to the shell the success or failure (with a relevant error message) of our processing. If we run the application ourselves, then this will be the HINSTANCE of the new process. If we break the processing, then we can assign to it any value greater than 32 in order to prevent the shell from displaying an error message box.

As an example, suppose that we decide to block *any* new process:

```
HRESULT Execute(LPSHELLEXECUTEINFO lpsei)
{
   return S_OK
}
```

No matter what parameters we receive, we immediately return S_OK. In this case, the shell finds a value of 0 in the hInstApp member and interprets the return value as an error code. It then displays an appropriate message box for that error number. Here's a screenshot:

Writing an IShellExecuteHook Handler

When it comes to writing COM servers, the Active Template Library (ATL) is a great resource. Having run the ATL COM AppWizard to generate a skeleton COM server called Hook, we can add a new class to it by choosing Simple Object:

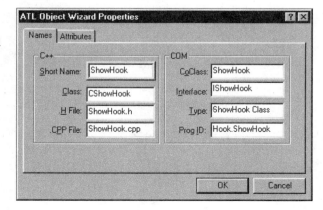

This new class, called CShowHook, should be derived from IShellExecuteHook. As already mentioned, this interface requires us to include shlobj.h. However, rather than deriving from IShellExecuteHook directly, we can define a generic implementation of the class, named (in the conventional ATL manner) IShellExecuteHookImpl:

```
// IShellExecuteHookImpl.h
//
/////////////////////////////////////////////////////////////////////
#include <AtlCom.h>
#include <ShlObj.h>
class ATL_NO_VTABLE IShellExecuteHookImpl : public IShellExecuteHook
{
public:

    // IUnknown
    STDMETHOD(QueryInterface)(REFIID riid, void** ppvObject) = 0;
    _ATL_DEBUG_ADDREF_RELEASE_IMPL(IShellExecuteHookImpl)

    // IShellExecuteHook
    STDMETHOD(Execute)(LPSHELLEXECUTEINFO lpsei)
    {
        return S_FALSE;
    }
};
```

The real CShowHook class is then declared like this:

```
#include "resource.h"
#include "comdef.h"
#include "IShellExecuteHookImpl.h"

/////////////////////////////////////////////////////////////////////
// CShowHook
class ATL_NO_VTABLE CShowHook :
    public CComObjectRootEx<CComSingleThreadModel>,
    public CComCoClass<CShowHook, &CLSID_ShowHook>,
    public IShellExecuteHookImpl,
    public IDispatchImpl<IShowHook, &IID_IShowHook, &LIBID_SHOWLib>
{
public:
    CShowHook()
    {
    }

    STDMETHOD(Execute)(LPSHELLEXECUTEINFO lpsei);

DECLARE_REGISTRY_RESOURCEID(IDR_SHOWHOOK)

DECLARE_PROTECT_FINAL_CONSTRUCT()

BEGIN_COM_MAP(CShowHook)
    COM_INTERFACE_ENTRY(IShowHook)
    COM_INTERFACE_ENTRY(IDispatch)
    COM_INTERFACE_ENTRY(IShellExecuteHook)
END_COM_MAP()

// IShowHook
public:
};
```

Now all that's missing is the implementation of the hook. Earlier, I outlined three possible applications of such hooks: tracing, authorization, and naming. Let's see the code necessary for all three of these.

```
HRESULT CShowHook::Execute(LPSHELLEXECUTEINFO lpsei)
{
    // Trace the program/file opened
    TCHAR szTime[50] = {0};
    GetTimeFormat(LOCALE_SYSTEM_DEFAULT, 0, NULL, NULL, szTime, 50);
    TCHAR szText[1024] = {0};
    wsprintf(szText, __TEXT("%s: %s  at %s"),
                                    lpsei->lpVerb, lpsei->lpFile, szTime);

    FILE *f;
    f = fopen(__TEXT("c:\\ShowHook.txt"), __TEXT("a+t"));
    fseek(f, 0, SEEK_END);
    fprintf(f, __TEXT("%s: %s  at %s\n\r"),
                                    lpsei->lpVerb, lpsei->lpFile, szTime);
    fclose(f);

    // Check the shortcuts list and run programs
    TCHAR szFileName[MAX_PATH] = {0};
    GetPrivateProfileString(__TEXT("GoldList"), lpsei->lpFile,
                    "", szFileName, MAX_PATH, __TEXT("c:\\showhook.ini"));
    if(lstrlen(szFileName))
    {
        lpsei->hInstApp =
                reinterpret_cast<HINSTANCE>(WinExec(szFileName, SW_SHOW));
        return S_OK;
    }

    // Prevent from doing anything if the name contains DEBUG
    strlwr(const_cast<LPTSTR>(lpsei->lpFile));
    if(strstr(lpsei->lpFile, __TEXT("debug")))
    {
        lpsei->hInstApp = reinterpret_cast<HINSTANCE>(42);
        return S_OK;
    }

    // Let it continue...
    return S_FALSE;
}
```

Editing the Registry Script

Before we analyze the code that's been added above, we need to do one more thing to make the server completely self-registering. This involves supplementing the registry script code that's provided by the Wizard, in order to add information specific to the shell execute hook.

Place this at the end of the file:

```
HKLM
{
   SOFTWARE
   {
      Microsoft
      {
         Windows
         {
            CurrentVersion
            {
               Explorer
               {
                   ShellExecuteHooks
                   {
                      val {4F43D133-2951-11D2-BC00-7CA506C10000} = s ''
                   }
               }
            }
         }
      }
   }
}
```

The hook is contained in `ShowHook.dll`, and registration of the *server* is mostly automatic, thanks to the Wizard code. What we've done here is to arrange that the hook's CLSID be correctly registered under the `ShellExecuteHooks` key.

How the Hook Works

Tracing is done by writing to disk the verb used, the name of the file acted upon, and the time of the call. The following picture shows the results. Notice that the log also includes traces of the activity during a reboot (`SysTray.exe`, for instance).

ShowHook.txt - Notepad

File Edit Search Help

```
open: C:\WINDOWS\EXPLORER.EXE  at 20.30.33
open: C:\WINDOWS\Application Data\Microsoft\Internet Explorer\Quick La
(null): regsvr32  at 20.31.06
(null): regsvr32  at 20.31.47
open: C:\WINDOWS\EXPLORER.EXE  at 20.31.54
Explore: E:\Book\SHELL\Text  at 20.31.59
Explore: E:\Book\SHELL\Text\Chap08  at 20.32.00
Explore: E:\Book\SHELL\Text\Chap08\Source  at 20.32.02
Explore: E:\Book\SHELL\Text\Chap08\Source\NewLink  at 20.32.03
Explore: E:\Book\SHELL\Text\Chap08\Source\Show  at 20.32.06
Explore: E:\Book\SHELL\Text\Chap08\Source\Show\Debug  at 20.32.07
(null): regsvr32  at 20.32.24
(null): C:\WINDOWS\SYSTEM\SysTray.Exe  at 20.35.20
(null): C:\WINDOWS\SYSTEM\Mgactrl.exe  at 20.35.20
(null): C:\Program Files\Matrox MGA PowerDesk\Color\Mgcctl95.exe  at 2
(null): C:\Programmi\WebSvr\Sistema\svctrl.exe  at 20.35.21
open: E:\UTILITY\EXPFOLD\Release\ExpFold.exe  at 20.35.21
open: D:\MsOffice\Office\FINDFAST.EXE  at 20.35.22
open: E:\Book\SHELL\Text\Chap08\Chapter 8.doc  at 20.35.37
open: C:\WINDOWS\Application Data\Microsoft\Internet Explorer\Quick La
open: D:\DevStudio\SharedIDE\bin\MSDEV.EXE  at 20.43.26
(null): D:\DEVSTU~1\SHARED~1\BIN\REGSVR32.EXE  at 20.48.45
```

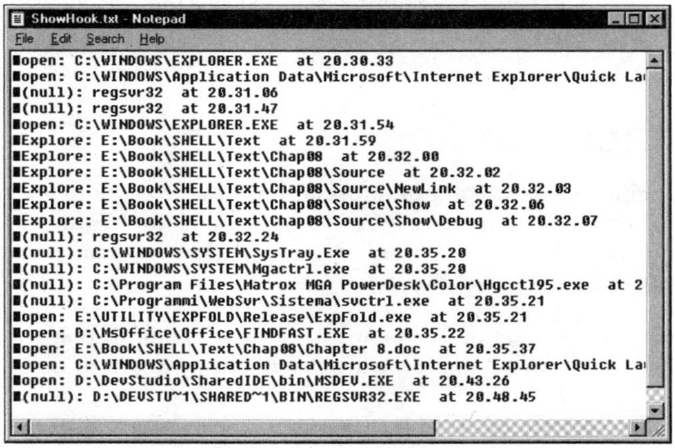

The code above also deals with naming – it attempts to recognize a list of key names, and then translate them into applications. The list is kept in a `.ini` file that's located in the root directory. Typical content of the file would be something like:

```
[GoldList]
reg=regedit.exe
tt=notepad.exe
AddNewHardware=control.exe sysdm.cpl,Add New Hardware
```

The words on the left are recognized by the hook and translated into the command lines on the right. This allows us to type AddNewHardware into the Run... box, for example, and the Wizard will start! I'll say more about the syntax for the Wizard in Chapter 11.

Finally, authorization is covered by the last part of the Execute() function, which prevents any folder or any file whose name contains the string "debug" from being opened. Note though that if we had forgotten to return a value greater than 32, we'd also have been presented with a nasty error message box. This is just a demonstration, but consider the fact that ShellExecute() is called very often throughout Explorer, and you should take great care over the size and duration of any custom code that you hook to it.

Summary

As usual, I've covered a lot of ground in this chapter and revealed several pitfalls along the way. I began with a discussion of WinExec(), moved on to CreateProcess(), and then dealt with ShellExecute(). After discussing the features and bugs of that function, I talked about FindExecutable(), which also has a few flaws.

Overall, ShellExecuteEx() seems to combine the silent power of CreateProcess() with the flexibility of ShellExecute(). Support for PIDLs and policies, and the possibility of hooking, makes ShellExecuteEx() my candidate for the title of "Best Windows Program Executor"!

As my argument developed, I covered:

- The features and bugs of ShellExecute() and FindExecutable()
- Why the Windows 98 Logo documentation recommends ShellExecute()/ShellExecuteEx() over CreateProcess()
- Where ShellExecuteEx() extends the functionality of ShellExecute()
- How to extend ShellExecuteEx() with hooking

Further Reading

A chapter with a wealth of information is the prelude to a wealth of further reading! If you want to know more about the new Logo Requirements for Windows 98 applications, you can check out the Platform SDK area of the MSDN Library. In particular, you might be interested in the Windows Programming Guidelines section.

For more information concerning the shell functions that we have examined in this chapter, here's a selection of Knowledge Base articles that may prove to be useful:

- **Article ID: Q94956:** *WinExec() Error Codes in Windows 3.0/3.1*
- **Article ID: Q67673:** *How to Determine When Another Application Has Finished*
- **Article ID: Q137572:** *How to Restart the Windows Shell Programmatically*
- **Article ID: Q145701:** *How to Close a Shelled Process When Finished under Windows 95*
- **Article ID: Q84456:** *TERMWAIT Spawns Task and Waits for its Termination*
- **Article ID: Q174156:** *Programmatically Launch the Default Internet Browser*
- **Article ID: Q140724:** *FindExecutable() Truncates Result at First Space in LFN*
- **Article ID: Q182807:** *Problems Using SEE_MASK_INVOKEIDLIST with ShellExecuteEx()*

If you're looking for an idea on how to write your own function to connect to the Internet, then you should take a look at Stuart Patterson's article *A GotoURL Function using ShellExecute()*, which appeared in the August 97 issue of WDJ.

If you're planning to experience the thrill of multi-monitor output, you would do well to begin by reading David Campbell's *How to exploit multi-monitor support in Memphis and Windows NT5.0*, MSJ, June 97.

Jeff Prosise explains how to get the context menu (and find out about the dynamic verbs of a file or a PIDL) in his *Wicked Code* column in the April 1997 issue of MSJ.

Finally, for the registry and policies, I recommend *Managing the Windows NT Registry*, by Paul Robichaux (O'Reilly). Despite the title, which implies that the book is specifically for NT, it turns out that the book is also relevant to Windows 9*x*. A quick and dirty example of policy management can also be found in an old article of mine, *Testing the Autoplay via the Floppy Drive* which appeared in WDJ, December 1996.

9

Icons and the Windows Taskbar

If you ask non-programming people to point out the best features of Windows, you can be sure that sooner or later they will mention the clarity of the icons as one of the most attractive aspects of the system. No matter that Windows 98 now supports esoteric things like the Universal Serial Bus and WDM (which looks more like the acronym of a new software conference than a common architecture for device drivers); icons still remain dear to people's hearts. You have to admit that Microsoft always gets the most out of its graphics people.

You need neither a passion for drawing nor an appreciation of fine art to realize that representing the simple (and not-so-simple) concepts that lie behind menu commands, using just a block of 32 x 32 pixels and 16 colors, is a great achievement. What I like most about Microsoft's icons is that even at the lowest resolution (16 x 16 pixels) they are clear and easily understood.

With the release of Windows 95, icons consolidated their already strong position in the Windows jigsaw. They multiplied too – this was the time when 16 x 16 and even 48 x 48 resolutions were introduced, with better support from the system for a larger number of colors. Icons that use 256 colors are now a common feature of many commercial products.

On a related theme, we should also consider the taskbar. It's certainly not the case that the taskbar is *only* concerned with icons, but it makes very good use of them, from program buttons, through the more recent quick-launch toolbars (introduced in shell version 4.71), to the tray area.

From the software writer's point of view, the best news from Microsoft has been the introduction of the `SHGetFileInfo()` function, the behavior of which we examined thoroughly in Chapter 4. Despite its name, this function is at its best when working with icons. Furthermore, with the introduction first of the Active Desktop and then Windows 98, a brand new interface has been introduced for working with the taskbar. The structure of the taskbar window (and of the desktop itself) has also altered considerably as a result of these changes.

In this chapter, I intend to:

❑ Provide an annotated overview of the functions you need to work with icons
❑ Demonstrate how to extract icons from modules
❑ Show the way to put and, above all, manage icons in the tray area
❑ Examine the new layout of the taskbar
❑ Explain the undocumented aspects of the new taskbar COM interfaces

Also in this chapter I'll write a function for browsing the icons contained in any executable file, and a piece of code that can automatically restart the shell and, more importantly, detect when the shell restarts. This latter point is directly related to a possible bug in the code of shell32.dll that manages tray icons.

What You Should Know About Icons

An icon can be used to identify any object that appears in the shell's namespace; it differs from a bitmap mainly due to the presence of a **bitmask**. When combined with the pixel layer, this mask gives the icon a kind of 'transparency' with respect to the underlying background. An icon can be a single resource or a group of related pictures that reproduce the same subject at different resolutions and color depths.

Throughout the Windows shell, icons are managed by the means of a COM interface called IExtractIcon, which we met in Chapter 5. IExtractIcon is implemented by the code that wraps namespace extensions, and for a file folder this code is in shell32.dll. However, you can provide your own IExtractIcon through a shell extension module in order that you may customize the shell's icons, and I'll show you how to do that in Chapter 15.

Windows provides a collection of standard icons that applications can load and use without the need to unload them again afterwards. These icons are identified by symbols with the prefix IDI_ that are defined in winuser.h – typical examples are IDI_ICONQUESTION and IDI_ICONSTOP, which you may have come across when using MessageBox().

When created or loaded, an icon is assigned a unique handle whose type is HICON. Many of the Win32 functions that work with icons require a handle of this kind. You have to release all the icons that you create or extract explicitly from your modules, but that is not the case for system icons like those mentioned above. Because they belong to the system, it frees them when it can.

Creating Icons

There are a variety of ways in which you can create icons. You can use an image editor and create a .ico file, or you can use a resource editor and compile icons in a .res file, together with the application's other resources. It's also possible to create icons programmatically, in which case the functions you might be interested in are:

❑ CreateIcon()
❑ CreateIconFromResource()
❑ CreateIconIndirect()

The best way to create icons from within the code of a program, however, is by means of one of the Windows 95 common controls: the **image list**.

Creating and Modifying Icons Programmatically

I showed you an example of how you could *modify* an existing icon programmatically by means of the image list control in Chapter 5. Specifically, I demonstrated how to combine two icons dynamically. The example produced the 'hand-held' folder icon that the system uses to denote that a given folder is shared.

Creating new icons is easy too. Broadly speaking, what you should do is put an icon or a bitmap into an image list control, and then read it back through `ImageList_GetIcon()`. For example, if you have an `HBITMAP`, then you can convert it to an icon with the following code:

```
HICON HBitmapToHIcon(HBITMAP hbm, int cx, int cy)
{
    HIMAGELIST himl = ImageList_Create(cx, cy, ILC_COLOR, 1, 1);
    int i = ImageList_Add(himl, hbm, NULL);
    HICON hIcon = ImageList_GetIcon(himl, i, ILD_NORMAL);
    ImageList_Destroy(himl);
    return hIcon;
}
```

This is a quite simple implementation; there are many other `ILC_` and `ILD_` flags that you could have exploited in the calls to `ImageList_Create()` and `ImageList_GetIcon()`, but I'll refer you to the MSDN Library documentation of these functions for further details. An application that obtains an icon this way must take care to free it when it is no longer needed.

Bitmaps and icons are much more alike than is commonly believed to be the case. You can extract a structure called `ICONINFO` from an `HICON` using the `GetIconInfo()` function:

```
BOOL GetIconInfo(HICON hIcon, PICONINFO piconinfo);
```

The structure renders an icon and is defined as follows:

```
typedef struct _ICONINFO
{
    BOOL    fIcon;        // TRUE if the structure refers to an icon
    DWORD   xHotspot;     // x-coordinate of the hotspot (See below)
    DWORD   yHotspot;     // y-coordinate of the hotspot (See below)
    HBITMAP hbmMask;      // Bitmask that makes the icon transparent
    HBITMAP hbmColor;     // Icon color bitmap
} ICONINFO;
```

As you can see, there are `HBITMAP`s inside any icon. `ICONINFO` serves a dual purpose: it is used to describe the internal structure of icons *and* cursors. The `fIcon` member distinguishes the actual type of the resource – it's `TRUE` for icons, and `FALSE` for cursors.

Don't be confused by the 'hotspot' member. Like cursors, icons have hotspots, but for the latter the hotspot is always at the center of its area. For cursors, the location of the hotspot may change. The most interesting parts of the structure, however, are the two `HBITMAP` members, because they mean that you have a system-provided means of converting an `HICON` to an `HBITMAP`. Here's a simple and direct wrapper:

```
HBITMAP HIconToHBitmap(HICON hIcon)
{
    ICONINFO ii;
    GetIconInfo(hIcon, &ii);
    return ii.hbmColor;
}
```

Drawing Icons

Despite the means available for creating icons programmatically, you will usually end up loading them from external files. There are several functions for doing this, but the most widely known are `LoadIcon()` and `LoadImage()`. I'll examine these and the others in a moment. Even when you're drawing icons, there are several methods you can use to place the icon on the screen. As usual, the best approach depends upon exactly what you need to do. The simplest solution is to call `DrawIcon()`:

```
BOOL DrawIcon(HDC hdc, int x, int y, HICON hIcon);
```

It's fast and easy to use, but it's not very flexible. Consider, though, that this function was introduced back when icons only existed at a resolution of 32 x 32, and in 16 colors. Now, there are so many types of icons that a simple function like this one just doesn't suffice. `DrawIcon()` *can* be used to draw small and large icons, provided that you hold a valid handle to them, but that's the limit of its versatility.

If you need to do more than `DrawIcon()` allows, a better approach is to use `ImageList_Draw()`. This function allows you to apply graphic filters, such as blending. The 'selected' or 'ghosted' icons that populate the Windows shell are realized with this technique.

Animated Icons

Animated icons have largely been superseded by animated GIFs and simple AVI files, but if you do come across a situation in which you need to use them, `DrawIconEx()` is the API function to employ. It also gives you the ability to stretch the icon to a desired size.

Extracting Icons from Files

You have a range of choices for extracting icons from files. You can use `ExtractIcon()` or `ExtractIconEx()`, as well as `ExtractAssociatedIcon()`, `LoadImage()` and `SHGetFileInfo()`. Let's compare and contrast these possibilities.

Function	Description
`ExtractIcon()`	Extracts a given icon from a file by specifying a zero-based index. The function always returns the large icon.
`ExtractIconEx()`	Works like `ExtractIcon()`, but can extract both large and small icons.

Function	Description
`ExtractAssociatedIcon()`	Returns the large icon associated with a given file or path
`SHGetFileInfo()`	Returns the large or small icons for a given file, path or PIDL, and can apply some graphic effects too, as described in Chapter 4.
`LoadImage()`	Extracts the icon from a given file at the desired resolution. This is the only way to get at, say, 48 x 48 icons.
`LoadIcon()`	Extracts the icon from the resources of a given executable file. The source file is identified by instance and not by name. The icon is identified by ID and not by index.

As you can see, in the descriptions I've differentiated between functions that *return* an icon, and functions that *extract* an icon. Members of the first group take the name of a file, folder or PIDL as input, and walk the registry for the default icon to load. They are `SHGetFileInfo()` and `ExtractAssociatedIcon()`. Functions in the second set want the name of a file (EXE, DLL, ICO, or similar) whose resources they will walk in order to find the specified icon, which is identified by a zero-based index.

The distinction between returning and extracting is essentially academic, since all the functions give you an `HICON` as a result, from slightly different input parameters. You decide to load and return or extract an icon depending on the information that you can give to the function.

`ExtractIcon()` requires a legacy `HINSTANCE` argument that its sister function `ExtractIconEx()` does not need. Consequently, the prototype of the latter seems more natural today:

```
HICON ExtractIcon(HINSTANCE hInst,
                  LPCTSTR    szFile,
                  UINT       nIconIndex);

UINT ExtractIconEx(LPCTSTR lpszFile,
                   int      nIconIndex,
                   HICON*   phiconLarge,
                   HICON*   phiconSmall,
                   UINT     nIcons);
```

As you can see, `ExtractIconEx()` allows you to get both large and small icons. Furthermore, it is also able to retrieve icons by their IDs. To do this, you should resort to a little trick and assign `nIconIndex` the *negative* value of the ID. For example, to get the icon with an ID of 1001 you need to pass −1001. Notice that this feature is a specific 32-bit enhancement, and isn't available for the 16-bit version of the function.

> *Of course, this technique won't work with icons that don't have a numeric ID. In those cases, you must refer to the icon by index.*

`ExtractAssociatedIcon()` is an earlier (and simpler) version of `SHGetFileInfo()`:

```
HICON ExtractAssociatedIcon(HINSTANCE hInst, LPTSTR lpIconPath, LPWORD lpiIcon);
```

This searches for the indexed icon in the specified file (or in its associated executable file) and always returns the large icon. The function checks whether `lpIconPath` addresses a file with embedded icons, and if successful extracts the icon indexed by `lpiIcon`. This is nearly identical to what `ExtractIconEx()` does. If `lpIconPath` doesn't contain icons, `ExtractAssociatedIcon()` attempts to locate the icon on a per-class basis. It figures out the type of the file by looking at the extension (BMP, DOC etc), and walks the registry for the default icon for *that* type.

```
WORD wID;
ExtractAssociatedIcon(hInst, __TEXT("c:\myfile.doc"), &wID);
```

The above code, for example, returns the icon associated with Word documents, provided that you have installed Microsoft Word. Interestingly, `lpiIcon` is an input/output parameter that will be set to the ID of the selected icon.

We carefully examined the features of `SHGetFileInfo()` in Chapter 4, but remember that it doesn't allow you to pick an icon from a file by number.

What About LoadImage() and LoadIcon()?

It's worth taking a moment to discuss `LoadImage()` and `LoadIcon()`. For years, the latter was the only way to access both application and system icons, and it has the advantage of a simple and easy-to-remember prototype:

```
HICON LoadIcon(HINSTANCE hInst, LPCTSTR szIconName);
```

Unfortunately, it doesn't allow you to load icons from an ICO file and requires the executable (DLL, EXE, OCX, DRV etc) to be loaded in memory to be able to extract icons. In fact, it locates the resources through an `HINSTANCE` handle. In this respect (and several others), `LoadImage()` is a great improvement. For example, it provides you with the ability to load an icon from a disk file, and at a size you request. If such an icon exists, it is loaded. Otherwise, the nearest icon is stretched to the required dimensions.

```
HICON hIcon = LoadImage(hInst, szIconName, IMAGE_ICON, 48, 48, LR_DEFAULTCOLOR);
```

The line of code above demonstrates how to load a 48 x 48 icon. Furthermore, the final parameter of `LoadImage()` can be used to apply filters to the icon's colors.

Loading System Icons

To load a system icon, such as the Windows logo or the question mark, you just need to pass `NULL` as the application instance:

```
HICON hIcon = LoadIcon(NULL, MAKEINTRESOURCE(IDI_WINLOGO));
```

You don't need to free this icon, because it belongs to the system and will be freed upon shutdown.

If you're not familiar with SDK programming, you should note that the `MAKEINTRESOURCE()` *macro serves the purpose of casting numeric IDs into strings, to fit the prototypes of the* `LoadXXX()` *functions that load resources.* `MAKEINTRESOURCE()` *is also used inside MFC code, but this is hidden from the programmer.*

The System's Image List

As long as the shell or your applications are using icons, the system caches them in order to provide quicker access and easier icon manipulation. This cache is implemented by means of an image list. You can get the handle to this through SHGetFileInfo() by specifying the SHGFI_SYSICONINDEX flag. If you want the list of small icons, just add the SHGFI_SMALLICON flag. (See Chapter 4 for details about this function.)

Which is the Best Way?

So, what's the best way to extract icons? In the light of my experience, I would recommend that you use ExtractIcon() if you just want to get icons from a file and provided that you don't need small icons. If you *do* need small icons, then you absolutely must use ExtractIconEx().

Going further up the chain, any time you need to know the icon that the shell has associated with a file object (a drive, a folder, a printer, an ordinary file, etc.), use SHGetFileInfo() instead.

LoadImage() is rather more complex than LoadIcon(), so I recommend that you resort to it only if you need an icon at a specified resolution, say 48 x 48.

> *This has been a fairly rapid overview of ground-level icon programming. If you need to get further into the details, you should refer to the MSDN Library.*

Assigning Icons to Dialog Boxes

If you're creating top-level windows, or more generally, if you can control the classes of your windows, then assigning icons is hardly an issue at all. You just have to set the appropriate member of the WNDCLASS structure, and make a call to RegisterClass(). If you want to handle small icons too, you should use WNDCLASSEX and RegisterClassEx() instead, but the idea is the same.

But what about dialog boxes? These have a system-defined class called WC_DIALOG (the value of this symbol is #32770), over which you have no control. Moreover, were you to change the icon assigned to this class, all the dialog boxes throughout the system would be affected. While this is not recommended because of the impact it may have on the whole system, you could change the icon of *all* dialogs by calling SetClassLong():

```
SetClassLong(hDlg, GCL_HICON, reinterpret_cast<LONG>(hIconNew));
```

The hDlg argument is a window handle that's used as an indirect reference to its class. In other words, the function changes the icon for the class to which the window belongs.

Fortunately, if you just want to change the icon of a single dialog, there are a couple of messages that allow you to do it: WM_SETICON and WM_GETICON. As the names suggest, the former lets you set the icon assigned to a particular dialog, while the latter reads the current HICON. You can call the following code at any time that suits your needs (but typically in response to the WM_INITDIALOG message):

```
SendMessage(hDlg, WM_SETICON, FALSE, reinterpret_cast<LPARAM>(g_hIconSmall));
SendMessage(hDlg, WM_SETICON, TRUE, reinterpret_cast<LPARAM>(g_hIconLarge));
```

The lParam argument of the message is the HICON, large or small. The wParam tells the system how to store and consider that icon – in practice, it denotes in which system image list the icon should be stored. It should be FALSE for small icons, and TRUE for large icons. Conversely, the following code shows how to *get* the icons (both large and small) *from* a dialog window:

```
HICON hIconSm = SendMessage(hDlg, WM_GETICON, ICON_SMALL, 0);
HICON hIconLg = SendMessage(hDlg, WM_GETICON, ICON_BIG, 0);
```

Browsing for Icons

The ability to browse for icons is a feature that could enrich many programs. Unfortunately, there's no documented way of generating a dialog like the one in this figure programmatically:

In case you're wondering, this dialog is the one that appears when you open the **Properties** dialog of a shortcut and click on <u>C</u>hange Icon…. The figure shows all the icons contained in Explorer.exe.

How hard would it be, then, to write a function (let's call it SHBrowseForIcon()) that works *like* the dialog in the picture? In fact, it's easier than it sounds, as I shall demonstrate in this Wrox AppWizard-based DLL project that I called SHHelper.

A SHBrowseForIcon() Function

I chose this prototype for the function and added it to SHHelper.h:

```
int SHBrowseForIcon(LPTSTR szFile, HICON* lphIcon);
```

SHBrowseForIcon() takes the name of the file to browse, and a pointer to a handle where the function will store the selected icon. On success, the function also returns the zero-based index of the icon you picked up; on failure, it returns -1.

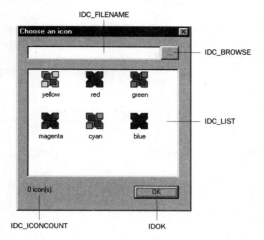

Of course, the function needs a dialog template, and the above screenshot shows what mine looks like – I gave it the identifier `IDD_BROWSEICON`. The behavior of `SHBrowseForIcon()` is intuitive, and can be summarized in the following steps:

- ❑ Create an image list to hold all the icons contained in the file
- ❑ Extract the icons and fill the image list
- ❑ Associate the image list with a list control, and fill the list control
- ❑ Get the currently selected icon, and go back to its index in the image list
- ❑ Extract the icon from the image list, and return

The code for the function looks like this:

```
int SHBrowseForIcon(LPTSTR szFile, HICON* lphIcon)
{
    // The function assumes default-sized icons (usually 32 x 32)
    int cx = GetSystemMetrics(SM_CXICON);
    int cy = GetSystemMetrics(SM_CYICON);

    lstrcpy(g_szFileName, szFile);
    g_himl = ImageList_Create(cx, cy, ILC_MASK, 1, 1);

    DialogBox(g_hThisDll,
              MAKEINTRESOURCE(IDD_BROWSEICON), GetFocus(), BrowseIconProc);

    // Free the image list
    ImageList_Destroy(g_himl);

    // Set the return values (the file might have changed)
    *lphIcon = g_hIcon;
    lstrcpy(szFile, g_szFileName);

    // This index has been set by the dialog procedure
    return g_iIconIndex;
}
```

Firstly, we create a global image list, specifying that we're interested in default-sized pictures (usually 32 x 32 pixels). Then, we display the dialog. Once the dialog is closed, we destroy the image list and set the return values – the selected icon (or NULL if the dialog has been canceled) and its index. In both cases, we make use of global variables that are set by the dialog's window procedure. Furthermore, since our dialog template provides a browsing button, the file from which the selected icon comes may not be the same as we get initially from the caller application. We return the file name too, using the same szFile buffer.

The code that follows comprises the dialog's window procedure, and some helper functions that it uses internally.

```
BOOL CALLBACK BrowseIconProc(HWND hDlg, UINT uiMsg, WPARAM wParam, LPARAM lParam)
{
    switch(uiMsg)
    {
    case WM_INITDIALOG:
        OnInitDialog(hDlg);
        break;

    case WM_COMMAND:
        switch(wParam)
        {
        case IDC_BROWSE:
            OnBrowse(hDlg);
            break;

        case IDCANCEL:
            EndDialog(hDlg, FALSE);
            return FALSE;

        case IDOK:
            DoGetIcon(hDlg);
            EndDialog(hDlg, TRUE);
            return FALSE;
        }
    }

    return FALSE;
}
```

```
void OnInitDialog(HWND hDlg)
{
    HWND hwndList = GetDlgItem(hDlg, IDC_LIST);
    SetDlgItemText(hDlg, IDC_FILENAME, g_szFileName);

    ListView_SetImageList(hwndList, g_himl, LVSIL_NORMAL);
    DoLoadIcons(hDlg, g_szFileName);
}
```

```
void OnBrowse(HWND hDlg)
{
    TCHAR szWinDir[MAX_PATH] = {0};
    TCHAR szFile[MAX_PATH] = {0};

    // Browse for files...
    OPENFILENAME ofn;
    ZeroMemory(&ofn, sizeof(OPENFILENAME));
    ofn.lStructSize = sizeof(OPENFILENAME);
```

```
    ofn.lpstrFilter = __TEXT("Icons\0*.exe;*.dll;*.ico\0");
    ofn.nMaxFile = MAX_PATH;
    GetWindowsDirectory(szWinDir, MAX_PATH);
    ofn.lpstrInitialDir = szWinDir;
    ofn.lpstrFile = szFile;
    if(!GetOpenFileName(&ofn))
        return;

    SetDlgItemText(hDlg, IDC_FILENAME, ofn.lpstrFile);
    DoLoadIcons(hDlg, ofn.lpstrFile);
    lstrcpy(g_szFileName, ofn.lpstrFile);
}
```

The heart of `SHBrowseForIcon()` lies in the `DoLoadIcons()` and `DoGetIcon()` functions. They extract the icons for filling the list control and get the selected icon when the user clicks the OK button respectively.

```
int DoLoadIcons(HWND hDlg, LPTSTR szFileName)
{
    TCHAR szStatus[30] = {0};

    // Get the number of icons
    int iNumOfIcons = reinterpret_cast<int>(
                              ExtractIcon(g_hThisDll, szFileName, -1));

    // Update user interface
    HWND hwndList = GetDlgItem(hDlg, IDC_LIST);
    ListView_DeleteAllItems(hwndList);
    wsprintf(szStatus, __TEXT("%d icon(s) found."), iNumOfIcons);
    SetDlgItemText(hDlg, IDC_ICONCOUNT, szStatus);

    // Fill the image list and the list view at the same time
    for(int i = 0 ; i < iNumOfIcons ; i++)
    {
        HICON hIcon = ExtractIcon(g_hThisDll, szFileName, i);
        int iIndex = ImageList_AddIcon(g_himl, hIcon);

        // Add to the list view
        LV_ITEM lvi;
        ZeroMemory(&lvi, sizeof(LV_ITEM));
        lvi.mask = LVIF_IMAGE;
        lvi.iItem = iIndex;
        lvi.iImage = iIndex;
        ListView_InsertItem(hwndList, &lvi);
    }

    return iNumOfIcons;
}
```

```
void DoGetIcon(HWND hDlg)
{
    HWND hwndList = GetDlgItem(hDlg, IDC_LIST);

    // Get the index of the list view's selected item
    g_iIconIndex = -1;
    int i = ListView_GetNextItem(hwndList, -1, LVNI_SELECTED);
    if(i == -1)
        return;
```

265

```
        g_iIconIndex = i;

        // Get information about the selected item
        LV_ITEM lvi;
        ZeroMemory(&lvi, sizeof(LV_ITEM));
        lvi.mask = LVIF_IMAGE;
        lvi.iItem = i;
        ListView_GetItem(hwndList, &lvi);

        // Get the image list index of the icon and return the HICON
        g_hIcon = ImageList_GetIcon(g_himl, lvi.iImage, 0);
    }
```

A quick (and bitter!) note about list views: I just don't understand the reason why they have such a quirky and bewildering programming interface – I'm referring in particular to the algorithm required to get the selected item. Of course, if you don't know the solution already (or who to ask!), the chances are that you'll resort to... owner-drawn list boxes.

Once we know the index of the selected list view item, we *could* avoid passing through the list view and the image list to get the HICON – we could re-call ExtractIcon() with the current filename and icon index instead. I chose the approach you see here in the belief that it is more efficient because we won't have to access a disk file again. If the system itself is dynamically maintaining an image list, we can reasonably hope that it is the best solution.

To compile and make the DLL usable, you now need to add an entry for SHBrowseForIcon() to the DEF file, and to complete the header and library file lists. The header files required for this project are shlobj.h, resource.h, commdlg.h and shellapi.h, while the libraries you need to link to are comctl32.lib and comdlg32.lib.

How to Call SHBrowseForIcon()

I shall use SHBrowseForIcon() in a real world example in Chapter 11, but to conclude this section, let's have a quick look at how an external application might call it:

```
int iIconIndex = SHBrowseForIcon(szFileName, &hIcon);
if(iIconIndex >= 0)
{
    ...
}
```

The Tray Notification Area

The **tray notification area** (TNA) is a window of class
`TrayNotifyWnd` that lies at the right hand edge of the taskbar
(when the taskbar is placed horizontally).

By default, the system places a child window containing the clock (class `TrayClockWClass`) in the
TNA. Some of the icons that appear by default in your TNA are set during system startup by a
program called `systray.exe`, which may add icons depending upon your hardware. Typically, it
adds an icon if you have a sound card, or the machine is a laptop. If you want your own icons to
appear in the TNA at startup, you have to write your own program to manage the TNA and place it
in the `Startup` folder.

> *We met the TNA briefly in Chapter 7, when we discussed a tool to create folders through Explorer by
> hitting a key. Here we'll delve deep into the details of how to manage icons in the TNA.*

Of course, there's a function to add or remove icons in the tray area programmatically; its name is
`Shell_NotifyIcon()`. An icon placed in the tray area can have an ID, tooltip text, a context menu
and a window with which to communicate and notify it of mouse events. You probably won't be
surprised to discover that we'll run into a couple of nasty bugs too.

Putting Icons in the Tray Notification Area

The `Shell_NotifyIcon()` function has the following prototype:

```
BOOL WINAPI Shell_NotifyIcon(DWORD dwMessage, PNOTIFYICONDATA pnid);
```

NOTIFYICONDATA is a structure that gathers all the data we want to use to configure the icon in the
tray notification area. The `dwMessage` parameter specifies the action we want to accomplish:

Action	Description
NIM_ADD	Add a new icon to the tray area
NIM_DELETE	Remove an existing icon from the tray area
NIM_MODIFY	Modify an existing icon in the tray area

Each icon is fully described by the following structure:

```
typedef struct _NOTIFYICONDATA
{
    DWORD cbSize;
    HWND  hWnd;
    UINT  uID;
    UINT  uFlags;
    UINT  uCallbackMessage;
    HICON hIcon;
    char  szTip[64];
} NOTIFYICONDATA, *PNOTIFYICONDATA;
```

267

Member	Description
cbSize	Must contain the size of structure.
hWnd	The handle of the window that will receive notification messages from the icon.
uID	The icon identifier – that is, a user-defined value that allows the caller application to identify the icon uniquely.
uFlags	Specifies what combination of the following members is used by the function: uCallbackMessage, hIcon and szTip, represented by the flags NIF_MESSAGE, NIF_ICON and NIF_TIP respectively. If you're using any of these members, remember to turn on the corresponding flag.
uCallbackMessage	ID of the message the icon will use to communicate with the hWnd window. Requires NIF_MESSAGE to be set in uFlags.
hIcon	Handle of the icon to be shown. It should be a small icon (16 x 16), but the system will automatically apply stretching, if needed. Requires NIF_ICON to be set in uFlags.
szTip	Text of up to 64 bytes in length for the icon's tooltip. Requires NIF_TIP to be set in uFlags.

With this knowledge, putting an icon in the tray notification area is a fairly simple task that you can accomplish like this:

```
NOTIFYICONDATA nid;
ZeroMemory(&nid, sizeof(NOTIFYICONDATA));
nid.cbSize = sizeof(NOTIFYICONDATA);
nid.hWnd = hWnd;
nid.uID = ICON_ID;
nid.uFlags = NIF_TIP | NIF_ICON | NIF_MESSAGE;
nid.uCallbackMessage = WM_MYMESSAGE;
nid.hIcon = hSmallIcon;
lstrcpyn(nid.szTip, __TEXT("This icon's been added by me!"), 64);
Shell_NotifyIcon(NIF_ADD, &nid);
```

Deleting an icon is much simpler, since you don't have to set any members other than uID and cbSize. You can modify any of the previously set arguments at any time in order to reflect changes in your applications. In this case, you would use NIM_MODIFY instead of NIM_ADD when calling Shell_NotifyIcon().

Outlook Express, for example, uses NIF_MODIFY to show a little animation when sending or receiving data. Similarly, the envelope icon that shows up when you have new unread e-mail is added using a NIM_ADD message, and then removed through NIM_DELETE.

Notifying Mouse Events

When discussing tray icons, an incorrect (but commonly accepted and understood) expression that you'll hear is, "The icon notifies the window of all the mouse events." In fact, all that's wrong is the subject of this sentence; we should say, "The TrayNotifyWnd window notifies the specified window of all the mouse-related events." The actual icons are drawn in the client area of the TrayNotifyWnd window. The size of this window changes according to the number of icons it contains, and the screen edge where the taskbar is docked.

If the TrayNotifyWnd window detects that the mouse is doing something that affects one of its icons, then it lets the window associated with the icon (the hWnd member of the NOTIFYICONDATA structure) know about it. In practice, when the mouse is moved, clicked or right-clicked over the bounding rectangle of the icon, the messages produced by the system are forwarded to the window.

Referring to the sample above, the message sent has the following form:

```
SendMessage(nid.hWnd, nid.uCallbackMessage, nid.uID, lParam);
```

The wParam argument of SendMessage() is the identifier of the icon on which the event originated, while lParam is the message code: WM_RBUTTONUP, WM_LBUTTONUP, WM_MOUSEMOVE and so on. Note that because of this, no information related to the original message (the mouse position, for example) is forwarded to the application's window. Here's how a window could handle the notifications it gets from a tray icon:

```
case WM_MYMESSAGE:
    if(wParam == ICON_ID)
    {
        switch(lParam)
        {
        case WM_RBUTTONUP:
            ShowContextMenu();
            break;
        case WM_LBUTTONUP:
            DoMainAction();
            break;
        }
    }
```

Normally, the window associated with a tray icon will do two things:

- ❑ Display a context menu in response to a right-click on the icon
- ❑ Execute a primary action when the user clicks on the icon. In most cases, this means displaying a dialog box

Conversely, the window has *nothing* to do in order to display the tooltip. Tooltips are handled transparently by the TrayNotifyWnd window.

Writing Tray Applications

A tray-based application has a slightly different layout from any other Windows program. It should still have a main window, but in most cases this is invisible. This window will receive and process events in the background, and possibly be displayed only after the user clicks or double-clicks the icon.

There's no rule that prevents an application from having a visible main window as well as a tray icon. However, you should use a tray icon as an indication to the user that your program is up and running behind the scenes – this is particularly applicable to programs that don't require a great deal of interaction with the user. The idea is that when necessary, you click on the tray icon and the user interface pops up for you to work with.

Tray applications might be seen as the Windows equivalent of the old MS-DOS TSR (Terminate and Stay Resident) programs. If you haven't had the pleasure of dealing with MS DOS programming, TSRs were applications that were idle from loading until you pressed a particular key combination. They then awoke and a dialog popped up.

Over the next few pages, I'll outline the basic code necessary for a simple tray application. In the `WinMain()` function, we first load the small icon to put into the tray area and then create the dialog to receive messages. Once we've set the icon (a task accomplished by `TrayIcon()`), we enter the loop that keeps our program alive and running. When we exit that loop, it's time to free the icon and terminate the application.

```
int WINAPI WinMain(HINSTANCE hInstance, HINSTANCE hPrevInstance,
                   LPSTR lpCmdLine, int nCmdShow)
{
    // Copy the instance handle to a global
    g_hInstance = hInstance;

    // Load the 16x16 icon to go into the tray
    HICON hSmallIcon = reinterpret_cast<HICON>(LoadImage(hInstance,
                         __TEXT("APP_ICON"), IMAGE_ICON, 16, 16, 0));

    // Create an invisible dialog to get messages from the icon
    HWND hDlg = CreateDialog(hInstance, __TEXT("DLG_MAIN"), NULL, APP_DlgProc);

    // Show the icon
    TrayIcon(hDlg, hSmallIcon, NIM_ADD);

    // Enter the loop to keep this program running
    MSG msg;
    while(GetMessage(&msg, NULL, 0, 0))
    {
        if(!IsDialogMessage(hDlg, &msg))
        {
            TranslateMessage(&msg);
            DispatchMessage(&msg);
        }
    }

    // Remove the icon and exit
    TrayIcon(hDlg, hSmallIcon, NIM_DELETE);
    DestroyWindow(hDlg);
    DestroyIcon(hSmallIcon);
    return 1;
}
```

What's different from a traditional Windows program? The answer is that you don't make the main window visible, and instead have to deal with the tray area. The next function shows how to do this. The value set in the `uFlags` field means that we wish to support a callback message, an icon and a tooltip.

The callback message is a user-defined message to be declared as an offset of `WM_APP`:

```
const int WM_EX_MESSAGE = (WM_APP + 1);
```

```
BOOL TrayIcon(HWND hWnd, HICON hIcon, DWORD msg)
{
   NOTIFYICONDATA nid;
   ZeroMemory(&nid, sizeof(NOTIFYICONDATA));
   nid.cbSize = sizeof(NOTIFYICONDATA);
   nid.hWnd = hWnd;
   nid.uID = ICON_ID;
   nid.uFlags = NIF_TIP | NIF_ICON | NIF_MESSAGE;
   nid.uCallbackMessage = WM_EX_MESSAGE;
   nid.hIcon = hIcon;
   lstrcpyn(nid.szTip, __TEXT("This icon's been added by me!"), 64);

   // Perform the specified operation on the icon
   return Shell_NotifyIcon(msg, &nid);
}
```

A typical example of a tray application is the Volume Control that's present on almost all Windows systems. When you click on the icon, the configuration dialog appears:

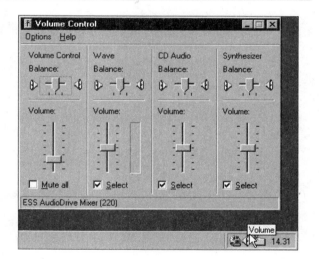

Pay Attention to the Context Menu

A common feature of tray applications is the context menu that appears after you right click on the icon. The following is a typical window procedure for the hidden window of a tray program.

```
BOOL CALLBACK APP_DlgProc(HWND hDlg, UINT uiMsg, WPARAM wParam, LPARAM lParam)
{
   switch(uiMsg)
   {
   case WM_COMMAND:
      switch(LOWORD(wParam))
      {
      case IDCANCEL:
         PostQuitMessage(0);
         return FALSE;
      }
      break;
```

```
    case WM_EX_MESSAGE:
        if(wParam == ICON_ID)
        {
            switch(lParam)
            {
            case WM_RBUTTONUP:
                ContextMenu(hDlg);
                break;
            }
        }
        break;
    }
    return FALSE;
}
```

When the specified message is received and the icon involved has been verified (this is important because the same application might add more icons), you can display a context menu. The context menu is managed entirely by the window associated with the icon and is not a feature of the system tray.

Displaying a context menu is not a problem; here's some vanilla code to do it:

```
void ContextMenu(HWND hwnd)
{
    HMENU hmenu = LoadMenu(g_hInstance, MAKEINTRESOURCE(IDR_MENU));
    HMENU hmnuPopup = GetSubMenu(hmenu, 0);
    SetMenuDefaultItem(hmnuPopup, IDOK, FALSE);

    POINT pt;
    GetCursorPos(&pt);
    TrackPopupMenu(hmnuPopup, TPM_LEFTALIGN, pt.x, pt.y, 0, hwnd, NULL);

    DestroyMenu(hmnuPopup);
    DestroyMenu(hmenu);
}
```

The code loads a menu from the application's resources, extracts the first popup menu and declares one default item to be drawn in bold with the call to `SetMenuDefaultItem()`.

When you right click on the icon, the context menu appears, as you would expect it to. Great! However, for this first run, you don't want to test any of the menu commands, so click outside the menu to cause it to disappear. You will find that the menu stubbornly remains in place, but disappears as soon as you move the mouse over its area. In other cases, you'll end up with a menu that hides nervously behind the taskbar:

This is a known bug (see *Further Reading*), but you can solve it by enclosing calls to `TrackPopupMenu()` or `TrackPopupMenuEx()` between a pair of calls to `SetForegroundWindow()`:

```
void ContextMenu(HWND hwnd)
{
    HMENU hmenu = LoadMenu(g_hInstance, MAKEINTRESOURCE(IDR_MENU));
    HMENU hmnuPopup = GetSubMenu(hmenu, 0);
    SetMenuDefaultItem(hmnuPopup, IDOK, FALSE);

    POINT pt;
    GetCursorPos(&pt);
    SetForegroundWindow(hwnd);
    TrackPopupMenu(hmnuPopup, TPM_LEFTALIGN, pt.x, pt.y, 0, hwnd, NULL);
    SetForegroundWindow(hwnd);

    DestroyMenu(hmnuPopup);
    DestroyMenu(hmenu);
}
```

This ensures that all the input gets redirected to our window, which can then dismiss the menu. The bug is in the code of the `TrayNotifyWnd` window, not in `TrackPopupMenu()` or our application.

How Many Icons are in the Tray Notification Area?

I'm not sure whether it would ever become an issue, but there's no documented way to discover programmatically how many icons are stored in the tray notification area. If it becomes important in your application, then you could try to get a result by examining the size of the `TrayNotifyWnd` window. This is not simple, though, because you have to take into account the different edges where the taskbar can be docked, and whether the clock is being shown. If the taskbar is vertically aligned then the icons are usually displayed below the clock, but if the taskbar is wide enough they will be drawn next to it. Furthermore, the icons can sometimes be drawn in a single column. You get the picture: the number of different possibilities is large, and overall it's a real mess.

Detecting When the Shell Restarts

If for any reason the shell is restarted, the icons in the tray notification area *aren't* restored. This is clearly due to a bug in shell code and, depending on how many icons you have in the tray, it might be rather bothersome. However, restarting the shell is not an operation we expect to do frequently. In my experience there are a couple of circumstances where it may be necessary: to recover an Explorer crash (a GPF), or to obtain a brand new instance of it during the test of a shell extension. In the former case, it's the system that recreates a new instance of the shell objects. In the latter case it's entirely down to us. We can do it either programmatically or manually.

If we need to restart the shell programmatically, we can employ the following (surprisingly simple) code:

```
void SHShellRestart()
{
    HWND hwnd = FindWindow(__TEXT("Progman"), NULL);
    PostMessage(hwnd, WM_QUIT, 0, 0);
    ShellExecute(NULL, NULL, __TEXT("explorer.exe"), NULL, NULL, SW_SHOW);
}
```

We first quit the shell's main window, and then run it again. When you launch `explorer.exe` it first verifies whether or not there's another running instance. If not, it creates the taskbar and initializes the Windows shell, otherwise it simply pops up the traditional browser.

Under Windows NT, the taskbar is created each time `explorer.exe` *is launched in an empty desktop. Even in Windows NT jargon, a desktop is exactly what you think it is: the on-screen work area with menus, icons, windows, hooks and running programs. What's different is that Windows NT lets you create multiple desktops and have them working at the same time.*

However, only one such desktop is visible to the user at a time. The screensaver, for example, runs in a separate desktop from the rest of your active programs. You can use API functions to create new desktops and switch among them – `CreateDesktop()` *and* `SwitchDesktop()` *are two of these. Windows 9x supports just one desktop.*

Is there a way to detect when the shell restarts? If so, an application that relies heavily on tray icons could restore them programmatically, simply by re-executing a piece of code. Happily, the Internet Client SDK provides the answer: each time the shell restarts and recreates the taskbar, it registers and broadcasts a message called `TaskbarCreated`.

Any application that is listening for this message, therefore, can restore its icons or do whatever else it may need to do in response to the shell restarting. The code required is straightforward: the program must register the same message, and store the value returned when it does so. This value is guaranteed to be valid and unique throughout the system and the session.

```
UINT g_uShellRestart;
g_uShellRestart = RegisterWindowMessage(__TEXT("TaskbarCreated"));
```

When you register a message that's already been registered by another module, you're actually returned the value assigned. In this way both modules know the message and can communicate through it.

A good time to do this registration is during the initialization of your application. Any action in response to the shell restarting must then be coded in the window procedure:

```
if(uiMsg == g_uShellRestart)
{
   ...
}
```

Note that this feature is only available with shell version 4.71 or higher. In my opinion, the presence of the `TaskbarCreated` message is an indirect confirmation (because a workaround is provided) of the bug that causes the tray icons to disappear on shell restarts that I mentioned earlier.

Restarting the Windows Shell

Earlier in this section, I demonstrated a simple function that you could call from your programs in order to restart the Windows shell. However it's also possible to do this 'manually' with the following steps:

- ❑ Press *Ctrl-Alt-Del*.
- ❑ Select Explorer from the Task Manager and kill it
- ❑ When the typical shutdown window appears, cancel the operation
- ❑ A few seconds later, the system will warn you that Explorer is not responding – kill the task
- ❑ A few more seconds, and finally the shell restarts with a brand new taskbar

Knowing how to restart the shell (manually or programmatically) becomes an important issue when it comes to developing shell extensions, because sometimes it's the only way to unload such a module and make it possible to recompile it during the edit/compile/debug cycle.

The Layout of the Taskbar

As I pointed out in Chapter 2, the layout of the taskbar changed with the advent of shell version 4.71. The main window is still `Shell_TrayWnd`, and it still has the Start button and the `TrayNotifyWnd` as child windows, but the difference is that the tab control window that shows the active tasks is contained in a **coolbar** window. This window shares the available space with a number of toolbar windows.

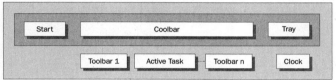

The new layout is presented in the above diagram. The toolbars 1 to n may be added to the coolbar using the taskbar's context menu, which you can obtain by right-clicking on the taskbar.

When a Window Goes in the Taskbar

The Windows taskbar is actually a tab control with a special `TCS_BUTTONS` style that gives each page a button-like look. What you see in the taskbar aren't buttons at all, but just tabs of a `SysTabControl32` window. (`SysTabControl32` is the official class name for a tab control.) To be absolutely precise, this is *not* directly owned by the taskbar – there's an `MSTaskSwWClass` window in the middle. This information can easily be verified through Spy++.

By default, the tabs of a tab control have no content – it's up to your code to fill them. The control itself is limited to notifying selection changes to its parent. In the case of the taskbar, the tabs display the icons and captions of some top-level windows.

What appears on the taskbar is not a list of *all* the processes running at a certain moment in time. To get this information, you should not rely on the taskbar, or on the Windows 95 Task Manager. Instead, you should resort to specialized tools like the Process Viewer that comes with Visual C++. In Chapter 15 I'll create a shell extension that uses the same logic as the Process Viewer to enumerate processes.

Not all processes have a window that goes in the taskbar, or put another way, not all windows are *eligible* to go in the taskbar. The taskbar only accepts:

- ❑ Ownerless, visible windows
- ❑ Owned, visible windows with the `WS_EX_APPWINDOW` extended style

The taskbar always rejects:

- ❑ Invisible windows
- ❑ Owned, visible windows with the `WS_EX_TOOLWINDOW` extended style
- ❑ Visible windows owned by an invisible window

Toggling the Visibility of the Taskbar

In Visual Basic, forms can have the `ShowInTaskbar` attribute. If you put Spy++ to work on a Visual Basic form with this attribute set, you'll find that the value of `ShowInTaskbar` evaluates to the state of the `WS_EX_APPWINDOW` bit. In other words,

```
Form1.ShowInTaskbar = True
```

means

```
DWORD dwStyle = GetWindowLong(Form1.hWnd, GWL_EXSTYLE);
dwStyle |= WS_EX_APPWINDOW;
SetWindowLong(Form1.hWnd, GWL_EXSTYLE, dwStyle);
```

On the other hand,

```
Form1.ShowInTaskbar = False
```

means

```
dwStyle = GetWindowLong(Form1.hWnd, GWL_EXSTYLE);
dwStyle &= ~WS_EX_APPWINDOW;
SetWindowLong(Form1.hWnd, GWL_EXSTYLE, dwStyle);
```

Flashing a Window

There are functions and techniques in the Windows SDK that survive for years in obscurity. Then, someone makes use of one of them in some well-known application and the poor function or technique has its moment of glory. This happened when owner-drawn menus were brought into the spotlight by Visual Studio 97 and Office 97, and now it's happening again for `FlashWindow()`, which is used to notify important but invisible messages in the Active Setup.

`FlashWindow()` is used to toggle the active/inactive color of a window's caption as if you were manually activating/deactivating it. When the window is iconic and displayed in the taskbar, the color of the button that renders the specified window changes.

```
BOOL FlashWindow(
    HWND hWnd,       // Handle to window to flash
    BOOL bInvert     // Flash status
);
```

The `hWnd` argument identifies the window to flash, while `bInvert`, if `TRUE`, denotes that you want to invert the color of the caption (active to inactive, and vice versa). If `FALSE`, the window caption is returned to its original status, be it active or inactive. `FlashWindow()` is used to inform the user that there's an important message window in the background.

This function might be very helpful, but as it stands it has a significant flaw. `FlashWindow()` is designed to flash only once, but you really need to do it repeatedly to capture the user's attention. (Remember that the flashing window is not in the foreground, so the user may not notice it.) Wouldn't it be nice to have a function that uses a timer to flash continuously for a few seconds?

276

A function to fulfil this role is unavailable on earlier platforms, but Windows 98 comes with a `FlashWindowEx()` function that fills the gap, and which makes flashing a window on the taskbar as easy as calling a single function:

```
BOOL FlashWindowEx(PFLASHWINFO pfwi);
```

The `FLASHWINFO` structure is declared as follows:

```
typedef struct
{
   UINT   cbSize;            // Size of the structure, in bytes
   HWND   hwnd;              // Window to flash
   DWORD  dwFlags;           // Flash status
   UINT   uCount;            // Number of times to flash
   DWORD  dwTimeout;         // Flash timeout
} FLASHWINFO, *PFLASHWINFO;
```

The Windows Taskbar

The Win32 API defines a few functions to create **application desktop toolbars** (**appbars**). These objects are rather like 'custom taskbars', and have their official representative in the Office Shortcut bar. It's useful for commercial products to be able to gather and make available their main functionality in a single, desktop-based window, and this is particularly true for suites of applications.

To help programmers deal with these objects, Microsoft has defined a programming interface for taskbars. Unfortunately, because the system taskbar is different from appbars, the use of the word 'taskbar' in this context seems a sure-fire way of bewildering people.

Attempts to differentiate taskbars from appbars are tricky, because the system taskbar and application desktop toolbars share the `SHAppBarMessage()` function:

```
UINT APIENTRY SHAppBarMessage(DWORD dwMessage, PAPPBARDATA pData);
```

However, it's not as bad as it sounds, because only a couple of the messages this function deals with are sent to the system taskbar, from which they simply retrieve information. One, `ABM_GETSTATE`, can tell us whether the Windows taskbar is currently 'autohiding', or always on top. The other, `ABM_GETTASKBARPOS`, retrieves the bounding area of the taskbar and the edge where it is aligned. We used this feature in Chapter 7 when we subclassed the Start button.

None of the other messages that can be issued through `SHAppBarMessage()` has anything to do with the system taskbar.

Getting the Taskbar's State Programmatically

Let's see exactly how to read the state of the system taskbar programmatically. As suggested above, to know whether the taskbar is in the 'always on top' or 'auto hide' state, we need to call `SHAppBarMessage()` specifying `ABM_GETSTATE` as the `dwMessage` argument. The return value is then a combination of the following constants:

- ❑ ABS_ALWAYSONTOP
- ❑ ABS_AUTOHIDE

To call `SHAppBarMessage()`, we need to know a bit about a structure called `APPBARDATA`, which is declared as follows:

```
typedef struct _AppBarData
{
    DWORD   cbSize;
    HWND    hWnd;
    UINT    uCallbackMessage;
    UINT    uEdge;
    RECT    rc;
    LPARAM  lParam;
} APPBARDATA, *PAPPBARDATA;
```

In fact, though, the structure is not very important when it comes to reading the taskbar's 'autohide' status, as the following code snippet demonstrates:

```
APPBARDATA abd;
ZeroMemory(&abd, sizeof(APPBARDATA));
abd.cbSize = sizeof(APPBARDATA);

rc = SHAppBarMessage(ABM_GETSTATE, &abd);
if(rc & ABS_ALWAYSONTOP)
{
    lstrcat(szText, __TEXT("always on top"));
}

if(rc & ABS_AUTOHIDE)
{
    lstrcat( szText, __TEXT("autohide"));
}
```

To get the current edge and the area occupied by the taskbar, we need the `ABM_GETTASKBARPOS` message. This time, the `SHAppBarMessage()` function fills in an `APPBARDATA` structure with useful information:

```
APPBARDATA abd;
ZeroMemory(&abd, sizeof(APPBARDATA));
abd.cbSize = sizeof(APPBARDATA);

SHAppBarMessage(ABM_GETTASKBARPOS, &abd);
switch(abd.uEdge)
{
case ABE_BOTTOM:
    lstrcat(szText, __TEXT("aligned at the bottom"));
    break;
case ABE_TOP:
    lstrcat(szText, __TEXT("aligned at the top"));
    break;
case ABE_LEFT:
    lstrcat(szText, __TEXT("aligned on the left"));
    break;
case ABE_RIGHT:
    lstrcat(szText, __TEXT("aligned on the right"));
    break;
}
```

The uEdge member will contain a constant that denotes the edge of the screen that the taskbar is currently docked at, while the rc member will hold the coordinates of the taskbar rectangle. The working area of the shell — that is, the screen minus all the docked taskbars and appbars — can be obtained via SystemParametersInfo(), specifying the SPI_GETWORKAREA flag.

We can also get information about another of the settings that's dealt with by the **Taskbar Properties** dialog: the clock. To determine whether the clock is displayed, you just need to get hold of the handle of its window and check the WS_VISIBLE flag.

```
// Get the taskbar window handle
hwndTaskbar = FindWindow(__TEXT("Shell_TrayWnd"), NULL);

// Get the tray window handle
hwndTray = FindWindowEx(hwndTaskbar, NULL, __TEXT("TrayNotifyWnd"), NULL);

// Get the clock window handle
hwndClock = FindWindowEx(hwndTray, NULL, __TEXT("TrayClockWClass"), NULL);
if(hwndClock)
{
    if(IsWindowVisible(hwndClock))
        lstrcat(szText, __TEXT("clock visible"));
    else
        lstrcat(szText, __TEXT("clock not visible"));
}
```

For the remainder of this chapter, I'll be putting together a program that highlights some of the theory we've discussed. To start it off, I'll use the Wrox AppWizard to create a dialog-based application called Taskbar that reads the state of the taskbar, and is also aware of the shell restarting. Here's its user interface:

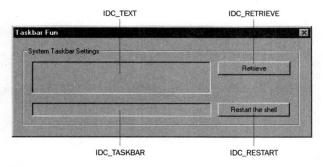

The **Retrieve** button will execute the various snippets of code you've seen so far and display the taskbar's position, its 'auto hide'/'always on top' status, and the clock settings. **Restart the shell** causes the shell to restart.

279

First of all, if we're going to detect when the shell is restarted, we need to register the `TaskbarCreated` message in `WinMain()`:

```
int APIENTRY WinMain(HINSTANCE hInstance, HINSTANCE hPrevious,
                     LPTSTR lpsz, int iCmd)
{
    // Code omitted for brevity

    g_uShellRestart = RegisterWindowMessage(__TEXT("TaskbarCreated"));

    // Run main dialog
    BOOL b = DialogBox(hInstance, "DLG_MAIN", NULL, APP_DlgProc);

    // Exit
    DestroyIcon(g_hIconLarge);
    DestroyIcon(g_hIconSmall);
    return b;
}
```

Here, `g_uShellRestart` is just a global variable of type `UINT`, as shown earlier. Next, add code to `APP_DlgProc()` to handle the **Retrieve** and **Restart** buttons being pressed, and to test for the shell restarting:

```
BOOL CALLBACK APP_DlgProc(HWND hDlg, UINT uiMsg, WPARAM wParam, LPARAM lParam)
{
    switch(uiMsg)
    {
    case WM_INITDIALOG:
        OnInitDialog(hDlg);
        break;

    case WM_COMMAND:
        switch(wParam)
        {
        case IDC_RETRIEVE:
            OnTaskbarSettings(hDlg);
            return FALSE;
        case IDC_RESTART:
            SHShellRestart();
            return FALSE;
        case IDCANCEL:
            EndDialog(hDlg, FALSE);
            return FALSE;
        }
        break;
    }

    // When the shell restarts...
    if(uiMsg == g_uShellRestart)
    {
        TCHAR szTime[50] = {0};
        TCHAR szMsg[MAX_PATH] = {0};
        GetTimeFormat(LOCALE_SYSTEM_DEFAULT, 0, NULL, NULL, szTime, 50);
        wsprintf(szMsg, __TEXT("The shell was last restarted at %s"), szTime);
        SetDlgItemText(hDlg, IDC_TASKBAR, szMsg);
    }

    return FALSE;
}
```

If the **Restart** button is pressed, the SHShellRestart() function that I defined earlier in the chapter is called, and the resulting TaskbarCreated message fulfills the if condition. When **Retrieve** is clicked, the OnTaskbarSettings() function is invoked:

```
void OnTaskbarSettings(HWND hDlg)
{
    TCHAR szText[MAX_PATH] = {0};

    APPBARDATA abd;
    abd.cbSize = sizeof(APPBARDATA);

    // Retrieve the taskbar edge
    SHAppBarMessage(ABM_GETTASKBARPOS, &abd);
    switch(abd.uEdge)
    {
    case ABE_BOTTOM:
        lstrcat(szText, __TEXT("aligned at the bottom\r\n"));
        break;
    case ABE_TOP:
        lstrcat(szText, __TEXT("aligned at the top\r\n"));
        break;
    case ABE_LEFT:
        lstrcat(szText, __TEXT("aligned on the left\r\n"));
        break;
    case ABE_RIGHT:
        lstrcat(szText, __TEXT("aligned on the right\r\n"));
        break;
    }

    // Retrieve the taskbar state
    DWORD rc = SHAppBarMessage(ABM_GETSTATE, &abd);
    if(rc & ABS_ALWAYSONTOP)
        lstrcat(szText, __TEXT("always on top\r\n"));
    if(rc & ABS_AUTOHIDE)
        lstrcat(szText, __TEXT("autohide\r\n"));

    // Retrieve the Show Clock option
    HWND hwnd1 = FindWindow(__TEXT("Shell_TrayWnd"), NULL);
    HWND hwnd2 = FindWindowEx(hwnd1, NULL, __TEXT("TrayNotifyWnd"), NULL);
    HWND hwndClock = FindWindowEx(hwnd2, NULL, __TEXT("TrayClockWClass"), NULL);
    if(hwndClock)
    {
        if(IsWindowVisible(hwndClock))
            lstrcat(szText, __TEXT("clock visible\r\n"));
        else
            lstrcat(szText, __TEXT("clock not visible\r\n"));
    }

    // Show settings
    SetDlgItemText(hDlg, IDC_TEXT, szText);
}
```

With these functions in place, and with a #include directive for resource.h, you should be able to compile and execute the application, and achieve results something like this:

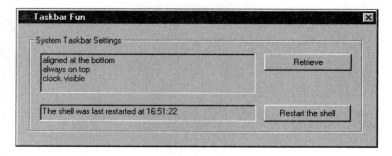

The other interesting setting of the system taskbar, the 'auto hide' attribute, appears to be impossible to set programmatically. If this can be done, the method of doing so is completely undocumented.

Hiding the Taskbar

As I mentioned earlier, the taskbar is an ordinary window that belongs to the shell process. It can be subclassed or hidden just like any other window throughout the system. I covered interprocess subclassing in Chapter 7, and demonstrated how browser helper objects and SHLoadInProc() can bring your code into the shell's address space.

If you try to subclass the taskbar without first injecting the code into the shell process, you won't be successful. This happens not because you can't subclass the taskbar or the Start button (or indeed any other system window), but because you haven't mapped your code into the shell's context. Subclassing the taskbar is no harder than subclassing the Start button (see Chapter 7).

However, there *are* things you can do with the taskbar simply by using the window handle. In general, you can safely send messages to another process window provided that you know its HWND, and you aren't required to use pointers. Let's see an example that demonstrates this point.

I've already demonstrated how to use FindWindow() to get hold of the taskbar handle. Once you've got it, hiding the taskbar is simply a matter of calling the right function:

```
void SHHideTaskbar(BOOL fHide)
{
    HWND hwndTaskbar = FindWindow(__TEXT("Shell_TrayWnd"), NULL);
    ShowWindow(hwndTaskbar, (fHide ? SW_HIDE : SW_SHOW));
}
```

SHHideTaskbar() hides or restores the taskbar window according to the Boolean value it receives. Note that this code works *despite* the fact that the taskbar belongs to another process.

The ITaskbarList Interface

A new COM interface appeared on the scene with the introduction of version 4.71 of the shell; its name is ITaskbarList. This is not an interface that you should implement in your own applications (in fact, it's implemented by the shell), but simply a programming interface for modifying the system taskbar.

There are two points to note about ITaskbarList. First, documentation for it *does* exist, but it's not brilliant. Second, it seems that the header file that contains the interface definition is missing, which means that if you want to use the interface, you'll have to write it yourself, which is exactly what I'll do in a moment.

What ITaskbarList Promises to Do

In a nutshell, ITaskbarList gives you the means to modify slightly the contents of one of the components of a Windows 9*x* taskbar: the **task list**. Through ITaskbarList, you can add new custom buttons to, and delete them from, the taskbar. The methods of the interface are described as follows:

Method	Description
ActivateTab()	The documentation says, "*Activates an item on the taskbar. The window is not actually activated; the window's item on the taskbar is merely displayed as active.*" I was unable to reproduce this behavior.
AddTab()	Add a new tab to the taskbar. The function requires an HWND, preferably one with the WS_CAPTION style to avoid blank tabs.
DeleteTab()	Deletes a tab that was previously added by AddTab(). The related window is unaffected by this operation.
HrInit()	Initializes some internal structures that will keep track of the tabs that you create. This method must be invoked only once, and before any other method in the interface.
SetActiveAlt()	The documentation says, "*Marks a taskbar item as active but does not visually activate it.*" I was unable to reproduce this behavior.

An IDL Definition for the Interface

The latest shlguid.h file defines a CLSID and an IID, but the formal definition of the ITaskbarList interface upon which your own implementation would be based is nowhere to be found! Given this, there are just two options: we can give up and get on with our lives, or we can be a bit more persistent and write an appropriate IDL file ourselves. By passing this through the MIDL compiler, we'll get a ready-to-use header.

```
// Taskbar.idl

import "oaidl.idl";
import "oleidl.idl";

//-----------------------------------------------------------------
//   Interface:  ITaskbarList
//-----------------------------------------------------------------
[
    local,
    object,
    uuid(56FDF342-FD6D-11d0-958A-006097C9A090),
    pointer_default(unique)
]
```

```
interface ITaskbarList : IUnknown
{
   HRESULT ActivateTab([in] HWND hWnd);
   HRESULT AddTab([in] HWND hWnd);
   HRESULT DeleteTab([in] HWND hWnd);
   HRESULT HrInit();
   HRESULT SetActiveAlt([in] HWND hWnd);
};
```

I added this file to my project and amended its settings to generate a header called
`ITaskbarList.h`. With this file in hand, we can turn our minds to starting to try some code:

```
#include <shlguid.h>

void OnAddTab(HWND hWnd)
{
   ITaskbarList* pTList = NULL;
   CoInitialize(NULL);

   CoCreateInstance(CLSID_TaskbarList, NULL, CLSCTX_SERVER,
                    IID_ITaskbarList, reinterpret_cast<void**>(&pTList));
   pTList->AddTab(hWnd);
   pTList->Release();

   CoUninitialize();
}
```

This is the barest minimum code you'll need to add a tab to the taskbar (I shall use an extended
version in the sample program). The documentation recommends that you give the window at least
the WS_CAPTION style, but any valid window, visible or not, is accepted.

Earlier in the chapter, I said that the taskbar rejects invisible windows. How does that fit with what's
written here? It's simple: ITaskbarList is the low-level interface that lets you program the tabs of
the taskbar. All the logic that guides the taskbar when it comes to creating new buttons is built on the
top of ITaskbarList. For this interface, windows and tabs just exist to be created, activated and
deleted — it knows nothing about the 'business rules' of the taskbar.

For a better understanding of the role played by ITaskbarList, let's see how to make use of it.

ITaskbarList Sample Program

To save work, I decided to extend the sample program I developed earlier by adding a couple of new
buttons to the main dialog — I labeled them **Add Tab** and **Delete Tab**, with identifiers IDC_ADDTAB
and IDC_DELETETAB respectively.

What remains to be done, for now at least, is fairly simple. First, we need to modify APP_DlgProc()
to deal with the buttons:

```
case WM_COMMAND:
   switch(wParam)
   {

   case IDC_ADDTAB:
      OnAddTab(hDlg);
      return FALSE;
```

```
            case IDC_DELETETAB:
                OnDeleteTab();
                return FALSE;

        case IDC_RETRIEVE:
            OnTaskbarSettings(hDlg);
            return FALSE;
        case IDC_RESTART:
            SHShellRestart();
            return FALSE;
        case IDCANCEL:
            EndDialog(hDlg, FALSE);
            return FALSE;
        }
        break;
```

Then, the two new message handlers need to be implemented to add and delete the new tab respectively. On the first occasion `OnAddTab()` is called, it creates the hidden window (I've arbitrarily chosen a button) that the tab will represent.

```
void OnAddTab(HWND hWnd)
{
    static BOOL bFirstTime = TRUE;
    ITaskbarList* pTList = NULL;

    HRESULT hr = CoCreateInstance(CLSID_TaskbarList, NULL, CLSCTX_SERVER,
                    IID_ITaskbarList, reinterpret_cast<void**>(&pTList));
    if(FAILED(hr))
        return;

    // Call the first time only
    if(bFirstTime)
    {
        bFirstTime = FALSE;
        pTList->HrInit();

        // Create a new button window (although any window class is fine)
        g_hwndButton = CreateWindow(__TEXT("Button"), __TEXT("Custom button..."),
                        WS_CAPTION | WS_SYSMENU | WS_VISIBLE,
                        -300, -300, 50, 50, hWnd, NULL, NULL, NULL);
    }

    pTList->AddTab(g_hwndButton);
    pTList->Release();
    ShowWindow(g_hwndButton, SW_HIDE);
}
```

```
void OnDeleteTab()
{
    ITaskbarList* pTList = NULL;

    HRESULT hr = CoCreateInstance(CLSID_TaskbarList, NULL, CLSCTX_SERVER,
                    IID_ITaskbarList, reinterpret_cast<void**>(&pTList));
    if(FAILED(hr))
        return;

    pTList->DeleteTab(g_hwndButton);
    pTList->Release();
}
```

To make this code work, you need to add a new global variable of type `HWND` to hold the handle of the new window. The COM libraries should also be initialized (and uninitialized) in `WinMain()`, like this:

```
    // Run main dialog
    CoInitialize(NULL);
    BOOL b = DialogBox(hInstance, "DLG_MAIN", NULL, APP_DlgProc);

    // Exit
    OnDeleteTab();
    CoUninitialize();
    DestroyWindow(g_hwndButton);
    DestroyIcon(g_hIconLarge);
    DestroyIcon(g_hIconSmall);
    return b;
}
```

Finally, you need `#include` directives for `ITaskbarList.h` and `shlguid.h`, and to link to `ole32.lib`. With this in place, you'll be able to get behavior like that shown in the screenshot below. A new button can be added and deleted, but it is lifeless. You can check and uncheck it endlessly, but nothing more will happen.

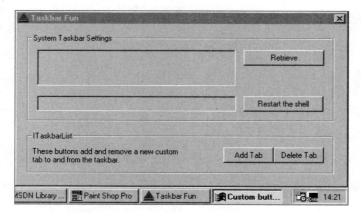

Taskbar-Window Communication

If a taskbar button were a real button, it would be quite easy to intercept any related events. Sadly, a taskbar button is actually just a page on a tab control, which makes things rather more difficult.

While puzzling over this problem, I found myself wondering exactly why the documentation for `ITaskbarList::AddTab()` "recommends" that the windows you pass to it have the `WS_CAPTION` style. Could it be that in certain circumstances, you can treat the taskbar button as if it's the caption of your window? To find out, I tried subclassing the window whose `HWND` was passed to `AddTab()`, and to my considerable relief it seems that my hunch was right.

It's true: some of the messages related to caption activity *are* forwarded to the window that the button represents. In other words, the window passed through `AddTab()` receives a `WM_ACTIVATE` message (and other non-client area related messages) when someone clicks on the corresponding taskbar button.

We can subclass that window like this (where `g_pfnOldProc` is a global variable of type `WNDPROC`):

```
void OnAddTab(HWND hWnd)
{
    static BOOL bFirstTime = TRUE;
    ITaskbarList* pTList = NULL;

    HRESULT hr = CoCreateInstance(CLSID_TaskbarList, NULL, CLSCTX_SERVER,
                        IID_ITaskbarList, reinterpret_cast<void**>(&pTList));
    if(FAILED(hr))
        return;

    // Call the first time only
    if(bFirstTime)
    {
        bFirstTime = FALSE;
        pTList->HrInit();

        // Create a new button window (although any window class is fine)
        g_hwndButton = CreateWindow(__TEXT("Button"), __TEXT("Custom button..."),
                        WS_CAPTION | WS_SYSMENU | WS_VISIBLE,
                        -300, -300, 50, 50, hWnd, NULL, NULL, NULL);
        g_pfnOldProc = SubclassWindow(g_hwndButton, ButtonProc);
    }

    pTList->AddTab(g_hwndButton);
    pTList->Release();
    ShowWindow(g_hwndButton, SW_HIDE);
}
```

Before we discuss the kinds of things it's possible to do once the button has been subclassed, I should say that the arguments I passed to `CreateWindow()` were chosen as a result of experimentation that revealed some very strange behavior. If the window you pass to `AddTab()` has a caption *and* the `WS_SYSMENU` style, then the button on the taskbar will show the icon as well. If the window is also visible, however, I ran into these problems:

❑   The application's main window loses the focus, with no way of regaining it
❑   The application's system menu is never displayed properly when its taskbar button is right-clicked

Another thing that happens when the window is visible on being added is that the new taskbar button is unselected, which is more like what we want. To get the best of both worlds, therefore, I initially placed the window off the screen. Then, once the new tab has been added, I hide it 'properly' with a call to `ShowWindow()`.

Setting up a Menu
Anyway, now that we know how communication between the taskbar and the window works, it's quite easy to set up and display a pop-up menu on the fly. The following procedure is the one I'll use to subclass the window (of class 'Button') that is associated with the new taskbar's button.

```
LRESULT CALLBACK ButtonProc(HWND hwnd, UINT uiMsg, WPARAM wParam, LPARAM lParam)
{
    switch(uiMsg)
    {
    case WM_ACTIVATE:
        if(LOWORD(wParam) == TRUE)
            OnButtonActivation();
    }
    return CallWindowProc(g_pfnOldProc, hwnd, uiMsg, wParam, lParam);
}
```

```
void OnButtonActivation()
{
    // Get the handle of the tab control
    HWND h0 = FindWindow(__TEXT("Shell_TrayWnd"), NULL);
    HWND h1 = FindWindowEx(h0, NULL, __TEXT("RebarWindow32"), NULL);
    HWND h2 = FindWindowEx(h1, NULL, __TEXT("MSTaskSwWClass"), NULL);
    HWND h3 = FindWindowEx(h2, NULL, __TEXT("SysTabControl32"), NULL);

    // Create a new popup menu
    HMENU hmenu = CreatePopupMenu();

    // Get the currently selected button in the tab control
    int i = TabCtrl_GetCurSel(h3);

    // If no tab is selected show a menu with a sole 'Close' item
    if(i == -1)
        AppendMenu(hmenu, MF_STRING, IDC_DELETETAB, __TEXT("&Close"));
    else
    {
        AppendMenu(hmenu, MF_STRING, IDC_RESTART, __TEXT("&Restart the shell"));
        AppendMenu(hmenu, MF_STRING, IDC_RETRIEVE,
                        __TEXT("Re&trieve Taskbar Settings"));
        AppendMenu(hmenu, MF_SEPARATOR, 0, NULL);
        AppendMenu(hmenu, MF_STRING, IDC_DELETETAB, __TEXT("&Delete Me"));
    }

    // Find out the position for the menu. It depends upon the taskbar's edge
    STARTMENUPOS smp;
    if(i == -1)
    {
        POINT pt;
        GetCursorPos(&pt);
        smp.ix = pt.x;
        smp.iy = pt.y;
        smp.uFlags = TPM_BOTTOMALIGN;
    }
    else
        GetMenuPosition(h3, i, &smp);

    // Display and then destroy the menu
    TrackPopupMenu(hmenu, smp.uFlags, smp.ix, smp.iy, 0, g_hDlg, 0);
    DestroyMenu(hmenu);
}
```

A different menu is displayed if there's no longer a currently selected item when the button is activated. As you can see, the menu items are given the same identifiers as other controls in the main program, so that you can cause the shell to restart or retrieve taskbar settings from a context menu as well as from the main dialog. For the call to TrackPopupMenu() to work properly, you'll need a final global variable of type HWND that you can set to the handle of the main dialog in OnInitDialog().

Determining the Menu Position

The final part of the application is concerned with the position of the pop-up menu (this is the function performed by `GetStartMenuPosition()` in the above code). Ultimately, this depends on the edge of the taskbar, and the relative position of the taskbar button. In practice, the algorithm to determine the correct position is very similar to the one I created in Chapter 7 for the Start menu – the `ABM_TASKBARPOS` message is relied upon to determine the edge of the taskbar. In this case, however, there's an additional difficulty: the *x* coordinate, which is always 0 for the Start menu, now depends on the position of the button.

```
struct STARTMENUPOS
{
    int  ix;
    int  iy;
    UINT uFlags;
};

typedef STARTMENUPOS* LPSTARTMENUPOS;

int GetMenuPosition(HWND hwndTab, int iItem, LPSTARTMENUPOS lpsmp)
{
    // Set and then reset the size to get current width and height of button
    long iItemSize = TabCtrl_SetItemSize(hwndTab, 0, 0);
    TabCtrl_SetItemSize(hwndTab, LOWORD(iItemSize), HIWORD(iItemSize));

    // Get the tab control rectangle
    RECT r;
    GetWindowRect(hwndTab, &r);

    // Retrieve the taskbar's edge
    APPBARDATA abd;
    abd.cbSize = sizeof(APPBARDATA);
    SHAppBarMessage(ABM_GETTASKBARPOS, &abd);
    switch(abd.uEdge)
    {
    case ABE_BOTTOM:
        lpsmp->ix = r.left + LOWORD(iItemSize) * iItem + 3;
        lpsmp->iy = abd.rc.top;
        lpsmp->uFlags = TPM_LEFTALIGN | TPM_BOTTOMALIGN;
        break;
    case ABE_TOP:
        lpsmp->ix = r.left + LOWORD(iItemSize) * iItem + 3;
        lpsmp->iy = abd.rc.bottom;
        lpsmp->uFlags = TPM_LEFTALIGN | TPM_TOPALIGN;
        break;
    case ABE_LEFT:
        lpsmp->ix = abd.rc.right;
        lpsmp->iy = r.top + HIWORD(iItemSize) * iItem + 3;
        lpsmp->uFlags = TPM_LEFTALIGN | TPM_TOPALIGN;
        break;
    case ABE_RIGHT:
        lpsmp->ix = abd.rc.left;
        lpsmp->iy = r.top + HIWORD(iItemSize) * iItem + 3;
        lpsmp->uFlags = TPM_RIGHTALIGN | TPM_TOPALIGN;
        break;
    }
    return 1;
}
```

In these calculations, the *x* coordinate is given by the left edge of the tab control window, plus an offset determined by the width of the buttons:

```
lpsmp->ix = r.left + LOWORD(iItemSize) * iItem + 3;
```

The item size is the same for all items, and obtained using a trick. When you set a new size, the current one is returned, so we can grab the width and height by setting and then immediately restoring the size. Width and height are packed into a `long` value, the low order word being the width.

We can't use `TabCtrl_GetItemRect()` for this purpose, because the code that's calling the tab control is part of another process. Windows, on the other hand, are global objects and accessible from any process. Everything works, and messages can be sent, provided that pointers aren't involved. Unfortunately, `TabCtrl_GetItemRect()` requires a buffer to return the actual rectangle.

If the taskbar is aligned vertically, the coordinate that may vary is *y*:

```
lpsmp->iy = r.top + HIWORD(iItemSize) * iItem + 3;
```

And to prove that it works, this final screenshot shows how the menu looks when the taskbar is right aligned:

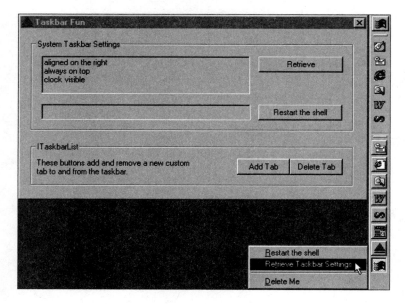

Summary

In this chapter, I began by looking at icons, and finished with a look at the new, but poorly documented, COM interface for the taskbar. Along the way I covered many aspects of Windows icons, in particular the functions that place icons in the tray notification area.

The code that handles tray icons has problems when the shell restarts, and while Microsoft hasn't solved them as such, it has recently introduced a message that can inform applications of an upcoming shell reboot. This sounds rather like a silent admission of guilt to me, but whether this is true or not, all existing applications are still affected. Ours, on the other hand, should be fine from now on!

I also tried to clarify some points about the system taskbar and application desktop toolbars (a.k.a. appbars). Finally, I put the `ITaskbarList` interface into action to modify the content of the taskbar.

To summarize the summary, this chapter provided:

- ❑ An overview of icons under Win32
- ❑ Advanced details about programming tray icons
- ❑ A description of a semi-clandestine message that informs you of any shell restart
- ❑ A comparison between taskbars and appbars
- ❑ A report of real-world experiences with `ITaskbarList`

Further Reading

Useful tips about icons can be found in Bret Pehrson's article in the April 98 issue of WDJ, *Rebuilding the Internal Shell Icon Cache.* In the same context, I can also point you to a more comprehensive MSDN piece by John Hornick, entitled *Icons in Win32,* which you'll find in the MSDN Library under Technical Articles | Windows Platform | User Interface.

Bitmaps and icons raise interesting issues if you look at them from the Visual Basic perspective as well. I contributed an article to the December 1997 edition of WDJ that demonstrates how to convert `HICON`s and `HBITMAP`s to Visual Basic pictures; it is called *Converting Icon/Bitmap Handles to Pictures in VB.*

An interesting example of shell programming that also involves icons may be found in the August 1998 issue of MIND. The piece, which appears in the *Cutting Edge* column that I usually run, concentrates mainly on Visual Basic code but does have a smattering of C++ as well.

Application desktop toolbars may be studied with the aid of Jeff Richter's article that appeared in the March 1996 issue of MSJ.

Finally, here's a list of related Knowledge Base articles:

- ❑ **Knowledge Base Article Q179363:** *Cover the Task Bar with a Window*
- ❑ **Knowledge Base Article Q142166:** *Taskbar Anomalies When Application Larger than the Screen*
- ❑ **Knowledge Base Article Q135788:** *Menus for Notification Icons Don't Work Correctly*
- ❑ **Knowledge Base Article Q97925:** *SetActiveWindow() and SetForegroundWindow() Clarification*
- ❑ **Knowledge Base Article Q149276:** *Use Icons with the Windows 95 System Tray*
- ❑ **Knowledge Base Article Q176085:** *Use the System Tray Directly from Visual Basic 5.0*

10

Windows Helper Libraries

The aspect of Windows 98 that I appreciate most of all is that it has (hopefully) put a definitive end to the long running saga of `comctl32.lib` and `shell32.lib` version numbers. The version of Internet Explorer 4 and the status of your Active Desktop settings are no longer an issue — with Windows 98, all libraries on all machines are aligned.

I fear, however, that this state of calm is only an illusion and that sooner or later we'll have to write wrapper code for creating slightly enhanced controls that show up late-breaking tweaks to the user interface. Still, let's enjoy the lull before that particular storm!

To enable us to appreciate the present, how about remembering the bad old days? In this chapter, I'll recall briefly the major problem that tormented programmers during the transition from Windows 95 to Windows 98. I'll also demonstrate what's new in the latest libraries. After that, the chapter will revolve around three groups of new helper functions that address the Recycle Bin, the registry and string manipulation.

Finally, I'll talk about what could be considered to be an open secret: an unofficially documented but officially unacknowledged function for formatting drives.

To summarize then, we're going to look at:

- ❑ Microsoft's answer to the shell versioning problem
- ❑ The Recycle Bin API
- ❑ An annotated overview of some new helper libraries for working with strings and the registry
- ❑ What's still undocumented in Windows 98

In particular, I'm aiming to show a useful and general technique for customizing and improving system dialogs. I will then apply this to the still officially undocumented `SHFormatDrive()` function, which is a helper routine that Explorer uses to format drives programmatically.

The Versioning Epidemic

This story begins when the first betas of Internet Explorer 3.0 hit the Web. People immediately noticed the flat and textured toolbars, and then more complicated (even resizable) objects with side handles. It wasn't exactly clear how they worked, but they were certainly cool, and so they became known as **coolbars**.

While preliminary copies wisely stopped short of installing new system DLLs, the final version of Internet Explorer 3.0 threw caution to the wind and overwrote comct132.dll. From that point on, unwary programmers began to use the brand new Internet Explorer 3.0 controls (mostly coolbars), in some cases creating applications that required IE 3.0 to be installed to work properly. Worse still, Microsoft refused for a long time to authorize distribution of the new version of comct132.dll, and it's still only relatively recently that they provided a self-extracting module that installs the latest control libraries on Windows 95 and Windows NT 4.0 machines.

So far, I've restricted the discussion to IE 3.0, but the problems have continued into later versions. In fact, the *coup de grâce* came with the shell update release of Internet Explorer 4.0, because when the Active Desktop starts getting involved, things become even more complicated. It's no longer a simple matter of whether to use a more or less cool control for the user interface. Now, many new functions have been added and documented as if they have always been part of Windows.

These problems are the reason why I've been making it very clear that this book assumes that you have Windows 98 or Windows 95/Windows NT 4.0 with Internet Explorer 4.*x* and Active Desktop installed. If you run some of the examples provided on a machine with different characteristics, the chances are that you will get a polite error message from the system, informing you that a particular function cannot be found in the shell library.

DLL Version Information

Many programmers have written utilities to determine which version of a given module a given machine is hosting. Here's a code fragment that shows how this information can be obtained from the VS_VERSIONINFO block stored in the module's resources:

```
DWORD dwLen = GetFileVersionInfoSize(szFile, &dwUseless);
LPVOID lpVI = malloc(dwLen);
GetFileVersionInfo(szFile, NULL, dwLen, lpVI);
VerQueryValue(lpVI, __TEXT("\\"), reinterpret_cast<LPVOID*>(&lpFFI), &iBufSize);
DWORD dwVer1 = lpFFI->dwFileVersionMS;
DWORD dwVer2 = lpFFI->dwFileVersionLS;
```

Here, lpFFI *is a pointer to a previously initialized* VS_FIXEDFILEINFO *structure. Of course, a module that doesn't expose a* VS_VERSIONINFO *resource doesn't expose any version information that an external program can read and check.*

In fact, Microsoft now provides this facility through a new DLL policy. Every system DLL is supposed to export a function called DllGetVersion() that returns its version number – internally, this function will execute code that is similar to the fragment shown above. Third-party library vendors are being encouraged to do the same in their own products.

Version Number of a System DLL

The idea of this policy is to provide a common and easy way for applications to know the version of the DLLs they're using, or that they expect to find. Of course, a program that wants to perform such checks can't attempt to import the function statically, because old DLLs won't support it. Instead, it must rely on dynamic loading.

Here's an example of how a program could check for the Active Desktop update:

```cpp
BOOL IsActiveDesktopInstalled()
{
   HINSTANCE hShell32 = LoadLibrary(__TEXT("shell32.dll"));
   if(!hShell32)
      return FALSE;
   else
   {
      DLLGETVERSIONPROC pFunc = reinterpret_cast<DLLGETVERSIONPROC>(
                           GetProcAddress(hShell32, __TEXT("DllGetVersion")));
      if(!pFunc)
      {
         FreeLibrary(hShell32);
         return FALSE;
      }
      else
      {
         DLLVERSIONINFO dvi;
         ZeroMemory(&dvi, sizeof(dvi));
         dvi.cbSize = sizeof(dvi);
         (*pFunc)(&dvi);

         // Shell version < 4 means NT 3.51
         if(dvi.dwMajorVersion < 4)
         {
            FreeLibrary(hShell32);
            return FALSE;
         }

         if(dvi.dwMajorVersion == 4)
         {
            // Active Desktop installed
            if(dvi.dwMinorVersion >= 71)
            {
               FreeLibrary(hShell32);
               return TRUE;
            }
         }
         else
         {
            // Higher than Windows 9x and NT 4.0
            FreeLibrary(hShell32);
            return TRUE;
         }
      }
   }
   FreeLibrary(hShell32);
   return FALSE;
}
```

The function loads shell32.dll and attempts to call a function called DllGetVersion(). If this fails, it's clear that the DLL is far older than the one installed by Active Desktop. Otherwise, it issues a call. The prototype of the function is:

```
HRESULT DllGetVersion(DLLVERSIONINFO* pdvi);
```

DLLVERSIONINFO is a structure defined in shlwapi.h like this:

```
typedef struct _DllVersionInfo
{
    DWORD cbSize;
    DWORD dwMajorVersion;
    DWORD dwMinorVersion;
    DWORD dwBuildNumber;
    DWORD dwPlatformID;
} DLLVERSIONINFO;
```

By using this structure, a program can even retrieve the build number and the target platform of a DLL. The dwMajorVersion and dwMinorVersion members are the first two items that form a version number; the build number is usually the third. To distinguish the target platform, you can check dwPlatformID against the following constants:

- ❑ DLLVER_PLATFORM_WINDOWS (0x01) – DLL built for all Windows platforms
- ❑ DLLVER_PLATFORM_NT (0x02) – DLL built specifically for Windows NT

All the structure and constants that you need to call this function are declared in shlwapi.h, the header file for the Shell Lightweight API that we'll be discussing further later in the chapter. To reiterate, *every* shell DLL installed by Active Desktop exposes the DllGetVersion() function.

Exposing the Version Number in your Own Functions

Every time you develop an executable module – an EXE, a DLL, or whatever – I strongly recommend that you incorporate some version information. This can be done either by defining the already-mentioned VS_VERSIONINFO structure in the module's resources, or through the DllGetVersion() function. Let's examine both cases.

Using VS_VERSIONINFO

The easiest way to provide applications and modules with version information is by defining a VS_VERSION_INFO resource type in the .rc file of the project (in fact, the Wrox AppWizard does exactly this). There's a resource editor screen for precisely this purpose, as the screenshot opposite clearly demonstrates:

The information above is ultimately stored in script form in the project's RC file, like this:

```
VS_VERSION_INFO VERSIONINFO
 FILEVERSION 1,0,0,1
 PRODUCTVERSION 1,0,0,1
 FILEFLAGSMASK 0x3fL
#ifdef _DEBUG
 FILEFLAGS 0x1L
#else
 FILEFLAGS 0x0L
#endif
 FILEOS 0x4L
 FILETYPE 0x1L
 FILESUBTYPE 0x0L
BEGIN
    BLOCK "StringFileInfo"
    BEGIN
        BLOCK "040904b0"
        BEGIN
            VALUE "CompanyName", "\0"
            VALUE "FileDescription", "\0"
            VALUE "FileVersion", "1.00.001\0"
            VALUE "InternalName", "VERSION\0"
            VALUE "LegalCopyright", "\0"
            VALUE "LegalTrademarks", "\0"
            VALUE "OriginalFilename", "VERSION.exe\0"
            VALUE "ProductName", "Version Checker\0"
            VALUE "ProductVersion", "1, 0, 0, 1\0"
        END
    END
    BLOCK "VarFileInfo"
    BEGIN
        VALUE "Translation", 0x409, 1200
    END
END
```

Using DllGetVersion()

In addition, you are encouraged to export a `DllGetVersion()` function from your own libraries. If everyone follows this guidline, it should lead to a standard way of identifying the version number of a module. Here's a typical implementation of `DllGetVersion()` that returns a version number of 1.0.

```
#include <shlwapi.h>

HRESULT DllGetVersion(DLLVERSIONINFO* pdvi)
{
    if(pdvi == NULL)
        return E_FAIL;

    ZeroMemory(pdvi, pdvi.cbSize);
    pdvi->dwMajorVersion = 1;
    pdvi->dwMinorVersion = 0;
    pdvi->dwPlatformID = DLLVER_PLATFORM_WINDOWS;

    return NOERROR;
}
```

A More General Function

As I've already mentioned, you can't expect to find `DllGetVersion()` implemented in every DLL on every Windows platform. While the steps Microsoft is taking to encourage its adoption are welcome, we need much more. Asking the DLL itself to disclose its version number sounds a bit strange to me, but on the other hand I guess it's easy to code and test.

In an ideal world, I would have liked a new system API function that could be used to *read* version information from any valid file. The low-level means to do this have been available since Windows 3.1, but attempting to cope with version functions can be bothersome, to say the least. However, I've written a general function that's capable of returning the version information of any executable file that exposes it, both as string and as an array of numbers. You can even use this function, which I've called `SHGetVersionOfFile()`, to read version numbers of 16-bit programs and DLLs, regardless of the vendor:

```
DWORD SHGetVersionOfFile(LPTSTR szFile,
                         LPTSTR szBuf, LPINT lpiBuf, int iNumOfFields)
{
    DWORD dwUseless = 0;
    UINT iBufSize = 0;
    VS_FIXEDFILEINFO* lpFFI = NULL;
    TCHAR s[MAX_PATH] = {0};

    DWORD dwLen = GetFileVersionInfoSize(szFile, &dwUseless);
    if(dwLen == 0)
    {
        if(szBuf)
            lstrcpy(szBuf, __TEXT("<unknown>"));
        return 0;
    }

    LPVOID lpVI = GlobalAllocPtr(GHND, dwLen);
    GetFileVersionInfo(szFile, NULL, dwLen, lpVI);
```

```
        VerQueryValue(lpVI, __TEXT("\\"),
                      reinterpret_cast<LPVOID*>(&lpFFI), &iBufSize);
   DWORD dwVer1 = lpFFI->dwFileVersionMS;
   DWORD dwVer2 = lpFFI->dwFileVersionLS;
   GlobalFreePtr(lpVI);

   // Fill return buffers
   if(szBuf != NULL)
   {
      wsprintf(s, __TEXT("%d.%d.%d.%d"),
               HIWORD(dwVer1), LOWORD(dwVer1), HIWORD(dwVer2), LOWORD(dwVer2));
      lstrcpy(szBuf, s);
   }

   if(lpiBuf != NULL)
   {
      for(int i = 0 ; i < iNumOfFields ; i++)
      {
         if(i == 0)
            lpiBuf[i] = HIWORD(dwVer1);
         if(i == 1)
            lpiBuf[i] = LOWORD(dwVer1);
         if(i == 2)
            lpiBuf[i] = HIWORD(dwVer2);
         if(i == 3)
            lpiBuf[i] = LOWORD(dwVer2);
      }
   }

   return dwVer1;
}
```

A version number consists of 4 numbers that are usually separated by dots. A typical example of a full version number would therefore be something like `4.71.2106.1`. The first two numbers (4 and 71 in this case) are known as the **major** and **minor version number** respectively.

There's nothing to prevent you from using only a portion of the version number, if that is all you require. I usually find that I need the version number in one of two formats — either as a string to display in a dialog or as separate numbers in order to perform checks easily.

The programming interface of `SHGetVersionOfFile()` is very flexible and tries to meet both requirements. The function's return value is the major version number, but the parameter list includes a pointer to a string in which it will return the information in the format `%d.%d.%d.%d`. You can pass `NULL` if you don't need a string.

`SHGetVersionOfFile()` accepts two additional arguments. The first one is a pointer to an array of integers, while the second specifies its size — it can contain up to 4 elements. Through this buffer, the caller can receive the various elements that make up the version number separately. This undoubtedly makes any further processing that you might want to do on the numbers more comfortable.

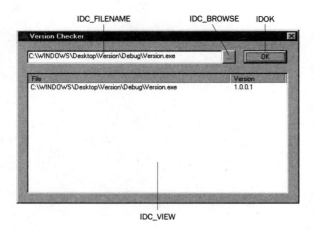

The screenshot above shows the interface of a program generated by the Wrox AppWizard that uses `SHGetVersionOfFile()`. Implementing it is largely a matter of writing handlers for the two buttons, a process that you ought to be getting familiar with by now! Here's `OnBrowse()`:

```
void OnBrowse(HWND hDlg, WPARAM wID)
{
    TCHAR szFile[MAX_PATH] = {0};
    TCHAR szWinDir[MAX_PATH] = {0};
    GetWindowsDirectory(szWinDir, MAX_PATH);

    OPENFILENAME ofn;
    ZeroMemory(&ofn, sizeof(OPENFILENAME));
    ofn.lStructSize = sizeof(OPENFILENAME);
    ofn.lpstrFilter = __TEXT("Executable\0*.exe;*.dll;*.drv;*.vxd\0");
    ofn.nMaxFile = MAX_PATH;
    ofn.lpstrInitialDir = szWinDir;
    ofn.lpstrFile = szFile;

    if(!GetOpenFileName(&ofn))
        return;
    else
        SetDlgItemText(hDlg, wID, ofn.lpstrFile);
}
```

Once you've chosen the file to interrogate, clicking on the OK button will invoke a function called `DoGetVersionInfo()`, which looks like this:

```
const int BUFSIZE = 1024;
const int MSGSIZE = 40;

void DoGetVersionInfo(HWND hDlg)
{
    TCHAR szTemp[MAX_PATH] = {0};
    HWND hwndList = GetDlgItem(hDlg, IDC_VIEW);
    GetDlgItemText(hDlg, IDC_FILENAME, szTemp, MAX_PATH);

    // Create the string for the list view
    TCHAR pszBuf[BUFSIZE] = {0};
```

```
    LPTSTR psz = pszBuf;

    lstrcpy(psz, szTemp);
    lstrcat(psz, __TEXT("\0"));
    psz += lstrlen(psz) + 1;

    // Get the version info
    TCHAR szInfo[MSGSIZE] = {0};
    SHGetVersionOfFile(szTemp, szInfo, NULL, 0);
    lstrcpy(psz, szInfo);
    lstrcat(psz, __TEXT("\0"));
    psz += lstrlen(psz) + 1;

    // Add the two column text
    AddStringToReportView(hwndList, pszBuf, 2);
}
```

To do its work, `DoGetVersionInfo()` uses `SHGetVersionOfFile()`, which we defined earlier in this chapter, and `AddStringToReportView()`, which you first saw back in Chapter 6. The latter's sister function, `MakeReportView()`, is used in `OnInitDialog()` to set up the list view:

```
void OnInitDialog(HWND hDlg)
{
    // Initialize the report view with 2 columns: File and Version
    HWND hwndList = GetDlgItem(hDlg, IDC_VIEW);
    LPTSTR psz[] = { __TEXT("File"), reinterpret_cast<TCHAR*>(350),
                     __TEXT("Version"), reinterpret_cast<TCHAR*>(95) };
    MakeReportView(hwndList, psz, 2);

    // Set the icons (T/F as to Large/Small icon)
    SendMessage(hDlg, WM_SETICON, FALSE, reinterpret_cast<LPARAM>(g_hIconSmall));
    SendMessage(hDlg, WM_SETICON, TRUE, reinterpret_cast<LPARAM>(g_hIconLarge));
}
```

Finally, you need to add `#include`s for `resource.h` and `comdlg.h`, link to `version.lib` and `comdlg32.lib`, and add a couple of new `case`s to the `switch` in `APP_DlgProc()`:

```
case WM_COMMAND:
    switch(wParam)
    {

    case IDC_BROWSE:
        OnBrowse(hDlg, IDC_FILENAME);
        return FALSE;

    case IDOK:
        DoGetVersionInfo(hDlg);
        return FALSE;

    case IDCANCEL:
        EndDialog(hDlg, FALSE);
        return FALSE;
    }
    break;
```

Once the application is running, you can type the name of the file to check in the edit field, or select it from the Open dialog that appears when you click on the ... button. The code tied to the OK button then attempts to read the version information from the specified file. The name of the file and the version string are then written in the report view below *unless* the file doesn't contain version information, in which case the string <unknown> is returned.

The Recycle Bin API

The Recycle Bin is a custom object that you find in the shell's namespace, right beneath the desktop. It can be seen as a temporary container for all the file objects that have been deleted using shell functions, from which files can be restored or definitively destroyed. It's important to keep in mind that only those file objects that you delete manually through the shell, or programmatically by means of the shell functions, go into the Recycle Bin. If you delete a file using DeleteFile(), or from the MS-DOS prompt, the file will be removed from the file system directly, with no further intervention required.

A specialized programming interface is needed for working with the Recycle Bin because deletion requests must be processed differently. In Chapter 3 we discussed the SHFileOperation() function, which was able to send deleted files to the bin. In the next section I'll examine two other, more recent, functions that allow us to empty the Recycle Bin, and also to send it some queries. These functions were introduced with version 4.71 of the shell.

Structure of the Recycle Bin

To elaborate on the definition of the last two paragraphs, the *namespace extension* through which the Recycle Bin is implemented lies on the desktop. The actual containers for the deleted files are located on each local drive, in a folder called Recycled.

Although you won't see it through the shell interface, each Recycled folder contains only the files deleted in that drive. In fact, if you open any of the Recycled folders on your system you will always see the same content, which is a list of *all* the deleted files from *all* your drives. If you look around these folders with a DOS-based tool instead, you should be able to see the logic that the Recycle Bin adopts.

```
MS-DOS Prompt

Auto

Microsoft(R) Windows 98
  (C)Copyright Microsoft Corp 1981-1998.

C:\WINDOWS>dir c:\recycled

 Volume in drive C is WIN98
 Volume Serial Number is 353B-7F55
 Directory of C:\RECYCLED

.              <DIR>         20/04/98   17:15 .
..             <DIR>         20/04/98   17:15 ..
DC0      BMP        59.978   19/10/98   16:19 DC0.BMP
DC1      BMP       134.458   04/11/98   10:12 DC1.BMP
        2 file(s)           194.436 bytes
        2 dir(s)        495.386.624 bytes free

C:\WINDOWS>dir e:\recycled

 Volume in drive E is STUDIO
 Volume Serial Number is 353B-6FFB
 Directory of E:\RECYCLED

.              <DIR>         20/04/98   16:40 .
..             <DIR>         20/04/98   16:40 ..
DE0      BMP        29.154   19/10/98   16:40 DE0.BMP
DE1      BMP        52.258   31/07/98   20:49 DE1.BMP
        2 file(s)            81.412 bytes
        2 dir(s)        799.080.448 bytes free

C:\WINDOWS>
```

The figure above shows the real content of two `Recycled` directories, on my C and E drives.

In fact, *any* deletion that occurs within the shell is divided into two non-consecutive steps. Initially, the shell just moves the file from its original location to the `Recycled` folder of the current drive. Once there, the file is renamed according to a convention that I will cover in the next section. When asked to list its contents, the Recycle Bin that you see on the desktop just collects the files from the various `Recycled` folders located on each local drive.

Renaming Convention

As the screenshot suggests, all the files in the Recycle Bin have a name that begins with D. The second character is the original drive letter, and what follows is a local, incremental number that is assigned to the file at time of deletion. The file retains its original extension.

While the `Recycled` folders themselves are hidden, the files marked for deletion have only the **Archive** attribute set. The link between the 'deleted' name and the original is stored on a drive-by-drive basis in a hidden file called `info2`. (Open an MS-DOS prompt, then go to any `Recycled` folder and type `dir /AH`.)

What if the `info2` file gets lost or damaged? That's no problem, because the deletion of this file doesn't affect the files to which it refers. Moreover, at each startup, Windows makes sure that an `info2` file exists if there are deleted files. If `info2` doesn't exist, Windows will create it on the fly.

Restoring a file therefore means moving it back to its original location, and reverting to its original name. If another file with the same name exists, a confirmation dialog box pops up. Deleting a file from the Recycle Bin simply means that it will 'really' be deleted.

The Recycle Bin View

The next picture illustrates what the Recycle Bin looks like through the Windows shell:

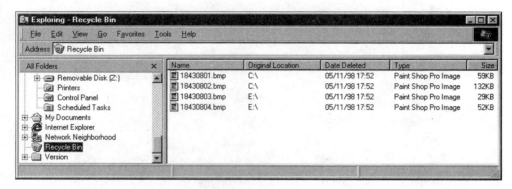

You can see that the shell view shows the real names of the deleted files – essentially, the shell is interpreting the names on our behalf. The filename you actually work with is not the same as the one displayed via the shell.

> *This behavior is an example of how a namespace extension can build a layer of abstraction over the physical content of a directory.*

Functions for Interacting with the Recycle Bin

Apart from SHFileOperation(), there are just two other shell functions for working with the Recycle Bin. They are:

- ❑ SHEmptyRecycleBin()
- ❑ SHQueryRecycleBin()

As its name suggests, the first of these destroys all the files contained in the various Recycled folders throughout the machine. The latter, on the other hand, retrieves the number of items in the Recycled directory of a specified drive, and the amount of memory that they occupy. Let's see the syntax in more detail, starting with SHEmptyRecycleBin().

```
HRESULT SHEmptyRecycleBin(HWND hwnd, LPCTSTR pszRootPath, DWORD dwFlags);
```

The hwnd argument denotes the parent window for any window or dialog box that the function should create. Depending on the value of pszRootPath, the function can empty the Recycled folder for a single disk, or all the disks – the argument is a path to the root directory of the drive on which to empty the folder. If you pass a fully qualified path, only the drive part will be taken into account. If the string is NULL, then the entire Recycle Bin is emptied, drive after drive.

The last argument can be used to specify some flags, as explained in the following table:

Flag	Description
SHERB_NOCONFIRMATION	Usually, the system displays a confirmation dialog box before proceeding with the operation. If this bit is set, the dialog is suppressed.
SHERB_NOPROGRESSUI	The shell also displays a dialog with a progress bar (shown below). If this bit is set, no dialog will be displayed.
SHERB_NOSOUND	If this bit is set, there will be no sound upon completion.

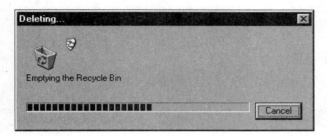

The SHQueryRecycleBin() function has the following prototype:

```
HRESULT SHQueryRecycleBin(LPCTSTR pszRootPath, LPSHQUERYRBINFO pSHQueryRBInfo);
```

The pszRootPath argument has the same features as it did for SHEmptyRecycleBin(): it should indicate the root directory of the drive for which information is to be retrieved. However, it can also be NULL or a fully qualified path. In the first case the system retrieves information for all the drives available, while in the latter case only the drive portion of the string is used.

The information retrieved is stored in a structure called SHQUERYRBINFO, which is defined like this:

```
typedef struct _SHQUERYRBINFO
{
    DWORD cbSize;
    __int64 i64Size;
    __int64 i64NumItems;
} SHQUERYRBINFO, FAR* LPSHQUERYRBINFO;
```

As usual, the cbSize member must be filled with the structure's size prior to issuing the call. After the call, i64Size will contain the total number of bytes occupied by the portion of the Recycle Bin specified in pszRootPath, and i64NumItems will hold the number of items marked for deletion. The latter two members are both 64-bit integers.

Helper Libraries

In semi-clandestine fashion, installing the Active Desktop stores a new, relatively small library on your disk called shlwapi.dll (the Shell Lightweight API). This DLL contains many functions that can (sometimes!) make a programmer's life much easier. Using this library is as easy as adding a #include for the header file shlwapi.h, and linking to the import library shlwapi.lib.

Let's see what this DLL can do for us. In the Internet Client SDK you will find quick descriptions of its functions, with short examples. This is usually sufficient, because many of the functions are self-explanatory. They are divided into three groups, which cover the following areas:

- ❑ The registry
- ❑ Strings
- ❑ Path string manipulation

I'll be using these functions in the following examples, but I won't provide exhaustive coverage of them. They are incredibly numerous and surprisingly simple, so I will point out what's new and most interesting about the functionality that you can expect from `shlwapi.dll`, rather than give an endless list of names and arguments. From shell version 4.71 on, these routines may be considered to be part of the Windows SDK.

The Registry Shell API

A great, and universally known, drawback of the Win32 Registry API is that you need to call three functions in order to get even the world's most useless and insignificant value! You have to open/create the key, do your reading or writing and then close the handle. To a greater or lesser extent, they mimic file operations. The new functions in the Registry *Shell* API are a step forward, because they save you the hassle of opening and closing the registry key each time you want a value.

Table of Functions in the Registry Shell API

The following table summarizes the most important of the new functions that you will find. They simplify the development of registry-based code, and increase productivity.

Function	Description
SHDeleteEmptyKey()	Deletes the entire sub-tree of an empty key, like Windows NT's RegDeleteKey()
SHDeleteKey()	Deletes a key and all its sub-trees, like Windows 95's RegDeleteKey()
SHDeleteValue()	Deletes a value
SHEnumKeyEx()	Enumerates the sub-keys of a given key
SHEnumValue()	Enumerates the values of a given key
SHGetValue()	Retrieves a value
SHOpenRegStream()	Returns the IStream interface to a registry value
SHQueryInfoKey()	Retrieves information about a given key
SHQueryValueEx()	Queries a registry key for a specific value
SHSetValue()	Sets a value

Manipulating Strings

High-level development tools have certainly provided us with useful ways of manipulating strings. If they choose, Windows programmers *can* rely on the facilities provided by the C runtime library, which includes things like `strstr()` and `strchr()`, but if we can get rid of the runtime library, we gain a smaller memory footprint. This is the reason why an increasing number of C runtime functions have an alias in a Windows library, and this list now includes `lstrcpy()`, `lstrcat()`, `wsprintf()` and `lstrcmp()`, to name just a few.

This trend is reinforced with `shlwapi.dll`, and we have new and interesting aliases such as `StrDup()`, `StrChr()`, `StrRChr()` and `StrStr()`. In addition, the library provides some timesaving and much-needed functions such as the two that convert a number into kilobytes, or into a time interval. `StrFormatByteSize()` is capable of taking 24102 and returning "23.5 KB" – it's even smart enough to convert to MB or GB, depending on the actual value that you pass. `StrTimeFromInterval()` can take a length of time in milliseconds and convert it into a string of minutes or hours.

To be critical for a moment, I'd say that we are *still* waiting for functions like Visual Basic's `Right$()` and `Mid$()`, although to be fair similar functionality is available with MFC's `CString` class, and with STL's `string` class.

Table of Functions for Manipulating Strings

The following table summarizes the most important of the new functions for manipulating strings. Notice that some of the functions have two versions, one of which is case sensitive. The function whose name ends with `I` is *not* case sensitive.

Function	Description
`ChrCmpI()`	Compares two characters (not case sensitive)
`StrChr()`, `StrChrI()`	First occurrence of a character in a string
`StrCmpN()`, `StrCmpNI()`	Compares the first *n* bytes of two strings
`StrDup()`	Duplicates a string
`StrFormatByteSize()`	Converts a numeric value in bytes to KB, MB or GB
`StrFromTimeInterval()`	Converts a numeric value in ms to a time interval
`StrNCat()`	Appends the specified number of characters
`StrPBrk()`	First occurrence of any of the characters in a given buffer
`StrRChr()`, `StrRStrI()`	Last occurrence of a character in a string
`StrSpn()`	Finds a substring entirely formed by a given set of characters

Table Continued on Following Page

Function	Description
StrStr(), StrStrI()	Searches for a substring
StrToInt(), StrToLong()	String to number conversion
StrToIntEx()	Decimal/Hexadecimal string to number conversion
StrTrim()	Remove leading and trailing blanks

Manipulating Path Strings

Although all of us continue to define them as strings, a path is *not* just a string. There will be few programs that you write where you won't have to reuse or rewrite a set of specialized functions for handling paths. I think that a function to add a backslash conditionally must be one of the top-ten most written functions in the history of modern computing! My own favorite macro for this purpose is contained in a single line of code:

```
#define ADDBACKSLASH(p)   lstrcat(p, (p[lstrlen(p) - 1] == 92 ? "\\" : ""))
```

The functions of shlwapi.dll sound really interesting, but sadly they won't help you to overcome really difficult problems. Their main benefit is for dealing with repetitive tasks. In Chapter 8, for example, we discussed the problems with spaces in long file names that cause FindExecutable() to fail. The list of path functions in the next section includes one for extracting arguments that appears to offer a solution, but unfortunately the function assumes that the first space is the end of the file name, which (as we have seen) is not always the case.

Table of Functions for Manipulating Path Strings

The following table summarizes many of the new functions for manipulating path strings. My favorites are PathCompactPathEx(), which provides you with a truncated path that fits in a given number of pixels, and (even better) PathSetDlgItemPath(), which exploits this function and automatically draws the path name to a child window identified by ID. Also useful are PathQuoteSpaces() and PathUnquoteSpaces(), which add and remove delimiting quotes if a path contains one or more spaces. This is just the kind of functionality that would prevent the bug in FindExecutable() (See Chapter 8).

Function	Description
PathAddBackslash()	Makes sure the path has a final backslash
PathAddExtension()	Makes sure the path has an extension
PathBuildRoot()	Builds a drive path from the drive number (0 = A, etc.)
PathCanonicalize()	Expands and properly replaces all the instances of . . and . that a path may contain
PathCombine()	Combine drive and directory path
PathCompactPath()	Truncates a path to fit a certain number of pixels

Function	Description
PathCompactPathEx()	Inserts ellipses to make a path fit a certain number of characters
PathCommonPrefix()	Compares two paths for a common prefix
PathFileExists()	Verifies that a file exists
PathFindExtension()	Gets the extension
PathFindFileName()	Gets the file name
PathFindNextComponent()	Gets the next item between two backslashes
PathGetArgs()	Returns the command line of a path
PathGetCharType()	Examines a given character with respect to the path. Is it a valid long file name character, is it a wildcard or is it a separator?
PathGetDriveNumber()	Gets the drive number. (0 = A, etc.)
PathIsDirectory()	Checks whether the given path is a directory
PathIsFileSpec()	Checks whether the given path contains separators (\, :)
PathIsRoot()	Checks whether the given path contains a root
PathIsSameRoot()	Checks whether two given paths share the same root
PathIsSystemFolder()	Checks whether the given path has the **System** attribute
PathIsUNC()	Checks whether the given path follows UNC conventions
PathIsURL()	Checks whether the given path is an URL
PathQuoteSpaces()	If a path contains a space, puts quotes around the path
PathRemoveArgs()	Removes the arguments
PathRemoveBackslash()	Makes sure there's no final backslash
PathRemoveExtension()	Makes sure there's no extension
PathRemoveFileSpec()	Makes sure there's no file or extension
PathRenameExtension()	Replaces the extension
PathSearchAndQualify()	Determines whether a path is correct and fully qualified
PathSetDlgItemPath()	Makes sure text of a control containing a path is correctly displayed in a child window

Table Continued on Following Page

Function	Description
PathSkipRoot()	Parses a path, starting from a directory
PathStripPath()	Removes the drive and directory
PathStripToRoot()	Leaves the drive only
PathUnquoteSpaces()	Makes sure the path has no delimiting quotes

The Case for SHFormatDrive()

Despite the fact that Windows 98 has shipped and a large part of the shell has been affected by recent changes, the documentation of a function called SHFormatDrive() is still poor. By combining the information here with the quick note in the MSDN Library and some articles that have appeared (see *Further Reading*), you can format disks programmatically.

What the Function Does

As its name suggests, SHFormatDrive() allows you to format a drive. In principle, you could try to format your C drive, were it not for the fact that the function (or rather, the system) prevents you from doing so! The official reason for this is that a drive with Windows or the swap file in use cannot be formatted. Whatever the merits of the argument, I'll limit my discussion here to floppies. The prototype (taken from the MSDN Library) is as follows:

```
DWORD WINAPI SHFormatDrive(HWND hwnd, UINT drive, UINT fmtID, UINT options);
```

Argument	Description
hwnd	Parent window of the dialog displayed
drive	ID of the drive to be formatted (0 = A, 1 = B, 2 = C, etc.)
fmtID	Should always be set to -1 at present
options	Type of formatting

For the type of formatting, we can choose from:

Value	Description
0	Quick format
1	Full format
2	Make system disk

The return code of the function is one of the following:

Return Code	Description
>0	Success
0	Wrong parameters passed
-1	Error while formatting
-2	Operation aborted
-3	Drive cannot be formatted

Now we have all that we need to call `SHFormatDrive()` and format our disks, like this:

```
irc = SHFormatDrive(hWnd, 0, -1, 0);
```

`SHFormatDrive()` is exported quite normally by `shell32.dll`, and `shell32.lib` contains its definition. What's missing (apart from a few lines of documentation!) is a declaration in `shellapi.h`. Since the function is defined in `shell32.lib`, you don't have to load it dynamically through `LoadLibrary()` and `GetProcAddress()` — you can just use its regular name.

Remember, though, that you'll have to add a declaration for the function *somewhere.* The one I gave above is fine, although using it from C++ will require you to declare it as having C linkage by using the `extern` keyword. See the code at the end of the section for clarification of this point.

SHFormatDrive() and Windows NT

Although the MSDN article doesn't mention it, the behavior of `SHFormatDrive()` is slightly different under Windows NT than it is under Windows 9*x*. In particular, the successful return code is 0 under NT, while it is greater than 0 under Windows 9*x*. In addition, the user interface is different, and there's a further confirmation message box that appears when you press OK to start formatting. See *Further Reading* for related articles.

The function is supported only on Windows NT 4.0 or higher. The version of the library that shipped with NT 3.51 has an entry for it, but it just returns –1. Furthermore, a 16-bit version of the function still exists in `shell.dll`.

A General Approach to Improving System Dialogs

Windows is still waiting for a well-documented function for formatting drives. Once we've figured out how to use `SHFormatDrive()`, we might be satisfied and stop there, but there's so much more that we can do! For example, I'm still wondering why the function doesn't allow us to set the disk label programmatically — doing it though `SetVolumeLabel()` seems like unnecessary extra effort. And what about a silent function that you can run *without* confirmation, and only stop when you need to?

You know that I must be working towards something! Because `SHFormatDrive()` is a dialog-based function, it offers us a place to hook onto and change anything we want about it. In fact, there's a general technique for so doing, which is:

❑ Install a `WH_CBT` hook just before calling the dialog-based function that you want to hook, because the first window of class `WC_DIALOG` created in that thread is the dialog in which we're interested
❑ Do whatever you want to do when intercepting the various events of the hook
❑ Uninstall the hook

The hook receives from the system a pointer to the `CREATESTRUCT` structure that contains information about the window to be created. We can modify its template, subclass it, modify its position or a combination of all three! The possibilities that the `WH_CBT` hook provides are numerous indeed.

The example program we will develop later in the chapter, whose dialog is shown in the figure below, exploits this technique to enable label setting and silent formatting in `SHFormatDrive()`. The options that you select on this dialog will be communicated directly to the `SHFormatDrive()` dialog by means of the hook.

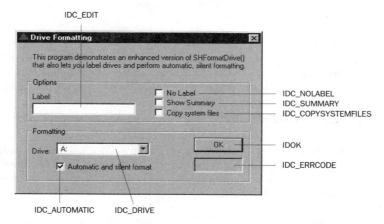

The **Drive** combo box lets you choose the drive to format (floppies only), while the **OK** button starts the operation. The various checkboxes allow the user to specify the behavior we're expecting the function to provide. The label under the **OK** button displays the value the function returns, while the **No Label, Show Summary**, and **Copy system files** checkboxes map some of the controls that populate the `SHFormatDrive()` dialog under Windows 9x. As you'll see shortly, the situation is a little different under Windows NT, and we'll be making a few runtime tweaks to the user interface.

Extending the Syntax of SHFormatDrive()

As a first step down the road to our sample application, I'll define a new function that will use `SHFormatDrive()` for much of its internal operation. Imaginatively called `FormatDrive()`, the function has the following prototype:

```
int FormatDrive(HWND hWnd, int iDrive, int iCapacity,
                int iType, LPFORMATDRIVESTRUCT lpfd);
```

The additional parameters are gathered together in the FORMATDRIVESTRUCT structure:

```
struct FORMATDRIVESTRUCT
{
    BOOL    bShowSummary;             // Unused under Windows NT
    BOOL    bNoLabel;                 // Unused under Windows NT
    BOOL    bCopySystemFiles;         // Unused under Windows NT
    BOOL    bAutomatic;               // Unused under Windows NT
    TCHAR   szLabel[11];
};

typedef FORMATDRIVESTRUCT* LPFORMATDRIVESTRUCT;
```

Many of these parameters are modeled on the layout of the dialog produced by SHFormatDrive() under Windows 9*x*, which looks like this:

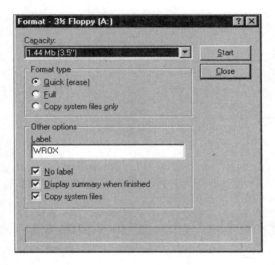

The bShowSummary, bNoLabel and bCopySystemFiles members match the analogous checkboxes in the system dialog box. szLabel will point to the new label required, while bAutomatic indicates that a silent and somewhat automatic process is required. This last feature doesn't have an analog in any of the dialog's controls, so its implementation is entirely my own.

The Windows NT Dialog Box

Unfortunately, the dialog produced by SHFormatDrive() under Windows NT is quite different, as the next figure shows:

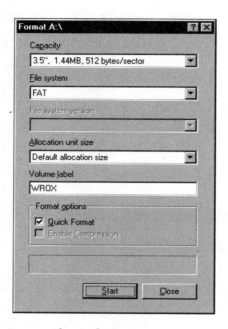

Not only are there are fewer controls, rendering our bShowSummary, bNoLabel and bCopySystemFiles structure members useless, but also the ID of the **Label** textbox is different. Spy++ reveals that it's ID_DLG_TEXTLABEL under Windows 9*x*, and ID_NT_DLG_TEXTLABEL under Windows NT. These inconsistencies will force us once again to detect on which platform we're running and execute conditional code as appropriate.

An Automatic Function for Formatting Drives

We're now in a position where we know the things our FormatDrive() function must do. It needs to establish what operating system it's running on, and to verify that the drive it has been called upon to format is removable. Then it has to squirrel away the additional parameters in global memory so that the hook can read them. After that it's just a matter of installing the hook, calling SHFormatDrive(), and uninstalling the hook again:

```
HHOOK g_hHook = NULL;            // CBT hook
BOOL g_bIsNT;                    // Are we on NT?
FORMATDRIVESTRUCT g_fd;          // Other options

LRESULT CALLBACK CBTProc(int, WPARAM, LPARAM);

extern "C" DWORD WINAPI SHFormatDrive(
                    HWND hwnd, UINT drive, UINT fmtID, UINT options);

// Format a drive calling the standard SHFormatDrive() function
int FormatDrive(HWND hWnd, int iDrive,
                int iCapacity, int iType, LPFORMATDRIVESTRUCT lpfd)
{
    // Read the platform for later use...
    OSVERSIONINFO os;
    os.dwOSVersionInfoSize = sizeof(OSVERSIONINFO);
```

```
    GetVersionEx(&os);
    g_bIsNT = (os.dwPlatformId == VER_PLATFORM_WIN32_NT);

    // Check the drive type
    TCHAR sz[5] = {0};
    wsprintf(sz, __TEXT("%c:\\"), 'A' + iDrive);
    BOOL bIsFloppy = (GetDriveType(sz) == DRIVE_REMOVABLE);
    if(!bIsFloppy)
        return -3;

    // Copy the additional parameters to global memory
    CopyMemory(&g_fd, lpfd, sizeof(FORMATDRIVESTRUCT));

    // Install the hook and call the function
    g_hHook = SetWindowsHookEx(WH_CBT, CBTProc, NULL, GetCurrentThreadId());
    int irc = SHFormatDrive(hWnd, iDrive, iCapacity, iType);
    UnhookWindowsHookEx(g_hHook);
    return irc;
}
```

This is obviously not the whole story, because, apart from a bit of elementary setup and checking, most of the actual work gets pushed off to the CBTProc() callback function that's installed and removed by the calls to SetWindowsHookEx() and UnhookWindowsHookEx() respectively. By dint of this code, CBTProc() will be called when the SHFormatDrive() dialog is about to be displayed, and that's the point at which we get to step in and make changes.

Setting Volume Labels

As you'll see when we get to the code, making the settings on the SHFormatDrive() dialog match the ones we specify in our application is a relatively easy task, but there are some other issues that CBTProc() needs to deal with.

For example, you might be thinking that to force the dialog to set a new disk label, it will be sufficient simply to put the desired text into the appropriate edit box. Unfortunately, this won't suffice because the contents of the box are actually read and utilized *only* if it has previously been edited. The dialog procedure ignores the box completely until it detects an EN_CHANGE notification message from it.

When you change the text in the control manually, this message gets sent automatically, but doing it from software doesn't have the same effect, so SetDlgItemText() alone isn't enough. In order to make the dialog believe that the text has been changed, we need to add a call to SendDlgItemMessage(), like this:

```
    SetDlgItemText(hDlg, iLabelID, szLabel);
    SendDlgItemMessage(hDlg, iLabelID, EM_SETMODIFY, TRUE, 0);
```

Here, the EM_SETMODIFY message serves the purpose of raising the EN_CHANGE notification.

Silent Formatting

Another problem with the SHFormatDrive() dialog (from the point of view of manipulating it programmatically) is that it always requires the user to click to confirm the operation. Ideally, we'd like to be able to skip this confirmation so that we can begin formatting the disk simply by clicking on a button in *our* application.

To do this, the software must simulate a click on the `SHFormatDrive()` dialog's **OK** button, and it can do so by posting a `WM_COMMAND` message to the dialog:

```
PostMessage(hDlg, WM_COMMAND, IDOK, 0);
```

There's additional complexity here: we must make sure to post the message only on the *first* occasion that the window is activated. Unfortunately, the `HCBT_ACTIVATE` event is also raised when the progress window closes, and the format dialog returns to the foreground.

In order to close the progress window programmatically (by using another message), we also need a way to detect when the formatting has been completed. The solution here is a timer that frequently checks the state of the **OK** button to see whether it is enabled – it is always disabled for the entire process of formatting. To know when to kill the timer, we just need to hook for the `HCBT_DESTROYWND` notification.

Further NT Problems

Unfortunately, this trick won't work under Windows NT because there's a further confirmation window before the format takes place. To try to work around this, we could consider hooking for the additional window as well, but for now I'm going to add support for 'automatic' operation to the list of things the application can't do under NT. Here, at last, is the code for `CBTProc()`:

```
HWND g_hwndDlg;                    // Dialog HWND
UINT g_idTimer;                    // Timer ID

void CALLBACK TimerProc(HWND, UINT, UINT, DWORD);

// CBT hook callback
LRESULT CALLBACK CBTProc(int iCode, WPARAM wParam, LPARAM lParam)
{
    static BOOL bFirstTime = TRUE;

    if(iCode < 0)
        return CallNextHookEx(g_hHook, iCode, wParam, lParam);

    // About to activate the dialog
    if(iCode == HCBT_ACTIVATE)
    {
        // Get a handle to the dialog
        g_hwndDlg = reinterpret_cast<HWND>(wParam);

        // Set the label edit box
        int iLabelID = (g_bIsNT ? ID_NT_DLG_TEXTLABEL : ID_DLG_TEXTLABEL);
        SetDlgItemText(g_hwndDlg, iLabelID, g_fd.szLabel);
        SendDlgItemMessage(g_hwndDlg, iLabelID, EM_SETMODIFY, TRUE, 0);

        // Check the option buttons
        CHECK(GetDlgItem(g_hwndDlg, ID_DLG_SHOWSUMMARY), g_fd.bShowSummary);
        CHECK(GetDlgItem(g_hwndDlg, ID_DLG_NOLABEL), g_fd.bNoLabel);
        CHECK(GetDlgItem(g_hwndDlg, ID_DLG_BOOTABLE), g_fd.bCopySystemFiles);

        // If not the first time, then must skip
        if(g_fd.bAutomatic && bFirstTime)
        {
            // Simulate a click on the Start button
            bFirstTime = FALSE;
```

```
                PostMessage(g_hwndDlg, WM_COMMAND, IDOK, 0);

            // Set the timer to detect when formatting ends
            g_idTimer = SetTimer(NULL, 1, 1000, TimerProc);
        }
    }

    // About to destroy the dialog
    if(iCode == HCBT_DESTROYWND)
    {
        // Reset first time flag and stop the timer
        bFirstTime = TRUE;
        if(g_fd.bAutomatic)
            KillTimer(NULL, g_idTimer);
    }

    return CallNextHookEx(g_hHook, iCode, wParam, lParam);
}
```

The `wParam` passed to the callback procedure is the handle of the window being activated, namely the dialog. Once you've got hold of that, accessing and modifying the content of the dialog controls is fairly straightforward. You need to know the IDs of the standard dialog controls (another job for Spy++!):

```
// IDs of Windows 9x standard dialog controls
const int ID_DLG_TEXTLABEL =        0x26;    // Edit box for label
const int ID_DLG_NOLABEL =          0x27;    // "No.Label" checkbox
const int ID_DLG_BOOTABLE =         0x28;    // "System files" checkbox
const int ID_DLG_SHOWSUMMARY =      0x29;    // "Show Summary" checkbox

// IDs of NT4 standard dialog controls
const int ID_NT_DLG_TEXTLABEL =     0x7007;  // Edit box for label
```

Then there's my handy little macro, `CHECK()`, which makes light of some repetitive calls to `PostMessage()`:

```
// Macro to post check messages more quickly
#define CHECK(h,b) \
        PostMessage(h, BM_SETCHECK, (b ? BST_CHECKED : BST_UNCHECKED), 0)
```

And finally, we have the `TimerProc()` callback function:

```
// Timer callback
void CALLBACK TimerProc(HWND hwnd, UINT uMsg, UINT idEvent, DWORD dwTime)
{
    HWND hwndOK = GetDlgItem(g_hwndDlg, IDOK);

    // Simulate the Close button being pressed
    if(IsWindowEnabled(hwndOK))
        PostMessage(g_hwndDlg, WM_COMMAND, IDCANCEL, 0);
}
```

As you can see, it watches for the **OK** button becoming enabled and then dismisses the dialog.

The Sample Program

All that remains now is to set up a Wrox AppWizard-generated application with the dialog that I showed you earlier in the chapter, and so that it uses the `FormatDrive()` function. Once you've added all the functions we've developed so far, you just need to add code to the `OnInitDialog()` and `OnOK()` functions:

```
#include "resource.h"

void OnInitDialog(HWND hDlg)
{
    // Read the platform...
    OSVERSIONINFO os;
    os.dwOSVersionInfoSize = sizeof(OSVERSIONINFO);
    GetVersionEx(&os);
    BOOL bIsNT = (os.dwPlatformId == VER_PLATFORM_WIN32_NT);

    // Disable some options if under NT
    if(bIsNT)
    {
        EnableWindow(GetDlgItem(hDlg, IDC_SUMMARY), FALSE);
        EnableWindow(GetDlgItem(hDlg, IDC_NOLABEL), FALSE);
        EnableWindow(GetDlgItem(hDlg, IDC_COPYSYSTEMFILES), FALSE);
        EnableWindow(GetDlgItem(hDlg, IDC_AUTOMATIC), FALSE);
    }

    // Fill the drive list
    HWND hwndCbo = GetDlgItem(hDlg, IDC_DRIVE);
    ComboBox_AddString(hwndCbo, __TEXT(" A:"));
    ComboBox_AddString(hwndCbo, __TEXT(" B:"));
    ComboBox_AddString(hwndCbo, __TEXT(" C:"));
    ComboBox_AddString(hwndCbo, __TEXT(" D:"));
    ComboBox_AddString(hwndCbo, __TEXT(" E:"));
    ComboBox_SetCurSel(hwndCbo, 0);

    // Set the icons (T/F as to Large/Small icon)
    SendMessage(hDlg, WM_SETICON, FALSE, reinterpret_cast<LPARAM>(g_hIconSmall));
    SendMessage(hDlg, WM_SETICON, TRUE, reinterpret_cast<LPARAM>(g_hIconLarge));
}

void OnOK(HWND hDlg)
{
    HWND hwndCbo = GetDlgItem(hDlg, IDC_DRIVE);
    int iDrive = ComboBox_GetCurSel(hwndCbo);

    FORMATDRIVESTRUCT fd;
    ZeroMemory(&fd, sizeof(FORMATDRIVESTRUCT));
    fd.bNoLabel = (IsDlgButtonChecked(hDlg, IDC_NOLABEL) == BST_CHECKED);
    fd.bShowSummary = (IsDlgButtonChecked(hDlg, IDC_SUMMARY) == BST_CHECKED);
    fd.bCopySystemFiles = (IsDlgButtonChecked(hDlg, IDC_ COPYSYSTEMFILES) ==
                        BST_CHECKED);
    fd.bAutomatic = (IsDlgButtonChecked(hDlg, IDC_AUTOMATIC) == BST_CHECKED);
    GetDlgItemText(hDlg, IDC_EDIT, fd.szLabel, 11);
    int irc = FormatDrive(hDlg, iDrive, -1, 0, &fd);

    TCHAR szBuf[MAX_PATH] = {0};
    wsprintf(szBuf, __TEXT("%d"), irc);
    SetDlgItemText(hDlg, IDC_ERRCODE, szBuf);
}
```

There's really very little to be said: `OnOK()` gets the values from the dialog, bundles them up into a `FORMATDRIVESTRUCT`, calls `FormatDrive()` and outputs the return value. What could be easier than that?

Summary

This chapter has presented some fairly new aspects of the Windows 9*x* shell. In fact, they're new not because they are relatively recent additions, but also because they are not widely known. With the usual well-documented provisos, everything you've seen in this chapter works under Windows 95 and Windows NT 4.0, as long you have installed Internet Explorer 4.0 and Active Desktop.

In this chapter, we examined:

- ❑ How to get the version number of a generic executable file
- ❑ The Recycle Bin API
- ❑ The Shell Lightweight Utility API
- ❑ An poorly-documented function for formatting drives
- ❑ A general technique for hooking and customizing system dialogs

In the book so far, we've been examining specific parts of the shell API. In this chapter, we have covered more minor aspects with a broader brush and completed the overview.

Starting with the next chapter, I'll begin to dig inside Explorer, its objects, its registry settings and its customization levels. In particular, I'll examine traditional components such as Control Panel, My Briefcase and Printers, as well as some new ones. Among these, the most noteworthy are Scriptable Shell Objects and the Windows Scripting Host.

Further Reading

A programmer's perspective of Windows 98 may be found in an article of mine that appeared in the July 98 edition of MIND, in the *Cutting Edge* column. A similar article by Matt Pietrek, entitled *A Programmer's Perspective on New System DLLs Features in Windows NT 5.0*, was published in the November and December 97 issues of MSJ.

I stated earlier that being able to leave the C runtime library out of the compiled code could improve performance and memory demand. Doubtful? Then check out two of Matt Pietrek's articles that appeared in the October 1996 issue of MSJ. One is in the *Under The Hood* column and specifically covers runtime library functions, while the other is called *Remove Fatty Deposits from Your Applications Using Our 32-bit Liposuction Tools*.

I wrote an article on `SHFormatDrive()` that appeared in the March 98 issue of WDJ, in which I endeavored to provide a uniform interface for dealing with the function, both under Windows 95 and Windows NT 4.0. Check it out; it's called *An Undocumented Function for Formatting Drives*.

Finally, as usual, here's a list of related Knowledge Base articles:

Article ID: Q158439: *Files with Long Extensions Bypass the Recycle Bin When Deleted*
Article ID: Q168570: *Files Do Not Show Up in Recycle Bin When Deleted*
Article ID: Q17169: *Differences Between the Recycle Bin and the Recycled Folder*
Article ID: Q136517: *How the Recycle Bin Stores Files*
Article ID: Q173688: *Call SHFormatDrive in Windows 95 and Windows NT*

11

Exploring the Shell

We'll now turn our attention away from the API and to the Windows Shell itself. My goal for this chapter and the rest of the book is to provide you with a clear and comprehensive understanding of how Explorer works, what objects make up the shell's namespace, and finally how you can customize and extend its characteristics and behavior.

The Windows Shell, also known as Explorer, is a collection of specialized modules that work together to form the shell's namespace and give it the ability to perform a lot of specialized tasks. These include such things as exploring a folder, showing a specific directory sub-tree, or loading an external module and communicating with it. Although the end result may be different, whenever these objects are invoked and displayed, it is always Explorer working away in the background.

In many cases, Explorer provides these services by communicating with a given program through its command line. It's therefore important to understand what Explorer expects from your applications if you want it to manage them effectively for you. (This topic will be covered in much more detail in Chapter 14.)

In this chapter, we'll be covering the following topics:

- ❑ Explorer's command line
- ❑ The `RunDll32` program that runs system dialogs
- ❑ The shell objects My Briefcase, Control Panel, Printers and Scheduled Tasks
- ❑ Scrap objects

The source code example for this chapter provides you with a tool that could well be useful to you in your everyday work. It brings together many of the topics we have covered in recent chapters, such as shortcuts and registry manipulation, and also addresses some new topics that we will be discussing in detail in the next few chapters.

This tool, called NewLink, provides an alternative and far more flexible way to create shortcuts, on the desktop or elsewhere. If you really like it, you can even install it as your default shortcut handler, replacing the standard Windows Wizard.

Explorer's Command Line

Explorer has a command line that can take four optional switches, and as a result there are several possible combinations:

```
explorer.exe [/n [, <folder>]]
             [/e [, <folder>]]
             [, /root, <object>]
             [[, /select], <sub object>]
```

Notice the use of commas in the command line structure. This is certainly an unusual thing to see, but it's not a mistake — that really is how it works! The following table explains what the switches mean:

Switch	Description
/n	Opens the specified folder in a new, single-paned view. A single-paned view looks like the windows you get in My Computer, and is based on a list view.
/e	Opens the specified folder in a new, double-paned view. This is the typical Explorer view, with the namespace in the left pane as a tree view, and the details in the right pane.
/root	Makes the specified folder the root of the tree view. Requires an /e view.
/select	Selects the specified item in the left pane (the tree view).

The simplest switch is the /select option, which is used to select a specific sub-item within the opened folder. Here's an example of the syntax:

```
explorer /e, /select, c:\windows
```

You need to use this flag in conjunction with /e, because the /select flag requires a tree view. There's no way to select an item in the right pane, or the folder in a single-pane view. When you use the /n and /e switches, you specify the folder name following a comma:

```
explorer /e, c:\
explorer /n, c:\
explorer c:\
```

The second and third of the command lines listed above produce identical results (a single-paned view) — in other words, /n is the default option.

The /root Switch

You'll often come across views that look like Explorer views, but which have a particular folder as the root node. You can open Explorer views like this by using the /e and /root switches together, thus:

```
explorer /e, /root, c:\windows
```

Note that when a view is opened with a root other than the Desktop, the user cannot navigate up the tree. If you run Explorer using c:\windows as the root, then you won't be able to access c:\ or any other directory at the same level in the tree as c:\windows.

Using Special Folders as the Root

Special folders, such as the Recycle Bin, don't have a one-to-one correspondence with file system folders. As we've discussed before, these **namespace extensions** are in-process COM servers, and as such are identified by a CLSID. The /root switch lets you specify a CLSID as the folder to be used, although a couple of constraints must be satisfied:

❑ The COM server must implement all the interfaces required for a namespace extension.
❑ You have to prefix the CLSID with :: to refer to it on Explorer's command line. The syntax ::{clsid} is handled as if it's an ordinary directory name.

Take the following line as an example:

```
explorer ::{645FF040-5081-101B-9F08-00AA002F954E}
```

This will open a new window on the Recycle Bin, and you'll be able to do exactly the same with your own custom folders. The following table contains the CLSIDs of a few of the folder objects you might find on your desktop, but note that not all the objects on the desktop are folders – Inbox and My Briefcase, for example, are applications.

CLSID	Object
645FF040-5081-101B-9F08-00AA002F954E	Recycle Bin
20D04FE0-3AEA-1069-A2D8-08002B30309D	My Computer
208D2C60-3AEA-1069-A2D7-08002B30309D	Network Neighborhood
871C5380-42A0-1069-A2EA-08002B30309D	Internet Explorer
645FF040-5081-101B-9F08-00AA002F954E	Recycle Bin
21EC2020-3AEA-1069-A2DD-08002B30309D	Control Panel
992CFFA0-F557-101A-88EC-00DD010CCC48	Dial-Up Networking
2227A280-3AEA-1069-A2DE-08002B30309D	Printers

Note that in this context, you can treat CLSIDs like traditional folders and combine them using slashes. For example, to access the `Printers` folder, which is a sub-folder of `My Computer`, you can use the following syntax:

```
explorer ::{20D04FE0-3AEA-1069-A2D8-08002B30309D}\
                              ::{2227A280-3AEA-1069-A2DE-08002B30309D}
```

What is rundll32.exe?

As I said a little earlier, the command line plays a primary role in the organization of Explorer. Many of the functions that you can execute on file objects are carried out through the command line. To help with this, Windows 9*x* and Windows NT 4.0 (and higher) come with a helper program called `rundll32.exe` that allows you to call a DLL-exported function directly from the command line. This utility is a simple wrapper built around the few API calls that are necessary to execute a DLL function dynamically.

The following pseudo-code shows you roughly what `rundll32` is doing:

```
void DoRunDll32(LPCTSTR szDllName, LPCTSTR szFuncName, LPCTSTR szCmdLine)
{
    // Load the library into memory
    HANDLE hLib = LoadLibrary(szDllName);

    // Get the address of the function we've been asked to execute
    FARPROC pFunc = GetProcAddress(hLib, szFuncName);

    // Execute the function using the pointer
    pFunc(GetFocus(), hLib, szCmdLine, SW_SHOW);

    // Free the library
    FreeLibrary(hLib);
}
```

In real life, all `rundll32` receives is a single string that it parses to extract the DLL and function names, plus any optional arguments for the function. The command line looks like this:

```
rundll32 dllname,funcname [arguments]
```

The DLL name and the function name must be comma-separated, *with no blanks between them*. If you call `rundll32` without specifying a fully qualified name for the DLL, it is searched for in all the standard paths, including the application's directory, the Windows directories, and the current directory.

A flaw of this program is that it doesn't usually return enough information in the case of errors. If the DLL function you're trying to call is missing (say, you mistyped its name), then it lets you know quite precisely what happened. However, if the function can be called but fails during execution, the chances are that you will have to guess the causes yourself!

The `rundll32` interface is often used to call into some little known system dialogs, and you can also use it to let other users call into your own DLLs. To be able to do so, all that matters is that the callable functions have a predefined prototype.

Functions Callable By rundll32.exe

In the pseudo-code above, look at the line that actually calls the DLL function. Rundll32 can *only* be used to call functions with the following prototype – it is made up of four parameters, of which the user sets only one:

```
void CALLBACK FuncName(HWND hwnd,                // Window handle
                       HINSTANCE hinst,          // Instance handle
                       LPTSTR lpszCmdLine,       // Command line
                       int nCmdShow);            // ShowWindow() parameter
```

The first parameter, hwnd, is used to give a parent to any dialog box that may be created by the function. In principle, this means that such dialogs will be modal with respect to the parent window. In practice, though, this parameter always evaluates to the desktop window (that is, hwnd is NULL), so any new window will be modeless with respect to all the other windows opened in the shell.

The second parameter is an HINSTANCE handle, which is the handle of the library, itself as returned by LoadLibrary(). The fourth parameter, nCmdShow, determines how the window will be displayed, and is always SW_SHOW when the function is called through rundll32.

The only 'controllable' parameter is the function command line lpszCmdLine, through which the function will receive its argument data. As an example, suppose you have a function that takes two numbers. Its definition might be:

```
void MyFunc(int iFirst, long lSecond)
{
    ...
}
```

To make this function callable through the rundll32 interface, it should be changed like this:

```
void MyFunc1(HWND hwnd, HINSTANCE hinst, LPTSTR lpszCmdLine, int nShow)
{
    int iFirst;
    long lSecond;

    // Parse the command line, and crack out the parameters
    ParseCommandLine(lpszCmdLine, &iFirst, &lSecond);

    // Call the function with the parameters we've extracted
    MyFunc(iFirst, lSecond);
}
```

Under Windows NT, the function to call is first searched with its Unicode name, then with the ANSI name, and finally as it is written. This means that a call to MyFunc() will be converted to calls to MyFuncW(), MyFuncA() and MyFunc(), in that order. Of course, in the case of Unicode calls the string will be passed in wide characters and evaluates to a LPWSTR rather than a LPSTR.

What you can do with rundll32.exe

rundll32 (and its 16-bit ancestor, called simply rundll) is used mainly to display system dialog boxes and to call DLL functions in situations where only a command line can be specified. Originally, it was a tool designed by Microsoft for internal use only, and the limited set of practices for which it was intended are obvious.

The program can save you from having to load and unload DLLs explicitly when you're testing code, and sometimes it can help you to check the dialogs exported from a DLL. On the other hand, it forces you to adopt a fixed syntax for function calls, and there's no mechanism for returning data to the caller. There is, however, one particular way in which you might want to use it.

You can use rundll32 to gain access to some of the system dialogs, including ones that aren't easily accessible due to lack of documentation. In many cases, this is by design and the *only* recommended (and documented) way to access such things is by using rundll32. As an example, let's consider the Add New Printer Wizard:

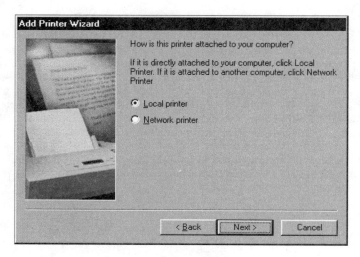

This Wizard is implemented and invoked by the system through a function located in sysdm.cpl, which by its extension we can identify as a Control Panel DLL. The documentation suggests that you call it like this:

```
rundll32.exe sysdm.cpl,InstallDevice_Rundll printer
```

Instead of a more 'natural' straight call to InstallDevice_Rundll(). This function takes the four parameters we've already discussed, and uses the word printer as an argument to decide what to do. In fact, although it is undocumented, you can use the same syntax to install a new modem or a monitor, simply by replacing the word printer with the modem or monitor.

A RunDll() Function

Many system dialogs and Wizards are *only* supposed to be invoked by using rundll32. This is probably because things could change in the future, in which event using rundll32 would shield you from the new details. It may also be that some aspects of these functions and dialogs are not meant to be completely public, and again, using an interface like rundll32 hides many of them.

The next listing shows a possible implementation of a C++ function that mimics what rundll32 does. As such it revisits our earlier pseudo-code example, adding error checking and a means of specifying the parent window:

```
void RunDll(HWND hwnd, LPCTSTR szDllName, LPCTSTR szFunc, LPCTSTR szCmdLine)
{
    HANDLE hLib = NULL;
    hLib = LoadLibrary(szDllName);
    if(hLib == NULL)
        return;
    FARPROC pFunc = NULL;
    pFunc = GetProcAddress(hLib, szFunc);
    if(!pFunc == NULL)
        pFunc(hwnd, hLib, szCmdLine, SW_SHOW);

    FreeLibrary(hLib);
}
```

By writing our own wrapper function in this way, we can pass any window we like as the parent of any child dialog, enabling us to display dialogs that really *are* modal. In the source code for this book that you can download from the Wrox web site, there's a sample application called RunXXX that uses a function just like this one.

Rundll32.exe Protection Faults

Of course, you can try to use rundll32 with functions not specifically designed to work with it, but you do so at your own risk – there can be problems. For instance, if you try to run a dialog, you may well find that a protection fault occurs when you close it. Try executing the following code from the Run dialog box:

```
rundll32 appwiz.cpl,ConfigStartMenu
```

The command will display a window that allows you to modify the content of the Programs menu:

When I close this dialog on my machine (which is running Internet Explorer 4.0), rundll32 produces this error:

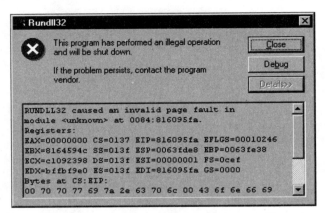

However, I've found out that if you issue the same command from within your own code, using a function like RunDll() above, it will work just fine!

This is just one example. If you search the MSDN Knowledge Base archive for 'rundll' *or* 'rundll32', *you'll find a number of articles describing various faults caused by* rundll32 *when exiting from dialogs.*

Commonly Used Commands

In some cases, these crashes stem from incorrect use of the function. If you ask rundll32 to execute a function that has a prototype other than the recommended one, you'll probably get an error. It's not possible to know exactly which exported functions are safely callable from rundll32, but you can be sure that a function will work if its name includes a self-explanatory RunDll prefix or suffix.

By delving into Knowledge Base articles, newsgroups, and several other places, I've put together a short list of calls that allow you to access otherwise undocumented system dialogs:

Dialog	Command line
Internet Properties	Rundll32 Inetcpl.cpl,LaunchInternetControlPanel
Remove Shortcuts/Folders	Rundll32 appwiz.cpl,ConfigStartMenu
Open With	Rundll32 shell32.dll,OpenAs_RunDLL file
Connect to *My Connection*	Rundll32 rnaui.dll,RnaDial *My Connection*
Make New Connection	Rundll32 RnaUI.dll,RnaWizard
Add Printer Wizard	Rundll32 sysdm.cpl,InstallDevice_Rundll printer
Install New Modem	Rundll32 sysdm.cpl,InstallDevice_Rundll modem
Install New Monitor	Rundll32 sysdm.cpl,InstallDevice_Rundll monitor
Add New Hardware Wizard	Control.exe sysdm.cpl,Add New Hardware

Internet Properties is the well-known tabbed dialog that appears if you double-click on the Internet applet from the Control Panel, or if you choose the View | Internet Options... menu of Internet Explorer, or even if you select Properties from the context menu associated with the Internet Explorer icon. Moving on, we saw the **Remove Shortcuts/Folders** dialog during our earlier experimentation, while **Open With** is the dialog that pops up when you try to open a file that hasn't got a default viewer.

Connect to is the dialog that lets you connect to the Internet through the specified dial-up networking applet. Note that you don't have to place the string that represents the connection in quotes, even if the name includes spaces. **Make New Connection** runs the system Wizard to add a new connection to the `Dial-Up Networking` folder. As I've already mentioned, the remaining **Add/Make** dialogs allow you to add a new modem, printer or monitor to the system's hardware configuration.

The last item in the table, **Add New Hardware Wizard**, is the default Wizard that scans your PC, searching for new plug-and-play hardware. As you can see, however, it is not tied to `rundll32` for execution. Instead, it relies on `control.exe`, which is the executable behind the Control Panel; I've included it here because it leads us on to a new topic: Explorer's constituent objects.

If you're running a non-English version of Windows, the Add New Hardware Wizard *command line won't work properly. You won't get an error message, but I can tell you that the problem is due to localization — instead of the string* Add New Hardware, *you should use its localized version. I'll say more about this topic later on.*

The Explorer's Objects

The figure below shows a view of the shell's namespace. All the folders you can see below the desktop are the objects that form the shell. `My Computer` and `Network Neighborhood` hold the details of the PC and its connections to the network. The `Internet Explorer` node is a virtual folder that represents the Internet. If a connection is present, you can expand it to see any web pages currently displayed as if they are ordinary files. The `Recycle Bin` and `My Briefcase` complete the desktop's list of objects.

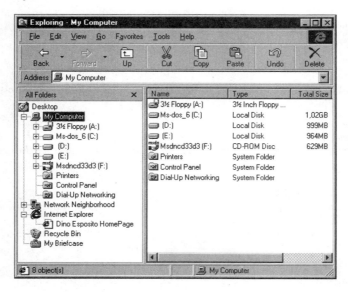

We talked about the Recycle Bin in Chapter 10: it's a virtual folder that collects the statuses of multiple physical folders distributed across all the local fixed drives. Each of these folders contains references to the files marked for deletion.

My Briefcase is an interesting but less well-known (and less frequently used!) feature that helps you keep files and directories synchronized when you need to use them on more than one PC. I'll have more to about this a little later on.

Under the node called My Computer there are some more special folders. From the programmer's point of view, the most interesting are:

- ❑ Printers
- ❑ Control Panel
- ❑ Dial-Up Networking
- ❑ Scheduled Tasks (Windows 98 and higher only)

Other special folders located under the Windows directory hold details of subscriptions, downloaded program files, and the history of visited sites.

The Control Panel

Control Panel is a sort of repository for dialogs that describe and configure hardware and software components. The system provides a number of these dialogs automatically, and you can also add your own. The Control Panel folder is a namespace extension that's filled by reading information from all the .cpl files found in the System directory. There's also a little executable called control.exe that simply asks the shell to open the folder, and then manages the activity of the user, notifying the applets accordingly.

Of course, for an application you write to be a Control Panel item, you need rather more than just a .cpl extension. First and foremost, the file must be a DLL, but it must also satisfy a number of additional requirements:

- ❑ It must export a function called CPlApplet()
- ❑ It must respond properly to certain messages
- ❑ It must provide an icon and a dialog box

The behavior of a Control Panel applet is entirely built around the configuration dialog that it displays – one applet, one dialog.

> *Despite the fact that today, the term **applet** is mostly used to describe little Java modules, it has been used for a long time in the Microsoft documentation to denote the components of the Control Panel.*

Developing Control Panel Applets

A Control Panel applet DLL must export a function called CPlApplet() that has the following prototype:

```
LONG CPlApplet(HWND hwndCPl,   // Handle of the parent window for the dialog
               UINT uMsg,      // Message received
               LONG lParam1,   // First argument specific for the message
               LONG lParam2);  // Second argument specific for the message
```

This function is basically the window procedure for the applet – the controlling application communicates with an applet by sending messages to this function. In particular, it may ask for the number of applets the DLL implements, as well as information about the icon, name and description of any given applet. Many `.cpl` files implement only a single applet, but there's nothing to prevent them from implementing more than that. The following table shows all the possible messages:

Message	Description
CPL_DBLCLK	The applet icon has been double-clicked, so the associated dialog should show up. The `lParam1` argument is the 0-based number of the applet in the DLL. This message is sent after `CPL_INQUIRE` and `CPL_NEWINQUIRE`. The `lParam2` argument contains the user data defined in the `lData` member of the `CPLINFO` structure. (See later.)
CPL_EXIT	This follows `CPL_STOP` and gets sent immediately before the applet is unloaded. It takes no parameters.
CPL_GETCOUNT	Asks the DLL to return the number of applets it implements. It is sent after `CPL_INIT` and takes no parameters.
CPL_INIT	Sent immediately after the applet is loaded. It takes no parameters.
CPL_INQUIRE	Used to get information about the applet. It is called only once and the information the applet returns is cached by the system. The `lParam1` argument is the 0-based number of the applet in the DLL. `lParam2` is a pointer to a `CPLINFO` structure that must be filled in.
CPL_NEWINQUIRE	Used for the same purpose as `CPL_INQUIRE`, it makes use of a different structure and can be sent more than once during the session. The `lParam1` argument is the 0-based number of the dialog in the DLL; `lParam2` is a pointer to a `NEWCPLINFO` structure that must be filled in.
CPL_SELECT	Obsolete and unsupported on all Win32 platforms.
CPL_STOP	Sent only once to denote that the dialog is going to be closed. The `lParam1` argument is the 0-based number of the dialog in the DLL. The `lParam2` argument denotes the user-defined data defined in the `lData` member of the `CPLINFO` structure.

As you can see, the `lParam1` argument is *always* the index of the dialog in the DLL, except in the case of messages that take no parameters. The `lParam2` argument, on the other hand, can have two meanings: it may represent a custom 32-bit buffer, or it might be a pointer to a data structure used to gather information about the dialog.

There are two messages used by the controlling application to get information about the dialog displayed by a given applet: `CPL_INQUIRE` and `CPL_NEWINQUIRE`. In these cases, `lParam2` points to one of two different structures – `CPLINFO` and `NEWCPLINFO` – which are defined as shown overleaf:

```
typedef struct tagCPLINFO
{
    int  idIcon; // Resource ID of the applet's icon
    int  idName; // Resource ID for the string with the dialog's short name
    int  idInfo; // Resource ID for the string with the dialog's description
    LONG lData;  // Data defined by the application
} CPLINFO;
```

```
typedef struct tagNEWCPLINFO
{
    DWORD dwSize;               // Size of the structure
    DWORD dwFlags;              // Currently ignored
    DWORD dwHelpContext;        // Currently ignored
    LONG  lData;                // Data defined by the application
    HICON hIcon;                // Handle of the applet's icon
    TCHAR szName[32];           // Short name of the dialog
    TCHAR szInfo[64];           // Description of the dialog
    TCHAR szHelpFile[128];      // Currently ignored
} NEWCPLINFO;
```

As you can see, despite different declarations, the structures contain the same information at this time. A Control Panel applet should answer at least one of the associated messages, and in most cases CPL_INQUIRE offers slightly better performance due to the caching of information. If any of the returned information is subject to change during the session, though, then you need to support CPL_NEWINQUIRE as well. In fact, the latter message is sent each time that the controller is about to use any of the applet's information. Another subtle difference is that CPLINFO requires the information to be stored in the applet's resources, whereas NEWCPLINFO returns them in ready-to-use buffers.

There might be circumstances in which you want to associate global status information with the applet — it's never *necessary*, but sometimes it can help, and this is where the lData member comes into play. The following listing shows a sample CPlApplet() function:

```
LONG CPlApplet(HWND hwndCPl, UINT uMsg, LONG lParam1, LONG lParam2)
{
    // Save the index of the dialog to consider
    int iDlgIndex = lParam1;

    switch(uMsg)
    {
    // Do any initialization that might be required
    case CPL_INIT:
        return 1;

    // Return the number of applets in this DLL
    case CPL_GETCOUNT:
        return g_iNumOfApplets;

    // Fill in the fields in the CPLINFO structure
    case CPL_INQUIRE:
        LPCPLINFO pCPL = reinterpret_cast<LPCPLINFO>(lParam2);
        pCPL->idIcon = g_iIconIndex;
        pCPL->idName = g_pszAppName;
        pCPL->idInfo = g_pszDesc;
        break;
```

```
    // Display the dialog on receipt of a double-click message
    case CPL_DBLCLK:
        DialogBox(GetModuleHandle(NULL),
                        MAKEINTRESOURCE(g_iDlgID), hwndCPl, pfnDlgProc);
        break;
    }

    return 1;
}
```

Running Control Panel Applets

The control.exe application that I mentioned earlier in this chapter is not the program behind the Control Panel folder, but simply a stub that invokes Explorer to display the contents of all the .cpl files it can find. In fact, Control Panel isn't a physical folder at all — the representation and all the work of managing it are dealt with by the namespace extension that implements the folder.

If you want to run a Control Panel applet from a program, the best approach is to use rundll32 to execute a function called Control_RunDLL() that's exported by the shell32.dll library:

```
rundll32.exe shell32.dll,Control_RunDLL applet.cpl
```

The above line will execute the applet called applet.cpl by sending a CPL_DBLCLK message to the CPlApplet() function exported by the DLL. You could also call Control_RunDLL() using the RunDll() wrapper function that we put together earlier, for example:

```
RunDll(hDlg, "shell32.dll", "Control_RunDLL", "desk.cpl,,3");
```

The output from this command is shown in the figure below:

The command calls the display applet (desk.cpl) and tells it to display its fourth tab (the 3 in the command line above refers to the fourth element in a 0-based counting system). This works because when you call a Control Panel applet through Control_RunDLL(), you can specify three parameters of which two are optional. The first argument is the name of the .cpl file, while the second argument is the 0-based number of the applet implemented in the DLL. This defaults to 0, and must be prefixed by @. The third argument is the 0-based index of the tab you want to select initially. Of course, this applies only to dialogs with multiple tabs, and once again defaults to 0.

With this explanation in mind, the above string desk.cpl,,3 must be read as, "Display the fourth tab in the first applet found in desk.cpl". As a further example, let's consider the sysdm.cpl module, which contains two applets: **System** and **Add New Hardware**. To display the second page of the first applet, which lists the peripherals installed on your system, you'd use this command line:

```
RunDll(hDlg, "shell32.dll", "Control_RunDLL", "sysdm.cpl,,1");
```

Which is equivalent to:

```
RunDll(hDlg, "shell32.dll", "Control_RunDLL", "sysdm.cpl,@0,1");
```

To start the **Add New Hardware** Wizard, on the other hand, you'd say:

```
RunDll(hDlg, "shell32.dll", "Control_RunDLL", "sysdm.cpl,@1");
```

This call reflects the fact that we're invoking the second applet in the DLL, which is not a tabbed dialog.

Control_RunDLL() vs. Control.exe

Earlier, I presented another way to run the **Add New Hardware** Wizard, using the control.exe program:

```
control.exe sysdm.cpl,Add New Hardware
```

While this approach certainly works, it has the significant drawback that the command line will vary according to localization, and this tends to make it inferior to the Control_RunDLL() solution. If you're running, say, the Italian version of Windows, the string will be Nuovo Hardware instead of Add New Hardware. This means that the command line must be changed to:

```
control.exe sysdm.cpl,Nuovo Hardware
```

The localized string has the ID 202 in the string list of the library sysdm.cpl and is also returned through the CPlApplet() interface.

RunDll32.exe and RunDll() Trade-offs

rundll32.exe and our function RunDll() provide the same functionality, and there are points in favor of both of them. The rundll32.exe program is a standard part of the operating system, and you can expect it to be updated in newer versions of Windows. This means that even if Microsoft changes rundll32's programming interface – the prototype required for functions to be called correctly – the program will still continue to work properly.

On the other hand, if you're developing 16-bit code under Windows NT, you don't have an equivalent 16-bit version of `rundll32`. (There's one called `rundll.exe` under Windows 9*x*.) More importantly, `rundll32` is a program that you can't control directly, and it always starts a new process. The `RunDll()` function, on the other hand, runs in the address space of the caller.

The Printers Folder

The `Printers` folder doesn't map to a real file system folder either – it's a virtual folder that provides access to the printing devices available on the system, such as printers and fax machines. When you install a new printer on your PC, a new file is created in a hidden subdirectory under `Windows`. This subdirectory plays the same role as the `Recycled` folders of the Recycle Bin that we examined in Chapter 10. The directory is called `PrintHood`, and its path can be retrieved using the `SHGetSpecialFolderPath()` API function.

> *We examined how to browse the contents of the* `Printers` *folder in Chapter 5, and we'll return to the subject in the next chapter, where we'll look at the new scriptable shell objects that offer much of the navigational functionality we built earlier through Automation.*

When talking about printers, we need to look at the `SHInvokePrinterCommand()` function, which lets you send commands to printer objects. This function is supported only by shell versions 4.71 and higher, and looks like this:

```
BOOL SHInvokePrinterCommand(HWND    hwnd,
                            UINT    uAction,
                            LPCTSTR lpBuf1,
                            LPCTSTR lpBuf2,
                            BOOL    fModal);
```

Parameter	Description
hwnd	Parent window for any dialog or window to be displayed by the function
uAction	Code that identifies the action to be performed on the printer. (See below)
lpBuf1	Buffer that contains additional information related to the action; this is invariably the name of the printer
lpBuf2	Buffer that contains additional information related to the action
fModal	If set to TRUE, the function must wait for the action to complete before returning

Invoking Printer Commands

The `uAction` parameter can take the values shown overleaf:

Command	Description
PRINTACTION_OPEN	Opens a window that displays the status of the printer
PRINTACTION_PROPERTIES	Displays the properties of the printer
PRINTACTION_TESTPAGE	Prints a test page
PRINTACTION_OPENNETPRN	The same as PRINTACTION_OPEN, but for network printers
PRINTACTION_NETINSTALL	Installs the specified network printer
PRINTACTION_NETINSTALLLINK	Creates a shortcut to the specified network printer; lpBuf2 points to the path for the shortcut

In all cases, lpBuf1 points to the name of the printer, be it local, network or shared. In the case of network printers, the name must follow the UNC format (\\server\printer). The lpBuf2 parameter, on the other hand, is used only with the PRINTACTION_NETINSTALLLINK flag.

Under Windows NT, a couple of other flags are supported for network printers only: PRINTACTION_SERVERPROPERTIES, which displays properties for the server, and PRINTACTION_DOCUMENTDEFAULTS, which shows the properties of the default document on this printer.

As usual, the Wrox AppWizard makes an excellent starting point for creating a quick application to test aspects of SHInvokePrinterCommand() and the web site code contains a basic example. As with its similarly named brethren, the header file that defines the function is shellapi.h.

What the Function Returns

The documentation states that the function returns non-zero values *if successful*, but try as I might, I was unable to make it return a value of zero. The function stubbornly returned TRUE even when I specified a non-existent printer. Depending upon the command you've executed, you may get an error message that tells you what has happened.

Dial-Up Networking

Dial-Up Networking is a virtual folder that collects all the available Internet and network connections. The associated functions are exported by rnaui.dll, and are called RnaDial() (for dialing a connection) and RnaWizard() (for setting up a new connection). They both support the rundll32 interface, and can therefore be run by the methods I described earlier in the chapter.

If you want to connect to the Internet without dealing with specific connections, you can resort to the WinInet API. In particular, the InternetAutoDial() function lets you connect through the default connection defined in the Dial-Up Networking folder.

Offline Browsing

Internet Explorer 4.0 introduced **offline browsing** – that is, a browse mode that accesses pages exclusively from a local cache. You can detect this state through the `InternetQueryOption()` function in the WinInet API, while the `InternetGoOnline()` function presents a dialog box with the options either to connect or to remain offline. All these topics are well covered in the Internet Client SDK documentation, and for more information about the WinInet API you should refer to *Further Reading*.

Scheduled Tasks

The **Task Scheduler** (or **scheduling agent**) is a module that was introduced under Windows 95 and Windows NT 4.0 with the Active Desktop update, and was then included in Windows 98. Its main purpose is to provide you with the ability to run specified tasks at particular times, or when predefined criteria are satisfied.

From the programmer's perspective, the Task Scheduler is a COM server that exposes the functionality to define a task and the trigger that causes it to execute. Basically, the Task Scheduler is a simple monitor application that spends all its time watching for certain combinations of date, day of week and time that have been marked as 'interesting', and then executes actions as required.

Windows NT Support for Scheduling

The scheduling agent introduced with shell version 4.71 is an application functionally similar to the `AT` command provided with Windows NT. What's different is that the `AT` command employs the NetSchedule API, while the agent exposes COM interfaces.

The Scheduling Agent

The scheduling agent under Windows 9*x* is the program `mstask.exe`, while under NT it is a service called `Schedule`. The agent isn't started by default unless you're running Windows 98, which also includes a special folder with which to keep track of the scheduled tasks. The Internet Client SDK provides several code examples that illustrate how to start and drive the agent.

The objects that the agent manages are the tasks. A task is basically an executable file, and each task can have one or more triggers that decide when it's time to execute.

The scheduling agent is a server application that manages all the defined tasks, launches them at the right time, and returns information about the time of last execution, the total number of executions and the like. The functionality of the scheduling agent is fully described by the `ITaskScheduler` interface.

Tasks and Triggers

A **task** is described by the `IScheduledWorkItem` and `ITask` interfaces, and these expose methods that are not very different from those you would find in a shortcut. You set up a task using information such as application name, working directory, parameters, priority, maximum allowed time of execution, and – most importantly – the trigger. `ITask` derives from `IScheduledWorkItem`, and is a more specialized version of that interface. There may be many different types of work items defined in the future, but at present only tasks are supported. A task can be a Win32 or Win16 application, an OS/2 or MS-DOS application, a batch file (`*.bat`), a command file (`*.cmd`), or indeed any file type properly registered with a handler application.

Triggers are events used to identify the right moment to run a work item. In many cases, a trigger is a unique time, such as "12:00:00 on December 3rd 1998". In other cases, it may be repeatable, such as "6:00:00 on the third Monday of each month". Triggers are manipulated using the `ITaskTrigger` interface and the `TASK_TRIGGER` structure, which defines the starting time of the task, its repetition frequency, and its parameters.

All the related interfaces and the structures involved with task scheduling are fully documented in the Internet Client SDK, and you should refer there for more detailed information and samples.

My Briefcase

`My Briefcase` is a Windows 95 utility designed to help users maintain multiple copies of the same documents on different computers. Once you've put a document in the `My Briefcase` folder, the software will take care of keeping the copy in the briefcase synchronized with the original.

This is useful when you are working between, say, a desktop PC and a laptop. You'll usually consider the copy on the desktop machine as the 'original', and replace it with the modified version that comes from the laptop. Then, just click on the file name in the `My Briefcase` folder to have it check and synchronize the copies:

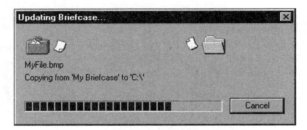

If one of the files has changed since the last synchronization operation, Windows automatically replaces the unmodified files with the modified copies. If *both* files appear to have been changed, then a merge operation will occur. The merge operation involves some interfaces that you can implement in order to handle merging your own documents:

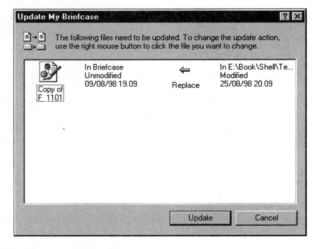

The objects that implement these interfaces are called **reconcilers**, and they are involved in determining whether two versions of the same file are aligned or not. If both have changed, the module can provide the means to merge the content to produce a new copy. This operation can be interactive or not, as required, and may leave residue files. Precisely how the merge works will depend upon the specific implementation of the reconciler.

Details about reconcilers can be found in the Internet Client SDK documentation, as well as in the Windows 95 Resource Kit.

Scrap Objects

Have you ever tried to select a piece of text from a Microsoft Word document and move or copy it onto the Windows desktop? Surprisingly, the mouse cursor changes to an encouraging arrow instead of a stop sign, meaning that you *can* drop that piece of Word document straight onto the desktop (or any other Windows folder)! When you do so, you create a **scrap object**:

Basically, you're looking at a *link* to an object. Scraps are files with .shs extensions that are automatically created when an object implementing IDataObject is dropped onto a folder or the desktop. To read scraps, there's a rundll32-compliant function exported by shscrap.dll. This library is located in the System directory and is not officially documented, because scrap support should be provided automatically if you create a fully-fledged OLE application. However, if you're interested in experimenting, shscrap.dll exports a function called OpenScrap_RunDLL() that you can use to open any .shs file.

A New Shortcut Handler

In this book so far, we've discussed a number of individual topics and discussed the ways to integrate particular features into your next application. In this chapter, however, we've started to explore the components of the shell, focusing mainly on folders and command lines. Now I'm going to present a significant example that uses many of the basic topics we've covered so far (shortcuts, icons, and folders) and looks ahead towards shell customization. We're going to assemble a tool similar to (but better than!) one of the standard Windows components, and then discover how to replace the standard component with our own.

If you try to create a shortcut by right-clicking on the desktop, or on any folder in Explorer, or by selecting the File | New | Shortcut menu, you'll be prompted with a Wizard that allows you to specify the target object and the name of the file you want to create. The target folder for the .lnk file is always assumed to be the folder from which the process started. There's no way to specify a description, or a hotkey, or even an icon, and neither can you decide where to create the shortcut.

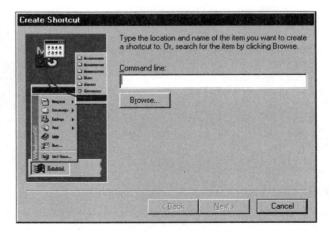

To work around all these limitations, we're going to build our own shortcut creator, and to make things even better we're also going to substitute it for the standard Windows shortcut Wizard. In this way, each time you right-click to create a new shortcut anywhere in the shell, our application will pop up instead of the standard dialog.

The User Interface

This new Wizard for creating shortcuts will provide fields for entering the target file object, a description, a hotkey and an icon. In addition, it will allow users to choose the path and name of the final shortcut. The path can be expressed in terms of an absolute drive and directory, or in terms of a special folder ID, such as Desktop, Send To, Programs, Start Menu, and a few others.

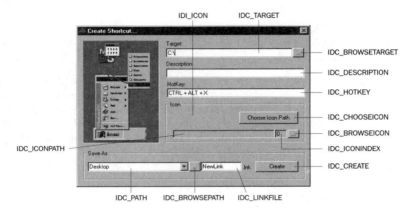

The above screenshot shows the user interface. The first edit box will contain the name of the target file, which you can browse for if you choose. The second edit box is for the shortcut's description, while the third specifies the key combination to be used to recall it.

The next area lets you choose an icon to associate with the shortcut. You can select both the source file (with the **Choose Icon Path** button) and the index of the icon within that file. We'll be making use of the SHBrowseForIcon() function that we defined back in Chapter 9 for this purpose.

In the **Save As** frame, you can type in the path name or pick up a predefined item in the combo box. Predefined items will be special folders such as Desktop, Send To, and the like. The right hand edit box will contain the file name for the shortcut without the .lnk extension and finally, to create the shortcut, you'll need to press the **Create** button to invoke SHCreateShortcutEx(), one of our functions from Chapter 6.

As ever, our starting point is a dialog-based application generated by the Wrox AppWizard – I called mine NewLink. When the program is called from the shell (I'll demonstrate how to do that shortly) it receives the name of a temporary file that the shell creates automatically before invoking the Wizard. This name is passed in as WinMain()'s lpsz argument, and since we aren't interested in it, our first action is to delete the file. We do, however, use its name for the output .lnk file.

The Old Functions

Once you have your dialog looking something like the one above, you can start coding with the WinMain() function, deleting the temporary file but saving the name away for future use:

```
int APIENTRY WinMain(HINSTANCE hInstance, HINSTANCE hPrevious,
                     LPTSTR lpsz, int iCmd)
{

    // Delete any temporary file created by the shell
if(lstrlen(lpsz))
DeleteFile(lpsz);

    // Save global data
    g_hIconLarge = static_cast<HICON>(
            LoadImage(hInstance, "APP_ICON", IMAGE_ICON,
            GetSystemMetrics(SM_CXICON), GetSystemMetrics(SM_CXICON), 0));
    g_hIconSmall = static_cast<HICON>(
            LoadImage(hInstance, "APP_ICON", IMAGE_ICON,
            GetSystemMetrics(SM_CXSMICON), GetSystemMetrics(SM_CXSMICON), 0));
    lstrcpy(g_szNewLinkName, lpsz);

    // Enable common controls
    INITCOMMONCONTROLSEX iccex;
    iccex.dwSize = sizeof(INITCOMMONCONTROLSEX);
    iccex.dwICC = ICC_WIN95_CLASSES;
    InitCommonControlsEx(&iccex);

    // Initialize COM for the SHCreateShortcutEx() function
    CoInitialize(NULL);

    // Run main dialog
    BOOL b = DialogBox(hInstance, "DLG_MAIN", NULL, APP_DlgProc);

    CoUninitialize()

    // Exit
    DestroyIcon(g_hIconLarge);
    DestroyIcon(g_hIconSmall);
    return b;
}
```

The dialog procedure calls handlers for all the new buttons:

```
case WM_COMMAND:
    switch(wParam)
    {
    case IDC_CREATE:
        DoCreateShortcut(hDlg);
        return FALSE;

    case IDC_BROWSEPATH:
        OnBrowse(hDlg, IDC_PATH);
        return FALSE;

    case IDC_CHOOSEICON:
        OnChooseIcon(hDlg);
        return FALSE;

    case IDC_BROWSETARGET:
        OnBrowse(hDlg, IDC_TARGET);
        return FALSE;

    case IDC_BROWSEICON:
        OnBrowse(hDlg, IDC_ICONPATH);
        return FALSE;
```

```
        case IDCANCEL:
            EndDialog(hDlg, FALSE);
            return FALSE;
    }
    break;
```

The last of our three predefined functions, `OnInitDialog()`, initializes all the controls in ways that are probably familiar to you by now:

```
void OnInitDialog(HWND hDlg)
{
    // Set the icons (T/F as to Large/Small icon)
    SendMessage(hDlg, WM_SETICON, FALSE, reinterpret_cast<LPARAM>(g_hIconSmall));
    SendMessage(hDlg, WM_SETICON, TRUE, reinterpret_cast<LPARAM>(g_hIconLarge));

    // Special folders available
    HWND hwndCbo = GetDlgItem(hDlg, IDC_PATH);
    int i = ComboBox_AddString(hwndCbo, "Desktop");
    ComboBox_SetItemData(hwndCbo, i, CSIDL_DESKTOP);
    i = ComboBox_AddString(hwndCbo, "Favorites");
    ComboBox_SetItemData(hwndCbo, i, CSIDL_FAVORITES);
    i = ComboBox_AddString(hwndCbo, "Programs");
    ComboBox_SetItemData(hwndCbo, i, CSIDL_PROGRAMS);
    i = ComboBox_AddString(hwndCbo, "My Documents");
    ComboBox_SetItemData(hwndCbo, i, CSIDL_PERSONAL);
    i = ComboBox_AddString(hwndCbo, "SendTo");
    ComboBox_SetItemData(hwndCbo, i, CSIDL_SENDTO);
    i = ComboBox_AddString(hwndCbo, "Start Menu");
    ComboBox_SetItemData(hwndCbo, i, CSIDL_STARTMENU);
    ComboBox_SetCurSel(hwndCbo, 0);

    // Initialize the hotkey control to prefix everything with Ctrl-Alt
    SendDlgItemMessage(hDlg, IDC_HOTKEY, HKM_SETRULES,
                       HKCOMB_NONE | HKCOMB_S | HKCOMB_A | HKCOMB_C,
                       HOTKEYF_CONTROL | HOTKEYF_ALT);

    SetDlgItemText(hDlg, IDC_TARGET, "C:\\");
    SetDlgItemText(hDlg, IDC_ICONINDEX, "0");

    // Handle any file name received through the command line
    if(lstrlen(g_szNewLinkName))
    {
        LPTSTR pszBuf = g_szNewLinkName;
        LPTSTR psz = strrchr(g_szNewLinkName, '\\');
        SetDlgItemText(hDlg, IDC_LNKFILE, ++psz);
        pszBuf[psz - pszBuf] = 0;
        SetDlgItemText(hDlg, IDC_PATH, pszBuf);
    }
    else
        SetDlgItemText(hDlg, IDC_LNKFILE, "NewLink");
}
```

The first action is to fill the combo box in the **Save As** frame with the names of the special folders where you might want to create shortcuts. We also associate some item data with each string, to make future processing easier. The next job is to initialize the hotkey control so that it will prefix everything with *Ctrl-Alt*, which is necessary for shortcuts. We then set the default values for the target string and the icon index, and use the filename passed on the command line as the basis for the link name.

The New Functions

The second handler function, and the first new function we're adding to the application, is called when any one of the three browse buttons that the dialog boasts is pressed. The second argument is used to differentiate between them:

```
void OnBrowse(HWND hDlg, WPARAM wItemType)
{
    // Browse for directory only...
    if(wItemType == IDC_PATH)
    {
        LPMALLOC pMalloc = NULL;
        TCHAR szDir[MAX_PATH] = {0};
        LPITEMIDLIST pidl = NULL;

        BROWSEINFO bi;
        ZeroMemory(&bi, sizeof(BROWSEINFO));
        bi.hwndOwner = hDlg;
        bi.lpszTitle = "Choose a folder:";

        pidl = SHBrowseForFolder(&bi);
        SHGetPathFromIDList(pidl, szDir);
        SetDlgItemText(hDlg, IDC_PATH, szDir);

        SHGetMalloc(&pMalloc);
        pMalloc->Free(pidl);
        pMalloc->Release();
        return;
    }

    // Browse for files...
    TCHAR szFile[MAX_PATH] = {0};
    OPENFILENAME ofn;
    ZeroMemory(&ofn, sizeof(OPENFILENAME));
    ofn.lStructSize = sizeof(OPENFILENAME);
    switch(wItemType)
    {
    case IDC_TARGET:
        ofn.lpstrFilter = "All files\0*.*\0";
        break;
    case IDC_ICONPATH:
        ofn.lpstrFilter = "Icons\0*.exe;*.dll;*.ico\0";
        break;
    }

    TCHAR szWinDir[MAX_PATH] = {0};
    ofn.nMaxFile = MAX_PATH;
    GetWindowsDirectory(szWinDir, MAX_PATH);
    ofn.lpstrInitialDir = szWinDir;
    ofn.lpstrFile = szFile;
    if(!GetOpenFileName(&ofn))
        return;

    SetDlgItemText(hDlg, wItemType, ofn.lpstrFile);

    // Show the first icon by default
    HICON hIcon = ExtractIcon(GetModuleHandle(NULL), ofn.lpstrFile, 0);
    SendDlgItemMessage(hDlg, IDI_ICON, STM_SETICON,
                       reinterpret_cast<WPARAM>(hIcon), 0);
}
```

If we're browsing for a path, we use the `SHBrowseForFolder()` API function to let the user find the path, display it in the appropriate edit control, and then return after tidying up.

If we're browsing for files, we fill in a filter string appropriate to the type of files we're looking for, and use this in a call to `GetOpenFileName()`. We display the filename in the appropriate edit control, and also arrange to display the first icon in the file by default.

The handler for the **Choose Icon Path** button simply uses the `SHBrowseForIcon()` function from Chapter 9 to select an icon from a file:

```
void OnChooseIcon(HWND hDlg)
{
    TCHAR szFileName[MAX_PATH] = {0};
    GetDlgItemText(hDlg, IDC_ICONPATH, szFileName, MAX_PATH);

    HICON hIcon;
    int iIconIndex = SHBrowseForIcon(szFileName, &hIcon);
    if(iIconIndex >= 0)
    {
        SetDlgItemText(hDlg, IDC_ICONPATH, szFileName);
        SetDlgItemInt(hDlg, IDC_ICONINDEX, iIconIndex, TRUE);
        SendDlgItemMessage(hDlg, IDI_ICON, STM_SETICON,
                        reinterpret_cast<WPARAM>(hIcon), 0);
    }
}
```

Once we've got all the data, the main work of the application is done in the handler for the **Create** button:

```
void DoCreateShortcut(HWND hDlg)
{
    TCHAR szTarget[MAX_PATH] = {0};
    TCHAR szDesc[MAX_PATH] = {0};

    // Get the hotkey
    SHORTCUTSTRUCT ss;
    ss.wHotKey = static_cast<WORD>(SendDlgItemMessage(
                                hDlg, IDC_HOTKEY, HKM_GETHOTKEY, 0, 0));

    // Get target and description
    GetDlgItemText(hDlg, IDC_TARGET, szTarget, MAX_PATH);
    GetDlgItemText( hDlg, IDC_DESCRIPTION, szDesc, MAX_PATH);
    ss.pszTarget = szTarget;
    ss.pszDesc = szDesc;

    // Get the icon
    TCHAR szIcon[MAX_PATH] = {0};
    GetDlgItemText(hDlg, IDC_ICONPATH, szIcon, MAX_PATH);
    ss.pszIconPath = szIcon;
    ss.wIconIndex = 0;

    // Determine shortcut file name
    // Get the target folder & final backslash
    HWND hwndCbo = GetDlgItem(hDlg, IDC_PATH);
    int i = ComboBox_GetCurSel(hwndCbo);
    DWORD nFolder = ComboBox_GetItemData(hwndCbo, i);

    TCHAR szPath[MAX_PATH]= {0};
```

```
    if(nFolder)
        SHGetSpecialFolderPath(hDlg, szPath, nFolder, FALSE);
    else
        GetDlgItemText(hDlg, IDC_PATH, szPath, MAX_PATH);

    if(szPath[lstrlen(szPath) - 1] != '\\')
        lstrcat(szPath, "\\");

    TCHAR szLnkFile[MAX_PATH] = {0};
    GetDlgItemText(hDlg, IDC_LNKFILE, szLnkFile, MAX_PATH);
    lstrcat(szPath, szLnkFile);
    lstrcat(szPath, ".lnk");

    // Create...
    SHCreateShortcutEx(szPath, &ss);
}
```

All we're doing here is gathering the information from the various controls on the screen and packing them into a SHORTCUTSTRUCT, prior to calling SHCreateShortCutEx() to actually do the work for us. (We defined the structure and function involved here in Chapter 6.) With this code in place, you just need to add the usual list of header files and libraries. On this occasion, we require #includes for resource.h, shlobj.h and commdlg.h, and links to ole32.lib and comdlg32.lib.

How to Replace the Windows Wizard

Wouldn't it be nice if we were able to replace the standard Windows Wizard for creating shortcuts with our own? In fact, it's not that hard to do, and as you might expect, the key to the enterprise lies in the registry. A shortcut is a .lnk file, so the first place to look is under this key:

```
HKEY_CLASSES_ROOT
    \.lnk
```

Beneath it, you'll find a key called ShellNew. When it comes to creating a new file of a given type from the shell – that is, through the <u>N</u>ew menu – Explorer always searches for a ShellNew key within the file class sub-tree.

Inside this key, the Command value gives the command line, and you should find that it's set to:

```
runDLL32 AppWiz.Cpl,NewLinkHere %2
```

Note the use of rundll32.exe to run a DLL function as a command-line instruction. To replace the standard Wizard, all we have to do is to change the Command value to execute our program, like this:

```
c:\Utility\NewLink\NewLink.exe %2
```

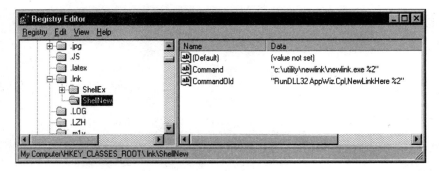

Notice that the final %2 is fundamental for the command line to work properly – remove or replace it and the dialog will never appear. When you next choose to create a new shortcut from the desktop, you'll find that our new dialog will appear.

The NewLink.exe program detects and uses the file name passed by the shell as an argument – before invoking the shortcut creator, the shell always creates an empty file and passes its name to the program. However, handling this file name is not a problem for us.

Editing the Registry

Replacing the default shortcut Wizard requires some editing of the registry, which you can either do manually through the Registry Editor, or programmatically with a script file. For example, you can restore the original situation simply by reassigning the original value to the Command entry with the following script:

```
; restore.reg
REGEDIT4

[HKEY_CLASSES_ROOT\.lnk\ShellNew]
"Command" = "RunDLL32 appwiz.cpl,NewLinkHere %2"
```

In just the same way, you could have used this script to install the handler in the first place:

```
; replace.reg
REGEDIT4

[HKEY_CLASSES_ROOT\.lnk\ShellNew]
"Command" = "c:\\utility\\newlink\\newlink.exe %2"
```

Make sure you always use double slashes when entering path names in .reg scripts, and remember to replace the path in the example with the actual path where the newlink.exe file lives!

Summary

Our first journey through the Windows shell ends here. We've looked at Explorer's command line and discovered an interesting utility program called `rundll32.exe`, which allows you to use DLL functions as command line instructions. While discussing the features of `rundll32.exe`, we also discovered how to access programmatically some system dialogs whose programming interface isn't documented, such as Add Printer Wizard, Add New Hardware, Make New Connection, and Open With.

The second part of the chapter discussed some special virtual folders that implement shell objects, such as Printers, Dial-up Networking, Scheduled Tasks, and My Briefcase. I provided an overview of this subject, and mentioned some sites and documents where you could find further information.

Finally, we looked at an example that used many of the topics we've covered so far in the book. The shortcut handler also provides a good introduction to the new topics we'll cover in Chapter 14, where I'll explain how your documents should be integrated into the system's shell.

In summary, therefore, this chapter covered:

- ❑ Explorer's command line.
- ❑ The RunDLL32 programming interface
- ❑ Accessing undocumented functions to display system dialogs
- ❑ A review of some virtual folders such as `Printers` and `My Briefcase`
- ❑ Scrap objects
- ❑ How to write and install a new, custom module to create shortcuts

In the next two chapters, we'll continue our exploration and discover two really useful aspects of the new Windows shell. The first involves the scriptable shell objects that give you programmatic access to any shell feature, from dialogs to folders, and from windows to shortcuts. After that, we'll focus on a very promising subsystem called Windows Scripting Host (WSH) that's supposed to bring the idea of DOS batch files into Windows land.

Further Reading

I've found interesting ideas on using `rundll32` in an article in Visual Basic Journal, the Italian version of Visual Basic Programmer's Journal (VBPJ). The author was Marco Losavio, and the article was published in the September 97 issue. (The article is in Italian with source code available at ftp://ftp.infomedia.it/pub/VBJ/vbj17disk.zip.)

The Internet Client SDK contains introductory and detailed documentation about the development of Control Panel applets. I also recommend the Internet Client SDK for getting more information about WinInet, the Briefcase, and the Scheduling Agent. Further explanation of `My Briefcase` can also be found in the Windows 95 Resource Kit.

I'd like also to mention a few articles about WinInet by Aaron Skonnard that appeared in MIND, December 97, and MSJ, June 98. The titles are *Dress your Applications for Success with WinInet* and *How to design reusable HTTP components by exploiting WinInet and COM* respectively. On the theme of scheduling agents, let me point you towards a piece by Jomo Fisher in the March 1998 edition of Windows Developer's Journal in March 98 called *The Windows 98 Scheduling Agent*.

The section in the Internet Client SDK about drag-and-drop also covers scrap objects, and provides you with a wider overview and hints about the internal machinery that makes them work. Finally, here's a list of useful Knowledge Base articles:

KB Article ID: Q130510: *Command-Line Switches for Windows Explorer*
KB Article ID: Q164787: *The Windows 95 Rundll and Rundll32 Interface*
KB Article ID: Q173039: *RUNONCE Key Is Processed Immediately When RUNDLL32 Is Called*
KB Article ID: Q166168: *Use RUNDLL32 to Debug Control Panel Applets*
KB Article ID: Q135068: *Starting a Control Panel Applet in Windows 95 or WinNT*
KB Article ID: Q177076: *How to Start the Add Printer Wizard at a Command Prompt*
KB Article ID: Q153383: *How to Use/Replace Windows 95 Hardware Wizard in Custom Code*

12
Scriptable Shell Objects

The new Windows shell has been enriched with a powerful new set of objects that provide you with full access to all the shell's main features via Automation. Internet Explorer 4.0 introduced these new COM objects in the latest version of `shdocvw.dll`, which is one of its core components.

These objects let you drive the shell and its folders from programs, and they are documented in the Internet Client SDK (now integrated into the Platform SDK). Because they are Automation servers, these objects can easily be used from programs written in Visual Basic, Delphi or C/C++. They can also be called from script code, including code from the Windows Scripting Host (WSH) environment, which we'll cover in the next chapter.

In this chapter, we'll look at the shell object model and rewrite one of samples that I presented back in Chapter 5. This will give us the opportunity to examine the true purpose of scriptable shell objects: they provide a way to simplify access to features of the shell, and the contents of shell folders. Along the way, we'll be covering:

- ❏ The Shell object model
- ❏ The `Folder` and `FolderItem` objects
- ❏ Helper objects to manage verbs and favorites
- ❏ Code examples written in both C++ and Visual Basic

The objects that we'll be describing provide an easy way to access the Windows shell and all its features programmatically. It has always been *possible* to enumerate the contents of a folder, but you needed a fairly deep knowledge of C++ programming. With the introduction of shell objects, it has become as easy as calling an Automation server. Unfortunately, the drawback to this is that in order to make life easier for Visual Basic and script programmers, it has been made more difficult for C and C++ programmers who now have to cope with VARIANT types and collections without the in-built help provided by Visual Basic.

The Best Language to Program the Shell

It seems that there's no middle path when it comes to accessing the shell's commands and properties – it is either really easy, or really hard. We saw something of this in Chapter 5, when we tried to enumerate the contents of a folder. We had to get the PIDL to the folder and the pointer to the right IShellFolder interface, and then by combining these two items we finally obtained an IEnumIDList interface that allowed us to enumerate the items in the folder. This isn't a very satisfactory solution, though, because, while it gets the PIDL to each element, it's up to you to convert that into a readable name.

This is the hard, low-level way to do the job, and of course it's a way only possible using languages like C and C++ that support pointers. Scriptable shell objects solve this problem by providing a way to program the shell with Visual Basic and scripting languages. If that was all they gave us, it would still be a real boon, but these new objects offer more than just a set of Automation interfaces.

Undocumented Shell Features

What makes shell objects really interesting for C++ programmers is that they provide the *only* documented way to access some shell features and dialogs. In addition, they provide a consistent programming interface to *all* the features of the shell, documented or not.

Many of the methods exposed by the shell objects address functionality we already know about, but which is accessible in several different ways. For example, to browse for folders you have a specific API function, while you have to resort to ShellExecute() to run the Find dialog, and to hand-coded routines to enumerate the content of a folder. These are all now available through shell objects.

Here's a list of the dialogs and functions that you can only access through the shell object model:

- ❑ The dialog that pops up when you click on Taskbar Settings from the Start menu
- ❑ The functions to minimize or restore all the open windows
- ❑ The functions to tile or cascade all the open windows
- ❑ The functions to suspend or 'undock' a PC
- ❑ The Run dialog
- ❑ The Find Computer dialog
- ❑ The system dialog to add folders or files to the Favorites list

Other functions exposed by the object model can also be accessed in other ways; these include:

- ❑ The dialog to browse for folders
- ❑ Opening or exploring a folder
- ❑ The date and time setup dialog
- ❑ Running a Control Panel applet
- ❑ The Find dialog
- ❑ Access to any system folder

The Shell Object Model

All the objects that actually form the shell's object model are implemented in `shdocvw.dll`. A quick but somewhat incomplete source of documentation for these objects is the Visual Basic Object Browser.

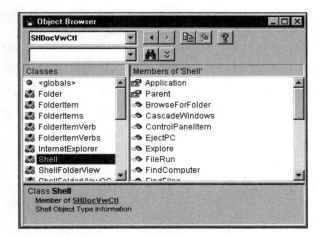

If you're using Visual Basic, the Object Browser can really help you to discover new features with which to experiment. I found out about the shell's object model by casually snooping around `shdocvw.dll` with the Object Browser. The next diagram shows this layout.

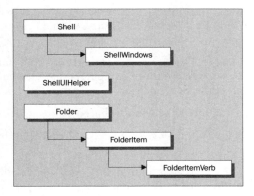

The easiest way to create an instance of the `Shell` object in Visual Basic is:

```
Dim o As Object
Set o = CreateObject("Shell.Application")
```

In C++, the equivalent code would be:

```
#include <comdef.h>
#include <exdisp.h>


CoInitialize(NULL);

IShellDispatch* pShellDisp = NULL;
HRESULT hr = CoCreateInstance(CLSID_Shell, NULL, CLSCTX_SERVER,
                IID_IShellDispatch, reinterpret_cast<LPVOID*>(&pShellDisp));
if(SUCCEEDED(hr))
{
    ...
}


CoUninitialize();
```

However, before going any further with programming topics, let's have a look at the methods exposed by the Shell object.

Method	Description
BrowseForFolder()	A simplified version of the SHBrowseForFolder() API function. It displays a tree-based window that lets you choose a folder. It differs from the API function in that it doesn't support the callback mechanism.
CascadeWindows()	Arranges all the top-level windows in cascading fashion.
ControlPanelItem()	Launches a Control Panel applet. The method takes the name of an existing CPL file and calls the Control_RunDLL() function we saw in the previous chapter.
EjectPC()	Undocks ('ejects') the computer from its docking station. This method only works on those computers that have an Eject command on the Start menu.
Explore()	Opens an Explorer-like window based on the specified folder.
FileRun()	Launches the Run dialog, as if you've clicked Run from the Start menu.
FindComputer()	Launches the Find Computer dialog, as if you've clicked Find I Computer from the Start menu.
FindFiles()	Launches the Find dialog, as if you've clicked Find I Files or Folders from the Start menu.
Help()	Displays a help window as if you've clicked Help from the Start menu.
MinimizeAll()	Clears the desktop and minimizes all the open windows (not just top-level windows). This method has the same effect as clicking the Show Desktop button on the taskbar (shell version 4.71 or higher), right-clicking on the taskbar and selecting Minimize All Windows, or pressing *Windows-M*.

Method	Description
NameSpace()	This takes a path name or a constant as input, and creates a folder object. We'll cover Folder objects later in this chapter.
Open()	Opens the specified folder as a separate window without an Explorer-like left-hand pane.
RefreshMenu()	Refreshes the Start menu to reflect possible changes.
SetTime()	Displays the dialog to set the current date and time. Calling this method is the same as double clicking on the clock icon in the tray area.
ShutdownWindows()	Launches the procedure to exit Windows, as if you've clicked on the Sh<u>u</u>t Down... command on the Start menu.
Suspend()	Suspends the computer. This method only works on those computers that have a Suspend command on the Start menu.
TileHorizontally()	Horizontally tiles all the currently open top-level windows.
TileVertically()	Vertically tiles all the currently open top-level windows.
TrayProperties()	Launches the Taskbar Properties dialog, as if you've clicked on <u>S</u>ettings	<u>T</u>askbar from the Start menu.
UndoMinimizeALL()	Undo any changes carried out by a previous call to MinimizeAll(), restoring the windows on the desktop. This method has the same effect as clicking the desktop button on the taskbar, right-clicking the taskbar and selecting <u>U</u>ndo Minimize All, or hitting *Shift-Windows-M*. Note the double uppercase L in the name!
Windows()	The documentation says that this, "Creates and returns a ShellWindows object that represents a collection of all of the open windows that belong to the shell". However, I have had problems producing this behavior.

As you can see, many of the methods are just equivalents of the commands you find on the Start menu and the taskbar's context menu, which just goes to show that the Shell object is providing the functionality of the Windows shell. Many of the methods are extremely simple and require no arguments at all; let's take a closer look at those that do.

Methods of the Shell Object

Before looking at the details of the methods that have input or output parameters, note that all the strings used in these roles are BSTRs and not LPSTRs. You can find Visual Basic documentation in the Internet Client SDK, but for the pure IDL-derived C++ header defining all the functions, look at the exdisp.h header that's installed with the latest version of the Internet Client SDK.

As usual for COM interface methods, all the functions return an HRESULT value that identifies the error code. Visual Basic hides these from the programmer, so anything that the Visual Basic documentation defines as a return value is actually an [out] parameter. In Visual Basic, any error condition raises an exception that you can handle with the On Error Goto construct.

BrowseForFolder()

This function returns a Folder object, and takes the following arguments:

- ❏ The handle of the parent window
- ❏ A string to be used as the title of the dialog
- ❏ Some options, which are the same as those used in SHBrowseForFolder()
- ❏ An optional folder to be used as the root for the browse operation

The folder to be used as the root must be specified as a VARIANT type, and can include a string or one of the CSIDL_XXX constants we met in Chapter 5. The prototype is:

```
HRESULT BrowseForFolder(
        long Hwnd, BSTR Title, long Options, VARIANT RootFolder, Folder** ppsdf);
```

The following code demonstrates how to call the method in C++ using both a CSIDL_XXX number and a string to identify the root folder. By adding a #include for atlbase.h to the top of a source file that contains this code, you get to use the ATL wrapper classes CComBSTR and CComVariant that make using BSTRs and VARIANTs so much easier in C++.

If you want to test these listings, you can plug them straight into the code for creating an instance of the Shell object that I presented earlier. Note that as always with COM, if you're not using the CComPtr<> class, you must Release() any pointers you have acquired before calling CoUninitialize().

```
#include <atlbase.h>

        // Set up pointer, VARIANT and BSTR
        Folder* pFolder = NULL;
        CComVariant vRoot(CSIDL_DRIVES);              // My Computer
        CComBSTR bstrTitle(__TEXT("My Computer:"));   // Dialog caption

        // Call the method
        HRESULT hr = pShellDisp->BrowseForFolder(
                reinterpret_cast<long>(hDlg), bstrTitle, 0, vRoot, &pFolder);

        // Release the pointer
        pFolder->Release();
```

Or...

```
        // Set up pointer, VARIANT and BSTR
        Folder* pFolder = NULL;
        CComVariant vRoot(__TEXT("c:\\"));            // The C Drive
        CComBSTR bstrTitle(__TEXT("My Disk C:"));     // Dialog caption
```

ControlPanelItem()

This function takes as input a string giving the name (file and extension) of the `.cpl` file to run, and again the string must be a BSTR. The prototype is:

```
HRESULT ControlPanelItem(BSTR szDir);
```

Here's an example in C++ that again uses a BSTR created with one of the overloaded CComBSTR class constructors:

```
CComBSTR bstr(__TEXT("desk.cpl"));
HRESULT hr = pShellDisp->ControlPanelItem(bstr);
```

Explore()

This method takes a VARIANT that specifies the folder to open. The VARIANT can contain a path name as well as one of the CSIDL_XXX constants. The prototype is:

```
HRESULT Explore(VARIANT vDir);
```

Here's an example:

```
// Set up the VARIANT
CComVariant vDir(CSIDL_HISTORY);              // History Folder

// Call the method
HRESULT hr = pShellDisp->Explore(vDir);
```

NameSpace()

This function takes two parameters, the first of which is a VARIANT that can be a path name or a predefined constant identifying a special system folder. The second parameter is an output argument that's filled by the method – a double pointer to a Folder object:

```
HRESULT NameSpace(VARIANT vDir, Folder** ppsdf);
```

Here's a code fragment to show it in action:

```
Folder* pFolder = NULL;
CComVariant vDir(CSIDL_STARTMENU);            // Start menu
pShellDisp->NameSpace(vDir, &pFolder);

// Do something with pFolder...

pFolder->Release();
```

Open()

As far as the syntax is concerned, this function is exactly the same as Explore(). The prototype is:

```
HRESULT Open(VARIANT vDir);
```

Windows()

This function takes no input parameters, but provides a pointer to an `IDispatch` interface as its output. This parameter will give you access to the collection of currently open windows. The prototype is:

```
HRESULT Windows(IDispatch** ppid);
```

Attributes of the Shell Object

The `Shell` object has just two attributes: `Parent` and `Application`. They are implemented through methods called `get_Parent()` and `get_Application()` respectively, which take a double pointer to `IDispatch` and return an `HRESULT`.

Invoking the Shell Object

From the programmer's perspective, the `Shell` object is important because it offers, among other things, a quick and easy way to access the contents of any folder. All the other functionality we listed above provides an interesting set of commands, but they tend not to be essential in most real-world applications. However, I'll now show you how to make calls to the `Shell` object, and in this context there are four things we need to discuss:

❑ Getting a pointer to the right interface
❑ The use of the `VARIANT` type
❑ The use of Unicode strings
❑ Accessing and using collections

I'll start by showing you how things work in languages like Visual Basic and scripting languages, and then we'll take a look at the C++ approach, which is a bit more complex. These examples show how to call:

❑ `BrowseForFolder()`
❑ `FindComputer()`
❑ `NameSpace()`

Using these as examples, I can present a complete overview of the techniques required to call the methods of the `Shell` object.

Using Visual Basic

In Visual Basic, you can use either **early** or **late binding**. That is, member names can be bound to dispatch identifiers (DISPIDs) at runtime (late binding) or at compile time (early binding), the latter of which makes calls into the interface faster. In early binding, you declare object variables with the appropriate types early, thereby informing the compiler about which methods, properties and events they support. For example:

```
Dim s As New Shell
```

By declaring s as a Shell and not as an Object, we've opted for early binding. This requires that you add a reference to the library to your project, so that the compiler can easily check all calls to the object. In the case of Shell objects, the library is shdocvw.dll. Here's how to store a reference to a library, and a short example of code that illustrates early binding with Visual Basic.

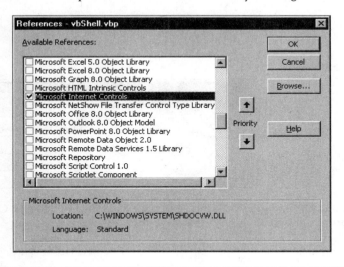

```
Dim s As New Shell
s.FindComputer
```

Late binding, on the other hand, means that we bind to the library at runtime. In the source code, we declare a generic Object variable that will be linked to the library of a specific object dynamically. The code looks like this:

```
Dim o As Object
Set o = CreateObject("Shell.Application")
o.FindComputer
```

In this case, we don't need to include references to anything. The following picture shows a demonstration application I put together using Visual Basic:

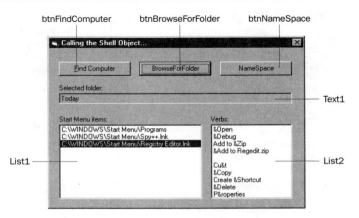

The form has three buttons to call the three functions I mentioned above. **Find Computer** is linked to this code:

```
' Finds a computer
Private Sub btnFindComputer_Click()
   Dim s As New Shell
   s.FindComputer
End Sub
```

Which causes the following dialog to appear:

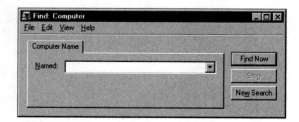

BrowseForFolder, on the other hand, displays the dialog that we examined in detail in Chapter 5. In this example, I arranged for it to browse the My Computer folder, like this:

```
' Navigates the History folder
Private Sub btnBrowseForFolder_Click()
On Error Resume Next
   Dim s As New Shell
   Dim f As Folder
   Dim fi As FolderItem

   Set f = s.BrowseForFolder(Me.hWnd, "My Computer:", 0, ssfDRIVES)
   Set fi = f.Items.Item

   ' Show the selected path in a textbox
   Text1.Text = fi.Path
End Sub
```

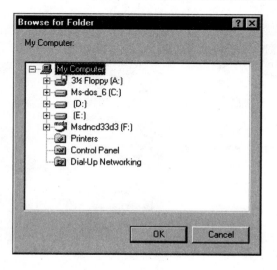

The method returns a reference to a Folder object, but if you want the path of the selected element, a Folder isn't sufficient. Instead, you have to use a FolderItem object, which exposes a Path property. (We'll talk more abou Folder and FolderItem later on.)

The special `ssfDRIVES` constant that you can see in the above listing is taken from a predefined enumeration type called `ShellSpecialFolderConstants`. The values of this enumeration are identical to the `CSIDL_XXX` constants we met in Chapter 5, but the type under discussion doesn't include *all* the constants that are defined in `shlobj.h`. The missing ones (not counting the 'COMMON' constants) are:

- ❑ CSIDL_HISTORY
- ❑ CSIDL_COOKIES
- ❑ CSIDL_INTERNET
- ❑ CSIDL_INTERNET_CACHE
- ❑ CSIDL_APPDATA
- ❑ CSIDL_ALTSTARTUP
- ❑ CSIDL_PRINTHOOD

However, should you need it, adding support for these is simply a matter of adding the following constant declarations:

```
Const ssfHISTORY = &H22
Const ssfCOOKIES = &H21
Const ssfINTERNET = &H1
Const ssfINTERNETCACHE = &H20
Const ssfAPPDATA = &H1A
Const ssfALTSTARTUP = &H1D
Const ssfPRINTHOOD = &H1B
```

Feel free to adopt any other names for the constants. The values come straight from the `shlobj.h` *header file.*

The last of the three buttons, **NameSpace**, opens and returns a `Folder` object that is based on the path name or the ID specified. Then, it enumerates the items in that folder, displaying them in the left-hand list box:

```
' Enumerates the content of the Start Menu folder
Private Sub btnNameSpace_Click()
    Dim s As New Shell
    Dim f As Folder
    Dim i As Integer
    Dim Item As FolderItem

    Set f = s.NameSpace(ssfSTARTMENU)
    For Each Item In f.Items
        List1.AddItem Item.Path
    Next
End Sub
```

The above code makes use of the `ssfSTARTMENU` constant, thereby retrieving the `Start Menu` folder. Notice how easy it is to walk the contents of a folder once you have a reference to a `Folder` object — it's as easy as setting up a `for` loop!

Chapter 12

Here's the code for the remainder of the Visual Basic project, showing the handlers for the other controls:

```
Option Explicit

    ' Add btnFindComputer_Click()

    ' Add btnBrowseForFolder_Click()

    ' Add btnNameSpace_Click()

' Displays the verbs for each folder item
Private Sub List1_Click()
    Dim s As New Shell
    Dim f As Folder
    Dim fi As FolderItem
    Dim fiv As FolderItemVerb
    Dim i As Integer

    Set f = s.NameSpace(ssfSTARTMENU)
    i = List1.ListIndex

    Set fi = f.Items.Item(i)

    List2.Clear
    For Each fiv In fi.Verbs
        List2.AddItem fiv.Name
    Next
End Sub
```

The final portion of the source code, which handles clicks on the left-hand list box, deals with using verbs, which we'll cover a little later on.

Using C++

Doing the same thing with C++ requires a little more work and increased lines of code, but the approach is basically the same. The first problem we encounter is making sure to include all the header files we need so that the project compiles and the CLSIDs are properly declared, but that's not usually *too* tricky provided that you keep your wits about you!

All the declarations needed for using the Shell object model can be found in exdisp.h. The following lines are sufficient to compile correctly a piece of software that makes use of the Shell object:

```
#include <windows.h>
#include <comdef.h>
#include <exdisp.h>
```

Make sure you have the most up-to-date versions, because the ones that come with compilers and other tools might not contain everything you need. For instance, Visual C++ 5.0 installs a version of exdisp.h in its include subdirectory that doesn't contain any of the required definitions for the shell's object model. The "correct" version of exdisp.h is installed with the Internet Client SDK, and is also distributed with Visual Studio 6.0.

364

The second problem is coping with the VARIANTs, which add a level of complexity to COM programming in C++. In Visual Basic, you can use either strings or numbers to identify a folder — this flexibility relies on the fact that VARIANTs can hold different data, but always expose the same interface. However, using the ATL wrapper class CComVariant goes a long way to making VARIANT use easier in C++.

The third difficulty you run into when doing low-level COM programming is enumerating collections. Support for doing this is built into Visual Basic, as demonstrated by code like this:

```
Dim pF As Folder
Dim pFI As FolderItem

For i = 0 to pF.Items.Count - 1
    Set pFI = pF.Items.Item(i)
    ' Do something
Next
```

> *Generally in Visual Basic, a* For...Each *construct is faster than a* For...Next *because it makes use of a hash algorithm to locate the ith item instead of scanning the items sequentially. However, I've used* For...Next *here because it maps more closely to the programming approach used in C++.*

Doing this in C++ is more long-winded, but it isn't really more complex. In trying to convert the fragment above to C++, we must consider three things:

- ❑ Getting the Items collection
- ❑ Getting the Count property
- ❑ Getting the ith element of the collection

To see how we can address these issues, let's consider a typical sample: enumerating the content of a folder. The NameSpace() method provides us with a reference to a Folder object:

```
Folder* pFolder = NULL;
CComVariant vDir(CSIDL_STARTMENU);
pShellDisp->NameSpace(vDir, &pFolder);
```

We know from the Internet Client SDK documentation that the Folder object has an attribute called Items whose type is FolderItems. Basically, FolderItems is a collection of elements of type FolderItem. (I know that I still owe you complete coverage of the Folder and FolderItem objects, but bear with me; we'll do that shortly.)

What we need to do, therefore, is to get a pointer to Items and then visit every item in the collection, performing an action for each one, such as adding an icon to a list view control.

```
long nLength;
FolderItems* pFIColl = NULL;
pFolder->Items(&pFIColl);                // Visual Basic: Folder.Items
pFIColl->get_Count(&nLength);            // Visual Basic: Folder.Items.Count
```

The lines above demonstrate how to get the pointer to the `FolderItems` collection, and its length. At this point, we could arrange a loop:

```
for(int i = 0 ; i < nLength ; i++)
{
    // Get the ith element from pFIColl and
    //  do something with it
}
```

The `FolderItems` object is a helper object; it exposes an interface that lets us browse a collection. In particular, it has an `Item()` member function that takes two arguments: a `VARIANT`, and a pointer to a `FolderItem` object.

```
for(int i = 0 ; i < nLength ; i++
{
    CComVariant varIndex(i);

    FolderItem* pFI = NULL;
    pFIColl->Item(varIndex, &pFI);

    //  do something with it

    pFI->Release();
}
```

You might be wondering why a function like `Item()`, which is intended to return a reference to the *i*th element of a given collection, needs a `VARIANT` argument instead of a simpler `int`, `UINT` or `long`. The answer is that collections usually allow you to access their elements by name as well as by index. Given this, it's clear that `Item` must be ready to accept both numbers and strings, hence the decision to use a `VARIANT`.

Once we have a pointer to a `FolderItem`, we have a pointer to a logical object that can tell us about a file contained in a folder. We can ask it for the path, the size or the date, like this:

```
CComBSTR bstr;
TCHAR szFile[MAX_PATH] = {0};
pFI->get_Path(&bstr);
wcstombs(szFile, bstr, MAX_PATH);
```

The filename can then be used to retrieve the icon for the document class and add an item to a list view control, which is exactly what we'll do in the sample C++ program I'll be presenting shortly. Before that, though, we need to take a closer look at `Folder` and `FolderItem`.

The Folder Object

A `Folder` object represents a shell folder that contains files or references to other types of objects. Usually, you don't create folders directly but rely on the `NameSpace()` function, which creates them starting from a path name or a virtual folder ID.

The `Folder` object exposes four properties, two of which are the well-known `Application` and `Parent`. The other two are `ParentFolder` and `Title`, whose purposes are (I hope!) self-explanatory.

This table lists the object's methods:

Method	Description
CopyHere()	Copies one or more file objects into the folder.
GetDetailsOf()	Returns column-based information about the specified folder item, the same way it would be displayed in a shell view.
Items()	The collection of FolderItem elements in the folder. This collection is of type FolderItems.
MoveHere()	The same as CopyHere, but moves files.
NewFolder()	Creates a new folder within the given folder.
ParseName()	Creates a FolderItem object from a name.

As you can see, the Folder object gives you the same basic functionality that you get when manipulating folders in Explorer.

More on Folder Object Methods

Let's look in more detail at the methods exposed by the Folder object. We've already mentioned Items(), which returns a pointer to a collection of FolderItem objects, and explained how the collection exports a property Count and a method Item() to help you enumerate the elements, but what about the rest?

CopyHere()

The method may be considered as a sort of wrapper around the API function SHFileOperation(). It copies one or more files (or file objects) from their original location to the current folder. The source files may be strings, a FolderItem object, or a collection of FolderItem objects. The operation can be controlled through the same flags that control SHFileOperation() (see Chapter 3).

The prototype of the CopyHere() function is:

```
HRESULT CopyHere(VARIANT vItem, VARIANT vOptions);
```

GetDetailsOf()

This method is intended to give programmers the same information that users can get from the right-hand pane in Explorer. Each folder may give you several columns of data; for file folders the columns contain:

- ❑ Name
- ❑ Size
- ❑ Date last modified
- ❑ Type
- ❑ Attributes

The function retrieves this information for a given folder item, based on the column index number. The only exception to this is for the infotip (the text of the tooltip that appears for some elements in the shell), which is assigned an ID number of −1. Column IDs are zero-based, so for ordinary file folders, for example, column 1 is the size. The information is always returned in the form of strings, so the prototype of the method is:

```
HRESULT GetDetailsOf(VARIANT vItem, int iColumn, BSTR* pbs);
```

Items()

Retrieves the collection containing all the folder items in the folder; the prototype is:

```
HRESULT Items(FolderItems** ppid);
```

The FolderItems collection has the following interface:

Method	Description
Item()	Allows you to walk the various elements of the collection. An element is a FolderItem object.

The collection also has a _NewEnum() method that has a special meaning. In fact, *every* collection object must expose a method named _NewEnum to let clients know that iteration capability is provided. The _NewEnum method returns a pointer to an object that supports the IEnumVARIANT interface.

MoveHere()

This method works the same way as CopyHere(), the only (and obvious) difference between them being that MoveHere() moves files instead of copying them. The prototype is:

```
HRESULT MoveHere(VARIANT vItem, VARIANT vOptions);
```

NewFolder()

This method creates a new subfolder in the specified folder. It takes two arguments: the name of the folder to be created, and a VARIANT that is currently unused. The prototype is:

```
HRESULT NewFolder(BSTR bName, VARIANT vUnused);
```

ParseName()

This method creates and returns a new FolderItem object using the name passed in as the first argument. The prototype is:

```
HRESULT ParseName(BSTR bName, FolderItem** ppid);
```

The FolderItem Object

The `FolderItem` object represents an element in a shell folder. It exposes two methods and a number of properties to let you know about the characteristics of the item. Let's start with a table of the properties.

Property	Description
Application	Retrieves the `IDispatch` interface of the object.
GetFolder	Retrieves the `Folder` object if the item is a folder.
IsBrowsable	Returns a Boolean value denoting whether the folder item can be browsed.
IsFileSystem	Indicates whether the folder item is a file system object.
IsFolder	Indicates whether the folder item is a subfolder.
IsLink	Indicates whether the folder item is a shortcut.
ModifyDate	Returns a `DATE` value with the date and time of the last update to the item. A `DATE` is an 8-byte floating-point number.
Name	Returns a string with the name of the item.
Parent	Retrieves the `IDispatch` interface of the parent of the item.
Path	Returns a string with the full path of the item.
Size	Returns an `unsigned long` value denoting the size in bytes of the item.
Type	Returns a string with the type of the item.

All these properties are read-only and implemented through methods called `get_XXX()`, where XXX is the name of the property. All these functions return HRESULTs and accept pointers to output variables to be filled with the data to return.

The methods exposed by `FolderItem` are:

- ❑ `InvokeVerb()`
- ❑ `Verbs()`

Both of these are related to working with the verbs supported by the item.

Invoking an Item's Verbs

We talked about verbs in Chapter 8, and `InvokeVerb()` executes a verb on the folder item. The method is declared this way:

```
HRESULT InvokeVerb(VARIANT vVerb);
```

While `Verbs()` has the following prototype:

```
HRESULT Verbs(FolderItemVerbs** ppfic);
```

The `VARIANT` you can pass to `InvokeVerb()` should be one of the strings returned by the `FolderItemVerbs` collection, which is accessible via the `Verbs()` method.

The FolderItemVerbs Collection

Here's the programming interface of the `FolderItemVerbs` collection:

Method	Description
Item()	Allows you to walk the collection, the elements of which are FolderItemVerb objects

In addition to this, there are three properties: `Application`, `Parent` and `Count`. The last of these, as you might expect, returns the number of items in the collection.

The FolderItemVerb Object

The interface of the `FolderItemVerb` object is extremely limited and contains just the method `DoIt()` that takes no arguments.

Method	Description
DoIt()	Executes the verb on the folder item

Apart from this, the `FolderItemVerb` has the usual `Application` and `Parent` properties, plus an attribute called `Name` that returns the actual verb name for the item:

```
HRESULT get_Name(BSTR* pbs);
```

The string returned here could contain an ampersand to indicate the menu item's accelerator key; the string is *exactly* what appears on the context menu. It seems that this programming interface is not so flexible after all! The `FolderItemVerbs` collection doesn't give you the real, absolute name of the verb, but just the string that appears on the context menu. In other words, the `FolderItemVerbs` collection provides you with a string like **&Open** instead of **Open**. Things get even worse with localized versions of Windows, because the string you have to pass to `InvokeVerb()` to execute a given command (say, `Open`) is what appears to the user, and *not* what is stored in the registry. In the Italian version of Windows, for example, you should call this to open a document:

```
InvokeVerb("&Apri");
```

> **As we discussed back in Chapter 8, a verb is a name for a command that applies to a certain class of files. It can be static (stored in the registry), or dynamic (added by a shell extension). A verb is a universal string and shouldn't be dependent upon localization, nor contain ampersands. So what we're calling a 'verb' here is slightly different from what we originally defined in Chapter 8.**

Accessory Objects

So far, we've examined the main (that is, most commonly used) objects in the shell's object model. However, there are secondary objects too. In particular, you might be interested in the ShellUIHelper object, which implements the IShellUIHelper interface derived from IDispatch. This interface lets you add directories or files to the Favorites folder.

I actually demonstrated this in Chapter 6 – after all, adding a new 'favorite' is just a matter of creating a new shortcut in a specified path. What ShellUIHelper can also do is call the system dialog for adding to Favorites:

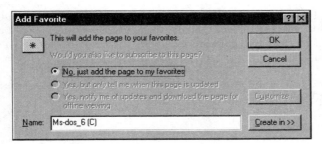

In addition, it allows you to handle channels, subscriptions and desktop components. (See the *Further Reading* section for more details.)

The ShellUIHelper Object

The ShellUIHelper object is also defined in the exdisp.h header file. The server is identified by CLSID_ShellUIHelper, and implements the IShellUIHelper interface, which exposes four methods:

Method	Description
AddChannel()	Adds a channel to the local list. It takes the URL to a channel definition (.cdf) file as input.
AddFavorite()	Adds a file or folder to the list of favorite folders. The two arguments it takes are the URL to the folder or file, and a VARIANT to describe the favorite.
AddDesktopComponent()	Adds a new desktop item by specifying its URL, the type (image or web site), and the initial position on the screen.
IsSubscribed()	Verifies whether we're subscribed to a certain URL or not.

AddChannel() accepts a URL to the CDF file for a channel and stores it locally. Its prototype is:

```
HRESULT AddChannel(BSTR URL);
```

AddFavorite() shows the default dialog for adding a new file or folder to the list of your favorites. It's declared this way, where the VARIANT argument is the descriptive name of the item:

371

```
HRESULT AddFavorite(BSTR URL, VARIANT* Title);
```

`AddDesktopComponent()` registers a new desktop item. It takes the URL and a string denoting the type of the component. This type can be the string 'image' or 'website', and is followed by four VARIANTs that specify the initial position of the item:

```
HRESULT AddDesktopComponent(BSTR URL, BSTR Type,
            VARIANT* Left, VARIANT* Top, VARIANT* Width, VARIANT* Height);
```

A desktop item is *not* a file placed in the desktop folder. Instead, it is a web page hosted in a floating frame or embedded in the HTML page that you can set as the desktop's background. The content of this page is the content of the specified URL. Usually, these URLs are specialized pages that just provide headlines and links to the actual data source. Each URL referred through a desktop item is automatically subscribed to.

Finally, the `IsSubscribed()` method returns a Boolean value according to whether we are subscribed to the specified URL or not.

```
HRESULT IsSubscribed(BSTR URL, VARIANT_BOOL* pBool);
```

See the *Further Reading* section for references on how to develop desktop items, understanding .cdf files, and manage channels and subscriptions.

Adding to Favorites

The following code fragment shows how to invoke the **Add to Favorites** system dialog from C++ code. As a reminder and a point of reference, the equivalent Visual Basic code is:

```
Dim s As New ShellUIHelper
s.AddFavorite "c:\"
```

For C++ programmers, adding the root of disk C to the `Favorites` folder requires this code:

```
void AddDiskCToFavorites()
{
    IShellUIHelper* pShellUI = NULL;

    // Creates the Shell UI Helper object
    HRESULT hr = CoCreateInstance(CLSID_ShellUIHelper, NULL, CLSCTX_SERVER,
                        IID_IShellUIHelper, reinterpret_cast<LPVOID*>(&pShellUI));
    if(FAILED(hr))
        return;

    // Sets the title of the item to add
    CComVariant vTitle(__TEXT("My C Drive"));

    // Causes the dialog to appear with the specified default settings
    CComBSTR bstrPath(__TEXT("c:\\"));
    pShellUI->AddFavorite(bstrPath, &vTitle);

    // Clean up
    pShellUI->Release();
}
```

Putting it all Together

We've now examined several objects implemented in the Internet Explorer 4.*x* DLL shdocvw.dll. These objects let you drive the shell from programs in a way that you haven't been able to do before. All the current examples that are around make use of Visual Basic as the programming environment, and I introduced a Visual Basic example earlier in the chapter. Now I'd like to present a demonstration application written in pure C++ code that shows how to deal with the shell's object model at a lower level of abstraction.

Once again, it's time to start up the Wrox AppWizard and create a dialog-based project; I called mine CppShell. Here's the dialog we're going to implement:

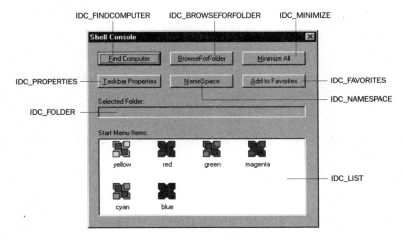

The following table describes what the six buttons on the dialog do:

Button	Action
Find Computer	Makes the Find Computer dialog appear.
Taskbar Properties	Makes the Taskbar Properties dialog appear.
BrowseForFolder	Browse the History folder. The selected item will be displayed in the text box below.
NameSpace	Gets a reference to the Start Menu folder and enumerates its content to the list view below.
Minimize All / Undo Minimize All	This button minimizes all the opened windows, as if we had pressed the *Windows-M* key combination. Then, the caption changes to Undo Minimize All, and the effect is identical to pressing *Shift-Windows-M* – that is, restoring the windows.
Add to Favorites	Causes the Add to Favorites dialog to appear.

As usual, implementing the application involves little more than writing handlers for the buttons. The following source code includes some of the fragments used in the discussion above, and portions of it appeared in my *Cutting Edge* column in the August 1998 issue of Microsoft Interactive Developer (MIND). The title of that article is *The Windows 98 Shell*.

First things first, we need to make sure that the COM libraries are initialized while our dialog is running, so add a couple of lines to `WinMain()` to that effect:

```
// Enable common controls
INITCOMMONCONTROLSEX iccex;
iccex.dwSize = sizeof(INITCOMMONCONTROLSEX);
iccex.dwICC = ICC_WIN95_CLASSES;
InitCommonControlsEx(&iccex);

// Initialize the COM libraries
CoInitialize(NULL);

// Run main dialog
BOOL b = DialogBox(hInstance, "DLG_MAIN", NULL, APP_DlgProc);

// Uninitialize COM
CoUninitialize();
```

Each of the buttons on the dialog will have its own handler function, so we can change `APP_DlgProc()` to reflect that fact:

```
case WM_COMMAND:
    switch(wParam)
    {
    case IDC_FINDCOMPUTER:
        OnFindComputer();
        return FALSE;

    case IDC_PROPERTIES:
        OnTaskbarProperties();
        return FALSE;

    case IDC_BROWSEFOLDER:
        OnBrowseForFolder(hDlg);
        return FALSE;

    case IDC_NAMESPACE:
        OnNameSpace(hDlg);
        return FALSE;

    case IDC_MINIMIZE:
        OnMinimizeAll(hDlg);
        return FALSE;

    case IDC_FAVORITES:
        OnAddFavorites();
        return FALSE;

    case IDCANCEL:
        EndDialog(hDlg, FALSE);
        return FALSE;
    }
    break;
```

There's nothing else for it; we'll just have to go through the handlers one at a time. Here's the first (and one of the simplest), `OnFindComputer()`:

```
void OnFindComputer()
{
    IShellDispatch* pShellDisp = NULL;

    HRESULT hr = CoCreateInstance(CLSID_Shell, NULL, CLSCTX_SERVER,
                        IID_IShellDispatch, reinterpret_cast<LPVOID*>(&pShellDisp));
    if(FAILED(hr))
        return;

    pShellDisp->FindComputer();
    pShellDisp->Release();
}
```

Equally easy is `OnTaskbarProperties()` — in fact, it just involves calling a different method of the `Shell` object:

```
void OnTaskbarProperties()
{
    IShellDispatch* pShellDisp = NULL;

    HRESULT hr = CoCreateInstance(CLSID_Shell, NULL, CLSCTX_SERVER,
                        IID_IShellDispatch, reinterpret_cast<LPVOID*>(&pShellDisp));
    if(FAILED(hr))
        return;

    pShellDisp->TrayProperties();
    pShellDisp->Release();
}
```

Gaining in complexity, `OnBrowseForFolder()` gets a pointer to the `Shell` object like the previous functions, but then goes on to call `BrowseForFolder()`, which retrieves a pointer to a `Folder` object:

```
void OnBrowseForFolder(HWND hDlg)
{
    TCHAR szTitle[MAX_PATH] = {0};
    IShellDispatch* pShellDisp = NULL;
    Folder* pFolder = NULL;

    HRESULT hr = CoCreateInstance(CLSID_Shell, NULL, CLSCTX_SERVER,
                        IID_IShellDispatch, reinterpret_cast<LPVOID*>(&pShellDisp));
    if(FAILED(hr))
        return;

    // Set the root of the namespace displayed
    CComVariant vRoot(CSIDL_HISTORY);

    // Displays the dialog
    CComBSTR bstrFolder(__TEXT("History Folder:"));
    hr = pShellDisp->BrowseForFolder(
                    reinterpret_cast<long>(hDlg), bstrFolder, 0, vRoot, &pFolder);
```

```
      if(pFolder)
      {
         // Get the display name of the selected item
         CComBSTR bstr;
         pFolder->get_Title(&bstr);

         // Convert it to ANSI and display
         wcstombs(szTitle, bstr, MAX_PATH);
         SetDlgItemText(hDlg, IDC_FOLDER, szTitle);
      }

      // Clean up
      pFolder->Release();
      pShellDisp->Release();
   }
```

If a valid `Folder` object is obtained, we call its `get_Title()` method and display the name of the folder on the dialog.

`OnNameSpace()` is much bigger, but that's really more to do with the code necessary for outputting icons to the list view than it is with the COM code. In operation, it's really quite straightforward, and the pattern of calls should be familiar to you by now:

```
void OnNameSpace(HWND hDlg)
{
   IShellDispatch* pShellDisp = NULL;
   Folder* pFolder = NULL;

   HRESULT hr = CoCreateInstance(CLSID_Shell, NULL, CLSCTX_SERVER,
                     IID_IShellDispatch, reinterpret_cast<LPVOID*>(&pShellDisp));
   if(FAILED(hr))
      return;

   // Set the folder to work with
   CComVariant vDir(CSIDL_STARTMENU);

   // Get the Folder object
   pShellDisp->NameSpace(vDir, &pFolder);

   // Prepare to enumerate the folder's content
   long nLength;
   FolderItems* pFIColl = NULL;
   pFolder->Items(&pFIColl);
   pFIColl->get_Count(&nLength);

   // Prepare the list view to fill
   HIMAGELIST himl = ImageList_Create(32, 32, ILC_MASK, 1, 1);
   HWND hwndList = GetDlgItem(hDlg, IDC_LIST);
   ListView_SetImageList(hwndList, himl, LVSIL_NORMAL);

   // Enumerate the folder items
   for(int i = 0 ; i < nLength ; i++)
   {
      // Get the ith folder item
      CComVariant varIndex(i);
      FolderItem* pFI;
```

```
        hr = pFIColl->Item(varIndex, &pFI);
        if(SUCCEEDED(hr))
        {
            CComBSTR bstr;
            TCHAR szFile[MAX_PATH] = {0};

            // Get the ANSI version of the ith item path
            pFI->get_Path(&bstr);
            wcstombs(szFile, bstr, MAX_PATH);

            // Add the item to the list view
            LV_ITEM lvi;
            ZeroMemory(&lvi, sizeof(LV_ITEM));
            lvi.mask = LVIF_TEXT | LVIF_IMAGE;
            lvi.pszText = szFile;
            lvi.cchTextMax = lstrlen(szFile);

            // Get the icon and add to the list view
            SHFILEINFO sfi;
            SHGetFileInfo(szFile, 0, &sfi, sizeof(SHFILEINFO), SHGFI_ICON);
            int iIconPos = ImageList_AddIcon(himl, sfi.hIcon);
            lvi.iImage = iIconPos;
            ListView_InsertItem(hwndList, &lvi);
        }
        pFI->Release();
    }

    pFIColl->Release();
    pFolder->Release();
    pShellDisp->Release();
}
```

We begin by creating a pointer to the `Shell` object, and then use that in a call to the `NameSpace()` function to get hold of a pointer to the `Start Menu` special folder. From there we can use the `Items()` method to obtain a pointer to the `FolderItems` object, and finally we acquire a `FolderItem` pointer with which to obtain the icons and path names. It really is just a matter of picking your way through the hierarchy of objects.

Just two functions to go now, and they're starting to get smaller again. Depending on a global, Boolean flag, `OnMinimizeAll()` calls one of two methods of the `Shell` object, and amends the caption on the button accordingly:

```
void OnMinimizeAll(HWND hDlg)
{
    IShellDispatch* pShellDisp = NULL;

    HRESULT hr = CoCreateInstance(CLSID_Shell, NULL, CLSCTX_SERVER,
                    IID_IShellDispatch, reinterpret_cast<LPVOID*>(&pShellDisp));
    if(FAILED(hr))
        return;
```

```
    // Use a global flag to remember the current status
    if(!g_bMinimized)
    {
        pShellDisp->MinimizeAll();

        // Change the button's caption
        SetDlgItemText(hDlg, IDC_MINIMIZE, "&Undo Minimize All");
        g_bMinimized = TRUE;
    }
    else
    {
        pShellDisp->UndoMinimizeALL();

        // Change the button's caption
        SetDlgItemText(hDlg, IDC_MINIMIZE, "&Minimize All");
        g_bMinimized = FALSE;
    }

    pShellDisp->Release();
}
```

Finally, `OnAddFavorites()` requires no new work at all, because we can just reuse the body of the `AddDiskCToFavorites()` function that I developed earlier in the chapter!

```
void OnAddFavorites()
{
    IShellUIHelper* pShellUI = NULL;

    // Creates the Shell UI Helper object
    HRESULT hr = CoCreateInstance(CLSID_ShellUIHelper, NULL, CLSCTX_SERVER,
                     IID_IShellUIHelper, reinterpret_cast<LPVOID*>(&pShellUI));
    if(FAILED(hr))
        return;

    // Sets the title of the item to add
    CComVariant vTitle(__TEXT("My C Drive"));

    // Causes the dialog to appear with the specified default settings
    CComBSTR bstrPath(__TEXT("c:\\"));
    pShellUI->AddFavorite(bstrPath, &vTitle);

    // Clean up
    pShellUI->Release();
}
```

That's all the code; but there's a whole slew of header files that you'll need to #include in order to get the project to compile – the list is comdef.h, exdisp.h, atlbase.h, shlobj.h, and good old resource.h. With these at the top of your file, the code will compile, link and run as described.

Summary

This chapter discussed scriptable shell objects from the points of view of both Visual Basic and C++. You can exploit them if you have Internet Explorer 4.*x* and Active Desktop installed under Windows 95 or Windows NT 4.0, or if you're running Windows 98 or higher. These objects are documented only in the Internet Client SDK (now part of the Platform SDK), and mainly for the benefit of the Visual Basic programmer. I've tried to make up for the lack of documentation for C++ programmers, particularly in the areas of:

- The functions of the Shell's object model
- The `Folder` and `FolderItem` objects
- `VARIANT`s and Unicode strings

Further Reading

For more detailed information on COM, you should consider some or all of:

- *Essential COM*, Don Box, Addison-Wesley, ISBN 0-201-63446-5
- *Inside COM*, Dale Rogerson, Microsoft Press, ISBN 1-57231-349-8
- *Professional DCOM Programming*, Richard Grimes, Wrox Press, ISBN 1-861000-60-X

At the time of writing, the scriptable shell objects were documented only in the Internet Client SDK. If you're looking for books or articles that can provide a different point of view, you may find the going rather tough.

The Windows 9*x* shell is covered in an article of mine that appeared in the *Cutting Edge* column of the August 1998 issue of MIND. The article provides an overview of the objects involved, and then builds an embeddable COM component (that is, an ActiveX control) that works as the Explorer's left-pane tree view. This control, which lets you choose a directory by expanding the nodes of a tree view, can be inserted in *any* ActiveX-compliant application. It is written in Visual Basic and has an interesting plus: it allows you to filter the directory names to display. In other words, you can use this filter to show your customers only a specified portion of the disk. This source code is available for download from MIND's web site at http://www.microsoft.com/mind.

Two related articles appeared in the MIND edition of July 1998. The first one is *Adding Internet Explorer Favorites to Your Application* by Scott Roberts, which discusses some undocumented functions for handling favorites and, above all, subscriptions. The second, Michael Heydt's *Incorporating the WebBrowser Control Into Your Program* touches on some advanced uses of the WebBrowser control.

In this chapter, we also had to consider some topics relating to the Internet and the Active Desktop. Once again, further information on channels and the CDF format can be found in the November 97 edition of MIND, in the *Cutting Edge* column, written by John P. Grieb. A high-level overview of subscriptions, channels, and Active Desktop components is in MSJ, October 1997, in an article entitled *A Preview of Active Channel and Active Desktop for Internet Explorer 4.0* by Nancy Cluts and Michael Edwards.

A tutorial on how to write Active Desktop components (*Creating an Active Desktop Component* by Josh Hochmann) appeared in MIND in May 98, and last but not least, many of these topics are covered in a single book: Wrox Press' *Professional IE4 Programming*, ISBN 1-861000-70-7.

13

The Windows Scripting Host

Many of today's Windows developers have previously programmed in the MS-DOS environment. Almost all have a soft spot for batch files, those text-based command files that allow you to combine multiple instructions in a single executable command. Batch files are easy to write, and follow a fairly simple syntax.

However, some people claim that the syntax of batch files is *too* simple. The interpreter of `.bat` files is smart enough to recognize some basic control elements, like `if`, but it's a long way from providing an up-to-date and powerful scripting environment.

Until now, though, Windows hasn't had a better mechanism – MS-DOS batch files are still considered as executable files in Windows. With the introduction of the **Windows Scripting Host** (**WSH**), though, things have finally changed. As I'll show in this chapter, the WSH provides support for much more complicated operations than you could perform with `.bat` files, and this is mainly due to the features of the embedded scripting engine.

In this chapter, I'll cover:

- ❑ The origins of Windows batch files
- ❑ The layout of the Scripting Host that provides a framework for shell scripting
- ❑ The WSH object model
- ❑ What you can do with the WSH
- ❑ How you can enhance the power of the WSH with new Automation objects

We will be using JScript and VBScript to write sample WSH applications, but provided that you have (and distribute) an appropriate ActiveX-compliant scripting engine, you could use any other scripting language.

Windows Batch Files — At Last

The idea behind the Windows Scripting Host is quite simple. It is an environment that works as the run-time engine for interpreting script files written in VBScript, JScript or any other script language. The only proviso is that each language should have a parsing module that's compatible with the Internet Explorer ActiveX scripting engine.

In practice, you write a single script file and the WSH runtime allows you to run it as if it were a batch file or a typical Win32 binary. It's therefore quite reasonable to consider .vbs and .js files as new kinds of executable files, where .vbs files are ASCII files that contain a piece of VBScript code, and .js files are their JScript equivalent.

What Can the WSH do for You?

To grasp the importance of the WSH, consider it as a tool that allows you to describe a series of operations programmatically, such as running external executables, or accessing Windows objects like shortcuts, folders and even the registry. With WSH, any repetitive task can be saved to a .vbs or .js file, and invoked with a simple double-click at a later time.

There are a number of advantages that WSH-based scripts have over batch files:

❑ They use more articulated and powerful programming languages that provide a variety of control flow structures, variables, subroutines and arrays that you don't find in DOS batch files.

> **These features will be further enhanced with the release of version 5.0 of the scripting engines, expected to ship with Internet Explorer 5.0. The major feature of the new scripting engines is a built-in mechanism to catch errors and recover from them in JScript, and a way to evaluate and execute code at runtime in VBScript.**

❑ A second (but no less important) fact that makes the WSH incomparably more powerful than batch files is the ability to access *any* registered COM server. First, this enables you to create instances of any existing COM server in your WSH application and control it as you wish. Second, you can design new COM servers specifically to extend the capabilities of the WSH run-time environment. In the remainder of the chapter, I'll examine both of these approaches.

Running Scripts at Startup

In MS-DOS based systems, it's common to have a custom batch file that runs at the end of autoexec.bat and performs some more specialized processing. In most cases, this consists of a keyboard-based menu that uses goto statements to move control to the required block of code. Well, the same effect can be obtained with the WSH. Once you've written the code to execute at startup, you can store it in the Startup folder and have it run during each user's logon.

Structure of the WSH Environment

The Windows Scripting Host environment is an integrated module that embeds an ActiveX scripting engine in the Windows shell. By implementing a handful of COM interfaces, you can give any Win32 application the ability to be driven by scripts. The application should be an Automation server that exposes its own objects to the outside world, and there are many examples in the literature of how to accomplish this. (See the *Further Reading* section for more information.)

In the Windows shell, there exists a program that is capable of interpreting VBScript and JScript source code. The underlying principle is the same as that which makes Internet Explorer able to run scripts from within HTML pages. Internet Explorer, Internet Information Server and the WSH manager embed a parsing module that is compatible with the ActiveX Scripting specifications.

The difference between these three applications is the object model that each imposes upon the hosted module. In other words, from the script's point of view, Internet Explorer and the WSH differ in the object model that they build around the same scripting engine.

> *Microsoft has released an ActiveX component called Script Control that works as an embeddable object that provides a scripting engine for your applications. As a result, you can register your own objects and have your program become scriptable automatically (assuming that your program already exposes Automation objects). The Script Control is available from Microsoft's scripting site:* http://msdn.microsoft.com/scripting.

How to Get the Windows Scripting Host

The Windows Scripting Host module is a standard part of the Windows 98 operating system. It is also available for Windows 95 and Windows NT 4.0, but it's not included with Internet Explorer 4.*x* and the Active Desktop. Instead, you can get it from Microsoft's scripting site (as above).

Installation is as simple as indicating a path where files must be stored. Basically, the WSH package is composed of a couple of executables, plus some COM modules that contain the objects that form the WSH object model.

The setup also registers two new classes of files: `.vbs` and `.js`. These are associated with some shell verbs, so that you can open (run) and edit such files.

What is the Host?

The Windows Scripting Host is composed of two files called `wscript.exe` and `cscript.exe`, which are located in the `Windows` and the `Windows\Command` directories respectively. The latter is a console application and runs inside a DOS window, while the former is a Windows program.

The Host Command Line

Both hosts share the same command line, which is:

```
wscript scriptfile [//options] [/arguments]
cscript scriptfile [//options] [/arguments]
```

The `options` here are listed in the table below; note that you need to use a double slash to prefix each one. Arguments to script files, on the other hand, must be prefixed with a single slash. The following command is an example of how to run a script file for a maximum of two seconds. Once this time has elapsed, the script terminates, whether the operation has actually completed or not:

```
wscript myfile.js //T:2
```

The `T` switch is one of several accepted by both hosts; indeed, the lists are almost identical, as the following table demonstrates:

Switch	Description
B	Runs the script in a non-interactive, batch mode. It suppresses all message boxes and anything that requires the user's intervention.
I	Runs the script in interactive mode and prompts the user if necessary. Execution terminates at the end of the code, and there is no limit on its duration. This is the default setting.
logo	A banner is shown at startup. This option is only valid for `cscript.exe` (for which it is the default setting), and is unsupported by `wscript.exe`.
nologo	Doesn't show a banner at startup. This option is only valid for `cscript.exe`, and is unsupported by `wscript.exe`.
T:nn	The script can run only for the specified time, expressed in seconds. The interruption is realized through a specific method of the ActiveX Scripting engine, and may be considered absolutely thread-safe.
?	Displays the program's usage.

From the command line standpoint, `cscript` and `wscript` are nearly the same and differ only in the `logo` and `nologo` switches. A script file run through the `cscript` module will always make a DOS window appear in the background.

Shell Support for Script Files

After the Windows Scripting Host has been installed, `.vbs` and `.js` files are recognized and properly handled by the shell. This means that you can double-click these files and have them run immediately from Explorer. This feature comes simply from having the `open` verb added to the registry, an approach that we saw in Chapter 11. Under this path:

```
HKEY_CLASSES_ROOT
   \.js
```

and this one:

```
HKEY_CLASSES_ROOT
   \.vbs
```

the `Default` value contains the name of the key that stores all the shell information – `Jsfile` and `Vbsfile` respectively. Following on, this path:

```
HKEY_CLASSES_ROOT
    \jsfile
        \shell
            \open
                \command
```

points to the command line that executes when you click a `.js` file, which is the same as the one specified for `.vbs` files:

Windows 9*x*:   `C:\WINDOWS\WScript.exe "%1" %*`
Windows NT: `C:\WINNT\System32\WScript.exe "%1" %*`

The `%1` stands for the file name, while the `%*` means that the program is also passed any command line arguments in the call. If you simply double-click on a VBScript or JScript file in Explorer, the *actual* command line will be:

```
C:\WINDOWS\WScript.exe filename
```

On the other hand, if you run the VBScript or JScript programmatically with `ShellExecute()` or `ShellExecuteEx()`, or even via the Run dialog box, you can specify additional parameters or options. For example, the following picture shows a way to invoke a JScript file passing arguments:

The context menus for JScript and VBScript files have *two* 'open' commands: **Open** runs `wscript.exe`, while **Open with MS-DOS Prompt** (**Open with Command Prompt** in NT) runs `cscript.exe`. Furthermore, JScript and VBScript files both have a custom property page, which is added to the **Properties** dialog:

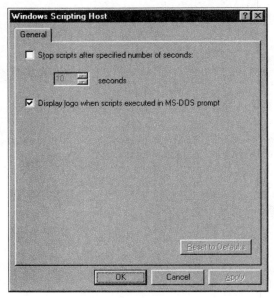

The page lets you set a fixed number of seconds as the maximum execution time. Any settings you change are saved to a `.wsh` file, which has the following format:

```
[ScriptFile]
Path=c:\myfile.js

[Options]
Timeout=2
DisplayLogo=1
BatchMode=0
```

In some senses, a `.wsh` file is a like a shortcut for script files. When they're dealing with these files, both `cscript` and `wscript` first try to extract the contents of the `Path` entry, and then run what they find. The `ScriptFile` section defines the target, while `Options` describe the status of the command line switches.

The Scripting Engine

The WSH uses the extension of the script filename to decide which parser to load. Logically, a `.vbs` extension means that the script was written in VBScript, while `.js` indicates JScript. The WSH natively supports only these two languages because they are the ones supported by the ActiveX scripting engine that ships with Internet Explorer. Provided that you have a valid parser for another scripting language at your disposal – Perl, for example – you can use it to write Windows batch files.

Registering New Scripting Engines

To register a new scripting engine, the following steps are required:

- ❑ Identify the extension of the files handled by the new engine. For example, `.pl` for Perl files.
- ❑ Create an entry for them in the registry similar to the format of those we discussed earlier.
- ❑ Add a `ScriptEngine` key whose `Default` value points to another key.
- ❑ This second key will contain the CLSID of the module implementing the ActiveX scripting parser for the new language.

So, continuing with the Perl example I've been using, the registry will include a key like this:

```
HKEY_CLASSES_ROOT
   \.pl
```

The `Default` value of this key will point to another key called, say, `plfile`, which will have a whole sub-tree of keys beneath it:

```
HKEY_CLASSES_ROOT
   \plfile
      \defaulticon
      \scriptengine
      \shell
         \open
         \edit
         \print
```

This comprises all the verbs needed (open, edit, print), the default icon, and a scriptengine key. The Default value of the latter should contain a reference to *another* key that will identify the parser. In this case, that could be PScript:

```
HKEY_CLASSES_ROOT
    \pscript
        \clsid
```

Under this key will be stored the CLSID of the module that contains the ActiveX scripting compliant parser for Perl.

Command Line Arguments

As I mentioned earlier, a WSH script can take command line arguments. You can specify these one after another, making sure that they are separated by blanks, and that strings with spaces that should be considered as a single parameter are enclosed in quotes. For example:

```
wscript ScriptFile.js First "Second Argument"
```

You can access the collection of command line arguments from within the script code by using a specialized collection object called WshArguments. (See *The WshArguments Object*.)

The WSH Object Model

There are a number of predefined objects used by the Windows Scripting Host, and together they form the **WSH object model**. They allow you to perform a range of actions anywhere in the Windows shell.

The main objects are WScript, WshShell and WshNetwork. The first comprises the WSH engine, while the other two represent the Windows shell and the network respectively. As you'll discover later on, WshShell is quite different from the Shell object we saw in the previous chapter.

WshShell and WshNetwork must be instantiated before use, but this step is unnecessary for WScript because it is an object that's implemented in both wscript and cscript. Consequently, it is already running when it's needed, and there's no need to re-instantiate it.

All the remaining objects are coded into another component called wshom.ocx, and need to be loaded each time you want to use them.

The WScript Object

This object is the root of the WSH's collection of objects. It provides properties and methods to get information about the command line arguments of the invoked script. Moreover, it lets you create new objects and terminate existing ones.

The following tables list the properties and methods supported by the WScript object.

Property	Description
Application	Retrieves the `IDispatch` pointer for the `WScript` object.
Arguments	Returns the collection of arguments for the scripts. The collection is a `WshArguments` object.
FullName	Retrieves the fully qualified name of the scripting host.
Interactive	Specifies whether the execution mode is 'interactive' or 'batch'. This is a read/write property, and undocumented. (See below.)
Name	Retrieves the name of the scripting host.
Path	Retrieves the path of the scripting host.
ScriptFullName	Retrieves the fully qualified name of the current script file.
ScriptName	Retrieves the file name of the current script file.
Version	Returns a string with the current version of the scripting host.

Method	Description
CreateObject()	Creates a new object with the specified ProgID.
DisconnectObject()	Releases the specified object.
GetObject()	Retrieves an object with the specified ProgID.
Echo()	Displays messages in a window (`wscript`) or a DOS box (`cscript`). It is affected by the status of the `Interactive` property. (See below.)
Quit()	Stops execution of the script.

`Interactive` is an undocumented, read/write property that accepts and returns a Boolean value. It is initially set with the value of the I command line switch, but you can change it programmatically. Interestingly, when `Interactive` is set to `False`, `WScript.Echo()` won't work, but you can still display messages through the methods of the `WshShell` object that we'll cover in a moment.

The method that's absolutely central to `WScript` is `CreateObject()`, which you can use to create new object instances. The prototype is:

```
WScript.CreateObject(sProgID, [sPrefix])
```

The `sPrefix` argument is a string used to identify the names of **event procedures** that are relevant to the object. We'll see this again in a later section dedicated to events.

`GetObject()` is defined like this:

```
WScript.GetObject(sPathname, [sProgID], [sPrefix])
```

It retrieves an object that's specified using either a filename or a ProgID. The `sPrefix` argument plays the same role as it did for `CreateObject()`.

Because the WSH exposes a `CreateObject()` *method, we're obviously supposed to use it to create new objects. However, using the straight VBScript* `CreateObject()` *or the JScript* `ActiveXObject()` *method works just as well. In fact, it turns out to be a bit faster because* `WScript`'s `CreateObject()` *method relies on its script counterpart.*

The WshShell Object

This object represents the Windows shell, but it's very different from the `Shell` object we examined in the previous chapter. It is missing quite a bit of functionality, but on the flip side it has a variety of additional methods too. Despite the similarity in their names, they should be considered as two very different components.

`WshShell` has just a couple of properties. One is called `Environment` and retrieves the collection of system environment variables, and the other property is `SpecialFolders`, which returns a collection of the shell's special folder names.

The methods span various functions: from shortcuts, through the registry and process spawning, to special folders. An instance of `WshShell` can be created using `WScript`, as follows:

```
Set s = WScript.CreateObject("WScript.Shell")
```

Here's the complete list of `WshShell` methods:

Method	Description
`CreateShortcut()`	Creates an empty `WshShortcut` or `WshUrlShortcut` object to be filled and saved as a shortcut or a URL shortcut, respectively.
`ExpandEnvironmentStrings()`	Expands variables enclosed by a pair of % symbols.
`Popup()`	Shows a message box. You can use this to display messages even if the `WScript.Interactive` property is set to `False`.
`RegDelete()`	Deletes a key or value from the registry.
`RegRead()`	Reads a key or value from the registry.
`RegWrite()`	Writes a key or value to the registry.
`Run()`	Launches and synchronizes an executable.

I'll focus on the registry functions in *Accessing the Registry*; in the meantime, let's quickly look at the `Run()` and `ExpandEnvironmentStrings()` methods. The prototype of `Run()` is as follows:

```
Run(sCommand, [iWindowType], [bWaitOnReturn])
```

Beyond the command line, you can specify the type of the output window (minimized, maximized, normal, hidden). Valid values are summarized below; as you can see, they are a subset of the SW_XXX constants:

Constant	Description
0	Hides the window (like SW_HIDE).
1	Displays the window and gives it the focus (like SW_SHOWNORMAL).
2	Minimizes the window and gives it the focus (like SW_SHOWMINIMIZED).
3	Maximizes the window and gives it the focus (like SW_MAXIMIZE).
4	Displays the window without giving it the focus (like SW_SHOWNOACTIVATE).
6	Minimizes the window without giving it the focus (Like SW_MINIMIZE).

If the bWaitOnReturn flag is set to True, it blocks the calling script until the spawned program has terminated. Any environment variable included in the command line string is automatically expanded.

The Run() method is implemented through a call to ShellExecuteEx(). This means that we can also pass it the name of a file that has a registered open verb. It also means that it silently supports any object implementing IShellExecuteHook that is installed. I'll say more about this later on, in the section called *Hooking a Program's Execution*.

The ExpandEnvironmentStrings() method takes and returns a string. The input string is text with environment variables enclosed in % symbols, while the output contains the expanded string.

```
sWinDir = ExpandEnvironmentStrings("Windows is at %WINDIR%")
```

If the environment string doesn't exist, the method returns an undefined object. Consequently, you should ensure that you get the outcome you require before proceeding.

Shortcuts and URL Shortcuts

The CreateShortcut() method receives a filename and returns objects whose type depends on the filename's extension. If the extension is .lnk, then the returned object is a WshShortcut, whereas if the extension is .url the returned object is a WshUrlShortcut. If any other extension is specified, you'll get a run-time script error. The basic difference between a shortcut and a URL shortcut is that the latter points to a remote URL. WshUrlShortcut is also a bit simpler than WshShortcut. (More details in the *Helper Objects* section.)

The WshNetwork Object

Remote printers and network connections are the subjects of this object. An instance of WshNetwork is created through WScript:

```
Set n = WScript.CreateObject("WScript.Network")
```

The following table provides a list of the methods that it supports:

Methods	Description
AddPrinterConnection()	Runs the Wizard to add a new printer connection.
EnumNetworkDrives()	Allows you to enumerate the network drives by returning a collection. (See Helper Objects.)
EnumPrinterConnections()	Allows you to enumerate all the printer connections by returning a collection. (See Helper Objects.)
MapNetworkDrive()	Establishes a connection with a network drive.
RemoveNetworkDrive()	Removes a connection with a network drive.
RemovePrinterConnection()	Removes a connection with a network printer.
SetDefaultPrinter()	Defines the new default printer. If it's a remote printer, you must specify its full UNC name (say, \\server\Printer XYZ).

There are also three properties for this object, whose roles are self-explanatory:

- ComputerName
- UserDomain
- UserName

Helper Objects

The WSH object model also includes six other **helper objects**. The first point to note about these is that you can't create any of them directly. They don't have a ProgID, and they can be used only when returned by methods/properties of other objects. The objects are:

Object	Returned by
WshArguments	WScript.Arguments
WshCollection	WshNetwork.EnumNetworkDrives(), WshNetwork.EnumPrinterConnections()
WshEnvironment	WshShell.Environment
WshShortcut	WshShell.CreateShortcut()
WshUrlShortcut	WshShell.CreateShortcut()
WshSpecialFolders	WshShell.SpecialFolders

Apart from WshShortcut and WshUrlShortcut, the others are all special types of collection. Thus their programming interfaces are pretty similar, at least syntactically.

The WshArguments Object

This collection comprises all the command-line arguments for a running script, and you get access to it through the Arguments property of the WScript object. The component has the usual properties of a collection: Item and Count. Item allows you to get the value of the ith argument (the list is zero-based), while Count returns the total number of arguments.

There's also a Length property that is maintained for compatibility purposes – it's equivalent to Count. The following VBScript code snippet shows how a script can display its command line.

```
For Each item In WScript.Arguments
    ' Displays the various items on the command line
    WScript.Echo item
Next
```

The WshCollection Object

This object is a generic collection, and is returned mainly by methods of WshNetwork.

The WshEnvironment Object

A reference to this object, which has a method called Remove() is returned by the WshShell.Environment property. Count, Length and Item let you walk the items of the collection.

The items in this collection are environmental variables, like WINDIR or PATH. While you can pass the Item member an index, it is particularly useful to call Item with strings that identify a variable by name:

```
Set s = WScript.CreateObject("WScript.Shell")
Set e = s.Environment
WScript.Echo e.Item("PATH")
WScript.Echo e.Remove("PATH")
```

The WshShortcut Object

WshShortcut is a component that allows you to define and save a .lnk shortcut to disk. Shortcut creation takes two steps: you first create a WshShortcut object, and then you must fill in its properties and save it to disk. The first stage is accomplished by the WshShell.CreateShortcut() function:

```
Set s = WScript.CreateObject("WScript.Shell")
Set lnk = s.CreateShortcut("mydiskc.lnk")
lnk.TargetPath = "c:\"
lnk.Save
```

When calling CreateShortcut(), you specify the name of the final .lnk file. Next, you fill in the various attributes of the shortcut and save it by calling WshShortcut.Save(). If you want to create a shortcut in a special folder, just get the path name and pass a fully-qualified name to CreateShortcut(). To obtain the physical path of a special folder, you should make use of the WshSpecialFolders object, which we'll see in a moment. Here's a full list of WshShortcut's properties:

Property	Description
Arguments	A string that contains the arguments of the shortcut's target.
Description	The shortcut's description string.
FullName	Retrieves the full path name of the .lnk file.
Hotkey	A string that contains the representation of the hotkey that starts the shortcut.
IconLocation	A string that contains the path and index of the icon location. Path and index are comma-separated. An example would be c:\windows\system\shell32.dll,13
TargetPath	This can be a folder, an executable, or a file to run using ShellExecute().
WindowStyle	Denotes the SW_XXX style of the window.
WorkingDirectory	The directory from which to start the executable.

The WshUrlShortcut Object

This works in the same way as WshShortcut, but supports only the following two properties:

Property	Description
FullName	Retrieves the full path of the .url file that contains the shortcut.
TargetPath	Retrieves the URL to which the shortcut points.

It also supports the Save() method to store the shortcut on disk.

The WshSpecialFolders Object

Finally, this object is a kind of wrapper built on top of the SHGetSpecialFolderPath() API function that we saw in Chapter 5. It's a collection that includes the Item, Count and Length members, with the same features we examined earlier. The following fragment demonstrates how to create a shortcut in the Favorites folder:

```
Set s = WScript.CreateObject("WScript.Shell")
sPath = s.SpecialFolders("Favorites")
sPath = sPath & "\mydiskc.lnk"
Set lnk = s.CreateShortcut(sPath)
lnk.TargetPath = "c:\"
lnk.Save
```

As you can see, it is a slightly different version of the previous sample that created a shortcut to c:\. A reference to WshSpecialFolders is returned by the WshShell.SpecialFolders property.

Accessing the Registry

The Windows Scripting Host also gives you the ability to access the registry smoothly, for reading or writing both keys and values. This is an important feature, because the ability to manipulate the registry really boosts and empowers your applications. As I have pointed out in previous chapters, the API for accessing the registry is cumbersome and designed at too low a level of abstraction, although things have improved with the lightweight API, which I looked at in Chapter 10.

The `WshShell` object contains three methods for programmatically modifying the status of the system registry. They are:

- ❏ `RegDelete()`
- ❏ `RegRead()`
- ❏ `RegWrite()`

The syntax of these methods is quite simple, and reminiscent of the syntax of the new `SHxxx()` functions we met in Chapter 10, rather than the original registry API. Basically, you are required to specify the key or the value on which to work, and the buffer from which to read or write.

Supported Types

The Win32 registry programming interface allows you to store and read a variety of different data types – see the Win32 documentation for details. However, the WSH object supports only the five most popular, which are:

- ❏ `REG_SZ` – strings
- ❏ `REG_DWORD` – 32-bit unsigned values
- ❏ `REG_BINARY` – binary data
- ❏ `REG_EXPAND_SZ` – strings that contain expandable macros such as `%WINDIR%`
- ❏ `REG_MULTI_SZ` – an array of null-terminated strings, doubly null-terminated (supported for reading but not writing)

In script code, all variables are treated as `VARIANT`s, while the registry methods listed above ultimately make use of the low-level registry API that requires a specific type. Consequently, some type conversions are necessary, but the `WshShell` object performs them automatically.

Deleting a Registry Entry

The `RegDelete()` method has the following syntax:

```
WshShell.RegDelete sKeyOrValue
```

There's no need to mention explicitly that a given string is a key or a value – just pass a fully qualified registry path to the function. If the path ends with a backslash, it is considered to be a key; otherwise it is handled as a value.

These WSH methods and the Win32 registry API have fundamentally different programming interfaces at this level. The Win32 registry API has different functions for dealing with keys and values. Furthermore, WSH methods want the root node, say `HKEY_LOCAL_MACHINE`, specified within the string and not as a separate parameter, as the Win32 API functions require.

Differences between Windows NT and Windows 9x

The `RegDelete()` method ends up calling the registry functions `RegDeleteKey()` and `RegDeleteValue()`, and while the latter works the same under Windows 9x and Windows NT, `RegDeleteKey()` exhibits different behavior on each. When a key is deleted in Windows 9x, its sub-tree is also removed. In NT, a key is deleted only if it is empty (that is, it has no child keys). This behavior is upheld by the `RegDelete()` method.

> *The number of values a key holds is irrelevant to the question of whether it is considered empty − a key can be deleted provided that it doesn't include sub-keys, even if it contains values.*

Reading from the Registry

To read from the registry, just call `RegRead()`, passing a fully qualified name that refers to a key or a value with the same logic as discussed above: a final backslash denotes a key, otherwise it's a value.

There's no need to specify the type of the data you want to read. It is sufficient that you declare a valid variable to store the result. It's always the object's infrastructure that takes care of getting the raw data and returning it, packaged as a `VARIANT`. The function works like this:

```
v = WshShell.RegRead(sKeyOrValue)
```

Getting System Information from the Registry

Here's a brief example (which I've called `system.vbs`) that reads version and registration information about the installed copy of Windows.

```
' SYSTEM.VBS
' Reads version and registration information from the registry
'-----------------------------------------------------------

' Create the WshShell object
Set s = WScript.CreateObject("WScript.Shell")

' Registry Path constants
RP_SYSTEM = "HKLM\System\CurrentControlSet\Control\ProductOptions\"
RP_PRTYPE = "ProductType"
RP_NTVERS = "HKLM\Software\Microsoft\Windows NT\CurrentVersion\"
RP_WINVER = "HKLM\Software\Microsoft\Windows\CurrentVersion\"

' System name constants
WIN_NTWORK = "Windows NT Workstation"
WIN_NTSERV = "Windows NT Server"

' Read about the product type
On Error Resume Next      ' Because the key doesn't exist under Win9x
sProdType = ""
sProdType = s.RegRead(RP_SYSTEM & RP_PRTYPE)

' Determine the OS version
select case sProdType
   case "WinNT"
      sRegPathVer = RP_NTVERS
      sBuf0 = WIN_NTWORK
      sBuf1 = s.RegRead(RP_NTVERS & "CurrentVersion") + "."
      sBuf2 = s.RegRead(RP_NTVERS & "CurrentBuildNumber")
      sBuf3 = s.RegRead(RP_NTVERS & "CSDVersion")
```

```
       case "ServerNT",  "LanManNT"
           sRegPathVer = RP_NTVERS
           sBuf0 = "Windows NT Server"
           sBuf1 = s.RegRead(RP_NTVERS & "CurrentVersion")
           sBuf2 = s.RegRead(RP_NTVERS & "CurrentBuildNumber")
           sBuf3 = s.RegRead(RP_NTVERS & "CSDVersion")
       case ""
           sRegPathVer = RP_WINVER
           sBuf0 = s.RegRead(RP_WINVER & "Version")
           sBuf2 = s.RegRead(RP_WINVER & "VersionNumber")
           sBuf3 = "----------------------"
end select

' Read registration info
sBuf4 = s.RegRead(sRegPathVer & "RegisteredOwner")
sBuf5 = s.RegRead(sRegPathVer & "RegisteredOrganization")

' Display the result
WScript.Echo sBuf0 + "   " + sBuf1 + sBuf2 + vbCrLf + _
             sBuf3 + vbCrLf + vbCrLf + _
             sBuf4 + vbCrLf + _
             sBuf5

' Close
WScript.Quit
```

The code relies only on registry information to ascertain the underlying platform. In Win32 code, almost all of this information would be returned by the GetVersionEx() function. Interestingly, however, there's an exception: that API function doesn't distinguish between the Workstation and Server editions of Windows NT. For this information, you need to access the registry. Let's see how the above code performs this trick.

Under Windows NT, the following registry path contains a value called ProductType:

```
HKEY_LOCAL_MACHINE
    \System
        \CurrentControlSet
            \Control
                \ProductOptions
```

If this key doesn't exist, then we're running Windows 95 or Windows 98. ProductType can contain three possible strings:

Value	Description
WinNT	Windows NT Workstation
ServerNT	Windows NT Server
LanManNT	Windows NT Server working as a primary or backup domain controller

Once you know the operating system, you can easily manage the differences in the registry structure between Windows and Windows NT. The most important is that version and registration information is stored under

```
HKEY_LOCAL_MACHINE
    \Software
        \Microsoft
            \Windows NT
                \CurrentVersion
```

under Windows NT, and

```
HKEY_LOCAL_MACHINE
    \Software
        \Microsoft
            \Windows
                \CurrentVersion
```

under Windows 9*x*. Other differences exist in the values each key provides. Both versions of the registry support `RegisteredOwner` and `RegisteredOrganization`, but Windows NT stores information about the installed service pack in the `CSDVersion` values, while `CurrentBuildNumber` stores the build number. This information isn't available under Windows 9*x*, where we have `Version` and `VersionNumber` values to store the actual operating system name and its full version number.

The following picture shows the output of the `system.vbs` script on my Windows 95 and Windows NT machines:

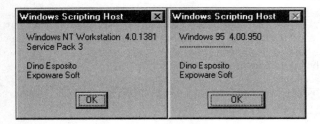

Note that you can use acronyms to refer to some of the registry root nodes. In the above example, I've used `HKLM` instead of `HKEY_LOCAL_MACHINE`. The other valid acronyms are:

Acronym	Equivalent Root Node
HKLM	HKEY_LOCAL_MACHINE
HKCR	HKEY_CLASSES_ROOT
HKCU	HKEY_CURRENT_USER

Of course, it's perfectly possible to access other nodes like `HKEY_USERS` and `HKEY_CURRENT_CONFIG`, but they don't have acronyms – you have to use their full names.

Writing to the Registry

You can write new content to the registry from within the WSH environment by using the `RegWrite()` method. The syntax is shown overleaf:

```
WshShell.RegWrite(sKeyOrValue, vValue, [iType])
```

The method automatically creates any missing keys that appear in the path. If you pass a key as the
sKeyOrValue argument, then the vValue content is written to the Default value of the key itself.

With iType, you can specify the type of the value you're about to write from one of the
aforementioned REG_Xxx types, with the exception of REG_MULTI_SZ. The default for this
parameter is REG_SZ, namely a string. This occurs even if you actually pass a number as the vValue
parameter.

```
Set s = WScript.CreateObject("WScript.Shell")
sRegPath = "HKLM\Software\Expoware Soft\"
s.RegWrite sRegPath & "Wsh\", "WSH examples"
```

Doing More with the Registry

If you need to extend the WSH programming interface for the registry, then you should consider
writing a new COM component that exposes the functionality you're missing. There are at least a
couple of things you might want to do with the registry that the current programming interface
doesn't allow.

Firstly, you may need to handle more data types. However, such a requirement would be quite
unusual, unless you need to handle little or big-endian numbers, or an array of strings.

Secondly, you might require your server to provide enumeration of keys and values. Further
possibilities are connecting to a remote registry, implementing a change notification mechanism, or a
save/restore key method. In general, by designing a COM server you can port to the WSH
everything that the Win32 API lets you do with the registry.

In the *Adding New Objects to the WSH* section of this chapter, I will write such a COM server, which
will provide key and value enumeration.

Scripting the Local File System

Scripts can't call into API functions, so they need specialized objects to provide access to the local file
system. Both VBScript and JScript come with some useful objects for working with files, folders and
drives. They are:

Scripting Object	Description
FileSystemObject	Manages file and folder operations, and creates text files
Folder	Returns information on a file system folder
Drive	Returns information on a drive
File	Returns information on a file
Dictionary	A high-performance collection object
TextStream	Renders an I/O stream of text

An updated version of these objects – the Microsoft Scripting Runtime – is available on Microsoft's scripting web site.

> *For more information about these objects, you should refer to the documentation in the MSDN Library.*

Because the Windows Scripting Host environment is somewhat closed, and something that will be used mostly on an intranet (or perhaps even on a standalone PC), concerns about unsafe access to the disk diminish in their importance. In light of this, `FileSystemObject` can be a really useful and quite powerful tool to use when programming the WSH.

Here's a short example showing what you can do with `FileSystemObject`. The following code displays a message box with the status of each drive in the system:

```
Set fs = CreateObject("Scripting.FileSystemObject")
Set dc = fs.Drives
For Each d in dc
   s = s & d.DriveLetter & " - "
   If d.DriveType = Remote Then
     n = d.ShareName
   ElseIf d.IsReady Then
     n = d.VolumeName
     n = n + vbCrLf + "Free: " + FormatNumber(d.FreeSpace/1024, 0) + " KB"
     n = n + vbCrLf
   Else
     n = n + vbCrLf
   End If
   s = s & n & vbCrLf
Next

WScript.Echo s
```

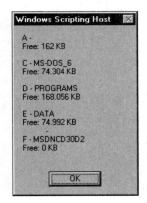

Accessing Existing Objects

The Windows Scripting Host is a fully COM-aware environment. This means that you can invoke and use any correctly registered COM server from the host. What I have described so far are the objects distributed with the WSH package, and in a certain sense, they form the WSH object model. However, in my opinion, what constitutes the WSH object model is somewhat debatable. The two viewpoints are:

❑ *Everything* that exposes an Automation interface can be called from the WSH, and may be considered part of its object model.

❑ The WSH object model is just a handful of interfaces that set up communication with the ActiveX scripting engine. Apart from the WScript object, everything else might be considered to be a related COM server, but not necessarily a part of the object model.

You can access any existing Automation server by using the WScript.CreateObject() method or, for more efficiency, VBScript's CreateObject() method. For example, you can drive the Shell objects we discussed in the previous chapter from WSH scripts. The following example shows how to display the taskbar property dialog from a WSH script:

```
Set s = WScript.CreateObject("Shell.Application")
s.TrayProperties
```

Of course, you can do exactly the same for your own COM servers (see *Adding New Objects to the WSH).*

Handling Events with the WSH

The typical way of handling events on the client side is by defining a procedure whose name follows a special convention. The name is composed of two elements: a prefix that identifies the object that raised the event, and the name of the event. This scheme is common in visual environments, such as Visual Basic, where the event that reveals a click on Button1 is handled through a procedure called Button1_Click.

With the WSH, things work the same way. If the server fires an event named Collapse, and the object that represents that server is called TreeViewNode1, then the client-side procedure that handles it is called TreeViewNode1_Collapse.

Defining an Event Handler

Normally, the name of an object is assigned automatically and modified via the Property Editor or some such tool. With the WSH, we can't rely on visual tools and need a programmatic way to assign an object its internal name.

When you create a new object with the WScript.CreateObject() call, it's possible to specify an optional parameter as well as the ProgID of the server:

```
WScript.CreateObject(sProgID, [sPrefix])
```

The `sPrefix` parameter is a string like `MyObj_` that will be used as the prefix for the procedure name of any event that is raised by the object being created (it takes the place of `TreeViewNode1_` in the example given in the previous section).

Steps to Creating an Event Handler

If you know that the server exposes events in which you might be interested, then it's necessary to specify the second parameter in the `WScript.CreateObject()` call. Once you've assigned a prefix to the object, you can handle any event with an appropriately named procedure. The prototype will be exactly that required by the event's syntax. In practice, the WSH environment composes the name of the procedure that *might* be the handler, and tries to locate it. If successful, the event is handled executing code on the caller's side.

Note that the prefix must be unique for every possible copy of the same object. Also, it's recommended that it end with an underscore character.

> *To support events in Windows Scripting Host sources, you* must *create your objects with* `WScript.CreateObject().`

Adding New Objects to the WSH

As we've seen, the Windows Scripting Host environment comes with a number of built-in objects, and these are intended to provide WSH users with a significant subset of the functionality available outside the WSH. For example, the network object allows you to know about remote printers and shared disks, while the shell component provides shortcut capabilities, environment variables, process launching and registry manipulation.

These objects are enough to get you started, but sooner or later you will need more objects. If the COM component you need exists on the machine, you can simply instantiate and use it, provided of course that you know its methods. Alternatively, you can write your own custom objects to extend the WSH object model, and this is what I'll do in the remainder of the chapter.

In particular, I'll be building an Automation server to provide support for areas in which the WSH is weak:

- ❑ Clipboard support
- ❑ Drive formatting
- ❑ Registry enumeration

In addition, I'll redesign and integrate into the WSH a couple of the examples we've built in previous chapters:

- ❑ How to browse for icons (Chapter 9)
- ❑ Using custom names to run programs or files (Chapter 8)

Arranging an ATL Automation Server

The WSH can call the methods of any COM Automation server, implemented in whatever language you choose. In this case I chose C++ and ATL, so to start it off, use the ATL COM AppWizard to create an in-process DLL project called WshMore.

Next, use the Object Wizard to add a simple ATL object called WshFun, ensuring that the interface is called IWshFun and that it's a dual interface. All we need to do now is fill in the functions. It should be a breeze!

Defining the Programming Interface

This interface is not going to be a model of good design – I just want to show you some of the things that it's possible to do. Here's a list of the functions that we'll be adding to the IWshFun interface over the next few sections:

Function	Area	Description
CopyText()	Clipboard	Copies a text string to the clipboard. Makes use of the CF_TEXT format.
PasteText()	Clipboard	Reads text from the clipboard. Makes use of the CF_TEXT format.
AddExecuteHook()	Shell Execute	Adds and removes entries from the .ini file used by the IShellExecuteHook module (see Chapter 8) to create new keyboard shortcuts for launching executables.
BrowseForIcon()	Icons	Displays the dialog I created in Chapter 9 to let you pick up an icon from a given file.
FormatDrive()	Drive	Opens up the system dialog for drive formatting.
FindFirstKey()	Registry	Given a base path, enumerates the first key.
FindNextKey()	Registry	Continues enumerating the keys of the above path.
FindFirstValue()	Registry	Given a base path, enumerates the first value.
FindNextValue()	Registry	Continues enumerating the values of the above path.

In the forthcoming sections, I'll examine these methods more closely by discussing their syntax, digging through their implementation details, and by providing examples of their use.

Clipboard Support

The clipboard is a system tool that can be used for temporary data storage, but scripting languages don't usually provide you with a means of handling it. As you know, the Windows clipboard is a kind of repository for data in a variety of formats, including custom ones. However, the methods I'll be writing make use only of the simplest format, CF_TEXT, which renders plain text.

The methods to be added are CopyText() and PasteText() and, as their names suggest, they let you copy text to, and read it from, the clipboard. Because the function declarations utilize BSTR strings, some string conversions inside the bodies of the methods need to be performed.

Copying Text

The syntax of IWshFun::CopyText() is:

```
HRESULT CopyText([in] BSTR bText);
```

This simply accepts the text to be copied, and always returns S_OK. The function takes a BSTR string as its input parameter, creates a memory handle to contain the data, packages it, and stores it on the clipboard.

```
STDMETHODIMP CWshFun::CopyText(BSTR bText)
{
    USES_CONVERSION;
    TCHAR pszText[MAXBUFSIZE] = {0};
    lstrcpy(pszText, OLE2T(bText));

    HANDLE hData = GlobalAlloc(GHND, MAXBUFSIZE);
    LPTSTR psz = static_cast<LPTSTR>(GlobalLock(hData));
    lstrcpyn(psz, pszText, MAXBUFSIZE);
    GlobalUnlock(hData);

    OpenClipboard(NULL);
    SetClipboardData(CF_TEXT, hData);
    CloseClipboard();

    return S_OK;
}
```

I defined MAXBUFSIZE as a constant equal to 32768, giving us a 32K buffer. I've also used ATL's OLE2T() macro to convert strings from BSTR to LPTSTR. Using CopyText() from within VBScript or JScript will mean writing code like this:

```
Dim o
Set o = WScript.CreateObject("WshMore.WshFun.1")
o.CopyText "I'm the IWshFun interface"
```

Reading Text

PasteText() is a method that retrieves any content in CF_TEXT format from the clipboard and returns it as a string. The method declaration is:

```
HRESULT PasteText([out, retval] BSTR* pbRetVal);
```

This method doesn't take any input parameters. Instead, the value placed in `pbRetVal` is passed to the script as the return value of the method. The listing below shows the implementation.

```
STDMETHODIMP CWshFun::PasteText(BSTR* pbRetVal)
{
    USES_CONVERSION;

    // Get a memory handle from the clipboard
    OpenClipboard(NULL);
    HANDLE hData = GetClipboardData(CF_TEXT);
    CloseClipboard();

    // Extract the content
    LPTSTR psz = static_cast<LPTSTR>(GlobalLock(hData));
    TCHAR pszText[MAXBUFSIZE] = {0};
    lstrcpyn(pszText, psz, MAXBUFSIZE);
    GlobalUnlock(hData);

    // Returns a BSTR
    *pbRetVal = T2BSTR(pszText);

    return S_OK;
}
```

I've created a `BSTR` by using the ATL macro `T2BSTR()`, which takes an ANSI string as input. Unless you're using ATL class wrappers like `CComBSTR` in your code, once you've called `PasteText()` you should free the `BSTR` with a call to `SysFreeString()`. Here's an example in plain C++:

```
IWshFun* pWshFun = NULL;
hr = CoCreateInstance(CLSID_WshFun, NULL, CLSCTX_INPROC_SERVER,
                          IID_IWshFun, reinterpret_cast<LPVOID*>(&pWshFun));
if(FAILED(hr))
    return;

BSTR bstr;
pWshFun->PasteText(&bstr);
MessageBox(GetFocus(), bstr, __TEXT("PasteText"), MB_OK);
pWshFun->Release();
SysFreeString(bstr);
```

And here's another example in VBScript:

```
Dim o, s
Set o = WScript.CreateObject("WshMore.WshFun.1")
s = o.PasteText
MsgBox s
```

Drive Formatting

Because the Windows Scripting Host is a scripting environment inside the Windows shell, and works in much the same manner as DOS batch files, accessing the file system is sometimes necessary. I've already introduced `FileSystemObject` as a good solution to this problem.

However, while `FileSystemObject` provides you with a huge collection of functions and properties, it isn't a tool for formatting disks. However, in Chapter 10, I covered `SHFormatDrive()` function in detail. As part of this example, I will provide access to it through a COM method. The prototype is shown at the top of the next page:

```
HRESULT FormatDrive([in] int iDrive);
```

For the sake of simplicity, I've discarded all the enhancements to the function that I made in Chapter 10, and as a consequence the source code for this method is pretty straightforward:

```
extern "C" int WINAPI SHFormatDrive(long, long, long, long);

STDMETHODIMP CWshFun::FormatDrive(int iDrive)
{
    int irc = SHFormatDrive(0, iDrive, 0, 0);
    return (irc < 0 ? S_OK : E_FAIL);
}
```

The function returns a Boolean value to denote the success or failure of the operation. In particular, it has a non-zero value if the function actually formats the disk, and zero otherwise (including the case where you cancel the dialog).

> *As we discussed in Chapter 10,* SHFormatDrive() *is included in the* shell32.lib *import library, but there isn't a proper entry in* shellapi.h *or any other header file. I have therefore added a declaration to the code, prefixing it with* extern "C" *to ensure compatibility.*

Here's an example of how to call the new method from within JScript code:

```
// Format drive A:
var o;
o = WScript.CreateObject("WshMore.WshFun.1");
o.FormatDrive(0);
```

To indicate the drive to format, you should use the common, zero-based notation: 0 is drive A, 1 is drive B, 2 is drive C, and so on.

Browsing for Icons

Creating shortcuts is a typical application of the WSH. An interesting function would be a system-provided dialog to let you visually choose the icon to assign to the shortcut. We've already discussed the source code necessary for such a dialog — see Chapter 9 for the details, and Chapter 11 for a concrete example of its use.

In this example, I'm going to show you how to make this functionality available to Windows Scripting Host applications. The method is:

```
HRESULT BrowseForIcon([in] BSTR bFile, [out, retval] BSTR* pbRetVal);
```

The bFile argument denotes the file to
browse for icons, which may be changed at
runtime by clicking the dialog's browse
button.

When you select an icon, the method returns a string with the name of the file and the index of the
selected icon, separated by a comma:

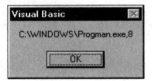

The source code of the method calls into SHHelper.dll (see code for Chapter 11), a helper library
that collects many of the functions we have built so far. This DLL contains the
SHBrowseForIcon() function, whose source code was developed in Chapter 9.

```
#include "shhelper.h"


STDMETHODIMP CWshFun::BrowseForIcon(BSTR bFile, BSTR* pbRetVal)
{
    USES_CONVERSION;
    TCHAR pszFile[MAX_PATH] = {0};
    lstrcpy(pszFile, OLE2T(bFile));

    HICON hIcon;
    int iIndex = SHBrowseForIcon(pszFile, &hIcon);
    if(iIndex >= 0)
    {
        TCHAR szBuf[MAX_PATH + 10] = {0};
        wsprintf(szBuf, __TEXT("%s,%d"), pszFile, iIndex);

        *pbRetVal = T2BSTR(szBuf);
        return S_OK;
    }
    return S_FALSE;

}
```

In this case, the ANSI-Unicode conversion is necessary because the `SHBrowseForIcon()` function requires an ANSI string. The following snippet shows how to call the `BrowseForIcon()` method from within VBScript code.

```
Dim o, s
Set o = WScript.CreateObject("WshMore.WshFun.1")
s = o.BrowseForIcon("shell32.dll")
MsgBox s
```

Registry Key Enumeration

As I mentioned earlier, the built-in registry support in the WSH doesn't include key and value enumeration. However, if you need to do something to a certain registry sub-tree, such methods can be really useful. I'll provide two different enumerators, one for keys and one for values.

The low-level Win32 API functions and the new shell utility API (see Chapter 10) have a similar approach to this issue. You need to specify an incrementing variable to identify the nth item, be that a key or a value. The `RegEnumValue()` and `SHEnumKeyEx()` functions are generic loops driven by a Boolean guard that interrupts at the end of the list of keys or values.

For my implementation, I shall take a slightly different approach by defining a couple of methods called `FindFirstXxx()` and `FindNextXxx()`. The prototypes are:

```
HRESULT FindFirstKey([in] long hk, [in] BSTR bRegPath,
                                        [out, retval] BSTR* pbRetVal);
HRESULT FindNextKey([out, retval] BSTR* pbRetVal);

HRESULT FindFirstValue([in] long hk, [in] BSTR bRegPath,
                                        [out, retval] BSTR* pbRetVal);
HRESULT FindNextValue([out, retval] BSTR* pbRetVal);
```

I've maintained the same syntax as the Win32 API, so registry paths are identified by root node and path in separate parameters. Note that the `WshShell` methods use a fully qualified path, which is parsed to get the root node. This technique makes it easier to use acronyms like `HKLM`.

The `IWshFun` interface requires you to pass an `HKEY` value (namely a `long`) and the remaining path as a string. Each pair of functions works together; the `FindNextXxx()` function continues on where `FindFirstXxx()` stops. In practice, all that changes is the index of the enumeration, which is set to 0 during the call to `FindFirstXxx()`, and increases by one for each call to `FindNextXxx()`. To keep the programming interface simple, the registry arguments are cached so they don't need to be specified each time.

Both enumerations have the same internal structure and are built on the top of two helper functions: `GetNthKey()` and `GetNthValue()`.

Enumerating Keys

The `GetNthKey()` function opens the specified key and extracts the nth child key, if any. This name is returned through the `pbRetVal` output argument. `SHEnumKeyEx()` (which is implemented in `shlwapi.lib`) is used simply because it uses fewer arguments than `RegEnumKeyEx()`.

```
DWORD CWshFun::GetNthKey(long hk, BSTR bRegPath, int iIndex, BSTR* pbRetVal)
{
USES_CONVERSION;
    TCHAR szRegPath[MAX_PATH] = {0};
    lstrcpy(szRegPath, OLE2T(bRegPath));

    HKEY hkey;
    RegOpenKeyEx(reinterpret_cast<HKEY>(hk),
                                    szRegPath, 0, KEY_ALL_ACCESS, &hkey);

    TCHAR szKey[MAX_PATH] = {0};
    DWORD dwSize = MAX_PATH;
    DWORD rc = SHEnumKeyEx(hkey, iIndex, szKey, &dwSize);
    if(rc == ERROR_SUCCESS)
        *pbRetVal = T2BSTR(szKey);
    RegCloseKey(hkey);
    return rc;
}
```

The skeleton of the `FindFirstKey()`/`FindNextKey()` enumeration is in a pseudo-loop that spans two functions and maintains state with a few global variables.

```
DWORD g_dwIndex = 0;
BSTR g_bRegPath;
LONG g_hk;


STDMETHODIMP CWshFun::FindFirstKey(long hk, BSTR bRegPath, BSTR* pbRetVal)
{
    g_dwIndex = 0;
    g_bRegPath = bRegPath;
    g_hk = hk;

    DWORD rc = GetNthKey(hk, bRegPath, g_dwIndex, pbRetVal);
    return (rc == ERROR_SUCCESS ? S_OK : S_FALSE);
}

STDMETHODIMP CWshFun::FindNextKey(BSTR* pbRetVal)
{
    g_dwIndex++;
    DWORD rc = GetNthKey(g_hk, g_bRegPath, g_dwIndex, pbRetVal);
    return (rc == ERROR_SUCCESS ? S_OK : S_FALSE);
}
```

`GetNthKey()` is called with an index of 0 during `FindFirstKey()`, and with an incremented value inside `FindNextKey()`. The registry path is saved for further use in `FindNextKey()`.

Enumerating Values

Enumerating values is an almost identical process. The `GetNthValue()` function relies on `SHEnumValue()` to list all the leaves of a specified key:

```
DWORD CWshFun::GetNthValue(long hk, BSTR bRegPath, int iIndex, BSTR* pbRetVal)
{
    USES_CONVERSION;
    TCHAR szRegPath[MAX_PATH] = {0};
    lstrcpy(szRegPath, OLE2T(bRegPath));

    HKEY hkey;
    RegOpenKeyEx(reinterpret_cast<HKEY>(hk),
                                  szRegPath, 0, KEY_ALL_ACCESS, &hkey);

    DWORD dwType = 0;
    TCHAR szKey[MAX_PATH] = {0};
    DWORD dwSize = MAX_PATH;
    DWORD rc = SHEnumValue(hkey, iIndex, szKey, &dwSize, &dwType, NULL, 0);
    if(rc == ERROR_SUCCESS)
        *pbRetVal = T2BSTR(szKey);
    RegCloseKey(hkey);
    return rc;
}
```

Note that SHEnumValue() can return the type of a given value, as well as the current content and its size. Pass NULL instead of &dwType if you aren't interested in this information.

The skeletons of FindFirstValue() and FindNextValue() are similar to the analogous functions for keys:

```
STDMETHODIMP CWshFun::FindFirstValue(long hk, BSTR bRegPath, BSTR* pbRetVal)
{
    g_dwIndex = 0;
    g_bRegPath = bRegPath;
    g_hk = hk;

    DWORD rc = GetNthValue(hk, bRegPath, g_dwIndex, pbRetVal);
    return (rc == ERROR_SUCCESS ? S_OK : S_FALSE);
}

STDMETHODIMP CWshFun::FindNextValue(BSTR* pbRetVal)
{
    g_dwIndex++;
    DWORD rc = GetNthValue(g_hk, g_bRegPath, g_dwIndex, pbRetVal);
    return (rc == ERROR_SUCCESS ? S_OK : S_FALSE);
}
```

Don't forget that to use the SHEnumKeyEx() and SHEnumValue() functions, you will need to link to shlwapi.lib to compile this code successfully.

Using Enumerators

Let's see how to make use of these enumerators in WSH applications. This sample is in VBScript, and demonstrates how to list the keys under

```
HKEY_LOCAL_MACHINE
    \Software
```

And the values of:

```
HKEY_LOCAL_MACHINE
    \Software
        \Microsoft
            \Windows
                \CurrentVersion
```

The script first enumerates the keys, and then incrementally composes a string to be displayed. Each string is separated by a couple of carriage return and linefeed characters (ASCII 13 + ASCII 10), which cause each key to appear on a different row. The same logic is then applied to the values of a given path.

```
' Some constants for Root Nodes
Const HKCR = &H80000000  ' HKEY_CLASSES_ROOT
Const HKCU = &H80000001  ' HKEY_CURRENT_USER
Const HKLM = &H80000002  ' HKEY_LOCAL_MACHINE
Const HKU  = &H80000003  ' HKEY_USERS
Const HKPD = &H80000004  ' HKEY_PERFORMANCE_DATA

Dim o, s, b
Dim sValues, sKeys
Set o = CreateObject("WshMore.WshFun.1")

' Enumerates keys
s = o.FindFirstKey(HKLM, "Software")
if Len(s) > 0 then
    b = True
    while b
        sKeys = sKeys + s + vbCrLf
        s = o.FindNextKey
        if Len(s) = 0 then
            b = False
        end if
    wend
end if
MsgBox sKeys

' Enumerates values
s = o.FindFirstValue(HKLM, "Software\Microsoft\Windows\CurrentVersion")
if Len(s) > 0 then
    b = True
    while b
        sValues = sValues + s + vbCrLf
        s = o.FindNextValue
        if Len(s) = 0 then
            b = False
        end if
    wend
end if
MsgBox sValues
```

To simplify things, I've defined some constants that map to the actual values of the registry root nodes. As you know, HKEY values are nothing more than longs, and the constants used here reproduce the exact values of some of them. These values have been taken from winreg.h, a file that you will find in the include directory of any Win32 compiler.

The following picture shows the two messages produced by the above code. The first window refers to keys, the second to values. Of course, the output depends upon the actual content of the registry, and upon the operating system. This screenshot was taken under Windows 95.

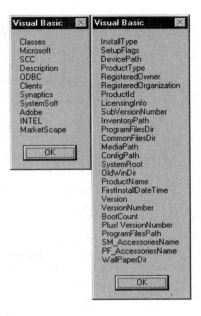

Hooking a Program's Execution

The final method that we'll add to the `IWshFun` interface provides a direct and programmatic way to add a keyboard shortcut to the `IShellExecuteHook` handler that I built in Chapter 8. By defining and properly installing a COM module that implements the `IShellExecuteHook` interface, you have the ability to hook on each command line that passes through the `ShellExecute()` and `ShellExecuteEx()` API functions. In particular, this means that you can gain control over each program launched via the system's Run dialog, or the `WshShell.Run()` method of the Windows Scripting Host.

In Chapter 8, I exploited this feature to add 'keyboard shortcuts' – to run `notepad.exe`, for example, you could type in *n* instead of the full path. Then, to launch Notepad, you simply call:

```
Set s = WScript.CreateObject("WScript.Shell")
s.Run "n"
```

It is the `IShellExecuteHook` handler that retrieves the list of mappings and resolves the specific command. My handler looks for the command in a file called `showhook.ini` located in the `c:` root directory. This file is a typical `.ini` file, with content like this:

```
[goldlist]
n=c:\windows\notepad.exe
```

The `IWshFun` method, `AddExecuteHook()`, just adds an entry to, or removes an entry from, this file:

```
HRESULT AddExecuteHook([in] BSTR bShortcut, [in] BSTR bExeFile)
```

Its source code is straightforward; it just calls `WritePrivateProfileString()`:

```
const LPTSTR EXECUTEHOOK = __TEXT("c:\\showhook.ini");
STDMETHODIMP CWshFun::AddExecuteHook(BSTR bShortcut, BSTR bExeFile)
{
    USES_CONVERSION;
    TCHAR szEntry[MAX_PATH] = {0};
    lstrcpy(szEntry, OLE2T(bShortcut));
    TCHAR szFile[MAX_PATH] = {0};
    lstrcpy(szFile, OLE2T(bExeFile));

    WritePrivateProfileString(__TEXT("goldlist"), szEntry,
                              (lstrlen(szFile) ? szFile : NULL), EXECUTEHOOK);
    return S_OK;
}
```

By specifying an empty string as the name of the file (the `bExeFile` argument), you cause the entry identified by `bShortcut` to be completely removed. Here's how to use the method:

```
Dim o
Set o = CreateObject("WshMore.WshFun.1")
o.AddExecuteHook "r", "regedit.exe"
```

The lines above add a new entry that launches the Registry Editor if you ask to run a program called `r`:

```
r=regedit.exe
```

The above example concludes our trip around the Windows Scripting Host environment.

Hints for Improving the WSH

The WSH is a system module that provides considerable assistance to both programmers and system administrators, but it is by no means perfect. In particular, there are a couple of areas where it is noticeably lacking. They are:

- ❑ User interface
- ❑ Code reusability

To build really useful and powerful scripts, you need a way to set up complex and articulate dialogs, and to have some kind of reusability mechanism. In this final section of the chapter, I'll discuss some ways to accomplish this. However, I'm not going to provide explicit solutions here, simply because such solutions (and the technologies involved) are a bit beyond the scope of this book (though I will, of course, provide exhaustive references).

Adding User Interface Support

Any serious development environment allows you to create and design dialogs. Without dialogs, it's difficult to get input from users and to make your applications more friendly and usable. WSH scripts are an improvement upon dear old MS-DOS batch files, but we also definitely need a replacement for old-fashioned, keyboard-based menus.

Creating dialogs

There are no facilities built into the WSH for creating a generic dialog, so you have to rely on features of the scripting language, or external objects. VBScript provides a function called InputBox() that lets you accept a string interactively. It's used like this:

```
strResult = InputBox(strMessage, strTitle, strDefault)
```

This function allows you to define the message that you wish to appear, the dialog's title in the caption bar, and the default value.

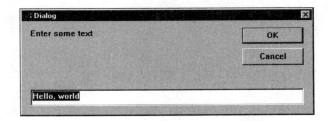

The above figure, for example, is produced by the following call:

```
InputBox "Enter some text", "Dialog", "Hello, world"
```

Unfortunately, this function is seldom enough. What's needed is an object that works as a generic dialog provider, and lets you specify a template for the interface. Furthermore, it should be so clever that it allows you to embed code to coordinate the various interface components, and to drive them. In other words, this object should be capable of interpreting the following pseudo-code:

```
dlg = CreateObject("Dialog.Provider");
dlg.SetDlgItemText("object1", text1);
dlg.SetDlgItemInt("object2", num1);
dlg.Show();
MessageBox(dlg.GetDlgItemText("object1"));
dlg.Close();
```

In addition, the dialog template must be easy to draw. A potential answer to this demand is Dynamic HTML, by using which you:

- ❑ Can use an attractive, HTML-based user interface
- ❑ Don't force people to learn a new scripting language to describe dialogs
- ❑ Can mix interface components and code
- ❑ Can design the dialog template with maximum ease and power
- ❑ Have a straightforward way to identify objects on the template
- ❑ Can update the content at any time

An example of such a component is given in my Cutting Edge article in the December 1998 issue of MIND.

To reinforce the idea, consider that the Internet Explorer 4.*x* Dynamic HTML object model presents a method called `showModalDialog()` that takes the name of an HTML page and displays it in a modal dialog. The About window of Internet Explorer 4.0 is built with the same logic. This dialog is based on the `ShowHTMLDialog()` function exported by `mshtml.dll` – the core of Dynamic HTML.

The alert() Dialog Box

Beware of a possible pitfall when using JScript with WSH applications. A common misconception is that JScript has a few functions for displaying standard dialogs, namely `alert()`, `prompt()`, and `confirm()`. Unfortunately, this is incorrect, since all these are actually methods of the Internet Explorer 4.0 `window` object. They aren't implemented in the JScript runtime engine, and consequently aren't available in the WSH. If you need to display some information, then use the `WScript.Echo()` or `WshShell.Popup()` methods.

Even though `alert()` is always associated with JSscript, it is just a window method that is every bit as accessible from VBScript:

```
<html>
<script language="VBScript" for="window" event="onload">
window.alert "Hello, world!"
</script>
</html>
```

Drag-and-Drop on WSH Files

A WSH file, be it a `.vbs` or a `.js` document, is often an application that takes its own set of parameters. Wouldn't it be nice if we could drop data onto the files and set the parameters that way? To enable drag-and-drop over files throughout the shell, a shell extension is required. I'll look at this in Chapter 15.

Reusability within the WSH

Another evident weakness of the WSH is its limited support for reusability. What is needed is the ability to write script code that is reusable and 'componentized'. The solution is a mix of COM and script, and goes under the name of **XML Scriptlets**.

An XML Scriptlet is a text file that follows the XML syntax. It describes a COM object, and embeds pieces of script code (VBScript or JScript). This code is interpreted and presented to the outside world as if it was binary COM code. In other words, the XML Scriptlet (which is made up of `<script>` tags) appears to be a regular Automation object to any COM-aware client, including the WSH! Thus, you can write Automation servers in pure VBScript or JScript, and solve the reusable script code problem.

Scriptlets and XML Scriptlets are covered in detail in my book Instant DHTML Scriptlets, *also published by Wrox Press, ISBN 1-861001-38X.*

Summary

The WSH is a desktop-level scripting engine that you can use to automate repetitive actions, following the logic of DOS batch files. By combining the power of today's scripting languages with the use of COM components, the WSH is ideally suited to making your applications richer and more user-friendly.

I haven't provided a full and detailed explanation of *all* the properties and methods of *all* the Windows Scripting Host objects – the Internet Client SDK already does a good job of that. Instead, I've tried to focus on the technology and the way in which you can use it.

At present, I see two main fields of application for the WSH: as an administration tool on Windows NT platforms, and as a user-development platform for both Windows 9*x* and Windows NT. This means that system administrators and end users could both take advantage of the built-in scriptable objects that the system provides, as well as those of third-party vendors. If you're selling a suite of related and integrated programs, you should think of providing objects to let your users automate tasks like putting together features that come from different programs.

In this chapter, I've covered:

- ❑ What the Windows Scripting Host is
- ❑ How to get it, and how it works
- ❑ The WSH object model
- ❑ How to access generic COM components
- ❑ How to write COM components to extend the WSH object model
- ❑ Hints on how to improve the WSH

Further Reading

Related articles and documentation about the Windows Scripting Host can be found in the MSDN library and in an article of mine called *Windows Scripting Host* that appeared in the June 1998 issue of MIND. In the printed version of the July/August 1998 issue of MSDN News, there is a centerfold with a diagram of the complete WSH object model.

There are a number of useful sources of information about script languages other than VBScript and JScript. For Perl, there's an article by Jeff Zado entitled *Active Scripting with Perl* in MIND, August 1997. Other references are available at http://www.mks.com. If you're interested in REXX support, look at http://service.software.ibm.com/dl/rexx/orexx-d, while late-breaking news about the ActiveX engine for Python is at http://www.python.org/windows. Because the WSH requires a good knowledge of scripting languages, you will find *Instant VBScript* by Alex Homer and Darren Gill, and *Instant Javascript* by Nigel McFarlane to be of use.

For XML Scriptlets, you can refer to an article entitled *Server Scriptlets* in MIND, May 1998. More recently I wrote an article for MSDN News called *Writing COM Objects with Scripting Languages*. It appeared in the November/December 1998 issue.

For information on hosting an ActiveX scripting module in your applications, read Don Box's *Say Goodbye to Macro Envy with the ActiveX Scripting Engine* in MIND, February 1997. It provides you with all the details and explanations you need. Steve Zimmerman covered the same topic from a different angle in the August 1997 issue of MIND, and I also recommend that you take a look at the SPRUUIDS sample available with the Internet Client SDK.

This chapter also included some ATL code, and to learn more about that I recommend *Beginning ATL COM Programming* (Wrox Press, ISBN 1-861000-11-1). A good overview of COM development with ATL, by Don Box, appeared in MSJ, May 97. Both show the joy that can be yours when you write your COM servers using ATL.

Finally, ATL necessarily points to IDL. If you are having problems with the various attributes of that language, then you may want to read *Understanding Interface Definition Language: A Developer's Survival Guide* by Bill Hludzinski, published in MSJ, July 1998.

14

Designing a Shell-Integrated Application

There are a number of facilities an application can provide to make it more integrated with the shell and the underlying system. In this way, the users can treat your documents and programs as they would the rest of the system. For instance, right clicking on a file to display a list of available functions is common nowadays. Windows provides each file with a default collection of functionality, such as Open With..., Properties, Copy and the like. Why not add more *specific* functions that are peculiar to *specific* documents? In order to do this, you have to customize the context menu of the document class.

Another example of an application that is well integrated with the shell might be the following: suppose that your program has the ability to create empty documents. Your users would appreciate an item in the system New menu to let them create a new document on the fly, in any folder. To do this, you have to enter some information in the system registry.

Of course, these are particular cases, and there are many other usability features that you, as a developer or an application designer, should take into account. In this chapter, we'll cover all those aspects of application design and development that help to integrate your software with the system's shell seamlessly, making your product that bit more professional. This includes:

- ❑ How to customize the context menu
- ❑ How to register a new file type
- ❑ How to design and programmatically handle a command line
- ❑ How to program customized Open dialogs

We'll design a document-based, fully-featured application that you might just find useful. The application will display and print all the kinds of metafiles that Windows supports, from the traditional (*.wmf), through placeable metafiles, right up to enhanced metafiles (*.emf). We'll apply all the theory we've previously discussed, and end up with full shell support for metafiles.

Shell-Integrated Applications

The first thing to be clear about is exactly what constitutes a shell-integrated application. When I use the phrase, I'm talking about a Win32, document-oriented program that provides at least a certain number of features that relate to the system's shell.

> *There's an excellent overview of this topic in an old MSJ article by Jeff Richter (see* Further Reading *for details).*

So much for the simple answer – let's now discuss the three groups of features that define a shell-integrated application. To me, shell support means:

- ❑ A registered icon and type name for any document the program handles
- ❑ A custom context menu for documents that the program handles
- ❑ Possibly one or more custom entries in the system's New menu
- ❑ A single-instance program
- ❑ A new entry in the Recent document folder for each opened document
- ❑ Full support for long file names, especially when it comes to user's documents

To these basic features, we could add the following ones, which are used less frequently:

- ❑ One or more custom entries on the system's Send To menu
- ❑ One or more custom entries on the Start and/or Programs menu
- ❑ One or more custom entries in the Favorites folder
- ❑ One or more new shortcuts on the desktop
- ❑ An application desktop toolbar to collect all the main functionality of the program
- ❑ Customized versions of some of the system's common dialogs
- ❑ Registering the application to start automatically when the user next logs on

A third group of features is today mostly restricted to the work of specialized installers, like InstallShield and WISE. They are:

- ❑ Copying shared files to a system-wide common path
- ❑ Installing the application under the Program Files folder
- ❑ Providing an uninstall program
- ❑ Exploiting the shell's **application path names** to define the paths where files can be found

This set of requirements comes from the guidelines for Windows logo compliance. However, at a higher level of abstraction they are rooted in what is, for the Windows world, a new idea: in order to open and use a document, the user should not need to know what program actually loads and displays it. Instead, they simply have to locate and double-click on the descriptive icon and name that have been allocated to that document. (In fact, depending on your Active Desktop settings, a single click might suffice to open a document from the shell!)

Documents and the Shell

With the release of Windows 95, documents gained a more central role in the system's shell. The document has become the actor, while the program that actually handles it is reduced to a mere executor. Even their location on the hard drive suggests a lowering of their status: programs get grouped under the `Program Files` folder, each one in its own sub-folder, with a sub-tree of directories in which DLLs and other helper files are stored. Many of these folders are hidden — further confirmation that programs have a secondary role with respect to documents.

Looking at the screenshot above, you can see that documents have their own specific icons and descriptions. Better than that, each document has a dedicated context menu from which you can execute a number of shell functions. Some of these could apply to any kind of document and therefore appear in all context menus, but others are particular to a single document type.

Basic Document Functions

The Windows shell provides a number of menu verbs for free, which are:

- ❑ Copy, Cut, Paste
- ❑ Delete
- ❑ Rename
- ❑ Create Shortcut
- ❑ Properties

In addition, there are always at least a couple of other menu commands. Either Open or Open With… will be there, but the two are mutually exclusive – the latter appears only if you have no program registered to open the document, and brings up the following dialog if selected:

The action of the Open command, on the other hand, depends upon what you store in the registry, as we'll discuss shortly.

The 'Send To' Command

The other command you'll always see in one form or another is Send To, which displays a sub-menu with a list of possible destinations for the selected document. A 'destination' is a program that will receive the given filename on the command line. The picture below, for example, shows how the Send To menu lets you set a file to be the attachment in a new e-mail message.

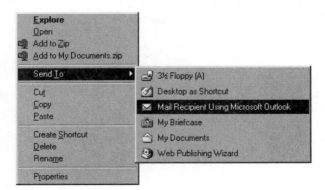

Through the commands I've listed in this section, the shell guarantees a minimum level of support for any kind of document you may have on your PC. It's up to you, as seasoned user or software engineer, to extend this basic behavior with more document-specific and appropriate features.

Registered Document Types

Everything that relates to the configuration of the shell is stored somewhere in the system registry, so any path you take to modify the shell's appearance or behavior must pass through it.

In order for the shell to recognize and properly handle a certain kind of document, it must be of a **registered type**. A type of document is identified by its file name extension, and all the registered document types are stored under the `HKEY_CLASSES_ROOT` registry node:

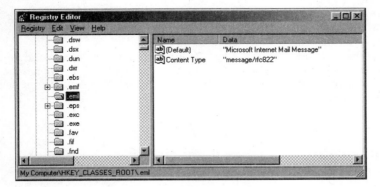

An entry for the file extension (`.ext`) points to another key under the same node whose name is stored in the `Default` value of `.ext`. In the above figure, for EML files (Microsoft Internet Mail Message, the Outlook Express e-mail file format), we have the value:

```
Microsoft Internet Mail Message
```

If you want to get at all the registered information for this type of document, you must start digging at:

```
HKEY_CLASSES_ROOT
    \Microsoft Internet Mail Message
```

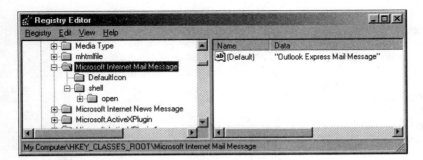

Under this key, you can store information that applies to three areas:

- ❑   The user interface
- ❑   The context menu
- ❑   Shell extensions

Shell User Interface for Documents

By the title of this section, I mean the collection of graphical attributes we might want to set for a document – these are typically the icon and the type name. The `DefaultIcon` key lets you assign an icon to identify all the files with this extension throughout the shell. The `Default` value of this key contains a string that looks something like this:

```
C:\PROGRAMS\THEPROG.EXE,0
```

> *Note once again that this information is not stored in the* `.ext` *key, but in the one that* `.ext` *points to.*

The string that identifies the default icon is made up of a full path name, a comma and an index number. The icon to be shown is the one with the given index in the given file – remember that an icon index always starts at zero. Furthermore, if the index is a negative number, then it denotes the resource ID instead, so for EML files the `DefaultIcon` string is:

```
C:\PROGRAM FILES\OUTLOOK EXPRESS\MSIMN.EXE,-4
```

And as we saw above, the `Default` value of the main key (`Microsoft Internet Mail Message` in the sample above) contains the string to be used as the type name of the document.

To modify these settings, you don't have to be an expert Windows programmer. Any seasoned Windows user could change the description of EML files, or the icon that represents them. However, inserting keys to register documents *programmatically* is completely different from manually modifying the registry. We need to focus on what your *software* should do to integrate its documents with the shell automatically.

Document-Specific Commands on the Context Menu

The key called `shell` can contain a number of sub-keys, each of which relates to a specific command that will appear on the document's context menu. The keys under `shell` are called **verbs** (in this case, the verb is `open`), and the `Default` values of the keys contain the string that will be shown on the context menu. If this value is not set, the name of the key itself is used.

So: we have a verb called `open`, but it's quite possible for the menu command to have a different name. Since we're discussing e-mail messages, how about having Read instead of Open on the menu? If you change the contents of the `Default` value and then bring up the context menu, you'll see the result:

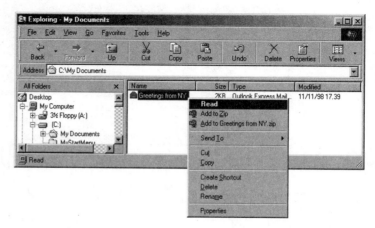

The context menu shows Read, but the actual behavior doesn't change at all, because that's established in the `Default` value of the `command` sub-key. Every verb must have a `command` sub-key that contains the executable's path and command line, plus any other necessary settings. It's very important to specify a valid command line with the proper switches, and a `%1` to denote the name of the file to work on:

```
C:\PROGRAM FILES\OUTLOOK EXPRESS\MSIMN.EXE" /eml:%1
```

The line above shows the command line for EML files on my machine – whether you see the same will depend upon whether you have installed Outlook Express.

Shell Extensions for Documents

By modifying the registry, you can add **static verbs** to the document's context menu. Any static verbs you define will always be displayed, and will always execute the same command line.

A more flexible and dynamic behavior can be obtained by using **shell extensions**, which we'll cover in the next chapter. For now, let's just say that a shell extension is a piece of code that runs in Explorer's address space and gets called each time Explorer needs to do some 'customizable' actions, such as painting an icon, or displaying a context menu. Your piece of code is given a chance to decide dynamically what menu items to add, and what to do in response to user clicks.

All the shell extensions for a given document class are listed under the `shellex` key, which is placed at the same level as the `shell` key.

How Programs are Affected

We've now touched upon a number of features that affect documents, and at the beginning of this chapter I stated explicitly that documents are the kings of the Windows shell. However, we can't get away from the fact that in the end, documents are still displayed through programs – the question is, how and to what degree are programs affected by our efforts at shell integration?

Well, there are two major points. First, users may click repeatedly to open different documents, or even multiple copies of the same document. When this happens, the program is called repeatedly, and so to avoid a proliferation of windows you may want to allow only a single running instance. Second, programs' command lines gain importance, because static verbs are usually implemented through switches on the command line. You should endeavor to expose the most important functions in a very modular way.

In Chapter 11, we covered the `RunDLL32` module, which represents a good way of calling DLL functions with a fixed prototype through a command line. In both these cases, the program's functions must be clearly isolated and easily callable from external modules.

When someone clicks on a document in the Windows shell, the program is called. Each time the program starts, it checks for other running copies of itself. If any are found, then one is passed the control and the command line, while the current instance quits. I'll say more about this later in the chapter, when I come to discuss the sample application.

MDI versus SDI

MDI and **SDI** are the two typical designs for file-based Windows applications. MDI stands for **Multiple Document Interface**, and denotes a program that can open several documents at the same time, displaying each in a separate window. SDI, on the other hand, is an acronym for **Single Document Interface** – an SDI program opens only one document at a time. Traditionally, major Windows applications have been MDI – the Office suite is a prime example of this. Applets such as Notepad and Paint, on the other hand, are SDI.

From the shell's point of view, the choice of MDI or SDI really isn't an issue. When you dig a little deeper, however, you begin to realize that to examine the difference between MDI and SDI is to open a window onto a much broader comparison: an application-centric versus a document-centric environment.

The MDI schema is governed by the application, which opens and manages the various 'child' documents. Conversely, the SDI interface is more document-centric: you see a single document surrounded by the tools that are available to utilize and modify it.

Since the launch of Windows 95, Microsoft has been recommending the development of SDI applications wherever possible, but it seems that most people – myself included – have paid little attention to that advice.

> *From the information available at the time of writing, it seems that the next version of the Office suite – Office 2000 – will employ an SDI interface. If confirmed by the final release, I think this development will herald a real change in Windows applications design.*

Creating New Documents

Whenever you right click on an Explorer window that's displaying the contents of a folder, you're presented with a menu like the one in the figure:

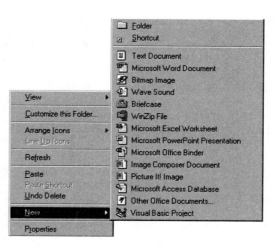

The **New** command lists all the document types that can be created via the shell. When you select one of the listed types of document, the shell calls the registered application and asks it to create a new document with a name that's formed from the type name of the document (as it appears in the menu), prefixed by the word New. For example, if you choose to create a new bitmap image, the file name will default to New Bitmap Image.bmp.

The New Menu

Each item that appears in the <u>N</u>ew menu (except for <u>F</u>older and <u>S</u>hortcut) has a related file class for which a `ShellNew` key exists, under the following registry path:

```
HKEY_CLASSES_ROOT
   \.ext
      \ShellNew
```

The contents of the `ShellNew` key determine what appears on the <u>N</u>ew menu, and what happens when someone clicks on it. When you think about it, there are actually four ways of creating a new document through the shell. You can create:

- ❑ Empty, zero-length documents
- ❑ Documents that are copies of a default document
- ❑ Documents whose contents come from binary data stored in the registry
- ❑ Documents created by special external programs, such as Wizards

Naturally enough, these options require different registry settings:

Value	Content
NullFile	The empty string.
FileName	The name of the file to be used as the template. Such files are assumed to reside in the `Windows\ShellNew` directory.
Data	A chunk of binary data, read from the registry.
Command	The command line needed to create the document.

The following screenshot shows the setup on my machine for BMP files:

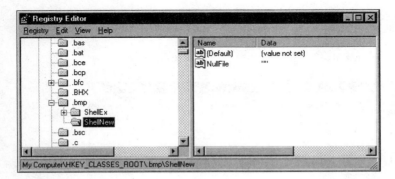

Normally, you'll want to use `NullFile` if your application can handle empty and zero-length files. `FileName` is the approach chosen by Word and Excel, and is useful if you have complex, compound files for which even empty files need a certain, minimal structure. In this case, you prepare a standard file (whether empty or not), save it to the `ShellNew` subdirectory of the `Windows` directory, and assign its name and extension to the `FileName` value. Each time someone attempts to create a new file of that type, a copy of the template is created. See Further Reading to get references about Office 97 file format specifications.

`Data` is a value that may contain binary data to be flushed to the newly created file, making this case little different from the one we've just been discussing. With `FileName`, the template is a separate file; with `Data`, it is a chunk of data stored in the registry.

We met the `Command` value in Chapter 11 while discussing replacing the standard handler for creating shortcuts. If this value is present, then the shell is limited to running the specified command line, and assuming that it will be able to create a new document of the required type. This option has been specifically created for Wizards and step-by-step document creation.

We'll now look at an example in which we add a command to the shell's <u>N</u>ew menu that will create a brand new HTML file with minimal content.

Creating New HTML Files

I'm assuming that you have a program on your PC that is registered to handle HTML files. When you need to create a new HTML document from scratch, you usually either:

❑ Run a visual HTML editor (Microsoft FrontPage, for example)
❑ Run Notepad or some other plain text editor

Like most of the rest of the Windows world, when I need to write an HTML page, I resort to Notepad. However, an HTML file is not just another ASCII file. It needs tags to delineate it as a valid document that a browser can successfully handle. A minimal HTML file may look like this:

```
<html>
<body>
</body>
</html>
```

Save this code to a file called, say, `html4.htm` and place it in your `Windows\ShellNew` (or `Winnt\ShellNew`) directory. Then, open the Registry Editor and add a `ShellNew` key to:

```
HKEY_CLASSES_ROOT
    \.htm
```

This newly created key must also be given a `FileName` string value:

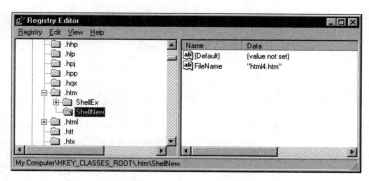

Once you have saved these settings, you should be able to right-click on the desktop and produce something like this:

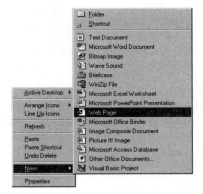

The picture shows what happened on my PC after I changed the description of the `htmlfile` registry key from the original string to **Web Page**. Any new file created from this menu item will be called `New Web Page.htm`.

Note that you can add an item to the <u>N</u>ew menu only if that file type is correctly registered.

Other Features

There are a couple of other features to take into account when it comes to design and coding a good shell-integrated application. They are:

❑ Storing a list of the directories where helper modules like DLLs can be found
❑ Arranging for an automatic re-run upon next logon

The first feature might seem to be more relevant to setup programs, but not all installers do exactly what you need, and in those cases you must write your own extensions and delve deep into registry paths.

The second feature is typical of Explorer and a few other applications. If the application is still running when you shut down the system, the shell will automatically restart it the next time that you log on. Let's see how to code this behavior.

Application Paths

Almost all Windows applications are composed of more than one file. Typically, there's an EXE file and one or more DLLs (not to mention all the system DLLs, such as `kernel32.dll` and `user32.dll`).

The helper DLLs must be copied somewhere by the installer. They can go in the program folder or elsewhere, but Microsoft strongly discourages you from copying DLLs to one of the main system folders, like `Windows` or `Windows\System`. If you do decide not to put them in the same directory as the EXE, the chances are that sooner or later you'll get an error message informing you that the system is unable to locate a given DLL.

Why then would you decide not to put the DLLs in the same folder as the EXE? Well, your application could be part of a suite in which many programs share the same helper DLLs. It's wasteful to give each component its own copy of the files, so instead you could create a common folder and place everything that's shareable in there. The problem now is making the shell aware of it – when you launch an application that needs a certain library, you must make sure that the path to the library is globally visible.

MS-DOS based programs (and Windows programs too) used to rely on the PATH environment variable. A similar, but shell-oriented replacement for this is the so-called **application path**. To use one, you should add the following registry key after installing your application (let's call it program.exe):

```
HKEY_LOCAL_MACHINE
   \SOFTWARE
      \Microsoft
         \Windows
            \CurrentVersion
               \App Paths
                  \Program.exe
```

The Default value of the key contains the full path name of the executable. If present, the Path value lists all the paths where any other files can be found:

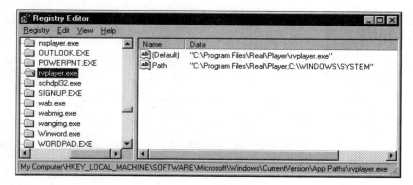

Automatic Startup of Applications

When a particular user logs on, Windows will attempt to read the following key:

```
HKEY_CURRENT_USER
   \Software
      \Microsoft
         \Windows
            \CurrentVersion
               \RunOnce
```

If the key exists, any programs whose names are stored in its values will be executed. After examination, all entries are deleted, so they are executed once and only once. We therefore have the ability to code applications that are capable of executing the next time a particular user logs on.

Note that this is only at the next *logon, not at each subsequent logon. Applications that are run every time a particular user logs on have entries under the* Run *key in the above location.*

Automatic execution is not totally a feature of the system; programs must cooperate in order for it to occur. In particular, a program must add itself (and/or any other application) to the RunOnce key, and the right moment to do this is in response to the WM_ENDSESSION message. Of course, it's *possible* to do this at any time, but since our goal is getting persistence across sessions, we should create the entry only if we're still running when the user shuts down the current session or logs off. This is when the WM_ENDSESSION message arrives.

The information about the application to be run should be entered in the registry in the following format:

```
ID = program name
```

You need to create a value whose content is the path name of the executable. The ID must be unique, but apart from that the name you give it is not too important. The next figure shows an example:

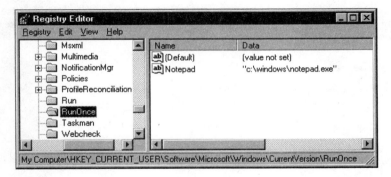

The entries are taken sequentially, in the same order that they were entered – that order doesn't necessarily coincide with the output of the Registry Editor, where the entries always appear in alphabetical order. The programs are spawned asynchronously, one after another. If you have a registry entry like the one shown above, you'll find that Notepad opens up on your desktop when you log on.

Another RunOnce Key

There's another, rather more powerful RunOnce key located under the following path:

```
HKEY_LOCAL_MACHINE
    \SOFTWARE
        \Microsoft
            \Windows
                \CurrentVersion
                    \RunOnce
```

The syntax for using this key is exactly the same as before, but there are three big differences in the way it works. They are:

❑ The contents of this key are considered when *any* user logs on.

❑ The various registered programs execute synchronously – the next entry runs only when the previous one has finished.

❑ The programs registered under this key execute *before* the programs registered under the same sub-key of the HKEY_CURRENT_USER node.

See Further Reading *for a reference to a document that details the Windows startup process.*

If you have a program registered under HKEY_LOCAL_MACHINE\...\RunOnce, then at the next logon or reboot, Notepad will appear on the desktop *before* the taskbar and the desktop icons. More importantly, you won't see them until you terminate the process by closing the window.

The Run Key

The Run key, which I mentioned briefly in the above discussion, also exists both under HKEY_LOCAL_MACHINE and HKEY_CURRENT_USER. Run and RunOnce follow identical logic, except that the latter deletes each line it reads from the registry. Items under the Run key are executed every time someone logs on.

The RunServices Keys

Under Windows 95 and Windows 98, there are two keys that allow you to simulate NT services – that is, modules that run *before* the user logs on. These keys are:

```
HKEY_LOCAL_MACHINE
    \SOFTWARE
        \Microsoft
            \Windows
                \CurrentVersion
                    \RunServices
                    \RunServicesOnce
```

Once again, their syntax is the same as the other keys we've been examining in this section. RunServices runs applications before *every* logon, while RunServicesOnce does the same thing for only the *next* logon. The programs are executed asynchronously, and might terminate after the user actually logs on. In any case, all the services must be executed before the system starts considering the RunOnce and Run keys.

The following table shows the exact order in which Windows considers the registry keys during the startup process:

Step	Key
1	HKLM\...\RunServicesOnce (unsupported under NT)
2	HKLM\...\RunServices (unsupported under NT)
3	User Logon. The user may log on before all the services start.

Step	Key
4	All the services started and the user logged on.
5	`HKLM\...\RunOnce`
6	All the registered programs completed.
7	`HKLM\...\Run`
8	`HKCU\...\Run`
9	Programs contained in the `Startup` folder for the current user.
10	`HKCU\...\RunOnce`

The Winlogon Key

If you simply need to display a message before any user logs on, you can exploit the entries of the following key:

```
HKEY_LOCAL_MACHINE
    \SOFTWARE
        \Microsoft
            \Windows
                \CurrentVersion
                    \Winlogon
```

The `LegalNoticeCaption` and `LegalNoticeText` values let you define the title and the text of a system message box that will appear before any user logs on.

Services in Windows 9x

Under Windows NT, you can write **services** to accomplish certain tasks that require special system privileges. An NT service is a Win32 application with a particular structure and behavior. Aside from the specific implementation details, the main features of a service can be summarized as follows:

- A service runs before any user logs on
- A service continues running even after a user logs off
- A service has no user interface and is not interactive
- A service gets special treatment from the operating system – for example, it can be started automatically and run under any user account, including the System account
- A service runs in a separate, virtual desktop, which is different from the desktop used by the applications
- A service can be stopped or paused

Windows NT has a special component called Service Control Manager (SCM) to manage the running services. Because this interface is very powerful, there's no need under Windows NT for registry keys like `RunServices` or `RunServicesOnce`. See *Further Reading* for more information about writing NT services.

The interesting thing from our point of view is that by exploiting the RunServices key you can simulate NT services, obtaining roughly the same behavior. A Windows 9*x* service is in every way a normal Win32 application (no matter whether it's a GUI or a console application) that's simply registered in the RunServices key to run before each logon.

By calling the RegisterServiceProcess() API function, you can register the current process (or any other running process) as a service, causing it to continue working even after the user has logged off. This function is not exposed through any import library, though, so you need to load it dynamically via GetProcAddress(), which is contained in kernel32.dll.

The following table lists the differences between Windows NT and Windows 9*x* services. A complete example of a Windows 95 service is referenced in *Further Reading*.

Windows NT Service	Windows 9*x* Service
Win32 application that exposes a ServiceMain() function	Traditional Win32 application
Runs before logon	If registered under RunServices, runs before logon
Continues running after logoff	If registered as a service with RegisterServiceProcess(), continues running after logoff
A GUI or console application with no user interface	A GUI or console application with no user interface
Can run under the System account	Unsupported
Runs in a separate desktop	Unsupported
Can be stopped or paused.	Can be stopped only by calling TerminateProcess()

That a service must have no user interface is not a system requirement, but simply a reasonable and strong recommendation.

Designing a Shell-Integrated Application

So far, we've examined the major points that make a real-world application integrate successfully with the shell. Now it's time to look at a concrete example, where we'll be translating all the principles and rules into practice.

The first requirement for a shell-oriented application is that it be a file-based program. This means that the application must, broadly speaking, work as a wrapper built around a certain kind of document. Its menus should faithfully render the actions you might want to make with the documents it handles. So, to design a shell-integrated application, it's important that you are clear which functions are to be exported through the shell.

Secondly, these functions must be coded in as modular a fashion as possible, and must be accessible through the command line, through a `RunDLL32` interface or by means of a shell extension. Let's see how this advice applies in a case study.

A Metafile Viewer

The application we will develop is a metafile viewer. I've chosen this example for two reasons:

- ❑ It is a significant, file-based application
- ❑ There's no system utility in Windows to view WMF and EMF files

To expand upon the second point, the only current way to view metafiles is to turn on the View | as Web Page option for the folder, and relying on the embedded thumbnail control. (Of course, it's not that hard to find a shareware utility out there, but it remains to be proven that such utilities offer an adequate level of shell support.)

My example is a simple, dialog-based application that allows you to choose, display, print and convert any valid Windows metafile. The screenshot below shows the initial appearance of the sample program, a Wrox AppWizard generated dialog-based application called `WMFView`:

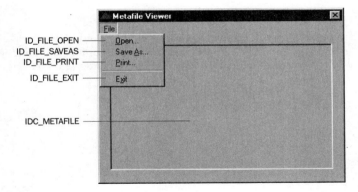

We'll first examine how to make the application operational in terms of actually being able to display metafiles, and then we'll see how to enhance its code to help with context menu customization.

Windows Metafiles and Enhanced Metafiles

A metafile is a collection of graphic instructions, called **records**, which execute one after another in order to produce a picture. Until the advent of Win32, there were two types of metafiles:

- ❑ Windows metafiles
- ❑ Placeable metafiles

The Office 97 clip art files, for instance, are all placeable metafiles, and both these types are given the usual `.wmf` extension.

> *Detailed coverage of metafiles is beyond the scope of this book, so you should resort to the MSDN Library for advanced and exhaustive articles. See also the* Further Reading *section.*

The file format of Windows metafiles changed with the advent of the Win32 platform. Win32 promotes the newer .emf format (enhanced metafiles), but continues to provide support (albeit of a rather poor kind) for the old WMF files.

This drawback aside, the API for enhanced metafiles is noticeably richer than the corresponding one for WMFs. Interestingly, among the Win32 common controls is one (the Picture control) that's capable of displaying an enhanced metafile, starting from its handle. Opening and displaying an EMF is therefore pretty straightforward, but unfortunately, doing the same for an old WMF file is not that easy. Thankfully, I discovered a tool for the purpose on the Microsoft web site at:

```
http://support.microsoft.com/download/support/mslfiles/enmeta.exe
```

I was therefore able to use this example as a reference while building my own metafile viewer.

Displaying a Metafile

The wmfview.exe program will recognize three types of metafile:

❑ Windows
❑ Placeable
❑ Enhanced

The first two are assumed to have a .wmf extension, while the last should have .emf. Whatever the original format of the currently opened file, the program *always* uses enhanced metafiles internally. The following code shows how to open and display a metafile, no matter what its original format.

```cpp
/////////////////////////////////////////////////////////////////////
// Needed to handle 16-bit placeable metafiles
#pragma pack(push)
#pragma pack(2)
typedef struct{
    DWORD       dwKey;
    WORD        hmf;
    SMALL_RECT  bbox;
    WORD        wInch;
    DWORD       dwReserved;
    WORD        wCheckSum;
} APMHEADER, *LPAPMHEADER;
#pragma pack(pop)
/////////////////////////////////////////////////////////////////////

// Gets the handle and displays the specified metafile
void DisplayMetaFile(HWND hwndMeta, LPTSTR szFile)
{
    // Get the metafile handle
    HENHMETAFILE hemf = GetMetaFileHandle(szFile);
    if(hemf == NULL)
    {
        MessageBox(NULL, __TEXT("Unable to handle the file."),
                                    szFile, MB_OK | MB_ICONSTOP);
        return;
    }

    // Free the old file and display the new one
    HENHMETAFILE hemfOld = reinterpret_cast<HENHMETAFILE>(
            SendMessage(hwndMeta, STM_GETIMAGE, IMAGE_ENHMETAFILE, 0));
```

```
      if(hemfOld)
         DeleteEnhMetaFile(hemfOld);

      // hwndMeta is a Picture control
      SendMessage(hwndMeta, STM_SETIMAGE, IMAGE_ENHMETAFILE,
                                   reinterpret_cast<LPARAM>(hemf));
      lstrcpy(g_szCurFile, szFile);
}
```

The `DisplayMetaFile()` function calls a helper named `GetMetaFileHandle()` to obtain a handle to the metafile at the location passed to it, deletes any metafile that is currently in place and then sends a message to the control to have it display the new metafile.

```
// Retrieves an HENHMETAFILE handle for the specified file
HENHMETAFILE GetMetaFileHandle(LPTSTR szFile)
{
    DWORD dwSize = 0;
    LPBYTE pb = NULL;

    // Try to read it as an EMF
    HENHMETAFILE hEMF = GetEnhMetaFile(szFile);
    if(hEMF)
        return hEMF;

    // Try to read it as a WMF
    HMETAFILE hWMF = GetMetaFile(szFile);
    if(hWMF)
    {
        dwSize = GetMetaFileBitsEx(hWMF, 0, NULL);
        if(dwSize == 0)
        {
            DeleteMetaFile(hWMF);
            return NULL;
        }

        // Allocate enough memory
        pb = new BYTE[dwSize];
        if(pb == NULL)
        {
            DeleteMetaFile(hWMF);
            return NULL;
        }

        // Get the metafile bits
        dwSize = GetMetaFileBitsEx(hWMF, dwSize, pb);
        if(dwSize == 0)
        {
            delete [] pb;
            DeleteMetaFile(hWMF);
            return NULL;
        }

        // Convert to EMF
        hEMF = SetWinMetaFileBits(dwSize, pb, NULL, NULL);
```

```
      // Clean up
      DeleteMetaFile(hWMF);
      delete [] pb;
      return hEMF;
   }

   // Try to handle the input as a placeable metafile
   HANDLE hFile = CreateFile(szFile, GENERIC_READ, 0, NULL,
                            OPEN_EXISTING, FILE_ATTRIBUTE_NORMAL, NULL);
   if(hFile == INVALID_HANDLE_VALUE)
      return NULL;

   // Read the file to a buffer
   dwSize = GetFileSize(hFile, NULL);
   pb = new BYTE[dwSize];
   ReadFile(hFile, pb, dwSize, &dwSize, NULL);
   CloseHandle(hFile);

   // Check to see if it is a placeable metafile
   if((reinterpret_cast<LPAPMHEADER>(pb))->dwKey != 0x9ac6cdd71)
   {
      // Don't know how to handle this...
      delete [] pb;
      return NULL;
   }

   // Create an enhanced metafile from the bits
   hEMF = SetWinMetaFileBits(dwSize, &(pb[sizeof(APMHEADER)]), NULL, NULL);

   delete [] pb;
   return hEMF;
}
```

The operation of `GetMetaFileHandle()` is made trickier by the fact that it has to deal with 'ordinary' metafiles as well as enhanced ones, and much of the code you see here is geared towards converting from the former to the latter on the fly. At the end, though, it just returns an enhanced metafile handle to the function that called it.

Printing and Converting a Metafile

The program will also let you print a metafile, or convert from WMF to EMF and vice versa. Printing is simply a matter of getting an appropriate print device context and playing the enhanced metafile to it.

```
void PrintMetaFile(LPTSTR szFile)
{
   // Get an EMF handle
   HENHMETAFILE hEMF = GetMetaFileHandle(szFile);
   if(hEMF == NULL)
      return;

   // Get a printer DC
   PRINTDLG pdlg;
   ZeroMemory(&pdlg, sizeof(PRINTDLG));
   pdlg.lStructSize = sizeof(PRINTDLG);
   pdlg.Flags = PD_RETURNDC;
```

```
    HDC hDC = NULL;
    if(PrintDlg(&pdlg))
        hDC = pdlg.hDC;
    else
        return;

    // Prepare document printing
    DOCINFO di;
    ZeroMemory(&di, sizeof(DOCINFO));
    di.cbSize = sizeof(DOCINFO);
    di.lpszDocName = "Printing EMF";

    // Start printing
    StartDoc(hDC, &di);
    StartPage(hDC);

    // Scale to fit the entire printed page
    RECT rc;
    SetRect(&rc, 0, 0, GetDeviceCaps(hDC, HORZRES), GetDeviceCaps(hDC, VERTRES));
    PlayEnhMetaFile(hDC, hEMF, &rc);

    // Clean up
    EndPage(hDC);
    EndDoc(hDC);
    DeleteDC(hDC);
    DeleteEnhMetaFile(hEMF);
}
```

Converting metafiles isn't any more complicated, as the following listing will demonstrate. The first of the three functions here, `SaveMetaFile()`, arranges for an EMF to be saved to a placeable WMF file (and vice versa) with the same name, but a different extension. In practice, each metafile is first converted to EMF (thanks to the `GetMetaFileHandle()` function), and then saved to disk as EMF or WMF.

```
void SaveMetaFile(LPTSTR szFile)
{
    TCHAR szOutputFile[MAX_PATH] = {0};
    HENHMETAFILE hEMF = GetMetaFileHandle(szFile);
    if(hEMF == NULL)
        return;

    // Determine the output format
    lstrcpy(szOutputFile, szFile);
    strlwr(szFile);
    if(strstr(szFile, ".emf"))
    {
        PathRenameExtension(szOutputFile, ".wmf");
        SaveToWMF(hEMF, szOutputFile);
    }
    else if(strstr(szFile, ".wmf"))
    {
        PathRenameExtension(szOutputFile, ".emf");
        SaveToEMF(hEMF, szOutputFile);
    }

    DeleteEnhMetaFile(hEMF);
}
```

The two helper functions, SaveToEMF() and SaveToWMF(), are very similar to one another and serve simply to save the metafile in one of two available forms:

```
void SaveToEMF(HENHMETAFILE hEMF, LPTSTR szFile)
{
    // Get memory to store the EMF bits
    DWORD dwSize = GetEnhMetaFileBits(hEMF, 0, NULL);
    LPBYTE pb = new BYTE[dwSize];

    // Get the EMF bits
    GetEnhMetaFileBits(hEMF, dwSize, pb);

    // Save to file
    HANDLE hFile = CreateFile(szFile, GENERIC_WRITE,
                        0, NULL, CREATE_NEW, FILE_ATTRIBUTE_NORMAL, NULL);
    if(hFile == INVALID_HANDLE_VALUE)
    {
        UINT rc = MessageBox(GetFocus(), "File exists. Overwrite?",
                                    szFile, MB_ICONQUESTION | MB_YESNO);
        if(rc == IDYES)
            hFile = CreateFile(szFile, GENERIC_WRITE,
                        0, NULL, CREATE_ALWAYS, FILE_ATTRIBUTE_NORMAL, NULL);
        else
        {
            delete [] pb;
            return;
        }
    }

    DWORD dwBytes;
    WriteFile(hFile, pb, dwSize, &dwBytes, NULL);
    CloseHandle(hFile);
    delete [] pb;
}
```

```
void SaveToWMF(HENHMETAFILE hEMF, LPTSTR szFile)
{
    // Get memory to store the WMF bits
    HDC hDC = GetDC(NULL);
    DWORD dwSize = GetWinMetaFileBits(hEMF, 0, NULL, MM_ANISOTROPIC, hDC);
    LPBYTE pb = new BYTE[dwSize];

    // Get the WMF bits from the EMF handle
    GetWinMetaFileBits(hEMF, dwSize, pb, MM_ANISOTROPIC, hDC);
    ReleaseDC(NULL, hDC);

    // Save to file
    HANDLE hFile = CreateFile(szFile, GENERIC_WRITE,
                        0, NULL, CREATE_NEW, FILE_ATTRIBUTE_NORMAL, NULL);
    if(hFile == INVALID_HANDLE_VALUE)
    {
        UINT rc = MessageBox(GetFocus(), "File exists. Overwrite?",
                                    szFile, MB_ICONQUESTION|MB_YESNO);
        if(rc == IDYES)
            hFile = CreateFile(szFile, GENERIC_WRITE,
                        0, NULL, CREATE_ALWAYS, FILE_ATTRIBUTE_NORMAL, NULL);
```

```
        else
        {
            delete [] pb;
            return;
        }
    }

    DWORD dwBytes;
    WriteFile(hFile, pb, dwSize, &dwBytes, NULL);
    CloseHandle(hFile);
    delete [] pb;
}
```

They might seem superfluous to this discussion, but the conversion functions are not just for show. Although Win32 primarily supports enhanced metafiles, you invariably end up dealing with lots of WMF files – mostly, placeable metafiles. An easy way of converting to and from the EMF format is therefore invaluable for an application such as this.

Assembling the Viewer

In order to bring together the disparate functions I've presented so far to create an application, we need somewhere to call them from. At this stage of development, the way I've chosen to do that is by associating a menu with the dialog (you can do that in the **Properties** context menu of the Visual C++ Resource Editor). Add the items that you saw in the screenshot at the beginning of this discussion, and then modify the WM_COMMAND handler in APP_DlgProc() like this:

```
    case WM_COMMAND:
       switch(wParam)
       {
       case ID_FILE_OPEN:
           OnOpen(hDlg);
           return FALSE;

       case ID_FILE_PRINT:
           OnPrint(hDlg);
           return FALSE;

       case ID_FILE_SAVEAS:
           OnSave(hDlg);
           return FALSE;

       case ID_FILE_EXIT:
       case IDCANCEL:
           EndDialog(hDlg, FALSE);
           return FALSE;
       }
       break;
```

At a stroke, the problem is reduced to the implementation of three relatively easy functions that call the routines we've already defined. Here's what they look like:

```
    void OnOpen(HWND hDlg)
    {
        TCHAR szFile[MAX_PATH] = {0};
```

```
      OPENFILENAME ofn;
      ZeroMemory(&ofn, sizeof(OPENFILENAME));
      ofn.lStructSize = sizeof(OPENFILENAME);
      ofn.lpstrFilter =
              "Metafiles\0*.?mf\0WMF\0*.wmf\0Enhanced\0*.emf\0All Files\0*.*\0";
      ofn.nMaxFile = MAX_PATH;
      ofn.lpstrFile = szFile;
      if(!GetOpenFileName(&ofn))
          return;
      else
      {
          HWND hwndMeta = GetDlgItem(hDlg, IDC_METAFILE);
          DisplayMetaFile(hwndMeta, ofn.lpstrFile);
          RefreshUI(hDlg, ofn.lpstrFile);
      }
  }
```

```
void OnPrint(HWND hDlg)
{
    if(lstrlen(g_szCurFile))
       PrintMetaFile(g_szCurFile);
    else
       Msg("There's no metafile currently opened.");
}
```

```
void OnSave(HWND hDlg)
{
    TCHAR s[1024] = {0};
    TCHAR szOutputFile[MAX_PATH] = {0};

    if(!lstrlen(g_szCurFile))
    {
        Msg("There's no metafile currently opened.");
        return;
    }

    // Ask for user's confirmation
    lstrcpy(szOutputFile, g_szCurFile);
    if(strstr(g_szCurFile, ".emf"))
       PathRenameExtension(szOutputFile, ".wmf");
    else if(strstr(g_szCurFile, ".wmf"))
       PathRenameExtension(szOutputFile, ".emf");

    wsprintf(s, "You're about to convert %s to %s.\nAre you really sure?",
                                     g_szCurFile, szOutputFile);
    UINT rc = MessageBox(hDlg, s, APPTITLE, MB_ICONQUESTION | MB_YESNO);

    // Proceed...
    if(rc == IDYES)
       SaveMetaFile(g_szCurFile);
}
```

As presented, these functions complete the application but for three things. First, APPTITLE is a global string constant that's used as the title of the dialog and is therefore equal to "Metafile Viewer". Second, g_szCurfile is a global character array that's used to store the name of the open metafile and should be set to the empty string in WinMain(). Third, RefreshUI() is a helper function that's used to add the name of the open metafile to the dialog title:

```
void RefreshUI(HWND hWnd, LPTSTR szFile)
{
    TCHAR szCaption[MAX_PATH] = {0};

    // Refresh the caption bar
    wsprintf(szCaption, "%s - %s", APPTITLE, szFile);
    SetWindowText(hWnd, szCaption);
}
```

With this last function in place and with the addition of the headers and libraries for the common dialogs and the Shell Lightweight API, you're now the proud owner of a serviceable application for displaying, printing and converting metafiles. On with the show!

Adapting the Application

What better way is there to print and convert metafiles than by using the document's context menu? In the functions assembled so far, we have three functions implemented in a modular way:

- ❑ Open
- ❑ Print
- ❑ Convert to

In other words, we have three static verbs to add to WMF and EMF documents. However, there are a few problems to solve in our application before we can claim successfully to have customized the context menu. First, we need to add command line support. Second, we need to register both EMF and WMF as system file classes – they are unknown file types by default.

Even after we've done all this, a third problem arises. Every click on a metafile will cause a new instance of the wmfview application to run. It would be better to have just one running instance, and send it any new document to be opened, printed or converted. Let's see how to solve each of these issues in turn.

The Importance of the Command Line

The application will support the following command lines:

```
wmfview.exe filename
wmfview.exe /p filename
wmfview.exe /s filename
```

The first one opens the specified file, while the other two print and convert the file, respectively. Having command line support will allow us to add new verbs to EMF and WMF documents easily. Let's see how this is coded:

```
int APIENTRY WinMain(HINSTANCE hInstance, HINSTANCE hPrevious,
                     LPTSTR lpsz, int iCmd)
{
    // This code is unchanged and omitted for brevity

    // Run main dialog
    BOOL b = DialogBoxParam(hInstance, "DLG_MAIN", NULL, APP_DlgProc,
                                reinterpret_cast<LPARAM>(lpsz));
```

```
    // Exit
    DestroyIcon(g_hIconLarge);
    DestroyIcon(g_hIconSmall);
    return b;
}
```

The WinMain() function passes the command line string that it receives to the dialog procedure through a call to the DialogBoxParam() API function. Any command line arguments are then processed in response to the WM_INITDIALOG message. Let's see how:

```
void OnInitDialog(HWND hDlg, LPARAM lParam)
{
    // Set the icons (T/F as to Large/Small icon)
    SendMessage(hDlg, WM_SETICON, FALSE, reinterpret_cast<LPARAM>(g_hIconSmall));
    SendMessage(hDlg, WM_SETICON, TRUE, reinterpret_cast<LPARAM>(g_hIconLarge));

    if(lstrlen(reinterpret_cast<LPTSTR>(lParam)))
        ParseCommandLine(hDlg, reinterpret_cast<LPTSTR>(lParam));
}
```

```
void ParseCommandLine(HWND hwnd, LPTSTR pszCmdLine)
{
    if(!lstrlen(pszCmdLine))
        return;

    // Get the first 2 (+ 1) chars from the command line (it's the switch)
    TCHAR pszSwitch[2] = {0};
    lstrcpyn(pszSwitch, pszCmdLine, 3);
    LPTSTR psz = pszCmdLine + lstrlen(pszSwitch) + 1;

    // Resolve any case by sending a custom message
    if(!lstrcmpi(pszSwitch, "/p"))
        SendMessage(hwnd, WM_EX_PRINTMETA, 0, reinterpret_cast<LPARAM>(psz));
    else if(!lstrcmpi(pszSwitch, "/s"))
        SendMessage(hwnd, WM_EX_SAVEMETA, 0, reinterpret_cast<LPARAM>(psz));
    else
        SendMessage(hwnd, WM_EX_DISPLAYMETA, 0,
                    reinterpret_cast<LPARAM>(pszCmdLine));
}
```

As you can see, the ParseCommandLine() function examines the command line, decides what to do and then sends a custom message to the application's window procedure. The custom messages are defined like this:

```
const int WM_EX_DISPLAYMETA = WM_APP + 1;
const int WM_EX_PRINTMETA   = WM_APP + 2;
const int WM_EX_SAVEMETA    = WM_APP + 3;
```

APP_DlgProc() gains a few more handlers that call some of the functions we've already defined, like this:

```
BOOL CALLBACK APP_DlgProc(HWND hDlg, UINT uiMsg, WPARAM wParam, LPARAM lParam)
{
    switch(uiMsg)
    {
    case WM_INITDIALOG:
        OnInitDialog(hDlg, lParam);
    break;
```

```
case WM_EX_DISPLAYMETA:
    DisplayMetaFile(GetDlgItem(hDlg, IDC_METAFILE),
                                reinterpret_cast<LPTSTR>(lParam));
    RefreshUI(hDlg, reinterpret_cast<LPTSTR>(lParam));
    break;

case WM_EX_PRINTMETA:
    PrintMetaFile(reinterpret_cast<LPTSTR>(lParam));
    break;

case WM_EX_SAVEMETA:
    SaveMetaFile(reinterpret_cast<LPTSTR>(lParam));
    break;
```

```
case WM_COMMAND:
```

You should now find that you're able to run the application and display, print and save metafiles from the command line just as you can by using the dialog menu.

Why a Single Instance Application?

The code shown above runs a new instance of the program at each invocation. Once we've added shell support for metafiles, we will be able to click on any WMF or EMF file we find and have `wmfview` pop up, showing us the file. The trouble is that a new copy of the program is launched not only when you ask to open a file, but also if you simply want to print or convert it. To avoid dozens of `wmfview` windows, we need to make this a single instance application.

Back in the days of Windows 3.*x*, the `hPrevious` argument of `WinMain()` was used to denote the existence of a previous instance of the application. On Win32 platforms, though, this argument is maintained for compatibility purposes only, and is always set to `NULL`. Unfortunately, this makes it a bit harder to figure out whether another copy of the same process is currently running, but there are still a few techniques available:

Technique	Description
`FindWindow()`	The API function `FindWindow()` returns the handle of the first window belonging to a given class and/or with a given title. It can therefore identify *our* window by class name and/or title.
`EnumWindows()`	The API function `EnumWindows()` enumerates all the existing, non-child windows. This is useful to allow further investigation whenever there may be multiple windows with the same class or title.
Process name	This technique requires you to enumerate all the active processes and check against the name of your program. (See *Further Reading*.)
Mutexes and Semaphores	If you want to limit the number of instances, you can also make use of synchronization constructs like mutexes and semaphores. Mutexes are fine for single-instance applications, while semaphores are better for allowing a fixed number of copies. (See *Further Reading*.)

Dialog-Based Single-Instance Application

In the case of `wmfview`, we have additional requirements that force us to adopt the `EnumWindows()` approach. For a start, the mutex and process name solutions are no good to us because we need to retrieve the handle of the previous *window* so that we can reuse it. Simply knowing that it exists doesn't help.

Secondly, although `FindWindow()` is the simpler of the remaining options, our program is dialog-based, so we don't have an easily-distinguished class name. Put another way, the class name of our program's main window is `#32770`, which is exactly the same as any other dialog box or dialog-based application, and `FindWindow()` stops after the first match. We could use the title to reduce the choices, but we'll be adding the name of the open file to the caption bar, making it highly variable.

All that remains, then, is the `EnumWindows()`-based approach. We'll enumerate the windows, and check the class name and the title for each one. For each dialog window, we'll verify that the title begins with the prefix we expect – that is, **Metafile Viewer**. To be absolutely sure we get the right window, we should also check the executable that created it.

> *Getting the name of the executable is harder than you might imagine, because there isn't a common approach for Windows 9x and Windows NT. You need to use the* `ToolHelp` *API functions under Windows 9x, and the* `PSAPI` *functions under Windows NT. Documentation about these two is available in the MSDN library; in addition, see* Further Reading *for articles that address the specific problem of identifying the program that created a given window.*

Once we actually have the `HWND` handle of the previous instance, we can bring it to the foreground and call `ParseCommandLine()`, passing the command line we received. Here's how to modify the code in `WinMain()`:

```
int APIENTRY WinMain(HINSTANCE hInstance, HINSTANCE hPrevious,
                     LPTSTR lpsz, int iCmd)
{
    // Is there another running instance of this?
    HWND hwnd = AnotherInstanceRunning();
    if(IsWindow(hwnd))
    {
        // Bring the previous window to the top
        if(IsIconic(hwnd))
            ShowWindow(hwnd, SW_RESTORE);
        SetForegroundWindow(hwnd);

        // Parse "this" command line but send messages to the prev. window
        ParseCommandLine(hwnd, lpsz);

        // Now we can exit
        return 1;
    }

    // Rest of the function as before
}
```

And here's `AnotherInstanceRunning()`, the function that actually used for the test. It calls `EnumWindows()`, and the callback function that we provide on this occasion stops only if it finds a window of the same class and with the same title as the one we're looking for.

```
HWND AnotherInstanceRunning()
{
    HWND hwndFound = NULL;
    EnumWindows(CheckRunningApps, reinterpret_cast<LPARAM>(&hwndFound));

    // hwndFound will get the handle of the matching window, if any
    return hwndFound;
}
```

```
BOOL CALLBACK CheckRunningApps(HWND hwnd, LPARAM lParam)
{
    TCHAR szClass[MAX_PATH] = {0};
    GetClassName(hwnd, szClass, MAX_PATH);
    if(!lstrcmpi(szClass, "#32770"))
    {
        TCHAR s[MAX_PATH] = {0};
        TCHAR szTitle[MAX_PATH] = {0};
        GetWindowText(hwnd, szTitle, MAX_PATH);

        lstrcpyn(s, szTitle, 1 + lstrlen(APPTITLE));
        if(!lstrcmpi(s, APPTITLE))
        {
            // Uses the buffer pointed by lParam to return the HWND
            HWND* lphwnd = reinterpret_cast<HWND*>(lParam);
            *lphwnd = hwnd;
            return FALSE;
        }
    }

    return TRUE;
}
```

Now that we finally have a single-instance application to view, print and convert metafiles, we can think about how to add some shell support.

Adding Shell Support

Typically, shell support means:

- ❑ Registering each file type the application handles
- ❑ Registering a default icon for each file type
- ❑ Adding a few verbs to the context menu
- ❑ Adding each opened document to the recent documents list

We've already seen how to register new file types and their icons, and I've arranged for the resources of `Wmfview.exe` to include specific icons for both metafiles and enhanced metafiles:

enhmeta

winmeta

The entries to be added to the system registry are contained in the following script:

```
REGEDIT4

; //////////////////////////////////////////////////
; // Register WMF and EMF file types

[HKEY_CLASSES_ROOT\.wmf]
@= "WinMetafile"

[HKEY_CLASSES_ROOT\WinMetafile]
@= "Windows Metafile"

[HKEY_CLASSES_ROOT\.emf]
@= "EnhMetafile"

[HKEY_CLASSES_ROOT\EnhMetafile]
@= "Enhanced Metafile"


; //////////////////////////////////////////////////
; // Register the icons for WMF and EMF

[HKEY_CLASSES_ROOT\WinMetafile\DefaultIcon]
@= "C:\\WmfView\\WmfView.exe,2"

[HKEY_CLASSES_ROOT\EnhMetafile\DefaultIcon]
@= "C:\\WmfView\\WmfView.exe,1"


; //////////////////////////////////////////////////
; // Add Open, Print and Save verbs to WMF

; Open
[HKEY_CLASSES_ROOT\WinMetafile\Shell\Open\Command]
@= "C:\\WmfView\\WmfView.exe %1"

; Print
[HKEY_CLASSES_ROOT\WinMetafile\Shell\Print\Command]
@= "C:\\WmfView\\WmfView.exe /p %1"

; Save To EMF
[HKEY_CLASSES_ROOT\WinMetafile\Shell\Save]
@= "&Convert to EMF"

[HKEY_CLASSES_ROOT\WinMetafile\Shell\Save\Command]
@= "C:\\WmfView\\WmfView.exe /s %1"


; //////////////////////////////////////////////////
; // Add Open, Print and Save verbs to EMF

; Open
[HKEY_CLASSES_ROOT\EnhMetafile\Shell\Open\Command]
@= "C:\\WmfView\\WmfView.exe %1"

; Print
[HKEY_CLASSES_ROOT\EnhMetafile\Shell\Print\Command]
@= "C:\\WmfView\\WmfView.exe /p %1"
```

```
; Save To WMF
[HKEY_CLASSES_ROOT\EnhMetafile\Shell\Save]
@= "&Convert to WMF"

[HKEY_CLASSES_ROOT\EnhMetafile\Shell\Save\Command]
@= "C:\\WmfView\\WmfView.exe /s %1"
```

Apart from assuming you've installed `WmfView.exe` in the `c:\wmfview` folder, the listing reveals a number of things that you need to be aware of when you're writing your own registry script. In particular:

- ❑ In REG scripts, the `@` symbol denotes the `Default` value
- ❑ It is very important that you use a *double* backslash in path names, and a *single* backslash for registry entries
- ❑ While writing REG scripts, remember never to break a registry path contained between brackets across two or more lines

By default, the name of the verb (in this case, any sub-key of the `Shell` key) is exactly what appears on the context menu. This works fine for `Open` and `Print`, but we don't want the string `Save` to represent the command for converting from EMF to WMF and vice versa. That's why we set the `Default` value of the `Save` verb to the custom string that we want to appear in the menu.

You can run the script by using the Registry | Import Registry File... menu item of the Registry Editor, by double-clicking on the REG file from the shell, or even programmatically, by executing the file with `ShellExecute()` as explained in Chapter 8. However you do it, when you restart Explorer, the result is shown in the next picture:

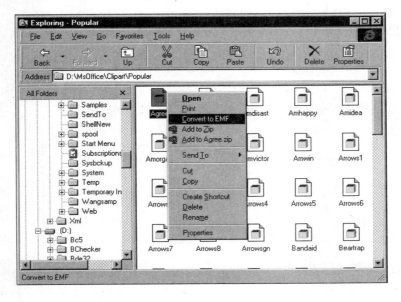

Changing the Default Menu Item

If present, the Open verb is always set as the default item for the context menu. The default item is drawn in bold, and is automatically selected by a double left click (or a single-click, depending upon your Active Desktop settings). The default item is *always* the first to appear in the context menu.

However, it's possible to reorder the items in the enhanced metafile context menu, for example, by setting the Default value in the following key:

```
HKEY_CLASSES_ROOT
    \EnhMetafile
        \Shell
```

Normally, this value contains an empty string, but if you set it to a comma-separated string whose tokens are the various verb names, then they'll be displayed in the order you specify, with the first one as the default item. It's not required that you include all the verbs in the list, so you can limit how many you reorder.

> **Remember that this technique works only for the *static* verbs defined in the Shell key.**

Adding Context Menu Items for any File

In the above screenshot, you may have noticed that there are two items related to WinZip. These are not specific to metafiles, and instead apply to all files (but not folders). For this reason, the items are not listed under the Shell key for WinMetaFile or EnhMetaFile. To add context menu items to *any* file type, simply add the verb under:

```
HKEY_CLASSES_ROOT
    \*
        \Shell
```

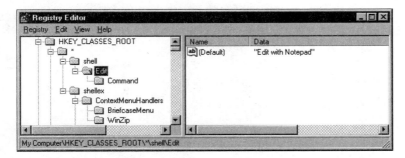

Sometimes, adding new items like this will remove the default style from the Open With... item. Note also that all the items you add here are always displayed before the Shell items that are specific to a particular type of file. However, this is evidently not the case for WinZip, so what's going on there?

If you want to avoid removing the current default item by adding new commands under `HKEY_CLASSES_ROOT\*\Shell`, the alternative is for you to define a shell extension, as WinZip and Briefcase do in the above figure. Shell extensions go under the `shellex` key, and if they are to apply to context menus, they require a further sub-key called `ContextMenuHandlers`. I'll cover this in detail in the next chapter.

If you need to add custom menu items to any folder or drive then the registry keys to consider are `HKEY_CLASSES_ROOT\Folder` *and* `HKEY_CLASSES_ROOT\Drive` *respectively.*

Give a Folder a Custom Icon

Suppose that you're writing a suite of applications that install under a common path. Wouldn't it be nice if that folder could have a custom icon? Look at this figure:

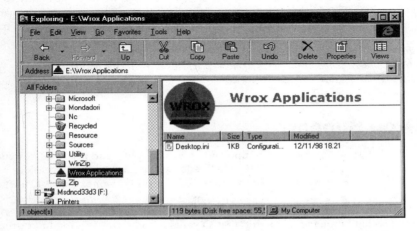

The `Wrox Applications` folder is a perfectly normal folder, but its icon is different. To get this behavior, just do the following:

❑   In the folder you want to customize, create an ASCII file called `desktop.ini`. You might want to make it hidden, but that's not strictly necessary. I'll discuss what you need to put in the file in a moment.

❑   Make the directory read-only. This can either be done programmatically or by the means of the **P**roperties dialog.

The `desktop.ini` file has a special meaning to Explorer — it represents a junction point between the shell and a piece of code that's meant to customize both the look and the behavior of the folder. In Chapter 16, I'll show you how to change the behavior of a folder through **namespace extensions**, but that will require `desktop.ini` to contain rather more information than we need here. To change the icon of a folder, you just need to add lines like these to the file:

```
[.ShellClassInfo]
IconIndex=0
IconFile=C:\WMFVIEW.EXE
```

The role of the entries is quite self-explanatory: `IconIndex` denotes the icon's index in the `IconFile` file, and so the combination of the two defines the icon to be displayed for that folder.

Note that as you change settings for the folder — especially those inherent to Web views — the contents of this file are automatically updated.

Adding Recent Documents is Free

The Win32 documentation says that if you want to add your documents to the system folder for recently used documents, then you need to issue a call to the `SHAddToRecentDocs()` function. Doing this works perfectly well, but I've noticed that sometimes you don't need to go even this far.

Once it has been registered to handle metafiles, you'll find that the `wmfview` application automatically saves any opened document to the folder, even though we *never* explicitly call `SHAddToRecentDocs()`. This is clearly a feature of the shell that applies only to applications that have registered their documents; for non-registered file types, you will still need the API function.

In fact, you don't necessarily have to open *a document. This behavior also applies when you print one, or indeed execute any of the verbs. However, when you recall the document from the* Documents *menu, the default verb always executes.*

Drag-and-Drop Support

Having drag-and-drop support for file-based applications is a big plus, and if you've designed your software carefully and integrated it well with the shell, adding this capability is as easy as assigning the WS_EX_ACCEPTFILES style to your main window and detecting the next WM_DROPFILES message.

The important thing is that you have a function that's available to be run as a modular procedure after such an event occurs. If you handle the command line as explained above, then adding shell drag-and-drop requires just the following additional code, which will be invoked in response to a WM_DROPFILES message:

```
case WM_DROPFILES:
    HandleFileDrop(hDlg, reinterpret_cast<HDROP>(wParam));
    break;
```

```
void HandleFileDrop(HWND hDlg, HDROP hDrop)
{
    TCHAR szFileName[MAX_PATH] = {0};

    // Since we are an SDI app, it doesn't make sense to receive
    //  more than one file, so extract only the first
    DragQueryFile(hDrop, 0, szFileName, MAX_PATH);
    SendMessage(hDlg, WM_EX_DISPLAYMETA, 0, reinterpret_cast<LPARAM>(szFileName));
    DragFinish(hDrop);
}
```

Customized Open Dialogs

Another interesting feature that shell-oriented applications can use is specialized versions of the system's common dialogs. The Win32 API describes what you need to do to customize any of the common dialogs, like Color, Font or Print, and you should refer to Microsoft's documentation for more details.

For our purposes, the most interesting dialogs are the Open/Save ones. Let's see an example of how to customize the Open dialog to add a few new buttons that work as bookmarks to specific paths. The figure below shows an example of customized dialog taken from Visual C++; notice in particular the Open as section with a label and a combo box.

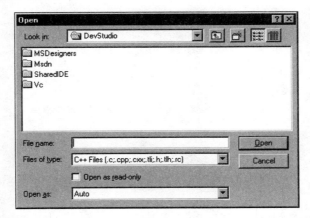

In the rest of this chapter, I'll demonstrate how to build a dialog that looks a little like the Open dialog of the upcoming Office 2000 products. Before this, however, I owe you an explanation of how dialog customization actually takes place.

Defining a New Template

The Open dialog allows you to define a non-standard template, although you don't have the same degree of freedom as was available in Windows 3.1. If you're using the Explorer-like layout, you're not allowed to hide controls that aren't needed. This behavior is by design, and I can't see a reliable way to work around it, apart from writing a new dialog from scratch.

To call the Open dialog, you need the GetOpenFileName() function, as shown below:

```
OPENFILENAME ofn;
TCHAR szFile[MAX_PATH] = {0};

ZeroMemory(&ofn, sizeof(OPENFILENAME));
ofn.lStructSize = sizeof(OPENFILENAME);
ofn.lpstrFile = szFile;
ofn.nMaxFile = sizeof(szFile);
ofn.lpstrFilter = __TEXT("All files\0*.*\0");
ofn.Flags = OFN_PATHMUSTEXIST | OFN_FILEMUSTEXIST | OFN_HIDEREADONLY;
GetOpenFileName(&ofn);
```

To enable customization, you need to add the following lines before the call is made:

```
ofn.lpTemplateName = MAKEINTRESOURCE(IDD_DIALOG);
ofn.lpfnHook = OpenDlgExProc;
ofn.Flags |= OFN_EXPLORER | OFN_ENABLEHOOK | OFN_ENABLETEMPLATE;
```

`ofn.lpTemplateName` points to a dialog template, and `ofn.lpfnHook` points to a window procedure that will handle messages for all the custom controls.

The controls that form the original dialog must be considered as a single control, so any template that you design must include the whole original dialog as a building block. In practice, this means using relative positioning for your additional controls. Look at this figure, in which the dialog template you can see has the Child style, and no border:

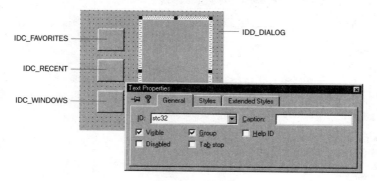

The highlighted component is a static control with an ID of `stc32`, which is a special constant that's defined in `dlgs.h`, one of the Visual C++ header files. It represents the standard Open dialog. You then place your controls around the component, and no matter what size you give the `stc32` control in the Resource Editor, the final window is properly resized, as shown in the figure. The next screenshot shows how the Open dialog that makes use of the above template will look at runtime; the dialog that you can see in the background betrays this as yet another Wrox AppWizard-generated application.

The standard dialog has been extended with a series of three buttons placed vertically on the left-hand side. So much for the look, but what about the behavior?

New Dialog Features

Apart from adopting the new look, what else should an Open dialog have in order better to customize the host application?

- ❑ Shortcuts to frequently-used paths are a good idea, and better still if they can be user-defined
- ❑ Tooltips on the new controls are another feature that improves the dialog's look and feel
- ❑ The dialog should be able to prevent deletion and renaming of the items in the folder

Bookmarks to Frequently Used Paths

Going back to the previous discussion, I've chosen to add a few buttons to store bookmarks to Favorites, Recent Documents and the Windows directory. The trickiest part of the code is working out programmatically how to get to a specified path, and the solution is to do it the same as you would manually. In other words, just set the File name edit box to the name of the path, and 'click' Open.

The IDs of all the controls used in the common dialogs are defined in the dlgs.h header file, but unfortunately this file doesn't assign intelligible mnemonics to the IDs. However, by combining the things you discover using Spy++ with the contents of dlgs.h, it's possible to figure out how they correspond. For the File name edit box, the ID is 0x0480, which is associated to a mnemonic constant called edt1. Calling this function from the window procedure that handles the button clicks will do the job we need:

```
#include <dlgs.h>
#include <shlobj.h>

void Goto(HWND hDlg, WORD wID)
{
    TCHAR szDir[MAX_PATH] = {0};
    LPITEMIDLIST pidl;

    // Retrieve the path to jump to
    if(wID == IDC_WINDOWS)
        GetWindowsDirectory(szDir, MAX_PATH);
    else
    {
        if(wID == IDC_FAVORITES)
            SHGetSpecialFolderLocation(hDlg, CSIDL_FAVORITES, &pidl);
        else
            if(wID == IDC_RECENT)
                SHGetSpecialFolderLocation(hDlg, CSIDL_RECENT, &pidl);

        SHGetPathFromIDList(pidl, szDir);
    }

    // Set a new path in the file name edit box
    HWND hdlgParent = GetParent(hDlg);
    SetDlgItemText(hdlgParent, edt1, szDir);
    SendMessage(hdlgParent, WM_COMMAND, IDOK, 0);
    SetDlgItemText(hdlgParent, edt1, "");
}
```

Notice from this code that the window handle your hook procedure receives is *not* the handle to the actual dialog window. This applies only to the Open dialog, and to get the real window you have to acquire a handle to the parent of the window that was passed to you:

```
HWND hdlgParent = GetParent(hDlg);
```

Once you've done that, you can safely obtain each child control of the Open dialog.

Icon and Tooltips for the Buttons

The new buttons each have an icon and tooltip. Here's how they are set:

```
void InitNewButtons(HWND hDlg)
{
    SHFILEINFO sfi;
    LPITEMIDLIST pidl = NULL;

    // Assign an icon to the Favorites button
    SHGetSpecialFolderLocation(hDlg, CSIDL_FAVORITES, &pidl);
    SHGetFileInfo(reinterpret_cast<LPTSTR>(pidl),
                            0, &sfi, sizeof(SHFILEINFO), SHGFI_PIDL | SHGFI_ICON);
    SendDlgItemMessage(hDlg, IDC_FAVORITES, BM_SETIMAGE, IMAGE_ICON,
                                        reinterpret_cast<LPARAM>(sfi.hIcon));

    // Assign an icon to the Recent Documents button
    SHGetSpecialFolderLocation(hDlg, CSIDL_PERSONAL, &pidl);
    SHGetFileInfo(reinterpret_cast<LPTSTR>(pidl),
                            0, &sfi, sizeof(SHFILEINFO), SHGFI_PIDL | SHGFI_ICON);
    SendDlgItemMessage(hDlg, IDC_RECENT, BM_SETIMAGE, IMAGE_ICON,
                                        reinterpret_cast<LPARAM>(sfi.hIcon));

    // Assign an icon to the Windows button
    SendDlgItemMessage(hDlg, IDC_WINDOWS, BM_SETIMAGE, IMAGE_ICON,
                            reinterpret_cast<LPARAM>(LoadIcon(NULL, IDI_WINLOGO)));

    // Set tooltips for each button
    SetTooltips(hDlg);
}
```

The icons are retrieved in different ways according to the specific icon needed. For special folders, like Favorites or Recent Documents, I relied on SHGetFileInfo(), while LoadIcon() was a help for the Windows logo. Each button has its own tooltip too:

```
void SetTooltips(HWND hDlg)
{
    // Creates a new tooltip control
    HWND hwndTT = CreateWindow(TOOLTIPS_CLASS, NULL, TTS_ALWAYSTIP, CW_USEDEFAULT,
                            CW_USEDEFAULT, CW_USEDEFAULT, CW_USEDEFAULT, hDlg,
                            NULL, GetModuleHandle(NULL), NULL);

    // Define the required tools, one for each button
    // Look in Favorites
    TOOLINFO ti;
    ZeroMemory(&ti, sizeof(TOOLINFO));
    ti.cbSize = sizeof(TOOLINFO);
    ti.uFlags = TTF_IDISHWND | TTF_SUBCLASS;
    ti.hwnd = hDlg;
    ti.uId = reinterpret_cast<UINT>(GetDlgItem(hDlg, IDC_FAVORITES));
```

```
        ti.lpszText = __TEXT("Look in Favorites");
        SendMessage(hwndTT, TTM_ADDTOOL, 0, reinterpret_cast<LPARAM>(&ti));

        // Look in Recent Documents
        ZeroMemory(&ti, sizeof(TOOLINFO));
        ti.cbSize = sizeof(TOOLINFO);
        ti.uFlags = TTF_IDISHWND | TTF_SUBCLASS;
        ti.hwnd = hDlg;
        ti.uId = reinterpret_cast<UINT>(GetDlgItem(hDlg, IDC_RECENT));
        ti.lpszText = __TEXT("Look in Recent documents");
        SendMessage(hwndTT, TTM_ADDTOOL, 0, reinterpret_cast<LPARAM>(&ti));

        // Look in Windows
        ZeroMemory(&ti, sizeof(TOOLINFO));
        ti.cbSize = sizeof(TOOLINFO);
        ti.uFlags = TTF_IDISHWND | TTF_SUBCLASS;
        ti.hwnd = hDlg;
        ti.uId = reinterpret_cast<UINT>(GetDlgItem(hDlg, IDC_WINDOWS));
        ti.lpszText = __TEXT("Look in Windows");
        SendMessage(hwndTT, TTM_ADDTOOL, 0, reinterpret_cast<LPARAM>(&ti));
    }
```

I create a new tooltip window and define five new tools, each one with its own text to display. In each of the blocks that defines a new tool, the uFlags field specifies that the uId field identifies a window handle (TTF_IDISHWND). This implies that the window, namely one of the buttons, is the area to which lpszText is assigned.

For a tip to appear, it's essential that the window that owns the area send proper mouse notifications to the tooltip window. The TTF_SUBCLASS flag causes the tooltip window to subclass the button automatically in order to send each message that's needed.

Tying the Code Together

To make all this code as reusable as possible, the following function is a wrapper built around the standard GetOpenFileName() API that takes as its input a pointer to a OPENFILENAME structure. If this structure contains a non-null template field, then the standard function is called. In other words, if the user has already required a custom folder, then the function does nothing but call the original routine. Otherwise, it replaces the standard dialog template with the one we've developed above.

```
#include <commdlg.h>

BOOL GetOpenFileNameEx(LPOPENFILENAME lpofn)
{
    // If the template is custom, revert to the standard dialog
    if(lpofn->lpTemplateName)
        return GetOpenFileName(lpofn);

    // Adjust the OPENFILENAME structure
    lpofn->hInstance = GetModuleHandle(NULL);
    lpofn->lpTemplateName = MAKEINTRESOURCE(IDD_DIALOG);
    lpofn->lpfnHook = OpenDlgExProc;
    lpofn->Flags |= OFN_EXPLORER | OFN_ENABLEHOOK | OFN_ENABLETEMPLATE;

    BOOL b = GetOpenFileName(lpofn);
    return b;
}
```

The callback used by the above function needs to handle just two messages. When WM_NOTIFY is received because the dialog has been constructed, InitNewButtons() must be called to set up the button icons and tooltips. If WM_COMMAND is the message, we check which button has been pressed and respond appropriately:

```
UINT CALLBACK OpenDlgExProc(HWND hDlg, UINT uiMsg, WPARAM wParam, LPARAM lParam)
{
    LPOFNOTIFY pN = NULL;
    switch(uiMsg)
    {
    case WM_NOTIFY:
        pN = reinterpret_cast<LPOFNOTIFY>(lParam);
        if(pN->hdr.code == CDN_INITDONE)
            InitNewButtons(hDlg);
        break;

    case WM_COMMAND:
        switch(LOWORD(wParam))
        {
        case IDC_FAVORITES:
        case IDC_RECENT:
        case IDC_WINDOWS:
            Goto(hDlg, LOWORD(wParam));
            break;
        }
        break;
    }
    return 0;
}
```

All that remains now is to call GetOpenFileNameEx() with appropriate arguments from the OnOK() function of the main application dialog. This will do the trick:

```
void OnOK(HWND hDlg)
{
    // Local data
    OPENFILENAME ofn;
    TCHAR szFile[MAX_PATH] = {0};

    ZeroMemory(&ofn, sizeof(OPENFILENAME));
    ofn.lStructSize = sizeof(OPENFILENAME);
    ofn.hwndOwner = hDlg;
    ofn.lpstrFile = szFile;
    ofn.nMaxFile = sizeof(szFile);
    ofn.lpstrFilter = "All files\0*.*\0";
    ofn.nFilterIndex = 1;
    ofn.Flags = OFN_PATHMUSTEXIST | OFN_FILEMUSTEXIST | OFN_HIDEREADONLY;

    if(GetOpenFileNameEx(&ofn))
        MessageBox(hDlg, ofn.lpstrFile, "Open", MB_OK | MB_ICONINFORMATION);
}
```

Prevent the Renaming of Items

By default, the Open dialog allows you to delete and rename the files it displays. This feature is provided by the system and there's no flag to prevent it. In many cases, however, you don't need it, and at that point it becomes extremely annoying. Let's see how you can turn it off.

The control that shows us the list of the files is a list view control with the `LBS_EDITLABELS` style. In order to get the behavior we want, we just have to turn this bit off. The hardest part of this process is getting hold of a handle to the list view.

```
void ModifyStyle(HWND hDlg)
{
    // Get the files' listview handle.
    HWND hwndDefView = GetDlgItem(GetParent(hDlg), lst2);
    HWND hwndListView = GetDlgItem(hwndDefView, 1);

    // Turn off the bit
    DWORD dwStyle = GetWindowLong(hwndListView, GWL_STYLE);
    dwStyle &= ~LVS_EDITLABELS;
    SetWindowLong(hwndListView, GWL_STYLE, dwStyle);
}
```

Our list view is child of a container window whose ID is `lst2` – another value taken from the `dlgs.h` header. The ID of the list view is 1; this information is mostly due to Spy++. The above function must be called each time the user changes a directory, because the list view is destroyed and recreated each time this happens. A good place to do this is therefore in response to the `CDN_FOLDERCHANGE` notification:

```
case WM_NOTIFY:
    pN = reinterpret_cast<LPOFNOTIFY>(lParam);
    if(pN->hdr.code == CDN_INITDONE)
        InitNewButtons(hDlg);
    if(pN->hdr.code == CDN_FOLDERCHANGE)
        ModifyStyle(hDlg);
    break;
```

Tips for Preventing File Deletion

Even if you subclass the list view, you won't be able to catch events that correspond to the *Delete* key. It's clear that Explorer traps the request for file deletion through a keyboard hook that processes the message, and then eats it.

Given this, the best way to trap the *Delete* key ourselves is to install our own keyboard hook, trap the message, and then break the hook chain in the same way Explorer does. This way, Explorer won't get the message, and will never attempt to delete the file. The hook should be installed before the call to `GetOpenFileName()`, and removed immediately afterwards. The modification to the code is minimal:

```
BOOL GetOpenFileNameEx(LPOPENFILENAME lpofn)
{
    // If the template is custom, revert to the standard dialog
    if(lpofn->lpTemplateName)
        return GetOpenFileName(lpofn);

    // Adjust the OPENFILENAME structure
    lpofn->hInstance = GetModuleHandle(NULL);
    lpofn->lpTemplateName = MAKEINTRESOURCE(IDD_DIALOG);
    lpofn->lpfnHook = OpenDlgExProc;
    lpofn->Flags |= OFN_EXPLORER | OFN_ENABLEHOOK | OFN_ENABLETEMPLATE;

    // Set a keyboard hook on the current thread
    g_hHook = SetWindowsHookEx(WH_KEYBOARD,
                                    HookProc, NULL, GetCurrentThreadId());
```

```
        BOOL b = GetOpenFileName(lpofn);

    // Remove the hook
    UnhookWindowsHookEx(g_hHook);
    return b;
}
```

The hook procedure that gets called each time a key is pressed within the **Open** dialog is very simple, and completes the code for this chapter:

```
LRESULT CALLBACK HookProc(int iCode, WPARAM wParam, LPARAM lParam)
{
    // Eat the DELETE key...
    if(wParam == VK_DELETE)
        return 1;

    // ...otherwise feel free to proceed
    return CallNextHookEx(g_hHook, iCode, wParam, lParam);
}
```

What *is* a Shell-integrated Application?

We've spent this chapter discussing the various aspects involved in integrating your application with the shell. We've found that there are a certain number of features that can be coded into an executable, including parsing command line parameters, and ensuring that there is only a single instance of the application. We have also come across many other features that are not necessarily tied to the main application, like file type registration and context menu improvements.

Basically, there are two levels of integration with the shell. The first one is somewhat cosmetic and aimed at the user interface: nice file type names, nice icons and new context menu items. The second level, however, touches the source code. It consists of certain global application design rules, but also many other little tricks, such as handling the WM_ENDSESSION message to cause the application to rerun automatically at the next logon, and adding shortcuts to the Favorites or Recent Documents folders.

Summary

In this chapter, I've demonstrated a complete Win32 application that attempts to integrate itself well with the system's shell. We examined what shell-integration means, what aspects to consider, and how to design or re-engineer your existing code to facilitate shell support for your documents. We also discussed customizing and extending the capabilities of **Open** dialogs.

In brief, the topics of this chapter have been:

- ❑ File classes and the information stored in the registry
- ❑ Context menu customization
- ❑ Creating new documents via the shell
- ❑ Application command lines
- ❑ How to write Win32, dialog-based, single-instance applications
- ❑ Customizing the **Open File** common dialog
- ❑ Principles to make your application shell-aware

However, I have kept hinting that shell extensions are the most flexible and powerful way to extend the capability and the behavior of the Windows shell, and now the wait is over! Shell extensions will be the subject of the next chapter.

Further Reading

A good source of information on the subject of shell integration is an old article by Jeff Richter that appeared in the April 1996 issue of MSJ. The title is *Fusing your Application to the System through the Windows 95 Shell*. Some programming topics that are inherent to the Windows shell are covered in the Microsoft Press book *Programming the Windows 95 User Interface*, written by Nancy Cluts (ISBN 1-556158-84-X). A digital version of the book is available in the MSDN Library.

If you're interested in discovering more about Office 97 file formats, check out the latest MSDN documentation. All the details are under `Microsoft Office Development\Office`.

NT services are given the comprehensive treatment they deserve in *Professional NT Services* by Kevin Miller (Wrox Press). Other sources of note include Jeff Richter's MSJ articles *Design a Windows NT Service to Exploit Special Operating System Facilities* (October 1997) and *Manipulate Windows NT Services by Writing a Service Control Program* (February 1998). Also take a look at *Why Do Certain Win32 Technologies Misbehave in Windows NT Services?* by Frank Kim, MSJ, March 1998. A primer on writing Windows 95 services can be found in the Windows Developer's Journal of May 1998. The article is called *NT-style Services for Windows 95*, and it was written by Dmitri Klementiev.

Identifying the process behind a given window can be a pretty difficult task, and I wrote an article on exactly this subject for the October 97 issue of WDJ. Called *Process Names from Window Handles*, it provides a solution that works both on Windows 9*x* and Windows NT 4.0. All the information you may desire on mutexes, semaphores and other kernel objects is available in Jeff Richter's best-selling *Advanced Windows*, from Microsoft Press (ISBN 1-572315-48-2).

Finally, we spent a portion of this chapter talking about Windows and enhanced metafiles without going down to the low-level details. If you want to know more, check out *Enhanced Metafiles in Win32* by Dennis Crain, an article on MSDN. To conclude, Knowledge Base article Q145999 points to a piece of code demonstrating the use of standard and enhanced metafiles.

Finally, and as ever, here are some useful Knowledge Base articles:

- ❑ **Knowledge Base Article Q179365:** *Run, RunOnce, RunServices, RunServicesOnce and Startup*
- ❑ **Knowledge Base Article Q137367:** *Definition of the RunOnce Keys in the Registry*
- ❑ **Knowledge Base Article Q174018:** *Description of the Windows 95 Startup Process*
- ❑ **Knowledge Base Article Q125714:** *How to Start an Application at Boot Time Under Windows 95*
- ❑ **Knowledge Base Article Q175030:** *Enumerate Applications in Win32*

15

Shell Extensions

When you're talking about Windows shell programming, **shell extensions** are one of the most important topics. Most of the coolest features that commercial applications deploy are implemented through shell extensions, and many features that are apparently down to the system are actually due to plugged-in extensions. The particularly exciting aspect of shell extensions is that they allow you to manipulate the shell as though your application is actually a part of it.

Another encouraging aspect of shell extensions is that Microsoft is using them sensibly. For example, the Find menu has grown from what it was under Windows 95 to what it has become under Active Desktop and Windows 98, and the new items have been added through shell extensions. Moving on, any bitmap item that appears on a document's context menu has been added using shell extensions. Further still, any additional page on a document's Properties menu is there by means of a shell extension as well, and the list could go on.

So, shell extensions are not only important building blocks for adding functionality to the shell, but also enable your programs to take advantage of the shell's features. In the previous chapter, I outlined what a typical Win32 program should do in order to integrate with the system. I spoke of context menus, icons, and a few other minor adjustments. All those changes, however, were static and defined once and for all. You can set them or remove them, but that's all you can do: there's nothing in between.

The final step towards a fully Windows-compliant application is therefore to take into account the possibility of writing one or more shell extensions. Notice that I said, "the possibility," here. In fact, although shell extensions are a powerful and flexible way to communicate with the shell, it's not the case that they're a must-have for you and your software.

In this chapter, I'll cover all the programming aspects of shell extensions, and provide you with some insightful samples. In particular:

❑ What shell extensions are, and how you work with them
❑ How to write shell extensions with C++ and ATL
❑ Ways of debugging shell extensions
❑ Using shell extensions to customize context menus, icons, and properties

The final part of the chapter will be dedicated to file viewers. Strictly speaking, these are not shell extensions, but they have a similar internal structure. A file viewer is a module that lets you get a quick preview of a given type of document without resorting to the application that creates and manages that type of file. A file viewer is usually linked to the Quick View item on the context menu.

Shell Extensions: Types and Tips

A shell extension is an in-process COM server that Explorer loads when necessary. Shell extensions are not a completely new idea; they owe more than a little to the File Manager add-ons that were introduced with Windows 3.1. However, shell extensions use the COM infrastructure instead of DLL functions, and give you a wider range of functionality.

What are Shell Extensions?

As mentioned above, a shell extension is an in-process COM server that implements COM interfaces. You write the module, register it in the registry, and run an instance of the Explorer window to test it. You should never have to worry about how, when or by whom your extension is called – it occurs automatically, provided that you have registered it correctly.

A shell extension is a DLL that can be located anywhere in your PC. Like any other COM server, it exports four global functions, through which a client module can identify, and connect to, the server:

❑ `DllGetClassObject()`
❑ `DllCanUnloadNow()`
❑ `DllRegisterServer()`
❑ `DllUnregisterServer()`

Beyond this, a shell extension must provide the usual COM paraphernalia, like a class factory and an implementation of `IUnknown`. Finally, it must implement the specific interfaces needed to interact with the shell.

Calling Shell Extensions

There are a number of events that Explorer recognizes as being customizable via client modules. Examples are when Explorer is about to show a context menu or a property page, draw an icon or drop a file over another. Put another way, when performing one of a particular set of tasks on any kind of document, Explorer looks for registered user modules before proceeding. If one is found, Explorer connects to it and invokes the required methods.

This scenario looks like the kind of callback mechanism described in any Windows programming primer. A callback is a function with a predefined prototype (and usually a "recommended" behavior) that a server module will invoke to let clients intervene in response to given events. A good example of this is provided by the Windows API enumeration functions. EnumWindows(), which we used in the last chapter, takes a pointer to a function with a fixed prototype and then invokes it, passing each window handle it finds. What occurs with shell extensions is conceptually pretty similar.

File Manager Add-ons

The file manager add-on mechanism just relied on callback functions. On being loaded, File Manager scanned its winfile.ini file looking for a DLL name in the AddOns section:

```
[AddOns]
MyExtension=C:\WINDOWS\SYSTEM\FMEXT.DLL
```

In that DLL, File Manager expected to find a function called FMExtensionProc(), whose prototype had to be:

```
LRESULT CALLBACK FMExtensionProc(HWND    hwnd,
                                 WORD    wMsg,
                                 LPARAM  lParam);
```

From this point on, File Manager began sending notification messages to the function so specified. By writing such a function, you could add new toolbar buttons, be notified of selection changes, modify menus, and other things. If you're interested, you should refer to the Internet Client SDK documentation for a detailed overview of what you can do. In particular, check out the Platform SDK\User Interface Services\Shell and Common Controls\Windows Shell API area.

From File Manager Add-ons to Shell Extensions

Now you have an idea of what happens when File Manager add-ons come into play, let's try to translate this idea into the world of shell extensions. Here are the main structural differences:

- ❑ Instead of a single callback function, we now have a COM interface
- ❑ Instead of an INI file, we now have a bunch of registry keys and values to associate our extensions with types of file
- ❑ Instead of a simple DLL, we now have a COM server

So, while some similarity cannot be denied, File Manager add-ons and shell extensions are very different things. For one thing, the scope of the technology has changed: File Manager add-ons are application-centric, because the messages exchanged rarely regard single files, and never distinguish between file types. Shell extensions apply separately to each type of file — in fact, they've been specifically designed to act this way.

How Explorer Calls Into Shell Extensions

To understand the interaction that takes place between Explorer and a shell extension, let's examine a real case. When we're finished, you should have a clear understanding of how things work, and why shell extensions have been designed the way they are.

As I mentioned earlier, before proceeding with one of a particular set of tasks, Explorer looks for registered modules somewhere in the registry. All the extensions it finds are loaded, and their methods are invoked accordingly. To enable a certain behavior, just register an appropriate module. To disable it, just unregister the same module.

The exact path in the registry to look in, and the programming interface of the extension, can vary quite a bit, depending on the event that causes Explorer to trigger the call.

Displaying a Context Menu

Let's consider a typical example: displaying the context menu for a certain type of file – bitmaps, perhaps. The procedure starts when the user right clicks on a BMP file in a shell view. The context menu is composed of different groups of items. First, there are the standard system items, like Copy, Cut, Create Shortcut, and Properties. Then there are the document-specific verbs that get added statically. Thirdly, there are the general verbs added for any file, regardless of type.

A fourth group of items will come from any context menu shell extension registered for the file type under consideration. In our case, these are bitmap files.

When Explorer creates the pop-up menu, it starts by adding all the standard items, and each item that comes from the registry. Then it looks under the ShellEx key for the relevant file type (if one exists), searching for a ContextMenuHandlers sub-key. For BMPs, this would be:

```
HKEY_CLASSES_ROOT
    \Paint.Picture
        \ShellEx
            \ContextMenuHandlers
```

The main key for bitmaps is Paint.Picture if Microsoft Paint is the program enabled to manage bitmaps. This is the default, unless you've installed some alternative graphics software.

Under the ContextMenuHandlers key, the Default value should contain the CLSID of the COM server that implements the extension. Once the CLSID is known, Explorer loads the module into its own memory space. This is accomplished by creating an instance of the server, and asking for the interface that deals with the extension in question. For context menus, this interface is IContextMenu, which comprises methods for adding a new item, retrieving its description string to display on the status bar, and executing some code in response to a user's click.

It works like this: Explorer first invokes IContextMenu::QueryContextMenu() to ask the module for new items to add. Each time the new item is selected, Explorer calls GetCommandString() to get a description to show on the status bar. Finally, when someone clicks the custom menu item, InvokeCommand() is run to provide run-time behavior.

The COM interface functions that get invoked by Explorer can provide a means of customizing items in the shell. In order for the interface to be visible to Explorer, though, it must be registered according to a rigorous schema. I'll be digging out these and other details later on in the chapter.

Types of Shell Extensions

I've mentioned repeatedly that shell extensions are loaded in response to a particular set of shell events. Consequently, there are a fixed number of different shell extensions, by which I mean a set of different COM interfaces that expose different functions in order to reflect the specific circumstances. Displaying a context menu is not the same as painting an icon, or displaying a Properties dialog box, so it should come as no surprise that there are different COM interfaces doing the work.

The types of shell extensions are:

Shell Extension	Interface	Description
Context Menu	IContextMenu	Allows you to add new items to a shell object's context menu.
Right Drag-and-drop	IContextMenu	Allows you to add new items to the context menu that appears after you right-drag-and-drop files.
Shell Icons	IExtractIcon	Lets you decide at runtime which icon should be displayed for a given file within a file class.
Property Sheet	IShellPropSheetExt	Lets you insert additional property sheet pages to the file class Properties dialog. It also works for Control Panel applets.
File Hook	ICopyHook	Lets you control any file operation that goes through the shell. While you can permit or deny them, you aren't informed about success or failure.
Left Drag-and-drop	IDropTarget	Lets you decide what to do when an object is being dropped (using the left mouse button) onto another one within the shell.
Clipboard	IDataObject	Lets you define how an object is to be copied to and extracted from the clipboard.

Writing Shell Extensions

It will come as no surprise that writing a shell extension is much the same as writing a COM in-process server. You have to provide the basic COM stuff, implement the interfaces, register the server properly, and then go on with testing and debugging. As with any other COM module you develop, there's a lot of pretty repetitive code that you rarely need to change once you've written it. This code lends itself well to being encapsulated in some C++ classes. Can you guess what's coming next?

Using ATL

Of course I'm going to recommend ATL as the best tool for developing shell extensions. After all, ATL is today the best tool for developing COM servers in C++, and that's exactly what shell extensions are. Microsoft's Active Template Library is a C++ framework specifically designed to simplify the development of COM modules, and it's far lighter than MFC.

Our First Shell Extension

It's high time we got down to looking at how to write a shell extension. They are really quite simple objects, so there's no point in developing a toy sample, even though this is our first one. We'll begin with an example that completes what we began in the previous chapter for Windows and enhanced metafiles; my goal is to show you how to add custom pages to the Properties dialog for both WMF and EMF files.

Adding Property Pages

Wouldn't it be nice if we could preview the metafile directly on the Properties dialog? Sure, you can get a nifty preview when you select the file in a folder with the View | as Web Page option turned on, but what if you don't know about or don't want that view? Furthermore, what if you're still running Windows 95 or Windows NT without the Active Desktop shell update?

The answer, of course, is a property sheet shell extension, which (like any other shell extension) will work fine even without Active Desktop and Internet Explorer 4.0.

Which Interfaces to Implement

Once the basic ATL code has been generated by the ATL COM AppWizard, the question that needs to be addressed is this: Which interfaces should be implemented in order to add property pages to a Properties dialog? In fact, there are two: `IShellPropSheetExt` and `IShellExtInit`. The first of these provides methods to add pages, while the latter takes care of initialization and establishes a connection between the shell and the extension. Both are defined in `shlobj.h`.

`IShellPropSheetExt` requires you to create a new property page using the API functions that deal with the common controls. This page is then passed to the shell through a callback function. In other words, when calling the methods of `IShellPropSheetExt`, the shell passes a pointer to a function that will be called back by the extension with the page as an argument. The interface has two methods, one of which is not implemented in most cases.

The single method of `IShellExtInit` receives the name of the file (or files) selected in the shell, and makes it available to the module. You can use any technique you want to store this name, but typically you'd just use a member variable. The initialization of a shell extension is a process that may vary quite a bit for different types of extensions, so making the mechanism as generic as possible is the key here.

Initialization of Shell Extensions

We need to spend a few moments discussing how shell extensions get initialized. In this context, 'initialization' means the procedure followed by Explorer to call the extension, passing the correct arguments. Basically, initialization may take one of three forms: no initialization at all, initialization via `IShellExtInit`, and initialization via `IPersistFile`. The method of initialization used depends upon the nature of the shell extension itself.

The following table shows how the various types of extensions get initialized. (Refer to the earlier table for a list of shell extension types.)

Initialization	Applies to	Description
No initialization at all	File Hook, Clipboard	The shell extension doesn't require any initialization step.
Via `IShellExtInit`	Context Menu, Property Sheet, Right Drag-and-drop	The shell extension works on all the selected files. Their names are passed in the same format as they are copied to the clipboard.
Via `IPersistFile`	Left Drag-and-drop, Icons	The shell extension works on a file regardless of whether it is selected. The name is passed as a Unicode string.

The startup process of a shell extension consists of calling one or more methods of the initialization interface. When Explorer detects an event that may trigger a shell extension, it knows which kind of extension might be registered, and how to initialize it. All it needs to do in addition is query for the appropriate interface.

My intention is to describe how `IShellExtInit` and `IPersistFile` work in detail as I demonstrate the shell extensions that need them, so let's begin by looking at `IShellExtInit`, the interface involved in property sheet shell extensions. (I'll cover `IPersistFile` in the section entitled Initializing the IconHandler Extension.)

The IShellExtInit Interface

The property sheet extension we're dealing with here is loaded by means of the `IShellExtInit` interface. This has a single method, called `Initialize()`, that Explorer invokes, passing the following three parameters:

Type	Parameter	Description
`LPCITEMIDLIST`	`pidlFolder`	Always NULL for property sheet extensions
`LPDATAOBJECT`	`lpdobj`	Points to an `IDataObject` that can be used to obtain the files currently selected
`HKEY`	`hkeyProgID`	The registry key for the file object involved

Because the same interface serves several types of extension, the first and third parameters can have different meanings according to the type being initialized. For property sheets, there are no folders involved, so the `pidlFolder` argument is unused. The `hkeyProdID` parameter is an HKEY handle to the registry key that contains information for the file object involved. For example, if the shell extension is working on WMF files, and you've worked through the examples in the last chapter, then `hkeyProgID` will be a handle to the following key:

```
HKEY_CLASSES_ROOT
   \WinMetafile
```

I'll cover what happens to these arguments for other types of shell extension later in the chapter.

For property sheet shell extensions, the most important argument is `lpdobj`, which contains a pointer to an object that implements `IDataObject`. This is a well-known interface that's employed in a number of user interface tasks. Basically, `IDataObject` defines the behavior of a block of data to be exchanged among running modules, and so clipboard and drag-and-drop operations are its main fields of application.

Copying or getting data to and from the clipboard the OLE way means storing and retrieving a pointer to an object that implements `IDataObject`. Likewise, when you drag-and-drop data using COM interfaces, the source and the target are exchanging data through `IDataObject`. Another way of looking at it is this: think of `IDataObject` as an evolution of the Windows handle – that is, a generic object for representing a block of memory containing data. The enhancements provide the ability to store:

- ❏ Data with a precise format, not just a generic "pointer to something"
- ❏ Data in storage media other than memory
- ❏ More blocks of data at the same time

`IDataObject` exposes methods to get, set and enumerate data. In particular, it makes use of structures like `FORMATETC` and `STGMEDIUM` that define the format and storage medium of the data. When you get a pointer to `IDataObject`, you can interrogate it to discover whether it contains data of a certain format on a certain medium. This latter point will become clearer in a moment, when I demonstrate how this applies to property sheet shell extensions. I also recommend that you look at the *Further Reading* section at the end of the chapter for references to books that cover the internals of `IDataObject`.

Let's switch back to property sheet shell extensions. In this case, the `IDataObject` object passed to `Initialize()` contains an `HDROP` handle. As we saw in Chapter 6, this handle contains a list of filenames that you can walk with functions like `DragQueryFile()`. For property sheet extensions, the list includes the names of all the files currently selected in the shell.

The **Properties** dialog pops up from the shell only if you right-click on one or more selected files and choose **Properties** from the resulting context menu. The list of selected files is passed to the shell extension via an object that implements `IDataObject`, and contains data in the `CF_HDROP` format. `CF_HDROP` is one of the standard clipboard formats, and data of this form is stored in a global memory handle called `HDROP`.

```
STGMEDIUM medium;
HDROP hDrop;

FORMATETC fe = {CF_HDROP, NULL, DVASPECT_CONTENT, -1, TYMED_HGLOBAL};
HRESULT hr = lpdobj->GetData(&fe, &medium);
if(SUCCEEDED(hr))
   hDrop = static_cast<HDROP>(medium.hGlobal);
```

The above snippet demonstrates how to retrieve the HDROP handle from an IDataObject pointer called lpdobj. GetData() takes the description of the data to retrieve through a FORMATETC variable and, if successful, returns it via a STGMEDIUM argument. FORMATETC is defined as follows:

```
typedef struct tagFORMATETC
{
    CLIPFORMAT        cfFormat;
    DVTARGETDEVICE*   ptd;
    DWORD             dwAspect;
    LONG              lindex;
    DWORD             tymed;
} FORMATETC, *LPFORMATETC;
```

The interesting members from our point of view are cfFormat and tymed, which address the data format and the type of storage medium respectively. In the snippet, therefore, CF_HDROP is the data format, while TYMED_HGLOBAL is a constant that denotes a global memory handle as the medium by which the data should be returned. Other possible storage media are disk files, metafiles, and pointers to IStorage or IStream objects.

Here and elsewhere in this chapter, I'm going to provide 'do-nothing' implementations of ATL classes whose functions I'll override when it comes to creating sample projects. The following listing is of a file called IShellExtInitImpl.h, which contains the most basic possible implementation of the IShellExtInit interface.

```
// IShellExtInitImpl.h

#include <AtlCom.h>
#include <ShlObj.h>

class ATL_NO_VTABLE IShellExtInitImpl : public IShellExtInit
{
public:

    // IUnknown
    STDMETHOD(QueryInterface)(REFIID riid, void** ppvObject) = 0;
    _ATL_DEBUG_ADDREF_RELEASE_IMPL(IShellExtInitImpl)

    // IShellExtInit
    STDMETHOD(Initialize)(LPCITEMIDLIST, LPDATAOBJECT, HKEY)
    {
        return S_FALSE;
    }
};
```

The IShellPropSheetExt Interface

The interface that provides methods for adding new property pages is `IShellPropSheetExt`. It exposes two functions (on top of the `IUnknown` functions): `AddPages()` and `ReplacePage()`. The first one takes the following parameters:

Type	Parameter	Description
LPFNADDPROPSHEETPAGE	lpfnAddPage	Points to a function that will actually add the page
LPARAM	lParam	Argument that has to be passed to the function specified by lpfnAddPage

`AddPages()` creates a new property sheet and calls the function whose address it received through `lpfnAddPage`. This callback function is defined by the shell, and has the following prototype:

```
BOOL CALLBACK AddPropSheetPageProc(HPROPSHEETPAGE hpage, LPARAM lParam);
```

The second argument is always passed by the shell, but getting the first one is the task of `AddPages()`. The callback function is called once for each registered property sheet shell extension, specifically when the shell is displaying the **Properties** dialog. `AddPages()` can add one or more pages, but if it does add multiple pages, it must create them and call the function pointed to by `lpfnAddPage` repeatedly.

`ReplacePage()`, the other method exposed by `IShellPropSheetExt`, is only used to replace property pages in Control Panel applets. I won't be implementing it in the sample we're constructing here, but the prototype is:

```
HRESULT ReplacePage(
    UINT                  uPageID,          // Index of page to replace
    LPFNADDPROPSHEETPAGE  lpfnReplacePage,  // Pointer to fn to replace page
    LPARAM                lParam);          // Additional argument for fn
```

In keeping with my earlier promise, the following listing is of `IShellPropSheetExtImpl.h`, a file that contains a basic implementation of `IShellPropSheetExt`:

```
// IShellPropSheetExtImpl.h

#include <AtlCom.h>
#include <ShlObj.h>

class ATL_NO_VTABLE IShellPropSheetExtImpl : public IShellPropSheetExt
{
public:
    TCHAR m_szFile[MAX_PATH];

    // IUnknown
    STDMETHOD(QueryInterface)(REFIID riid, void** ppvObject) = 0;
    _ATL_DEBUG_ADDREF_RELEASE_IMPL(IShellPropSheetExtImpl)
```

```
    // IShellPropSheetExt
    STDMETHOD(AddPages)(LPFNADDPROPSHEETPAGE, LPARAM)
    {
        return S_FALSE;
    }

    STDMETHOD(ReplacePage)(UINT, LPFNADDPROPSHEETPAGE, LPARAM)
    {
        return E_NOTIMPL;
    }
};
```

Adding a New Property Page

To start off the project proper, create a new ATL DLL project called `WMFProp` and add a simple
object called `PropPage`. After the skeleton of the ATL component has been generated, we need to
make some changes to the new object's header file, `PropPage.h`:

```
// PropPage.h : Declaration of the CPropPage

#ifndef __PROPPAGE_H_
#define __PROPPAGE_H_

#include "resource.h"              // main symbols
#include <comdef.h>                // Standard interface GUIDs
#include "IShellExtInitImpl.h"     // IShellExtInit
#include "IShellPropSheetExtImpl.h" // IShellPropSheetExt

BOOL CALLBACK PropPage_DlgProc(HWND, UINT, WPARAM, LPARAM);

/////////////////////////////////////////////////////////////////////
// CPropPage
class ATL_NO_VTABLE CPropPage :
    public CComObjectRootEx<CComSingleThreadModel>,
    public CComCoClass<CPropPage, &CLSID_PropPage>,
    public IShellExtInitImpl,
    public IShellPropSheetExtImpl,
    public IDispatchImpl<IPropPage, &IID_IPropPage, &LIBID_WMFPROPLib>
{
public:
    CPropPage()
    {
    }

DECLARE_REGISTRY_RESOURCEID(IDR_PROPPAGE)

DECLARE_PROTECT_FINAL_CONSTRUCT()

BEGIN_COM_MAP(CPropPage)
    COM_INTERFACE_ENTRY(IPropPage)
    COM_INTERFACE_ENTRY(IDispatch)
    COM_INTERFACE_ENTRY(IShellExtInit)
    COM_INTERFACE_ENTRY(IShellPropSheetExt)
END_COM_MAP()
```

```
// IPropPage
public:
    STDMETHOD(Initialize)(LPCITEMIDLIST, LPDATAOBJECT, HKEY);
    STDMETHOD(AddPages)(LPFNADDPROPSHEETPAGE, LPARAM);
};

#endif //__PROPPAGE_H_
```

The interface methods for which an implementation is required are `Initialize()` and `AddPages()`. I've also declared a static member function called `PropPage_DlgProc()`, which is needed to define the behavior of the page being added — it will be the window procedure of the new page.

Code for Initialize()

The `Initialize()` method looks like this:

```
HRESULT CPropPage::Initialize(
            LPCITEMIDLIST pidlFolder, LPDATAOBJECT lpdobj, HKEY hKeyProgID)
{
    if(lpdobj == NULL)
        return E_INVALIDARG;

    // Initialize common controls (Property Sheets are common controls)
    InitCommonControls();

    // Get the name of the selected file from the IDataObject
    // Data is stored in the CF_HDROP format
    STGMEDIUM medium;
    FORMATETC fe = {CF_HDROP, NULL, DVASPECT_CONTENT, -1, TYMED_HGLOBAL};
    HRESULT hr = lpdobj->GetData(&fe, &medium);
    if(FAILED(hr))
        return E_INVALIDARG;
    HDROP hDrop = static_cast<HDROP>(medium.hGlobal);

    if(DragQueryFile(hDrop, 0xFFFFFFFF, NULL, 0) == 1)
    {
        DragQueryFile(hDrop, 0, m_szFile, sizeof(m_szFile));
        hr = NOERROR;
    }
    else
        hr = E_INVALIDARG;

    ReleaseStgMedium(&medium);
    return hr;
}
```

Because property sheets are common controls, we need to initialize the appropriate library. This also means that you have to `#include commctrl.h` and import the `comct132.lib` library.

After getting hold of the selected files by the technique I described earlier in this section, I check how many there are. For the sake of simplicity, if there is more than one file selected, I just exit the function; that's what this code does:

```
if(DragQueryFile(hDrop, 0xFFFFFFFF, NULL, 0) == 1)
{
    ...
}
```

When called as above, `DragQueryFile()` returns the number of selected files. The next line then extracts the first and only file (it has an index of 0) and stores its name in the `m_szFile` buffer:

```
DragQueryFile(hDrop, 0, m_szFile, sizeof(m_szFile));
```

Finally, when all this activity is complete, it's time to release the storage medium by issuing a call to `ReleaseStgMedium()`.

Code for AddPages()

The code for `AddPages()` is as follows:

```
HRESULT CPropPage::AddPages(LPFNADDPROPSHEETPAGE lpfnAddPage, LPARAM lParam)
{
    lstrcpy(g_szFile, m_szFile);

    // Fill out the PROPSHEETPAGE structure needed to create a new page
    PROPSHEETPAGE psp;
    ZeroMemory(&psp, sizeof(PROPSHEETPAGE));
    psp.dwSize = sizeof(PROPSHEETPAGE);
    psp.dwFlags = PSP_USEREFPARENT | PSP_USETITLE | PSP_DEFAULT;
    psp.hInstance = _Module.GetModuleInstance();
    psp.pszTemplate = MAKEINTRESOURCE(IDD_WMFPROP);
    psp.pszTitle = __TEXT("Preview");
    psp.pfnDlgProc = PropPage_DlgProc;
    psp.lParam = reinterpret_cast<LPARAM>(g_szFile); // Custom data for dlgproc
    psp.pcRefParent = reinterpret_cast<UINT*>(&_Module.m_nLockCnt);

    // Create the new page
    HPROPSHEETPAGE hPage = ::CreatePropertySheetPage(&psp);

    // Add the page to the property sheet
    if(hPage != NULL)
    {
        if(!lpfnAddPage(hPage, lParam))
            ::DestroyPropertySheetPage(hPage);
        return NOERROR;
    }
    return E_INVALIDARG;
}
```

The new page contains a dialog that must have neither caption nor border, and the `pszTemplate` member of the `PROPSHEETPAGE` structure is set to contain its ID in the above code. I designed my dialog to contain a single `Picture` control with the `SS_ENHMETAFILE` style that I called `IDC_METAFILE`; adding a dialog template to the project resources is always necessary for a property sheet shell extension.

However, a dialog requires a dialog procedure to handle all the controls it includes. In the example here, `PropPage_DlgProc()` simply responds to `WM_INITDIALOG` and draws the metafile, for which purpose I've used the functions that I defined in the previous chapter. Since the dialog procedure can't access the members of the class, I pass the name of the file to be displayed through the `lParam` field of the `PROPSHEETPAGE` structure, and the dialog procedure receives a pointer to this data structure as the `lParam` argument of the `WM_INITDIALOG` message.

```
BOOL CALLBACK PropPage_DlgProc(
                        HWND hwnd, UINT uiMsg, WPARAM wParam, LPARAM lParam)
{
    switch(uiMsg)
    {
    case WM_INITDIALOG:
        HWND hwndMeta = GetDlgItem(hwnd, IDC_METAFILE);
        LPPROPSHEETPAGE lppsp = reinterpret_cast<LPPROPSHEETPAGE>(lParam);
        DisplayMetaFile(hwndMeta, reinterpret_cast<LPTSTR>(lppsp->lParam));
        return FALSE;
    }
    return FALSE;
}
```

Registering Shell Extensions

As I said earlier, a shell extension won't work if you fail to register it correctly: Explorer will not be able to find the module to load. Each and every shell extension is tied to a certain file object, be that a file type (say, EMF), or a generic object (like `Folder`). Thus, when you're registering a shell extension, you need to consider whether you need to add information to install the file type as well. This is not necessary if you're writing shell extensions for system file types like BMP, TXT, `Folder` or *. However, for custom file types (say, XYZ), or file types that are not defined by default (as is the case for EMF and WMF), you should make sure that the registration information has already been entered.

Assuming that the file types involved *are* correctly registered, I still need to add a few lines to the standard registry script produced by the ATL Wizard. These lines will associate the shell extension with the file type or types that it will work with. In this case, the shell extension must be tied to both WMF and EMF files. In the last chapter, I registered these types under the following keys:

```
HKEY_CLASSES_ROOT
    \WinMetafile
```

for WMFs, and

```
HKEY_CLASSES_ROOT
    \EnhMetafile
```

for EMFs.

A shell extension must be registered under the `shellex` sub-key of the specified file class's key. Under `shellex`, you'll need to create additional keys to group the various types of extensions, and these have specific names. To register a property sheet shell extension, you should create a key called `PropertySheetHandlers`, under which you can list the CLSID of all the property sheet shell extensions for that file class.

> *In case that sounds a little strange, there are shell extension types that allow you to define multiple servers for the same file class, to be called sequentially. For instance, it's perfectly possible to have three COM servers implementing three different extensions to the context menu for bitmap files. This is true for all the shell extension types except those that handle the clipboard and dragging-and-dropping with the left button, but I'll wait until discussing these types later in the chapter before saying more on this issue.*

The following listing shows how the default registry script should be changed to register a property sheet shell extension correctly.

```
HKCR
{
    WMFProp.PropPage.1 = s 'PropPage Class'
    {
        CLSID = s '{0D0E3558-8011-11D2-8CDB-505850C10000}'
    }
    WMFProp.PropPage = s 'PropPage Class'
    {
        CLSID = s '{0D0E3558-8011-11D2-8CDB-505850C10000}'
        CurVer = s 'WMFProp.PropPage.1'
    }
    NoRemove CLSID
    {
        ForceRemove {0D0E3558-8011-11D2-8CDB-505850C10000} = s 'PropPage Class'
        {
            ProgID = s 'WMFProp.PropPage.1'
            VersionIndependentProgID = s 'WMFProp.PropPage'
            ForceRemove 'Programmable'
            InprocServer32 = s '%MODULE%'
            {
                val ThreadingModel = s 'Apartment'
            }
            'TypeLib' = s '{0D0E354B-8011-11D2-8CDB-505850C10000}'
        }
    }

    WinMetafile
    {
        Shellex
        {
            PropertySheetHandlers
            {
                {0D0E3558-8011-11D2-8CDB-505850C10000}
            }
        }
    }

    EnhMetafile
    {
        Shellex
        {
            PropertySheetHandlers
            {
                {0D0E3558-8011-11D2-8CDB-505850C10000}
            }
        }
    }
}
```

The next picture illustrates the state of the registry after the registration of enhanced metafiles. Notice the presence of *three* property sheet shell extensions. If we have other shell extensions for enhanced metafiles – to manage the context menu, for example – they will be registered in the same way but under a new sub-tree, located at the same level as PropertySheetHandlers.

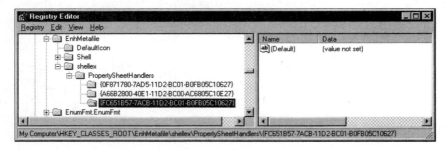

Now that the shell extension is registered correctly, you should be able to right-click on EMF or WMF files and get behavior something like this:

Testing Shell Extensions

So far, we've written and registered a shell extension. Now it's time to see if everything works as it ought to. The only way to run a shell extension is to start up Explorer and perform the action that causes the shell extension to come into play, but it can be tricky to convince Explorer that your extension exists!

In certain cases, you will need to log off or even restart the machine to cause the shell to load the updated version of your extension. In other cases, a simple shutdown of Explorer is fine, and you can use the Taskbar utility we built back in Chapter 9 to do so. I have also experienced circumstances in which pressing *F5* suffices, but there appears to be no method that will *always* work, other than rebooting the machine.

See the section entitled A Shell Extension Developer's Handbook *at the end of this chapter for more discussion on this topic.*

These little difficulties aside, suppose now that you're running your extension. Things get complicated when you detect an error and need to debug the code to find the point at which the problem is occurring. Debugging a shell extension is not an intuitive task, and we need to examine carefully how to proceed.

The first step is to set `explorer.exe` as the executable for the debug session. This is necessary because a shell extension is a DLL and not a stand-alone executable. Note that you need to specify the full path to Explorer:

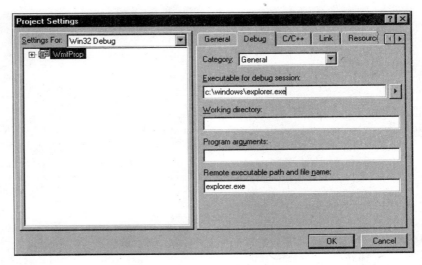

The next step is to make sure that you have the shell extension project open in the Visual C++ IDE. The trick is to stop the shell and then cause a new instance of it to run under the debugger, which is harder than it sounds.

If you simply run the debugger, you cause a new Explorer window to appear, but this doesn't mean that a new shell process has started. For debugging to take place, you first need to terminate the shell process without terminating the other processes on the machine. Then, next time you run the debugger, it will actually create a new, 'debuggable' shell process.

To stop the shell, you can programmatically send a `WM_QUIT` message to the only window of class `Progman`. (I covered this technique in Chapter 9.) To do it manually, follow this procedure:

❑ Select Sh<u>u</u>t Down... from the Start menu and click Cancel while holding down *Ctrl-Alt-Shift*. It's not an easy thing to do, but it works! When you do this, the taskbar disappears and you'll feel abandoned by the system, but don't be tempted to reboot the machine! There's nothing wrong and everything is under control.

❑ Use the *Alt-Tab* keys to bring the Visual C++ window to the top, and run the debugger. Now the taskbar will be visible again. It's a brand new shell process running under the Visual C++ debugger.

❑ Now do what you would do to debug any program: click on the <u>B</u>uild I Start <u>D</u>ebug I <u>G</u>o menu item. When the Explorer window shows up, perform an action that will cause the shell extension to load. In the sample we've been discussing so far, you could select a WMF file, right-click, and open the Properties dialog box.

The breakpoints you've put in the code are now detected as usual, and cause processing to stop when they're hit. When you've finished debugging, double clicking on the desktop will bring the Task Manager window to the foreground:

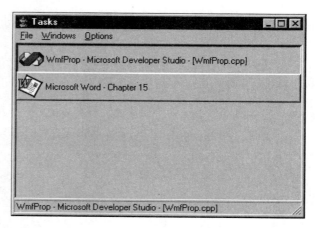

Choose File | Run, launch Explorer, and everything will be restored to the way it was before. I agree that it's not exactly the kind of thing you'd want to do every day, but it does work.

Interestingly, Control Panel applets – which always comprise a series of tabbed pages – don't run in Explorer's address space. This means that you can't use the technique described above to debug them. Instead, you should specify rundll32.exe *as the executable for the debug session. (See* Further Reading *for more details.)*

Debugging under Windows NT

If you want to do your testing under Windows NT, then I recommend that you add a value under the following key:

```
HKEY_CURRENT_USER
    \Software
        \Microsoft
            \Windows
                \CurrentVersion
                    \Explorer
```

The value to be added is called DesktopProcess, and it must be a REG_DWORD value set to 1. If you set it and then log on again, you'll find that the Windows NT shell is divided into two parts – the desktop, the taskbar and the tray area run in a separate process from folders and files. When you run Explorer from within the Visual C++ environment now, you really are starting a new process that you can debug. Moreover, any crashes won't affect the stability of the system desktop.

Unloading a Shell Extension

Another interesting topic of shell extension testing is determining when a shell extension is going to be *unloaded*. Like any COM object, a shell extension is the target of a continuous stream of unloading requests issued through DllCanUnloadNow(). Depending on its internal reference count, the module can decide whether it may be unloaded.

There is no automatic mechanism that removes a module whose reference count has become zero from memory, and so the sooner Explorer calls `DllCanUnloadNow()`, the sooner an unused shell extension is unloaded. Note that an unloaded shell extension also means that the module can safely be recompiled, which is a pretty important aspect to consider during the development process of a shell extension.

By default, Explorer attempts to unload a shell extension every ten seconds or so. The documentation claims that you can make such attempts more frequent by setting the `Default` value of the following key to 1:

```
HKEY_LOCAL_MACHINE
    \Software
        \Microsoft
            \Windows
                \CurrentVersion
                    \Explorer
                        \AlwaysUnloadDll
```

In my tests on machines running Windows 95/NT with Active Desktop and higher, I didn't see a great deal of difference — attempts to unload the shell extension appeared to be a *bit* more frequent, which I discovered by dumping the time of each unloading attempt to a file. With the retail version of Windows 95, however, there was a really substantial difference: ten *minutes* with `AlwaysUnloadDll` set to 0, against ten *seconds* with it set to 1.

More on Property Page Shell Extensions

The above example only worked if you had a single file selected, but there's nothing to preventing us from adding a separate property sheet for each selected file, like this:

The changes required to the code aren't major, and it's even possible to make it so that you can run both extensions at the same time — Explorer will manage them sequentially. The only drawback is that you may have additional copies of some property pages. Let's see what changes we need to make.

Modifying the Code to Support Multiple Selection

The first and most obvious thing to do is change the class declaration of the shell extension to make it reflect the fact that we no longer have a single file to keep track of, but a list of file names. This list has an upper limit, though, because prsht.h (the header file for property sheets) limits the number of pages on any one sheet to 100. The mnemonic constant name is MAXPROPPAGES.

That said, it's very unlikely you'll manage to fit 100 pages on a single tab control — I've noticed the control never exceeds six rows of pages, giving a more reasonable maximum of 30-35 pages. Here, then, is the new version of IShellPropSheetExt.h:

```
// IShellPropSheetExtImpl.h (Multi-selection version)
//
////////////////////////////////////////////////////////////////////
#include <AtlCom.h>
#include <ShlObj.h>

class ATL_NO_VTABLE IShellPropSheetExtImpl : public IShellPropSheetExt
{
public:
    TCHAR m_aFiles[MAXPROPPAGES][MAX_PATH];
    int m_iNumOfFiles;

    // IUnknown
    STDMETHOD(QueryInterface)(REFIID riid, void** ppvObject) = 0;
    _ATL_DEBUG_ADDREF_RELEASE_IMPL(IShellPropSheetExtImpl)

    // IShellPropSheetExt
    STDMETHOD(AddPages)(LPFNADDPROPSHEETPAGE, LPARAM)
    {
        return S_FALSE;
    }

    STDMETHOD(ReplacePage)(UINT, LPFNADDPROPSHEETPAGE, LPARAM)
    {
        return E_NOTIMPL;
    }
};
```

The code in the implementations of both Initialize() and AddPages() also changes slightly. Here is the new Initialize():

```
HRESULT CPropPage::Initialize(
                LPCITEMIDLIST pidlFolder, LPDATAOBJECT lpdobj, HKEY hKeyProgID)
{
    if(lpdobj == NULL)
        return E_INVALIDARG;

    // Initialize common controls
    InitCommonControls();

    // Get the data in CF_HDROP format
    STGMEDIUM medium;
    FORMATETC fe = {CF_HDROP, NULL, DVASPECT_CONTENT, -1, TYMED_HGLOBAL};
    HRESULT hr = lpdobj->GetData(&fe, &medium);
    if(FAILED(hr))
        return E_INVALIDARG;
    HDROP hDrop = static_cast<HDROP>(medium.hGlobal);
```

```
        // Get the number of selected files
        m_iNumOfFiles = DragQueryFile(hDrop, 0xFFFFFFFF, NULL, 0);

        // Normalize it to the maximum number allowed
        m_iNumOfFiles = (m_iNumOfFiles >= MAXPROPPAGES ?
                                             MAXPROPPAGES : m_iNumOfFiles);

        // Extract and manage all the selected files
        for(int i = 0 ; i < m_iNumOfFiles ; i++)
            DragQueryFile(hDrop, i, m_aFiles[i], MAX_PATH);


    ReleaseStgMedium(&medium);
    return hr;
}
```

Now all the files are stored in an array of filenames. They will be processed one after another in `AddPages()`:

```
    HRESULT CPropPage::AddPages(LPFNADDPROPSHEETPAGE lpfnAddPage, LPARAM lParam)
    {
        for(int i = 0 ; i < m_iNumOfFiles ; i++)
        {
            // Check if the selected file is a metafile
            LPTSTR p = PathFindExtension(m_aFiles[i]);
            if(lstrcmpi(p, __TEXT(".WMF")) && lstrcmpi(p, __TEXT(".EMF")))
                continue;

            // Allocate the string to pass. Will be freed in the dlgproc.
            LPTSTR psz = new TCHAR[MAX_PATH];
            lstrcpy(psz, m_aFiles[i]);

            // Strip path and extension for the title
            LPTSTR pszTitle = PathFindFileName(m_aFiles[i]);
            PathRemoveExtension(pszTitle);


            // Fill out the PROPSHEETPAGE structure
            PROPSHEETPAGE psp;
            ZeroMemory(&psp, sizeof(PROPSHEETPAGE));
            psp.dwSize = sizeof(PROPSHEETPAGE);
            psp.dwFlags = PSP_USEREFPARENT | PSP_USETITLE | PSP_DEFAULT;
            psp.hInstance = _Module.GetModuleInstance();
            psp.pszTemplate = MAKEINTRESOURCE(IDD_WMFPROP);
            psp.pszTitle = pszTitle;
            psp.pfnDlgProc = PropPage_DlgProc;
            psp.lParam = reinterpret_cast<LPARAM>(psz);
            psp.pcRefParent = reinterpret_cast<UINT*>(&_Module.m_nLockCnt);

            HPROPSHEETPAGE hPage = ::CreatePropertySheetPage(&psp);

            // Add the page to the property sheet
            if(hPage != NULL)
                if(!lpfnAddPage(hPage, lParam))
                    :: DestroyPropertySheetPage(hPage);
        }
        return NOERROR;
    }
```

There are a few things to note about this version of AddPages(). First of all, I've set the title of the property page to the name of the file without path and extension, by using some of the functions from shlwapi.dll that I covered in Chapter 10. Of course, this makes it necessary to #include <shlwapi.h>, and to link to shlwapi.lib.

Second, one of the comments in the listing refers to having to delete in the dialog procedure the pointer that was allocated with new in the for loop, and so PropPage_DlgProc() now looks like this:

```
BOOL CALLBACK PropPage_DlgProc(
                        HWND hwnd, UINT uiMsg, WPARAM wParam, LPARAM lParam)
{
    switch(uiMsg)
    {
    case WM_INITDIALOG:
        HWND hwndMeta = GetDlgItem(hwnd, IDC_METAFILE);
        LPPROPSHEETPAGE lppsp = reinterpret_cast<LPPROPSHEETPAGE>(lParam);
        DisplayMetaFile(hwndMeta, reinterpret_cast<LPTSTR>(lppsp->lParam));
        delete [] reinterpret_cast<LPTSTR>(lppsp->lParam);
        return FALSE;
    }
    return FALSE;
}
```

Finally, the function now distinguishes WMF/EMF files from other types – it accepts the former and discards the latter. When a number of files are selected, you can't be sure that they will all be of the same type. That means when you right-click to get the **Properties** dialog, you won't necessarily be selecting a file of the expected type, and so there's no guarantee that your extension will be used. For example, if you select an EMF and a BMP file, and ask for the **Properties** dialog by right clicking on the BMP file name, you'll get the dialog for the BMP. On the other hand, if all your files are metafiles, or if you right-click on a metafile, here's what you could get:

Context Menu

When it comes to adding new items to a context menu, shell extensions are the most flexible technique because they give you total control over events. In the previous chapter, I examined a means of achieving the same task based on registry manipulation, but that involved an external piece of code coming into play. With shell extensions, you run a piece of code that communicates *directly* with the shell, receiving and returning information. If you write and register a context menu shell extension, you'll be given a chance to specify a menu item string, a status bar description and a behavior *every time the menu is displayed*. If you really want to, you can change them each time programmatically, without having to modify anything in the registry.

Implementing IContextMenu

Arranging a context menu shell extension means writing a COM server that implements the `IContextMenu` interface. Apart from this change, you don't need to do anything else that I haven't already described in the previous example. `IContextMenu` has three functions, over and above the three of `IUnknown`:

- ❏ `GetCommandString()`
- ❏ `InvokeCommand()`
- ❏ `QueryContextMenu()`

They retrieve a description for the menu item, execute some code in response to a click, and add a new command to the menu respectively.

Help Text for the New Item

`GetCommandString()` has a prototype like this:

```
HRESULT GetCommandString(
    UINT   idCmd,        // ID of the menu command that needs a description
    UINT   uFlags,       // Specifies what to do (see later)
    UINT*  pwReserved,   // Reserved. Always set to NULL
    LPSTR  pszName,      // Buffer to receive the string retrieved (Max 40)
    UINT   cchMax        // Actual length of the string retrieved
);
```

The valid `uFlags` for `GetCommandString()` are:

Flag	Description
GCS_HELPTEXT	The shell requires a descriptive string for the item
GCS_VALIDATE	The shell simply wants to know whether an item with this ID exists and is valid
GCS_VERB	The shell requires the language-independent name for the verb the menu item represents

As I explained earlier in the book (check out Chapter 8 in particular), a **verb** is a name that renders a command. Verbs can be executed through functions like `ShellExecute()` and `ShellExecuteEx()`.

When you add new menu items statically through the registry, the name of the key you create is the language-independent verb; the command behind it is hidden in a Command sub-key. When you add items dynamically, you should implement InvokeCommand() to provide a behavior (like the Command key does), and respond properly to the GCS_VERB flag to let the shell know about the verb of your new command.

Note that any help text you pass in will be truncated after 40 characters, although passing a longer string doesn't break anything but the text itself.

A Behavior for the New Item

InvokeCommand() is the method called when the user clicks on a custom context menu item. The prototype is:

```
HRESULT InvokeCommand(LPCMINVOKECOMMANDINFO lpici);
```

The CMINVOKECOMMANDINFO structure looks like this:

```
typedef struct _CMINVOKECOMMANDINFO
{
    DWORD   cbSize;
    DWORD   fMask;
    HWND    hwnd;
    LPCSTR  lpVerb;
    LPCSTR  lpParameters;
    LPCSTR  lpDirectory;
    INT     nShow;
    DWORD   dwHotKey;
    HANDLE  hIcon;
} CMINVOKECOMMANDINFO, *LPCMINVOKECOMMANDINFO;
```

Let's examine it in more detail.

Member	Description
cbSize	The size of the structure.
fMask	A bitmask to enable the dwHotkey and hIcon members, and to prevent any UI action, like message boxes (See later).
hwnd	Parent window of the menu.
lpVerb	A DWORD given by the ID of the command (with 0 in the high word), or a string denoting the verb to execute (See later).
lpParameters	Always NULL if the interface is called from the shell (See later).
lpDirectory	Always NULL if the interface is called from the shell (See later).
nShow	An SW_ constant to pass to ShowWindow() if a new application is started.
dwHotKey	The hot key to be assigned to an application started by the command. Ignored if fMask turns off its specific bit (See later).
hIcon	Icon to be assigned to an application started by the command. Ignored if fMask turns off its specific bit (See later).

The legal values for `fMask` are:

Values	Description
CMIC_MASK_HOTKEY	The `dwHotKey` member is valid
CMIC_MASK_ICON	The `hIcon` member is valid
CMIC_MASK_FLAG_NO_UI	No action that may affect the user interface (creating windows or message boxes, for example) should be taken

The `lpVerb` member is a 32-bit value, and its content can be determined in two ways. It *might* be the result of a call to

```
lpVerb = MAKEINTRESOURCE(idCmd, 0);
```

Here, `idCmd` is the ID of the menu item, but `lpVerb` can also denote the name of the verb to execute. In this case, the high-order word isn't zero, and the value is really a pointer to a string.

Like the other shell-related interfaces, `IContextMenu` can also be called from outside the shell, without a corresponding UI action over a shell element. Once you have an `IShellFolder` pointer, for example, you can ask it for an `IContextMenu` interface on the folder or the file object it's bound to. Then you can invoke a verb programmatically, using `IContextMenu` without going through the shell. In cases like this, `lpParameters` and `lpDirectory` might not be `NULL`.

More likely, you'll use `ShellExecuteEx()` to call a verb added dynamically by a shell extension. In this case, you can specify additional parameters and a working directory through the interface of the function, and these are the arguments that end up filling `lpParameters` and `lpDirectory`. (See Chapter 8 for details about `ShellExecuteEx()`.)

Adding a New Item

While it's creating the context menu for a given file object, the shell asks any registered context menu shell extension to add its own items by calling `QueryContextMenu()`. The prototype of this function is:

```
HRESULT QueryContextMenu(
    HMENU hmenu,        // Handle of the menu to which items are to be added
    UINT  indexMenu,    // Zero-based index of the first item to be added
    UINT  idCmdFirst,   // Lowest available command ID for the new item
    UINT  idCmdLast,    // Highest available command ID for the new item
    UINT  uFlags        // Attributes that affect the context menu
);
```

When adding a new menu item, the shell indicates the position at which the first item will be added, as well as the range of values from which to pick up the command ID. Here's a code snippet that shows the typical way to insert a new item from within `QueryContextMenu()`:

```
idCmd = idCmdFirst;
lstrcpy(szItem, ...);
InsertMenu(hMenu, indexMenu++, MF_STRING | MF_BYPOSITION, idCmd++, szItem);
```

Of all the documented flags available for the uFlags argument, we really only need to worry about two here: CMF_NORMAL and CMF_DEFAULTONLY. The others are not significant for a 'simple' shell extension, and apply mostly to namespace extensions (which I'll cover in the next chapter). However, here's the complete list:

Flags	Description
CMF_CANRENAME	If set, a namespace extension should add a Rename item.
CMF_DEFAULTONLY	The user double-clicked, so a namespace extension can add its default item. A shell extension shouldn't do anything, and in fact it should avoid adding items if this flag is set.
CMF_EXPLORE	Set when the Explorer tree window is open.
CMF_INCLUDESTATIC	Ignored by shell extensions.
CMF_NODEFAULT	The menu shouldn't have a default item. Ignored by shell extensions, but namespace extensions should refrain from defining a default item.
CMF_NORMAL	No special situation. Shell extensions can add their items.
CMF_NOVERBS	Ignored by shell extensions. Used for the Send To menu.
CMF_VERBSONLY	Ignored by shell extensions. Used for shortcut objects' menus.

You might be wondering why shell extensions should ignore flags that are useful to namespace extensions, or apply to special menus like Send To, or shortcuts. Isn't IContextMenu an interface for shell extensions?

Actually, the answer is no. IContextMenu is a generic COM interface for providing the functionality of a context menu. Almost all of the system menus can be extended by registering a context menu handler in the appropriate area of the registry – the shell loads it and thereby provides the possibility of adding and managing custom items. Thus, IContextMenu can be used to work outside the Explorer window as well, and I'll show you an example of this later on in the chapter. A namespace extension is a customized shell view, directly involved in providing a context menu to the user, so IContextMenu affects namespace extensions too.

The Return Value of QueryContextMenu()

Like other COM functions, QueryContextMenu() returns an HRESULT value. In many cases you use predefined constants, but just occasionally you need to format a specific return value. QueryContextMenu() is one of the functions that requires you to do this.

As you probably know, an HRESULT is a 32-bit value whose bits are split into three components: severity, facility, and code. QueryContextMenu() wants you to return a special value for the code, and zeros elsewhere. Specifically, you should return the number of menu items added. To format an HRESULT, the MAKE_HRESULT() macro is extremely helpful:

```
return MAKE_HRESULT(SEVERITY_SUCCESS, FACILITY_NULL, idCmd - idCmdList);
```

A Dependency List for Executables

Let's put everything you've learned about context menus so far into practice. When you walk through Explorer, you come across hundreds of executables. Wouldn't it be nice if someone could tell you what libraries those programs reference? The list of the modules statically referenced by a program is known as its **dependency list**. (See *Further Reading*.)

By scanning the binary format of a Win32 executable (and assuming a good understanding of the Win32 Portable Executable format), it's possible to extract the names of all the DLLs an application needs. In this example, we're going to implement a tool for this purpose as a context menu for EXE or DLL files.

Before going any further, let's clarify a few things. Firstly, the tool won't need to run the application – it will limit itself to examining the bytes. Secondly, it will be capable of retrieving only those DLLs *explicitly* imported in the code. This is because only DLLs that are statically linked to the project leave a footprint in code; if a program loads a DLL dynamically through LoadLibrary(), the DLL is not referenced in the import table, and we can't trace it.

Creating a Context Menu Extension

I'm not going cover the nitty-gritty details of how to get the dependency list of a Win32 executable, because it's a pretty complex topic that lies at the margins of this book's scope. If you're interested, see the *Further Reading* section for a list of books and articles that cover the subject at the lowest level of detail. In this example, I'll be using a shortcut that takes advantage of a relatively new system DLL called ImageHlp. This library doesn't expose a specific function to get the file names, but by making clever use of one of its routines, there are ways to work it out.

To begin, use the ATL COM AppWizard to create a DLL project called Depends, and add a new simple object called ExeMenu, accepting all the default options. This will be the object that implements the interfaces required for a context menu shell extension: IContextMenu and IShellExtInit. Here are the changes you need to make to the main header file, ExeMenu.h:

```
#include "resource.h"              // Main symbols
#include "IContextMenuImpl.h"      // IContextMenu
#include "IShellExtInitImpl.h"     // IShellExtInit
#include "DepListView.h"           // Dialog
#include <comdef.h>                // Interface IDs

/////////////////////////////////////////////////////////////////////////////
// CCExeMenu
class ATL_NO_VTABLE CExeMenu :
    public CComObjectRootEx<CComSingleThreadModel>,
    public CComCoClass<CExeMenu, &CLSID_CExeMenu>,
    public IShellExtInitImpl,
    public IContextMenuImpl,
    public IDispatchImpl<IExeMenu, &IID_IExeMenu, &LIBID_DEPENDSLib>
{
public:
    CExeMenu()
    {
    }
```

```
        TCHAR m_szFile[MAX_PATH];          // Name of the executable
        CDepListView m_Dlg;                // Dialog that shows the results

        // IContextMenu
        STDMETHOD(GetCommandString)(UINT, UINT, UINT*, LPSTR, UINT);
        STDMETHOD(InvokeCommand)(LPCMINVOKECOMMANDINFO);
        STDMETHOD(QueryContextMenu)(HMENU, UINT, UINT , UINT, UINT);

        // IShellExtInit
        STDMETHOD(Initialize)(LPCITEMIDLIST, LPDATAOBJECT, HKEY);

    DECLARE_REGISTRY_RESOURCEID(IDR_EXEMENU)

    DECLARE_PROTECT_FINAL_CONSTRUCT()

    BEGIN_COM_MAP(CExeMenu)
        COM_INTERFACE_ENTRY(IExeMenu)
        COM_INTERFACE_ENTRY(IDispatch)
        COM_INTERFACE_ENTRY(IShellExtInit)
        COM_INTERFACE_ENTRY(IContextMenu)
    END_COM_MAP()

    // IExeMenu
    public:
    };
```

The `CExeMenu` class derives from `IShellExtInitImpl` and `IContextMenuImpl`, two ATL classes that provide basic implementations of the `IShellExtInit` and `IContextMenu` interfaces. The `IShellExtInitImpl.h` header file is identical to the one we used in the previous example, while `IContextMenuImpl.h` looks like this:

```
// IContextMenuImpl.h

#include <AtlCom.h>
#include <ShlObj.h>

class ATL_NO_VTABLE IContextMenuImpl : public IContextMenu
{
public:

    // Data
    TCHAR m_szFile[MAX_PATH];

    // IUnknown
    STDMETHOD(QueryInterface)(REFIID riid, void** ppvObject) = 0;
    _ATL_DEBUG_ADDREF_RELEASE_IMPL(IContextMenuImpl)

    // IContextMenu
    STDMETHOD(GetCommandString)(UINT, UINT, UINT*, LPSTR, UINT)
    {
        return S_FALSE;
    }

    STDMETHOD(InvokeCommand)(LPCMINVOKECOMMANDINFO)
    {
        return S_FALSE;
    }
```

```
    STDMETHOD(QueryContextMenu)(HMENU, UINT, UINT , UINT, UINT)
    {
        return S_FALSE;
    }
};
```

Once again, the implementations here are minimal, to say the least. In other situations, you might want to prepare more effective classes and increase the quantity of reusable code, but this will suffice for our purposes. All that remains now is to provide the code for the various functions of the two interfaces involved, and all that goes in ExeMenu.cpp:

```
// QueryContextMenu
HRESULT CExeMenu::QueryContextMenu(
        HMENU hmenu, UINT indexMenu, UINT idCmdFirst, UINT idCmdLast, UINT uFlags)
{
    // This shell extension is intended to provide a 'Dependency List'
    //  item on the context menu for EXE files.
    UINT idCmd = idCmdFirst;

    // Add the new item
    InsertMenu(hmenu, indexMenu++, MF_STRING | MF_BYPOSITION,
                                        idCmd++, __TEXT("Dependency &List"));

    return MAKE_HRESULT(SEVERITY_SUCCESS, FACILITY_NULL, idCmd - idCmdFirst);
}

// InvokeCommand
HRESULT CExeMenu::InvokeCommand(LPCMINVOKECOMMANDINFO lpcmi)
{
    // Creates a modal dialog to display the information
    lstrcpy(m_Dlg.m_szFile, m_szFile);
    m_Dlg.DoModal();
    return S_OK;
}

// GetCommandString
HRESULT CExeMenu::GetCommandString(
        UINT idCmd, UINT uFlags, UINT* pwReserved, LPSTR pszText, UINT cchMax)
{
    // We don't care about the command ID, since we have a single item
    if(uFlags & GCS_HELPTEXT)
        lstrcpyn(
            pszText, __TEXT("Displays all the DLLs needed by the module"), cchMax);
    return S_OK;
}

// Initialize
HRESULT CExeMenu::Initialize(
                LPCITEMIDLIST pidlFolder, LPDATAOBJECT lpdobj, HKEY hKeyProgID)
{
    if(lpdobj == NULL)
        return E_INVALIDARG;

    // Get the data as CF_HDROP
    STGMEDIUM medium;
    FORMATETC fe = {CF_HDROP, NULL, DVASPECT_CONTENT, -1, TYMED_HGLOBAL};
    HRESULT hr = lpdobj->GetData(&fe, &medium);
    if(FAILED(hr))
        return E_INVALIDARG;
```

```
        // Get the name of the selected file
        DragQueryFile(reinterpret_cast<HDROP>(medium.hGlobal), 0, m_szFile, MAX_PATH);

        ReleaseStgMedium(&medium);
        return hr;
    };
```

As you can see, the code for `Initialize()` is nearly identical to what we had in the same function for our earlier property pages example.

Initializing a Context Menu Extension

I said earlier that the role of the parameters of `Initialize()` were different for different types of shell extensions. For context menu extensions, the `pidlFolder` argument is a PIDL for the folder that contains the selected file objects. These file objects are pointed to by `lpdobj` through the `IDataObject` interface that we met in the last example. The `hKeyProgID` parameter specifies the file class of the selected file object, and if several objects are selected, it refers to the one that has the focus.

Getting an Executable's Dependency List

My goal for this extension is that when the user clicks on the Dependency List menu item:

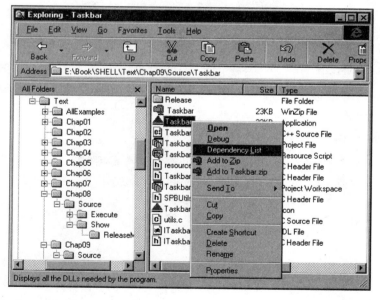

The shell will call into the `InvokeCommand()` method that causes a dialog to pop up. In the screenshot, notice the text on the status bar, which is the string we provided through `GetCommandString()`.

I added a dialog using the ATL Object Wizard, giving it the name `DepListView` and adding a public data member called `m_szFile` to hold the filename:

```
enum {IDD = IDD_DEPLISTVIEW};
TCHAR m_szFile[MAX_PATH];
```

The initialization of the dialog then takes place in its `OnInitDialog()` method, which requires `shlobj.h` and `windowsx.h` to be included at the top of `DepListView.h`:

```cpp
LRESULT CDepListView::OnInitDialog(
                    UINT uMsg, WPARAM wParam, LPARAM lParam, BOOL& bHandled)
{
    // Prepare the listview. Uses functions defined in previous chapters
    HWND hwndList = GetDlgItem(IDC_LIST);
    LPTSTR pszCols[] = {__TEXT("Library"), reinterpret_cast<TCHAR*>(280),
                        __TEXT("Version"), reinterpret_cast<TCHAR*>(103)};
    MakeReportView(hwndList, pszCols, 2);

    // Set the file name using an ellipsis if it's too long
    TCHAR szTemp[60] = {0};
    PathCompactPathEx(szTemp, m_szFile, 60, '\\');
    SetDlgItemText(IDC_FILENAME, szTemp);

    // Get the size of the import table
    int iNumOfBytes = GetImportTableSize(m_szFile);
    if(iNumOfBytes <= 0)
        return 0;

    // Get the COM allocator and reserve some memory
    LPMALLOC pM = NULL;
    SHGetMalloc(&pM);
    LPTSTR psz = static_cast<LPTSTR>(pM->Alloc(iNumOfBytes));
    if(psz == NULL)
    {
        ::MessageBox(0, __TEXT("Not enough memory!"), 0, MB_ICONSTOP);
        pM->Release();
        return 0;
    }
    ZeroMemory(psz, iNumOfBytes);

    // Access the import table
    int iNumOfLibs = GetImportTable(m_szFile, psz);
    if(iNumOfLibs <= 0)
    {
        pM->Release();
        return 0;
    }

    int i = 0;
    while(i < iNumOfLibs)
    {
        // p formats a null-separated string for the list view
        TCHAR buf[2048] = {0};
        LPTSTR p = buf;

        lstrcpy(p, psz);
        lstrcat(p, __TEXT("\0"));
        p += lstrlen(p) + 1;
```

```
        // Get the version info
        TCHAR szInfo[30] = {0};
        SHGetVersionOfFile(psz, szInfo, NULL, 0);
        lstrcpy(p, szInfo);
        lstrcat(p, __TEXT("\0"));
        p += lstrlen(p) + 1;

        // Add the string
        AddStringToReportView(hwndList, buf, 2);

        // Next library
        psz += lstrlen(psz) + 1;
        i++;
    }

    pM->Release();

    return 1;
}
```

First, we format the report list view by adding a couple of columns to host the file name and the version number. Second, we read in the import table for the executable module and format a NULL-separated string. In order to arrange the dialog you can see here, I've reused some of the functions that we developed in earlier chapters – in particular, MakeReportView() and AddStringToReportView() from **Chapter 6** and SHGetVersionOfFile() from **Chapter 10**.

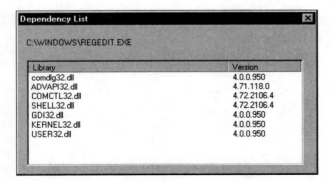

The picture shows the final dialog, which is composed of a report list view whose identifier is IDC_LIST, and a text label named IDC_FILENAME.

Notice also that I've utilized the PathCompactPathEx() function from shlwapi.dll to force the file name to a fixed number of characters – it inserts an ellipsis automatically to cut text off when it gets too long.

I said earlier that I wasn't going to go into detail about exactly how we get the dependency list, but there are a few things about the process that are worth mentioning. The ImageHlp API, which is available on both Windows 9x and Windows NT 4.0, provides functions to work on the memory image that an executable module produces. There are functions to walk the symbols, to map it into memory, and so on. (See the documentation in the MSDN Library for more information.)

In particular, we're interested in a function called `BindImageEx()`, which allows you to get the virtual address of any function that the executable imports from external libraries. Interestingly (from our point of view), the function accepts a callback routine to which it passes the name of each DLL it meets. By hooking these calls, we can easily figure out how many bytes are required to hold the entire list of names (`GetImportTableSize()`), and arrange a NULL-separated string with all the names (`GetImportTable()`).

We're going to provide these functions by means of a simple DLL, the header file for which (`DepList.h`) looks something like this, and should be `#include`'d at the top of `DepListView.h`:

```
#include <windows.h>
#include <imagehlp.h>

// Returns the bytes required to hold the names of the DLLs
int APIENTRY GetImportTableSize(LPCTSTR pszFileName);

// Fills the specified buffer with the name of the DLLs
int APIENTRY GetImportTable(LPCTSTR pszFileName, LPTSTR pszBuf);
```

The greater part of the source code, of course, comes in `DepList.cpp`:

```
#pragma comment(lib, "imagehlp.lib")
#include "DepList.h"

/*-------------------------------------------------------------*/
//                  GLOBAL section
/*-------------------------------------------------------------*/

// Data
LPTSTR* g_ppszBuf = NULL;
int g_iNumOfBytes = 0;
int g_iNumOfDLLs = 0;

// Callbacks
BOOL CALLBACK SizeOfDLLs(IMAGEHLP_STATUS_REASON, LPSTR, LPSTR, ULONG, ULONG);
BOOL CALLBACK GetDLLs(IMAGEHLP_STATUS_REASON, LPSTR, LPSTR, ULONG, ULONG);

/*-------------------------------------------------------------*/
// Procedure...: GetImportTableSize()
/*-------------------------------------------------------------*/
int APIENTRY GetImportTableSize(LPCTSTR pszFileName)
{
    g_iNumOfBytes = 0;

    // Bind to the executable
    BindImageEx(BIND_NO_BOUND_IMPORTS | BIND_NO_UPDATE,
                const_cast<LPTSTR>(pszFileName), NULL, NULL, SizeOfDLLs);
    return g_iNumOfBytes;
}
```

The prototype of `BindImageEx()` is as follows:

```
BOOL BindImageEx(DWORD                        dwFlags,
                 LPSTR                        pszFileName,
                 LPSTR                        pszFilePath,
                 LPSTR                        pszSymbolPath,
                 PIMAGEHLP_STATUS_ROUTINE pfnStatusProc);
```

You have to specify the filename you want to work with in `pszFileName`, and this may or may not include a path. If not, you can use `pszFilePath` to specify a root path in which to search for `pszFileName`. More importantly, this function accepts a callback routine in `pfnStatusProc` that gets invoked while the function binds to the specified executable. Here's the prototype of this callback:

```
BOOL CALLBACK BindStatusProc(IMAGEHLP_STATUS_REASON Reason,
                              LPSTR                  ImageName,
                              LPSTR                  DllName,
                              ULONG                  Va,
                              ULONG                  Parameter);
```

The only parameters I'm interested in are `Reason` and `DllName`. The purpose of the second of these is obvious, while the first one lets you filter the numerous calls made to the function for the ones you're actually interested in. I only want to know how many bytes are needed to store all the modules referred, and which modules these are. `SizeOfDLLs()` is a callback function that returns the size of the file import table, and `GetDLLs()` returns a NULL-separated string obtained by concatenating the names of all the modules bound by the call to `BindImageEx()`. This string is then combined with version information to produce the output you can see in the previous screenshot.

```
/*------------------------------------------------------------*/
// Procedure...: GetImportTable
/*------------------------------------------------------------*/
int APIENTRY GetImportTable(LPCTSTR pszFileName, LPTSTR pszBuf)
{
    g_ppszBuf = &pszBuf;
    g_iNumOfDLLs = 0;

    // Bind to the executable
    BindImageEx(BIND_NO_BOUND_IMPORTS | BIND_NO_UPDATE,
            const_cast<LPTSTR>(pszFileName), NULL, NULL, GetDLLs);
    return g_iNumOfDLLs;
}


/*------------------------------------------------------------*/
// Procedure...: SizeOfDLLs()
// Description.: Callback for calculating the size of DLLs
/*------------------------------------------------------------*/
BOOL CALLBACK SizeOfDLLs(IMAGEHLP_STATUS_REASON Reason,
            LPSTR ImageName, LPSTR DllName, ULONG Va, ULONG Parameter)
{
    if(Reason == BindImportModule || Reason == BindImportModuleFailed)
        g_iNumOfBytes += lstrlen(DllName) + 1;
    return TRUE;
}


/*------------------------------------------------------------*/
// Procedure...: GetDLLs()
// Description.: Callback for packaging a string
/*------------------------------------------------------------*/
```

```
BOOL CALLBACK GetDLLs(IMAGEHLP_STATUS_REASON Reason, LPSTR ImageName,
                      LPSTR DllName, ULONG Va, ULONG Parameter)
{
   if(Reason == BindImportModule || Reason == BindImportModuleFailed)
   {
      lstrcpy(*g_ppszBuf, DllName);
      *g_ppszBuf += lstrlen(*g_ppszBuf) + 1;
      g_iNumOfDLLs++;
   }
   return TRUE;
}
```

Finally, the functions are exported by the `DepList.def` file:

```
EXPORTS
   GetImportTableSize      @1
   GetImportTable          @2
```

At this point, provided that you're set up with all the appropriate import libraries, you should be able to compile and link the code we've put together so far. We're not quite out of the woods yet, though.

Registering the Extension

This listing shows the modifications that need to be added to the end of the ATL script code in `ExeMenu.rgs` in order to register our shell extension.

```
Exefile
{
   Shellex
   {
      ContextMenuHandlers
      {
         {20349851-699F-11D2-9DAF-00104B4C822A}
      }
   }
}
Dllfile
{
   Shellex
   {
      ContextMenuHandlers
      {
         {20349851-699F-11D2-9DAF-00104B4C822A}
      }
   }
}
}
```

With these changes in place, you'll find that next time you start the shell, the context menu generated by right clicking on DLL or EXE files will have the new Dependency List item we've been working towards.

Adding a New Find Menu

Another interesting use we can make of context menu
extensions is to customize the list that appears next to
the Find menu. For example, we could add a tool that
lets us find all the currently running processes under
Windows 9*x* and Windows NT.

Provided that
we have a valid
context menu,
adding a new
'find' utility is
just a matter of
writing a few
pieces of
information to
the registry:

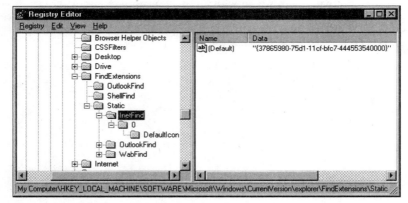

Under the Static key you can see, we need to add a new key called, say, FindProcess, and make
it the root of a new sub-tree. The Default value of this key must be the CLSID of the context menu
extension. Below that, the Default value of the key named 0 is the string to be displayed in the
menu. Finally, by adding a sub-key called DefaultIcon to the 0 key, you can assign an icon to the
item.

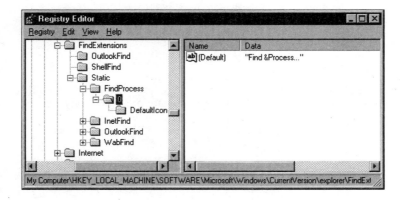

With a little thought, you'll realize that this is a strange and rather minimal shell extension. We don't need any initialization, because there's no file to work with. We don't need a description, because there's no status bar. We don't even need to add a new item explicitly, because the shell does this when it reads the registry. In fact, why we need a shell extension to customize the Find menu at all is a mystery to me!

> *Because the Find menu is also available through Explorer, you might think that a description is necessary, but a quick examination of the items already in the menu will show you that this is not the case. The complexity of creating a context menu shell extension reduces to implementing only the* `InvokeCommand()` *method that actually runs the 'find' utility.*

Configuring the Registry

Writing a context menu shell extension that works as a new 'find' utility takes very little effort, as the following code demonstrates. Here are the four interface methods that required rather more effort when we implemented them in `ExeMenu.h`:

```
// QueryContextMenu
HRESULT CProcess::QueryContextMenu(
        HMENU hmenu, UINT indexMenu, UINT idCmdFirst, UINT idCmdLast, UINT uFlags)
{
    return S_OK;
}

// InvokeCommand
HRESULT CProcess::InvokeCommand(LPCMINVOKECOMMANDINFO lpcmi)
{
    m_Dlg.DoModal();
    return S_OK;
}

// GetCommandString
HRESULT CProcess::GetCommandString(
        UINT idCmd, UINT uFlags, UINT* pwReserved, LPSTR pszText, UINT cchMax)
{
    return S_OK;
}

// Initialize
HRESULT CProcess::Initialize(
            LPCITEMIDLIST pidlFolder, LPDATAOBJECT lpdobj, HKEY hKeyProgID)
{
    return S_OK;
};
```

A little more complicated is the script that's required for configuring the registry. Note that what follows extends and does *not* replace the original script. This code should be added at the bottom of the RGS file that ATL writes for you.

```
HKLM
{
    Software
    {
        Microsoft
        {
            Windows
            {
                CurrentVersion
                {
                    Explorer
                    {
                        FindExtensions
                        {
                            Static
                            {
                                FindProcess = s '{977DA8D2-41D5-11D2-BC00-AC6805C10E27}'
                                {
                                    0 = s 'Find &Process...'
                                    {
                                        DefaultIcon = s '%MODULE%,0'
                                    }
                                }
                            }
                        }
                    }
                }
            }
        }
    }
}
```

Finding the Running Processes

Enumerating the running processes requires different techniques under Windows 9x and Windows NT 4.0 – the former provides a valuable set of functions in ToolHelp.dll, while the latter does not. Under Windows NT, you have to resort to a quite different library called PSAPI.dll.

PSAPI.dll ships with Windows NT 4.0, but it isn't always copied to your hard drive during installation. Nevertheless, on the Visual C++ CD you will find the two files you need to use PSAPI, namely psapi.h and psapi.lib.

I'm not going to cover the details of this procedure here because they are beyond the scope of the book. However, I'll list some resources in the *Further Reading* section at the end of the chapter, and the source code on the Wrox web site includes a project that incorporates all this material.

IContextMenu2 and IContextMenu3

With the introduction of Internet Explorer 4.0, two new context menu interfaces have been added, both of which are improvements over IContextMenu. More precisely, IContextMenu2 can be considered an extension of IContextMenu, while IContextMenu3 (which requires Internet Explorer 4.01) enhances IContextMenu2.

Both interfaces, however, only have one more function than IContextMenu. To add to the confusion, the 'extra' function in IContextMenu2 is called HandleMenuMsg(), while the one in IContextMenu3 is called HandleMenuMsg2(). The prototypes are similar:

```
HRESULT HandleMenuMsg(UINT    uMsg,
                      WPARAM  wParam,
                      LPARAM  lParam);

HRESULT HandleMenuMsg2(UINT     uMsg,
                       WPARAM   wParam,
                       LPARAM   lParam,
                       LRESULT* plResult);
```

These new interfaces extend IContextMenu by providing support for owner-drawn (and bitmapped) context menus. In particular, HandleMenuMsg() lets you intercept and handle three system messages:

- ❑ WM_INITMENUPOPUP
- ❑ WM_MEASUREITEM
- ❑ WM_DRAWITEM

The last two of these only come into play if you have owner-drawn menu items. For its part, HandleMenuMsg2() adds a fourth message to the list of the mirrored messages: WM_MENUCHAR. Documentation on this subject may be found in the Internet Client SDK.

Right-hand Drag & Drop

The Windows shell provides the possibility of dragging and dropping files from one directory to another, but if you hold down the *right* mouse button as you perform the operation, the behavior is modified: you are prompted with a menu. It's not the most-used feature of Windows, but it allows you to decide what to do after dragging a set of file objects:

Windows provides a typical menu for this operation, as shown in the figure. It also considers what operations are valid as a result of the action — you won't get the Move Here item if you're dropping in the same folder as the source, for example. Accordingly, right-hand drag-and-drop doesn't support keyboard modifiers like *Ctrl* or *Shift* that allow you to change the result of the operation on the fly. All the *available* options are listed in the final menu.

You can add custom items here too — an ordinary context menu extension will suffice. However, even though drag-and-drop handlers and context menu handlers are the same thing from a programming standpoint, they differ quite a bit when it comes to registration.

Registering Drag & Drop Handlers

Right-hand drag-and-drop handlers don't work on the basis of file types, so you can't install them to work on ZIP files alone, for example. They only apply to directories. A typical registration script is the following, in which I'm registering a right-hand drag-and-drop handler to work on the contents of directories.

```
HKCR
{

    Directory
    {
        Shellex
        {
            DragDropHandlers
            {
                RightDropDemo = s '{20349851-699F-11D2-9DAF-00104B4C822A}'
            }
        }
    }

}
```

The first thing to note is that your registry entry goes under the DragDropHandlers key, instead of ContextMenuHandlers. Furthermore, you need to create a specific sub-key and set its Default value to the CLSID. The name of the sub-key doesn't actually matter, as Explorer will enumerate the entire contents of the DragDropHandlers tree.

As usual, the first method called in the extension is IShellExtInit::Initialize(), and here you can perform a check on the types of the files selected. The input arguments respectively give you the PIDL of the target folder where the user dropped, the data object (from which you can retrieve the files being acted upon) and the registry key that contains information about the type of the file with the focus.

By arranging a check on the file extensions, you can avoid doing work on any file types for which it would be undesirable or unnecessary to do so. This approach is completely different from what we have been doing so far. For drag-and-drop handlers, you register all your shell extensions in the same tree, and during initialization you can decide whether the files selected are of interest. To abort a shell extension, simply return E_FAIL from Initialize(). Here's an example in which I assume a class called CDropExt that implements IContextMenu and IShellExtInit.

```
STDMETHODIMP CDropExt::Initialize(
                LPCITEMIDLIST pidlFolder, LPDATAOBJECT lpdobj, HKEY hkeyProgID)
{
    FORMATETC fe = {CF_HDROP, NULL, DVASPECT_CONTENT, -1, TYMED_HGLOBAL};
    STGMEDIUM medium;

    HRESULT hr = lpdobj->GetData(&fe, &medium);
    if(FAILED(hr))
        return E_FAIL;
```

```
    TCHAR szFile[MAX_PATH] = {0};
    HDROP hdrop = static_cast<HDROP>(medium.hGlobal);

    // Get the number of dragged files
    UINT cFiles = DragQueryFile(hdrop, 0xFFFFFFFF, NULL, 0);

    // Process the files one after another
    for(int i = 0 ; i < cFiles ; i++)
    {
        // Get the ith file name
        DragQueryFile(hdrop, i, szFile, MAX_PATH);

        // Check the extension and return E_FAIL to stop
    }

    return S_OK;
}
```

In the code above, I scan the list of dragged files (obtained through `IDataObject`), get the name of each file in turn and check the extension to decide whether or not it is of a supported type.

Right-hand drag-and-drop handlers work on the files that are the *source* of a drag-and-drop operation, provided that the operation is carried out with the right-hand mouse button. This is different from the `DropHandler` sample that I'll show later on in the chapter, which applies to the *target* of a drop action.

If you take a look at the contents of the registry on your PC, you'll find that no program registers drag-and-drop extensions for a given file type, as occurs for context menu handlers. WinZip, one of the very few 'must-have' utilities, works in exactly this way: its shell extension is always in the background when you 'right-drop' files, but it only pops up if you drop a ZIP file.

Assigning Dynamic Icons

The property sheets and context menus we've examined so far are two of the more exciting and generally useful applications of shell extensions, but they are definitely not the only ones. In this section, I'll be delving deep inside **dynamic icons**. In other words, I'll show how to have different icons for different files that are essentially of the same type.

Think about EXE files. Each time you met one of them in a shell view, the icon displayed is *not* a generic icon for that file type, but an icon that belongs to the file itself (unless, of course, the EXE doesn't contain an icon). This is true for ICO files as well.

In fact, this has been a feature of the shell ever since Windows 95, so it's quite likely that you've never given it much thought. Nevertheless, the dynamic assignment of icons to files of a certain type is a precise behavior that the shell provides through shell extensions.

I'm going to present an example in which I'll be showing you how to apply the technique to BMP files. Don't worry, I'm not talking about providing a 16 x 16 pixel preview of any bitmap you may have – it would be a painful activity to crunch an 800 x 600 true color picture down to the size of a small icon! What I have in mind is to exploit the icon to provide information about the bitmap at a glance. How about having a different icon to reflect the palette size of the BMP file?

Different Icons for Different Color Depths

Basically, I'm going to distinguish four cases and assign a different icon to each one:

- Monochromatic bitmaps
- 16 colors (4-bit)
- 256 colors (8-bit)
- True color bitmaps (24-bit or greater)

The idea is that we'll define an `IconHandler` shell extension (named after the key you place in the registry) and let it examine the color table of each bitmap file, in order to return the correct icon for Explorer to display. An `IconHandler` shell extension requires you to implement the following COM interfaces:

- `IExtractIcon`
- `IPersistFile`

The first of these is intended to facilitate the communication between your module and Explorer. In other words, Explorer will call methods of the `IExtractIcon` interface to ask for the icon to display with the file loaded through the `IPersistFile` interface.

> Notice that since this extension doesn't apply only to selected files but to *any* file, initialization is carried out via `IPersistFile` rather than `IShellExtInit`.

Initializing the IconHandler Extension

The `IPersistFile` interface is composed of six functions above the three of `IUnknown`, with the following prototypes:

```
HRESULT GetClassID(LPCLSID lpClsID);
HRESULT IsDirty();
HRESULT Load(LPCOLESTR pszFileName, DWORD dwMode);
HRESULT Save(LPCOLESTR pszFileName, BOOL fRemember);
HRESULT SaveCompleted(LPCOLESTR pszFileName);
HRESULT GetCurFile(LPOLESTR* ppszFileName);
```

You'll be pleased to know that for the purposes of shell extensions, you don't have to implement all of these methods. In fact, the `Load()` method will suffice; for all the others, we'll just return `E_NOTIMPL`. `Load()` lets us store the name of the bitmap file for which the icon is necessary, so all we have to do is convert the file name from Unicode to ANSI, and save it to a data member for further use.

Retrieving the Icon

There are two possible ways for Explorer to get the icon to display, and each passes through a method of `IExtractIcon`. The methods are:

- `GetIconLocation()`
- `Extract()`

The first of these is intended to return the path and index of the icon to use, together with some flags that instruct the shell how to handle it. Explorer calls the second, on the other hand, in order to give the extension a chance to extract the icon itself. Let's have a look at them in more detail, starting with GetIconLocation():

```
HRESULT GetIconLocation(
    UINT   uFlags,        // The reasons for which an icon is needed
    LPSTR  szIconFile,    // Buffer to contain the path name of the icon
    INT    cchMax,        // Size of the above buffer
    LPINT  piIndex,       // Ptr to an int that will contain the icon index
    UINT*  pwFlags);      // Sends information to the shell about the icon
```

The uFlags argument is not especially useful for our purposes here, but it may be helpful if you're working with folders instead of bitmaps, or with files in general — one of the things it lets you know is whether the icon is required in the 'open' state.

The other 'flag' parameter, pwFlags, allows us to tell the shell about the points listed below:

Flag	Description
GIL_DONTCACHE	Prevents Explorer from storing the icon in its internal cache.
GIL_NOTFILENAME	The information passed through szIconFile and piIndex don't evaluate to a <path, index> pair.
GIL_PERCLASS	The icon should be used for *any* document of the class. This flag is no use in our case, because we want to obtain the exact opposite! However, Microsoft itself recommends that you use the registry if you want to assign the same icon to all the files of a class. (See Chapter 14 for details.)
GIL_PERINSTANCE	The icon is assigned to a specific document. Each document of the class has its own icon. This is just what I want to obtain.
GIL_SIMULATEDOC	The icon is needed to create a document icon.

When Explorer needs to display an icon for a file, it first looks for a registered IconHandler extension. If it finds one, it initializes the module with the given file by calling the IPersistFile::Load() function. Next, it asks the extension to provide a path name and an index for the icon by calling IExtractIcon::GetIconLocation(). Explorer now expects to receive all the information it needs to retrieve the icon; if GetIconLocation() fails, the shell goes on as if the extension had never been found.

If GetIconLocation() succeeds, it should return S_OK. If it returns S_FALSE, the shell will use the default icon specified in the DefaultIcon registry key.

When GetIconLocation() returns, Explorer examines the pwFlags argument. If the GIL_NOTFILENAME bit is turned on, it assumes that the extension wants to extract the icon itself. It invokes the Extract() method, passing in the things it received through szIconFile and piIndex. From Extract(), Explorer expects to receive a pair of HICONs for the small and large icon. It's defined like this:

```
HRESULT Extract(
    LPCSTR pszFile,       // Value ret'd by GetIconLocation through szIconFile
    UINT    nIconIndex,   // Value ret'd by GetIconLocation through piIndex
    HICON* phiconLarge,   // Ptr to an HICON to receive the lge icon handle
    HICON* phiconSmall,   // Ptr to an HICON to receive the sml icon handle
    UINT    nIconSize);   // Desired size of the icon in pixels. Low word
                          //  for the large icon; high word for the small icon
```

This function must ensure that Explorer gets handles to a large and a small icon for the file. More importantly, the function should return S_FALSE to prevent Explorer from extracting the icon itself. In most cases, you don't need to implement Extract(), but even then you should arrange for it to return S_FALSE rather than E_NOTIMPL.

Details of the Example

To demonstrate this technique, we're going to create an ATL DLL project called BmpIcons. The following picture shows the icons that I used to identify the various bitmaps, but of course you're free to come up with your own:

The four icons are for monochromatic, 16-, 256-, and true-color bitmaps respectively; I added them to my project as resource files with the names BmpMono.ico, Bmp16.ico, Bmp256.ico and Bmp24.ico respectively.

Next, add a simple ATL object called Icon to the project. The CIcon class this generates will need to inherit from both IExtractIconImpl and IPersistFileImpl, two ATL classes that provide a basic implementation for the IExtractIcon and IPersistFile interfaces:

```
// IExtractIconImpl.h

#include <AtlCom.h>
#include <ShlObj.h>

class ATL_NO_VTABLE IExtractIconImpl : public IExtractIcon
{
public:

    // IUnknown
    STDMETHOD(QueryInterface)(REFIID riid, void** ppvObject) = 0;
    _ATL_DEBUG_ADDREF_RELEASE_IMPL(IExtractIconImpl)

    // IExtractIcon
    STDMETHOD(Extract)(LPCSTR, UINT, HICON*, HICON*, UINT)
    {
        return S_FALSE;
    }

    STDMETHOD(GetIconLocation)(UINT, LPSTR, UINT, LPINT, UINT*)
    {
        return S_FALSE;
    }
};
```

For our purposes, Extract() as defined here is fine — we don't need to override it in the source code for CIcon. The situation when we turn to considering IPersistFile is even better, because we can put everything into the 'Impl' class, making it highly reusable:

```
// IPersistFileImpl.h

#include <AtlCom.h>

class ATL_NO_VTABLE IPersistFileImpl : public IPersistFile
{
public:
    TCHAR m_szFile[MAX_PATH];

    // IUnknown
    STDMETHOD(QueryInterface)(REFIID riid, void** ppvObject) = 0;
    _ATL_DEBUG_ADDREF_RELEASE_IMPL(IPersistFileImpl)

    // IPersistFile
    STDMETHOD(GetClassID)(LPCLSID)
    {
        return E_NOTIMPL;
    }

    STDMETHOD(IsDirty)()
    {
        return E_NOTIMPL;
    }

    STDMETHOD(Load)(LPCOLESTR wszFile, DWORD /*dwMode*/)
    {
        USES_CONVERSION;
        lstrcpy(m_szFile, OLE2T(wszFile));
        return S_OK;
    }

    STDMETHOD(Save)(LPCOLESTR, BOOL)
    {
        return E_NOTIMPL;
    }

    STDMETHOD(SaveCompleted)(LPCOLESTR)
    {
        return E_NOTIMPL;
    }

    STDMETHOD(GetCurFile)(LPOLESTR*)
    {
        return E_NOTIMPL;
    }
};
```

The declaration of our shell extension looks like this:

```
#include "resource.h"
#include "IPersistFileImpl.h"
#include "IExtractIconImpl.h"
#include <comdef.h>

/////////////////////////////////////////////////////////////////////////////
// CIcon
class ATL_NO_VTABLE CIcon :
    public CComObjectRootEx<CComSingleThreadModel>,
    public CComCoClass<CIcon, &CLSID_Icon>,
    public IExtractIconImpl,
    public IPersistFileImpl,
    public IDispatchImpl<IIcon, &IID_IIcon, &LIBID_BMPICONSLib>
{
public:
    CIcon()
    {
    }

DECLARE_REGISTRY_RESOURCEID(IDR_ICON)

DECLARE_PROTECT_FINAL_CONSTRUCT()

BEGIN_COM_MAP(CIcon)
    COM_INTERFACE_ENTRY(IIcon)
    COM_INTERFACE_ENTRY(IDispatch)
    COM_INTERFACE_ENTRY(IPersistFile)
    COM_INTERFACE_ENTRY(IExtractIcon)
END_COM_MAP()

// IExtractIcon
    STDMETHOD(GetIconLocation)(UINT, LPSTR, UINT, LPINT, UINT*);

// IIcon
public:

private:
    int GetBitmapColorDepth();
};
```

Now we just need to give a body to `GetIconLocation()`, which is the core function for icon handlers. I've also added a private helper function called `GetBitmapColorDepth()`.

```
HRESULT CIcon::GetIconLocation(
        UINT uFlags, LPSTR szIconFile, UINT cchMax, LPINT piIndex, UINT* pwFlags)
{
    // We store ourselves the icons
    ::GetModuleFileName(_Module.GetModuleInstance(), szIconFile, cchMax);

    // Analyze the bitmap color table
    int iBitCount = GetBitmapColorDepth();
    if(iBitCount < 0)
        return S_FALSE;

    switch(iBitCount)
    {
    case 1:
        *piIndex = 0;                    // Monochrome
        break;
```

```
    case 4:
        *piIndex = 1;              // 16 colors
        break;

    case 8:
        *piIndex = 2;              // 256 colors
        break;

    default:
        *piIndex = 3;              // True color
    }

    *pwFlags |= GIL_PERINSTANCE | GIL_DONTCACHE;
    return S_OK;
};
```

```
int CIcon::GetBitmapColorDepth()
{
    // Read file header
    HFILE fh = _lopen(m_szFile, OF_READ);
    if(fh == HFILE_ERROR)
        return -1;

    BITMAPFILEHEADER bf;
    _lread(fh, &bf, sizeof(BITMAPFILEHEADER));

    BITMAPINFOHEADER bi;
    _lread(fh, &bi, sizeof(BITMAPINFOHEADER));
    _lclose(fh);

    // Returns
    return bi.biBitCount;
};
```

With this, the source code for the shell extension is complete, but we still have to consider the thorny issue of registration. Like any shell extension, if you miss something while registering it, you'll be unable to put the extension to work properly.

Registering the Icon Handler

An icon handler shell extension follows the same pattern as other shell extensions, although once again it uses a different key. On this occasion, you need to create an `IconHandler` key under the `ShellEx` key of the involved document class. For bitmaps (and provided that you use Microsoft Paint to open them), the key is:

```
HKEY_CLASSES_ROOT
    \Paint.Picture
        \ShellEx
            \IconHandler
```

Then, set the `Default` key to the object CLSID, and this time you should also set the `DefaultIcon` key to %1, to let Explorer know that the icon should be determined on a file-by-file basis. Normally, the `DefaultIcon` key contains a comma-separated string with a filename and an icon index.

Here's the non-standard portion of the ATL-generated script:

```
HKCR
{
    // Object registration

    Paint.Picture
    {
        DefaultIcon = s '%%1'
        ShellEx
        {
            IconHandler = s '{A2B00480-425A-11D2-BC00-AC6805C10E27}'
        }
    }
}
```

Note that for the DefaultIcon *key to take on the value* %1*, we need to use a double percentage sign (*%%*).*

To make sure that everything's working properly, it's safest to restart the system or log off. Notice that the old value of the DefaultIcon key is overwritten, so you might want to keep a note of it somewhere for safe keeping. Finally, here's how the shell extension changes your view of the shell:

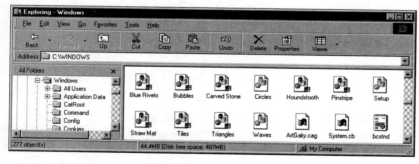

You can't have more IconHandler extensions for the same file class. If you register more, only the first one is considered.

Monitoring Folders through ICopyHook

A dream for many programmers is the ability to write a utility to monitor what's going on in the file system. There may be many reasons for this, but testing applications, debugging and just plain curiosity are certainly among them.

In Chapter 7 we discussed notification objects, which notify your application when something changes in the file system or within a specified folder. Unfortunately, under Windows 95 and Windows 98 there's no way to know *which* files caused the notification to be raised. In other words, you know that *something* changed in the watched folder, but then it's completely up to you to figure out exactly what happened. Under Windows NT, things are a little better thanks to a platform-specific function called ReadDirectoryChangesW().

Even though a number of Windows NT 4.0 functions have been ported to the Windows 9x platform with Windows 98, `ReadDirectoryChangesW()` *is not among them. Instead, functions like* `MoveFileEx()`, `CreateFiber()` *and* `CreateRemoteThread()` *are now available under Windows 98.*

Help is at hand: the Windows shell documents an interface called `ICopyHook` that can be employed to perform similar tasks. Basically, it lets you monitor any copy, move, rename or delete operations that occur within a folder. At first sight, it looks really exciting, but unfortunately there are three serious shortcomings that limit the usefulness of this extension:

❑ It only applies to folders and printers, not to file types
❑ It only allows you to permit or deny the operation, not to perform it yourself
❑ It only lets you know about the beginning of an operation, not about its end

For my next example, I'm going to create an ATL project that demonstrates how to implement this interface to build up a directory-watching tool.

Implementing ICopyHook

For this example I created a DLL project with the ATL COM AppWizard and called it `Copy`, accepting all the default options. Once it had been generated, I used the Object Wizard to add a simple ATL object called `Monitor`, and made these changes to the header file `Monitor.h`:

```
#include "resource.h"
#include "ICopyHookImpl.h"

/////////////////////////////////////////////////////////////////////
// CMonitor
class ATL_NO_VTABLE CMonitor :
    public CComObjectRootEx<CComSingleThreadModel>,
    public CComCoClass<CMonitor, &CLSID_Monitor>,
    public IShellCopyHookImpl,
    public IDispatchImpl<IMonitor, &IID_IMonitor, &LIBID_COPYLib>
{
public:
    CMonitor()
    {
    }

DECLARE_REGISTRY_RESOURCEID(IDR_MONITOR)

DECLARE_PROTECT_FINAL_CONSTRUCT()

BEGIN_COM_MAP(CMonitor)
    COM_INTERFACE_ENTRY(IMonitor)
    COM_INTERFACE_ENTRY(IDispatch)
    COM_INTERFACE_ENTRY_IID(IID_IShellCopyHook, CMonitor)
END_COM_MAP()
```

```
    // ICopyHook
public:
    STDMETHOD_(UINT, CopyCallback)(HWND hwnd, UINT wFunc, UINT wFlags,
                        LPCSTR pszSrcFile,  DWORD dwSrcAttribs,
                        LPCSTR pszDestFile, DWORD dwDestAttribs);

    // IMonitor
public:
    };
```

You've probably already noticed that the COM map is a little different from the rest of our examples so far because of the new COM_INTERFACE_ENTRY_IID() macro, which I'll discuss in a moment. The CMonitor class is derived from IShellCopyHookImpl, which in turn inherits from ICopyHook:

```
#include <AtlCom.h>
#include <ShlObj.h>

class ATL_NO_VTABLE IShellCopyHookImpl : public ICopyHook
{
public:

    // IUnknown
    STDMETHOD(QueryInterface)(REFIID riid, void** ppvObject) = 0;
    _ATL_DEBUG_ADDREF_RELEASE_IMPL(IShellCopyHookImpl)

    // ICopyHook
    STDMETHOD_(UINT, CopyCallback)(HWND hwnd, UINT wFunc, UINT wFlags,
                        LPCSTR pszSrcFile,  DWORD dwSrcAttribs,
                        LPCSTR pszDestFile, DWORD dwDestAttribs);
    };
```

Having seen the earlier examples, most of this procedure should already be looking pretty familiar. The ICopyHook interface requires you to implement a single function called CopyCallback(), which is basically just a filter built on top of SHFileOperation() (see Chapter 3). It 'catches' all the operations that go through that function, and your implementation can permit or refuse them to take place. Not surprisingly, the prototype of CopyCallback() looks rather like SHFileOperation().

```
UINT CopyCallback(
    HWND    hwnd,           // Parent of any window displayed by handler
    UINT    wFunc,          // The operation to carry out (see Ch 3)
    UINT    wFlags,         // Attributes of the operation (see Ch 3)
    LPCSTR  pszSrcFile,     // Source file for the operation
    DWORD   dwSrcAttribs,   // DOS attributes of the source file
    LPCSTR  pszDestFile,    // Target file for the operation
    DWORD   dwDestAttribs); // DOS attributes of the target file
```

CopyCallback() returns an UINT that evaluates to one of the typical MessageBox() return constants: IDYES, IDNO, IDCANCEL. Depending on the value returned, the operation will continue, be rejected, or be canceled respectively. Rejection means that just this one operation won't execute, whereas cancellation, on the other hand, means that all pending operations will also be canceled.

What's ICopyHook's IID?

While developing my first `CopyHook` extension, I took it for granted that the interface ID of `ICopyHook` would be `IID_ICopyHook`, so I was surprised when the compiler started complaining about an undeclared identifier. Curiously, the IID of `ICopyHook` is not `IID_ICopyHook`, but `IID_IShellCopyHook`.

This fact posed a little problem with ATL code that declares the COM map of the server object. After you've added a new `Monitor` object to an ATL project, the code in the header file looks like this:

```
BEGIN_COM_MAP(CMonitor)
    COM_INTERFACE_ENTRY(IMonitor)
    COM_INTERFACE_ENTRY(IDispatch)
END_COM_MAP()
```

The COM map is responsible for your object's implementation of `QueryInterface()`, and so in order to expose the `ICopyHook` interface, and as we've been doing in the other examples up to this point, I added a line like this:

```
BEGIN_COM_MAP(CMonitor)
    COM_INTERFACE_ENTRY(IMonitor)
    COM_INTERFACE_ENTRY(IDispatch)
    COM_INTERFACE_ENTRY(ICopyHook)
END_COM_MAP()
```

As I've said, this is what caused the compilation error. To fix it, I had to inform ATL that the interface to expose is `ICopyHook`, but that its IID *isn't* `IID_ICopyHook`. Fortunately, the designers of ATL have pre-empted this problem, and there's a `COM_INTERFACE_ENTRY` macro for dealing with exactly this kind of situation:

```
BEGIN_COM_MAP(CMonitor)
    COM_INTERFACE_ENTRY(IMonitor)
    COM_INTERFACE_ENTRY(IDispatch)
    COM_INTERFACE_ENTRY_IID(IID_IShellCopyHook, CMonitor)
END_COM_MAP()
```

This macro tells ATL to use the vtable of the class named in the second parameter as the implementation of the interface identified by the first parameter, which is exactly what we need.

Logging the Operations

The extension we're going to create here will simply compose and output strings to a log file. The strings will include the names of the source and target files, the type of operation, and the time at which it took place. Here's the implementation of `CopyCallback()`:

```
UINT CMonitor::CopyCallback(HWND hwnd, UINT wFunc, UINT wFlags,
                            LPCSTR pszSrcFile,  DWORD dwSrcAttribs,
                            LPCSTR pszDestFile, DWORD dwDestAttribs)
{
    TCHAR szTime[50] = {0};
    GetTimeFormat(LOCALE_SYSTEM_DEFAULT, 0, NULL, NULL, szTime, 50);

    FILE* f = NULL;
    f = fopen(__TEXT("c:\\monitor.log"), __TEXT("a + t"));
    fseek(f, 0, SEEK_END);
```

```
    switch(wFunc)
    {
    case FO_MOVE:
        fprintf(f, __TEXT("\n\n\rMoving:\n\r[%s] to [%s]\n\rat %s"),
                                pszSrcFile, pszDestFile, szTime);
        break;

    case FO_COPY:
        fprintf(f, __TEXT("\n\n\rCopying:\n\r[%s] to [%s]\n\rat %s"),
                                pszSrcFile, pszDestFile, szTime);
        break;

    case FO_DELETE:
        fprintf(f, __TEXT("\n\n\rDeleting:\n\r[%s] \n\rat %s"),
                                        pszSrcFile, szTime);
        break;
    }

    fclose(f);

    // Do not hamper the normal flow
    return IDYES;
}
```

Registering a CopyHook Extension

To register a `CopyHook` extension, you need to create a `CopyHookHandlers` key under the `ShellEx` key of the type of file you want to hook. Below `CopyHookHandlers`, create a new key with any name you like — the shell simply enumerates all the sub-keys it finds. The `Default` value of this one should point to the CLSID of the extension.

Here's how the ATL registry script code changes, (I've chosen to identify our custom key by the name `Monitor`):

```
HKCR
{
    // Object registration

    Directory
    {
        ShellEx
        {
            CopyHookHandlers
            {
                Monitor = s '{7842554E-6BED-11D2-8CDB-B05550C10000}'
            }
        }
    }
}
```

In this case, we're registering the extension to work on directories. You can try to register it to apply to file types (like `exefile`), but the shell will never invoke the extension if you do. This behavior is by design.

Here's a typical log file:

```
monitor - Notepad                                   _ □ ✕
File  Edit  Search  Help

■Copying:
■[E:\Source\Copy\Debug] to E:\Source\Copy\Debug]
■at 19.18.27

■Deleting:
■[E:\Source\Copy\Copy of Debug]
■at 19.19.17

■Moving:
■[E:\Text\Copy of Other Figures] to [E:\ZIP\Copy of Other Figures]
■at 19.20.27

■Deleting:
■[E:\RECYCLED\DE1]
■at 19.21.17
```

Monitorable Objects

Despite my warning about files, directories are not the only objects that can be monitored by a
`CopyHook` extension – printers and drives can be watched as well. To hook on printers, you need to
register your server under the `HKEY_CLASSES_ROOT\Printers` key; this is the trick that allows
some printer managers to pop up with their own user interface each time you print.

The Internet Client SDK documentation claims that you can register a `CopyHook` extension under
the * key, which might lead you to believe that this is a way to monitor operations on files, but sadly
this is untrue. In my experience, there is no way to hook for single files being copied or moved.

More on Copy Hooking

I said earlier that the shell doesn't notify your extension about the result (success, failure, abort) of the
hooked operation. However, since you know the directories involved in the operation, you could try
to detect it yourself by using a notification object (see Chapter 7). By installing such an object on both
the source and the target path, you would know when something changes in either. Then, through
simple checks, you could discover how things went. For a copy, for example, you could verify
whether the target directory contains a file with the same name as the source.

> *Actually, it's not* quite *that easy, because* `SHFileOperation()` *(which lies behind the hook)
> can allow files to be renamed on collision, so the system assigns the target a different name from
> the source. The principle, though, is sound.*

I started investigating `CopyHook` extensions when I was developing a product whose basic document
was composed of a collection of files. If my customers wanted to manage documents through the shell
(and not just through the program), they had to remember the inner structure of the document and be
sure to copy or delete *all* its components. My idea was to hook on copy, move, rename and delete
operations, and then to make sure that *all* relevant files were affected by changes to any *one* of them.
As I've explained, though, this seems to be impossible, and so the program I was developing ended
up using compound files and OLE structured storage instead.

Dropping Data over a File

A common feature of Win32 programs is the ability to select files from Explorer's window, drop them over the client area of a program, and have it detect and handle the data received. I've presented examples of this feature in earlier chapters, particularly in Chapter 6.

What I'll try to do here is a bit different. I want to be able to handle the same drop event when its target is a single file of a certain type in the Explorer window or the Windows desktop. Once again, the first example that comes to mind is WinZip: if you try to drag-and-drop one or more files over an existing `.zip` file, you'll notice that the mouse cursor changes to the typical 'add' cursor (an arrow with a plus sign). As soon as you drop, the file is compressed and added to the archive. This behavior is obtained through another type of shell extension: `DropHandler`.

The DropHandler Extension

A `DropHandler` extension derives from `IDropTarget` and `IPersistFile`, and must be registered under:

```
HKEY_CLASSES_ROOT
    \<FileClass>
        \ShellEx
            \DropHandler
```

Where `<FileClass>` is obviously the name that identifies the types of documents to which you want the extension to apply.

As usual, the `Default` value should be the CLSID of the server. Note that `DropHandler` *doesn't* allow multiple handlers to be in operation for the same file type at the same time. This is also hinted at by the fact that the name of the registry key is not plural.

The IDropTarget Interface

Before going on with a couple of examples, have a look at the methods of `IDropTarget`. They are all invoked after the drag-and-drop has started, and when the mouse moves around a possible target:

Method	Description
DragEnter()	The mouse entered a possible target that should decide whether data can be accepted or not
DragOver()	The mouse is moving over a possible target
DragLeave()	The mouse left the drop area
Drop()	The drag-and-drop has finished

In general, a possible target for an OLE drag-and-drop operation is a window (or a portion of a window) that registered itself through the `RegisterDragDrop()` function. When the module that originates and governs the drag-and-drop (the source) detects a window underneath the mouse, it verifies whether drag-and-drop support exists. If it does, the source gets a pointer to the `IDropTarget` interface exposed by the window and starts invoking the above methods.

Under the hood, this simply means checking whether the HWND *has a certain property that contains the pointer to the* IDropTarget *interface. By 'property' here, I mean a 32-bit data handle attached to a window via the* SetProp() *API function.*

DragEnter() gets called when the mouse enters an area that's a potential target. An IDropTarget interface is always associated with a window, but by coding DragEnter() properly, you can treat *any* area as a possible drop target. The prototype of the method is:

```
HRESULT IDropTarget::DragEnter(LPDATAOBJECT pDO,
                               DWORD        dwKeyState,
                               POINTL       pt,
                               DWORD*       pdwEffect);
```

It receives a pointer to an IDataObject interface that contains the data being dragged. The other parameters are a 32-bit value to denote the state of the keyboard, the position of the mouse in screen coordinates, and a buffer to fill with the effect allowed for the operation. In other words, the method is expected to analyze the incoming data, the mouse position and the state of the keyboard in order to determine whether it can accept the drop. By this means, you can accept drops over only a certain area of the window. (You need to convert the position to client coordinates before doing so.)

DragOver() is called when the mouse is moved over the target area. This method is meant to provide 'real-time' information about the drag-and-drop operation – as the mouse moves, the final effect may change. The prototype considers the state of the keyboard and the position of the mouse:

```
HRESULT IDropTarget::DragOver(DWORD  dwKeyState,
                              POINTL pt,
                              DWORD* pdwEffect);
```

Once again, you let the source know about the expected effect via the 32-bit output buffer pdwEffect. Of course, DragOver() is called more frequently (and always later) than DragEnter(), and so the effect set by DragOver() can overwrite the one set by DragEnter().

DragLeave() is a very simple method that's invoked to let the target know when the mouse has exited its area. The prototype is straightforward:

```
HRESULT IDropTarget::DragLeave();
```

The final method, Drop(), gets called when the data has been released over the target. This is clearly the most important function of all, and I'll have more to say about it shortly.

In order to create an ATL component, I need the IPersistFileImpl.h header that was used in the last example, and a similar file providing a base class for IDropTarget:

```
// IDropTargetImpl.h

#include <AtlCom.h>

class ATL_NO_VTABLE IDropTargetImpl : public IDropTarget
{
```

```
public:

    // IUnknown
    STDMETHOD(QueryInterface)(REFIID riid, void** ppvObject) = 0;
    _ATL_DEBUG_ADDREF_RELEASE_IMPL( IDropTargetImpl )

    // IDropTarget (optimized for shell drag-and-drop)
    STDMETHOD(DragEnter)(LPDATAOBJECT pDO, DWORD dwKeyState,
                                        POINTL pt, DWORD *pdwEffect)
    {
        STGMEDIUM sm;
        FORMATETC fe;

        // Do we accept this type of data?
        ZeroMemory(&sm, sizeof(STGMEDIUM));
        ZeroMemory(&fe, sizeof(FORMATETC));
        fe.tymed = TYMED_HGLOBAL;
        fe.lindex = -1;
        fe.dwAspect = DVASPECT_CONTENT;
        fe.cfFormat = CF_HDROP;
        if(FAILED(pDO->GetData(&fe, &sm)))
        {
            fe.cfFormat = CF_TEXT;
            if(FAILED(pDO->GetData(&fe, &sm)))
            {
                // Reject the drag-and-drop
                *pdwEffect = DROPEFFECT_NONE;
                return E_ABORT;
            }
        }

        // The default action is to copy data...
        *pdwEffect = DROPEFFECT_COPY;
        return S_OK;
    }

    STDMETHOD(DragOver)(DWORD dwKeyState, POINTL pt, DWORD* pdwEffect)
    {
        // Do not accept keyboard modifiers
        *pdwEffect = DROPEFFECT_COPY;
        return S_OK;
    }

    STDMETHOD(DragLeave)()
    {
        return S_OK;
    }

    STDMETHOD(Drop)(LPDATAOBJECT pDO, DWORD dwKeyState,
                                        POINTL pt, DWORD* pdwEffect);
};
```

Admittedly, this basic implementation is optimized for the use I want to make of it. In fact, I coded into this header file the actual behavior for all the methods but `Drop()`. The non-generic things about this class are:

❑ The target only accepts data in plain text format. The format name is CF_TEXT, one of the standard Windows clipboard formats.

❑ The target only supports 'copy' and no other operation like 'link' or 'move'.

Handling the Drop Event on TXT files

The first example I'll show you consists of handling text being dropped onto TXT files. The idea is that the dropped data (a file or plain text) will be added to the bottom of the target file. Start by creating a DLL project called `DropText` with the ATL COM AppWizard, and then use the Object Wizard to create a simple object called `StrAdd`. The ATL object under examination is declared as follows:

```
#include "resource.h"        // main symbols

#include "IPersistFileImpl.h"
#include "IDropTargetImpl.h"
#include <ComDef.h>

/////////////////////////////////////////////////////////////////////////////
// CStrAdd
class ATL_NO_VTABLE CStrAdd :
    public CComObjectRootEx<CComSingleThreadModel>,
    public CComCoClass<CStrAdd, &CLSID_StrAdd>,

    public IDropTargetImpl,
    public IPersistFileImpl,

    public IDispatchImpl<IStrAdd, &IID_IStrAdd, &LIBID_DROPTEXTLib>
{
public:
    CStrAdd()
    {
    }

DECLARE_REGISTRY_RESOURCEID(IDR_STRADD)

DECLARE_PROTECT_FINAL_CONSTRUCT()

BEGIN_COM_MAP(CStrAdd)
    COM_INTERFACE_ENTRY(IStrAdd)
    COM_INTERFACE_ENTRY(IDispatch)

    COM_INTERFACE_ENTRY(IDropTarget)
    COM_INTERFACE_ENTRY(IPersistFile)

END_COM_MAP()

// IDropTarget
public:
    STDMETHOD(Drop)(LPDATAOBJECT, DWORD, POINTL, LPDWORD);

// IStrAdd
public:

private:
    HDROP GetHDrop(LPDATAOBJECT);
    BOOL GetCFText(LPDATAOBJECT, LPTSTR, UINT);

};
```

The most interesting part of the code is what happens when the drop occurs, and this is defined in the source for the `Drop()` method that's shown next:

```
#include "stdafx.h"
#include "DropText.h"
#include "StrAdd.h"

#include <shlwapi.h>

// Constants
const int MAXBUFSIZE = 2048;        // Size of text to retrieve
const int MINBUFSIZE = 50;          // Size of text to be shown


///////////////////////////////////////////////////////////////////////////
// CStrAdd

HRESULT CStrAdd::Drop(
          LPDATAOBJECT pDO, DWORD dwKeyState, POINTL pt, LPDWORD pdwEffect)
{
   // Get the CF_HDROP data object
   HDROP hdrop = GetHDrop(pDO);
   if(hdrop)
   {
      // Consider only the first file in case of multiple selection
      TCHAR szSrcFile[MAX_PATH] = {0};
      DragQueryFile(hdrop, 0, szSrcFile, MAX_PATH);
      DragFinish(hdrop);

      // Check whether it is a TXT file
      LPTSTR pszExt = PathFindExtension(szSrcFile);
      if(lstrcmpi(pszExt, __TEXT(".txt")))
      {
         MessageBox(GetFocus(),
            __TEXT("Sorry, but you can only drop TXT files!"),
            __TEXT("Drop Files..."),
            MB_ICONSTOP);
         return E_INVALIDARG;
      }


      // Confirmation before concatenating...
      TCHAR s[2 * MAX_PATH] = {0};
      wsprintf(s, __TEXT("Would you add \n%s\nat the bottom of\n%s?"),
                                            szSrcFile, m_szFile);
      UINT rc = MessageBox(GetFocus(), s,
                      __TEXT("Drop Files..."), MB_ICONQUESTION | MB_YESNO);
      if(rc == IDNO)
         return E_ABORT;
   }
   else
   {
      TCHAR szBuf[MAXBUFSIZE] = {0};
      GetCFText(pDO, szBuf, MAXBUFSIZE);

      TCHAR s[MAX_PATH + MINBUFSIZE] = {0};
      TCHAR sClipb[MINBUFSIZE] = {0};
      lstrcpyn(sClipb, szBuf, MINBUFSIZE);
      wsprintf(s, __TEXT("Would you add\n[%s...]\nat the bottom of\n%s?"),
                                            sClipb, m_szFile);
      UINT rc = MessageBox(GetFocus(), s,
                      __TEXT("Drop Files..."), MB_ICONQUESTION | MB_YESNO);
```

```
        if(rc == IDNO)
            return E_ABORT;
    }

    // TO DO: Concatenate the text...

    return S_OK;
}
```

The function supports text and filenames, so you can drop either another TXT file selected within Explorer, or a piece of text taken from a text editor or a word processor, including Word, Notepad, WordPad, or even the Visual C++ Editor.

The first check performed by `Drop()` regards the type of the data being dropped. If the `GetHDrop()` method returns a valid handle, then the data is in CF_HDROP format and must be accessed through `DragQueryFile()`. In this case, the function only deals with the first file, discarding all the others in case of multiple selection, but this decision was taken only for the sake of simplicity – there's nothing to prevent you doing something more complex. The code also checks the extracted filename for a TXT extension by using the now familiar `PathFindExtension()` function from `shlwapi.dll`.

```
// Extracts an HDROP from a LPDATAOBJECT
HDROP CStrAdd::GetHDrop(LPDATAOBJECT pDO)
{
    STGMEDIUM sm;
    FORMATETC fe;

    // Check for CF_HDROP data
    ZeroMemory(&sm, sizeof(STGMEDIUM));
    ZeroMemory(&fe, sizeof(FORMATETC));
    fe.tymed = TYMED_HGLOBAL;
    fe.lindex = -1;
    fe.dwAspect = DVASPECT_CONTENT;
    fe.cfFormat = CF_HDROP;
    if(FAILED(pDO->GetData(&fe, &sm)))
        return NULL;
    else
        return static_cast<HDROP>(sm.hGlobal);
}
```

If the data dropped is not in CF_HDROP format, then the `Drop()` method attempts to extract plain text from it by using the helper function `GetCFText()`. If successful, it fills a buffer with a maximum number of bytes.

```
// Extracts CF_TEXT from a LPDATAOBJECT
BOOL CStrAdd::GetCFText(LPDATAOBJECT pDO, LPTSTR szBuf, UINT nMax)
{
    STGMEDIUM sm;
    FORMATETC fe;

    // Check for CF_TEXT data
    ZeroMemory(&sm, sizeof(STGMEDIUM));
    ZeroMemory(&fe, sizeof(FORMATETC));
    fe.tymed = TYMED_HGLOBAL;
    fe.lindex = -1;
    fe.dwAspect = DVASPECT_CONTENT;
    fe.cfFormat = CF_TEXT;
```

```
        if(FAILED(pDO->GetData(&fe, &sm)))
            return FALSE;
        else
        {
            LPTSTR p = static_cast<LPTSTR>(GlobalLock(sm.hGlobal));
            lstrcpyn(szBuf, p, nMax);
            GlobalUnlock(sm.hGlobal);
            return TRUE;
        }
    }
```

That brings the C++ code required for the technicalities of the extension to a conclusion, and once again it's time to think about registration. It's all a matter of knowing where to put the appropriate entries:

```
HKCR
{
    // Object registration

    txtfile
    {
        Shellex
        {
            DropHandler = s '{AE62DAAC-509C-11D2-BC00-AC6805C10E27}'
        }
    }
}
```

The following picture shows the confirmation message boxes that appear when you drop a TXT file or plain text over a TXT file in the Windows shell:

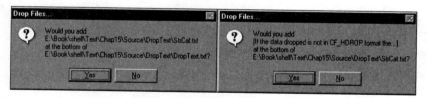

You'll surely have noticed that I didn't actually implement the code for concatenating the text, but the important part of this code is the *detection*, not the execution.

Adding Shell Support to Script Files

In Chapter 13, I covered the Windows Scripting Host object model. At the end of the chapter, during a discussion about ways of improving the WSH environment, I mentioned the possibility of writing a shell extension to drop parameters over a VBScript or JScript file. Now it's time to unravel the mystery and see how to achieve that.

The shell extension I need is a `DropHandler` that must be associated with VBS and JS files. The code layout is absolutely identical to the previous example: an ATL COM object implementing both `IPersistFile` and `IDropTarget`, reusing the same basic interface implementations. The things that need to change are the registration script and — of course — the code for the `Drop()` method.

The Project and the Registration Script

Let's get the easy stuff out of the way. I created a project called VBSDrop, added a simple object called WSHUIDrop, and made the following changes to the RGS script:

```
HKCR
{
    // Object registration

    vbsfile
    {
        Shellex
        {
            DropHandler = s '{E671DB13-4D41-11D2-BC00-AC6805C10E27}'
        }
    }

    jsfile
    {
        Shellex
        {
            DropHandler = s '{E671DB13-4D41-11D2-BC00-AC6805C10E27}'
        }
    }
}
```

Dropping Parameters over Script Files

The example I'm going to present shows how you can pass parameters to a VBS or JS script file through the shell. The idea is that you select data — filenames in the Explorer window, for example — and drop them onto a script file that will receive them through the command line. The sample uses filenames and the CF_HDROP format, but as I've already shown, this is not a limitation: you can handle strings as well.

The Drop() function I'll present here extracts the various file names you dropped over the VBS or JS file, and creates an itemized string in which each space-separated item is a fully-qualified file name. If a path name contains spaces of its own, then it gets put in quotes. For this last operation, I exploit yet another function from the seemingly limitless shlwapi.dll library: PathQuoteSpaces() encloses a path string in quotes if it contains long filenames that include spaces.

When the string is ready it must be passed as an argument to the script file and executed, and this is just what ShellExecute() has been designed to do. In the following call, the name of the script file has been saved in the m_szFile data member of the CWSHUIDrop class during the initialization of the shell extension:

```
ShellExecute(GetFocus(), __TEXT("open"), m_szFile, pszBuf, NULL, SW_SHOW);
```

To run a VBS or JS file, you simply have to execute the open verb. The pszBuf variable constitutes the command line parameters for the file.

```
/////////////////////////////////////////////////////////////////////
// A portion of this code also appeared in the December 1998 issue of MIND

HRESULT CWSHUIDrop::Drop(
            LPDATAOBJECT pDO, DWORD dwKeyState, POINTL pt, LPDWORD pdwEffect)
{
    // Get the CF_HDROP data object
    HDROP hdrop = GetHDrop(pDO);
    if(hdrop == NULL)
        return E_INVALIDARG;

    // Get the Shell memory handler
    LPMALLOC pMalloc = NULL;
    SHGetMalloc(&pMalloc);

    // Allocate enough memory for the final string to be composed
    int iNumOfFiles = DragQueryFile(hdrop, -1, NULL, 0);
    LPTSTR pszBuf = static_cast<LPTSTR>(
                            pMalloc->Alloc((1 + MAX_PATH) * iNumOfFiles));
    LPTSTR psz = pszBuf;
    if(!pszBuf)
    {
        pMalloc->Release();
        return E_OUTOFMEMORY;
    }
    ZeroMemory(pszBuf, (1 + MAX_PATH) * iNumOfFiles);

    // Get the dropped filenames and compose the string
    for(int i = 0 ; i < iNumOfFiles ; i++)
    {
        TCHAR s[MAX_PATH] = {0};
        DragQueryFile(hdrop, i, s, MAX_PATH);
        PathQuoteSpaces(s);
        lstrcat(pszBuf, s);
        lstrcat(pszBuf, __TEXT(" "));
    }
    DragFinish(hdrop);

    // Run the script, passing the dropped files as a command line argument
    ShellExecute(GetFocus(), __TEXT("open"), m_szFile, pszBuf, NULL, SW_SHOW);

    pMalloc->Release();
    return S_OK;
}
```

To see the global effect of this code, consider the following JScript code:

```
/////////////////////////////////////////////////////////////////////
// JScript sample for shell DropHandler
// It simply displays what it receives on the command line

var shell = WScript.CreateObject("WScript.Shell");
var sDrop = "Arguments received:\n\n";

if(WScript.Arguments.Length > 0)
{
    for(i = 1 ; i <= WScript.Arguments.Length ; i++)
        sDrop += i + ") " + WScript.Arguments.Item(i - 1) + "\n";
    shell.Popup(sDrop);
}
```

```
else
    shell.Popup("No argument specified.");

WScript.Quit();
```

This code, which I placed in a file called `jsdrop.js`, examines its command line and displays a message box listing the various parameters on separate rows. In the next figure, I'm trying to drop a few files over it:

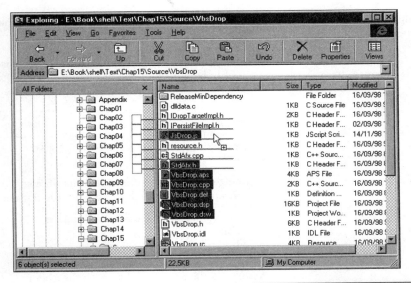

Thanks to our new `DropHandler` shell extension, the result is the following message box:

DataHandler Shell Extensions

We're almost at the end of our odyssey through the world of Windows shell extensions, but before we finish, there's time for a few words about *another* extension type that touches on *another* common aspect of the user interface: the clipboard. If you want to gain control over a copy-and-paste operation that involves files of a certain type, then you should write a `DataHandler` extension.

Suppose, for example, that you want to change the way a BMP file is copied to the clipboard when someone presses *Ctrl-C*. By default, the shell copies the name of the file in `CF_HDROP` format. If you want the *image* to go to the clipboard in `CF_BITMAP` format, then you need to write a `DataHandler` extension.

The COM Interfaces Involved

To write a `DataHandler` shell extension, you need to implement `IPersistFile` and `IDataObject`. Registration of an extension of this type requires a new `Default` value for:

```
HKEY_CLASSES_ROOT
    \<FileClass>
        \ShellEx
            \DataHandler
```

As usual, the value you set should be the CLSID of the server, while `<FileClass>` is the name that identifies the types of documents to which you want the extension to apply.

`IDataObject` is responsible for transferring data throughout the clipboard, and contains several methods. For our purposes here, however, you only have to implement the ones I've marked with an asterisk.

Method	Description
*GetData()	Retrieves the data associated with the given object
GetDataHere()	Similar to `GetData()`, but the function also receives the storage medium to store the data in
*QueryGetData()	Determines whether the required data is available
GetCanonicalFormatEtc()	Lists the formats supported by the object
*SetData()	Associates the specified data with the given object
EnumFormatEtc()	Enumerates the formats to use to store data with the object
DAdvise()	Connects a sink object to know when data changes
DUnadvise()	Disconnects a sink object
EnumDAdvise()	Enumerates the sinks currently connected

`DataHandler`, like `IconHandler` and `DropHandler`, doesn't allow multiple handlers to be in operation for the same file type at the same time. This means, for example, that if you copy the image bits to the clipboard for a BMP file, then you lose the ability to copy the name – unless of course you write an extension that does both these things!

A Shell Extension Developer's Handbook

In this chapter, we've used ATL to create a number of shell extensions – in fact, it's become something of a habit. In the following step-by-step procedure, I've summarized exactly what you need to do in order to create, compile and test your shell extensions with ATL.

- ❑ Create a new ATL project using the ATL COM AppWizard.
- ❑ Add a new simple object
- ❑ If one is not already available, write an `IxxxImpl.h` file for each interface you need to implement. You need to define a new class that inherits from the interface and provides a basic behavior for each method. You can also add attributes or private members, if required.
- ❑ Modify the new object class's header file. In particular, have it inherit from all the `IxxxImpl` classes you defined in the previous step. Add the interfaces to the object's COM map, and add declarations for all the interface methods that you need to override.
- ❑ Modify the ATL registry script to accomplish shell extension registration. Normally, the Wizard only generates the code necessary to register the server.
- ❑ Add the code for the overridden methods.
- ❑ Compile the project and make sure the registration went as expected. If you're not sure, repeat the registration by calling `regsvr32.exe`.
- ❑ Before testing the functionality, make sure the code is properly loaded into the shell. This is an operation that can vary depending upon the type of the shell extension. For context menus and property sheets, refreshing the Explorer windows is enough. Icon handlers and copy hooks, on the other hand, require you to log off or even to reboot.

Version 4.71 of the shell releases DLLs after a few seconds' inactivity, so having to reload the DLL after recompilation shouldn't be an issue *except* in the case of copy hooks. These are active all the time, so to recompile them you must first unregister the server, and then either log off or reboot.

File Viewers

To conclude this chapter, let's have a look at some modules that aren't shell extensions, but which play a similar role. **File viewers** (also known as 'quick viewers') are COM in-process servers that add functionality to document types through the system shell: they plug into Explorer and provide a quick view of the content of a certain type of file. For example, the Word Viewer lets you see Word documents but is far smaller and less powerful than the full Word program.

The user can neither modify nor execute special functions on a file that's opened with a quick viewer; the goal is simply to provide a read-only document preview without having to launch the application normally associated with the file. In order to give your documents full integration with the shell, file viewers must be considered as well as shell extensions.

File viewers rely on a special component that's been available since shell version 4.0, but which is not always installed by default – on one of my PCs, the component doesn't even appear as an option! In the end, I managed to install it by copying files from another PC and manually entering the keys to the registry. Anyway, I hope you're luckier than I was, and can get Windows Setup to install the component for you. Once it's in place, a Quick View item will appear on the context menu for files:

Windows comes with a number of interesting file viewers. One of them provides a useful view of all the symbols that a Win32 executable (DLL or EXE) exports and imports. Here it is in action on `winword.exe`:

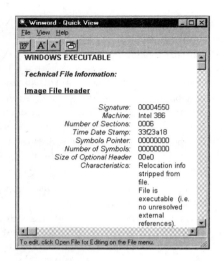

Starting a Quick View

When you click on Quick View, Windows launches the `quikview.exe` program, which is a kind of manager for file viewers. It doesn't do anything itself; instead, it loads and interfaces with the COM module responsible for actually displaying the contents of the file.

From our point of view, the biggest difference between file viewers and shell extensions is that the main program is not `explorer.exe` but `quikview.exe` — file viewers don't run in Explorer's address space. Apart from that, there's a new COM interface to cope with (`IFileViewer`), and registration follows a different logic. In a nutshell, though, it's fair to say that when it comes to loading and unloading file viewers, `quikview.exe` works quite a lot like Explorer.

The important thing about file viewers is that rather than having different applications for different types of files, there is just one main module that manages different COM extensions. These external plug-ins provide the actual viewing functionality, and they are all registered under:

```
HKEY_CLASSES_ROOT
    \QuickView
```

When you take a look, you'll find that there's a key for each supported file type. Here's a screenshot of a typical Windows 9x registry:

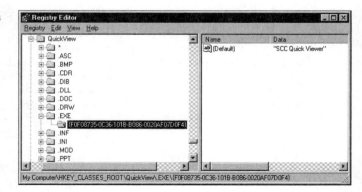

Each specific file extension key has a sub-key containing the CLSID of the COM server that provides the display. By default, all the supported file types are implemented in sccview.dll, whose CLSID is {F0F08735-0C36-101B-B086-0020AF07D0F4}.

How a Quick Viewer Gets Called

Either a click on the context menu or a command line like 'quikview filename' will cause the quick view manager to start. It examines the file extension, and scans the QuickView registry area searching for a CLSID. If successful, it creates an instance of the COM server and begins to deal with the interfaces this object must implement.

When the user requires a new quick view window, the manager looks at the state of the Replace Window toolbar button:

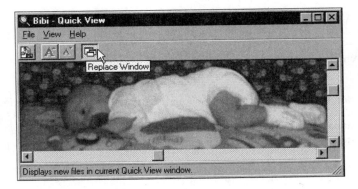

If it is set, then the same window and instance is used. Otherwise, a new instance of the viewer appears. A quick viewer must also support drag-and-drop, as you'll see shortly.

Writing a Quick Viewer

A quick viewer is an in-process COM module that implements three interfaces:

- ❑ IPersistFile
- ❑ IFileViewer
- ❑ IFileViewerSite

IPersistFile serves the purpose of loading the specified file. The manager just queries the module for IPersistFile, and calls the Load() method. A typical file viewer will then open the file and convert its content to a viewable format. If the file is a metafile, for example, then IPersistFile::Load() might want to create an HENHMETAFILE handle. Since a file viewer only ever takes 'read' actions, there's no need to implement the IPersistFile interface in its entirety, and writing code for the Load() method alone should work fine.

Showing the File

The IFileViewer interface is composed of three functions:

- ❑ PrintTo()
- ❑ Show()
- ❑ ShowInitialize()

529

Everything necessary to draw the content must go in `ShowInitialize()`. It must create an invisible window, and fill its client area with the file to display. In fact, this function should do everything that's needed to display the file, short of turning on the `WS_VISIBLE` style of the created window. In other words, `ShowInitialize()` is required to work on a kind of off-screen buffer.

`ShowInitialize()` should take care of everything to do with the user interface of the file viewer. This means:

- ❑ Creating the main window (if required)
- ❑ Creating and initializing the toolbar and the status bar
- ❑ Setting up menus and accelerators
- ❑ Creating the (initially invisible) window to host the content
- ❑ Resizing the windows properly

When the task has been completed successfully, it's the turn of `Show()`. Among other things, this method makes the window visible and enters a message loop.

From this brief description, you can see that a quick viewer is much more than a plug-in module. In fact, it's really a complete document/view application compiled inside a DLL. The command menus you can see, any font changes, and even starting the default application to open the file must all be handled inside the DLL.

A quick viewer should support drag-and-drop, and so the window must have the `WS_EX_ACCEPTFILES` flag. This may cause a situation where the viewer is currently displaying a document of type BMP, for example, and the user drops, say, a TXT file over the window. How can a viewer designed for bitmaps manage a text file properly?

To manage a case such as this, there's a lot of work done behind the scenes. Once I've explained it, it will be clear why the `IFileViewer` has both `ShowInitialize()` and `Show()` methods. The first method is called just to make sure that everything necessary to show the file is available – if it fails, the currently displayed document remains unchanged, as though you had never tried to open another file. This feature helps to make the entire quick view application look 'monolithic', instead of being (as it is) a collection of separate components.

When the `Show()` method is called, the quick viewer receives a `FVSHOWINFO` structure as its single argument:

```
typedef struct
{
    DWORD      cbSize;
    HWND       hwndOwner;
    int        iShow;
    DWORD      dwFlags;
    RECT       rect;
    LPUNKNOWN  punkRel;
    OLECHAR    strNewFile[MAX_PATH];
} FVSHOWINFO, *LPFVSHOWINFO;
```

This is used not only to pass information in, but also to return data back to the `quikview.exe` program. When a file is dropped, the quick viewer receives the usual `WM_DROPFILES` message. If the file can't be handled, then the module should do the following:

- ❑ Set `strNewFile` to the actual file name
- ❑ Turn on the `FVSIF_NEWFILE` bit in the `dwFlags` field
- ❑ Save its `IUnknown` pointer to `punkRel`
- ❑ Set `rect` to the current size of the window
- ❑ Exit the message loop

The important thing is that because you don't have to destroy a window, flickering and abrupt changes in the user interface are avoided. The `FVSHOWINFO` structure that you return is passed unchanged to the new (and appropriate) viewer for the new file.

`quikview.exe` invokes this new viewer (in our example, it will handle TXT files) and calls its `ShowInitialize()` method to prepare the display. Note that at this stage we still have the same bitmap on the screen, even though a completely different module is working under the hood. When the TXT quick viewer has finished loading and rendering the text, `quikview.exe` calls the `Show()` method, passing the `FVSHOWINFO` structure that was returned by the BMP quick viewer's `Show()` method. This structure contains the exact area the window should occupy, the name of the open file, and the `IUnknown` pointer of the previous (and still visible) quick viewer. `Show()` can display its window such that the previous one is completely covered.

At this point, the old window is still 'behind' the new one, and in fact the `Show()` method still has one more duty to perform. If it finds that the `FVSIF_NEWFILE` flags is set, then it must get the `punkRel` field of `FVSHOWINFO` and call `Release()` to free the old quick viewer.

Pinning

The third interface we have to deal with is `IFileViewerSite`, which has two quite easy methods:

- ❑ `GetPinnedWindow()`
- ❑ `SetPinnedWindow()`

A quick view window is said to be **pinned** when its **Replace Window** button is selected. This state causes the manager to direct all requests for new quick viewers to that window. If a window is pinned, then a click on the context menu is equivalent to dropping a file onto that window.

`GetPinnedWindow()` returns the handle of the window currently pinned (remember that you may have many quick viewers open at the same time), while `SetPinnedWindow()` moves that attribute to a new window. Their prototypes are simply:

```
HRESULT GetPinnedWindow(HWND*);
HRESULT SetPinnedWindow(HWND);
```

The logic behind pinning can be summarized this way:

- ❑ `SetPinnedWindow()` always fails if another window is pinned
- ❑ You always need to unpin the currently pinned window yourself – this is done by calling `SetPinnedWindow()` with a `NULL` argument

To let you know whether your window should start pinned, FVSHOWINFO includes the
FVSIF_PINNED flag in its dwFlags member. Given this, the most sensible way to pin a window is
by means of a couple of lines like these:

```
SetPinnedWindow(NULL);
SetPinnedWindow(hwnd);
```

Writing and Registering a File Viewer

Writing a file viewer is not the simple task it might seem, and in *Further Reading* I've put together the
best list of references I could find to help you. Once you've written it, however, registering it is
completely straightforward. Assuming that you've arranged a file viewer for .ext files, here's the key
change for the registry:

```
[HKEY_CLASSES_ROOT\QuickView\.EXT\<CLSID>]
@="EXT File Viewer"
```

Where <CLSID> should of course be changed to reflect the actual CLSID. Furthermore, don't forget
to register the server, as you would do with any other COM server. If you're using ATL to create the
object, then add the following lines to the RGS script file:

```
{
    QuickView
    {
        .ext
        {
            <CLSID> = s 'description'
        }
    }
}
```

Summary

This chapter has covered shell extensions at great length. We've examined their integration with
Explorer, the logic behind them, and their implementation. We also developed several examples that
showed the various types of shell extensions in action. In particular, we looked at:

- ❑ How to add custom property pages to the Properties dialog
- ❑ How to add custom menu items to a document's context menu
- ❑ How to add custom menu items to the system's Find menu.
- ❑ How to draw custom icons for each document of a certain type
- ❑ How to monitor changes in any folder in the system
- ❑ How to handle drag-and-drop onto files in the shell

I also provided an annotated review of the techniques available to extend the way Explorer copies
data to the clipboard, and handles drag-and-drop. Finally, I introduced you to file viewers, focusing
on the programming aspects that could give you problems.

Further Reading

With so many subjects covered, there's plenty of additional material that may interest you. To start, the first article on shell extensions that I saw was by Jeff Prosise, and appeared in the March 1995 edition of MSJ. Called *Integrate your Applications with the Windows 95 User Interface Using Shell Extensions*, the article is still valid as it presents a basic understanding of shell extensions with easy-to-understand examples.

The world's simplest code examples (many of which use MFC) for anything that relates to the shell are in Nancy Cluts' book, *Programming the Windows 95 User Interface*. Originally published by Microsoft Press, this book is now available in the Books section of the MSDN Library that comes with Visual C++.

Any topics that require serious knowledge of COM and OLE can be faced better after a look at Kraig Brockschmidt's *Inside OLE* (Microsoft Press) and Don Box's *Essential COM* (Addison-Wesley). Also David Chappell's *Understanding ActiveX and OLE* (Microsoft Press) can be very helpful. For more information about programming using ATL, the Wrox Press books *Beginning ATL COM Programming* (Grimes et al) and *Professional ATL COM Programming* (Grimes) are highly recommended.

Also in this chapter, I presented some code that enumerates the modules required by an executable, and the code on the web site includes an example that retrieves the list of running processes under Windows 9*x* and NT. To help here, I think that just about everything to do with the binary format of Win32 executables has been covered at one time or another in one of Matt Pietrek's *Under The Hood* columns in MSJ. In particular, I recommend the February 97 column, where he explains in detail how to follow the chain of imported libraries. Additional references may be found in his book, *Windows 95 System Programming Secrets* (IDG).

Regarding the enumeration of processes, I can suggest two articles. One is my own, and appeared in the October 97 issue of WDJ under the title *Process Names from Window Handles*. It explains how to get back to the name of the process that created a given window from an HWND. On the same theme, Pietrek's August 98 MSJ column is devoted to a similar topic. These two articles have in common a unified approach that hides the different system support for enumeration in Windows 9*x* and NT 4.0.

Finally, we come to file viewers. You'll find mention of these in the Cluts book I've already referenced, which is acceptable as a primer, but if you really need insights, tips, and even a complete case study, you must look at the series of three articles from Paul Dilascia that appeared in MSJ in January, March and June 1997. They will give you a precise idea of the circumstances in which you should enrich your application with file viewers. The series also covers using palettes, fonts, and hooking with MFC. The article that focuses specifically on file viewers is the final one, which I recommend as the *de facto* guide to programming file viewers.

When it comes to writing your first file viewer, I suggest you take the FileView example that comes with Visual C++ (look in the Samples\SDK\Win32 folder), compile it, and then make changes to that code. You risk consuming too much time by trying to write a file viewer from the ground up. Another helpful idea that stands out from the Dilascia articles is that you should think about setting up a framework that simplifies the development of file viewers, and the author provides one based on MFC.

Finally, to conclude this chapter, here some useful KB articles:

- ❑ **Knowledge Base Article Q138942:** *Debug a Windows Shell Extension*
- ❑ **Knowledge Base Article Q183106:** *Debug Control Panel Property Sheet Extensions*
- ❑ **Knowledge Base Article Q135986:** *How to Add a Custom Find Utility to the Start Menu*
- ❑ **Knowledge Base Article Q175030:** *Enumerate Applications in Win32*

16

Namespace Extensions

Explorer uses a hierarchical structure to represent many of the objects that form the system – files, folders, printers, network objects, and so on. These objects combine to define a **namespace**, which is a closed collection of symbols or names in which any given symbol or name can be successfully resolved. Resolving a name inside a namespace means successfully associating a given name with some concrete information that it represents.

The Explorer takes care of collecting all these objects together, communicating with them, and displaying their contents in what has now become the typical, two-pane window, with a tree view on the left and a list view on the right.

What makes things really interesting and exciting is that Explorer supports an interface that lets your code plug into this mechanism and add completely new, custom objects. In fact, Windows itself comes with a number of these **namespace extensions**, examples of which include the Dial-Up Networking, My Briefcase, and My Computer folders. In this chapter, I'm going to explain how the entire namespace machinery works, and walk you through the code as painlessly as possible.

Namespace extensions really are a huge topic. While it's not that hard to find articles about them, many of these satisfy only one of the above two commitments. Either they explain the basics, providing a mostly code-free overview of the whole mechanism, or else they concentrate on the code, discussing tricks and approaches, but don't provide an overall explanation of how namespace extensions work. Here's the running order of the things I'm going to cover:

❑   An overview of namespace extensions
❑   Installing a namespace extension
❑   Writing a complete namespace extension to browse the hierarchy of all the currently open windows
❑   Rules for defining custom PIDLs
❑   Exploiting namespace extensions to host custom applications in Explorer

Namespace extensions are built on a concept that is not particularly complex on its own. However, the extreme richness of details, programming approaches, implementation features, and required know-how makes writing them a far-from-trivial task. Even once you have an extension up and running, you're still a long way from finishing it. There are so many additional features you can add that the time and effort required for completion could double by the time you're done.

To be fair, a bare namespace extension is really no more complicated than the shell extensions we saw in the previous chapter. The trouble is that in most cases, a bare namespace extension is quite useless.

An Overview of Namespace Extensions

The world's easiest definition of a namespace extension is the following:

> **A namespace extension is a way of allowing external and custom information to be integrated in the Windows Explorer.**

By 'integrated', I basically mean that the information is displayed and handled in the same way that any other standard information would be. A synonym for 'namespace extension' might be 'custom-drawn folder' – a namespace extension includes the code to access and render the data, and the plumbing to integrate with the Explorer. The last of these is quite a standard piece of code, although encapsulating it in a collection of classes, for example, is still something of a challenge. (Are you listening, Microsoft?)

The information you want Explorer to display may or may not be related to a physical directory – consider the Dial-up Networking folder that has information about Internet connections, for example, or the Printers folder that contains details of the installed printers. There are also examples of namespace extensions that show file data in a non-standard fashion, like the Recycle Bin or the Temporary Internet Files folder.

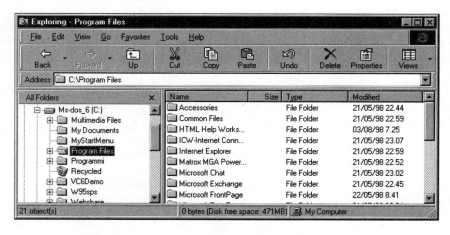

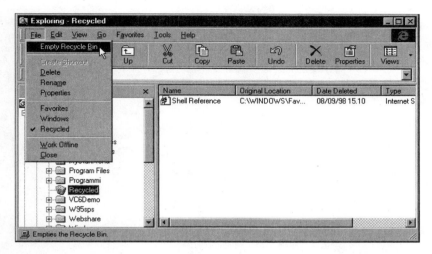

We can identify three levels of differences between the namespace extension and the 'ordinary' folder:

- ❑ The view, that is, the contents of Explorer's right-hand pane
- ❑ The menu (and possibly the toolbar)
- ❑ Other minor graphical changes, such as the icon in the tree view and custom text on the status bar

Most important of these is the custom content displayed in the view. Although the Recycle Bin uses a list view to display its content, this is only a choice — in your extensions, you can use any kind of window you like (although list views are probably the most flexible windows you can employ).

What Does Writing a Namespace Extension Mean?

A namespace extension renders a custom folder in Windows Explorer. It's an in-process COM object that the shell detects, provided that you have registered it correctly. A namespace extension implements a bunch of interfaces that Explorer will call back to get everything it needs to set up a proper view of the folder. Typically, Explorer requires:

- ❑ A folder manager object, through which it will ask its questions
- ❑ A window to display the folder's content
- ❑ An object to enumerate the various items contained in the folder
- ❑ A means of identifying the various items in the folder uniquely
- ❑ A collection of accessory functions to customize its user interface

This figure illustrates the architecture of Explorer:

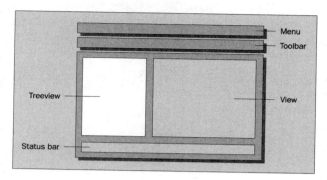

And the next figure shows how this relates to namespace extensions:

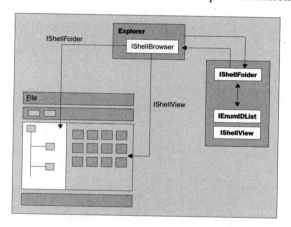

When Explorer detects the presence of a namespace extension (and I'll explain exactly how it does that later on), it loads the COM server that implements it and asks for an interface called IShellFolder. This interface works as a folder manager, and has the task of providing Explorer with everything it needs. In other words, it's a kind of proxy between Explorer and the rest of the extension.

When Explorer needs to display the contents of the view, it asks IShellFolder for a view object. Similarly, when it's time to display nodes in the tree view, it asks to enumerate the content and looks for the folder and subfolder attributes. Once again, all this is done through the IShellFolder interface.

When a namespace extension is loaded, Explorer also gives it a chance to update the user interface. All the events that may be of interest to the extension are notified by calling an appropriate function in one of the defined interfaces.

Put another way, writing a namespace extension means being ready to answer any incoming call from Explorer, and answering a call means implementing a certain function in a particular COM interface. As you might imagine, there's a minimal set of interfaces and functions that must be supported in order for the extension to be well integrated.

The Inner Structure of Explorer

Explorer is a program that relies entirely on shell and namespace extensions to put flesh on its skeleton that's made up of an empty framework with a tree view, a list view and a few other controls. Everything that actually gets displayed comes from outside the `explorer.exe` file. The standard extensions are implemented in `shell32.dll`, and this makes them system code of a sort, but they're definitely namespace extensions nevertheless.

Explorer scans the registry for installed components and opens communications with any of them, whether they were written by you or provided with the operating system.

Namespace Extensions vs. Shell Extensions

In principle, shell extensions and namespace extensions are very similar indeed. Both need registration to be detected and invoked, both are in-process COM servers implementing a fixed number of interfaces and both allow customization of the shell. What's quite different is the final effect they produce: a namespace extension adds a new folder to Explorer, while a shell extension is limited to working on file types.

Primary Interfaces

Now that we have some understanding of what's going on when namespace extensions come into play, let's see in more detail what *really* happens. This gives us a chance to look at the interfaces and at some of the function prototypes as well. Later in the chapter I'll be using this information to construct our examples. The interfaces a namespace extension is absolutely required to implement are:

- ❏ IShellFolder
- ❏ IPersistFolder
- ❏ IEnumIDList
- ❏ IShellView

The first two of these evaluate to what I earlier termed a "folder manager". IEnumIDList is what I called an "enumerator", while IShellView is mainly intended to provide a window for the view that will replace the standard list view.

Spanning across these four major interfaces (plus some other minor ones), there's the concept of a PIDL. I explained exactly what a PIDL is and how it is implemented in Chapter 2, but I can summarize here: a PIDL is an identifier that unambiguously identifies an item in a folder, and across the whole of the shell's namespace. A PIDL is something that's specific to a type of folder, and so when you're writing a 'custom folder', you should provide a 'custom PIDL' too! Although there are a few basic rules to follow when it comes to doing this, there's no general way of designing PIDLs, and they depend mostly upon the content they help to render. I'll have much more to say on this subject later in the chapter.

There are some other, optional, COM interfaces that a namespace extension can implement, and for a real-world extension exactly how 'optional' they are is open to question. IContextMenu and IExtractIcon, for example, are very often required to assign custom context menus and icons to single items.

In the following sections, I'll present tables that list all the functions defined by the various interfaces. If you can reasonably avoid implementing them, their names will appear in Italics. To avoid implementation, and to let Explorer know what you're up to, just return an error code of `E_NOTIMPL`.

An Activation Timeline

Before we depart on our tour of the interfaces, here's something to keep in mind for when we do so. To give you a picture of the communication that goes on during the process of getting a namespace extension displayed in Explorer, I've drawn up this timetable of events:

- ❑ Explorer detects the namespace extension through a **junction point**, and gets its `CLSID`.
- ❑ An instance of it is created, and Explorer queries for the `IShellFolder` interface.
- ❑ Explorer asks the object implementing `IShellFolder` to return a pointer to the `IShellView` interface on a view object.
- ❑ A pointer to `IShellBrowser` is passed to the view object, allowing it to manipulate Explorer's menu and toolbar. The view object also receives a pointer to `IShellFolder`.
  - ❑ Explorer asks the `IShellFolder` object to return an object to enumerate the content of the folder. This object will implement the `IEnumIDList` interface.
  - ❑ Explorer walks the list of elements contained in the folder. For each one it gets the `PIDL` and draws it according to its role and characteristics.

This is what happens when you select the namespace extension's node in Explorer's tree view. When you click to expand it, Explorer does the following:

- ❑ It asks `IShellFolder` to return an object to enumerate the content of the folder.
- ❑ It displays only those elements that have the 'folder' attribute. If they also have the 'has subfolders' attribute, 'plus' nodes are drawn.
- ❑ It asks `IShellFolder` to provide the icon to display near each node in the tree view. (In fact, it will receive a pointer to the `IExtractIcon` interface.)
- ❑ It asks `IShellFolder` to provide the text to be displayed for each item.
- ❑ It asks `IShellFolder` to provide the context menu for each item.

The Folder Manager

`IShellFolder` derives from `IPersistFolder`, which in turn inherits from `IPersist`. The functions of `IPersistFolder` allow Explorer to initialize the new folder, telling it where is located in the namespace. The `IShellFolder`-specific functions constitute a programming interface by means of which Explorer can ask for a view, an enumerator object, or a child subfolder. Furthermore, an `IShellFolder` object must be capable of providing the attributes of each single item it contains, comparing two such items, and returning their display names. Items are identified through `PIDL`s.

The IPersistFolder interface

The following table presents the functions of IPersistFolder:

Function	Description
GetClassID()	Returns the CLSID of the object. This method comes from IPersist.
Initialize()	Allows the folder to initialize itself. The method is passed a PIDL identifying the location of the folder in the namespace; this may or may not be relevant to the folder. If it is, it should be cached for further use, otherwise the method will simply return S_OK.

You will usually implement both of these methods, whose prototypes and typical (minimal) code follow:

```
STDMETHODIMP CShellFolder::GetClassID(LPCLSID lpClassID)
{
    *lpClassID = CLSID_WinView;
    return S_OK;
}

STDMETHODIMP CShellFolder::Initialize(LPCITEMIDLIST pidl)
{
    return S_OK;
}
```

The snippet is taken from the example that I'll cover in greater detail later in the chapter. For now, you need to know that CLSID_WinView should be a constant that identifies the CLSID of your own extension, and CShellFolder is the name of a C++ class that derives from IShellFolder and IPersistFolder.

You never call the methods of IPersistFolder directly. Instead, the system calls them during the process that binds it to your folder.

The IShellFolder interface

The IShellFolder interface exposes the ten functions listed below:

Function	Description
BindToObject()	This is the way by which the shell asks the module to open a subfolder, if any. This method is passed a PIDL and should simply create a new folder object based on the PIDL received.
BindToStorage()	At present, the shell never invokes this method, so just return E_NOTIMPL.
CompareIDs()	Takes two PIDLs and should decide their order — that one is greater than the other, or that they are equal.

Table Continued on Following Page

Function	Description
CreateViewObject()	Creates and returns the IShellView object that will provide the content for the right-hand pane.
EnumObjects()	Creates and returns the IEnumIDList object that will provide enumeration of items.
GetAttributesOf()	Returns a family of attributes for the specified item – whether it can be renamed or copied; whether it requires a ghosted icon; whether it's a folder or has subfolders. The valid constants have mnemonic names beginning with SFGAO_. Check the documentation for a complete list.
GetDisplayNameOf()	Returns the name to be used to render the item in the folder, the address bar, or for parsing purposes. The application for which the item's name is needed is one of the arguments passed. The value comes from the SHGNO enumerated type. (See later.)
GetUIObjectOf()	By means of this method, Explorer asks for a specified interface that has to do with the UI. It's a kind of highly specialized QueryInterface().
ParseDisplayName()	Returns a PIDL given a display name. The display name, however, is not *necessarily* what appears in the shell view or in the address bar. It is what GetDisplayNameOf() returns when the SHGDN_FORPARSING flag is set.
SetNameOf()	Assigns a new display name to a given object. The name is to be used in the address bar, in folders, and for parsing purposes.

I explained display names in Chapter 4, but briefly, it is the name used to render the item within the shell. In most cases, this display name coincides with the actual file name, although if the folder doesn't contain files it must be necessarily something else. There are three types of display names that are to be used in three different contexts, and they all come from the following enum type:

```
typedef enum tagSHGDN
{
    SHGDN_NORMAL = 0,                        // Name relative to the desktop
    SHGDN_INFOLDER = 1,                      // Name relative to the folder
    SHGDN_INCLUDE_NONFILESYS = 0x2000,       // Also non-file system objects
    SHGDN_FORADDRESSBAR = 0x4000,            // Used for address bar
    SHGDN_FORPARSING = 0x8000,               // Used for parsing
} SHGNO;
```

While each item is uniquely identified by a PIDL, it can be rendered with different names in different situations. To return the display name for any case, you implement GetDisplayNameOf(). This function receives a parameter whose value is a combination of the SHGNO values. In particular, the function might be required to return an absolute (SHGDN_NORMAL) or a relative name (SHGDN_INFOLDER). In the former case, you'd return a display name relative to the desktop, while in the latter a name relative to the parent folder is required.

In addition to this, there may be more flags that say more about the use the shell will make of the name, giving you a chance to adjust it properly, if needed. When the name is being shown in the address bar, SHGDN_FORADDRESSBAR will be set; when you detect SHGDN_FORPARSING, it means that the name will be passed to ParseDisplayName() to convert it to a PIDL. You may need to include special information to facilitate this task.

The SHGDN_INCLUDE_NONFILESYS bit is simply informational, and lets the method know that the caller also wants non-file system objects. If the PIDL passed is not for a file system object and this bit is not set, the method should fail.

> By means of IShellFolder, Explorer can get any information about the extension it may need in order to host it properly. Any required interface is obtained through the methods of this interface: the shell view, the context menu, the icon handler, and the item enumerator.

Interface	Obtained through
IShellView	CreateViewObject()
IContextMenu	GetUIObjectOf()
IExtractIcon	GetUIObjectOf()
IEnumIDList	EnumObjects()

Enumeration of Items

You write a namespace extension in order to embed a custom folder in the shell. This 'virtual' (rather than physical) folder may have contents that you want to display in a non-standard fashion. Alternatively, it may have non-standard contents that you want to display as if it *was* a list of file objects. A hypothetical folder called My Hardware, for example, could contain references to the various devices attached to the system. This information might be presented as a list view, in which the devices are rendered as items.

Whatever the specifics of the content, it's likely that it will be composed of a collection of elements, although nobody outside the namespace extension is necessarily aware of that fact. Nevertheless, Explorer needs to enumerate these objects in order to draw the tree view, for example.

To allow external modules to walk through the content of a custom folder, a namespace extension should implement the IEnumIDList interface. This is a collection of functions that provides any module with the ability to enumerate the various items of any folder. This interface is highly generic, and a module can communicate with it without knowing anything about the content or the organization of the folder itself.

The IEnumIDList Interface

The `IEnumIDList` interface exposes four functions for moving back and forth within a given collection.

Function	Description
Next()	Returns the specified number of items in the collection. Each item found is identified via a PIDL.
Skip()	Skips over a specified number of items.
Reset()	Moves the current pointer to the top of the list.
Clone()	Duplicates an object.

The key function is `Next()`, whose prototype looks like this:

```
HRESULT IEnumIDList::Next(ULONG          celt,
                          LPITEMIDLIST*  rgelt,
                          ULONG*         pceltFetched);
```

The first argument to the function specifies the number of items to retrieve, and PIDLs to these items will be stored by the function into the `rgelt` array. The total number of elements actually copied is then stored in the third argument, `pceltFetched`. An enumerator object manipulates (or acts as if it manipulates) a linked list of all the items. A full implementation, therefore, should store a pointer to the current item and move it by as many items as `Next()` retrieves.

The `Skip()` method also moves forward the item pointer by the number passed as its argument, but it doesn't actually retrieve or read their content as it does so:

```
HRESULT IEnumIDList::Skip(ULONG celt);
```

`Clone()` and `Reset()` are helper methods for the object, and below you'll find a couple of typical implementations of them:

```
STDMETHODIMP CEnumIDList::Reset()
{
   m_pCurrent = m_pFirst;
   return S_OK;
}

STDMETHODIMP CEnumIDList::Clone(IEnumIDList** ppEnum)
{
   return E_NOTIMPL;
}
```

Usually, the methods of this interface are built on top of a linked list that is filled during initialization of the class that implements it. Each item of the list points to a PIDL.

The Importance of the PIDL

With the `IEnumIDList` functions, anyone can navigate through the content of any folder. In a namespace extension, an object implementing `IEnumIDList` is returned as the result of a call to `IShellFolder::EnumObjects()`. However, a generic interface for enumerating items is not enough to identify each folder item correctly, and this is where PIDLs fit in.

As I explained back in Chapter 2, a PIDL is a pointer to a collection of `SHITEMID` structures. It allows you easily and unequivocally to identify a relative or absolute route to any given object in a folder. Such a route is said to be "relative" if it begins with the folder that contains the item, and "absolute" if it is a series of references that starts from the Desktop and goes straight to the object. A PIDL always identifies the element uniquely throughout the entire shell.

Defining a good PIDL is clearly a central issue for any namespace extension. A PIDL should be a collection of pieces of data, each of which refers to a folder or a subfolder encountered in the path from the Desktop down to the item. The structure of a PIDL depends upon the data you want the folder to render, and deciding how to organize the PIDL is ultimately up to the programmer, but there are few recommendations to consider:

❑　The PIDL should be allocated through the shell's memory allocator (`IMalloc` interface). This allows Explorer to free it. A PIDL is not an object but just a block of memory: once you've passed it to Explorer, it must be able to free it without nasty side effects.

❑　PIDLs can be saved to and then read from persistent storage media, such as disk files. This implies that all the information needed must be found sequentially. No pointers and no references to external data should be present.

❑　Since PIDLs can be persisted, you might want to consider using signatures and a version number so that you can always recognize your PIDL at any time, and guarantee backward compatibility. Of course, if that's not an issue for your application, you don't need to do it.

A PIDL is an array of `SHITEMID` structures:

```
typedef struct _SHITEMID
{
    USHORT cb;
    BYTE abID[1];
} SHITEMID, *LPSHITEMID;
```

`cb` is the size of the entire structure, including itself. The `abID` member marks the beginning of a sequence of data that can be structured in any way you want. As an example, consider the following `PIDLDATA` structure:

```
typedef struct _PIDLDATA
{
    TCHAR szSignature[SIGNSIZE];
    WORD wVersion;
    TCHAR szFileName[MAX_PATH];
    BYTE icon[ICONFILESIZE];
} PIDLDATA, *LPPIDLDATA;
```

This is a possible way of rendering the data that forms a filename PIDL – it's a chunk of data that's pointed by the abID field of the SHITEMID structure, and there are a couple of things to notice about it. Firstly, the strings have been included with all their characters, because for the reasons explained above you can't use a pointer to a string. The TCHAR[] buffer ensures that all the content is stored sequentially. Secondly, I'm assuming the need to store an icon, and you can't use an HICON as that also evaluates to a block of memory stored elsewhere. Instead, you need to serialize all the bytes that form the icon image.

The Shell View

The view object is undoubtedly the most interesting part of any namespace extension. A large part of the code you write for namespace extensions works in the background, silently communicating with Explorer. You never see it clearly in action.

However, the view object creates and manages a window – the **shell view**. A shell view is an ordinary window, with ordinary styles and a window procedure. The view object is what ends up embedded in the Explorer's right pane, displaying the contents of the folder selected in the left pane's tree view.

The view object exposes the methods of the IShellView interface to work with the shell view and deal with anything relating to the folder's user interface, message loop, and merging of menus and toolbars. The IShellView interface derives from IOleWindow.

The IShellView Interface

The following are the functions you should implement in order to support the IShellView interface.

Function	Description
AddPropertySheetPages()	Allows you to add custom pages to the Folder Options... dialog box.
CreateViewWindow()	Creates and returns a window to be embedded in Explorer's right pane. It should be a borderless dialog.
DestroyViewWindow()	Destroys the previous window.
EnableModeless()	Not currently used by Explorer. Simply return E_NOTIMPL.
EnableModelessSV()	Not currently not used by Explorer. Simply return E_NOTIMPL.
GetCurrentInfo()	Returns the current settings for the folder through a FOLDERSETTINGS structure. (See Chapter 5.)
GetItemObject()	Returns a pointer to the interface for the context menu or clipboard, given a set of items. Mostly invoked by common dialogs.
Refresh()	Causes the folder's content to be redrawn.
SaveViewState()	Saves the state of the view. (More on this later.)

Function	Description
SelectItem()	Changes the selection state of one or more items.
TranslateAccelerator()	Translates any key hit when the focus is on the extension. Return S_OK to prevent Explorer from translating again.
UIActivate()	Invoked when the activation state changes – when the folder is activated or deactivated, for example. (See later.)
GetWindow()	Returns the view's window handle. This method is inherited from IOleWindow.
ContextSensitiveHelp()	The folder should enter or exit the context sensitive help mode and handle all messages differently. Not usually implemented in a namespace extension. This method is inherited from IOleWindow.

A view object is sometimes given the opportunity to save its state to persistent storage. When this can be done, Explorer calls SaveViewState(). Now, this process can be a little tricky, so although you could probably figure out several other ways of making the settings of a folder persistent, the recommended one is to save it to a stream. A pointer to an IStream object is returned by the GetViewStateStream() method of the IShellBrowser interface, but just a minute... where did *that* interface come from?

In fact, this interface is implemented by Explorer, but there's no obvious function for getting hold of it. Instead, a pointer to it is passed to the shell view in CreateViewWindow()'s parameter list, and it would therefore be sensible to store it for further use in the extensions you write.

The upshot of all this is that in the SaveViewState() function, there will be code something like the following:

```
IStream* pstm;
pSB->GetViewStateStream(STGM_WRITE, &pstm);
pstm->Write(&data, sizeof(data), NULL);
```

With GetViewStateStream(), you can get hold of a stream into which you may write your state settings, such as column widths, icons, and anything else that may apply to your extension. To read the state back again, we follow the same approach, but this time open the view stream for reading:

```
IStream* pstm;
pSB->GetViewStateStream(STGM_READ, &pstm);
pstm->Read(&data, sizeof(data), NULL);
```

Code like this would normally appear in CreateViewWindow(), after you've constructed the shell view window itself. There's no need to close this stream yourself, because the task will be accomplished directly by Explorer.

Talking to Explorer: IShellBrowser

In one of my earlier diagrams, I outlined that Explorer uses the methods of `IShellFolder` to initiate the creation process for a new folder. The things it gets from `IShellFolder` (namely, pointers to `IShellView` and other interfaces) can interact with Explorer through `IShellBrowser`, which is an interface implemented with the precise goal of making communication between Explorer and namespace extensions easier.

`IShellBrowser` exposes several functions (see the documentation for details), but you will use it in your extensions for two main purposes:

- ❑ Getting the view state stream
- ❑ Interacting with Explorer's menu and toolbar

We've already considered the first of these, so let's look now at the steps required to modify menus and toolbars in order to add items specific to our own namespace extensions.

Modifying Explorer's Menu

A folder, even a custom folder, is always a folder. This means that it has the usual menu and toolbar that any other folder has. Or rather, it has the usual menu and toolbar unless it decides to change them!

A folder will make its changes to Explorer's menu and toolbar when it gets the focus, and will remove them whenever it loses it. The activation state for a folder is notified through the `UIActivate()` method:

```
HRESULT IShellView::UIActivate(UINT uState);
```

The `uState` argument can assume one of three possible values:

Flag	Description
SVUIA_ACTIVATE_FOCUS	The folder now has the focus
SVUIA_ACTIVATE_NOFOCUS	The folder is selected but doesn't have the focus
SVUIA_DEACTIVATE	The folder no longer has the focus

A folder has the focus when the system focus belongs to one of the view's child elements. If the folder is selected only in the left pane, then we have the circumstances in which `SVUIA_ACTIVATE_NOFOCUS` comes into play. For each of these different activation states, you can have different menus and toolbars to display in the Explorer's user interface, and all these changes are usually accomplished in `UIActivate()`.

To change the menu – regardless of whether you want to add a brand new popup menu, or simply add or remove items from existing ones – you always have to create a new, empty, top-level menu. The code for creating a new menu is simply:

```
hMenu = CreateMenu();
```

Then you just ask the shell to fill it the normal way. The code required is:

```
OLEMENUGROUPWIDTHS omw = {0, 0, 0, 0, 0, 0};
m_pShellBrowser->InsertMenusSB(hMenu, &omw);
```

The OLEMENUGROUPWIDTHS is a data structure, formed by an array of six longs, which comes into play when a container and an embedded object have to share a menu. (For more information about this you can refer to the Visual C++ or MSDN documentation about OLE in-place editing.)

Basically, the menu of Explorer (and of every OLE container) is divided into six logical groups, each of which can contain as many individual popup menus as required. The groups are:

Group Name	Position	Controlled by
File	0	Explorer (Container)
Edit	1	Namespace Extension (Object)
Container	2	Explorer (Container)
Object	3	Namespace Extension (Object)
Window	4	Explorer (Container)
Help	5	Namespace Extension (Object)

There's not necessarily a one-to-one relationship between group names and popup menus, either for the number or for the names. In other words, the first menu of the File group can variously contain:

- ❑ A single popup menu called File
- ❑ A couple of popup menus called, say, Property and Edit
- ❑ A popup called File and another one named, say, Directory
- ❑ For that matter, any other possible combination

The number of individual popup menus that each group contains is stored at the corresponding position in the OLEMENUGROUPWIDTHS structure. This is also referred as the **width** of the menu group.

By calling InsertMenusSB(), you're asking the shell to fill its own portion of the shared menu. As the table shows, the container and the object – in this case, Explorer and the namespace extension – are responsible for three groups each. In the case of Explorer, after calling this:

```
OLEMENUGROUPWIDTHS omw = {0, 0, 0, 0, 0, 0};
m_pShellBrowser->InsertMenusSB(hMenu, &omw);
```

The menu is as follows:

Menu	Group
File	File
Edit	File
View	Container
Go	Container
Favorites	Container
Tools	Container
Help	Window

The `OLEMENUGROUPWIDTHS` structure contains {2, 0, 4, 0, 1, 0}, and you can use these values as offsets to place any new popup menu correctly. To add your own items or popups, use traditional Win32 functions like `InsertMenuItem()`, `DeleteMenu()`, or indeed any function that lets you modify the structure of a menu.

> *Be aware that* `AppendMenu()`, `InsertMenu()`, `ModifyMenu()` *and a few other menu functions have been declared obsolete with the Win32 API. They are still supported and work fine but code that makes use of them is not guaranteed to continue working with future versions of Windows. Use the newer* `InsertMenuItem()` *function instead.*

In general, a hosted object should be a good citizen and not remove items or popups set by the container. In the same way, it should avoid invading the space reserved for the container by placing its popups in a group managed by the container. However, these rules are intended to apply to generic OLE containers, and if Explorer defines, say, an empty Edit menu, then in my opinion there's no reason to leave it there when your folder gets selected. Another circumstance in which I think you can break the rules is when you want to add a custom About command. In this case, I'd replace the standard item with my own, even if this means removing the item added by Explorer.

The shell assigns unique identifiers to its popup menus in order to let you do your editing work by command instead of by position. The `shlobj.h` header file defines constants like these to help identify the Explorer's popups by command:

- ❑ FCIDM_MENU_FILE
- ❑ FCIDM_MENU_EDIT
- ❑ FCIDM_MENU_VIEW
- ❑ FCIDM_MENU_FAVORITES
- ❑ FCIDM_MENU_TOOLS
- ❑ FCIDM_MENU_HELP

As you can see, an analogous constant for the Go menu is missing. If you look at the `shlobj.h` header file, you'll find other similar constants, but they aren't relevant to modifying a menu from a namespace extension.

The IDs of the items to be added must lie in the range 0x0000 to 0x7FFF, the extremes of which evaluate to the constants FCIDM_SHVIEWFIRST and FCIDM_SHVIEWLAST respectively. Once you've changed the menu according to your needs, you have to save it all with a call to:

```
m_pShellBrowser->SetMenuSB(hMenu, NULL, hwndView);
```

Curiously, SetMenuSB() is documented as if it takes only two arguments:

```
HRESULT SetMenuSB(HMENU hmenuShared, HOLEMENU holemenuReserved);
```

But it actually requires a third argument:

```
HRESULT SetMenuSB(
    HMENU     hmenuShared,           // Shared menu
    HOLEMENU  holemenuReserved,      // Currently ignored by Explorer
    HWND      hwndActiveObject       // Handle to the view's window
);
```

The first argument is the menu that's shared between Explorer and the namespace extension, the second is currently ignored, while the last is the handle of the window that renders the folder. To understand *why* the second argument is currently ignored, I need to make a little digression on how OLE in-place editing works when it comes to sharing a menu between containers and objects.

The methods of IShellBrowser that work with menus and toolbars stem from similar methods employed by IOleInPlaceFrame, an interface implemented by OLE containers. From one point of view, Explorer is a specialized container for namespace extensions, so let's draw some comparisons. After modifying the menus, a typical object hosted by an OLE container would need to fill out its own portion of the OLEMENUGROUPWIDTHS structure and then create what's called a 'OLE menu descriptor'. In fact, there's a function to do exactly this, with the following prototype:

```
HOLEMENU OleCreateMenuDescriptor(
    HMENU                 hmenuShared,      // Combined menu
    LPOLEMENUGROUPWIDTHS  lpMenuWidths      // Updated OLEMENUGROUPWIDTHS
)
```

Next, it passes this HOLEMENU handle to SetMenu(), which is a method very similar to SetMenuSB(). The prototype is:

```
HRESULT SetMenu(HMENU hmenuShared, HOLEMENU holemenu);
```

Inside this function, the container ends up calling OleSetMenuDescriptor(), which is responsible for setting up the dispatching code for the messages generated by the menus. In practice, the function installs a hook, detects menu messages, and then dispatches them to the right window − be that the container's or the object's. To understand *which* window a given message is targeted to, the hook simply looks at the position of the menu that generated it. It resolves any doubt by comparing that position to the values in the OLEMENUGROUPWIDTHS structure referred to by HOLEMENU.

At present, Explorer uses different logic to dispatch messages, and needs neither an HOLEMENU nor that the client should fill out the OLEMENUGROUPWIDTHS structure completely. When you call SetMenuSB(), Explorer sets a hook to intercept messages, and the messages to be dispatched to the active view window (the hwndActiveObject parameter seen above) are recognized via their IDs, and not through the position of the menu.

You'll make all these changes to the menu when the activation state is different from
`SVUIA_DEACTIVATE`. When the user deactivates the folder, you have to restore the previous
situation. To do this, just remove the menu by calling into `IShellBrowser::RemoveMenusSB()`:

```
m_pShellBrowser->RemoveMenusSB(hMenu);
DestroyMenu(hMenu);
```

Modifying Explorer's Toolbar

To manipulate the toolbar, you first need its window handle, and this is another service that
`IShellBrowser` can provide – the function you need is called `GetControlWindow()`, and it just
returns an `HWND`. However, the documentation discourages sending messages directly to this window,
so for forward-compatibility purposes you should use `SendControlMsg()`, yet another of
`IShellBrowser`'s methods:

```
HRESULT IShellBrowser::SendControlMsg(UINT      id,
                                      UINT      uMsg,
                                      WPARAM    wParam,
                                      LPARAM    lParam,
                                      LRESULT*  pret);
```

It looks like an ordinary `SendMessage()` function, with two differences: the `id` argument to identify
which control you're addressing (toolbar or status bar), and `pret` to get the value returned by the
message you're sending. Use the `FCW_TOOLBAR` constant to address the toolbar.

> *Refer to the Visual C++ or MSDN documentation for details about the structures and the
> messages needed to deal with toolbars.*

At this point, you can send messages to add as many buttons you want. Sounds easy? Well, that
depends – adding a button to a toolbar is not a trivial task. A toolbar button has a bitmap, so first of
all you have to register a new bitmap in the toolbar. Here's a code snippet that shows how to do it:

```
TBADDBITMAP tbab;
tbab.hInst = g_hInstance;     // Set the module that contains the bitmap
tbab.nID = IDB_TOOLBAR;       // Bitmap ID in the module's resources

m_pShellBrowser->SendControlMsg(FCW_TOOLBAR, TB_ADDBITMAP,
                    1, reinterpret_cast<LPARAM>(&tbab), &lNewIndex);
```

`TBADDBITMAP` is a structure that contains just two members to identify a bitmap. Once you've set
these to the module that contains the bitmap in its resources and the appropriate ID, you pass the
structure down to the toolbar via a `TB_ADDBITMAP` message. This message can actually accept a
whole array of structures, so the `wParam` argument of the message (1 in the snippet above) is the size
of the array, while `lParam` is a pointer to its first element. `lNewIndex` is a buffer that will contain
the return value of the message, and this is important because it turns out to be the index of the
image in the toolbar's global bitmap. All the bitmaps that come together to form a toolbar are stored
as a single bitmap in which the small images are concatenated side by side.

Exactly the same technique is required for adding a text label to the button. (Text labels are required for buttons going into Explorer's toolbar.)

```
m_pShellBrowser->SendControlMsg(FCW_TOOLBAR, TB_ADDSTRING,
                    NULL, reinterpret_cast<LPARAM>(szLabel), &lNewString);
```

The message involved this time is TB_ADDSTRING, whose lParam argument is a pointer to the string. Here lNewString will contain an index that helps the toolbar to identify the text label.

Once we've registered a new bitmap *and* a new string with the toolbar, it's time to declare a TBBUTTON structure that renders a button.

```
TBBUTTON tbb;
ZeroMemory(&tbb, sizeof(TBBUTTON));
tbb.iBitmap = lNewIndex;
tbb.iCommand = IDM_FILE_DOSOMETHING;
tbb.iString = lNewString;
tbb.fsState = TBSTATE_ENABLED;
tbb.fsStyle = TBSTYLE_BUTTON;
```

At long last, we can send the message that sets a new button:

```
m_pShellBrowser->SetToolbarItems(&tbb, 1, FCT_MERGE);
```

If you're feeling brave, you can follow the low-level road by sending messages directly to the toolbar, although I should point out once again that Microsoft discourages this technique:

```
m_pShellBrowser->SendControlMsg(FCW_TOOLBAR, TB_INSERTBUTTON,
                    0, reinterpret_cast<LPARAM>(&tbb), NULL);
```

This line adds a new button to the beginning of the toolbar, as the first button. This approach is actually somewhat more powerful than the one we've been examining because it allows you to add buttons *anywhere*. Adding them with SetToolbarItems() means they're *always* at the end of the toolbar.

Even if there's no explicit advice on this subject in the documentation, in my opinion, you should remove any buttons you've added when the folder loses the focus. The only option you have here is to use SendControlMsg(), regardless of the technique used to add the button in the first place:

```
TBBUTTON tbb;
m_pShellBrowser->SendControlMsg(FCW_TOOLBAR, TB_GETBUTTON,
                        0, reinterpret_cast<LPARAM>(&tbb), NULL);
if(tbb.idCommand == IDM_FILE_RUN)
    m_pShellBrowser->SendControlMsg(FCW_TOOLBAR, TB_DELETEBUTTON, 0, TRUE, NULL);
```

Before deleting the button, make sure it's the button you want to remove! Checking against the command ID is a reliable technique for doing this.

Accessing Explorer's Status Bar

The interface we used above for the toolbar can also be used to set custom text on the status bar; the ID to identify the status bar during calls to `IShellBrowser::SendControlMsg()` is `FCW_STATUS`. In this way, you are completely free to send messages and format the status bar at your leisure. However, if you simply want some text to appear there, I suggest that you use another of `IShellBrowser`'s helper functions, `SetStatusTextSB()`:

```
m_pShellBrowser->SetStatusTextSB(wszText);
```

The only drawback of this function (if you're developing ANSI-based software) is that it absolutely requires Unicode strings, and you have to do the conversion on your own.

Additional Interfaces

While using Explorer, you can activate context menus for each item, drag-and-drop them, or even copy them to the clipboard. Once again, this is not a behavior built into Explorer, but a feature provided by the folders themselves. More precisely, it's provided by the namespace extension that manages the folder's appearance and behavior. Who knows better than the folder itself what its items actually represent, and how to handle them?

While the folder carries out the specific action of packaging data or preparing the menu, the *trigger* is still Explorer. It detects the action of a user, and asks the namespace extension to provide data to be copied to the clipboard or dragged-and-dropped.

The right pane of Explorer is drawn entirely by the view object, but the namespace extension has no control over what goes on in the left pane. Nevertheless, even in the tree view, a user can invoke a context menu or open the sub-tree that displays the list of subfolders inside a given folder. Who is providing that context menu, and the icons to fill the tree view? As always, it's the namespace extension acting upon Explorer's requests.

It will come as no surprise at all that the namespace extension does this by implementing a handful of additional COM interfaces: `IContextMenu`, `IDataObject`, and `IExtractIcon`. Each of the pieces of functionality I've mentioned depends on one of these interfaces. If the interface is missing, the functionality isn't available.

Getting Pointers to Additional Interfaces

We saw several examples of shell context menus in the last chapter, so you should already have a pretty good idea of how to implement the `IContextMenu` interface. The implementation of `IContextMenu` from within a namespace extension is roughly the same as it is for shell extensions — what changes is the initialization procedure. When the user right-clicks in Explorer's tree view, the shell attempts to get a pointer to the folder's implementation of `IContextMenu`. If something valid is returned, the context menu appears. Otherwise, the operation is rejected.

The means by which Explorer gets a pointer to `IContextMenu` is the
`IShellFolder::GetUIObjectOf()` method, and here's a typical implementation:

```
STDMETHODIMP CShellFolder::GetUIObjectOf(HWND hwndOwner, UINT uCount,
    LPCITEMIDLIST* pPidl, REFIID riid, LPUINT puReserved, LPVOID* ppvReturn)
{
    // Clears the buffer to return data
    *ppvReturn = NULL;

    // Fails if the interface is required for >1 PIDLs
    if(uCount != 1)
        return E_FAIL;

    // Check the riid against the additional interfaces implemented
    // IExtractIcon
    if(IsEqualIID(riid, IID_IExtractIcon))
    {
        CExtractIcon* pei;
        pei = new CExtractIcon(pPidl[0]);          // First item of pPidl array
        if(pei)
        {
            pei->AddRef();                         // Increment the ref count
            pei->QueryInterface(riid, ppvReturn);  // QI implies inc ref count
            pei->Release();                        // Decrement the ref count
            return S_OK;
        }
        return E_OUTOFMEMORY;
    }

    // IContextMenu
    if(IsEqualIID(riid, IID_IContextMenu))
    {
        CContextMenu* pcm;
        pcm = new CContextMenu(pPidl[0]);
        if(pcm)
        {
            pcm->AddRef();
            pcm->QueryInterface(riid, ppvReturn);
            pcm->Release();
            return S_OK;
        }
        return E_OUTOFMEMORY;
    }

    // Check for other possible interfaces...

    return E_NOINTERFACE;
}
```

Again, this code snippet comes from the example that we'll start discussing shortly, in which
`CShellFolder` is the C++ class that implements the `IShellFolder` interface. Likewise,
`CExtractIcon` and `CContextMenu` provide implementations for `IExtractIcon` and
`IContextMenu`.

Let's have a look at the prototype of this method. `hwndOwner` is the handle of the window to be used
as the parent for any dialog or window to be displayed. The method receives an array of PIDLs
(`pPidl`), the size of which is passed in `uCount`. The interface required, `riid`, applies to all the
elements of this array.

There are some interfaces that simply can't work on multiple PIDLs at the same time — a context menu, for example, always refers to a single item, and the same is true for icons. An IDataObject, on the other hand, can be used for copying to the clipboard or for dragging a collection of items. In the above example we're implementing only IContextMenu and IExtractIcon, so we check the number of PIDLs passed in as a first measure.

In a namespace extension, we don't need to derive the classes that implement shell interfaces from IShellExtInit or IPersistFile. Within a namespace extension, the interfaces use PIDLs to identify the items to work on unambiguously. The PIDL is one of the arguments the shell passes to GetUIObjectOf(), and so the most reasonable thing to do is to have the class constructor accept a PIDL. In this way, you can initialize your context menu *and* let it know what item it refers to in one go.

Context Menus

Of the three functions included in the IContextMenu interface, you need only implement InvokeCommand() and QueryContextMenu(), avoiding GetCommandString() if you so choose. The implementation of the methods follows the rules I outlined in the previous chapter.

Custom Icons

Implementing IExtractIcon is suggested if you want to gain control over the icons actually displayed in the panes of Explorer for the items in the folder. As explained in Chapter 15, you can use two methods to pass icons to the shell: GetIconLocation() and Extract(). These are mutually exclusive in that if one succeeds, the other doesn't get called. GetIconLocation() is expected to return the path name of the file with the icon to extract, and the index of the icon. The actual extraction is then up to shell. Conversely, Extract() does the job itself and returns an HICON for both the large and the small icon.

Drag & Drop

If you want to support drag-and-drop for the items of your folder, you just need to implement the appropriate interfaces. In particular, you'll need IDropTarget in order to decide what to do when items are dropped.

Copying to Clipboard

Operations that copy to the clipboard and package data to drag and drop all pass through the IDataObject interface. This is a general interface for providing data in various formats to be moved between applications across the system, although Windows itself manages the actual storage of the data. What you have to do is to provide your own format and your own data.

The Concept of Folders

Writing a namespace extension means that you have some kind of content that you want to render using Explorer's document-centric and hierarchical logic. This means that you have to start thinking of your content in terms of folders, subfolders, and items. Sometimes, this turns out to be really easy and straightforward. At other times, it takes a while before you realize how to proceed. In a few cases, it turns out to be quite impossible to do. The concept of a folder — and having clear in your mind what a folder is in *your* context — is central to developing namespace extensions.

A namespace extension is the main folder, a kind of root directory. Its content may or may not be divided up into other subfolders and items. The simplest case is when you have no folders and no items to display, in which event you are just inserting an application into Explorer's frame. I'll have more to say on this topic later on.

You have to declare to Explorer what your folders are, and whether they have subfolders. Be sure to be accurate when doing this, because it may affect the way the shell handles your extension. In practice, all the items you declare to be folders will be displayed in the tree view as sub-nodes of the parent folder. If you declare that a folder has subfolders, then Explorer makes it an expandable node in the tree view.

Explorer asks an extension to enumerate its content by calling `IShellFolder::EnumObjects()`, and this function is called *every time* Explorer needs to enumerate a portion of the folder. It *isn't* just called once to get a pointer to the enumerator object. Here's a typical implementation:

```
STDMETHODIMP CShellFolder::EnumObjects(
                HWND hwndOwner, DWORD dwFlags, IEnumIDList** ppEnumIDList)
{
    *ppEnumIDList = NULL;

    // m_pidl is a member of CShellFolder for storing the PIDL of this
    // folder. You'd have filled it in the class constructor.
    *ppEnumIDList = new CEnumIDList(m_pidl, dwFlags);
    if(*ppEnumIDList == NULL)
        return hr;

    return S_OK;
}
```

In almost any implementation of `IShellFolder`, you will define a `m_pidl` data member to store the PIDL to the folder. (The shell passes in this PIDL when it binds to the folder via `IPersistFolder`.)

What's important here is that `EnumObjects()` receives a `DWORD` that denotes what kinds of items the shell wants the enumerator to provide. In other words, `dwFlags` works like a filter that the shell asks to be applied to whatever `IEnumIDList::Next()` returns.

Of course, it's up to you to decide whether this flag is meaningful for your own custom folder. Nothing prevents you from simply ignoring the flag, but you do so at your own risk.

Folder Attributes

The values that `dwFlags` can assume come from the `SHCONTF` enumerated type, which is defined like this:

```
typedef enum tagSHCONTF
{
    SHCONTF_FOLDERS = 32,
    SHCONTF_NONFOLDERS = 64,
    SHCONTF_INCLUDEHIDDEN = 128,
} SHCONTF;
```

It tells you whether it wants folders, folders and items, and if hidden items should be included too. Under normal circumstances the shell won't ask your folder to enumerate items only, but if it's reasonable in your scenario, you can return only items when you think that's appropriate.

What do we have to do to declare our items as folders? Well, we have just to answer properly when the shell asks for the attributes of a certain item. This is done through the `IShellFolder::GetAttributesOf()` method, and the next listing shows a basic implementation of that:

```
STDMETHODIMP CShellFolder::GetAttributesOf(
                UINT uCount, LPCITEMIDLIST aPidls[], LPDWORD pdwAttribs)
{
    *pdwAttribs = 0xFFFFFFFF;

    for(UINT i = 0 ; i < uCount ; i++)
    {
        DWORD dwAttribs = 0;
        if(IsThisAFolder(aPidls[i]))
            dwAttribs |= SFGAO_FOLDER;
        if(HasSubFolders(aPidls[i]))
            dwAttribs |= SFGAO_HASSUBFOLDER;
        *pdwAttribs &= dwAttribs;
    }

    return S_OK;
}
```

Of course, `IsThisAFolder()` and `HasSubFolders()` are fictitious functions that you should replace with your own routines — I just put them there to illustrate the kind of template the code for `GetAttributesOf()` should have. The function is called with an array of PIDLs, and you should specify global attributes for them all.

The attributes you see here aren't the only ones you can set. Refer to Chapter 4 for a complete list of the `SFGAO_XXX` *constants.*

Flavors of Namespace Extensions

A namespace extension is not just about code. Depending on what you actually store in the registry during installation, it may present itself in slightly different ways. For this reason, you'll often hear of two types of namespace extensions: **rooted** and **non-rooted**.

The difference between the two is not in the code but in the registry entries — the interfaces to implement and the behavior to follow remain the same. What changes is the Explorer view that hosts it. In this section we're going to examine rooted and non-rooted extensions in detail, and decide when to choose each.

Rooted Extensions

Basically, a rooted extension is a custom folder with its own root. This means that you can't navigate to an upper level, or jump to a parallel node at the same depth. A rooted extension shows just its own sub-tree, and the content is completely isolated from the rest of Explorer's namespace. For a concrete example of this, see the screenshot shown here.

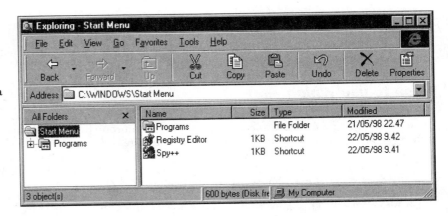

It shows the window that appears when you're about to change settings in the taskbar's Start menu. The Start Menu node is the root of the tree, and the Up One Level button is disabled so that you can't move to a higher level in the overall namespace.

The figure doesn't show a custom extension, but simply a rooted view. A rooted namespace extension is a custom folder *with* a rooted view.

Non-rooted Extensions

Non-rooted extensions are exactly the opposite of rooted extensions. They don't have a fixed root, and allow you to navigate the whole of Explorer's hierarchy. Non-rooted extensions are perfectly and seamlessly integrated into the shell's namespace. Note that the same namespace extension might be accessed and used in both ways, providing indirect confirmation of a previous statement: 'rooted' and 'non-rooted' are attributes that apply to the view rather than to the folder, be it custom or not.

Rooted vs. Non-rooted

Let's try to summarize some points. You have a custom folder – that is, a namespace extension. You have the opportunity to make it accessible through two possible views: rooted and non-rooted. In the former case, the view shows the folder as a stand-alone object, and you see a limited portion of the shell's namespace. In the latter case, Explorer's view encompasses all the folders, including our custom one, and so we can move back and forth among folders.

We can create shortcuts that open the same folder with both views. As explained in Chapter 11, all we have to do is specify the /root switch on Explorer's command line:

```
explorer /root, ::{clsid}
```

This, for example, opens a rooted namespace extension identified by the CLSID. By adding a /e switch, you can require also the tree view in the left pane.

```
explorer /e, ::{clsid}
```

The above command, opens the traditional Explorer view with the specified folder selected and opened. This is a non-rooted view.

When to use Which

Let me repeat just once more that from the code's point of view, there's absolutely no difference between writing a rooted extension and writing a non-rooted extension. In fact, the attributes would be more correctly applied to the view than to the extension itself. But when should you use a rooted or a non-rooted view for making your namespace extension accessible? I think this topic is open to debate, but in general you should think about using rooted views when the content of the folder really does stand alone, almost like an application.

Despite all these extensions you can write, Explorer is still basically a file manager, so you should consider adopting a rooted view for any extension that doesn't work on file system elements. Non-rooted views, on the other hand, are a good choice when it comes to presenting information that relates to files and directories in a custom fashion. A good example of this is the Temporary Internet Files folder, which collects in four hidden directories all the files you have silently downloaded during Internet sessions. When you open the folder, you don't see references to the four subfolders, but only to the files.

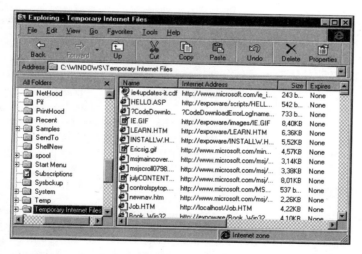

Discussing rooted and non-rooted views brings us straight to another important point in the development of namespace extensions. This aspect, unlike some of the others, has a decisive impact on how your extension will work and be used.

Junction Points

Writing a namespace extension is only half the story; you know that we need to enter some registry information too. Sometimes, however, we need to do even more than that. Depending on what we set in the registry, and on what the extension actually does, we may need an odd thing called a **junction point**.

In a nutshell, a junction point is the means by which we have to link our folder to the shell's namespace. This isn't actually a new *concept* — junction points were around when we were talking about shell extensions, but I didn't mention them in Chapter 15 because they were dealt with automatically by the registry information we provided for shell extensions. With namespace extensions, it's a bit different.

First and foremost, a namespace extension is a COM in-process server, so it needs to be properly registered under `HKEY_CLASSES_ROOT\CLSID`. In addition, it may need some specific registration information (we'll discuss exactly what it looks like later) that serves the purpose of setting the behavior and the appearance of the folder.

What's still to be clearly defined is how a namespace extension links to the shell. In other words, where should the folder be located in the shell's hierarchy? We didn't have this problem for shell extensions (like context menu handlers, for example) because a shell extension is a dynamic object. It gets called only when it's needed, and unloaded a few seconds after its reference count falls back to zero.

A namespace extension, on the other hand, is a folder, and a folder *should* have a location in the shell. This location is called a **junction point**. From another point of view, we could say that a junction point is the means of accessing a namespace extension. There are four ways to do this:

❑ Associating the namespace extension with a file type (if applicable)
❑ Using a directory with a very specific content
❑ Using a directory with a specific name
❑ Associating it with one of the existing namespaces

Let's examine each option in detail.

Using a File Type

Even though it would be a bit unusual (in my opinion, at least!), you might think of writing a namespace extension to let your users navigate through the content of your documents. In this case, your extension will be tied to a file type, and linked to the default item on the context menu. Consider this as a demonstration that a namespace extension is not really very different from a shell extension!

Personally, though, I'd say that if you have a type of document that lends itself to being browsed, it's better to define an external viewer as we did for metafiles in Chapter 14. The clear advantage of using an external viewer is that you save all the COM jiggery-pokery and the namespace extension skeleton. The disadvantage is that you create another process, while a namespace extension runs in the same address space as Explorer. (This might also be seen as an advantage, however, since separate processes give you better crash-resistance.)

To use a file type as the junction point, you need to create a new verb on the document class's context menu:

```
HKEY_CLASSES_ROOT
    \YourDocument
        \ShellEx
            \NewVerb
                \Command
```

In this tree, `YourDocument` and `NewVerb` are both customizable. If you want to add a namespace extension to walk the content of an HTML file, the registry entries would be:

```
HKEY_CLASSES_ROOT
    \htmfile
        \ShellEx
            \Browse
                \Command
```

In this case, we've chosen to call the verb `Browse`, and this will automatically add an item called `Browse` to the `.htm` context menu. (We saw this in Chapter 14.) To associate the namespace extension with the HTML files, the command line will be:

```
explorer /root, {CLSID}, %1
```

See Further Reading *for information on how to get hold of a couple of samples that use this technique.*

There are some kinds of files that work as 'containers' of different types of information, and it's possible that you might think of these in terms of folders and subfolders. An example of this can be found in HTML files (containing collections of objects, images, tables, and so on), which you could browse as if they were directories. What could be better than a namespace extension in this situation? In this case, though, we must necessarily use a rooted extension, as Explorer doesn't support browsing into files from the tree view.

Using a Directory

Normally, you link a namespace extension to the shell using a directory. The idea is very simple. Since a namespace extension is a custom folder, you just create an ordinary folder with an ordinary name, and associate it with your extension to provide the non-standard behavior. There are two equivalent ways to get this accomplished.

The desktop.ini File

The first technique requires you to create a new directory wherever you can, and give it the name you want. Then, make it read-only and create a hidden file called `desktop.ini`. Typical content for this file is:

```
[.ShellClassInfo]
CLSID={CLSID}
```

This is telling Explorer to refer to the CLSID you've specified for any information it may need about displaying that folder. You can change the display name of this folder by setting the `Default` key of the CLSID under this path:

```
HKEY_CLASSES_ROOT
    \CLSID
        \{CLSID}
```

Likewise, to set a custom icon, just add a `DefaultIcon` key under the same path:

```
HKEY_CLASSES_ROOT
    \CLSID
        \{CLSID}
            \DefaultIcon
```

The `Default` value of this key will address the location and the index of the icon using the usual syntax:

```
"filename, index"
```

A Special Folder Name

An even simpler (although probably less well known) technique requires you to create a folder and give it a particular name. No other operation is needed. The folder is automatically created with the read-only attribute, and is displayed with the icon and the title you set in the registry as described above. The name the folder should have has the form:

```
YourFolderName.{CLSID}
```

Like this, for example:

```
Wrox Web Site.{04051965-0fcc-11ce-bcb0-b3fd0e253841}
```

Here, the visible name of the folder will be 'Wrox Web Site', and the CLSID should of course reference a valid namespace extension.

Relying on Existing Namespaces

The Windows shell provides a collection of namespace extensions; among them are `My Computer`, `Network Neighborhood`, and a few others. It's possible for you to place your own namespace extensions beneath one of these existing special folders. In particular, you might want to add it directly to `My Computer`, or to the Desktop namespace. Doing this automatically links the extension to the shell, and you don't need to take any other action. Here's an example of how to add a namespace extension to the `My Computer` node:

```
HKEY_LOCAL_MACHINE
    \Software
        \Microsoft
            \Windows
                \CurrentVersion
                    \Explorer
                        \MyComputer
                            \NameSpace
                                \{CLSID}
```

The `Default` value of `{CLSID}` should point to the string you want the Explorer to display. The other default namespaces you can always rely on to be present are:

- Desktop (`Desktop`)
- Network Neighborhood (`NetworkNeighborhood`)
- Internet Explorer (`Internet`)

By simply replacing the `MyComputer` entry in the above path with the text in parentheses, you can move your extension to the desired namespace.

What you can do with a Namespace Extension

So far, we've discussed namespace extensions from an architectural point of view. I've explained how they work, and some basic ideas to keep in mind when approaching them. We also touched on the hot topic of installation.

Now it's time to start thinking about concrete and useful applications of this technology. If you look at the directories in your PC, you'll see many folders with custom icons. There are Subscriptions, Downloaded Program Files, Temporary Internet Files, Scheduled Tasks, Channels, Software Updates... the list goes on. Basically, Windows gives us a namespace extension every time there's some information to be displayed that logically can be represented by one or more nested folders. The information involved must be collectable in a single, main, folder, and it must relate to the system. It would be better yet if it were based on files.

This is just one way to think about namespace extensions. Another one moves the focus to applications. You could think about creating your own folder in the shell and reserving a sub-folder for each application your company ships. In these sub-folders you could host the entire application, or information about it, or (more simply still) just an Internet shortcut.

Designing Our Namespace Extension

Following the points outlined in the first part of this chapter, we need to provide consistent answers to a number of questions. We want to add a node to Explorer that lets us browse the hierarchy of currently opened windows. If you know Spy++, a utility that comes with Visual C++, then it's easy to imagine what we're aiming to do: basically, we want much of the Spy++ functionality built into the Windows shell. By expanding, say, a Windows View node, we want to be able to obtain a complete list of all the top-level windows. By expanding each of these nodes, we want to be able to find out about all the constituent windows of the upper-level window.

What we need to determine is:

- Whether this application includes the concept of a 'folder'
- How to build the PIDL
- How to enumerate the items
- How to present the information to the user
- Which additional functionality to provide

In the remainder of the chapter, I'll try to address all these points.

What's a Folder Here?

In a windows hierarchy we have just one kind of item: windows. This is different from what the situation would be if we were writing a namespace extension for viewing the registry. In that case, we would have folders (the registry keys) and items (the keys' values).

However, a Windows View extension is composed only of windows. If a given window has children, then it might be considered a folder. What's a sub-folder? A sub-folder is a window with a parent, at least one child and at least one grandchild.

Designing a Custom PIDL

Designing a PIDL is a very important part of namespace extension development. In this particular case, though, we get rather lucky. We don't need to concatenate data components to get a unique identifier to a window, because we've already got HWNDs. We'll be using a straight HWND as our PIDL, and this makes it absolutely certain that we'll be able to identify any item of the folder unambiguously.

How to Build a Window Enumerator

Another central item of namespace extensions is the enumerator object that has the task of returning the various items that the folder or the sub-folder contains. And we're lucky again, because windows are a system component for which the SDK provides great support. To enumerate windows, we have just to call EnumChildWindows() and store the result somewhere in a private data structure.

Designing the View

For a programmer, the key pieces of information about a window are its HWND, its title, and above all its window class name. The view we create should therefore allow you to see all this information at the same time. A report list view appears to be the best choice; we can give it four columns:

- ❑ An indication of whether the window has children
- ❑ The HWND of the window
- ❑ The name of the class the window belongs to
- ❑ The current title of the window

To facilitate viewing, we can adopt different icons to reflect whether the window has children – this is a way to distinguish between folder windows and item windows. Furthermore, adding some sorting capability would be helpful.

We also want the folder to provide information about a window through its context menu, which will require us to implement the IContextMenu interface as well.

Implementing Our Namespace Extension

To create this namespace extension, I used the structure of the source code that Microsoft provides for the Registry View extension as a basis. The Registry View extension is shown in this figure:

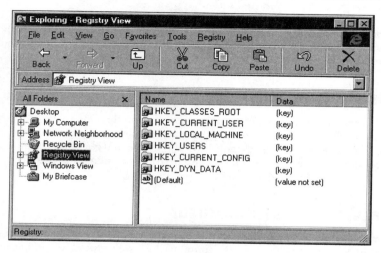

The source code for the RegView *example that adds the registry as a new folder in Explorer comes with the Internet Client SDK, and is available on your Visual C++ disks. You can find it at* Samples\SDK Samples\Windows UI Samples\Shell Samples\RegView, *and I recommend that you dig it out now so that you're better able to follow this discussion.*

Common Features of Registry View and Windows View

As mentioned earlier, I've used the Microsoft sample source code as a basis because it really is a rich, realistic example. It shows you:

❑ How to design a fairly complex namespace extension that inserts itself into Explorer's namespace
❑ How to code and manage a PIDL, and embed real-world data in it
❑ How to handle and organize sub folders
❑ How to add accessory features like modified menus and different icons
❑ How to place it on the desktop and store additional and helpful information in the registry

I maintained the structure of the code, trying to make it work with another type of data, with different features. The example employs pure C++ code, so I maintained it. All the COM paraphernalia is as it was in the original. Similarly, I kept the management code for PIDLs – encapsulating everything in a single manager class appeared to be a good choice to me. I just changed the format of the data, and adapted some class members to it.

Both the extensions (Microsoft's and mine) employ a list view as the window in which to display the folder's content, although mine is a little simpler. It doesn't support multiple views (large icons, small icons, and list) but only the report view. On the other hand, it does provide sorting capabilities and some enhancements to the user interface of the list view (full row selection, auto tracking, column drag-and-drop).

Moving on, both extensions make changes to Explorer's menu and support different icons for different items. In addition, Windows View implements context menus for both the left and the right pane. Speaking of user interface features, I should add that mine can be deleted, is visible from common dialogs, and displays a tooltip when the mouse hovers over it on the desktop.

Apart from the choice of maintaining the C++ skeleton and the organization of PIDL-related code, what remains – the largest part of the code – has a pretty standard form. The actions it implements couldn't sensibly be done in a radically different way, and so its suitability as a model for when you come to writing your own namespace extensions stands.

The Windows View Project

The project is composed of the following main classes, all of which also exist in the Registry View project:

Class	Interfaces	Description
CShellFolder	IShellFolder, IPersistFolder	Defines the behavior of the folder manager, which is the module that implements a bridge between Explorer and the extension.
CEnumIDList	IEnumIDList	Enumerates the windows that are part of the view.
CShellView	IShellView	Provides the view that will occupy Explorer's right pane.
CExtractIcon	IExtractIcon	Returns the icon to be used by Explorer.
CContextMenu	IContextMenu	Returns the menu items to be used by Explorer for the context menu.

Aside from these classes that implement the requisite COM interfaces, our project will contain another important class that will provide the main functions for managing the PIDL: CPidlMgr.

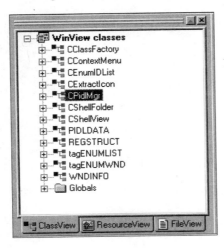

The PIDL Manager Class

As we've discussed, this namespace extension will use window handles as PIDLs, but we still need a layer of code to wrap the HWND and provide a programming interface that conforms to the PIDL specification and is consistent with the expectations of the shell.

To accomplish all the tasks that involve PIDLs, we need to define a PIDL manager class. Any class that needs to handle PIDLs will create an instance of this object.

```
#ifndef PIDLMGR_H
#define PIDLMGR_H

#include <windows.h>
#include <shlobj.h>

// Data structure for PIDLs
struct PIDLDATA
{
    // Add a signature and a version number here if backward compatibility
    //  is a real issue for you. Also add other data that's required to
    //  identify the elements of your folder.
    HWND hwnd;
};

typedef PIDLDATA* LPPIDLDATA;

extern HINSTANCE g_hInst;
extern UINT g_DllRefCount;

/*-------------------------------------------------------------------*/
//    CPidlMgr class definition
/*-------------------------------------------------------------------*/
class CPidlMgr
{
public:
    CPidlMgr();
    ~CPidlMgr();

    LPITEMIDLIST Create(HWND);
    LPITEMIDLIST Copy(LPCITEMIDLIST);
    void Delete(LPITEMIDLIST);
    UINT GetSize(LPCITEMIDLIST);

    LPITEMIDLIST GetNextItem(LPCITEMIDLIST);
    LPITEMIDLIST GetLastItem(LPCITEMIDLIST);

    BOOL HasChildren(HWND);
    BOOL HasChildrenOfChildren(HWND);
    HWND GetData(LPCITEMIDLIST);
    DWORD GetPidlPath(LPCITEMIDLIST, LPTSTR);

private:
    LPMALLOC m_pMalloc;
    HWND GetDataPointer(LPCITEMIDLIST);
    static BOOL CALLBACK WindowHasChildren(HWND, LPARAM);
};

typedef CPidlMgr* LPPIDLMGR;

#endif  // PIDLMGR_H
```

The `CPidlMgr` class defines methods to create, delete, copy, and navigate through a PIDL. Furthermore, the class includes a data member for storing a reference to the shell allocator object returned by `SHGetMalloc()`.

The key functions in this class are:

❑ `Create()`, to build a new PIDL
❑ `HasChildren()`, to decide whether a window is a 'folder'
❑ `GetData()`, to disassemble a PIDL in order to extract useful information
❑ `GetPidlPath()`, to return the display name of the PIDL

The others are largely helper functions that play a secondary role with respect to the above four. Let's examine each of these methods in detail.

Creating a PIDL

Associating a PIDL with an `HWND` doesn't mean that we can simply use an `HWND` wherever a PIDL is required. A PIDL is a structure that must expose a standard interface to let Explorer navigate it, whatever it may contain internally. The `HWND` is therefore just the *content* of the PIDL, and consequently creating the PIDL means building up the wrapper that encloses the handle.

As I explained earlier in the book, a PIDL is a pointer to a list of `SHITEMID` variables. To start off, then, we defined a `PIDLDATA` structure that's the kind of thing pointed to by the `abID` member of the `SHITEMID` structure:

```
struct PIDLDATA
{
    HWND hwnd;
};

typedef PIDLDATA* LPPIDLDATA;
```

This is a generic way to proceed: create a custom structure and fill it with any data you need to identify the item inside the folder that actually contains it. It's not necessary for a single PIDL to be *globally* unique, as in the case of `HWND`s. The important thing is that each PIDL is unique *within its subfolder*. Global uniqueness is achieved by concatenating the various PIDLs that form the path from the Desktop to the item. In other words, things work in much the same way as they work with files and directories. You can have two files with the same name in different directories, or with the same path in different drives, but you're still definitely addressing different objects.

In this specific example, we don't need to use more than an `HWND` to identify a folder item. In other circumstances, you might need more information, but that just requires adding new fields to the `PIDLDATA` structure you can see here.

When it comes to creating a new `PIDL`, you must allocate enough memory for it via the `IMalloc` interface. This is to make it possible for the shell to free `PIDL`s. The `IMalloc` interface is returned by `SHGetMalloc()`, which is called in `CPidlMgr`'s class constructor. The actual amount of memory to allocate must be equal to the size of the PIDL itself, plus the size of an empty structure. The following line defines the correct size:

```
USHORT uSize = sizeof(ITEMIDLIST) + sizeof(PIDLDATA);
```

As you can see, it's given by the size of an ITEMIDLIST, plus the size of the data that represents the item. In addition, you can't forget the final, null, ITEMIDLIST that lets the shell know that the chain of PIDLs is finished:

```
LPITEMIDLIST CPidlMgr::Create(HWND hwnd)
{
    // Global size of the PIDL, including SHITEMID
    USHORT uSize = sizeof(ITEMIDLIST) + sizeof(PIDLDATA);

    // Also allocate memory for the final, null, ITEMIDLIST
    // Note that we must use IMalloc to get new memory
    LPITEMIDLIST pidlOut = reinterpret_cast<LPITEMIDLIST>(
                           m_pMalloc->Alloc(uSize + sizeof(ITEMIDLIST)));
    if(pidlOut)
    {
        LPITEMIDLIST pidlTemp = pidlOut;

        // Prepares the PIDL to be filled with actual data
        pidlTemp->mkid.cb = uSize;
        LPPIDLDATA pData = reinterpret_cast<LPPIDLDATA>(pidlTemp->mkid.abID);

        // Fill the PIDL
        pData->hwnd = hwnd;

        //
        // Add more fields here if required...
        //

        // A PIDL of size 0 means the end of the chain
        pidlTemp = GetNextItem(pidlTemp);
        pidlTemp->mkid.cb = 0;
        pidlTemp->mkid.abID[0] = 0;
    }

    return pidlOut;
}
```

A PIDL must be a flat sequence of bytes, which means that you can't use pointers. If you try to do this, the pointer will be considered as a 32-bit number, and the reference to the address will be lost.

Extracting Information from a PIDL

All the shell API functions manipulate PIDLs, and every item or folder is referred in terms of PIDLs. However, it should always be possible to extract from the PIDL the information you actually need to process. In this case you need to know the HWND, and whether the window has children.

```
BOOL CPidlMgr::HasChildren(HWND hWnd)
{
    // Determine whether a window has children
    HWND h = GetWindow(hWnd, GW_CHILD);
    return (h != NULL);
}
```

```
HWND CPidlMgr::GetData(LPCITEMIDLIST pidl)
{
    if(!pidl)
        return NULL;
```

```
    // Get the last item of the PIDL to make sure we get the right HWND
    //  in case of multiple nesting levels
    LPITEMIDLIST p = GetLastItem(pidl);

    LPPIDLDATA pData = reinterpret_cast<LPPIDLDATA>(p->mkid.abID);
    return pData->hwnd;
}
```

As you know, a PIDL is a pointer to a list of structures composed of two members, the first of which indicates the size of the member that follows it. In this way, Explorer knows the exact number of bytes it needs to skip in order to walk the chain correctly. Likewise, a namespace extension can get the number of bytes and so interpret the structures properly. To make things simpler, a PIDL manager class should define some functions to allow 'walking':

```
LPITEMIDLIST CPidlMgr::GetNextItem(LPCITEMIDLIST pidl)
{
    if(pidl)
        return reinterpret_cast<LPITEMIDLIST>((reinterpret_cast<LPBYTE>(
                        const_cast<LPITEMIDLIST>(pidl))) + pidl->mkid.cb);
    else
        return NULL;
}
```

```
LPITEMIDLIST CPidlMgr::GetLastItem(LPCITEMIDLIST pidl)
{
    LPITEMIDLIST pidlLast = NULL;

    // Get the PIDL of the last item in the list
    if(pidl)
    {
        while(pidl->mkid.cb)
        {
            pidlLast = const_cast<LPITEMIDLIST>(pidl);
            pidl = GetNextItem(pidl);
        }
    }
    return pidlLast;
}
```

Another important task for a PIDL manager class is to provide the display name of the object. A PIDL is just a binary sequence of bytes, and for this reason the shell will, when needed, ask the folder manager (the object implementing IShellFolder) to provide a display name for each item. It's therefore reasonable that somewhere (and where if not in a PIDL manager class?) there should be a piece of code capable of taking a PIDL and returning a displayable string.

In general, this function will walk the list referenced by the PIDLs and create a string incrementally. If you're browsing into folders and sub-folders, then the innermost item has a PIDL that takes into account all the parent folders. Normally, then, you should provide an overall string. (Once again, think about files and directories, and consider the path name as the display name.) The idea is that you decide what to show for a single PIDL, and then walk the chain concatenating the various pieces, separating them by commas, semicolons, slashes or whatever.

```
DWORD CPidlMgr::GetPidlPath(LPCITEMIDLIST pidl, LPTSTR lpszOut)
{
    HWND hwnd = GetData(pidl);

    TCHAR szClass[100], szTitle[100];
    GetWindowText(hwnd, szTitle, 100);
    GetClassName(hwnd, szClass, 100);

    // Add a description to the desktop window (of class "#32769")
    if(!lstrcmpi(szClass, __TEXT("#32769")))
        lstrcpy(szClass, __TEXT("Desktop"));

    // Return a string in the form "title [class]"
    if(lstrlen(szTitle))
        wsprintf(lpszOut, __TEXT("%s [%s]"), szTitle, szClass);
    else
        wsprintf(lpszOut, __TEXT("[%s]"), szClass);

    // Return the size of the string
    return lstrlen(lpszOut);
}
```

As you can see from the above code, though, things are easier in this case because in returning the name of the current window, we don't need to take into account the list of the windows we traversed to reach it. We just discover the HWND and return the proper information. However, we're passed a PIDL, so the first thing to do is convert it to a window using GetData(). Then we return a formatted string containing the title and class of the window. This string will be shown in the address and status bar each time the window is selected. The GetPidlPath() method will be called by the folder manager in its GetDisplayNameOf() method.

All the classes in our namespace extension need to deal with PIDLs, so each will include a data member of type LPITEMIDLIST, and an instance of the PIDL manager.

The Windows Enumerator

Let's now examine the major features of the enumerator. This is a class derived from IEnumIDList that provides access to the list of the windows that are open throughout the system at the time the class is created. To function, it defines an internal list of PIDLs and uses it to store all the 'folder' items. When the class constructor is called, all the items in the folder that's passed as an argument are enumerated and added to the list. It's on this list, then, that interface methods like Next() will work. Regardless of the implementation details, this is generic behavior for any class implementing the IEnumIDList interface.

```
CEnumIDList::CEnumIDList(HWND hwnd, DWORD dwFlags, HRESULT* pResult)
{
    if(pResult)
        *pResult = S_OK;

    m_pFirst = NULL;
    m_pLast = NULL;
    m_pCurrent = NULL;
```

```
    // Creates the PIDL manager
    m_pPidlMgr = new CPidlMgr();
    if(!m_pPidlMgr)
    {
        if(pResult)
            *pResult = E_OUTOFMEMORY;
        delete this;
        return;
    }

    // Get the shell's memory manager
    if(FAILED(SHGetMalloc(&m_pMalloc)))
    {
        if(pResult)
            *pResult = E_OUTOFMEMORY;
        delete this;
        return;
    }

    // Creates the list of the items
    if(!CreateEnumList(hwnd, dwFlags))
    {
        if(pResult)
            *pResult = E_OUTOFMEMORY;
        delete this;
        return;
    }

    m_ObjRefCount = 1;
    g_DllRefCount++;
}
```

The above listing shows the code for the class constructor, which receives the handle of the window to enumerate and the flags to take into account. The flags were specified by the shell in the call to `IShellFolder::EnumObjects()`, as I explained earlier in the chapter.

In the `CreateEnumList()` method, the list is created by enumerating the windows with the `EnumChildWindows()` SDK function. If the base window is NULL, then it means that we've been requested to enumerate the topmost window, which is the Desktop. There are no other windows at this level, and hence no need to enumerate, so I simply obtain the handle of the desktop window through `GetDesktopWindow()` and add a new item to the list. In other cases, I enumerate the child windows and create new items when necessary:

```
typedef struct tagENUMWND {
    LPARAM lParam;
    HWND hwndParent;
    DWORD dwFlags;
} ENUMWND, FAR* LPENUMWND;
```

```
BOOL CEnumIDList::CreateEnumList(HWND hWndRoot, DWORD dwFlags)
{
    // Get the desktop window
    if(hWndRoot == NULL)
    {
        // If we must consider the root window (the desktop), we don't need to
        //  enumerate anything. Just get the desktop HWND and add a new
        //  element to the list. This is what's done by NewEnumItem().
        hWndRoot = GetDesktopWindow();
        NewEnumItem(hWndRoot);
        return TRUE;
    }

    // Enumerate the child windows of the specified window
    ENUMWND ew;
    ew.lParam = reinterpret_cast<LPARAM>(this);
    ew.hwndParent = hWndRoot;
    ew.dwFlags = dwFlags;

    // We need a function that only considers immediate children of the
    //  specified window. We're not interested in children of children. We'll
    //  correct this aspect of EnumChildWindows' behavior in callback code.
    EnumChildWindows(hWndRoot, AddToEnumList, reinterpret_cast<LPARAM>(&ew));
    return TRUE;
}
```

```
BOOL CALLBACK CEnumIDList::AddToEnumList(HWND hwndChild, LPARAM lParam)
{
    LPENUMWND lpew = reinterpret_cast<LPENUMWND>(lParam);

    // Avoid windows that aren't children of the specified window's parent.
    // This test is meant to skip over all those windows that aren't
    //  immediate children of the window whose children we're enumerating.
    // This check is due to a feature of EnumChildWindows() that enumerates
    //  not just children but also grandchildren. We avoid grandchildren.
    HWND h = GetParent(hwndChild);
    if((h != NULL) && (h != lpew->hwndParent))
        return TRUE;

    // We stored the pointer to the class in the lParam argument
    CEnumIDList* pEnumIDList = reinterpret_cast<CEnumIDList*>(lpew->lParam);

    // IMPORTANT: This is where we decide what's a 'folder' and what's a
    // 'leaf'. For windows, this rests on whether they have children.

    // Explorer wants non-folder items
    if(lpew->dwFlags & SHCONTF_NONFOLDERS)
        return pEnumIDList->NewEnumItem(hwndChild);

    // Explorer wants folder items
    if(lpew->dwFlags & SHCONTF_FOLDERS)
    {
        // If it has no children, drop it because it has already been added.
        if(!pEnumIDList->m_pPidlMgr->HasChildren(hwndChild))
            return TRUE;
        else
            pEnumIDList->NewEnumItem(hwndChild);
    }
    return TRUE;
}
```

```
BOOL CEnumIDList::NewEnumItem(HWND hwndChild)
{
    LPENUMLIST pNew = NULL;
    pNew = reinterpret_cast<LPENUMLIST>(m_pMalloc->Alloc(sizeof(ENUMLIST)));
    if(pNew)
    {
        // Create the new PIDL for the new element
        pNew->pNext = NULL;
        pNew->pidl = m_pPidlMgr->Create(hwndChild);

        // Is this the first item in the list?
        if(!m_pFirst)
        {
            m_pFirst = pNew;
            m_pCurrent = m_pFirst;
        }

        // Add the new item to the end of the list
        if(m_pLast)
            m_pLast->pNext = pNew;

        // Update the last item pointer
        m_pLast = pNew;
        return TRUE;
    }
    return FALSE;
}
```

For our purposes, the `EnumChildWindows()` function has a flaw that we should try to work around. It returns *all* the windows that are children of a specified window, even if they are actually children of children, when all we want are the immediate children. However, `EnumChildWindows()` can be passed a callback function that will do work on each of the enumerated windows. In our example, this function (I've called it `AddToEnumList()`) begins by performing a check against the actual parent of the enumerated window, and rejects it if the parent doesn't match the expected window.

For each window, we need to create a PIDL and add its address to the list; in the above listing, this is done by the helper function `NewEnumItem()`. Notice also that the callback function takes care of enumerating windows according to what the shell requests: only folders, or folders and items together.

Getting the Next Items

Once the list of windows has been created, returning the next *n* items to the caller is as easy as walking the list and filling an array. Notice that we're required to create and return a new copy of the PIDL. The shell will use them, and then they'll be freed.

```
STDMETHODIMP CEnumIDList::Next(
                DWORD dwElements, LPITEMIDLIST apidl[], LPDWORD pdwFetched)
{
    DWORD dwIndex;
    HRESULT hr = S_OK;

    if(dwElements > 1 && !pdwFetched)
        return E_INVALIDARG;
```

```
    for(dwIndex = 0 ; dwIndex < dwElements ; dwIndex++)
    {
        // Is this the last item in the list?
        if(!m_pCurrent)
        {
            hr = S_FALSE;
            break;
        }

        // Copy PIDLs
        apidl[dwIndex] = m_pPidlMgr->Copy(m_pCurrent->pidl);
        m_pCurrent = m_pCurrent->pNext;
    }

    // Returns the number of fetched items
    if(pdwFetched)
        *pdwFetched = dwIndex;
    return hr;
}
```

The Folder Manager

The class that works most tightly with the shell is the one that implements the `IShellFolder` interface. It has to create the enumerator and the view, and it must bind to subfolders by creating a new instance of the `CShellFolder` class. It has also to provide display names for each PIDL, and pointers to additional interfaces like `IContextMenu` and `IExtractIcon`.

`BindToObject()` is the method used to bind to a subfolder. It simply creates a new class derived from `IShellFolder` and passes the received PIDL as an argument to the constructor. The result is that a new child shell folder object is created.

```
STDMETHODIMP CShellFolder::BindToObject(
            LPCITEMIDLIST pidl, LPBC pbcReserved, REFIID riid, LPVOID* ppvOut)
{
    CShellFolder* pShellFolder = new CShellFolder(this, pidl);
    if(!pShellFolder)
        return E_OUTOFMEMORY;

    HRESULT hr = pShellFolder->QueryInterface(riid, ppvOut);
    pShellFolder->Release();
    return hr;
}
```

The following snippet shows how the folder object creates its view and enumerator objects. For the enumerator, we first need to extract the `HWND` of the window to enumerate. Then we can create the enumerator object:

```
STDMETHODIMP CShellFolder::CreateViewObject(
                            HWND hwndOwner, REFIID riid, LPVOID* ppvOut)
{
    CShellView* pShellView = new CShellView(this, m_pidl);
    if(!pShellView)
        return E_OUTOFMEMORY;
```

```
      m_pShellView = pShellView;
      HRESULT hr = pShellView->QueryInterface(riid, ppvOut);
      pShellView->Release();
      return hr;
}
STDMETHODIMP CShellFolder::EnumObjects(
                HWND hwndOwner, DWORD dwFlags, LPENUMIDLIST* ppEnumIDList)
{
      // hwndOwner is just the HWND to use as the parent for any message box
      HRESULT hr;
      *ppEnumIDList = NULL;

      HWND hWnd = m_pPidlMgr->GetData(m_pidl);
      *ppEnumIDList = new CEnumIDList(hWnd, dwFlags, &hr);
      if(*ppEnumIDList == NULL)
          return hr;

      return S_OK;
}
```

For display names, the folder manager ends up calling into the PIDL manager class, but needs to convert the string to Unicode characters before returning it. `GetDisplayNameOf()` actually returns a `STRRET`, which is a data structure that's a union of three possible data types for rendering a string: Unicode string, ANSI string, offset to a string (see Chapter 5). In this case, I've chosen to use Unicode strings:

```
STDMETHODIMP CShellFolder::GetDisplayNameOf(
                LPCITEMIDLIST pidl, DWORD dwFlags, LPSTRRET lpName)
{
      TCHAR szText[MAX_PATH] = {0};

      // Get the name to display in the left pane, address bar, etc
      m_pPidlMgr->GetPidlPath(pidl, szText);

      // Must convert string to Unicode, so allocate a wide character string
      int cchOleStr = lstrlen(szText) + 1;
      lpName->pOleStr = reinterpret_cast<LPWSTR>(
                        m_pMalloc->Alloc(cchOleStr * sizeof(WCHAR)));
      if(!lpName->pOleStr)
          return E_OUTOFMEMORY;

      lpName->uType = STRRET_WSTR;
      mbstowcs(lpName->pOleStr, szText, cchOleStr);
      return S_OK;
}
```

In my opinion, however, the most interesting part of the folder manager's activity comes when it's time to compare items, and to return attributes for an item.

Comparing Items

Comparing items is a relatively simple bit of functionality to implement, but it has tremendous importance. If you can't be absolutely sure to implement it correctly, it's better for you to state explicitly that you do not support it. At an early stage of the development of this namespace extension, I used a partial implementation of the `IShellFolder::CompareIDs()` method, and you have no idea how many errors and misleading bits of behavior I had to cope with! Worse still, they seemed to have very little to do with the item comparison routine. Only when I decided to arrange it properly did things – almost magically – suddenly start to work properly.

The `CompareIDs()` member function receives two PIDLs from the shell, and must return a value denoting which item is greater. A (non-zero) positive value indicates that the first is greater than the second, while a negative value denotes the opposite. A null value should be returned when the items are equal.

As you can easily verify yourself from the online documentation, `CompareIDs()` also takes a third parameter, `lParam`, which is meant to denote the sorting rule to apply. By convention, a value of 0 means that you have to sort the folder's content by name, while non-zero values denote folder-specific rules. In this application, `CompareIDs()` gets called when the user clicks on *any* column of the header control at the top of the list view. (This is typical behavior for Explorer-like user interfaces.) We're handling this event in shell view code, so it's completely up to us decide what to pass through `lParam`.

In this implementation, I've decided to ignore `lParam`, opting instead to use a data member of the `CShellFolder` class (`m_uSortField`) to denote how to sort the content. The reason for this is that I need to keep track of the currently sorted field, so a data member would be needed anyway. Furthermore, I want to be able to sort in either ascending or descending order – if a column is already sorted, then clicking to sort again will reverse the order. This listing shows exactly how I did it:

```
STDMETHODIMP CShellFolder::CompareIDs(
                  LPARAM lParam, LPCITEMIDLIST pidl1, LPCITEMIDLIST pidl2)
{
    // This function is always called with lParam set to 0. By convention,
    //  this means "sort by name"; other non-zero values are usually meant to
    //  indicate specific folder-sorting rules. Note that here I'm using the
    //  m_uSortField data member as a 'replacement' for lParam.

    HWND hwnd1 = m_pPidlMgr->GetData(pidl1);
    HWND hwnd2 = m_pPidlMgr->GetData(pidl2);

    // Sorting by CHILDREN
    if(m_uSortField == 1 || m_uSortField == -1)
    {
        int fChildren1 = m_pPidlMgr->HasChildren(hwnd1);
        int fChildren2 = m_pPidlMgr->HasChildren(hwnd2);

        if(fChildren1 < fChildren2)
            return m_uSortField;
        else if(fChildren1 > fChildren2)
            return m_uSortField * -1;
        else
            return 0;
    }

    // Sorting by CLASS
    if(m_uSortField == 2 || m_uSortField == -2)
    {
        // BUFSIZE is a symbolic constant set to 100
        TCHAR szClass1[BUFSIZE];
        TCHAR szClass2[BUFSIZE];
        GetClassName(hwnd1, szClass1, BUFSIZE);
        GetClassName(hwnd2, szClass2, BUFSIZE);
        return m_uSortField * lstrcmpi(szClass1, szClass2);
    }
```

```
       // Sorting by TITLE
       if(m_uSortField == 4 || m_uSortField == -4)
       {
           TCHAR szTitle1[BUFSIZE];
           TCHAR szTitle2[BUFSIZE];
           GetWindowText(hwnd1, szTitle1, BUFSIZE);
           GetWindowText(hwnd2, szTitle2, BUFSIZE);
           return m_uSortField * lstrcmpi(szTitle1, szTitle2);
       }

       // sorting by HWND
       if(hwnd1 < hwnd2)
           return m_uSortField;
       else if(hwnd1 > hwnd2)
           return m_uSortField * -1;
       else
           return 0;
   }
```

This function will let us sort the items in the view in four ways: by children, by class, by handle and by title. Furthermore, by making `m_uSortField` negative or positive and multiplying the result of the comparison by its value, we can alter the order of sorting. Depending on the logic of the comparison in question, we either compare HWNDs or resort to `lstrcmpi()` to compare strings.

Folder Attributes

Returning the correct folder attributes is vital to having your namespace extension work properly within Explorer. When you open the main node, for example, you expect to see all the folders it contains. In terms of windows, when you expand the node that relates to the desktop window, you should see all the top-level windows *and* all the windows with no parent, but *no others*. When you then click on one of this second set of windows, you want to see all the children of that window.

The `GetAttributesOf()` method is expected to return the correct attributes for a group of items identified by their PIDLs. To assign attributes, use the SFGAO_XXX constants that we met in Chapter 4. Remember that you might be passed several PIDLs at a time, and the attributes apply to them all.

```
STDMETHODIMP CShellFolder::GetAttributesOf(
                UINT uCount, LPCITEMIDLIST aPidls[], LPDWORD pdwAttribs)
{
    *pdwAttribs = -1;

    for(UINT i = 0 ; i < uCount ; i++)
    {
        DWORD dwAttribs = 0;

        // Is this item a window?
        HWND hwnd = m_pPidlMgr->GetData(aPidls[i]);
        if(IsWindow(hwnd))
        {
            // Assign here all the styles you want the items to have in common
            // Of course, it's then up to you to manage them properly.
            if(m_pPidlMgr->HasChildren(hwnd))
            {
                dwAttribs |= SFGAO_FOLDER;
                if(m_pPidlMgr->HasChildrenOfChildren(hwnd))
                    dwAttribs |= SFGAO_HASSUBFOLDER;
```

```
                    }
                }
                *pdwAttribs = dwAttribs;
            }
        return S_OK;
    }
```

The `GetAttributesOf()` function receives a list of PIDLs for which to retrieve the attributes. I said that every window that has child windows is a folder, so it's easy to determine when the `SFGAO_FOLDER` attribute should be indicated. If we stop there, though, the shell neglects to make the node expandable, making it impossible to browse beyond the first level. Thus, we need to indicate not only if a specified node has children, but also if any of these children has its own children. If the answer to this question is yes, we can set the `SFGAO_HASSUBFOLDER` flag as well.

Leaping back into the PIDL manager class for a moment, the `HasChildrenOfChildren()` function simply enumerates the child windows and checks whether any of them has children:

```
BOOL CPidlMgr::HasChildrenOfChildren(HWND hWnd)
{
    // Determine whether a window has children
    BOOL b = FALSE;

    EnumChildWindows(hWnd, WindowHasChildren, reinterpret_cast<LPARAM>(&b));
    return b;
}
```

```
BOOL CPidlMgr::WindowHasChildren(HWND hwnd, LPARAM lParam)
{
    BOOL* pB = reinterpret_cast<BOOL*>(lParam);

    // If the window is a child window then the returned HWND isn't NULL
    HWND h = GetWindow(hwnd, GW_CHILD);
    *pB = (h != NULL);          // TRUE if at least one grandchild exists
    return(h == NULL);          // Needs to return FALSE to stop enumeration
}
```

There are a few points to clarify about this code. To check whether a given window has grandchildren, I have to enumerate all its child windows. `EnumChildWindows()` is the API function that does just this. Like any other enumeration, it starts with the first window and finishes with the last one. Each window found is passed for further processing to the specified callback function, which in this case is `WindowHasChildren()`.

The point is that we need to know whether or not there's *at least one* grandchild, so once we've found the first one, we can stop the enumeration by returning `FALSE` from the callback function. On the other hand, we also need a way to notify the calling function `HasChildrenOfChildren()` that the enumeration finished because a grandchild has been found. The Boolean value passed to `EnumChildWindows()` serves as a return buffer for this result:

```
EnumChildWindows(hWnd, WindowHasChildren, reinterpret_cast<LPARAM>(&b));
```

A simpler approach would require us always to set the `SFGAO_HASSUBFOLDER` flag each time we set `SFGAO_FOLDER`, and things would work perfectly well but for a little bug: all the nodes would appear to be expandable, whether or not they had subfolders. By doing things properly, we'll have a tree view that looks like this:

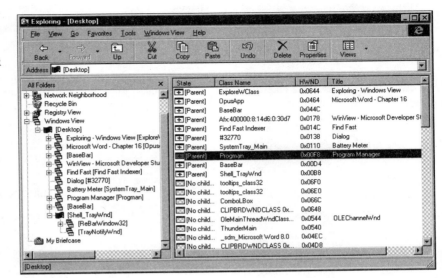

The Window View

Essentially, a view is a window. Normally, you create a pair of windows: a parent window containing a child. The child is what the user sees, and what they interact with. The view we create here will be a window of a custom class, in order to avoid subclassing. Another technique you can use requires you to define a modeless dialog with some constituent controls.

In this case, the child window is a list view, which I chose in order to try and make it look like the traditional folder views. It takes care of responding to some of messages coming from the system, including such important messages as `WM_CREATE`, `WM_SIZE`, `WM_SETFOCUS`, and `WM_NOTIFY`.

Note that when you create the class that implements the view, `WndProc()` (the window-procedure of the view window) must be a static member. Of course, a static member doesn't get the `this` pointer, and therefore can't access other members of the class, so we need to find another way to pass the `this` pointer down to the `WndProc()` code. My solution was to pass `this` as the last argument to `CreateWindowEx()` when creating the view window in `IShellView::CreateViewWindow()`:

```
hWnd = CreateWindowEx(0, NS_CLASS_NAME, NULL,
                 WS_CHILD | WS_VISIBLE | WS_CLIPSIBLINGS,
                 prcView->left, prcView->top,
                 prcView->right - prcView->left,
                 prcView->bottom - prcView->top,
                 m_hwndParent, NULL, g_hInst, this);
```

This causes the pointer to be passed to the window procedure through the `WM_NCCREATE` message. However, accessing `this` in a static member of the class isn't enough: we also need to make it 'persistent' across the various calls we're going to make to the window procedure. A typical solution to this problem is to store the pointer in the window's extra bytes — a 32-bit buffer associated with each window and at the full disposal of the programmer. This code shows how to set it:

```
SetWindowLong(hWnd, GWL_USERDATA, reinterpret_cast<LONG>(pThis));
```

While the next line shows how to read it back:

```
CShellView* pThis = reinterpret_cast<CShellView*>(
                            GetWindowLong(hWnd, GWL_USERDATA));
```

Once we have the pThis pointer, we can start calling all the public members of the class from within a procedure that is not a class member. (A static class member belongs to the class from a syntactical point of view, but it's actually a global function attached to the class.) Here's the code for the view's window procedure:

```
LRESULT CALLBACK CShellView::WndProc(
                    HWND hWnd, UINT uMsg, WPARAM wParam, LPARAM lParam)
{
    CShellView* pThis = reinterpret_cast<CShellView*>(
                            GetWindowLong(hWnd, GWL_USERDATA));

    switch(uMsg)
    {
    case WM_NCCREATE:
        {
            LPCREATESTRUCT lpcs = reinterpret_cast<LPCREATESTRUCT>(lParam);
            pThis = reinterpret_cast<CShellView*>(lpcs->lpCreateParams);
            SetWindowLong(hWnd, GWL_USERDATA, reinterpret_cast<LONG>(pThis));
            pThis->m_hWnd = hWnd;
        }
        break;

    case WM_CONTEXTMENU:
        return pThis->OnContextMenu();

    case WM_MENUSELECT:
        return pThis->OnMenuSelect(LOWORD(wParam));

    case WM_SIZE:
        return pThis->OnSize(LOWORD(lParam), HIWORD(lParam));

    case WM_CREATE:
        return pThis->OnCreate();

    case WM_SETFOCUS:
        return pThis->OnSetFocus();

    case WM_KILLFOCUS:
        return pThis->OnKillFocus();

    case WM_ACTIVATE:
        return pThis->OnActivate(SVUIA_ACTIVATE_FOCUS);

    case WM_COMMAND:
        return pThis->OnCommand(GET_WM_COMMAND_ID(wParam, lParam),
                            GET_WM_COMMAND_CMD(wParam, lParam),
                            GET_WM_COMMAND_HWND(wParam, lParam));

    case WM_NOTIFY:
        return pThis->OnNotify(wParam, reinterpret_cast<LPNMHDR>(lParam));
    }
    return DefWindowProc(hWnd, uMsg, wParam, lParam);
}
```

To guarantee perfect alignment between selected items and the status of both menus and toolbars, dealing with `WM_SETFOCUS` and `WM_KILLFOCUS` is particularly important:

```
LRESULT CShellView::OnSetFocus()
{
    // Tell the browser we have the focus
    m_pShellBrowser->OnViewWindowActive(this);

    OnActivate(SVUIA_ACTIVATE_FOCUS);
    return 0;
}
```

```
// OnKillFocus
LRESULT CShellView::OnKillFocus()
{
    OnActivate(SVUIA_ACTIVATE_NOFOCUS);
    return 0;
}
```

We create the list view during the `WM_CREATE` message, and resize it properly during `WM_SIZE` in order to have the view cover the entire available area.

Style of the List View

The list view has the following styles set upon creation in response to `WM_CREATE`:

```
WS_TABSTOP      WS_VISIBLE      WS_CHILD            WS_BORDER
LVS_SINGLESEL   LVS_REPORT      LVS_SHAREIMAGELISTS
```

In addition, since we're addressing Windows 95 with Active Desktop as our minimum platform, we can add some of the new list view styles. These must be set through a new macro, and are called **extended styles**.

```
BOOL CShellView::CreateList()
{
    DWORD dwStyle = WS_TABSTOP | WS_VISIBLE | WS_CHILD | WS_BORDER |
                        LVS_SINGLESEL | LVS_REPORT | LVS_SHAREIMAGELISTS;

    // Create the list view
    m_hwndList = CreateWindowEx(WS_EX_CLIENTEDGE, WC_LISTVIEW, NULL, dwStyle,
                                0, 0, 0, 0, m_hWnd,
                                reinterpret_cast<HMENU>(ID_LISTVIEW),
                                g_hInst, NULL);

    if(!m_hwndList)
        return FALSE;

    // Set some extended styles
    DWORD dwExStyle = LVS_EX_TRACKSELECT | LVS_EX_UNDERLINEHOT |
                        LVS_EX_FULLROWSELECT | LVS_EX_HEADERDRAGDROP;
    ListView_SetExtendedListViewStyle(m_hwndList, dwExStyle);
    return TRUE;
}
```

The new styles set by these flags mean that the selection now follows the mouse, the entire line is selected (not just the first item), and we can move the columns using drag-and-drop. Here's the source code that runs after the creation of the list view. It defines four columns and fills the list with the items:

```
BOOL CShellView::InitList()
{
    TCHAR szString[MAX_PATH] = {0};

    // Empty the list view
    ListView_DeleteAllItems(m_hwndList);

    // Initialize the columns
    LV_COLUMN lvColumn;
    lvColumn.mask = LVCF_FMT | LVCF_WIDTH | LVCF_TEXT | LVCF_SUBITEM;
    lvColumn.fmt = LVCFMT_LEFT;
    lvColumn.pszText = szString;

    lvColumn.cx = g_nColumn1;
    LoadString(g_hInst, IDS_COLUMN1, szString, MAX_PATH);
    ListView_InsertColumn(m_hwndList, 0, &lvColumn);
    RECT rc;
    GetClientRect(m_hWnd, &rc);

    lvColumn.cx = g_nColumn2;
    LoadString(g_hInst, IDS_COLUMN2, szString, MAX_PATH);
    ListView_InsertColumn(m_hwndList, 1, &lvColumn);

    lvColumn.cx = g_nColumn3;
    LoadString(g_hInst, IDS_COLUMN3, szString, MAX_PATH);
    ListView_InsertColumn(m_hwndList, 2, &lvColumn);

    lvColumn.cx = g_nColumn4;
    LoadString(g_hInst, IDS_COLUMN4, szString, MAX_PATH);
    ListView_InsertColumn(m_hwndList, 3, &lvColumn);

    ListView_SetImageList(m_hwndList, g_himlSmall, LVSIL_SMALL);
    return TRUE;
}
```

The list view is then filled by getting the information from the folder's enumerator and using its Next() method. The enumerator is built through the view's m_pSFParent member, a pointer to IShellFolder that was acquired and stored during construction.

```
void CShellView::FillList()
{
    LPENUMIDLIST pEnumIDList = NULL;

    // Get the enumerator object for the folder. EnumObjects() is called
    //  through the pointer received via the CShellView constructor.
    HRESULT hr = m_pSFParent->EnumObjects(
                    m_hWnd, SHCONTF_NONFOLDERS | SHCONTF_FOLDERS, &pEnumIDList);
    if(SUCCEEDED(hr))
    {
        LPITEMIDLIST pidl = NULL;

        // Stop redrawing to avoid flickering
        SendMessage(m_hwndList, WM_SETREDRAW, FALSE, 0);
```

```
        // Add items
        DWORD dwFetched;
        while((pEnumIDList->Next(1, &pidl, &dwFetched) == S_OK) && dwFetched)
        {
            LV_ITEM lvi;
            ZeroMemory(&lvi, sizeof(LV_ITEM));
            lvi.mask = LVIF_TEXT | LVIF_IMAGE | LVIF_PARAM;
            lvi.iItem = ListView_GetItemCount(m_hwndList);

            // Store PIDL to the HWND, using the lParam member for each item
            HWND h = m_pPidlMgr->GetData(pidl);
            lvi.lParam = reinterpret_cast<LPARAM>(m_pPidlMgr->Create(h));

            // Column 1: state (set image too)
            TCHAR szState[30] = {0};
            if(m_pPidlMgr->HasChildren(h))
            {
                lvi.iImage = 0;
                LoadString(g_hInst, IDS_CHILDREN, szState, 30);
            }
            else
            {
                lvi.iImage = 1;
                LoadString(g_hInst, IDS_NOCHILDREN, szState, 30);
            }
            lvi.pszText = szState;

            // Add the item
            int i = ListView_InsertItem(m_hwndList, &lvi);

            // Fill the subitem 2: HWND
            TCHAR szBuf[MAX_PATH] = {0};
            wsprintf(szBuf, __TEXT("0x%04X"), h);
            ListView_SetItemText(m_hwndList, i, 2, szBuf);

            // Fill the subitem 3: Title
            GetWindowText(h, szBuf, MAX_PATH);
            ListView_SetItemText(m_hwndList, i, 3, szBuf);

            // Fill the subitem 1: Class
            GetClassName(h, szBuf, MAX_PATH);
            ListView_SetItemText(m_hwndList, i, 1, szBuf);
        }

        // Sort the items by HWND initially
        ListView_SortItems(
            m_hwndList, CompareItems, reinterpret_cast<LPARAM>(m_pSFParent));

        // Redraw the list view
        SendMessage(m_hwndList, WM_SETREDRAW, TRUE, 0);
        InvalidateRect(m_hwndList, NULL, TRUE);
        UpdateWindow(m_hwndList);
        pEnumIDList->Release();
    }
}
```

Notice that we're taking a copy of the PIDL of an item in the list view, and storing it in the `lParam` member of that item. If you're wondering why we need to do that, well, just be patient... we'll need it later!

Sorting by Columns

When we click on one of the headers in the list view, we want to cause items in the view to be sorted using the `IShellFolder::CompareIDs()` method in the background. It's possible to sort on any of the columns, but actually arranging for it to get done is another task for us. Firstly, we need to detect when the user clicks on any of the columns, but that's the easy part: the event is notified to the view through a `WM_NOTIFY` message. We can intercept it in the main window procedure and handle it using the following code.

```
LRESULT CShellView::OnNotify(UINT CtlID, LPNMHDR lpnmh)
{
    switch(lpnmh->code)
    {
    case NM_SETFOCUS:
        OnSetFocus();
        break;

    case NM_KILLFOCUS:
        OnDeactivate();
        break;

    case HDN_ENDTRACK:
        g_nColumn1 = ListView_GetColumnWidth(m_hwndList, 0);
        g_nColumn2 = ListView_GetColumnWidth(m_hwndList, 1);
        g_nColumn3 = ListView_GetColumnWidth(m_hwndList, 2);
        g_nColumn4 = ListView_GetColumnWidth(m_hwndList, 3);
        return 0;

    case HDN_ITEMCLICK:
        {
            NMHEADER* pNMH = reinterpret_cast<NMHEADER*>(lpnmh);

            // Have we to reverse the order?
            if(m_pSFParent->m_uSortField == 1 + pNMH->iItem)
                m_pSFParent->m_uSortField = (-1) * (1 + pNMH->iItem);
            else
                m_pSFParent->m_uSortField = 1 + pNMH->iItem;

            ListView_SortItems(m_hwndList, CompareItems,
                                        reinterpret_cast<LPARAM>(m_pSFParent));
        }
        return 0;

    case LVN_ITEMACTIVATE:
        {
            LV_ITEM lvItem;
            ZeroMemory(&lvItem, sizeof(LV_ITEM));
            lvItem.mask = LVIF_PARAM;

            LPNMLISTVIEW lpnmlv = reinterpret_cast<LPNMLISTVIEW>(lpnmh);
            lvItem.iItem = lpnmlv->iItem;
            ListView_GetItem(m_hwndList, &lvItem);
            m_pShellBrowser->BrowseObject(
                            reinterpret_cast<LPITEMIDLIST>(lvItem.lParam),
                            SBSP_DEFBROWSER | SBSP_RELATIVE);
            return 0;
        }
    }
    return 0;
}
```

The WM_NOTIFY message is mainly used to handle the resizing of the columns (HDN_ENDTRACK), clicks on the column headings (HDN_ITEMCLICK), and even double-clicks (or single clicks if you have set the Web-style option for all folders) on a single item (LVN_ITEMACTIVATE).

To sort on a particular field, we have just to click the heading. What the system then passes to our procedure is the 0-based index of the column. If this value (pNMH->iItem) coincides with the value of m_uSortField (that is, with the 1-based index of the column currently sorted), then we reverse the order. In our code, this is simply a matter of multiplying the value of m_uSortField by -1. In combination with the IShellFolder::CompareIDs() method I showed you earlier, this simple operation will give us the desired result.

```
if(m_pSFParent->m_uSortField == 1 + pNMH->iItem)
    m_pSFParent->m_uSortField = (-1) * (1 + pNMH->iItem);
else
    m_pSFParent->m_uSortField = 1 + pNMH->iItem;
```

In order to actually sort the list view, we must call

```
ListView_SortItems(m_hwndList, CompareItems,
                   reinterpret_cast<LPARAM>(m_pSFParent));
```

Here, CompareItems() is a user-defined, global function that ends up calling IShellFolder::CompareIDs():

```
int CALLBACK CompareItems(LPARAM lParam1, LPARAM lParam2, LPARAM lpData)
{
    CShellFolder* pFolder = reinterpret_cast<CShellFolder*>(lpData);
    if(!pFolder)
        return 0;

    return pFolder->CompareIDs(0, reinterpret_cast<LPITEMIDLIST>(lParam1),
                              reinterpret_cast<LPITEMIDLIST>(lParam2));
}
```

The next figure shows a view in which items are sorted by HWND in descending order:

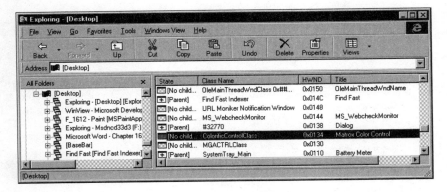

By clicking on, say, the `Class Name` column, we get the following result:

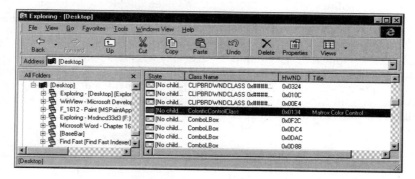

Browsing for Windows

In any given folder view, you will usually have sub-folders and 'leaf' windows. When it's dealing with 'real' folders, Explorer's user interface lets you browse into a sub-folder by double-clicking it. Now that we're writing a namespace extension, however, even this feature is not automatic and we have to implement it ourselves. There are two points to resolve:

❑ Getting the PIDL for the selected list view item
❑ Opening a new folder

The PIDL of the item is easy to get, because we deliberately stored it with the item. (I told you that would come in handy!) Here's how to get it, in code that again comes from the `LVN_ITEMACTIVATE` handler in the `CShellView::OnNotify()` function:

```
LV_ITEM lvi;
ZeroMemory(&lvi, sizeof(LV_ITEM));
lvi.mask = LVIF_PARAM;

LPNMLISTVIEW lpnmlv = reinterpret_cast<LPNMLISTVIEW>(lpnmh);
lvi.iItem = lpnmlv->iItem;
ListView_GetItem(m_hwndList, &lvi);
m_pShellBrowser->BrowseObject(
                    reinterpret_cast<LPITEMIDLIST>(lvi.lParam),
                    SBSP_DEFBROWSER | SBSP_RELATIVE);
```

First, we prepare a `LV_ITEM` structure to be filled by `ListView_GetItem()`. In the `mask` member, we set a flag that denotes the type of information we need – the `lParam` value associated with the item. Once we have that, we can call `IShellBrowser::BrowseObject()`, passing the PIDL to browse to. Notice particularly the second parameter of the method:

```
HRESULT IShellBrowser::BrowseObject(LPCITEMIDLIST pidl,
                                    UINT          wFlags);
```

This `UINT` number is intended to drive the behavior of `BrowseObject()`. The first flag we specified, `SBSP_DEFBROWSER`, means that we want the new folder opened with the same options as the current view: no new window, no different view settings. This is certainly the most common option for functions calling this method.

The second flag, SBSP_RELATIVE, instructs the function to consider the PIDL as being relative to the current folder. In this case, this is the only sensible option because we stored a relative PIDL in the item's lParam member – it refers only to a specific window, and forgets any information that relates to its parents. For this reason, using SBSP_ABSOLUTE would produce a new, empty folder.

Giving it a User Interface

Once our namespace extension has the focus, it may change both the menu and the toolbar of Explorer. The changes should be issued when the extension receives the focus, and dismissed when it loses the focus.

The IShellView::UIActivate() method gets called by the shell to notify your extension that it has been activated *or* deactivated, and so it's in this function that we'll make the changes to the menu and modify other user interface settings. In the code below, we also take care of the status bar, and this would be the right place to enter the changes to the toolbar that I covered earlier in the chapter.

```
STDMETHODIMP CShellView::UIActivate(UINT uState)
{
    // Exit if the state hasn't changed since last time
    if(m_uState == uState)
        return S_OK;

    // Modify the menu
    OnActivate(uState);

    // Modify the status bar
    if(uState != SVUIA_DEACTIVATE)
    {
        TCHAR szName[MAX_PATH] = {0};

        // Add more parts if needed... as is, it's equivalent to SB_SIMPLE
        int aParts[1] = {-1};

        // Set the number of parts
        m_pShellBrowser->SendControlMsg(FCW_STATUS, SB_SETPARTS, 1,
                                reinterpret_cast<LPARAM>(aParts), NULL);

        m_pPidlMgr->GetPidlPath(m_pidl, szName);
        m_pShellBrowser->SendControlMsg(FCW_STATUS, SB_SETTEXT, 0,
                                reinterpret_cast<LPARAM>(szName), NULL);
    }
    return S_OK;
}
```

The status bar is a strip that's usually placed at the bottom of a top-level window – in this case, Explorer. It can be divided into parts, each with their own appearance settings (inset, flat, raised). To set the parts of the status bar, use the SB_SETPARTS message that takes an array of integers to denote the right edges of the various parts (the lParam argument) and another integer to denote the number of parts to deal with (the wParam argument).

The values for the array represent the right edge of each section *expressed in client coordinates*. If one of the values is −1 (as in our example), then that part is meant to extend up to the right edge of the host window. A status bar with a single part is actually more simply defined with the SB_SIMPLE message that causes any existing part to be removed. Using an array of parts like this:

```
int aParts[1] = {-1};
```

and sending the SB_SIMPLE message would produce the same effect as the above code. However, if I'd done that here, you wouldn't have seen the details!

Menu Modifications

Modifying the menu is an operation that requires three steps, as I outlined earlier. First, you need to create a new menu, and then you pass it to Explorer together with a menu descriptor. The shell then fills the menu in a standard way, and at this point you're given a chance to modify it.

In our case, we need to add a new Windows View top-level menu. Furthermore, we don't want the Edit menu (because that wouldn't make any sense for a list of open windows), and we want to change the Help | About... window.

```
LRESULT CShellView::OnActivate(UINT uState)
{
    // Has state changed since the last time we were called?
    if(m_uState == uState)
        return S_OK;

    // Destroy all our previous changes to the menu
    OnDeactivate();

    // If active...
    if(uState != SVUIA_DEACTIVATE)
    {
        // Step 1: create a new menu
        m_hMenu = CreateMenu();
        if(m_hMenu)
        {
            // Step 2: Share it with the shell through a menu group descriptor
            OLEMENUGROUPWIDTHS omw = {0, 0, 0, 0, 0, 0};
            m_pShellBrowser->InsertMenusSB(m_hMenu, &omw);

            // Step 3: Change the menu
            // Step 3.1: Build and insert the 'Windows View' top level menu
            TCHAR szText[MAX_PATH] = {0};
            LoadString(g_hInst, IDS_MI_WINVIEW, szText, MAX_PATH);

            MENUITEMINFO mii;
            ZeroMemory(&mii, sizeof(MENUITEMINFO));
            mii.cbSize = sizeof(mii);
            mii.fMask = MIIM_SUBMENU | MIIM_TYPE | MIIM_STATE;
            mii.fType = MFT_STRING;
            mii.fState = MFS_ENABLED;
            mii.dwTypeData = szText;
            mii.hSubMenu = BuildWinViewMenu();
            if(mii.hSubMenu)
                InsertMenuItem(m_hMenu, FCIDM_MENU_HELP, FALSE, &mii);
```

```
        // Step 3.2: Get the Help menu and merge
        ZeroMemory(&mii, sizeof(MENUITEMINFO));
        mii.cbSize = sizeof(MENUITEMINFO);
        mii.fMask = MIIM_SUBMENU;
        if(GetMenuItemInfo(m_hMenu, FCIDM_MENU_HELP, FALSE, &mii))
            MergeHelpMenu(mii.hSubMenu);

        // Step 3.3: Remove the Edit menu
        DeleteMenu(m_hMenu, FCIDM_MENU_EDIT, MF_BYCOMMAND);

        // Step 3.4: If we have the focus, add items to the File menu
        if(uState == SVUIA_ACTIVATE_FOCUS)
        {
            // Get the File menu and merge
            ZeroMemory(&mii, sizeof(MENUITEMINFO));
            mii.cbSize = sizeof(MENUITEMINFO);
            mii.fMask = MIIM_SUBMENU;
            if(GetMenuItemInfo(m_hMenu, FCIDM_MENU_FILE, FALSE, &mii))
                MergeFileMenu(mii.hSubMenu);
        }

        // Set the new menu
        m_pShellBrowser->SetMenuSB(m_hMenu, NULL, m_hWnd);
    }
}

// Save the current state
m_uState = uState;
return 0;
}
```

Notice how we have to refer to system menus by using the predefined constants from `shlobj.h`. For example, to add a new menu before the Help menu, I used:

```
InsertMenuItem(m_hMenu, FCIDM_MENU_HELP, FALSE, &mii);
```

With this call, `InsertMenuItem()` inserts a new item before the menu specified in the second parameter. `BuildWinViewMenu()` is a helper function that looks like this:

```
HMENU CShellView::BuildWinViewMenu()
{
    HMENU hSubMenu = CreatePopupMenu();
    if(hSubMenu)
    {

        TCHAR szText[BUFSIZE] = {0};
        MENUITEMINFO mii;

        // Add "Properties" to "Windows View"
        LoadString(g_hInst, IDS_MI_PROPERTIES, szText, BUFSIZE);
        ZeroMemory(&mii, sizeof(MENUITEMINFO));
        mii.cbSize = sizeof(MENUITEMINFO);
        mii.fMask = MIIM_TYPE | MIIM_ID | MIIM_STATE;
        mii.fType = MFT_STRING;
        mii.fState = MFS_ENABLED;
        mii.dwTypeData = szText;
        mii.wID = IDM_WIN_PROPERTIES;
```

```
        // Add at the end of the menu
        InsertMenuItem(hSubMenu, static_cast<UINT>(-1), TRUE, &mii);

        // Add "Process View" to "Windows View"
        LoadString(g_hInst, IDS_MI_PROCESSVIEW, szText, BUFSIZE);
        ZeroMemory(&mii, sizeof(MENUITEMINFO));
        mii.cbSize = sizeof(MENUITEMINFO);
        mii.fMask = MIIM_TYPE | MIIM_ID | MIIM_STATE;
        mii.fType = MFT_STRING;
        mii.fState = MFS_ENABLED;
        mii.dwTypeData = szText;
        mii.wID = IDM_WIN_PROCESS;

        // Add at the end of the menu
        InsertMenuItem(hSubMenu, static_cast<UINT>(-1), TRUE, &mii);
    }
    return hSubMenu;
}
```

By default, the new items under the File menu (and any toolbar buttons we create) must appear only if the extension has the focus. If the item is selected only in the right pane, it still *doesn't* have the focus, so you have to wait before merging your custom items into the File menu. When the extension loses the focus, good manners dictate that we should remove all our footprints:

```
void CShellView::OnDeactivate()
{
    if(m_uState != SVUIA_DEACTIVATE)
    {
        if(m_hMenu)
        {
            m_pShellBrowser->SetMenusSB(NULL, NULL, NULL);
            m_pShellBrowser->RemoveMenusSB(m_hMenu);
            DestroyMenu(m_hMenu);
            m_hMenu = NULL;
        }
        m_uState = SVUIA_DEACTIVATE;
    }
}
```

Displaying Help Text

The following figure shows the new menu in Explorer when the Windows View extension is active.

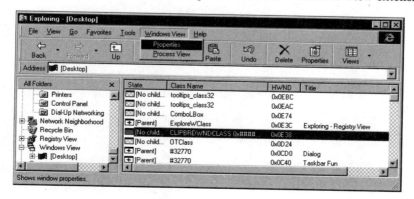

Notice the help text that appears in the status bar. To enable this feature, you simply have to handle the `WM_MENUSELECT` message in your window procedure, just as you would in good old SDK Windows programming. There are two methods to set text on the status bar. You can send messages directly to the window using `SendControlMsg()`, or you can set text yourself by calling `SetStatusTextSB()`. `IShellBrowser` exposes both of these functions, although the documentation recommends that you use the latter. While this is reasonable (the method is a wrapper for the bare status bar messages and won't change in the future), it also poses a problem, and is actually inadequate when you have to deal with status bars with multiple parts: `SetStatusTextSB()` doesn't allow you to specify which part you want to set. In addition, as I mentioned earlier in the chapter, `SetStatusTextSB()` requires Unicode strings.

Associating a Context Menu with Items

The shell searches for a context menu automatically, by looking for the `IContextMenu` interface. For this example I implemented it and added two items, the first of which copies the display name of the window to the clipboard, while the second shows a dialog with some window properties:

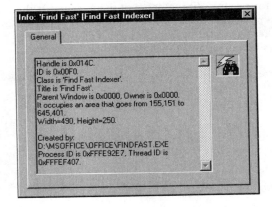

As you can see, the information that this dialog conveys includes the name of the executable that created the window, and the icon. To get the icon, in particular, I used the following code:

```
// Returns a copy of the large/small icon for the specified window, or a
//  standard icon if there's no icon for the window class it belongs to.
HICON GetWindowIcon(HWND hwnd, BOOL fBig)
{
    HICON hIcon = NULL;

    // First search for the icon assigned to the window class. If no icon is
    //  found, then I try to get the icon assigned to the specific window via
    //  WM_SETICON. In case of further failure, a standard icon is returned.
    if(fBig)
    {
        // A large icon is required
        hIcon = reinterpret_cast<HICON>(GetClassLong(hwnd, GCL_HICON));
        if(hIcon == NULL)
            hIcon = reinterpret_cast<HICON>(
                            SendMessage(hwnd, WM_GETICON, ICON_BIG, 0));
    }
    else
    {
        hIcon = reinterpret_cast<HICON>(GetClassLong(hwnd, GCL_HICONSM));
        if(hIcon == NULL)
            hIcon = reinterpret_cast<HICON>(
                            SendMessage(hwnd, WM_GETICON, ICON_SMALL, 0));
    }
```

```
        if(hIcon == NULL)
            hIcon = LoadIcon(g_hInst, MAKEINTRESOURCE(IDI_PARWND));

        // Return a copy of the icon
        return CopyIcon(hIcon);
    }
```

First, we check the icon of the class, but if no icon is found then we try sending a WM_GETICON message to the window instead. If this approach also fails, then we use a standard icon. Whatever the result, we return a copy of the icon rather than the original. The caller is then responsible for freeing the icon.

As for finding out the name of the executable that created a given window, we're using a trick that was presented in an article of mine that appeared in WDJ. (See *Further Reading* for more details.) It makes use of the ToolHelp API under Windows 9x, and the PSAPI library under Windows NT 4.0. This topic was also touched upon in Chapter 15.

Associating a context menu with the items is as easy as implementing the functions of the IContextMenu interface:

```
STDMETHODIMP CContextMenu::InvokeCommand(LPCMINVOKECOMMANDINFO lpcmi)
{
    WORD wCmd = LOWORD(lpcmi->lpVerb);

    switch(wCmd)
    {
    case 1:                          // Properties
        ShowProperties();
        break;

    case 0:                          // Copy
        CopyTextToClipboard();
        break;
    }

    return S_OK;
}
```

```
STDMETHODIMP CContextMenu::GetCommandString(UINT, UINT, UINT*, LPSTR, UINT)
{
    return E_NOTIMPL;
}
```

```
STDMETHODIMP CContextMenu::QueryContextMenu(HMENU hmenu,
            UINT indexMenu, UINT idCmdFirst, UINT idCmdLast, UINT uFlags)
{
    UINT idCmd = idCmdFirst;

    // Add the new items, loading strings from resources
    TCHAR szItem[BUFSIZE] = {0};
```

```
    LoadString(g_hInst, IDS_MI_COPY, szItem, BUFSIZE);
    InsertMenu(hmenu, indexMenu++, MF_STRING | MF_BYPOSITION, idCmd++, szItem);
    LoadString(g_hInst, IDS_MI_PROPERTIES, szItem, BUFSIZE);
    InsertMenu(hmenu, indexMenu++, MF_STRING | MF_BYPOSITION, idCmd++, szItem);

    return MAKE_SCODE(SEVERITY_SUCCESS, FACILITY_NULL, idCmd - idCmdFirst);
}
```

All this works fine in Explorer's *left* pane. If you want to catch right clicks on the view (that is, the *right* pane), then you have to do it all by yourself. Detecting the WM_CONTEXTMENU message in the view window procedure is the way to go. Once you've detected this message, you can create a menu on the fly, loading the template from the resources. Alternatively, if you have the IShellFolder pointer available in the view class, you can call GetUIObjectOf() and have the IContextMenu interface help you to compose the menu to display. In this case, however, you now have to distinguish *which* pane has called the menu: left or right. In general, I think that the solution adopted in our example – creating a new menu on the fly if the view is right-clicked on – is better. Note that there's no support for context menus in Microsoft's Registry View sample.

Code for a Better Context Menu

Although the above code certainly works, it doesn't consider all the possible attributes of the file object to which the menu applies. For example, if the folder item has the SFGAO_CANRENAME bit set, then the context menu should provide a Rename command (localized if needed).

The uFlags argument of the IContextMenu::QueryContextMenu() method can assume a number of values, which we partially considered in Chapter 15. Some of them now need revisiting in the light of namespace extensions.

Flag	Description
CMF_EXPLORE	The menu is displayed in Explorer's tree view window. Add an Explore command
CMF_RENAME	The file object can be renamed. Add a Rename command.
CMF_DEFAULTONLY	A namespace extension should add only the default item, if any.
CMF_NODEFAULT	A namespace extension shouldn't define any item as the default.

More precise code can be obtained by adding little code snippets to the previous QueryContextMenu() implementation like this one, which checks for the CMF_CANRENAME flag and then adds a new command to the menu.

```
    if(uFlags & CMF_CANRENAME)
    {
        LoadString(g_hInst, IDS_MI_RENAME, szItem, BUFSIZE);
        InsertMenu(
                hmenu, indexMenu++, MF_STRING | MF_BYPOSITION, idCmd++, szItem);
    }
```

To handle this command, you can send messages directly to the tree view using `SendControlMsg()` and the constant `FCW_TREE`. For the `Explore` command's implementation, on the other hand, you can use `ShellExecuteEx()`, passing the file object PIDL as the target file object.

In general, your implementation of `QueryContextMenu()` should take all the possible flags into account, but they don't always all make sense. In our example, it's a bit of a problem to figure out what should be 'edited' for windows — only the window title comes to my mind.

Associating an Icon with Items

`IExtractIcon` is a useful interface that lets you associate icons with folder items, but once again it only works for the icons to be displayed in the *left* pane. The reason is the same as it was for context menus: the shell can't know when the custom view may need an icon. The icons that appear in the list view are decided explicitly by the code that fills in the list view.

For the icons to be shown in the address bar and in the nodes of the tree view, you need to implement the functions of `IExtractIcon`:

```
STDMETHODIMP CExtractIcon::GetIconLocation(UINT uFlags,
            LPTSTR szIconFile, UINT cchMax, LPINT piIndex, LPUINT puFlags)
{
    *puFlags = GIL_DONTCACHE | GIL_PERINSTANCE;
    return S_FALSE;
}
```

```
STDMETHODIMP CExtractIcon::Extract(LPCTSTR pszFile, UINT nIconIndex,
                    HICON* phiconLarge, HICON* phiconSmall, UINT nIconSize)
{
    HWND hwnd = m_pPidlMgr->GetData(m_pidl);
    if(hwnd == GetDesktopWindow() ||
                        hwnd == FindWindow(__TEXT("shell_traywnd"), NULL))
    {
        *phiconLarge = LoadIcon(NULL, MAKEINTRESOURCE(IDI_WINLOGO));
        *phiconSmall = LoadIcon(NULL, MAKEINTRESOURCE(IDI_WINLOGO));
        return S_OK;
    }

    *phiconLarge = LoadIcon(g_hInst, MAKEINTRESOURCE(IDI_WINVIEW));
    *phiconSmall = LoadIcon(g_hInst, MAKEINTRESOURCE(IDI_WINVIEW));
    return S_OK;
}
```

We use the same icon in all cases but two: when the window is the desktop, or the taskbar. In these cases, we use an icon that looks like the Windows logo. As explained in Chapter 9, the window class for the taskbar is `shell_traywnd`, which I discovered after a little rummaging with Spy++.

When using icons in a namespace extension, you should also consider using `IShellIcon` rather than `IExtractIcon`, since it is the fastest way to get icons. Unfortunately, though, it doesn't have the power to go with it. `IShellIcon` exposes a single function called `GetIconOf()`:

```
HRESULT IShellIcon::GetIconOf(LPCITEMIDLIST pidl,
                    UINT          flags,
                    LPINT         lpIconIndex);
```

The `flags` argument plays the same role as the first argument of the `GetIconLocation()` method of the `IExtractIcon` interface. The legal values are `GIL_FORSHELL` and `GIL_OPENICON`. (See Chapter 15.) The function is expected to return an index in its `lpIconIndex` parameter that must be relative to the system's icon image list. If the icon to return is not in the system's image list, it's the responsibility of the developer to insert it before returning the index. Of course, you should make sure that you only add it once!

What makes `IShellIcon` competitive is that you don't need to create an instance of it every time an icon is needed. Instead, when you implement it you automatically have the shell asking it to return an index in the system image list for a given `PIDL`. There's only one instance of it running in the entire session, working as a kind of server that takes a `PIDL` and returns an icon index.

With `IExtractIcon`, on the other hand, you have an interface that renders a single, individual icon to appear somewhere in the shell folders. This means that you need a new instance of it each time you deal with a different icon. When it comes to drawing the icon of an item in the tree view, Explorer first searches for `IShellIcon` and resorts to `IExtractIcon` through `GetUIObjectOf()` only if it fails to find it.

Installing a Namespace Extension

At this point of the discussion, we've finished and compiled our namespace extension. The next step is installing and putting it to work. We need to do a few things:

❑ Register the namespace extension as a COM server, specifying the apartment threading model, the icon, and the name of the extension
❑ Register it as an approved extension, to have it to work under Windows NT too
❑ Define your junction point with the rest of the system

The first two points are easy to cope with:

```
REGEDIT4

; It's absolutely necessary that you write the registry entries on the same line...

; Register the server and its threading model
[HKEY_CLASSES_ROOT\CLSID\{F778AFE0-2289-11d0-8AEC-00A0C90C9246}\InProcServer32]
@= "C:\\WinView\\winview.dll"
"ThreadingModel" = "Apartment"

; Register the name of the extension
[HKEY_CLASSES_ROOT\CLSID\{F778AFE0-2289-11d0-8AEC-00A0C90C9246}]
@= "Windows View"

; Register the icon
[HKEY_CLASSES_ROOT\CLSID\{F778AFE0-2289-11d0-8AEC-00A0C90C9246}\DefaultIcon]
@= "C:\\WinView\\winview.dll,0"

; Register the extension under NT
[HKEY_LOCAL_MACHINE\SOFTWARE\Microsoft\Windows\CurrentVersion\ShellExtensions\Appr
ved\{F778AFE0-2289-11d0-8AEC-00A0C90C9246}]
@= "Windows View"
```

Here, `{F778AFE0-2289-11d0-8AEC-00A0C90C9246}` is the CLSID of our namespace extension, as defined in `Guid.h`.

The last of the three items in my list is really up to you. In this case, our extension has nothing to do with files, so it wouldn't make sense to register it for a given document class. A much better idea would be to use a directory as the junction point; by creating a folder called `My Windows.{F778AFE0-2289-11d0-8AEC-00A0C90C9246}`, you could achieve the following result:

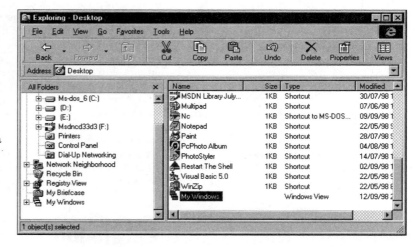

In the end, though, I decided on another approach: putting the extension inside the `Desktop` namespace.

```
HKEY_LOCAL_MACHINE
    \Software
        \Microsoft
            \Windows
                \CurrentVersion
                    \Explorer
                        \Desktop
                            \NameSpace
                                \{F778AFE0-2289-11d0-8AEC-00A0C90C9246}
```

I've simply created a new key under `NameSpace` with the CLSID of the extension. This is sufficient to have an icon appear on the desktop as well as a new node in Explorer's tree view.

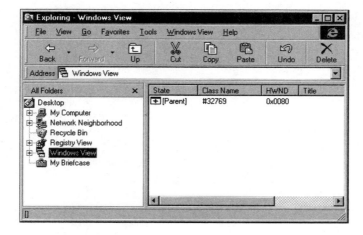

There is, however, another setting that we should save: the default flags for the folder. We do this by storing a new `ShellFolder` key under this path:

```
HKEY_CLASSES_ROOT
   \CLSID
      \{F778AFE0-2289-11d0-8AEC-00A0C90C9246}
         \ShellFolder
```

The `Attributes` entry then assumes the value of `SFGAO_FOLDER | SFGAO_HASSUBFOLDER`:

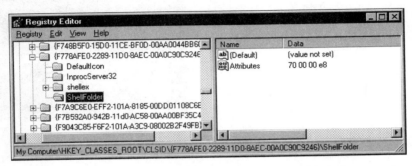

This is just the beginning of the things you can do with this `ShellFolder` key; I'll tell you about more of them in a moment.

A Node on the Desktop

The Windows desktop contains some icons that refer to special system folders. With the above technique, you too can add a brand new system folder that behaves however you want it to. The Windows View icon is neither a shortcut nor a program copied directly into the `Desktop` directory. It's just a custom, system folder that's located on the desktop. If we open it now, we get a rooted view:

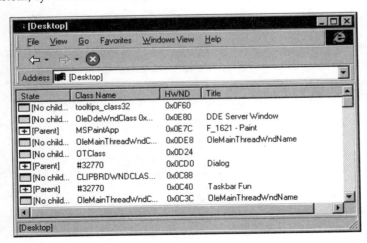

Adding an InfoTip

You have certainly noticed that almost all the system folders that appear on the desktop can have a tooltip (we're supposed to call it an **infotip**) when the mouse lingers over them for a moment. The figure shows what I mean for Network Neighborhood:

In case you're wondering exactly how an infotip is different from a tooltip, I'll tell you: it's simply a matter of naming. The word 'tooltip' is composed of 'tool' and 'tip', and the effect is meant to be of a help string for a tool. 'Datatip', 'titletip', and 'infotip' are all synonyms for tooltips that address tips for data in a window, titles in a report view or a tree view, and items in a list view.

Is it possible to add infotips to our own namespace extensions? Of course it is! After reading the documentation available I formed the opinion that the means of getting such infotips must be the new IQueryInfo interface, but in fact there's a far simpler and more reliable technique. All you have to do is add a new value to the CLSID key in the registry. In our case, this means:

```
HKEY_CLASSES_ROOT
  \CLSID
    \{F778AFE0-2289-11d0-8AEC-00A0C90C9246}
```

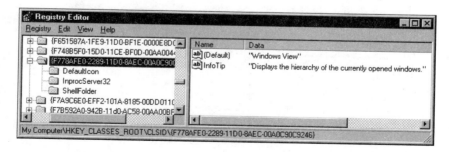

The value must be called `InfoTip`, and its content is the string that will be displayed:

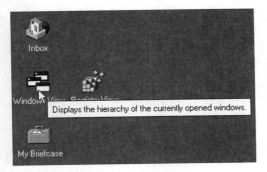

I didn't find any Knowledge Base article, official or any documentation (official or unofficial) about this. I simply reasoned it out by looking at the registry values for `My Computer` – a desktop namespace extension that sports this feature. The same namespace extension also has the feature that I'm going to describe in the next section.

Adding a Removal Message

While developing this extension, there was a point at which I wanted to remove it from my desktop and reinstall it. Automatically, I right-clicked the icon on the desktop searching for a <u>D</u>elete command... but there was nothing there! Never mind (I thought), I'll drop it onto the Recycle Bin instead. Again, no joy. Since I really wanted it removed, manual intervention in the registry was in order.

Before removing the `{CLSID}` key in the above path, I had a look at the information stored for the other system folders on my PC's desktop: Inbox, Registry View, and Recycle Bin. In particular, the Inbox item had defined an interesting value string: `Removal Message`. Immediately, I turned back to the desktop and right-clicked on Inbox. It had the <u>D</u>elete command, and selecting it produced a dialog box containing the removal message that had been set in the registry.

Making a Folder Deletable

Now we know how to set up a custom deletion message, but how is the <u>D</u>elete command on the folder's context menu enabled? Once again, it's all to do with folder attributes and the `Attributes` key in the registry that we discussed just a couple of sections ago. To make a folder deletable, just tell the shell about it by adding the `SFGAO_CANDELETE` attribute! I changed the default value for the folder attributes to be stored in the registry, and re-registered the extension to apply the changes immediately. The figure illustrates the final result.

Additional Attributes for a Folder

It didn't take much extra research to realize that you can make the folder support **Rename** and **Properties** context menu items by adding other values to the `Attributes` entry, such as `SFGAO_CANRENAME` and `SFGAO_HASPROPSHEET`. Renaming is completely handled by the system – all the user has to do is click the icon or press *F2* while keeping the icon selected.

Implementing a **Properties** command is a little more work. What's needed is a COM module that provides an `IShellPropSheetExt` interface, just like the shell extensions we saw in Chapter 15. When you click on the standard **Properties** item, the system automatically searches for that interface on the clicked object. You need to register it in the typical `Shellex\PropertySheetHandlers` key under:

```
HKEY_CLASSES_ROOT
   \CLSID
      \{CLSID}
```

Browsing a Custom Folder

A custom folder rendered through a namespace extension is not necessarily displayed in an **Open** or a **Save As** common dialog. To make this possible, you need to declare the folder as being part of the file system, because these dialogs only allow file system folders to be displayed. The trick is to add another couple of `SFGAO_XXX` constants: `SFGAO_BROWSABLE` and `SFGAO_FILESYSTEM`.

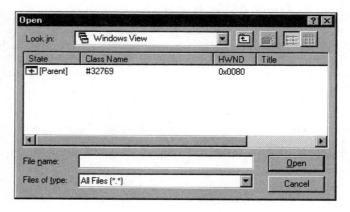

However, even if we succeed in displaying the folder in the standard **Open** dialog, it's not much use because the folder doesn't respond to solicitations and never goes further than one level. Worse still, the dialog is completely deaf to double clicking and the *Enter* key.

There's an interface that seems to be involved with displaying custom folders in common dialogs with the same power and capability as an ordinary file folder: `ICommDlgBrowser`. However, it's implemented *by* the common dialogs. Unfortunately, at this time, Microsoft doesn't support any third party namespace being browsed by these dialogs. To see and select items from a custom folder, then, you need to resort to the `SHBrowseForFolder()` function we met in Chapter 5.

Putting this Example to Work

Once you've successfully downloaded and recompiled this sample from the web site, all you have to do to install the extension is register the component. The necessary settings have been hard-coded into the module's `DllRegisterServer()` function. After calling `regsvr32.exe` on the DLL generated by the compiler, refreshing Explorer should be enough to make everything work as described.

Uninstalling the Sample

If you want to uninstall the example, the simplest method is to right click the icon on the desktop and choose <u>D</u>elete. This will remove the CLSID key from the `Desktop` node in the registry. If you wish, you can also do it manually through the Registry Editor:

```
HKEY_LOCAL_MACHINE
    \Software
        \Microsoft
            \Windows
                \CurrentVersion
                    \Explorer
                        \Desktop
                            \NameSpace
                                \{F778AFE0-2289-11d0-8AEC-00A0C90C9246}
```

Remove the last item in the above key, then turn back to the desktop and press *F5* to refresh the screen. I have to say, though, that following the menu-driven approach is preferable. When you select <u>D</u>elete, the following message will appear:

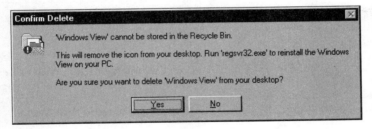

Confirm, and the icon will disappear from the desktop. Notice that the deletion procedure looks absolutely like any other system folder deletion. What happens is identical to the sequence of events when you try to remove the Internet Explorer 4.0 icon from your desktop, for example.

Summarizing Namespace Extensions

Namespace extensions were introduced in the retail versions of Windows 95 and Windows NT 4.0, and the rules for writing them haven't changed with the advent of the Active Desktop. However, starting with shell version 4.71, you can write namespace extensions that are capable of switching between two view modes: **classic** and **web view**.

The classic view is the typical, standard view that you see on machines where version 4.0 of the shell is installed. In case of file folders, the system renders the classic view through a list view. A Web view, on the other hand, is an HTML-based view of the same content. The challenge for the programmer is not only to create these two views, but also to make them interchangeable.

When you're writing namespace extensions, you should consider adding the capability of supporting web views. The means that allows the users to toggle between classic and web views is Explorer's View | as Web Page menu.

In the remainder of this chapter, I'll describe two techniques to combine your folders with HTML. Firstly, I'll provide you with an overview of web views and the design issues they pose when it comes to planning and realizing a web view namespace extension. Secondly, I'll show how you can use the existing shell view architecture to customize the template used for displaying data in an ordinary folder. This is a feature enabled by the Customize this Folder... command on the folder's context menu.

What's a Web View?

With Active Desktop on Windows 95 and Windows NT 4.0, and in Windows 98 and later, the **web view** for folders has been introduced. Basically, this is a Dynamic HTML page that includes the classic view as a component, plus some other sundries like a GIF image and a thumbnail view control. Trying to produce a more formal definition, I'd say firstly that:

> A 'classic view' for a namespace extension is the window used to show the contents of the folder.

Now we have that definition, a web view is:

> A 'web view' for a namespace extension is a browser window showing a Dynamic HTML page that includes the classic view as a component.

Once you have a working namespace extension, adding web view support is a matter of exposing its view window (the classic view) as a component to be embedded in a Dynamic HTML page. Furthermore, you must be ready to switch between the two views, and as if that weren't enough it could be that in the future, the number of views to consider might be more than two.

The typical shell view already provides four different views of the same data: large and small icons, details and list. However, these are just capabilities of the common control used to present the data – the list view – and aren't strictly due to the code that provides the folder's behavior. A web view is a bit different because it really requires *different* windows and components to come into play. These new actors must fit into the existing scenario and integrate with it well.

From the standpoint of namespace extensions, using a web view requires a couple of updated interfaces: IShellView2 and IPersistFolder2. Today, these are completely supported only in the version of the shell that comes with Internet Explorer 4.01 and Windows 98 or higher. A Web-enabled namespace extension has all the characteristics we've seen so far, plus the ability to support the View | as Web Page menu command. When this command is issued, the extension is expected to show the same content as before, but using a HTML template to do so.

The ability to switch between two views poses a number of additional problems and slightly modifies the global architecture of a namespace extension. At the time of writing, documentation on this subject is only just beginning to appear. For the best of it, refer to the Platform SDK editions released in late 1998. In this section, I'll try to give an annotated overview of what's going on with web views.

I expect a great deal of documentation to be produced about this topic in the months to come, and I should stress that what I'm covering here is compatible with shell version 4.71. Even more changes are in order with Windows 2000, so stay tuned and check both MSDN and the Platform SDK frequently!

The Shell View ID

If you look at the source code of the latest `shlobj.h` header file, you'll find the following declaration:

```
typedef GUID SHELLVIEWID;
```

It doesn't look much, but this refers to a new concept in namespace extensions: the **shell view ID**. This is a unique number that identifies a *kind* of shell view, and in most cases it will be the same as the CLSID of the COM object implementing the extension.

This new identifier is used by the functions of the `IShellView2` interface to switch among the possible views. In practice, when you check and uncheck the Web View option on the browser's menu or toolbar, Explorer calls `IShellView2::CreateViewWindow2()` with a different shell view ID to let you have a classic or a web view.

The Default View

Internally, `CreateViewWindow2()` must distinguish and actually create different view windows. Interestingly, though, it *can't* return different window handles to the Explorer. In other words, Explorer won't talk to the specific view, regardless of whether it's the list view or an instance of the WebBrowser control. Instead, it always deals with the same window, which is called the **default view**. This window is of the `SHELLDLL_DefView` class.

The next picture shows the difference between the piles of windows that are involved when the same folder is viewed through a classic or a web view. Notice that the default view appears in both:

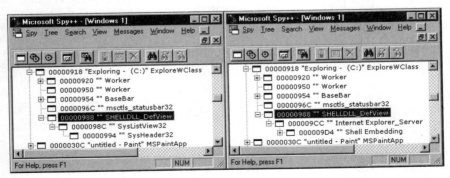

The left picture involves a classic view, while the one on the right is a web view of the same folder. `Internet Explorer_Server` is the window class name of the WebBrowser control. We can deduce that a Web-enabled namespace extension must create its web view window as a sister of the classic view window. The next picture shows the relationship between Explorer and the views:

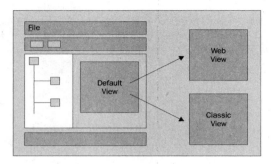

The default view should begin by hosting one of the available views (typically, the classic view). From then on, each time that Explorer calls into `CreateViewWindow2()`, the namespace extension should get the shell view ID and display the specific view identified by that ID inside the default view window.

New Functions in IShellView2

There are four new functions in `IShellView2`:

Function	Description
`CreateViewWindow2()`	Allows you to switch among different views, including the web view and the classic view.
`GetView()`	Returns the shell view ID of a view specified by a predefined constant. At the moment there are only two possibilities for this constant: the default view `SV2GV_DEFAULTVIEW` and the current view `SV2GV_CURRENTVIEW`.
`HandleRename()`	Allows you to change the PIDL of a given item. It receives a PIDL and replaces it with the new one.
`SelectAndPositionItem()`	This function takes a PIDL, some flags, and a pointer to a `POINT` structure. It serves the purpose of letting you select an item and place it wherever you want in the view. This is reasonable if you have a completely custom, HTML-based view for the folder.

For input, the `CreateViewWindow2()` method takes only a pointer to a structure called `SV2CVW2_PARAMS`, defined as follows:

```
typedef struct _SV2CVW2_PARAMS
{
    DWORD                    cbSize;
    IShellView*              psvPrev;
    FOLDERSETTINGS const*    pfs;
    IShellBrowser*           psbOwner;
    RECT*                    prcView;
    SHELLVIEWID const*       pvid;
    HWND                     hwndView;
} SV2CVW2_PARAMS;
```

Let's compare this to the parameter list of `IShellView::CreateViewWindow()`.

```
HRESULT CreateViewWindow(LPSHELLVIEW        pPrevView,
                         LPCFOLDERSETTINGS  lpfs,
                         LPSHELLBROWSER     psb,
                         LPRECT             prcView,
                         HWND*              phWnd);
```

As you can see, the structure includes arguments of exactly the same types, plus the shell view ID and the typical `cbSize` member. Clearly, `CreateViewWindow2()` is a refinement of the `CreateViewWindow()` that has been made in light of the introduction of web view support. Apart from the `cbSize` field, which mostly serves Microsoft's internal purposes, the shell view ID is the only relevant change.

What's New in IPersistFolder2

The `IPersistFolder2` interface extends `IPersistFolder` by adding a new function called `GetCurFolder()`. It has the following prototype:

```
HRESULT IPersistFolder2::GetCurFolder(LPITEMIDLIST* ppidl);
```

It uses its single 'out' parameter to return the PIDL of the current object, making available to the outside world the PIDL of the folder currently being viewed. In practice, it will be the same PIDL that was passed to the `IPersistFolder::Initialize()` method when the namespace extension was initially loaded.

How a Web View is Structured

If you want to arrange a web view of a given folder, you must do at least the following:

❑ Define a default view object as a container of other view objects
❑ Define a classic view object to provide the standard view with folder items
❑ Define a web view object that includes the classic view as a component

Your default view should be ready to return a classic or a web view object, according to the shell view ID it receives. Furthermore, the web view must contain a WebBrowser control that navigates to the Dynamic HTML page providing the template. This template should include the classic view object as an ActiveX component. If that sounds confusing, here's a figure that should clear things up a little:

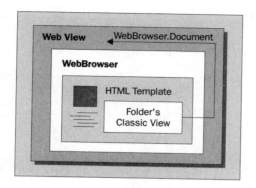

Getting in Touch with the Classic View Object

As the diagram shows, the web view object hosts a WebBrowser control that points to a Dynamic HTML page. This page, in turn, hosts the classic view as a component via its CLSID. The thing is, the web view needs to be able to drive the classic view object. For example, it needs to instruct the view to show the correct folder content. To manage this, the web view object needs to get the `Document` property from the WebBrowser by calling `IWebBrowser2::get_Document()`.

```
HRESULT IWebBrowser2::get_Document(IDispatch** ppDisp);
```

The `Document` object is the root of the Dynamic HTML object model. When an ActiveX document is hosted in an ActiveX container like WebBrowser, the `Document` property returns the entry point to the document's object model. (Internet Explorer 4.*x* treats HTML files like ActiveX documents.)

By enumerating the collection of `<OBJECT>` tags in the page, you should be able to get the `IDispatch` interface pointer for the classic view object. The classic view is embedded in the Dynamic HTML template by the means of an `<OBJECT>` tag, more or less like this:

```
<object classid="clsid:{...}"></object>
```

Since the web view object knows the CLSID of the classic view object, it can easily determine which of the enumerated objects is the right one. Once you've got the `IDispatch` pointer, you have the means to let the web view and the classic view communicate. (See *Further Reading* for a couple of references about Web views and Dynamic HTML programming from C++.)

The Template of a Web View

A web view is characterized by an HTML page. This page can reside wherever you find it comfortable: it could be a file located in same path as the DLL that actually implements the extension, or it could be stored in a system folder. There's a system folder for templates that we saw in Chapter 5, and we'll meet it again in a moment. The common feature, though, is that you have to deal with a separate file that may cause problems if for any reason it goes missing.

A better solution for web views is to embed the HTML file in the extension's resources, and then create temporary local copies or read it directly from there by exploiting the power of the res:// protocol. This URL protocol lets you load an HTML file (and in general, any Win32 resource) directly from an executable's resources. In this way, you can embed the HTML template in the resources and forget any problem with it. For example, if in the namespace extension's resources you have a line like this:

```
MYTEMP.HTT HTML      "myTemp.htt"
```

you can ask WebBrowser to navigate to a URL called:

```
res://<dll_path>/MYTEMP.HTT
```

At this point, though, there's another potential problem: How do you handle all the sundries like GIFs, controls, and scriptlets? The simple rule is that *everything* that can be identified through a separate filename is embedded in the resources and can be referred to in an HTML page through the res:// protocol. See *Further Reading* for more references about res://.

> The res:// *protocol is also used under the hood by the version of MFC that comes with Visual C++ 6 to implement some features of the* CHtmlView *class, which is a wrapper for* WebBrowser.

Firing Events

Unless your namespace extension is very unusual, its user interface always has something to select. This is a typical situation in which a classic and a web view need to communicate. Due to HTML, things are normally resolved as follows. The classic view is embedded as a component that fires events — say, SelectionChanged. The script code defined in the template for the web view intercepts these notifications and responds appropriately.

From Custom to Customized Folders

A web view is a way to render a folder in a custom manner. The person who changes the way a given folder is rendered is the programmer, and once the extension has been installed, the user can only switch between the classic and the web view.

Ordinary file folders have their web views provided by the system, and interestingly these views can be customized. In other words, once you've switched to the web view for a normal directory, you can change the template of the web view radically. This process is called **folder customization**.

> If you want to allow folder customization on your own extensions, then simply keep visible the HTML templates that drive them. Otherwise, hide them by embedding the files in the executables' resources and use the res:// protocol to retrieve them later.

Folder customization in itself is not a namespace extension, but it could be seen as an over-simplified imitation. Actually, that's a little harsh: sometimes, a customized folder may really work as a console for presenting data in a custom fashion. However, don't forget that a customized folder is based on a simple HTML template, and that relies entirely on the file folder web view extension to live and work.

Folder Customization

With shell version 4.71, any user is given the opportunity to customize the layout of each folder. If you right-click on the folder and choose the <u>C</u>ustomize this Folder... item, what appears is the following picture:

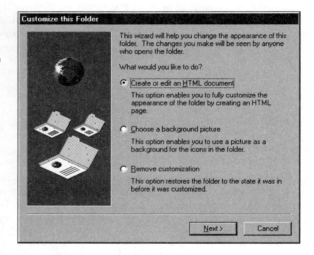

The Wizard is very simple and ends up opening `Notepad` with a file called `folder.htt`. A `.htt` file is an HTML file that defines the layout of the folder. If you accept and save the contents of the standard file, the view will look like this:

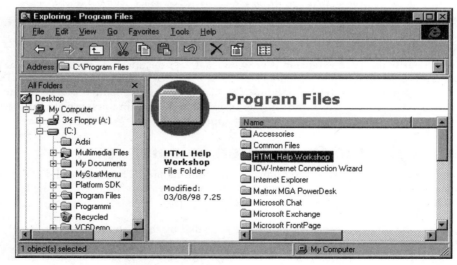

The structure of this page is rendered in the diagram below:

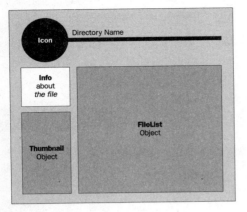

As you can imagine, the page is not static: a large part of its content is determined dynamically. The directory name, the icon, the file information, and the preview are all generated at runtime. In particular, the page embeds three ActiveX controls: one for extracting the icon, one for providing a preview of the currently selected file (only a few types are supported), and one for the actual file list. The directory name, on the other hand, is given by the macro `%THISDIRNAME%` that is expanded at runtime. (More later.)

> *I wasn't able to reuse the* `FileList` *component outside this context, but I succeeded in importing the thumbnail viewer into Visual Basic applications.*

The Default Template

At the end of the customization process, each folder contains a hidden file called `folder.htt` that is responsible for the look and the behavior of the folder itself. What the Wizard copies to the specified directory is only the default template, which follows the schema outlined above. You can modify and even rewrite it from scratch, introducing any HTML element you want: frames, tables, images, scriptlets, Java applets, and so forth.

The default template is taken from the `Windows\Web` directory, where all the standard HTML templates are located. If you look there, you'll find templates for some system folders that are used to show a slightly different layout: My Computer (`mycomp.htt`), Printers (`printers.htt`), Control Panel (`controlp.htt`), the Desktop (`deskmvr.htt`) and template of the page (`safemode.htt`) used when Active Desktop is cautiously turned off due to a system error. (If you've never seen that page, you've been really lucky!)

From this, you can deduce that a name of `folder.htt` is not a hard-and-fast rule for all folders. Let's see in a bit more detail what's going on in the folder once you've completed the customization Wizard.

The Desktop.ini File

Initially, the Wizard creates two hidden files in the folder: `folder.htt` and `desktop.ini`. I've already talked about the former, so let's have a closer look at the latter. `Desktop.ini` is not a new name for us because we met it earlier in this chapter, while covering the junction points for a namespace extension.

In general, `desktop.ini` is a folder-based informational file where Explorer and programmers add what they need to remember for that folder. Here's a typical content for that file:

```
[ExtShellFolderViews]
Default={5984FFE0-28D4-11CF-AE66-08002B2E1262}
{5984FFE0-28D4-11CF-AE66-08002B2E1262}={5984FFE0-28D4-11CF-AE66-08002B2E1262}

[{5984FFE0-28D4-11CF-AE66-08002B2E1262}]
PersistMoniker=file://folder.htt

[.ShellClassInfo]
ConfirmFileOp=0
```

The exact meanings of the various entries are still to be announced by Microsoft, but one thing is certain: if you change the name of the `.htt` file, Explorer will search the new one. That CLSID must identify the modules that load the HTT file.

The contents of this file aren't fixed. For example, try checking the Enable thumbnail view box on the folder's Properties dialog:

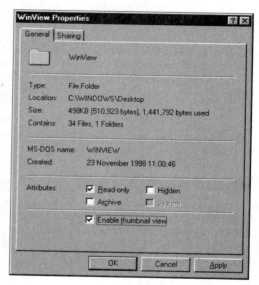

The content of `desktop.ini` will change like this:

```
[ExtShellFolderViews]
Default={5984FFE0-28D4-11CF-AE66-08002B2E1262}
{5984FFE0-28D4-11CF-AE66-08002B2E1262}={5984FFE0-28D4-11CF-AE66-08002B2E1262}
{8BEBB290-52D0-11d0-B7F4-00C04FD706EC}={8BEBB290-52D0-11d0-B7F4-00C04FD706EC}

[{5984FFE0-28D4-11CF-AE66-08002B2E1262}]
PersistMoniker=file://folder.htt

[.ShellClassInfo]
ConfirmFileOp=0

[{8BEBB290-52D0-11d0-B7F4-00C04FD706EC}]
MenuName=T&humbnails
ToolTipText=T&humbnails
HelpText=Displays items using thumbnail view.
Attributes=0x60000000
```

Furthermore, a new Thumbnails menu item appears under View. This item sets a new view like the one in this figure:

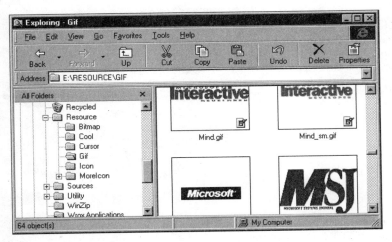

When the web view is on, Explorer searches in the current directory for the file specified in the `PersistMoniker` entry of `desktop.ini`. In case of failure the view is reset. You can give the file any name, provided that the extension is `.htt`. Curiously, if you use another extension – `.htz`, say – then you'll experience a side effect:

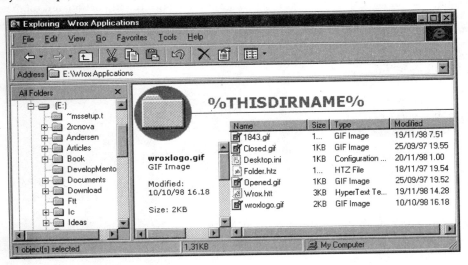

The name of the directory – the macro `%THISDIRNAME%` – isn't expanded if the template file has an extension other than `.htt`. This happens even if you simply rename a file without touching its source code.

Note that you can specify any protocol to access the `.htt` file, not just the `file://` indicated in the `desktop.ini` file. For example, you might want to use a file located somewhere on your intranet, in which case you should use `http://`.

Creating a New Template

To see folder customization in practice, let's see an example of some completely custom code that replaces the standard `folder.htt` template. The picture illustrates the structure of the HTT file:

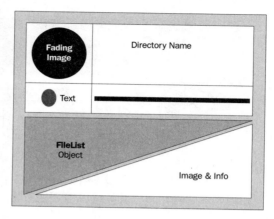

The page is split into two parts. The top part is further subdivided into four areas by the means of a 2x2 table that contains a GIF image and the directory name on the first row, and a bitmap button and a horizontal line on the second.

The bottom part of the page is entirely occupied by the file list, or by some other information. What's important is that these two sections are mutually exclusive. The bitmap button decides which to display accordingly to the user's clicks. In practice, the button toggles the file list on and off. You aren't always required to include the file list, and if necessary you can completely hide the actual contents of a folder, obtaining a result that looks like a namespace extension is in operation.

The template I'm using is nothing special, except for the use of a few Dynamic HTML techniques. In more detail, I'm going to employ:

❑ Image fading
❑ 3D graphics effects
❑ Event handling
❑ Hot-tracking text (changing color when the mouse passes over it)

The picture shows
the final intended
result:

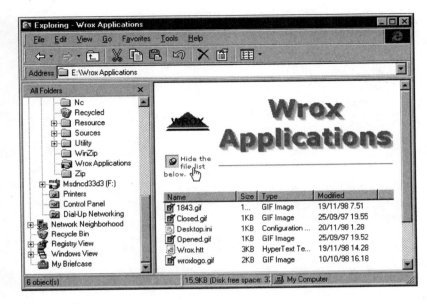

Let's have a look at the source code for `wrox.htt`:

```
<html>
<head>
<style>
.Title {font-Size: 38; font-Family: Verdana; font-Weight: bold; color: #808080;
        text-align: center;filter:Shadow(Color=#909090, Direction=135);}
.Small {font-Size: 10; font-Family: Verdana;}
.BookInfo {font-Size: 16; font-Family: Verdana;}
.HiliteSmall {font-Size: 10; font-Family: Verdana; color=red; cursor: hand;}
.Panel {background-color: #C0C0C0;}
.Fade {filter: alpha(opacity=0);}
</style>
</head>

<script language="JScript">
var strHide = "Hide the file list below.";
var strShow = "Show below the file list.";

// Activate the fading
function init()
{
   logo.flashTimer = setInterval("fade()", 100);
}

// Actually varies the opacity of the image producing fade-in effects
function fade()
{
   if (logo.filters.alpha.opacity < 100)
      logo.filters.alpha.opacity = logo.filters.alpha.opacity + 10;
   else
      clearInterval(logo.flashTimer);
}
```

```
// When the mouse exits a page component...
function mouseout()
{
   obj = event.srcElement
   if(obj.id == "msg")
      obj.className = "Small";
}

// When the mouse is over a page component...
function mouseover()
{
   obj = event.srcElement
   if(obj.id == "msg")
      obj.className = "HiliteSmall";
}

// When the mouse is clicked...
function mouseclk()
{
   // If the event isn't due to certain elements...
   if(event.srcElement.id != "toggle" && event.srcElement.id != "msg")
   {
      return;
   }

   // Toggle on/off the file list
   if(toggle.visible == 1)
   {
      toggle.src = "closed.gif";
      msg.innerHTML = toggle.outerHTML + strShow;
      toggle.visible = 0;
      FileList.width = 1;
      FileList.height = 1;
      book.style.display = "";
   }
   else
   {
      toggle.src = "opened.gif";
      msg.innerHTML = toggle.outerHTML + strHide;
      toggle.visible = 1;
      FileList.width = "100%";
      FileList.height = 200;
      book.style.display = "none";
   }
}
</script>

<body onload="init()" onmouseover="mouseover()"
                      onmouseout="mouseout()" onclick="mouseclk()">
   <table><tr>
     <td width=20%>
        <img src="Wroxlogo.gif" width=80 class="fade" id="logo">
     </td>
     <td class=Title>%THISDIRNAME%</td>
   </tr>
```

```
    <tr>
        <td class="Small" id="msg">
            <img src="opened.gif" visible=1 align=left
                                alt="Toggles the file list" id="toggle">
            </img>
            Hide the file list below.
        </td>
        <td><hr></td>
    </tr>
    </table>
    <br>

    <div class="Panel">
        <div id="book" style="display:none">
            <img src="1843.gif" align=left></img>
            <span class="BookInfo">
                <b>Visual C++ Windows Shell Programming</b><br>
                <i>Dino Esposito</i><br>1-861001-84-3<br>Wrox Press, 1998
            </span>
        </div>
        <object id="FileList"
            width=100% height=200
            classid="clsid:1820FED0-473E-11D0-A96C-00C04FD705A2">
        </object>
    </div>
</body>
</html>
```

The file list is exposed as an ActiveX control called `FileList`. It has its own set of properties, methods and events that I completely ignored in this example, but the standard `folder.htt` file makes considerable use of them. This object is documented in the Platform SDK; search for an object called `WebViewFolderContents`.

Although this book certainly isn't about Dynamic HTML, a few words about some of the techniques used in this code are in order. The fade-in effect is obtained by assigning a special style to the `<IMG>` tag, which defines an opacity coefficient that is incremented every 100 milliseconds. The shadowed text isn't a bitmap, but just a string drawn with some graphic effects. Again, it's just a style whose parameters require the color and the direction of the light.

By assigning IDs to page elements, you can control each of them via script code very well. This means that you can also detect and handle events for a specific element — say, a click on a particular bitmap. Finally, the hot-tracking effect is just a matter of detecting the right events. I've simply written two procedures to change the text color (more accurately, to change the class name for the style) when the mouse enters and exits the area of the elements for which highlighting is important.

Hosting Applications through Namespace Extensions

To conclude this chapter on namespace extensions, let's see how we can take advantage of them to host real applications in Windows Explorer. Frankly, there's nothing new to learn: a namespace extension is a module that allows you to customize a folder, and we've already seen how to create special folders and link them to namespace extensions. All that's missing is the application.

The key is the view object. A view object is a window, and sometimes it can be a dialog template. Given this, any dialog-based application is eligible to be embedded in a custom folder. This is even more reasonable if you consider that you can modify both menus and toolbars at your leisure.

This kind of namespace extension really is simple, because you don't have to worry about items, PIDLs, icons, context menus and the like. All the functionality will be delivered by the application that's hosted in the view; the namespace extension must provide only the folder manager, and the basic behavior to create the view.

The URL Folder Example

An example of this minimal approach is the URL Folder example that you can download from our Web site. It is a dialog with a button that opens a browser window onto the Wrox Press web site. However, it's a dialog whose controls are handled in a custom window procedure, and therefore a prototype of an embeddable application. The next figure shows how it will look once you've installed it by running the .reg file that's included:

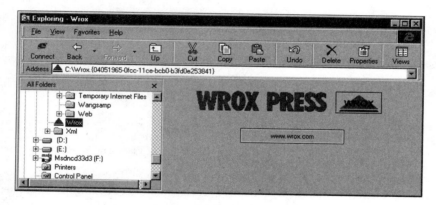

Summary

In this chapter we've examined the aspects of a namespace extension. In my opinion, namespace extensions are the very essence of shell programming: they allow your code to work tightly with Explorer, and allow an unmatched level of customization.

For all that, namespace extensions are quite complex too. It's not so much their intrinsic trickiness that's the problem, as it is the combination of several other factors. Among these are the number of interfaces you have to implement, as well as all the interfaces (and the functions within those interfaces) you aren't strictly *required* to support, but that are necessary to have a module work properly. The continuous updates to the Windows shell (I really hope that Windows 98 improves matters), and the lack of documentation, complete this awkward scenario.

Yet again, the documentation is worth a little more discussion. Often, I've blamed it for being poor or incomplete, but in this case the major thing that has been lacking for a long time is not so much good explanations but worthwhile examples. Only since the creation of the Internet Client SDK, have we had a truly interesting and insightful example of a non-rooted extension.

This chapter has covered:

- ❑ All the interfaces necessary to have a namespace extension work properly
- ❑ How to create and manage PIDLs
- ❑ How to map all the theory to a concrete and non-trivial scenario
- ❑ How to modify Explorer's user interface
- ❑ How to enrich a namespace extension with undocumented features such as infotips and removal messages
- ❑ An overview of web view extensions
- ❑ Tips on how to host applications inside Explorer
- ❑ Folder customization and HTML template files
- ❑ Employing Dynamic HTML to get interactive folders in a snap

Further Reading

The first article I ever read about namespace extensions was *Extending the Windows Explorer with Namespace Extensions* by David Campbell, which appeared in the July 1996 issue of MSJ. This is a good article that provides an overview of all the aspects you must know about. It includes one of Microsoft's standard samples (CabView), but doesn't discuss it thoroughly, so you aren't given the possibility to apply the theory to source code immediately.

Moving on, I wrote an article on namespace extensions for the February 1998 edition of MIND, entitled *Shell Support for DHTML*. It presents an example in which I walk into the content of an HTML file, exploiting the DHTML object model. In practice, I did what you need to do to implement communication between the views in a web view extension.

These articles, however, have a common peculiarity that might almost be described as a flaw: they present namespace extensions that work only on a specific file type. They have the structure of a namespace extension, but they could have been implemented as external viewers as well. The drawback is that examples like these don't explain clearly enough how to add a new, expandable and hierarchical node to the Explorer, when this is probably the main reason to write a namespace extension.

The CabView example I mentioned earlier opens a .cab file like a folder, and lets you navigate into it. It now comes as one of the Win32 SDK examples, and you can find it on the MSDN library disks that come with Visual C++. The first really great example of namespace extensions is the RegView example that comes with the Internet Client SDK. It adds the registry as a new folder in the Explorer, and you can find it at Samples\SDK Samples\Windows UI Samples\Shell Samples\RegView. A similarly worthwhile demo is SampView, in the latest Platform SDK.

Todd Daniell, Brian Daigle, Doug Bahr, and Dave Mims wrote the excellent *Implementing a Web View Namespace Extension Using Active Directory Services* in MSJ, August 1998, and I recommend it if you have dealing with web view extensions in mind. Despite the title, the article really has little to do with ADSI; it's just that the authors attempt to provide a custom view of an ADSI folder. In other words, ADSI in that article plays the same, secondary role as the EnumChildWindows() API does in our Windows View demonstration.

Furthermore, let me point you to another couple of articles of mine whose content relates to topics touched upon in this chapter. The first one is *Pluggable Protocols* (MIND, January 1999), in which I show how to take advantage of the Internet Explorer pluggable protocols and discuss in detail the `res://` protocol. The second article, *Active Desktop: The Shell and Beyond* (MIND, March 1998), contains a discussion of what you can do with Active Desktop's folder customization.

The final part of the chapter revolved around a bit of Dynamic HTML. If you'd like to learn more about that, I recommend *Professional IE4 Programming* or for more advanced topics, my *Instant DHTML Scriptlets* (both Wrox Press). To conclude, as usual, here are some interesting Knowledge Base articles:

- ❏ **Knowledge Base ID Q183860:** *Support Dropping of Items on Your Namespace Root*
- ❏ **Knowledge Base ID Q179911:** Implement Explore and Open in a Namespace Extension
- ❏ **Knowledge Base ID Q179900:** Support Renaming of Items in the Windows Explorer Tree
- ❏ **Knowledge Base ID Q182379:** Support Toolbar Item Text in a Shell Namespace Extension

Final Thoughts

This is the end of the book. In these 16 chapters, I've tried to address all the topics that are relevant to a Win32 programmer when he or she has to cope with the Windows shell. How successful have I been? Asked a similar question, someone once answered that real expertise only comes when you have made all the possible mistakes. Working with the Windows shell over the last couple of years has taught me a lot. Several times, I have thought that I was in front of the world's biggest bug in the system code. Almost as many times, it turned out to be a bug of my own. In these pages, I have collected all the problems I've had, and all the solutions I've found.

There's no doubt that working with the shell is hard. It's a mixture of COM and API, C and C++, and some of the documentation has been written only with Visual Basic in mind. The documentation isn't great, but it's not *that* poor, and I'm increasingly of the opinion that this is mostly due to the combined effect of vague descriptions and complex behaviors.

I really do hope that you stuck with this book, passing intrepidly from cover to cover. The final thing I'll do by way of explanation is to answer a question that was asked by a couple of my reviewers, and that may have crossed your mind too: Why is this book a mixture of C and C++, with a pinch of ATL, but no MFC? Well, my goal was to be faithful to a famous sentence by Albert Einstein, who recommended that things should always be kept as simple as possible, but no simpler. MFC has its merits, to be sure, but in the end you just have to trust that it knows what it's doing. Presenting code at a lower level allowed me to touch on all the steps required, case by case. I don't know how you feel about it, but I believe that once you have grasped the underlying technology – whatever it is – you're capable of facing anything that's been constructed upon it.

Things never stop where they are. There's always a new goal to achieve. The shell is evolving, and hopefully this book will evolve too. When I was ten or so, I used to watch UFO and Martians on TV. "Windows 2000 Enterprise" was more likely to be the name of a futuristic spaceship than an operating system, but then who cares about operating systems when he's ten? I imagined the year 2000 as a time when we'd be living in an all-automatic world, eating colorful pills, and moving by the power of thought.

In the same way, Windows 2000 has been touted as the mother (or the father?) of all operating systems: fully plug-and-play, fast as light, with built-in support for thought-reading devices. All or none of that may be true, but we can be sure that Windows 2000 *will* bring us lots of new things to study, enhancements, some bug fixes, and other changes. Inevitably, some of these things will affect the shell, so stay tuned for reading more in the next millennium!

A Programmer's Toolkit

Many of the examples in this book use the Active Template Library (ATL), which has a Wizard of its own for generating repetitive or boilerplate code automatically. In many other cases, however, such as testing API functions, we don't use ATL because there is no need for templates and frameworks. This fact doesn't mean it wouldn't be helpful to have a Wizard for generating the code for a simple dialog-based applet, or for the world's simplest dynamic-link library. To that end, I decided to build my own AppWizard – after all, it's quite an easy task, and the benefits are considerable.

The Custom AppWizard

Since version 4.0, Visual C++ has allowed us to write our own AppWizards. We can either modify the existing Wizards or write a new one from scratch, specifying the number of steps and the options that best suit our needs.

> *Custom AppWizards can only be created using the Professional and Enterprise editions of Visual C++. The Standard edition does not support this feature, but never fear: if you have this version of the software, you can download the compiled code for the AppWizard we'll generate in this chapter from the Wrox web site.*

The user interface of Windows 95 has many Wizards. They're used to detect your hardware, to add a printer, to connect to the Internet, and so on. However, these Wizards are a bit different from the AppWizards in Visual C++, and it's interesting to compare the two.

In both cases, we're faced with a sequence of dialogs, but an AppWizard is completely integrated with the surrounding infrastructure, so you can't use it outside Visual C++. You can't use the MFC AppWizard as a stand-alone program, nor can you connect it to another vendor's Win32 IDE. Worse than that, though, you can't even connect an AppWizard created with Visual C++ 5.0 to one generated by a previous version! This means that what I shall create here will need to be recompiled in order to be successfully attached to Visual C++ 4.2 or lower. An AppWizard generated with Visual C++ 5.0 should compile under Visual C++ 6.0, as our WroxWiz project demonstrates. The reverse is also true, although Visual C++ 6.0 provides a slightly richer programming interface that may affect backwards compatibility. So far, however, I haven't experienced any problems.

A traditional Wizard, on the other hand, is an instance of one of the Windows 95 common controls – namely, the **Property Sheet** – that is simply a sequence of windows that you can call and create anywhere that a Win32 dialog is acceptable. A Property Sheet control is the same as a Tab Control except that you access its child tabs sequentially and in a predefined order, rather than all tabs being available at the same time.

Why Can't an AppWizard Stand Alone?

Having an AppWizard live only in the Visual C++ IDE is not really a problem. These Wizards come into play when you hit *Ctrl-N* or select the File | New... menu. That is, they are expected to run in the middle of a sequence of steps. You choose the type of the project, type in the name and the folder, and go to the next step. At that point, you see the first page of the Wizard with its familiar navigation bar (Back, Next, etc.).

The steps before the first page of the Wizard, and after the last, transfer control of Visual C++ to the AppWizard and then return control to Visual C++ once the AppWizard has completed its task. Because of this, the C++ class that implements an AppWizard relies heavily on the framework, and this makes it difficult – impossible, even – to make such code run in a stand-alone manner. After all, the final goal of the Wizard is simply to generate a new Visual C++-compliant project.

A Quick Tour of a Custom AppWizard

An AppWizard is a DLL with the rather unusual extension .awx. They are commonly located in the Common\MSDev98\Bin\IDE subdirectory of Visual Studio, although custom AppWizards are stored in Common\MSDev98\Template. If you have the Standard edition of Visual C++, this is where you should install the file you can download.

The first step to creating your own AppWizard is to generate a new project using the Custom AppWizard, as shown:

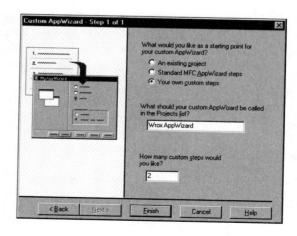

There are three ways to create a new AppWizard. You can clone an existing custom AppWizard, base your Wizard on the standard MFC AppWizard, or define a completely new one from scratch. I've chosen the third option.

Once you've worked your way through the Wizard, a new project opens up, which should look like the one shown in the following screenshot:

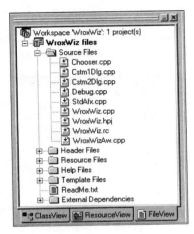

I've chosen to create a Wizard that has two custom steps. The files `Cstm1Dlg.cpp` and `Cstm2Dlg.cpp`, which you can see in the FileView shown above, render the dialogs for these steps.

At this point, our work begins. Basically, we're required to customize the look of the various steps, and define the options that control the code to be generated. An **option** is a kind of environment variable that stores one or more of the user's preferences. If you wanted comments in the code, for example, or certain functionality to be included, an option would be set to indicate this. From the implementation's point of view, an option is just an entry in a dictionary. The main AppWizard class, `CWroxWizAppWiz`, inherits a data member from `CCustomAppWiz` that's an instance of the MFC class `CMapStringToString`. This member, called `m_Dictionary`, is used to store all the options.

Aside from the dictionary, **templates** play an important role. In this context, a template is a custom resource type that contains the basis of a file (whether binary or text-based) to be generated by the AppWizard. In practice, for each file you want to create, you need a template. These files are then parsed by Visual C++ and added to the new project.

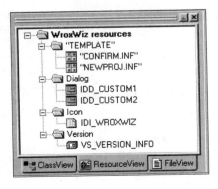

The important feature of the templates is that they can contain macros that the parser (a component of the compiler) will expand. This is the means by which the options that you have selected are incorporated into the final code. There is also basic support for conditional statements, to make the process of generating the source code straightforward, easy to understand, and simple to modify.

The Wrox AppWizard

What we need to do now is add to this skeleton in order to create the Wrox AppWizard that will be available from the Projects tab of the Visual C++ New dialog, as shown below:

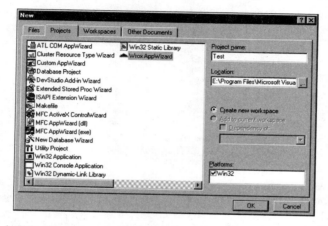

In this section I shall be focussing on the features required by the Wrox AppWizard. If you require more information about using the Custom AppWizard please refer to the *Further Reading* section.

The following listing is the main header file, `WroxWizAw.h`. It defines the `CWroxWizAppWiz` class, which will be used by Visual C++ to invoke our AppWizard. The Custom AppWizard generated most of the code; we've just added some Wizard-wide data members:

```
// WroxWizAw.h : header file
//

class CDialogChooser;

// All function calls made by mfcapwz.dll to this custom AppWizard (except for
// GetCustomAppWizClass - see WroxWiz.cpp) are through this class. You may
// choose to override more of the CCustomAppWiz virtual functions here to
// further specialize the behavior of this custom AppWizard.
class CWroxWizAppWiz : public CCustomAppWiz
{
public:
    virtual CAppWizStepDlg* Next(CAppWizStepDlg* pDlg);
    virtual CAppWizStepDlg* Back(CAppWizStepDlg* pDlg);

    virtual void InitCustomAppWiz();
    virtual void ExitCustomAppWiz();
    virtual void CustomizeProject(IBuildProject* pProject);
```

```
    // Custom data
    CBitmap m_bmpPicture;
    CBitmap m_bmpLogo;

protected:
    CDialogChooser* m_pChooser;
};

// This declares the one instance of the CWroxWizAppWiz class. You can access
// m_Dictionary and any other public members of this class through the
// global WroxWizaw. (Its definition is in WroxWizaw.cpp.)
extern CWroxWizAppWiz WroxWizaw;

//{{AFX_INSERT_LOCATION}}
// Microsoft Visual C++ will insert additional declarations immediately before //
the previous line.

#endif
// !defined(AFX_WROXWIZAW_H__39CCE78B_3CDB_11D2_9DAF_00104B4C822A__INCLUDED_)
```

The class declared above is the main class of our Wizard. Everything you want the Wizard to preserve from page to page, and any information or custom data that you wish to associate with the class, can be defined here as additional data members. For example, I've defined a couple of CBitmap members so that the Wrox logo and the Wizard picture (the image that is often placed on the left-hand side of the dialog) can be used. You'll need to make sure they get loaded into the process at runtime by placing these calls the CWroxWizAppWiz::InitCustomAppWiz() function in WroxWizAw.cpp:

```
    // TODO: Add any other custom AppWizard-wide initialization here.
    // Load pictures
    m_bmpPicture.LoadBitmap(IDB_IMAGE);
    m_bmpLogo.LoadBitmap(IDB_WROXLOGO);
```

CDialogChooser is another class generated by the Custom AppWizard; it takes care of moving back and forth among the pages of your AppWizard. The dialog chooser is the component that calls the correct method as you click on the <Back or Next> buttons. The main Wizard class doesn't handle such events directly — it relies on this intermediate class. Usually, you don't need to change anything about it, unless you need to impose a completely custom logic for progressing through the Wizard.

You should concentrate your efforts on the files that provide the actual implementations for the various dialogs, the first of which looks something like this:

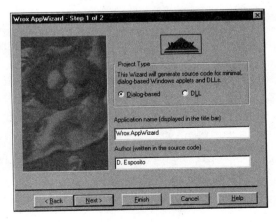

The two radio buttons are called `IDC_DIALOG` and `IDC_DLL`, while the edit boxes are
`IDC_APPNAME` (for the title bar) and `IDC_AUTHOR` (for the author's name). I'm going to arrange that
the entries you can see above are the defaults, so add these lines to `WroxWiz.h`:

```
// TODO: You may add any other custom AppWizard-wide declarations here.
const TCHAR AW_DEFAULT_APPNAME[] = _T("Wrox AppWizard");
const TCHAR AW_DEFAULT_AUTHOR[] = _T("D. Esposito");
```

These will become entries in the dictionary with the names `APPNAME` and `AUTHOR`. The other two
options to be set on this step will be represented by the names `TYPE_DIALOG` and `TYPE_DLL`. I have
chosen to use Boolean entries instead of having a single `TYPE` because the parser won't allow us to
test against a value, only whether a given entry exists or not.

Those files that implement the steps of the Wizard are named `CstmXDlg.cpp`, where **X** identifies the
*x*th step. Here's the start of the code behind the first step (`Cstm1Dlg.cpp`):

```
// Cstm1Dlg.cpp : Implementation File
//

#include "stdafx.h"
#include "WroxWiz.h"
#include "cstm1dlg.h"
#include "WroxWizaw.h"
#include "Chooser.h"          // For LAST_DLG

#ifdef _PSEUDO_DEBUG
#undef THIS_FILE
static char THIS_FILE[] = __FILE__;
#endif

/////////////////////////////////////////////////////////////////////////////
// CCustom1Dlg dialog

CCustom1Dlg::CCustom1Dlg()
    : CAppWizStepDlg(CCustom1Dlg::IDD)
{
    //{{AFX_DATA_INIT(CCustom1Dlg)
    m_szAppName = AW_DEFAULT_APPNAME;
    m_szAuthor = AW_DEFAULT_AUTHOR;
    //}}AFX_DATA_INIT

    WroxWizaw.m_Dictionary[_T("APPNAME")] = AW_DEFAULT_APPNAME;
    WroxWizaw.m_Dictionary[_T("AUTHOR")] = AW_DEFAULT_AUTHOR;
    WroxWizaw.m_Dictionary[_T("TYPE_DIALOG")] = _T("Yes");
}


void CCustom1Dlg::DoDataExchange(CDataExchange* pDX)
{
    CAppWizStepDlg::DoDataExchange(pDX);
    //{{AFX_DATA_MAP(CCustom1Dlg)
    DDX_Text(pDX, IDC_APPNAME, m_szAppName);
    DDV_MaxChars(pDX, m_szAppName, 40);
    DDX_Text(pDX, IDC_AUTHOR, m_szAuthor);
    DDV_MaxChars(pDX, m_szAuthor, 40);
    //}}AFX_DATA_MAP
}
```

```
// This is called whenever the user presses Next, Back, or Finish with this step
// present. Do all validation & data exchange from the dialog in this function.
BOOL CCustom1Dlg::OnDismiss()
{
    if (!UpdateData(TRUE))
        return FALSE;

    // TODO: Set template variables based on the dialog's data.
    WroxWizaw.m_Dictionary[_T("APPNAME")] = m_szAppName;
    WroxWizaw.m_Dictionary[_T("AUTHOR")] = m_szAuthor;

    return TRUE;    // return FALSE if the dialog shouldn't be dismissed
}
```

As you can see, I've used ClassWizard to add data members for the two edit boxes, and altered the lines in the constructor to initialize them to my default values. I've also written code to create entries in the dictionary that are set in the constructor and altered when the dialog is dismissed.

Next, you need to add handlers for the radio buttons, and perform some trivial initialization in `OnInitDialog()`. Here's the code for the second half of `Cstm1Dlg.cpp`, with the important aspects highlighted:

```
BEGIN_MESSAGE_MAP(CCustom1Dlg, CAppWizStepDlg)
    //{{AFX_MSG_MAP(CCustom1Dlg)
    ON_BN_CLICKED(IDC_DIALOG, OnDialog)
    ON_BN_CLICKED(IDC_DLL, OnDll)
//}}AFX_MSG_MAP
END_MESSAGE_MAP()


/////////////////////////////////////////////////////////////////////////////
// CCustom1Dlg message handlers

BOOL CCustom1Dlg::OnInitDialog()
{
    CAppWizStepDlg::OnInitDialog();

    // Local data
    CStatic* pStatic = NULL;

    // Bitmap initialization
    pStatic = static_cast<CStatic*>(GetDlgItem(IDC_IMAGE));
    pStatic->SetBitmap(static_cast<HBITMAP>(WroxWizaw.m_bmpPicture));
    pStatic = static_cast<CStatic*>(GetDlgItem(IDC_WROXLOGO));
    pStatic->SetBitmap(static_cast<HBITMAP>(WroxWizaw.m_bmpLogo));

    // Radio button initialization
    CheckRadioButton(IDC_DIALOG, IDC_DLL, IDC_DIALOG);
    return TRUE;    // return TRUE unless you set the focus to a control
                    // EXCEPTION: OCX Property Pages should return FALSE
}

void CCustom1Dlg::OnDialog()
{
    WroxWizaw.m_Dictionary.RemoveKey(_T("PROJTYPE_DLL"));
    WroxWizaw.m_Dictionary[_T("TYPE_DIALOG")] = _("Yes");
    WroxWizaw.m_Dictionary.RemoveKey(_T("TYPE_DLL"));
    GetDlgItem(IDC_APPNAME)->EnableWindow(TRUE);
```

```
        // We make sure the chooser knows the Wizard has 2 steps
        // This is in case we passed for the next handler.
        SetNumberOfSteps(LAST_DLG);
    }

    void CCustom1Dlg::OnDll()
    {
        WroxWizaw.m_Dictionary[_T("PROJTYPE_DLL")] = _T("Yes");
        WroxWizaw.m_Dictionary[_T("TYPE_DLL")] = _T("Yes");
        WroxWizaw.m_Dictionary.RemoveKey(_T("TYPE_DIALOG"));

        GetDlgItem(IDC_APPNAME)->EnableWindow(FALSE);

        // Tell the chooser the Wizard now has just 1 step. This
        // causes the Next> button to gray, skipping the Common Controls page.
        SetNumberOfSteps(1);
    }
```

The code in `OnInitDialog()` just deals with displaying the bitmaps that add a little color to the Wizard, and setting the initial state of the radio buttons. The button handlers set and remove the appropriate entries in the dictionary. If you're watching carefully, you'll have noticed an extra entry called `PROJTYPE_DLL`, – I'll talk about this a little later on.

The second step will let you choose whether you want the code to include built-in support for the Windows common controls. If so, the Wizard will generate a project that includes the necessary header file (`commctrl.h`), import library (`comct132.lib`), and the code to initialize the DLL. You can arrange for the code to deal with the Windows 95 controls alone, or with the new ones introduced with Active Desktop and Windows 98 as well.

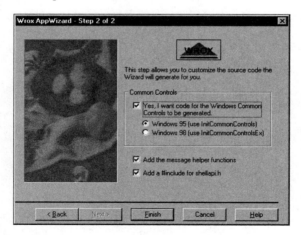

You'll have noticed that in the `OnDll()` and `OnDialog()` handlers for the first step, I included a call to `SetNumberOfSteps()`, which is a global function declared in `customaw.h`. As the name suggests, this function informs the dialog chooser of the total number of steps the Wizard should have. When the dialog chooser's internal counter reaches the last page, the **Next>** button is grayed. My design for this AppWizard dictates that if you choose to create a DLL you can't set any options on the second page, and judicious use of `SetNumberOfSteps()` allows us to fool the chooser and skip that step. As soon as you select the **DLL** option, the **Next>** button will gray and you must either finish the process or change the option.

Returning now to the second step, the states of the first three of these controls are stored in the dictionary with entries called USECC, USECC95 and USECC98. USECC is tied to the checkbox, while the others are linked to the radio buttons.

Also on this step you can ask the Wizard to generate a #include for shellapi.h, and to add some helper functions for handling error messages to the project. These functions will be written around well-known APIs such as FormatMessage() and MessageBox(), and are covered in detail in Chapter 3.

The first part of the source code for Cstm2Dlg.cpp (the second step) is shown below:

```cpp
// Cstm2Dlg.cpp : Implementation File
//

#include "stdafx.h"
#include "WroxWiz.h"
#include "cstm2dlg.h"
#include "WroxWizaw.h"

#ifdef _PSEUDO_DEBUG
#undef THIS_FILE
static char THIS_FILE[] = __FILE__;
#endif

/////////////////////////////////////////////////////////////////////////////
// CCustom2Dlg dialog


CCustom2Dlg::CCustom2Dlg()
    : CAppWizStepDlg(CCustom2Dlg::IDD)
{
    //{{AFX_DATA_INIT(CCustom2Dlg)
        // NOTE: the ClassWizard will add member initialization here
    //}}AFX_DATA_INIT

    WroxWizaw.m_Dictionary[_T("USECC")] = _T("Yes");
    WroxWizaw.m_Dictionary[_T("USECC95")] = _T("Yes");
    WroxWizaw.m_Dictionary[_T("ADDUTILS")] = _T("Yes");
    WroxWizaw.m_Dictionary[_T("ADDSHELLAPI")] = _T("Yes");
}


void CCustom2Dlg::DoDataExchange(CDataExchange* pDX)
{
    CAppWizStepDlg::DoDataExchange(pDX);
    //{{AFX_DATA_MAP(CCustom2Dlg)
        // NOTE: the ClassWizard will add DDX and DDV calls here
    //}}AFX_DATA_MAP
}

// This is called whenever the user presses Next, Back, or Finish with this step
// present. Do all validation & data exchange from the dialog in this function.
BOOL CCustom2Dlg::OnDismiss()
{
    if (!UpdateData(TRUE))
        return FALSE;

    return TRUE;    // return FALSE if the dialog shouldn't be dismissed
}
```

This part of the code is even easier than for the first step — it simply involves setting entries in the dictionary appropriately. However, there are more button handlers this time around, and `OnInitDialog()` has to be implemented to perform the same tricks as before:

```
BEGIN_MESSAGE_MAP(CCustom2Dlg, CAppWizStepDlg)
    //{{AFX_MSG_MAP(CCustom2Dlg)
    ON_BN_CLICKED(IDC_WIN95, OnWin95)
    ON_BN_CLICKED(IDC_WIN98, OnWin98)
    ON_BN_CLICKED(IDC_USECC, OnUsecc)
    ON_BN_CLICKED(IDC_UTILS, OnUtils)
    ON_BN_CLICKED(IDC_SHELLAPI, OnShellapi)
    //}}AFX_MSG_MAP
END_MESSAGE_MAP()


/////////////////////////////////////////////////////////////////////////////
// CCustom2Dlg message handlers

BOOL CCustom2Dlg::OnInitDialog()
{
    CAppWizStepDlg::OnInitDialog();

    // Local data
    CStatic* pStatic = NULL;

    // Bitmap initialization
    pStatic = static_cast<CStatic*>(GetDlgItem(IDC_IMAGE));
    pStatic->SetBitmap(static_cast<HBITMAP>(WroxWizaw.m_bmpPicture));
    pStatic = static_cast<CStatic*>(GetDlgItem(IDC_WROXLOGO));
    pStatic->SetBitmap(static_cast<HBITMAP>(WroxWizaw.m_bmpLogo));

    // Radio and check button initialization
    CheckDlgButton(IDC_USECC, TRUE);
    CheckDlgButton(IDC_UTILS, TRUE);
    CheckDlgButton(IDC_SHELLAPI, TRUE);

    CheckRadioButton(IDC_WIN95, IDC_WIN98, IDC_WIN95);
    return TRUE;      // return TRUE unless you set the focus to a control
                      // EXCEPTION: OCX Property Pages should return FALSE
}

void CCustom2Dlg::OnWin95()
{
    WroxWizaw.m_Dictionary[_T("USECC95")] = _T("Yes");
    WroxWizaw.m_Dictionary.RemoveKey(_T("USECC98"));
}

void CCustom2Dlg::OnWin98()
{
    WroxWizaw.m_Dictionary[_T("USECC98")] = _T("Yes");
    WroxWizaw.m_Dictionary.RemoveKey(_T("USECC95"));
}

void CCustom2Dlg::OnUsecc()
{
    BOOL bState = IsDlgButtonChecked(IDC_USECC);

    GetDlgItem(IDC_WIN95)->EnableWindow(bState);
    GetDlgItem(IDC_WIN98)->EnableWindow(bState);
```

```
    if(bState)
        WroxWizaw.m_Dictionary[_T("USECC")] = _T("Yes");
    else
        WroxWizaw.m_Dictionary.RemoveKey(_T("USECC"));    // Key must be removed
}

void CCustom2Dlg::OnUtils()
{
    BOOL bState = IsDlgButtonChecked(IDC_UTILS);

    if(bState)
        WroxWizaw.m_Dictionary[_T("ADDUTILS")] = _T("Yes");
    else
        WroxWizaw.m_Dictionary.RemoveKey(_T("ADDUTILS"));    // Key must be removed
}

void CCustom2Dlg::OnShellapi()
{
    BOOL bState = IsDlgButtonChecked(IDC_SHELLAPI);

    if(bState)
        WroxWizaw.m_Dictionary[_T("ADDSHELLAPI")] = _T("Yes");
    else
        WroxWizaw.m_Dictionary.RemoveKey(_T("ADDSHELLAPI"));
}
```

You'll see at once that none of these handlers is particularly tricky — it's always just a matter of manipulating the dictionary, and checking and enabling controls.

System Macros

Apart from the dictionary entries that you can define yourself, there are a few made available by the Visual C++ environment. As I explained earlier, the main custom AppWizard main class inherits from CCustomAppWiz. This class is the one that actually takes care of defining the dictionary object that, upon construction, contains the mappings for a standard set of environmental strings. Amongst others, there are:

Macro	Description
ROOT	The name of the project.
FULL_DIR_PATH	The full path to the project.
PROJTYPE_DLL	"Yes" if you want a DLL to be generated. By default, Visual C++ creates a project for an executable.

Interestingly, the ROOT entry can be expressed with lower case letters: Root and root. I'll show you how this can be useful later on.

The backward compatibility of custom AppWizards is affected by the fact that Visual C++ 6 defines many new macros. However, almost all of these macros are only useful if your AppWizard is based on the MFC AppWizard. In the other two cases I mentioned earlier, backward compatibility with Visual C++ 5 should be guaranteed. Among the new Visual C++ 6.0-specific macros, those in the following table are worthy of note. All render Boolean values and address various types of project.

Macro	Description
PROJTYPE_OCX	"Yes" if your project creates an ActiveX control
PROJTYPE_CON	"Yes" if your project creates a Win32 console application
PROJTYPE_LIB	"Yes" if your project creates a static library

Finalizing the Process

After you've completed the Wizard and clicked on Finish, you'll be presented with a dialog that summarizes what you've done so far:

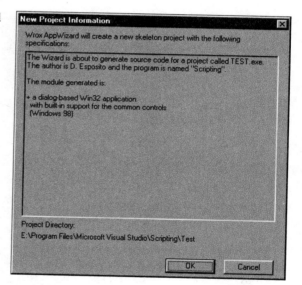

The text for this message is entirely up to you. The Visual C++ engine looks for a "TEMPLATE" custom resource named confirm.inf in your project's RC file. The content of this file is then parsed and displayed in the above dialog, so you can embed macros in order to reflect the options the user selected. This is the file that was used to generate the above dialog – it's not hard to see how it works:

```
$$IF(TYPE_DLL)
The Wizard is about to generate source code for a project called $$ROOT$$.dll.
The author is $$AUTHOR$$.
$$ELSE
The Wizard is about to generate source code for a project called $$ROOT$$.exe.
The author is $$AUTHOR$$ and the program is named "$$APPNAME$$".
$$ENDIF
```

```
The module generated is:

$$IF(TYPE_DIALOG)
+ a dialog-based Win32 application
$$IF(USECC)
   with built-in support for the common controls
$$IF(USECC98)
   (Windows 98)
```

```
$$ELIF(USECC95)
   (Windows 95)
$$ENDIF
$$ENDIF
$$ENDIF

$$IF(TYPE_DLL)
+ a Win32 DLL
$$ENDIF
```

`confirm.inf` is one of two files that are absolutely central to custom AppWizards; the other is `newproj.inf`. The latter is a kind of 'makefile' that assembles the various template resources and builds a Visual C++ project. The content of `newproj.inf` serves as input for the parser. From it, the parser will know which files are to be parsed, added to the project, or simply moved to the project folder verbatim. By embedding macros in `newproj.inf`, you can control the way the files are generated.

To show you what I mean, here's the `newproj.inf` file to be used by our Wizard:

```
$$// newproj.inf = template for list of template files
$$// format is 'sourceResName' \t 'destFileName'
$$//   The source res name may be preceded by any combination of
                                   '=', '-', '!', '?', ':', '#', and/or '*'
$$//       '=' => the resource is binary
$$//       '-' => the file should not be added to the project
                  (all files are added to the project by default)
$$//       '!' => the file should be marked exclude from build
$$//       '?' => the file should be treated as a help file
$$//       ':' => the file should be treated as a resource
$$//       '#' => the file should be treated as a template (implies '!')
$$//       '*' => bypass the custom AppWizard's resources when loading
$$//    if name starts with / => create new subdir

$$//    Dialog-based Win32 app
$$IF(TYPE_DIALOG)

a_main.cpp        $$root$$.cpp
+a_main.rc        $$root$$.rc
$$IF(ADDUTILS)
a_utils.cpp       utils.cpp
a_utils.h         SPBUtils.h
$$ENDIF
a_main.h          $$root$$.h
:=a_main.ico      $$root$$.ico

$$//    Win32 DLL
$$ELIF(TYPE_DLL)
```

```
d_main.cpp      $$root$$.cpp
d_main.def      $$root$$.def
d_main.h        $$root$$.h

$$ENDIF
```

The comments that were placed in the file explain that each line intended for the parser *must* have the format:

```
[symbols]TemplateName \t FileName
```

That is, the name of the template followed by a single tab character, and then the name of the target file. The symbols go at the beginning of each line, either individually or in combination; the following table provides a fuller explanation of the commands implied by each:

Symbol	Action
' '	The empty string means, "Parse and add the resulting file to the project."
–	The file won't be added to the project, but it will be copied and used correctly.
=	The file is intended to be binary. It must not be parsed but just copied.
!	The file won't be included in the list of files to build.
?	The file is treated as a help file, built differently, and added to the **Help Files** folder of the project.
:	The file is considered as a resource and added to the **Resource Files** folder.
#	The file is considered as a template and added to the **Template Files** folder. In addition, this flag implies '!'
*	The resource actually processed is not taken from the current project resources but from the MFC AppWizard resources (provided that a resource with the relevant name exists).

Visual C++ 5 syntax is slightly different but still supported by Visual C++ 6 for backward compatibility purposes. For instance, the + symbol (not mentioned in the documentation but still supported, with the same meaning) denoted that the specified resource must be added to the project. With Visual C++ 6.0 the perspective has changed: all the files are added by default, unless you explicitly prohibit this by using the – flag. New Wizards should avoid using +, but if it is used the project will be generated correctly.

Similarly, it is not strictly necessary to prefix resources such as icons or bitmaps with :. If you omit it, the file still goes in the **Resource Files** folder and gets treated as a resource. Again, this has been done for the sake of backward compatibility, but new Wizards should use : to denote a resource.

Of course, the most important aspects of any AppWizard are the files that it actually produces. In the case of our Wizard, we have two options: a Win32 dialog-based application, or a DLL. Let's take a look at the output of the Wizard, and how we can alter it using templates and macros.

A Minimal Dialog-based Application

If you choose the Dialog-based option from the first page of the Wizard, then you can expect it to build a Win32 project with no MFC support. The files generated will be:

- [Root].cpp
- [Root].h
- [Root].ico
- [Root].rc

And potentially:

- utils.cpp
- SPBUtils.h

Obviously, [Root] stands for the actual name of the project. As I stated earlier, we can write 'Root' in either upper or lower case, or with only the first letter capitalized − if 'Root' is not all capitals the project name will be printed in lower case letters. At least four files will be generated, so we must have (at least) four templates in the Wrox AppWizard resource file, WroxWiz.rc.

Here's the code that will produce [Root].cpp, which is contained in the template resource called "A_MAIN.CPP":

```
/********************************************************************
*
*   Project.....:   $$APPNAME$$
*   Application.:   $$ROOT$$.exe
*   Module......:   $$ROOT$$.cpp
*   Description.:   Application main module
*   Compiler....:   MS Visual C++
*   Written by..:   $$AUTHOR$$
*   Environment.:   Windows 9x/NT
*
********************************************************************/


/*----------------------------------------------------------------*/
//                      PRAGMA section
/*----------------------------------------------------------------*/
// Force the linker to add the following libraries.
#ifdef _MSC_VER

#pragma comment(lib, "kernel32.lib")
#pragma comment(lib, "user32.lib")
#pragma comment(lib, "gdi32.lib")
#pragma comment(lib, "shell32.lib")
$$IF(USECC)
#pragma comment(lib, "comctl32.lib")
$$ENDIF

#endif
```

```
/*----------------------------------------------------------------*/
//                           INCLUDE section
/*----------------------------------------------------------------*/
#include "$$root$$.h"
$$IF(USECC)
#include <commctrl.h>
$$ENDIF
$$IF(ADDSHELLAPI)
#include <shellapi.h>
$$ENDIF


/*----------------------------------------------------------------*/
//                           GLOBAL section
/*----------------------------------------------------------------*/
// Data
HICON g_hIconLarge;
HICON g_hIconSmall;

// Functions
void OnInitDialog(HWND);
void OnOK(HWND);

// Callbacks
BOOL CALLBACK APP_DlgProc(HWND, UINT, WPARAM, LPARAM);


/*----------------------------------------------------------------*/
// Procedure....: WinMain()
// Description..: Entry point in any Windows program
// Input........: HINSTANCE, HINSTANCE, LPSTR, int
// Output.......: int
/*----------------------------------------------------------------*/
int APIENTRY WinMain(HINSTANCE hInstance, HINSTANCE hPrevious,
                     LPTSTR lpsz, int iCmd)
{
   // Save global data
   g_hIconLarge = static_cast<HICON>(
            LoadImage(hInstance, "APP_ICON", IMAGE_ICON,
            GetSystemMetrics(SM_CXICON), GetSystemMetrics(SM_CXICON), 0));
   g_hIconSmall = static_cast<HICON>(
            LoadImage(hInstance, "APP_ICON", IMAGE_ICON,
            GetSystemMetrics(SM_CXSMICON), GetSystemMetrics(SM_CXSMICON), 0));
$$IF(USECC)
$$IF(USECC98)
   // Enable common controls
   INITCOMMONCONTROLSEX iccex;
   iccex.dwSize = sizeof(INITCOMMONCONTROLSEX);
   iccex.dwICC = ICC_WIN95_CLASSES;
   InitCommonControlsEx(&iccex);
$$ELIF(USECC95)
   // Enable common controls
   InitCommonControls();
$$ENDIF
$$ENDIF
```

```
    // Run main dialog
    BOOL b = DialogBox(hInstance, "DLG_MAIN", NULL, APP_DlgProc);
    // Exit
    DestroyIcon(g_hIconLarge);
    DestroyIcon(g_hIconSmall);
    return b;
}


/*----------------------------------------------------------------*/
// Procedure....: APP_DlgProc()
// Description..: Responds to all messages sent to the dialog
// Input........: HWND, UINT, WPARAM, LPARAM
// Output.......: BOOL
/*----------------------------------------------------------------*/
BOOL CALLBACK APP_DlgProc(HWND hDlg, UINT uiMsg, WPARAM wParam, LPARAM lParam)
{
    switch(uiMsg)
    {
    case WM_INITDIALOG:
        OnInitDialog(hDlg);
        break;

    case WM_COMMAND:
        switch(wParam)
        {
        case IDOK:
            OnOK(hDlg);
            return FALSE;

        case IDCANCEL:
            EndDialog(hDlg, FALSE);
            return FALSE;
        }
        break;
    }

    return FALSE;
}


/****************************************************************
*
*   Internals:
*      - OnOK()
*      - OnInitDialog()
*
****************************************************************/

/*----------------------------------------------------------------*/
// Procedure...: OnOK()
// Description.: Do something
// INPUT.......: HWND
// OUTPUT......: void
/*----------------------------------------------------------------*/
void OnOK(HWND hDlg)
{
    return;
}
```

```
/*--------------------------------------------------------------*/
// Procedure...: OnInitDialog()
// Description.: Initialize the dialog
// INPUT.......: HWND
// OUTPUT......: void
/*--------------------------------------------------------------*/
void OnInitDialog(HWND hDlg)
{
    // Set the icons (T/F as to Large/Small icon)
    SendMessage(hDlg, WM_SETICON, FALSE, reinterpret_cast<LPARAM>(g_hIconSmall));
    SendMessage(hDlg, WM_SETICON, TRUE, reinterpret_cast<LPARAM>(g_hIconLarge));
}


/*  End of file: $$root$$.cpp  */
```

The other template files that make up this AppWizard are shown at the end of the appendix, though you can, of course, download the project (along with the rest of the book's source code) from the Wrox Press web site.

As you can see, there are a number of macros within the code, enclosed between $$ symbols. The parser replaces these macros with their content before including them in the target file. In the case of conditional statements, the syntax is $$IF(macro), where the macro must simply exist for the expression to be true. To remove a macro, just use the RemoveKey() method of the dictionary.

If we now use our Wizard to create a new project called Demo, checking the option for the Windows 98 common controls, the result will be similar to that shown in the next figure:

You can see how $$AUTHOR$$, $$ROOT$$, and $$APPNAME$$ are correctly expanded. Note also the presence of the #include line for commctrl.h. All that remains to be done is compiling the code!

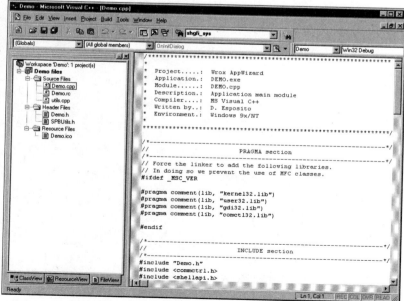

A Generic DLL

The Wrox AppWizard also allows you to create a minimal, generic DLL, composed only of the
`DllMain()` function, the header (`.h`), and the definition file (`.def`). The files generated will be:

- ❏ [Root].cpp
- ❏ [Root].h
- ❏ [Root].def

The [Root].cpp template is significantly simpler than the equivalent one for the Win32 dialog-
based application. It can be found in the "D_MAIN.CPP" template resource.

```
/************************************************************
*
*   Application.:   $$ROOT$$.dll
*   Module......:   $$root$$.cpp
*   Description.:   DLL main module
*   Compiler....:   MS Visual C++
*   Written by..:   $$AUTHOR$$
*
******************************/

/*---------------------------------------------------------*/
//                      PRAGMA section
/*---------------------------------------------------------*/
#ifdef _MSC_VER
    #pragma comment(lib, "kernel32.lib")
    #pragma comment(lib, "user32.lib")
    #pragma comment(lib, "gdi32.lib")
    #pragma comment(lib, "shell32.lib")
#endif

/*---------------------------------------------------------*/
//                      INCLUDE section
/*---------------------------------------------------------*/
#include "$$root$$.h"

/*---------------------------------------------------------*/
//                      GLOBAL section
/*---------------------------------------------------------*/
HINSTANCE g_hThisDll;

/*---------------------------------------------------------*/
// Procedure....: DllMain()
// Description..: Library main function
// Input........: HINSTANCE, DWORD, LPVOID
// Output.......: int
/*---------------------------------------------------------*/
int APIENTRY DllMain(HINSTANCE hInstance, DWORD dwReason, LPVOID lpReserved)
{
    switch(dwReason)
    {
    case DLL_PROCESS_ATTACH:
        g_hThisDll = hInstance;
        break;
    }
    return TRUE;
}

/*  End of module: $$Root$$.cpp  */
```

In the last few sections, I've attempted to provide you with an understanding of what a Custom AppWizard is in the context of Visual C++, and how you can create your own. However, the AppWizard isn't central to the topic of this book, and while you should now have a good idea of how it works, there are certainly a number of points that are worthy of further coverage. For suitable references, take a look at the *Further Reading* section at the end of the appendix.

To close here, the screenshot shows a list of all the template resources in the `WroxWiz` project.

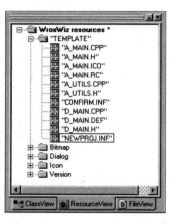

The Rest of the Code

The code for each of the templates (other than those already shown) is given below. Don't forget to add an icon file as well, though!

`"A_MAIN.H"`:

```
/********************************************************************
 *
 *    Project.....:    $$APPNAME$$
 *    Application.:    $$ROOT$$.exe
 *    Module......:    $$ROOT$$.h
 *    Description.:    Application main header
 *    Compiler....:    MS Visual C++
 *    Written by..:    $$AUTHOR$$
 *    Environment.:    Windows 9x/NT
 *
 ******************************************/


// Prevent multiple inclusions
#define WIN32_LEAN_AND_MEAN
#define STRICT

#ifndef _APP_DEFS_
#define _APP_DEFS_
```

```
/*------------------------------------------------------------*/
//                      INCLUDE section
/*------------------------------------------------------------*/
#include <windows.h>
#include <windowsx.h>
$$IF(ADDUTILS)
#include "SPBUtils.h"
$$ENDIF

#endif    // _APP_DEFS_


/*  End of file: $$root$$.h  */
```

"A_MAIN.RC":

```
/***********************************************************************
 *
 *   Project.....:  $$APPNAME$$
 *   Application.:  $$ROOT$$.exe
 *   Module......:  $$ROOT$$.rc
 *   Description.:  Application resources
 *   Compiler....:  MS Visual C++
 *   Written by..:  $$AUTHOR$$
 *   Environment.:  Windows 95
 *
 ******************************/

/*------------------------------------------------------------*/
//                      INCLUDE section
/*------------------------------------------------------------*/
#ifndef __BORLANDC__
#include <winres.h>
#endif

/*------------------------------------------------------------*/
// Version
/*------------------------------------------------------------*/
VS_VERSION_INFO VERSIONINFO
 FILEVERSION 1,0,0,1
 PRODUCTVERSION 1,0,0,1
 FILEFLAGSMASK 0x3fL
#ifdef _DEBUG
 FILEFLAGS 0x1L
#else
 FILEFLAGS 0x0L
#endif
 FILEOS 0x4L
 FILETYPE 0x1L
 FILESUBTYPE 0x0L
```

```
   BEGIN
      BLOCK "StringFileInfo"
      BEGIN
         BLOCK "040904b0"
         BEGIN
            VALUE "CompanyName", "\0"
            VALUE "FileDescription", "\0"
            VALUE "FileVersion", "1.00.001\0"
            VALUE "InternalName", "$$ROOT$$\0"
            VALUE "LegalCopyright", "\0"
            VALUE "LegalTrademarks", "\0"
            VALUE "OriginalFilename", "$$ROOT$$.exe\0"
            VALUE "ProductName", "$$APPNAME$$\0"
            VALUE "ProductVersion", "1, 0, 0, 1\0"
         END
      END
      BLOCK "VarFileInfo"
      BEGIN
         VALUE "Translation", 0x409, 1200
      END
   END


   /*-------------------------------------------------------------------*/
   // Icon
   /*-------------------------------------------------------------------*/
   APP_ICON                       ICON    DISCARDABLE    "$$root$$.ico"

   /*-------------------------------------------------------------------*/
   // Design Info
   /*-------------------------------------------------------------------*/
   #ifdef APSTUDIO_INVOKED
   GUIDELINES DESIGNINFO DISCARDABLE
   BEGIN
      "DLG_MAIN", DIALOG
      BEGIN
         LEFTMARGIN, 7
         RIGHTMARGIN, 234
         TOPMARGIN, 7
         BOTTOMMARGIN, 103
      END
   END
   #endif    // APSTUDIO_INVOKED


   /*-------------------------------------------------------------------*/
   // DLG_MAIN
   /*-------------------------------------------------------------------*/
   DLG_MAIN DIALOGEX 0, 0, 240, 110
   STYLE DS_MODALFRAME | DS_CENTER | WS_POPUP | WS_CAPTION | WS_SYSMENU
   CAPTION "$$APPNAME$$"
   FONT 8, "MS Sans Serif"
   BEGIN
      DEFPUSHBUTTON    "OK",IDOK,184,7,50,14
      PUSHBUTTON       "Cancel",IDCANCEL,184,24,50,14
   END


   /*  End of file: $$root$$.rc  */
```

"A_UTILS.CPP":

```cpp
#include "spbutils.h"


/*--------------------------------------------------*/
// Procedure....: Msg()
// Description..: Show a message box
/*--------------------------------------------------*/
void WINAPI Msg(char* szFormat, ...)
{

    va_list argptr;
    char szBuf[MAX_PATH];
    HWND hwndFocus = GetFocus();

    // init va_ functions
    va_start(argptr, szFormat);

    // format output string
    wvsprintf(szBuf, szFormat, argptr);

    // read title and show
    MessageBox(hwndFocus, szBuf, NULL, MB_ICONEXCLAMATION | MB_OK);
    // close va_ functions
    va_end(argptr);
    SetFocus(hwndFocus);
}


/*--------------------------------------------------*/
// Procedure....: SPB_SystemMessage()
// Description..: Formats a standard error message
/*--------------------------------------------------*/
void WINAPI SPB_SystemMessage(DWORD dwRC)
{

    LPVOID lpMsgBuf;
    DWORD rc;

    rc = FormatMessage(FORMAT_MESSAGE_ALLOCATE_BUFFER |
                       FORMAT_MESSAGE_FROM_SYSTEM |
                       FORMAT_MESSAGE_IGNORE_INSERTS,
                    NULL, dwRC,
                    MAKELANGID(LANG_NEUTRAL, SUBLANG_DEFAULT),
                    reinterpret_cast<LPTSTR>(&lpMsgBuf), 0, NULL);

    Msg("%s:  %ld.\n\n\n%s:\n\n%s", "This is the error code", dwRC,
         "This is the system's explanation", (rc == 0 ? "<unknown>" : lpMsgBuf));
    LocalFree(lpMsgBuf);
}
```

"A_UTILS.H":

```
/*********************************************************************
 *
 *  Project.....:  Shell Programming Book Utility Library
 *  Application.:  SPBUTIL.dll
 *  Module......:  SPBUtils.h
 *  Description.:  Utility header
 *  Compiler....:  MS Visual C++
 *  Written by..:  D. Esposito
 *  Environment.:  Windows 9x/NT
 *
 *********************************************************************/

// Prevent multiple inclusions
#define WIN32_LEAN_AND_MEAN
#define STRICT

#ifndef _SPB_UTILS_
#define _SPB_UTILS_
#ifdef __cplusplus
extern "C" {
#endif

/*------------------------------------------------------------------*/
//                          INCLUDE section
/*------------------------------------------------------------------*/
#include <windows.h>
#include <windowsx.h>

/*------------------------------------------------------------------*/
//                          PROTOTYPE section
/*------------------------------------------------------------------*/
// Error Messages
#include <stdarg.h>

void WINAPI Msg(char* szFormat, ...);
void WINAPI SPB_SystemMessage(DWORD dwRC);

#ifdef __cplusplus
}
#endif

#endif    // _SPB_UTILS_
```

"D_MAIN.DEF":

```
LIBRARY           $$ROOT$$


EXPORTS
; function number
```

"D_MAIN.H":

```
/***************************************************************
 *
 *    Application.:    $$ROOT$$.dll
 *    Module......:    $$root$$.cpp
 *    Description.:    Library header
 *    Compiler....:    MS Visual C++
 *    Written by..:    $$AUTHOR$$
 *
 *****************************/

/*-----------------------------------------------------------*/
//                     INCLUDE section
/*-----------------------------------------------------------*/
#define WIN32_LEAN_AND_MEAN
#define STRICT

#include <windows.h>
#include <windowsx.h>


/*-----------------------------------------------------------*/
//                     INCLUDE section
/*-----------------------------------------------------------*/
extern HINSTANCE g_hThisDll;


/*-----------------------------------------------------------*/
//                     PROTOTYPES section
/*-----------------------------------------------------------*/
// TODO:: list here all the constants, macros, typedefs, ...
// TODO:: list here all the exported functions



/*  End of file: $$Root$$.h  */
```

Further Reading

To learn more about AppWizards I recommend that you read an article by Walter Oney that appeared in the Microsoft Systems Journal (MSJ), in March 1997. Its title is *Pay No Attention to the Man Behind the Curtain! Write Your Own C++ AppWizards.*

I too have written an article on the subject, and curiously it was published in the same month as Walter Oney's (March 1997). It appeared in the now defunct Windows Tech Journal, under the title *A New Assistant.*

If you're interested in the wider field of customizing the Visual C++ environment, then you can take a look at Steve Zimmerman's *Extend Developer Studio 97 with Your Own Add-Ins, Macros, and Wizards,* which appeared in MSJ, September 1997.

All these articles address the Visual C++ 5.0 environment, but much of the information is still relevant to Visual C++ 6.

Index A

Symbols

_makepath(), 235
_NewEnum(), 368
_splitpath(), 235

A

ActiveXObject(), 389
AddChannel(), 371
AddDesktopComponent(), 372
AddFavorite(), 372
AddPages(), 472, 474, 475, 482, 483, 484
AddTab(), 286, 287
alert(), 414
APP_DlgProc(), 75, 112, 156, 168, 280, 284, 301, 374

B

BindImageEx(), 495
BindImageEx()(), 496
BindToObject(), 113, 115, 578
BitBlt(), 204
BrowseForFolder(), 358, 360, 375
BrowseObject(), 590

C

Clone(), 546
CloseHandle(), 164
CoCreateInstance(), 141
CoInitialize(), 141, 153
CompareIDs(), 110, 579, 580, 588, 589
confirm(), 414
ContextMenu(), 182
Control_RunDLL(), 335, 336
ControlPanelItem(), 359
CopyCallBack(), 512
CopyFile(), 38

CopyHere(), 367
CoUninitialize(), 153, 185, 358
CPlApplet(), 332, 334, 335, 336
CreateDC(), 228
CreateDesktop(), 274
CreateDialog(), 181
CreateFiber(), 511
CreateIcon(), 256
CreateIconFromResource(), 256
CreateIconIndirect(), 256
CreateObject(), 389, 400
CreateProcess(), 222, 223, 224, 229, 231, 238, 239, 247
CreateRemoteThread(), 511
CreateViewWindow(), 549, 609
CreateViewWindow2(), 607, 608, 609
CreateWindow(), 287

D

DeleteFile(), 38, 302
DeleteMenu(), 552
DialogBox(), 153, 181
DialogBoxParam(), 444
DllCanUnloadNow(), 184, 185, 464, 480
DllGetClassObject(), 184, 189, 211, 464
DllGetVersion(), 294, 296, 298
DllMain(), 184
DllRegisterServer(), 186, 187, 188, 464, 605
DllUnregisterServer(), 189, 464
DoIt(), 370
DoSearchPath(), 112
DragEnter(), 517
DragFinish(), 149, 156
DragLeave(), 517
DragOver(), 517
DragQueryFile(), 149, 156, 470, 475, 521
DragQueryPoint(), 149, 156
DrawIcon(), 204, 258
DrawIconEx(), 258
Drop(), 517, 518, 520, 521, 523

Index B

COMDeveloper

COMDeveloper is the new subscription newsletter about programming in the Component Object Model environment from Wrox Press. This document is addressed to experienced developers and is brought to you by leading Authors, Coders, Consultants and Pundits who're working and researching at the bleeding edge of these technologies. This is NOT 10 pages of lightweight editorial with some advertisements thrown in for good measure - each issue will contain detailed and challenging articles essential for working programmers and will be of a quality and depth you'd expect from an expert tutorial.

Subscribe and you'll receive 10 issues per year packed with investigative, explanatory, exhaustive and esoteric journeys into COM challenges. Some typical topics will be:

- Class Factories – how to use them effectively
- Expressing business objects in COM & ATL
- COM custom marshaling techniques
- Free threading challenges
- Attribute / declarative programming – the ATL enhancements
- COM+ internals

COM is rapidly growing into the distributed object development model of choice. The structural services of Queuing, Transactions and Directory are being refined and addressed on a continuous basis. Developing and distributing your COM component code can be a liberating and frustrating experience. COM+ is another step along the object brick road…you need to get the newsletter that is all about these issues and much much more.

Get your free trial issue today

We're not asking you to hand over the money now. Order your free trail issue now and see for yourself. When you receive the invoice, you can write 'Cancel' on it or pay just $199 for the next 10 issues. It's that easy.

Cancel at any time

If you don't find COM Developer to be everything we claim it is, you can cancel at any time and receive a refund for the remaining issues of your subscription.

Beginning Object Oriented Analysis and Design

Author: Jesse Liberty
ISBN: 1861001339
Price: $34.95 C$48.95 £32.49

Beginning Object-Oriented Analysis and Design is a tutorial about planning and designing a software product or project in a practical way, before getting involved with writing code. Using OOA&D, a programmer can develop a concrete blueprint or model of their software using the standard modeling language, UML. From the UML model, the programmer can successfully code the objects described. This can be done in any OO-capable language, although C++ is used as an example.

Going beyond the methodology and the modeling language, the book talks about the entire process of professional software development. *Beginning Object-Oriented Analysis and Design* is written in a straightforward manner that should be readily accessible to anyone developing software.

Instant UML

Authors: Pierre–Alain Muller
ISBN: 1861000871
Price: $34.95 C$48.95 £32.49

UML is the Unified Modeling Language. Modeling languages have come into vogue with the rise of object-oriented development, as they provide a means of communicating and recording every stage of the project. The results of the analysis and design phases are captured using the formal syntax of the modeling language, producing a clear model of the system to be implemented.

Instant UML offers not only a complete description of the notation and proper use of UML, but also an introduction to the theory of object-oriented programming, and the way to approach object-oriented application development. This is UML in context, not a list of the syntax without rhyme or reason.

This book is relevant to programmers of C++, VB, Java and other OO-capable languages, users of Visual Modeler (which comes with the Enterprise Edition of Microsoft's Visual Studio) and novice users of Rational Rose and similar UML-compliant tools.

Beginning ATL COM Programming

Authors: Various
ISBN: 1861000111
Price: $39.95 C$55.95 £36.99

This book is for fairly experienced C++ developers who want to get to grips with COM programming using the Active Template Library. The Beginning in the title of this book refers to COM and ATL. It does not refer to Programming.

We don't expect you to know anything about COM. The book explains the essentials of COM, how to use it, and how to get the most out of it. If you already know something about COM, that's a bonus. You'll still learn a lot about the way that ATL works, and you'll be one step ahead of the COM neophytes.

Neither do we expect you to know anything about ATL. ATL is the focus of the book. If you've never touched ATL, or if you've been using it for a short while, but still have many unanswered questions, this is the book for you.

Professional MFC with Visual C++ 5

Author: Mike Blaszczak
ISBN: 1861000146
Price: $59.95 C$83.95 £56.49

Written by one of Microsoft's leading MFC developers, this is the book for professionals who want to get under the covers of the library. This is the 3rd revision of the best selling title formerly known as 'Revolutionary Guide to MFC 4' and covers the new Visual C++ 5.0 development environment.

This book will give a detailed discussion of the majority of classes present in Microsoft's application framework library. While it will point out what parameters are required for the member functions of those classes, it will concentrate more on describing what utility the classes really provide. You will learn how to write a few utilities, some DLLs, an ActiveX control and even an OLE document server, as well as examining Microsoft's Open Database Connectivity (ODBC) and Data Access Objects (DAO) strategies. At the very end of the book, you'll take a look at what the Microsoft Foundation Classes provide to make programming for the Internet easier.

There's a CD_ROM included which has the complete book in HTML format - now you can use any browser to read your book on the road.

Professional ATL COM Programming

Authors: Dr. Richard Grimes
ISBN: 1861001401
Price: $59.99 C$89.95 £45.99

For experienced Visual C++ programmers with experience of COM and ATL (Active Template Library) The coverage throughout, is for the latest ATL version 3.0 and as such is essential reading for getting the most out of your COM servers.

Author, Richard Grimes - famous for his definitive text on DCOM, has applied all his specialist knowledge of ATL usage in the field to give you *the* book on ATL architecture and usage. If you've ever looked at Wizard-generated ATL code and wondered what's behind it. If you've ever wondered how it works, why it's implemented in that way and the options for customising and extending it – then the answer is in these pages. You will learn all about the plumbing behind ATL via example code that will be useful in your own projects. You should read this if you wish to: debug, get the right factory, thread, marshal, use Windows classes, use connection points, sink events, build composite controls and understand the COM object wizard.

Professional COM Applications with ATL

Authors: Sing Li and Panos Economopoulos
ISBN: 1861001703
Price: $49.99 C$69.95 £45.99

This book examines how and why you should use COM, ActiveX controls and DNA Business Objects, and how these components are linked together to form robust, flexible and scalable applications.

A key part of the book is the extended case study in which we produce a distributed events calendar that fits Microsoft's Distributed interNet Applications (DNA) model. This three-tier application uses flexible browser-based controls for the client user interface, business objects on both client and server to process the required information efficiently and Universal Data Access to perform the queries and updates. It depends on the support for component-based development now available for Windows NT server.

The additions and changes to this book make it both significant and relevant to readers of the first edition, Professional ActiveX/COM Control Programming.

Beginning NT Programming

Author: Julian Templeman
ISBN: 1861000170
Price: $39.99 C$59.95 £36.99

This book is designed to lay bare the guts of NT programming. In order to do this, it concentrates on programming at a system level, using the Win32 API, rather than the Windows GUI. You'll learn about structured exception handling, how threads and processes work and how to deal with NT's filing system. You'll also learn about how to write NT Services, deal with the NT security system programmatically and implement inter-process communication.

If you're already familiar with C++, and are keen to take your first steps in writing NT system applications, or to add NT-specific features to your applications, then this is the book for you.

Professional NT Services

Author: Kevin Miller
ISBN: 1861001304
Price: $59.99 C$83.95 £55.49

Professional NT Services teaches developers how to design and implement good NT services using all the features and tools supplied for the purpose by Microsoft Visual C++. The author develops a set of generic classes to facilitate service development, and introduces the concept of *usage patterns* — a way of categorizing the roles that services can fulfil in the overall architecture of a system. The book also gives developers a firm grounding in the security and configuration issues that must be taken into account when developing a service.

To date, the treatment of NT services has been sketchy and widely scattered. This book is aimed at bringing the range of relevant material together in an organized way. Its target readership is C/C++ Windows programmers with experience of programming under Win32 and basic knowledge of multithreaded and COM programming. At an architectural level, the book's development of usage patterns will be invaluable to client-server developers who want to include services as part of a multi-tiered system.

Visual C++ Windows Shell Programming Registration Card

Name _____

Address _____

_____

_____

City_____ State/Region _____

Country_____ Postcode/Zip _____

E-mail _____

Occupation _____

How did you hear about this book? _____

☐ Book review (name) _____

☐ Advertisement (name) _____

☐ Recommendation _____

☐ Catalog _____

☐ Other _____

Where did you buy this book? _____

☐ Bookstore (name)_____ City _____

☐ Computer Store (name) _____

☐ Mail Order _____

☐ Other _____

What influenced you in the
purchase of this book?

☐ Cover Design

☐ Contents

☐ Other (please specify) _____

How did you rate the overall
contents of this book?

☐ Excellent   ☐ Good

☐ Average   ☐ Poor

What did you find most useful about this book? _____

What did you find least useful about this book? _____

Please add any additional comments. _____

What other subjects will you buy a computer
book on soon? _____

What is the best computer book you have used this year?

*Note: This information will only be used to keep you updated
about new Wrox Press titles and will not be used for any other
purpose or passed to any other third party.*

WROX PRESS INC.

Wrox writes books for you. Any suggestions, or
ideas about how you want information given in
your ideal book will be studied by our team.
Your comments are always valued at Wrox.

Free phone in USA 800-USE-WROX
Fax (312) 397 8990

UK Tel. (0121) 706 6826   Fax   (0121) 706 2967

Computer Book Publishers

NB. If you post the bounce back card below in the UK, please send it to:
Wrox Press Ltd. 30 Lincoln Road, Birmingham, B27 6PA

BUSINESS REPLY MAIL
FIRST CLASS MAIL   PERMIT#64   CHICAGO, IL

POSTAGE WILL BE PAID BY ADDRESSEE

WROX PRESS
1512 NORTH FREMONT
SUITE 103
CHICAGO IL 60622-2567